The Diary of George Templeton Strong

YOUNG MAN
IN NEW YORK
1835–1849

The DIARY of
George Templeton Strong

YOUNG MAN
in NEW YORK
1835—1849

EDITED BY

ALLAN NEVINS

AND

MILTON HALSEY THOMAS

THE MACMILLAN COMPANY

New York : 1952

PREFACE

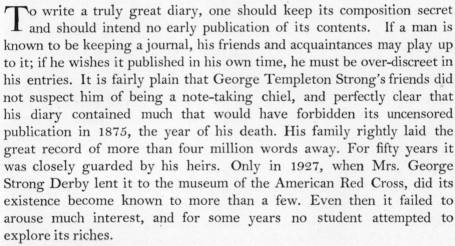

To write a truly great diary, one should keep its composition secret and should intend no early publication of its contents. If a man is known to be keeping a journal, his friends and acquaintances may play up to it; if he wishes it published in his own time, he must be over-discreet in his entries. It is fairly plain that George Templeton Strong's friends did not suspect him of being a note-taking chiel, and perfectly clear that his diary contained much that would have forbidden its uncensored publication in 1875, the year of his death. His family rightly laid the great record of more than four million words away. For fifty years it was closely guarded by his heirs. Only in 1927, when Mrs. George Strong Derby lent it to the museum of the American Red Cross, did its existence become known to more than a few. Even then it failed to arouse much interest, and for some years no student attempted to explore its riches.

A natural train of circumstances drew the diary to the attention of the present editors. Mr. Henry Waters Taft late in life began a history of the law firm which, founded in 1818 by George Washington Strong and John Wells, had during the next century engaged the talents of the diarist George Templeton Strong, his partners Marshall S. Bidwell and Charles E. Strong, and his successors John L. Cadwalader, George W. Wickersham, and Mr. Taft himself. In writing his history, Mr. Taft learned of the diary and obtained permission from John R. Strong of New York and Hasket Derby II, now of Portland, son and grandnephew of the diarist, to use it. His interesting volume on the record of this brilliant line of

[v]

attorneys, entitled *A Century and a Half at the New York Bar, Being the Annals of a Law Firm*, was privately printed in 1938. In that year Mr. Taft mentioned to President Nicholas Murray Butler of Columbia University that he had temporary possession of a diary containing a wealth of information on Columbia affairs, and Dr. Butler conveyed word of the find to the editors.

George Templeton Strong III, of Larchmont, New York, whose father John R. Strong died in 1941, and Hasket Derby II willingly consented to the publication of the journal, giving the editors complete freedom in their treatment of it.

The diary, kept in uniform blank-books, is now bound in four morocco volumes, fourteen by nine inches in size, which contain an aggregate of more than 2,250 pages. The number of words is perhaps nearer four and a half million than four million. Strong wrote his record in a minute hand, no larger than the type of our footnotes, beautifully regular, fine-lined, and clear. Hardly a hundred times in these volumes have we found a word undecipherable. At first the diarist used quill pens, whose deficiencies he often bewailed, and when gold pens grew popular in the 1850's he doubtless turned to them. Ordinarily he made his entries just before going to bed, first at his parents' home on Greenwich Street and later at his own residence on Gramercy Park. It is one merit of the record that he kept it up to date, seldom indulging in John Quincy Adams's practice of deferring it until a day of leisure enabled him to write in the arrears. His impressions were thus kept vivid; many a concert, political meeting, or evening party was described an hour after it ended.

The task of the editors has been both onerous and fascinating, sometimes irritating, frequently exhilarating. The first requisite was a drastic reduction of the bulky record. All diaries inevitably contain much that is ephemeral and trivial: comments on the weather, notes on random walks and pointless episodes, mentions of unidentifiable or uninteresting people, and jottings of commonplace ideas. We have not only excluded such dull matter, but have omitted prosy theological disquisitions, dealt sternly with lectures, sermons, and vestry sessions, and kept the notation of routine legal business to a minimum. In two fields we have held our selections within strict limits in the expectation that future books of a special nature will do ampler justice to the materials. Strong's interest in Columbia, as student, alumnus, and trustee, is well illustrated in these volumes; but enough remains unused to fill a valuable supplementary monograph. And though we give numerous excerpts from his discriminating criticism of concerts, oratorios, and operas, again an interesting volume of musical comment could—and some day will—be compiled from the diary.

With these two exceptions, these pages contain, we believe, the parts of Strong's narrative of greatest interest to the general public. We have tried to include all that bears significantly upon the cultural, social, and political history of the times. Many interesting personal entries, dealing with the diarist's family circle, have been left out; but these would make another kind of story.

In preparing the diary for publication, our fundamental rule has been to treat it precisely as any conscientious publishing house would treat an important manuscript by a living author. The text has been carefully respected; so far as words and sentence structure go, except for a few insertions of an article or preposition, the record stands exactly as Strong wrote it. But spelling and punctuation have been made fairly consistent, conforming to modern usage; orthography of proper names has been corrected and made uniform; Greek phrases have been put into English; abbreviations like "Col: Coll:" have been written out; and minor errors like the use of "farther" for "further" have been corrected. Omissions within entries have been indicated by the usual ellipses, but in the interest of space-saving and appearance of the printed page, especially in the Civil War volume, we have avoided an excess of dots and allowed selected passages to appear as entire entries.

Fidelity to the text has, of course, involved the retention of many outspoken passages. Strong had a way of indulging, sometimes semi-humorously, sometimes quite seriously, in heated attacks on individuals, groups, and societies; he used the diary now and then to blow off steam. His violent assaults upon Yankees, Negroes, Southern rebels, Britons, Irishmen, Frenchmen; his scathing remarks about conservative Columbia trustees, Roman Catholics, Low-Church Episcopalians, Jews, Unitarians, Presbyterians, and other sects; his contemptuous excoriation of many of the cruder manifestations of social and political democracy—all this gives salt to the great document he left. Sometimes the salt may seem a little stinging. But if hasty and unfair judgments are included, it is not because the editors approve them, but because they have historical value.

A final word is perhaps needed upon the apportionment of editorial labor and upon some debts incurred by the editors. This undertaking required help from many hands and a pooling of many energies for over a decade. Mr. Thomas is responsible for the selection of materials and editorial work in the first volume, Mr. Nevins for the selections and editorial work in the other three; but both editors have toiled over all parts of the diary. They have been given invaluable aid by Mrs. Jean W. Conti, whose broad knowledge, quick eye, and passion for accuracy have benefited the volumes from end to end. For help in a task of deciphering, copying, and verification which at times seemed endless the editors must thank a number of workers, but most notably Miss Sylvia Black, Miss Virginia Mergenthaler, and Miss Virginia Kraft. Grants from the Carnegie Corporation for enlarged microprints of the diary, and from the Dunning Fund of Columbia University for secretarial work have been of marked assistance. The biographical introduction is the work of Mr. Nevins; the indexes, which contain a careful identification of many persons casually mentioned in the diary, were prepared by Mr. Thomas.

Much painstaking editorial help has been furnished by Miss Susan Prink, and much general assistance by Mr. H. S. Latham and Mr. Charles E. Cuningham, of The Macmillan Company, while the editors especially wish to thank Mr. George P. Brett, Jr., the head of that publishing house, for his willingness to undertake, in the interest of history, so extensive and costly an enterprise.

ALLAN NEVINS

MILTON HALSEY THOMAS

Columbia University
January, 1952

GEORGE TEMPLETON STRONG

The Man and the Diarist

ON Sunday evening, October 4, 1835, a slender, fair-haired youth of
fifteen sat before the fire in the well-furnished living room of a
handsome brick house at 108 Greenwich Street in New York, plunged in
pleasant meditation. The family had just risen from what they called the
tea-table (though they now drank coffee on Sunday nights) and from an
adjoining room came the noise of a servant clearing away dishes. His
mother and his half-sister Mary Amelia were reading by the light of an
Argand lamp. His father, a busy lawyer, had slipped upstairs to the library
and was deep in a favorite Greek text. A little later two aunts would
probably come in from No. 110 next door, or an uncle from Murray
Street, but for the present the lad could mull over an ambition which had
seized him. He had determined to keep a diary!—for his life seemed
crowded with interesting experiences and sensations. He had but recently
returned from an active summer on the north shore of Long Island; next
day he would begin his sophomore year at Columbia; he was buying old
coins, devouring books, and scanning city sights and personages critically.
He pictured himself busy scribbling in some huge folio volume like a
bank ledger, another Evelyn, another Pepys. The moment made such an
impression that thirty years later he could vividly recall all the details
for an anniversary record, October 5, 1865.

Next day the vision was realized. A sizable blank book was procured,
and evening found the youth bent over it, recording how he had scurried
eight blocks up Church Street to the long three-storied college building,
arriving so early that he had a two-hour wait for faculty and classmates,
and how he had spent the rest of an exciting day. Not far away that

evening another diarist, fifty-four-year-old Philip Hone, former mayor of the city, was describing the rival Whig and Democratic celebrations of the battle of the Thames, and recording a street shindy between the city watch and some roisterers headed by the Marquis of Waterford, whose yacht lay in the Hudson.

I

A queer New York that little city of 1835 was, reflected Strong thirty years later. Bond Street marked the northern limit of the town; pigs still served as public scavengers; and William H. Aspinwall's house in College Place was esteemed the most luxurious and imposing in the city. The more fashionable residences were still to be found around the Battery, along Broadway (where the great Astor House was just being built between Vesey and Barclay Streets), and on Greenwich Street as far north as Cortlandt. Many merchants still lived over their stores in Pearl Street, where also were found a number of boardinghouses for out-of-town dealers who came from Ohio and Illinois by stage coach, or from Norfolk and Charleston by schooner. A marked northward drift of population was evident, however, and "uptown" lots (for example, around St. Mark's-in-the-Bowery, at Second Avenue and Eleventh Street) were fetching prices that astonished observers. When the great fire of 1835 (of which Strong furnished some boyish impressions) gave the city an extensive "burned district," Mayor Cornelius Lawrence and his associates seized the opportunity to widen a number of streets.

Already, however, New York—with fully 250,000 people in 1835—thought itself metropolitan. It had an infant railroad: the Harlem line was opened in 1834 as far north as the village of Yorkville, on the Boston Post Road at present-day Eighty-fifth Street. It had busy packets plying to Europe, and within half a dozen years the first Cunard steamers would tie it to Liverpool. An enterprising popular press was born when, on May 6, 1835, five months before Strong began his diary, James Gordon Bennett issued the first New York *Herald* from his cellar office at 20 Wall Street; young Strong must often have seen the ugly little Scot hurrying about the downtown streets for news. Five theatres were active in the fall of 1835, and New Yorkers who saw Junius Brutus Booth at the Bowery Theatre in *Othello* or the various actors who followed James Sheridan Knowles at the Park Theatre could hardly complain of poor fare. With Bryant editing the *Evening Post*, Irving issuing this year his *Tour on the Prairie*, and Fenimore Cooper frequently appearing on visits from Cooperstown, New York was up to this time more distinguished in literature than Boston. For ten years the city had been lighted by gas below Canal Street, and now the Manhattan Company was fast extending its gas mains uptown.

Still, the city remained sufficiently compact to be ideal ground for a diarist, who could see everything and know almost everybody by sight. The college sophomore beginning his record halfway through Jackson's second term could almost daily see the merchants who had made New York powerful: the Howlands, the Aspinwalls, the philanthropic Gideon Lee and Robert Lenox, the public-spirited Stephen Whitney and J. Phillips Phoenix. Now and then he might even see the fabulous John Jacob Astor. He knew by sight some of the great bankers, like Samuel Ward of Prime, Ward & King, and the great shipping men like Preserved Fish and Moses H. Grinnell. He must early have become familiar with the burly figure of Cornelius Vanderbilt, and with the tall Samuel B. Ruggles who, in 1835, was helping launch the Erie Railroad. He could easily walk to all the sights of the little city: to the eleven markets; to the Brooklyn ferry; to the few uptown churches, such as St. John's-in-the-Fields, which had been built on Varick Street in Jefferson's Administration; to Union Square, laid out only three years earlier; and to Peter Stuyvesant's pear tree just above Astor Place. Any public occurrence, such as the popular demonstrations brought on by the hard times of 1837–1838, was under his very eyes.

It was indeed a curious little city when the diary began. It was still so well-knit geographically and simple in manners that few families kept a two-horse carriage; probably not more than twenty-five. It still for the most part burned wood—though the Strongs used coal in open grates—and every fall hundreds of sloops, descending the Sound and the Hudson, filled the East and North River slips with their cargoes of oak, elm, and hickory. It had no police, a small corps of watchmen nightly patrolling the streets and pounding the curbs with their clubs as every hour struck. Milkmen from Long Island, carrying tin cans yoked across their shoulders, cried their prices from door to door. Some of the churches still fastened chains across the fronting streets during Sunday services. Porters with leather shoulder-straps, brass license plates, and heavy hand-carts stood at the business corners ready to fetch and carry. Householders were responsible for keeping the walks and streets before their premises clean, while fire-fighting was left to crews of more and more disorderly and quarrelsome volunteer firemen. Class lines between rich and poor were increasingly evident, and the feeling of the old stock against immigrants was sometimes fiercely expressed; but on the whole the community was remarkably homogeneous and harmonious.

From the first the diarist found a fascination in his task. His parents doubtless encouraged him; he had plenty of inborn tenacity—"he is certainly not wanting in resolution and energy," wrote his father in 1837; and he soon found the journal a companion. Particularly must his father have been friendly to the undertaking, for George Washington Strong was a remarkable letter-writer, showed a marked predilection for literature, and was keenly interested in all that the son did.

II

The diarist's ancestry on the paternal side has a good deal of interest. The Strong family had migrated from England to Massachusetts, and thence to Long Island. When the Revolution opened, Selah Strong of Setauket (the diarist's grandfather) sat in the Provincial Congress, 1775–1776; later he became a captain in the Continental Army; and after the war he was state senator and judge of the court of common pleas in Suffolk County. As old Judge Strong died in 1815, George Templeton Strong never saw him. This was a pity, for all accounts present him as a clearheaded man of much personal force. When Robert Fulton's *Clermont* made her first regular trip on the Hudson from New York to Albany, September 4, 1807, Judge Strong, then about seventy, was on board.

The family had enough means to send George Washington Strong, father of the diarist, to Yale, where he was graduated in 1803. He made a remarkable impression upon some of his classmates, four of whom wrote him a letter (November 25, 1806) in which they declared that he was a "veray parfit gentil knight"—that, "endowed with a strong mind and brilliant imagination, which your impregnable regard for virtue has served to strengthen, we have ever beheld in you a model, which to imitate, would be to establish an unblemished Character." The model young man had already mastered the elements of law. On November 21, 1805, he signed the roll in New York as attorney just below Washington Irving, who had appeared the same day; and within five years he became a counselor-at-law—that is, was admitted to practice in the higher courts. He soon built up a varied clientele, appearing in no fewer than 1,334 cases before the end of 1817. This figure gives us the rather impressive average of 120 new cases a year. Among his early clients were the Union Bank and the New York Sugar Refining Company. In Embargo days he did a large admiralty business, and later became especially proficient in the law relating to estates, realty titles, trusts, and wills.

In 1818, two years before the diarist was born, George Washington Strong had formed a partnership with an older and more distinguished lawyer, a graduate of Princeton and one-time friend of Alexander Hamilton—John Wells. It was a brief connection, ended by Wells's untimely death in the late summer of 1823. But brief as it was, it did a good deal to shape the character of the law office into which George Templeton Strong ultimately came. The father, writing a brother-in-law just after his partner's death, declared that Wells was "the first man, beyond all dispute, in this State"; that "no death since that of Hamilton has been so severely felt and universally deplored"; and that "I did not know before that I loved him so intensely or that the Public without a solitary exception esteemed him so highly." A large body of lawyers, meeting at City Hall, took steps to erect a monument which, crowned with a lifelike bust of Wells, stands today in St. Paul's Chapel. Chancellor Kent, in a memorial gathering at Albany, paid tribute to the attorney as one who "has been pouring instruction over my mind for fifteen years." The tradition of John Wells's profound learning and professional rectitude lingered in the law office; and we may be sure, too, that the elder Strong often spoke to his son of Wells's keen interest in historical and literary studies, of the grace and dignity of his manners, and of his religious devotion.

George W. Strong at once set about finding another partner, and after some fruitless negotiations with John Duer, later a well-known judge, formed a connection with George Griffin, undoubtedly one of the ablest lawyers of the city. James W. Gerard, who knew the bar of 1815–1820 well, said later that its seven most eminent members were then Thomas Addis Emmet, John Wells, George Griffin, Cadwallader D. Colden, Josiah Ogden Hoffman, David B. Ogden, and Samuel Jones. Like Strong, Griffin was a Yale man, class of 1797; like him, he was a man of broad reading, devoted to learning for its own sake—he eventually retired to give himself time for inquiries into theology, a field in which he produced four books. Gerard tells us that he was "full of ambition and zeal, a man of the most industrious habits and brilliant imagination, with a great command of powerful language." He undoubtedly lent strength and prestige to what was now one of the best law firms in New York. He, too, added to the traditions of the office.

It speaks well for George W. Strong that he was able to command such partners as Wells and Griffin; and indeed, by the 1820's he was counted one of the ablest lawyers of the East. In 1809 he had married Angelina Lloyd, a second cousin on his mother's side and a daughter of John Lloyd, Jr., of Huntington, Long Island. They had lived at 37 Sugarloaf (later Franklin) Street, where two daughters, Eloise Lloyd and Mary Amelia, were born. After only five years of married life, Mrs. Strong had died in September, 1814, at the age of twenty-nine. Strong continued to live in Franklin Street. In 1819 he brought a new bride there, Eliza Catherine Templeton, a daughter of Oliver Templeton of New York. This new union also produced two children, John Wells Strong, who died in infancy, and George Templeton Strong, who was born on January 26, 1820. In 1822 the family removed to 108 Greenwich Street.

I I I

It is not difficult to reconstruct many of the surroundings and appurtenances of George Templeton Strong's childhood. Greenwich Street, which in colonial days had been the shore road to Greenwich Village, began at Battery Place and ran northward to merge into Ninth Avenue just below Fourteenth Street. Lined with comfortable brick houses, it commanded here and there, across Washington and West streets, a glimpse of the Hudson. The Strongs' house, on the west side, just off Rector Street, was so close to Battery Park, then a favorite resort for band concerts and summer-evening sociability, that as a child George must often have been taken there to play; while as an active urchin he knew all the ships moored at the West Street wharves.

Every morning his father, green bag in hand, would walk over to the law office, first in Pine Street and then in Wall (with a brief sojourn on Exchange Place after the great fire of 1835). As this was but a ten minutes' stroll, George must often have accompanied him, and early have become familiar with legal forms, wafers, ledgers, and foolscap briefs. He naturally heard much talk, as he grew up, about the legal luminaries of the city: about Chancellor Kent, Thomas Addis Emmet, Ogden Hoffman, Daniel Lord, Caleb B. Riggs, and their peers. Some of these men occasionally came to the house. Benjamin F. Butler, later Attorney-General under President Van Buren, who was as witty and wise as he was shrewd, was in particular a warm friend of the elder Strong. And whenever the partner Griffin came to dinner, the boy would hear fragments of talk about the spectacular legal battles of the day: about Daniel Lord's case of Aymar and Aymar *v.* Astor, which led to Lord's lucrative legal connection with the John Jacob Astor family, or about Ogden Hoffman's brilliant argument in the Helen Jewett murder case of 1836, which obtained the dubious acquittal of the girl's paramour Robinson.

The diarist's father was an extremely busy man, who toiled even to the injury of his health. Of middle height, rather heavily built, he had a large head, bald on top but framed at the sides with thick curling brown-gray hair. His features showed strength rather than refinement: a massive jaw, stern in repose, a Roman nose, and a domelike forehead. But he had unusually brilliant and expressive eyes, which frequently lighted up with humor, while his mouth easily broke into a smile; his face could become delightfully sunny. Kindliness was one of his principal traits, and it was said that he never spoke ill of any living man. Earnest, conscientious, and able, he was modest to a fault, never seeking office or public notice. He regarded Chancellor Kent as the greatest jurist of the day, pronouncing him "a perfect giant in the law," and taking pleasure in his vigorous dogmatism. When in 1823 Kent's son entered the office as a student, Strong felt highly complimented. He also greatly respected Story and Marshall, although the latter did not make a deep impression upon him until he read the decision in the famous case of Gibbons *v.* Ogden. Among lawyers the elder Strong gave first place to Daniel Webster, writing in 1827 that the Supreme Court in Washington shared this opinion. He made a distinction here between the crowning eminence that sprang from high intellectual power and the lesser eminence that came as the fruit of erudition:

You mistake my former letter [he wrote his brother-in-law on December 31, 1827] if you infer from it that I think Mr. Webster's greatness consists in his *law knowledge.* I think far differently. Chancellor Kent, Judge Story, and men of that class, are *great* for their law knowledge. Chief Justice Marshall is and Chief Justice Parsons, Mr. Pinkney and Mr. Wells *were, great* in another sense; that is, in their arguments they relied not so much on books as on the resources of their own minds. Greatness in this latter sense is esteemed *greater* than in the former. Take almost any case, either of law or of fact, and if all that is said on it be taken from the books, it will cut but a sorry figure. I suppose Chancellor Kent could cite offhand fifty cases to Webster's one on any given subject, and yet, before either court or jury, the odds in favor of Webster would be great indeed. . . .

"I know," the elder Strong confessed in 1827, "I have labored too hard both bodily and mentally. This, I hope, has not proceeded from a love of filthy lucre, but rather from a disposition to do, and to do properly, such professional business as has been confided to me." Yet amid his toils he did not fail to take some time for exercise and amusement. Paying $200 for a mare in 1824, he resolved to rise early and get ten miles of horse-back exercise before going to office or court. In this he was consciously imitating some of the great jurists of England, who rode twelve or fifteen miles before breakfast and then worked unjaded until midnight. Lord Mansfield, for example, who won his fame when he went on the bench after the age of fifty, preserved his health by this means. "He lived nearly twenty miles from London," wrote Strong, "and besides riding backwards and forwards every day, was in the almost daily habit of chasing foxes before breakfast." The mare proved well worth all the lawyer paid for her. Formerly a hard day's work had left him utterly fatigued by ten or eleven at night. Now he could labor from eight to four daily at his office, and then go into a tedious referee's case which occupied him even until midnight, without being tired.

Among little George Templeton Strong's earliest memories were those of his father rising at half-past five, lighting a fire, and riding off at a hard gallop—sometimes as far north as Bloomingdale, where Columbia University now stands. Before long the lawyer methodically used the horse to acquaint himself with all parts of town. He would canter out to Greenwich Village, or up to Corlear's Hook, or along the Bowery. "I had no adequate conception before of the extent of the city," he wrote on October 20, 1824. He intended, if possible, to master every nook of it. "There are perhaps fifty miles of streets through the thickly-settled parts of the city, and it will take me a good while to become so familiar with them as to carry them in my mind's eye. The information itself will be useful to me, and I feel an ambition (perhaps rather silly as all ambition generally is) to become better acquainted with the geography of the City than any other person in it, and I am now in a fair way to succeed." Here perhaps was the source of one of the diarist's abiding interests, the social geography and changing lineaments of New York.

In summer the Strongs usually went to Whitestone, Long Island, boarding at some convenient house overlooking Flushing Bay. Young George became very fond of this area, bathing, berrying, fishing, and in time doing a little amateur geologizing. Farther out on Long Island were numerous relatives of the Strongs; and the diarist's father was co-guardian, with his brother-in-law John Nelson Lloyd, of a large farm at Lloyd's Neck, the legal title to which was held by George Washington Strong's children by his first wife. These farther reaches also became well known to the boy. Sometimes the family made a brief excursion up the Hudson to West Point, or into the Catskills, and during the cholera summer of 1832 they took refuge at Wilton, Connecticut.

I V

Little George, taught at first by his mother, proved a precocious student. On February 14, 1824, when just over four years of age, he was reported by his father to be reading Thomas Day's *Sandford and Merton* at the rate of six to ten pages daily. At six years he had nearly completed a history—perhaps Mercy Warren's—of the American Revolution; "and it is literally true," boasted his father, "that he knows and has at his command more facts connected with it than I do." In consequence, he had given up his original ambition of running a Hudson River steamboat and wanted to be a soldier. Before he was seven, George seemed to his father (who tried hard to be restrained in praise) the most learned boy of his years in New York. "He studies reading, writing, history, and botany with his mother, astronomy and grammar under Eloise, and Latin under me." An uncle pronounced him a perfect prodigy. Late in 1826 the youngster entered his first school, and by the third day was head of his class. "His ambition is highly excited," commented the father, "and he has begun upon the *high pressure principle*." At nine he took the first prize in his school; "and the boy who took the second," wrote the elder Strong, "was fifteen years old."

No doubt the abundance of books in the home, the good table talk, and the careful tuition by the parents did much to explain George's rapid progress. "I consider the education of children as of inconceivable importance," wrote the conscientious lawyer in 1834, "and I have endeavored to spare no labor or expense in reference to my own." When the boy was eight his father paid $260 for a handsome piano. The lad soon evinced "a great passion" for music. He learned to play both piano and organ by ear well enough to give himself much pleasure. Just before he was twenty-one his mother gave him an organ costing $1,250, "a most splendid piece of furniture." From an early period he read widely; when he was eight he fell head over ears in love, as he long after recalled, with Fair Margaret of *The Lay of the Last Minstrel*. Moreover, his father's tastes gave the house a studious atmosphere.

When in 1832 the before-mentioned cholera epidemic raged in New

York, sending thousands in flight to the country and keeping others within doors, the elder Strong resumed, partly as pastime, partly as discipline, the Greek he had dropped since college. It so fascinated him that half a dozen years later he wrote that his addiction resembled a drunkard's passion for the bottle. During these six years, he stated, "I have read Aesop's *Fables* twice, Jacob's *Greek Reader* twice, the Septuagint three times, the *Iliad* twice, the *Odyssey* once, *Graeca-Major* and *Minora*, all Xenophon's writings, Herodotus, and the Greek Testament, which latter I have read thro I know not how many times. I believe this language to be the most philosophical and perfect, and at the same time the most difficult, of any that ever existed. . . . There is no comparison between reading the Greek Testament and the English translation, as it regards the understanding of an author. There are innumerable beauties in the former which cannot be discovered in the latter." The lawyer enjoyed Greek so much, in fact, that he had to limit his week-day reading to a stated quantity; but on Sunday, he confessed, "I indulge myself in reading as much as I please." As the son was just launched in his classical studies at this time, it meant a great deal to him to have his father pursuing them with so much ardor.

In the fall of 1832 George began work in the Grammar School attached to Columbia College. The standards of this institution were as high as those of the Boston Latin School. Charles Anthon, the formidable professor of Greek and Latin in Columbia College, had taken charge as Rector two years earlier, and had placed both the scholarly requirements and discipline on a thoroughly sound basis. George was one of two hundred boys. "He stands in the utmost dread of his teachers," reported the father on December 5, 1833, "and knows very well that if he neglects a single lesson he will get a good whipping for it." In his first year the youth was taught by some of the dozen masters assisting the great "Bull" Anthon, but in his second he got into the highest class, and recited directly to that dignitary. His father thought him better grounded in Greek and Latin than most Yale graduates had been in the old days.

"I spend every evening with him at his studies from six to ten," recorded the lawyer, "and this is the first winter since I have been in business, that I have omitted coming to the office in the evening. My labor on the whole is substantially increased by this course, but I consider George's education as of so much importance, and the present such an interesting part of his life, that I deem it my duty to make the sacrifice. He is very fond of his studies, particularly of the languages, as a proof of which I might mention that for his amusement he spends his leisure hours in reading Sophocles' Tragedies and Lucian's Dialogues in the original Greek."

Yet the lad differed from ordinary student prodigies in that, far from confining himself to his course, he read both discursively and voraciously, devouring book after book on a wide range of subjects. At fifteen he took the final examinations of the Grammar School along with thirty-three other boys, some of them brilliant and several three years older than himself. In the tests on the ancient classics, he scored 158 points, while the next student below him had only 44! His schoolmates, emerging into the College Green afterwards, gave him three cheers—evidence that he was well liked. George came home feeling the cock of the walk. But this test, demurred the scrupulous father, was not quite fair. "It depended too much on good luck, self-possession, and a quick apprehension. George also had a decided advantage in having read so many of his *old books*, which are not studied in College. The first book selected was one which he had not only read before, but which he had written out the entire translation of. He had the candor to mention this, and it was laid aside, and for this I give him more credit than for anything else." The elder Strong refrained from praising him. And when in the other examinations George failed of first place, the father read him a lesson:

George [he writes] failed in obtaining the *General Testimonial*, which, as I understand, means the first scholar, and got only the certificate as to the classics. He is, I have no doubt, very much mortified at this result, and I am somewhat disappointed. He, however, contends that he would prefer the one he has got to all the rest. In this I differ from him, and aim at impressing on his mind two important and salutary lessons as to the result; the one is of humility, and the other is that he is to study his lessons more and other books less. He studies as hard as I desire, but heretofore it has been almost anything and everything other than his lessons.

V

It was decided to enter George in Columbia College; partly no doubt because it was conveniently near, but also because the elder Strong disliked the theological doctrines of the Rev. Nathaniel W. Taylor, then dominant at his own college, Yale. Almost wrecked by the Revolution, Columbia (the former King's College) had recovered but slowly and could be called small, straitened, and conservative. Its instruction, however, if of the eighteenth century cast, was thorough, and its student body consistently represented the best families of the city. When George entered at fourteen, in the fall of 1834, the president was William A. Duer, an accomplished lawyer who had resigned a judgeship five years before to take charge of the college. He had long been a close friend of Washington Irving; he had been a partner of Edward Livingston, who wrote a criminal code for Louisiana and was termed by Sir Henry Maine the first legal genius of his time; and he had served with credit in the legislature. A man of wide reading and contacts, Duer systematically broadened the teaching at Columbia, encouraging science and the modern languages. He knew every one of the students (diminished to little over a hundred by the recent opening of New York University) and certainly came to know George well.

The faculty, if small, possessed more distinction than Strong's boyish diary might suggest. Anthon was not only the most prominent classical scholar of his day in America, but a teacher of great power and energy. The Rev. John McVickar, another ripe scholar, held the chair of moral philosophy, rhetoric, belles-lettres, and philosophy—and as if this were not enough, was a pioneer in teaching political economy. Dr. Henry James Anderson was professor of mathematics and astronomy. James Renwick, son of a wealthy New York merchant and son-in-law of the rich Henry Brevoort, taught natural and experimental philosophy and chemistry, at the same time giving much attention to engineering work, both public and private. These men had much force of personality. Duer, a portly man of medium height with high bald brow and piercing eyes, who not only kept a sharp eye on discipline but himself oversaw the freshman work in composition and lectured to seniors on constitutional jurisprudence, had a commanding presence. The tall, spare, handsome McVickar, nervous in his movements and irascible of temper, had a strutting consciousness of his learning, his college dignities, and his position in the Episcopal Church. He loved to tell how he had visited Scott at Abbotsford and Wordsworth at Rydal Bank. Renwick had the look of a busy man of affairs, which he was. But it was "Bull" Anthon, tall, broad-shouldered, and massive, his deep-set black eyes as pugnacious as his strong jaw, a recluse who devoted himself to his books, his sisters, and his classes, whose personality made the deepest impression on young George Strong.

The youth grew; so did the diary. Particularly did George profit from constant use of the college library, then open on Saturdays from twelve to three for the borrowing of books. It is safe to say that few such detailed records of the development of a lad from fifteen to eighteen have ever been kept as that which Strong faithfully set down. And in the background was the youthful, fast-growing city of Mayors Cornelius Lawrence and Aaron Clark, and the exuberant young nation (though much chastened by the panic of 1837) of Presidents Jackson and Van Buren. There were changes meanwhile at home. When George was fourteen his sister Eloise, who had become a much-courted belle, married a wealthy young Boston attorney, Elias Hasket Derby, of the famous shipping family. He was homely, we are told, but a man of fine character and even excessive industry. Derby owned a 600-acre island in Lake Winnepesaukee, and at least once in these years George visited it. George's father, refusing a professorship of law in New York University, began in 1838 to make preparations for receiving the young man into the office.

When commencement approached in 1838, Anthon thought George entitled to rank first in his class—the lad having given continued preference to classics and literature. The rest of the faculty, however, ranked another student first and George second. "I hope," wrote the father, "he will learn from his defeat a lesson at least of humility." George duly read a Latin Salutatory. He had expressed some desire to make his own way in the world. Journalism, science, and teaching all had attractions for him. But his father, now approaching sixty and wishing to reduce his toils, insisted that he give law a trial. In October, 1838, George therefore set to work at the Wall Street office as student and clerk, beginning a career which was not to terminate until in 1873 he retired from practice to take the comptrollership of Trinity Corporation. The elder Strong had lately dissolved his partnership with George Griffin, which had lasted since 1823, and with the son Francis Griffin, who had entered the office about 1830 and had become a partner six years later. Able though the Griffins were, association with them had become a little irksome. George Griffin's immersion in theological studies had begun to interfere with his law work, while Francis Griffin sometimes displayed an excitability and sharpness of temper which led Strong to fear that the two sons might not work amicably in the same office.

V I

Thus it was that, in the fall of 1838, the eighteen-year-old George began copying legal papers and studying Blackstone, Coke, Kent, and the dreary Graham in a three-room suite in Wall Street. At almost the same time his father contracted a new partnership with one of the most interesting attorneys of the period, Marshall S. Bidwell—a man who had just arrived in New York under dramatic circumstances. In this era not yet forty, Bidwell had passed through stirring experiences. The son of an attorney-general of Massachusetts, who had absconded to Upper Canada, he had been admitted to the bar, entered parliament, and risen swiftly to be speaker and a leader of the Liberal Party. At this time Upper Canada was ruled by a small privileged group of merchants, churchmen, and Tory politicians. Bidwell headed a group of moderate reformers, while a combative Scot, William Lyon Mackenzie, rallied a body of more radical malcontents. An explosive situation developed. Just as Lord Melbourne's Government sent word to the Tory Governor, Sir Francis Bond Head, that he should appoint the brilliant Bidwell chief justice of the Court of Queen's Bench, Mackenzie launched the rebellious outbreak of 1837. Though Bidwell had no part in this lawless movement, he was a republican in principle, and the governor took advantage of the crisis to force him to leave the Province. He reached New York as the hero of a political persecution.

Fortunate it was for the Strongs that they could seize upon this talented attorney. The Supreme Court and Court of Chancery, disregarding all rules, at once admitted Bidwell to practice. The elder Strong, besought by friends to take him on trial for ten days, found that he was a man of extraordinary talents and attainments. "He will become one of the first lawyers in this State," Strong exclaimed to his brother-in-law. Bidwell was soon figuring in important cases; for example, in the libel suit brought by Fenimore Cooper against W. L. Stone of the *Commercial Advertiser*, he represented the novelist. As in Canada, he became a great favorite among his legal brethren. A big, impressive man—indeed, he grew positively elephantine—he was kindly, witty, and generous. He soon showed his public spirit by becoming active in the American Bible Society, the New-York Historical Society, the Lenox Library, and other organizations. He formed a close friendship with the great lawyer Daniel Lord. As a student, George Templeton Strong was as much under his tutelage as that of his father. The office, after a brief lull following the panic, became busier than ever. While the elder Strong continued to give his chief attention to probate cases, the drafting of legal instruments, and the preparation of opinions, Bidwell specialized in the law of real property, trusts, and wills, young Strong learning much from both.

In no long time the father pronounced George by far the best clerk he had ever employed. The young man showed just those qualities of fierce application and conscientious attention to details which were indispensable to success. "Should no misfortune befall him," wrote the elder Strong, "he bids fair to make a useful member of society." If George still thought of literary pursuits, he cast fewer longing glances behind him, making his diary, reading, and music his only ties with the arts.

Full admission to the bar came more easily than he had anticipated. He had been troubled by nightmare dreams of some examiner demanding of him: "Mr. Strong, what is the law touching the impounding of pigs taken damage feasant?" Whenever he took up the Revised Statutes to memorize those parts which were *terra incognita*, he always fell into a gentle slumber. He did not like to burden his memory with petty facts. But visiting Utica in July, 1841, to get admitted to the common law bar, he found the three committeemen, Comstock, Hill, and Tracy, amiably weak. "Such a farce of an examination, such an asinine set of candidates, and such prodigiously uncomfortable timber benches," wrote the aspirant, "I never met with before." Thence he proceeded to Saratoga, home of Reuben Hyde Walworth, Chancellor of the State, to be made a solicitor. After some difficulty in obtaining an audience with this distinguished man, he found him very affable and was made a solicitor "in no time." After the required three-year interval he became a counselor-at-law (that is, entitled to practice in the higher courts) in 1844, when he took two examinations described at some length in this volume. Throughout life he felt the keenest interest in broad principles of the law, but little patience with its minutiae.

Naturally, his early years in the office of Strong and Bidwell (which in 1845 became Strong, Bidwell, and Strong) demanded much otiose, irritating toil over routine matters. The succession of old ladies who, coming to have their wills executed, made capricious demands, exasperated him. On December 31, 1839, a certain Mrs. Monroe insisted that he write her will in duplicate, for she wished the two instruments in the same hand. "Darn her picter!" exclaimed the diarist. "If any more old women's wills come into the office, I shall certainly secure an early passage to Texas." Two years later the aged Mrs. Alexander Hamilton was in to see him "about the fortieth alteration of her will and divers other responsibilities." As 1845 begins we find him complaining of the endless work on small legal papers. "I've got to bestir myself or be swallowed up in a kind of snowbank of mortgages, subpoenas, depositions and polyonymous botherations, that are drifting in and banking up faster and faster." Next year the firm won an important case, Bidwell and Griffin making arguments which young Strong thought capital, and quite overthrowing Daniel Lord, who as he saw defeat closing in on him grew testy and waspish. The victory, however, had its penalties. "And now," groaned the young lawyer. "I've got to work like a dragon for a little while, to get up the accumulating arrearage of six-penny jobs that have been postponed to this suit."

The happier side of his early legal career was the opportunity of watching some of the great men of the bar pleading in court, and of making the acquaintance of the principal judges. It was diverting in Robinson's "sperm oil case" in 1841 to see "O'Conor and Bidwell and Lord pitch it into one another till they're tired." He took professional delight in hearing Griffin in 1843 deliver a masterly argument, "clear and cogent almost to demonstration." And in no great time he progressed from the dreary tasks of deed-making and will-writing to the trial of important issues in court. In the spring of 1849 he came to the rescue of the rich merchant Moses Taylor, the victim of a $40,000 judgment taken by default through the use of sharp practice. The opposing lawyer, apologizing and trying to explain, offered to compromise. Strong declined, "with an expression of my opinion which I think Mr. B. will not request his executors to engrave on his tombstone, or quote in his obituary"; and he began vigorously drawing up affidavits and certificates to get the judgment vacated. He was then twenty-nine. Two years later he had great fun writing an elaborate brief in a case of constructive fraud. "I have *never* taken up a case of magnitude before," he writes, "and I now see that the investigation of law in reference to particular cases is the only way to learn the science." And at the age of thirty-two he was pleased when, in Higgins *v.* Nostrand, he delivered a two-and-a-half-hour argument which was "greatly commended by Bidwell."

But he remained primarily an "office lawyer," specializing in realty and probate cases, and seldom making forensic appearances in court. As such, his returns from practice would seem to have been satisfactory. When only twenty-eight, he noted in his diary that up to that time he had made nearly $2,500 a year, the equivalent of thrice that sum a century later, and that he expected to make much more.

The death of his father on June 27, 1855, at the age of seventy-two, was a blow which the diarist felt deeply. The founder of the firm had worked at his accustomed desk down to his brief final illness. In later years, to be sure, he had taken more time for reading and study, and had devoted several days a month to his duties as head of the commission for the public school fund. His integrity, practical wisdom, kindliness, and idealism had made him universally respected. Strong noted in his diary the widespread regret manifested, even in the most hurried of cities, for this beloved citizen. "With good reason: learning—judgment—candor—integrity—justice— charity and kindliness—courtesy to rich and poor—[were] all combined in him. How many have I heard of who spoke of him as the best man they ever knew." He felt, he added, like a child who had lost his way in the streets. No longer could he confide in his father's judgment and ability, setting right every embarrassment and conquering every difficulty. Never was there a juster man. "But his justice was stern and rigorous only against himself. For the faults and frailties of others, he had silence—or sincere pity—or (if the case could possibly bear it) a genial laugh. Never was there a laugh so hearty and kindly as his—especially when some scapegrace was its object."

VII

Already Strong had founded his own home. Early in 1848 he had begun the courtship of Ellen Ruggles, the only daughter of Samuel Bulkley Ruggles, which is so charmingly recorded in this volume. It endured for three anxious, feverish, enraptured months—and then Ellen gave her consent. On May 15, 1848, the ceremony was performed in Grace Church, Ellen behaving like a "heroine"; and it was followed by a "reception— slight déjeuner—and soirée dansante, all very jolly and brilliant." The couple moved the next year into a house built for them by Strong's father at 74 East Twenty-first Street. It was a pleasant district, for Union Square was only half a dozen blocks to the southwest, Madison Square even closer on the northwest, and Gramercy Park at the door; and it was destined to become a historic area, for within a narrow circle were the residences at various times of Washington Irving, Bayard Taylor, Chester A. Arthur, Samuel J. Tilden, the Cary sisters, Horace Greeley, and Peter Cooper and Abram S. Hewitt, and the birthplace of Theodore Roosevelt. Ruggles himself lived on Union Square.

Never, as the diary proves, was there a happier or more harmonious union. Ellen, a handsome woman of literary and musical tastes, and of more marked social inclinations than the diarist, made a devoted wife and mother. In the spring of 1849, after the loss of a stillborn girl baby, she almost died of puerperal fever, only assiduous nursing by her husband and grandmother pulling her through. That harrowing episode Strong always remembered with pain, and the loss of his infant daughter he poignantly felt. Three sons were born to them: John Ruggles (1851), George Templeton, Jr. ("Temple") (1856), and Lewis Barton (1860); youngsters who were both a constant trial and a constant joy after the manner of boys, and in whose education George Templeton Strong took the same painstaking interest that his father had given to his own. The comfortable, unpretentious house on Twenty-first Street required a corps of servants that now seems fabulous: a cook, a waiter who also acted as butler, and two or more maids. Its upkeep sometimes strained the owner's resources. But, filling it full of books and sheet music, buying some good paintings, and offering friends good food and good talk, the Strongs made it a congenial center for a select circle of people of cultivation and breeding—a few of them also people of fashion.

Here they constantly entertained such close friends as George C. Anthon, son of the rector of St. Mark's and nephew of the old Columbia professor; Lewis Morris Rutherfurd, the astronomer; Ogden Hoffman, the lawyer; George William Curtis, journalist and author; Richard Grant White, Shakespearean scholar and critic; Wolcott Gibbs, the chemist; John W. Ehninger, the artist; Theodore Winthrop; various Episcopal churchmen; and a number of musicians, both amateur and professional. Sunday evening became an understood reception period, with sometimes a score of guests. The circle inevitably changed. George Anthon had a causeless quarrel with Strong and dropped out, leaving a painful void; Wolcott Gibbs was called to Harvard; Theodore Winthrop was killed at Big Bethel. To replace these men new friends appeared, none more valued for a time than Frederick Law Olmsted. The diarist, who had inherited his father's solitary tastes, accustomed himself to a good deal of company, and enjoyed an occasional evening at the Century Club, though it is plain that he greatly valued those quiet evenings on which he could read or devote himself to the Ross microscope, or play the piano, or silently go over a score by Mozart or Beethoven with Ellen. His home, whatever his troubles outside, was always a fortress of happiness.

It would be difficult to exaggerate the stimulation and warmth which Strong found also in the household of S. B. Ruggles, five minutes' walk from his own. At the time of the marriage, Ruggles, then forty-eight, was one of the most prominent citizens of New York. He was the principal champion of the use and enlargement of the Erie Canal; an original promoter, as already noted, of the Erie Railroad; and a founder (1839) of the Bank of Commerce. Columbia College had made him a trustee in 1836.

A staunch Whig, he had served in the Assembly. He had reaped large profits from shrewd deals in real estate as the city grew northward; and out of these realty operations had come his establishment (1831) of Gramercy Park, for which he turned forty-two lots over to five trustees. Moses Yale Beach in the 1845 edition of his *Wealthy Citizens of New York* had listed him as worth $250,000, and though this was an exaggeration, he was rich enough to contribute a handsome stone front and bay windows to the house built for the Strongs.

A restless, exuberant man, Ruggles was always on fire with some enthusiasm—usually some plan for the benefit of the city, state, or nation. He had the face of an idealist rather than a man of affairs: a great forehead circled by abundant, curly brown hair, bright, eager, blue eyes, a mobile mouth. Tall and handsome, he moved with quick energy. He was an optimist whose sanguine temperament more than once led him into trouble; a philanthropist, more intent on benefiting others than increasing his own fortune; a great believer in his own church, his own adopted college, his own city and state, all of which owe him more than they have been wont to acknowledge. Hamilton Fish once told John W. Burgess that Ruggles "could throw off more brilliant and pregnant ideas in a given moment than any man I ever saw." At Ruggles's fireside Strong found a large-minded wisdom and an inspiration to public service which gave him more breadth and maturity; and after 1855 he also found in Ruggles a second father. Nothing is more striking in Strong's long diary than the mingled affection and esteem for "Mr. Ruggles" (he is always mentioned in formal terms) which pervades it.

It is clear, too, that Ruggles soon felt for Strong all the affection usually given to a son. A tragic bereavement facilitated the young man's adoption into the family circle. John Rathbone Ruggles, elder son of the philanthropist, went to California in 1849 and the next year died on his return voyage. As the diary shows, Strong was with Ruggles when the news came. A younger son, James Francis ("Jem") Ruggles, survived to fight in the Civil War, to marry Grace Baldwin, and to give Ruggles grandchildren. The Ruggles family was closer to the inner circle of New York "society"— the Astors, Schermerhorns, Stuyvesants, Lenoxes, Brevoorts, and others —than the Strongs had been, so that after the marriage the diarist saw more of the wealthy aristocracy of the town. The two households kept stated feasts together, the Ruggleses always going to the Strongs for Thanksgiving and the Strongs to the Union Square house for Christmas;

and seldom a day passed without some members of the two families seeing each other.

After the death of the elder Strong the law firm was at first continued under the name of Bidwell and Strong. It was proper that Bidwell's name should come first. In 1855 he was fifty-six, and Strong only thirty-five; in learning he had only half a dozen equals in New York; and his prestige and experience gave him a commanding place. None of the regular clients dropped out. "I can't help a feeling of surprise that anyone should stick to me now," wrote the diarist, adding: "God enable me to fill my new place and make me equal to the new duties and responsibilities thus suddenly cast on me." For several years Strong was responsible for running the office and handling most out-of-court work, while Bidwell looked after most of the courtroom pleading.

Then in 1856 the style of the firm was altered to Strong, Bidwell, and Strong. This change signalized the entrance of Charles E. Strong, or "Charley," a cousin of the diarist, into the firm as junior partner. Four years younger than the diarist, and a graduate of Amherst, "Charley" had been carefully trained in the office for a dozen years and had been a member of the bar since 1846. For the remainder of George Templeton Strong's active career he was to be a tower of strength to the firm. He is not known ever to have tried a case in court; but Henry Taft has described him as "a great conveyancer in the broadest sense of that term," and "an ideal family counselor." He was a genial, kindly gentleman, widely read, socially popular, and happy to work hard in various charitable organizations and public institutions.

Only three years after Strong's marriage, his father-in-law suffered a terrible financial catastrophe. He had undertaken to build a number of warehouses on the Atlantic Docks in Brooklyn, to be leased to the government for $60,000 a year, and had borrowed about $325,000, giving mortgages on the warehouses as security. When some dissatisfied creditors refused to renew their notes, on May 23, 1851, he had to suspend payments. His anguish was sad to behold. Strong, doing his utmost to organize practical aid, was wrung by the sorrow of the sensitive man. "It is with keen remorse, bitter self-reproach, a sense of defeat, of disgrace—of indignation at himself for projects which seemed demonstrably certain of success six months ago—all preying on him so fiercely that, were it not for the incessant exertions his affairs demand just now and the constant strain on his mind to devise help for those whom his fall is likely to shatter, I should fear much for the effect of this on his physical frame." The situation was made more difficult by the wild charges which Francis Griffin, trained in the Strong law office, brought against Ruggles. This hot-tempered lawyer had endorsed Ruggles's notes to the amount of $70,000; he declared that he had been deceived as to the facts, though actually he was protected by mortgages normally worth $80,000; and giving way to vindictive rage, he invented outright lies. Ruggles, thought Strong, should have repelled the falsehoods with more asperity.

With the aid of his son-in-law and many friends, Ruggles finally extricated himself—ruined. In the summer of 1851 he bought a tin sign, put an advertisement in the press, and resumed the practice of law. William B. Astor, James Gore King, and other wealthy admirers helped him extend his notes. Francis Griffin, seeing that he would get his money back and more, began to acknowledge that he had been hasty and unjust, but he died before he could make public retraction. By 1853 Ruggles was on his feet again, though he continued burdened by debt down to the eve of the Civil War. Happily for his family, his wife had a considerable property inherited from her father and brother.

VIII

The city grew, reaching a population of half a million by 1850 and eight hundred thousand by 1860, creating Central Park, opening the Astor Library, and sending Columbia College up to Forty-ninth Street. The diary grew with Strong's activities and with the city. Its character changed, too, as his social circle widened, as he accepted various public responsibilities, and as the struggle between North and South became more intense, finally culminating in civil conflict.

Strong's election to the position of trustee of Columbia College in 1853 opened an important new chapter in his life. The post threw him into close association with President Charles King, son of Rufus King, a big hearty man of great dignity and polished manners who had come to the leadership of the college after a varied mercantile and editorial career. It also brought him into constant relations with twenty-odd fellow members of the board, of whom about one-third were men of sufficient distinction to be included long afterwards in the *Dictionary of American Biography*. They numbered Clement Clarke Moore, son of the second Episcopal bishop of New York, a grave, sweet-tempered man whose name is immortalized by his verses on St. Nicholas; the redoubtable Gardiner Spring, pastor of the Brick Presbyterian Church and a Puritan of Puritans; Ogden Hoffman, the greatest criminal lawyer of his time in New York, a genial, indolent, brilliant man; Senator Hamilton Fish, whose great qualities neither Strong nor anybody else fully comprehended until, at the age of sixty, he became Secretary of State under Grant; Gouverneur Morris Ogden, a peculiarly stubborn conservative, whose hostility to change led Strong to term him "that dense, impenetrable, and dangerous King of the Pachyderms," but who was honest and in his way intelligent; and the former professor, Henry James Anderson, whom Strong characterized as an indecisive, unenterprising prodigy of acquirements in all branches of learning.

It was an interesting body of men—and a very discordant body, as the resounding controversy over Wolcott Gibbs promptly showed.

No one saw more clearly than Strong the weaknesses of Columbia in 1853, or criticized them more unsparingly. The college had utterly failed to keep pace with the development of the community or the expansion of knowledge. Its course of study was archaic, its discipline that of a high school, its library puny and ill-managed, its scientific equipment contemptible, and its spirit narrow, church-bound, and timid. The trustees not merely failed to win the support of wealthy citizens or to capitalize on the affection of the alumni; they actually repelled offers of help or accepted gifts with chilling reluctance. Indeed, the first money gift from an alumnus was not received until 1857, and came not from an Episcopalian but a Jew, Sampson Simson. Strong at once aligned himself with the minority group led by Ruggles—a group which wished to enlist the support of New Yorkers, modernize the curriculum and equipment, make the students responsible for their own behavior and application, and develop enough new departments to convert the college into a university. The year after he joined the board it was split asunder by the bitter fight against the appointment of Wolcott Gibbs, a Unitarian, to a scientific chair. Beyond question Gibbs possessed superior qualifications. Beyond question, too, the letter and spirit of the college charter and the state laws forbade the exclusion of any person from the privileges or offices of Columbia on account of his religious tenets. President King was wholeheartedly behind Gibbs. So were a large body of fellow-alumni—he was of the class of 1841. But a phalanx of five clergymen, abetted by such reactionaries as Ogden and William Betts ("Log of Logs"), defeated the eminent scientist and elected a man of whom Columbia came to be thoroughly ashamed. It was a victory for what Strong called "the Boeotian fogyism, the abyss of inert, stolid, obstructive, obstinate, mulish, wilful stupidity," that was crippling the college.

Yet if the battle was lost, the campaign was ultimately won. Ruggles and Strong wrote a brilliant pamphlet, moderate in its tone but devastating in its logic, entitled *The Duty of Columbia College to the Community . . .*, which, scattered far and wide by Moses H. Grinnell and a body of alumni, won general approval. They pointed out that George II had chartered King's College in New York and Göttingen in Hanover at almost the same time; that Göttingen in a little German town had a faculty of a hundred distinguished men, a splendid library, more than 1,500 students, and world-wide influence; and that Columbia, seated in a rich city, had but six professors, 140 students, a pitiful library, and no influence whatever. The fight to reinvigorate the college was at once resumed. Step by step, with Ruggles and Strong always in the van, the institution was given elements of strength and growth. At times Strong became discouraged; in 1857 he wrote, "The diagnosis is very bad indeed." But the progressive element never gave up.

In the diary we can follow their gains, one by one. The School of Law was established in 1856, with Strong one of its founders. In 1857 the college removed to the new Forty-ninth Street site. Next year Theodore W. Dwight, the thirty-six-year-old grandson of the famous President Timothy Dwight of Yale, was brought from Hamilton College to take charge of the Law School, becoming its very soul. Strong greatly admired him as man and teacher. In 1858 Ruggles reported eight resolutions for organizing a postgraduate course, the first vigorous (though at first unsuccessful) step toward university standing. Then in 1863–1864 Strong threw himself with boundless zeal into Thomas Egleston's plan for a School of Mines; and when this new engineering branch was brought to a standstill for lack of apparatus and laboratory supplies, he was one of the small group which furnished the $3,000 needed for a start.

The 1850's also found the diarist giving faithful service to Trinity and to the Episcopal Church in general. Strong's father had been an elder in the Presbyterian Church, and George as a youth had attended services at the Scotch (or Second) Presbyterian Church with his father and sister Mary quite as often as he had gone to St. Paul's Chapel with his mother. In college, however, under the teaching of John McVickar, he had become a violent High Churchman. The Oxford Movement which R. H. Froude, John Keble, J. H. Newman, and others originated in England as a protest against Low Church and Broad Church Anglicanism quickly spread to America, and Strong, reading *Tracts for the Times* with passionate enthusiasm, became one of its devotees. This was the period of the long rectorship of the Rev. William Berrian at Trinity, the erection (1841–1846) of the beautiful new church of which Richard Upjohn was architect, and of a steady growth at Trinity in wealth and influence. On Ascension Day in 1846 Strong saw Bishop Samuel A. McCoskry of Michigan consecrate the new building. He labored as vestryman, gave Dr. Berrian loyal support, helped pass the contribution plates on Sunday, lent advice, whenever asked, on church music, and took a lively interest in the General Conventions and the proceedings of the House of Bishops.

IX

All of Strong's other public services paled, however, beside his Civil War activities in the Sanitary Commission. As the North went to war in 1861 his interests, previously local, became national—and his diary broadened into a stirring national record. He had awakened rather slowly to the sectional crisis. In the fall of 1860 he had been delighted by the Republican victory at the polls, and in December horrified and angered by the secession of South Carolina. Then he had followed with bated breath the exit of other cotton states, the vacillations of the weak Buchanan, and the sharp struggle of the loyal John A. Dix, Jeremiah Black, and Edwin M. Stanton against Southern traitors in the Cabinet. Early in 1861, as Lincoln passed through New York on his way to the capital, Strong had a momentary glimpse of the great rail-splitter's face. The diarist never for a moment doubted that secession must be met, if necessary, by force. He read Lincoln's inaugural with praise for the clank of metal in its lines. Then he was lifted into a new world when, in his fervent style, he wrote: "Saturday, April 13, 1861. Here begins a new chapter of my journal, entitled *'WAR— EXSURGAT DEUS.'*"

In the first pages of his Civil War journal a feeling of exultation predominates. The Southern attack and the President's call for 75,000 men aroused the city in a way that Strong, depressed by weeks of vacillation, uncertainty, and treasonable talk, found electrifying. "Change in public feeling marked, and a thing to thank God for," he writes. "We begin to look like a united North." Bennett's *Herald* and James Brooks's *Express* suddenly retracted their disloyal views and turned to patriotism. Mayor Fernando Wood came out with a proclamation—"The cunning scoundrel sees which way the cat is jumping," commented Strong. Visiting Governor's Island, the diarist talked with three hundred raw recruits and heard a farm lad from near Rochester declare: "I voted for Abe Lincoln, and as there is going to be trouble, I might as well *fight* for Lincoln." He induced the rector and vestry of Trinity to hoist the national flag on the church tower; "The biggest thing that has happened in New York in *my* day," exclaimed one onlooker. On April 18, while he was on business at City Hall, a roar rolled down Broadway. The Sixth Massachusetts was marching through on the way to Washington. "Immense crowd. Immense cheering. My eyes filled with tears. . . . God be praised for the unity of feeling here. . . . If it only lasts, we are safe." And a few days later, after the Baltimore outbreak, he was heartened to see the fighting demeanor of some Irish-American recruits leaving for the front. "When they were told they were to have not only the regulation arms but revolvers and bowie knives, too, they danced and yelled with delight. 'We can fix that Baltimore crowd. Let 'em bring their pavin' stones; we boys is sociable with pavin' stones!' "

War it was; and how should the forty-one-year-old lawyer serve his country? The answer came with that wonderful organization, the Sanitary Commission, the great civilian organization for dealing with wounds and sickness in the field and alleviating the horrors of war behind the lines. A committee under the Rev. Henry Whitney Bellows, representing New York medical men, the New York hospitals, and the Women's Central Association of Relief, went to Washington. They found the medical staff of the army an antiquated, incompetent, bureaucratic body, utterly unfit to meet the crisis; they discovered the War Department filled with confusion, demoralization, and ignorance; they learned that the army camps lacked the first elements of sanitation. Sweeping reforms and a powerful popular organization to prevent disease, supply ambulances and medicines, equip hospital boats, help recruit surgeons, inspect camps, and care for the maimed, were needed at once. A great clergyman and a great physician, Dr. Bellows and Dr. William H. Van Buren, labored frenziedly to create the Sanitary Commission. They obtained due powers from President Lincoln and Secretary of War Cameron. They forced a weak Surgeon-General, Dr. Finley, to abandon his opposition. They gathered a strong body of Commissioners—Alexander Dallas Bache, Wolcott Gibbs, Dr. Elisha Harris, Dr. Cornelius R. Agnew, and others. They established a nation-wide machinery for collecting supplies and money. And at their second meeting, in June, 1861, they added to their body George Templeton Strong.

He came in as treasurer and member of the small executive group which directed the Commission throughout the war. How he threw himself into the arduous labors of this indispensable agency; how he helped raise and disburse $4,925,000 in cash and direct the application of an immense amount of donated material and labor; how he visited encampments and battlefields; how he conferred with Lincoln, Stanton, McClellan, and Grant; how he supported and advised the farsighted Frederick Law Olmsted, who became chief executive officer; how, without a cent of compensation, he spent half his time in committee meetings and field errands, the diary modestly discloses. A letter to S. B. Ruggles dated from Washington, September 8, 1861, suggests the desperate urgency of the need which the Sanitary Commission met, and the spirit in which Strong worked:

We have been actively at work, sitting from ten A.M. till ten P.M. with only a couple of hours' interval, and with committee business to attend to besides. The necessity for the commission is more apparent than ever, and I devoutly trust the financiers of New York and Boston will provide us with the ways and means. The Medical Department here is imbecile beyond expression. Take this for an instance. The authorities admit that there may be a great battle here at any moment and that they may be suddenly called upon, any day, to provide for five thousand wounded men. Now can you believe that they have not on hand at this moment medicines, beds, or hospital room for *three hundred*? And more marvelous still, that they cannot be induced to take a solitary step toward supplying the deficiency? They say, "In the Mexican War we had not a wagon-load of reserve stores"; "If there's *a battle* we'll send to New York for medicine," and like imbecilities. Meantime typhus and other diseases are appearing with great force in the camp near Alexandria—and if McClellan made a forward move of five miles with half the troops across the river, the Regimental Hospitals would have to be emptied into the General Hospitals, which are unable to accommodate a quarter of them.

I mention this not as suggestive that the Commission should undertake to supply what Government is bound to furnish, but as showing the utter idiocy of the [Army] Medical Bureau and the importance of sustaining an organization to keep them up to their work and apply the hot end of the poker to the Surgeon-General. Fortunately we have the coöperation of McClellan's Medical Director (Tripler), and on Saturday we addressed a very stiff remonstrance about this non-feasance to the President, to Cameron, and to General Scott. If the evil be not promptly cured, I think we shall make an open issue with the Department. In that case I shall ask you to help us with a newspaper war before the people. But we ought to keep quiet a day or two yet, and see if our remonstrance produces any effect.

Tripler has taken an important step already (on our application, between ourselves). He has appointed a board to examine all volunteer surgeons, and oust all who are without proper qualifications. As I happen to know of one surgeon whose medical education has been acquired only in a *barber* shop, and of another who prescribes nothing but ipecac and

Epsom salts, I am not surprised to learn that this order has created some muttering. We shall want all the money we can get.

Five months later, on February 3, 1862, Strong was able to record that the Sanitary Commission had received $700,000 at its central office alone, besides three or four million dollars' worth of stores given to its depots. "It has become a 'big thing,' has this Sanitary Commission, a considerable fact in the history of this people and of this war."

But in becoming a big thing, in combating epidemics of smallpox, typhoid, and dysentery, in succoring the wounded on every battlefield, and in forcing the wretched Medical Bureau to reorganize its methods and personnel, the Commission made many enemies. Its war with the imperious, jealous, irascible Stanton gave drama to its record. The Commission, forcing Finley out of office, had brought in as Surgeon-General a comparatively young man of great force of character, scientific capacity, keenness of intellect, and originality of method, Dr. William A. Hammond. As imperious and immovable as Stanton, he gave the Secretary little deference—and Stanton hated him. Strong records a dialogue in the spring of 1862 between Bellows and Stanton. The Secretary confessed that he was no friend of the Commission, and in fact detested it.

"But why, Mr. Stanton, when it is notoriously doing so much good service, and when the Medical Department and the whole army confide in it and depend on it as you and I know they do?"

"Well," growled the Secretary, "the fact is the Commission wanted Hammond to be Surgeon-General and I did not. I did my best with the President and with the Military Committee of the Senate, but the Commission beat me and got Hammond appointed. I'm not used to being beaten and don't like it, and therefore, I am hostile to the Commission."

Hammond was forced out of office—though not until he had done his work. The high-strung Frederick Law Olmsted, his health impaired by toil and anxiety, resigned to take charge of the Mariposa mines in California—though not until he, too, had achieved great results. But Strong toiled till the end of the war and beyond, discharging every duty. His law office had to be kept going, and "diligent in Wall Street" remained a familiar diary entry. He continued to give a great deal of time to Columbia College, where Frederick A. P. Barnard replaced Charles King as president in 1864; the creation of the School of Mines in particular costing him much labor and anxious thought. He was one of the eight founders of the Union League Club of New York, established early in 1863 to "cultivate a profound national devotion" and "strengthen a love and respect for the Union," and he became one of the strongest pillars of that organization. But it was the Sanitary Commission to which he gave most liberally of his time and energy. Throughout most of the conflict the executive committee, with Strong, Bellows, Wolcott Gibbs, and Cornelius Rea Agnew as its backbone, met every day at three o'clock to transact business, often laboring into the night; and no member was more constant in attendance than this busy attorney.

Indeed, it is evident that during the war few men in the country toiled harder than Strong, or with less thought of reward. Financier and lawyer in one, he kept his accounts with meticulous care. "No public corporation of the widest relations," said Dr. Bellows later, "could have had a finer system of checks and balances, a closer periodical examination by disinterested auditors of vouchers filed and systematized." An all too typical day, Monday, February 6, 1864, found him working a long morning at his law office; seizing a hasty lunch; attending a meeting of the library committee of the Columbia trustees; catching a street car to 823 Broadway for a Sanitary Commission session; eating a quick supper; and then hurrying off to the Trinity vestry.

X

The post war era was in many ways a period of adversity and depression for the diarist. Like countless other professional or salaried men, he suffered cruelly from the inflation which raged 1865–1873, finding it almost impossible to make ends meet. His legal revenues decreased, for he had lost touch with clients during the conflict, and as he later confessed, "never got myself thoroughly into legal harness again." Then, too, in this era of the Tweed Ring, the Erie scandals, Black Friday, and the corruption represented by Judges Barnard and Cardozo, he was disheartened by "the progressive debasement of Bar and Bench." He took charge of some important cases: the argument of the Seamen's Savings Bank against some dirty, blackmailing legislation at Albany, the debt-recovery case of Carter *v.* Taylor, the partition of the great Schermerhorn family estate, the case in the Federal Supreme Court of the Bank for Savings *v.* Field, and others. But he no longer felt his early zest for practice.

Fortunately, he had efficient partners in the learned Bidwell and the alertly industrious Charles E. Strong. The latter was, as always, a boon companion as well as an able business associate. The former was a walking arsenal of knowledge. "Instead of studying up a question," Strong tells us,

"I usually went to Bidwell and received from him an offhand abstract of all the cases bearing on it and all the considerations on either side. He loved law as a pure science, and this sometimes led him to advise according to strict logical principles, when it was clear and certain that any jury and any court would assuredly decide otherwise. . . . He loved to insist on the logical inference from a rule of law, no matter what might follow." Fortunately, also, the diarist had a private income now of more than $5,000 a year.

Despite frequent attacks of dyspepsia and sick headache, Strong refused to falter in his public labors. He wrote a financial history of the Sanitary Commission which was striking for its analytical insights as well as its compressed statement of facts. Encouraged by a brisker spirit among the Columbia trustees and by the genuine vision of President Barnard, he worked with unabated enthusiasm to develop the School of Mines and improve that Law School which was rather the possession and preserve of the gifted Theodore W. Dwight than an arm of the college. New professors had come in: the erudite and egotistical Francis Lieber in political science, Charles Murray Nairne in philosophy and literature, and Charles Davies in mathematics. Particularly did Strong find joy in two exceptional men—Charles F. Chandler, who not only gave the department of chemistry new breadth and power, but became an invaluable municipal servant, and Thomas Egleston who with the aid of Francis L. Vinton and others lifted the School of Mines to a high level. Although the diarist did not live to see a true university born, he did see Columbia brought to the verge of its sudden amazing renascence.

In music he was responsible for a noteworthy innovation. During his boyhood New York had possessed a society for ecclesiastical music, mentioned by Philip Hone. Strong had always taken a special interest in religious compositions, and had long thought that Trinity and other churches fell short of a proper musical standard. Out of a series of Sunday musical soirées at his house, much enjoyed by the select circle invited, sprang a resolve to found a Church Music Association. A committee was formed; a series of concerts was planned; Ellen adroitly brought New York society behind the undertaking; and for several years the performances scored both an artistic and a popular success. Difficulties with first one and then another conductor wrecked the enterprise, but not until it had done something to elevate taste in this field. Meanwhile, Strong had been elected and reëlected president of the Philharmonic Society.

In 1872 two heavy blows befell the diarist. On October 22, Elias G.

Drake, Jr., who had worked in the law office for seventeen years and had lately been advanced to a partnership, announced his impending resignation. "The change involves trouble and work and new arrangements," wrote Strong, "and fills me, in my present morbid condition, with horror and dismay." Two days later Bidwell, sitting at his desk, fell dead of apoplexy. Strong was horrified by the sad event. "For thirty-four years," he wrote sorrowfully, "I have entered the office daily and said, 'Good morning, Mr. Bidwell,' and this morning I walked in, to see him lying dead." He acknowledged that at 68 Wall Street they had "all leaned on him, *too much for our own good.*" No longer did Strong have any heart for his legal practice. He took one more large case, that of the Associated Savings Banks against the national government. But when in December the Trinity Church vestry, through John Astor, asked him to accept the comptrollership just vacated by General John A. Dix, he gave his consent.

"It seems like a dream," noted the conscientious man, "that I should be free to keep away from Wall Street tomorrow without an uneasy conscience, and a feeling that someone might think me a malingerer or a shirk."

His days of comparative leisure, however, were to be few. His complaints of ill-health grew more frequent. Though he did not know it, he had been attacked by tumor of the mesenteric gland, accompanied by enlargement of the liver. In June, 1875, he was confined to his house, seriously ill. His sense of humor remained with him to the last; he could write almost gaily of his Strassburg-goose liver, and of nausea which "left me as weak as a sea-anemone at low water." On Wednesday, July 21, he died, and two days later was buried from Trinity Church. The pallbearers were men frequently mentioned in this diary—John Jacob Astor, John J. Cisco, William C. Schermerhorn, Henry Parish, John Taylor Johnston, George C. Anthon, Dr. Cornelius R. Agnew, and Wolcott Gibbs; and among the mourners who crowded the church were ex-Governor John A. Dix and President Ulysses S. Grant.

XI

The qualities of a great diarist are both rare and peculiar. A Pepys or Evelyn, a Wesley or Parson Woodforde, a John Quincy Adams or Philip Hone, must first of all have a distinct and interesting personality. Even in this voluminous record, not all the remarkable personal qualities of George Templeton Strong are revealed. He was a man of deep, unaffected modesty. "His nature was essentially private," wrote his friend Henry W. Bellows; "his studies were his own reward; his ambition was distinct from public recognition or applause." Joined with this modesty was an ingrained shyness. As Bellows added, he was "always a little distant, requiring the advance to come from others." When on the retirement of Charles King his associates talked of making him president of Columbia, he shrank from the idea of letting himself even passively seek the office. "It would be a positive degradation to which I would not submit"—and he quickly and decisively withdrew his name. Fruitfully as he labored for Columbia, for Trinity, for the Society Library, for the Philharmonic, and for the Sanitary Commission, he took care that only small groups of insiders should know how much he did. He was happiest withdrawn from the public gaze, living with his books, his music, his family, his religion, and his own rich nature. He sought only his own approval. As the diary shows, he had an almost morbid tendency to worry, a trait that he seems to have inherited from his father; and his worry sometimes produced severe fits of melancholia.

His standards were exact, his sense of duty was high, and his punctiliousness was unfaltering. It would be hard to find an unfair note in the whole diary. Even at the height of the Wolcott Gibbs controversy he wrote: "Personal feeling influences me but little." When the question arose of buying Foxe's *Book of Martyrs* for the Columbia Library, he was for getting it—but for also buying S. R. Maitland's *Letters* to show its worthlessness. Himself always a gentleman, he was quick to perceive any deficiency of gentlemanliness in others; for example, we may note his remarks on Richard Grant White and on the rich Griswold Gray. A certain fastidiousness went with this quality. At William B. Astor's on the last day of January, 1861, Strong was astounded to see Fernando Wood in a white cravat and evening dress; having taken a new wife and an opera box, Wood was trying to attain social station. "But I do not think I should invite him to this house," comments Strong, "were I twenty William B. Astors, or had he married twenty Miss Drake Millses."

Yet he had a hearty sense of democracy, evident in the large number of his plain self-made friends and in his praise of certain democratic institutions. He was caustic in his denunciation of demagogy and corruption, but in the essential soundness of the American system he but seldom and briefly lost faith. The most interesting, and at the same time the most moving, of all the many stories in the long diary, is the story of the slow but steady conversion of Strong from an initial distrust of Abraham

Lincoln to a wholehearted admiration of both the man and the statesman, until in 1865 he declared that history would place the homely rail-splitter, whose name was Faithful and True, on a pedestal as high as, if not higher than, that of Washington.

And however conscious of standards, however fastidious, Strong had no trace of priggishness. A rich vein of fun runs through all his long record. He wrote in 1851 of the Columbia Trustees as the "Board of Incurables which dozes periodically over the affairs of that institution." At about the same time the furor over Jenny Lind amused him. "Lindo-mania unabated; it's a prevalent morbid passion for assuming the form of an ass for the privilege of drinking in her sweet voice through the pre-ternaturally prolonged ears of the deluded victims of the terrible new disorder." A little later he spoke of Father Ruggles as "cathedral mad, as though bitten by a rabid transept." His sense of fun often expressed itself in epigram, as when he wrote of the Southern abuse of Ben Butler for his rough work in Louisiana: "quite right that rats should hold terriers un-constitutional and scandalous." Frequently it found vent in witty phrase-making. The opposition trustees in the Gibbs case offered "rhinoceral resolutions"; the Draft Riots were a combination of "rabbledom and rebeldom"; Jeff Davis in 1865 was the "fugaceous Confederate rebel pseudo-President." And how Strong loved to salt his diary with good stories; for example, the story of what a soldier of the boastful John Pope said when the tale of Samson's slaughter with the jawbone of an ass was read to him, and the story of the statistician who was aghast because the medical historians of the war, in listing the fevers from which troops had suffered, had omitted one of the commonest of all these diseases—puerperal fever!

Of enthusiasm, too, Strong always had more than his full allotment. His passion for those musicians he loved, such as Beethoven, Mozart, Bach, and Handel, is as fervently expressed as his contempt for most of Verdi, and his detestation of Liszt. He had a strong romantic vein, which found one expression, especially in early life, in an intense delight in nature, and another in his exuberant joy in Keats and Ruskin, in Turner's "Slave Ship" and other romantic paintings, and in such books as Gil-christ's *Life of Blake*. In boyhood he was all enthusiasm for old coins and medals; at another stage, marine life and aquaria delighted him; later still, the Ross microscope opened a new world; and after the war he became a rapt devotee of mineralogy. These passions, giving color to his life, impart their hues also to the diary. And throughout his career he was an ardent collector and reader of books. When Dr. James Wynne published his *Private Libraries of New York* in 1860, he listed Strong as owner of one of the thirty-one important collections. He had some fine illuminated manuscripts; a copy of the *Nuremberg Chronicle* (1493); Cicero's *Cato Major* printed by Benjamin Franklin; and a number of volumes from Charles Lamb's library, including a copy of Ben Jonson with Lamb's notes, and an edition of Donne's *Poems* with numerous holograph notes by Coleridge.

It is one requirement of a great diarist that he give us a rounded picture of his own world. In doing this vivid descriptive talent is a help; and Strong can be very vivid at times, as in his magnificent reproduction of the scenes in New York following Appomattox. The principal qualities necessary, however, are a daily renewed interest in human life and activity; a sense of a clearly realized social sphere revolving about the diarist as center; an ability to blend personal emotion with a record of passing events and scenes; an appreciation of the importance of picturesque details; and a belief that the writer's existence is, or can be made, a harmonious whole. That Strong was an artist who was consciously trying to render his own city, his own time, and his own personality in such form that later generations could comprehend them, and who put painstaking effort into this task as into everything else that he did, is clearly evident. The diary was plainly written for posterity, and the author justly regarded it—hurried though many entries had to be—as one of his public services. The reader who follows this great record from 1835 to 1875 will find himself magically transported back to a bygone republic and a bygone era, to witness a dramatic march of events, and to study a sweeping panorama of social and political change; and he will find that his guide in this adventure is one of the most cultivated, sincere, intelligent, highminded, and delightful gentlemen that New York ever produced.

ALLAN NEVINS

CONTENTS

Preface   *page v*

George Templeton Strong: The Man and the Diarist,
by ALLAN NEVINS   *page ix*

Dramatis Personae   *page xlix*

1835   *page 1*
RETURN TO COLLEGE · SCIENTIFIC INTEREST · A STUDENT ROW ·
JOINS PHILOLEXIAN · GREAT FIRE OF 1835

1836   *page 10*
THE LEARNED MR. WELFORD · MURDER OF HELEN JEWETT · BOOK
AUCTIONS · GENERAL BERTHEMY · NEW HAMPSHIRE TRIP · JOINS
ΑΔΦ · VISIT TO PHRENOLOGIST

1837   *page 48*
PERSECUTION OF DR. BARBER · SAMUEL WARD'S LIBRARY · COLUM-
BIA SEMI-CENTENNIAL · PANIC IN WALL STREET · BOSTON TRIP ·
QUEEN VICTORIA BEGINS HER REIGN · SUMMER AT WHITESTONE

1838   *page 80*
JOINS SOCIETY LIBRARY · ARRIVAL OF *SIRIUS* AND *GREAT WEST-
ERN* · LOCKHART'S *SCOTT* · MR. BIDWELL · GRADUATED FROM
COLUMBIA · BEGINS STUDY OF LAW

1839   *page 97*
WAR TALK · OXFORD TRACTS · J. Q. ADAMS'S SPEECH · NAHANT
TRIP · REBUILDING OF TRINITY · JOHN MASON'S WILL · ANTI-
RENT TROUBLES

1840   *page 121*

LEXINGTON DISASTER · FIRE IN STRONG HOME · UNITARIANISM · QUEEN VICTORIA'S WEDDING · HARRISON CAMPAIGN · ARRIVAL OF THE *BRITANNIA* · ELECTION

1841   *page 156*

MR. LLOYD'S INSANITY · DEATH OF PRESIDENT HARRISON · BAR EXAMINATION · SARATOGA · ADMITTED SOLICITOR IN CHANCERY · GENERAL CONVENTION

1842   *page 173*

MRS. STUART'S TRIAL · ERECTION OF TRINITY CHURCH · MESMERISM · FIRST APPEARANCE IN COURT · DORR'S REBELLION · CROTON WATER CELEBRATION · COLT'S LAST DAYS · *SOMERS* MUTINY

1843   *page 197*

THE MILLERITE DELUSION · ARTHUR CAREY'S ORDINATION · VISITS TO ALBANY AND THE CATSKILLS · THE CROTON WATER CASE

1844   *page 223*

NATIVE AMERICAN RIOTS IN PHILADELPHIA · POLK DEFEATS CLAY · TRIAL OF BISHOP ONDERDONK

1845   *page 253*

BISHOP ONDERDONK CONVICTED · ACADEMY OF DESIGN · DOWNTOWN FIRES · PROFESSOR LONGFELLOW

1846   *page 272*

TRINITY CHURCH CONSECRATED · NEW HAVEN AND THE WINTHROP WEDDING · THE ANTI-RENT MOVEMENT

1847   *page 287*

CAMPAIGNS IN MEXICO · CENTURY CLUB · NORTHWARD GROWTH OF CITY · WHIG VICTORY IN NEW YORK

1848 *page 308*

POLK'S PEACE TREATY · MISS ELLEN RUGGLES · COURTSHIP · MAR-
RIAGE AND HONEYMOON · TWENTY-FIRST STREET HOUSE · CALI-
FORNIA GOLD MANIA

1849 *page 341*

MACAULAY'S *ENGLAND* · PECUNIARY WORRIES · ELLEN'S ILLNESS ·
THE ASTOR PLACE RIOT · CHOLERA EPIDEMIC · A HOUSEWARMING

Index *page 367*

ILLUSTRATIONS

Endpaper:
New York, looking east and south from the steeple of St. Paul's Chapel, 1848. From a colored aquatint drawn by J. W. Hill, engraved by Henry Papprill, and published by H. I. Megarey. *Courtesy of Harry Shaw Newman.*

GEORGE TEMPLETON STRONG   10
Inscribed by the subject: "George Templeton Strong I, while a student at Columbia College, *circa* 1838. His appearance led to the nickname 'Black Hawk', among his college friends, referring to an Indian chief, then much talked of." *From a watercolor drawing owned by George Templeton Strong III of Larchmont, N. Y.*

THE STRONG RESIDENCE, 108 GREENWICH STREET   11
Nos. 110 (residence of Aunts Olivia and Jane Templeton) and 112 beyond; Carlisle Street is the cross street in the distance. From a charcoal drawing made in 1950 by Edward Punnett Chrystie. *Courtesy of Kenneth Holcomb Dunshee.*

COLUMBIA COLLEGE   42
The College building and College Green from Church Street. From the earliest surviving photograph of Columbia, taken about 1853 by Victor Prévost. *Columbiana Collection, Columbia University.*

CITY HALL PARK AND THE CROTON WATER FOUNTAIN   43
The "dolorous City Hall Bell" (5 July 1837) was housed in the small structure visible at the left of the tower in this engraving. From *American Scenery, Illustrated*, by T. Addison Richards, N.A. (New York, 1854).

PARK PLACE FROM BROADWAY   74
Colman's Literary Rooms, "that rascally citadel of humbug" (7 January 1837), on the corner; Columbia College in the next block, beyond Church Street; the Hudson in the distance. From a drawing by A. J. Davis, engraved by Fenner Sears & Co., London; published 1 August 1831 by Hinton, & Simpkin & Marshall. *Columbiana.*

ST. JOHN'S CHAPEL AND PARK   75
Varick Street looking south from Laight Street towards Beach; photographed in the winter of 1866–67 as the park was being destroyed for the erection of the Hudson River R.R. freight house. *Courtesy of the New-York Historical Society.*

WILLIAM ALEXANDER DUER   106
From a painting by an unidentified artist; owned by Columbia University.

The Reverend JOHN McVICKAR
From a photograph taken about 1859. *Columbiana.*

CHARLES ANTHON 107
From a photograph taken about 1861. *Columbiana.*

JAMES RENWICK
From a painting by an unidentified artist. *Photograph in Columbiana.*

GEORGE WASHINGTON STRONG 234
"The old gentleman"; from a portrait by Daniel Huntington. *Courtesy of Cadwalader, Wickersham & Taft, owners; Frick Art Reference Library photograph.*

EEL-SPEARING AT SETAUKET (1845), and BOYS CAUGHT
NAPPING IN A FIELD (1848) 235
These well-known paintings by William Sidney Mount were commissioned by George Washington Strong, and represent scenes in his youth. The former is now owned by the New York State Historical Association, Cooperstown, N.Y., and the latter by the Brooklyn Museum; they are reproduced here by courtesy of these institutions.

ELIAS HASKET DERBY and his son RICHARD HENRY DERBY 266
From a daguerreotype made about 1854. *Courtesy of Dr. Richard Derby of Oyster Bay, L.I., son of Dr. R. H. Derby.*

STRONG AND PROFESSOR ANTHON IN THE COLUMBIA
CHAPEL, and THE ATT'Y 267
Drawings by G. T. S. in the Diary.

THE GREAT FIRE OF 1835 298
The burning of the Merchants' Exchange, 16 December 1835. From a lithograph by Alfred Hoffy, published by H. R. Robinson. *Courtesy of the Home Insurance Company.*

THE GREAT FIRE OF 1845
View from Broad and Stone Streets, 19 July 1845. From a lithograph by Nathaniel Currier. *Courtesy of the Home Insurance Company.*

The Right Reverend BENJAMIN TREDWELL ONDERDONK,
Bishop of New York 299
Engraved by W. L. Ormsby from a photograph by Brady. *Columbiana.*

The Right Reverend JONATHAN MAYHEW WAINWRIGHT,
Provisional Bishop of New York
Wood-engraving by Leslie from *Gleason's Pictorial Drawing-Room Companion* (Boston), 11 November 1854.

TRINITY CHURCH 330
Second edifice, built in 1788 and torn down in 1839; from a drawing by A. J. Davis, engraved by Eddy. *Columbiana.*
Present edifice, built 1842–46; from a drawing by the architect, Richard Upjohn, engraved by J. N. Gimbrede. *Columbiana.*

Mrs. GEORGE TEMPLETON STRONG 331
From a photograph in the Diary, dated July 1864.

Mrs. PHILO RUGGLES
Mrs. Strong's "indomitable grandmamma"; from a photograph in the Diary, dated January 1864.

DRAMATIS PERSONAE

HENRY JAMES ANDERSON (*Harry*), graduate of Columbia (1818) and the College of Physicians and Surgeons, was professor of mathematics in Strong's time; later they were on the board of trustees together. Strong summed him up in one long, breathless sentence October 7, 1836.

CHARLES ANTHON (*Bull, Taurus, Charley*, etc.), Jay Professor of the Greek and Latin Languages at Columbia, the best-known member of the faculty of his time and something of a terror to the students, was the son of a German-born surgeon-general in the British army long stationed at Detroit, and a French mother. He was graduated from Columbia in 1815, practised law briefly, and in 1820 began his long teaching career at the college, to which he added in 1830 the rectorship of the Columbia Grammar School. A powerful, irascible man, he was a self-taught classicist who never married, shunned society, and over a period of forty years turned out an incredible number of grammars, lexicons, dictionaries, and heavily-annotated editions of Greek and Latin authors.

GEORGE CHRISTIAN ANTHON, Columbia 1839, son of the rector of St. Mark's and nephew of Bull, with whom he did not get along, was Strong's frequent companion and chess-antagonist in college and later. He joined the students in Strong's office for a time, but later abandoned the law for teaching.

NATHANIEL WILLIAM CHITTENDEN (1816–1885) was one of Strong's closest friends in early life. He came from Ulster County, and was in Alpha Delta Phi and Philolexian at Columbia with him. Chittenden took his degree in 1837, studied law in the Strong office, practised a few years in New York City, and went to San Francisco in the pioneer days, becoming one of the leading lawyers, specializing in land titles. He acquired and developed large tracts of land in the Pajaro Valley, and amassed a large fortune; he never married.

The CLASS of 1838 at COLUMBIA: Frederic Anthon, Edward Anthony, Mancer Mark Backus, Thomas Colden Cooper, Richard Henry

Douglass, Isaac Vanderbeck Fowler, John Hone, Philip Hone, Jr., Benjamin Tredwell Kissam, John Mason Knox, Jeremiah Larocque, Alfred Mersan Loutrel, William Brinckerhoff Moffat, Benjamin Romaine, William Edward Snowden, Charles Spear, George Templeton Strong, William Riggin Travers, Francis Marion Ward, Henry Hall Ward. *Temporary members:* Thomas Amerman, Henry Anthony Waldburg Barclay, James Leworthy Berrien (Princeton 1838), John King Duer, Thomas Addis Emmet, John Beekman Fish, Charles B. Freeman, Theodore Gordon, Alexander Henriques, John J. Hunt, I. Wilmot Johnson, Divie Bethune McCartee (M.D., Pennsylvania 1840), Joseph H. Procter, Henry Feltus Quackenbos (M.D., Coll. P. & S. 1841), Lewis Van Antwerp, Cornelius Isaac Van Wyck (Princeton 1839), James Witherspoon.

HENRY AUGUSTUS CRAM (1818–1894), Princeton 1837, had taken the Grand Tour and attended the Harvard Law School before he entered the Strong office in 1840; at first George was dubious about "his moustache, his *distingué* air, and the exquisite cut of his coat," but soon revised his opinion and they became good friends. He was afterward a prominent New York lawyer.

ELIAS HASKET DERBY (1803–1880), Harvard 1824, third of the name in the great Salem family of merchant shipowners to achieve eminence, he studied law in Boston with Daniel Webster, specialized in railroad cases, and was later connected with numerous railroad enterprises in New England. On September 14, 1834, he married Eloise Lloyd Strong, half-sister of George, and of their seven children, five survived. Strong was devoted to his Boston relatives, paying them many delightful visits.

WILLIAM ALEXANDER DUER (*Prex, Praeses*) had been a midshipman in the navy, a lawyer in New York and Rhinebeck, a student of the Spanish civil law with Edward Livingston in New Orleans, a New York assemblyman, and a judge of the Supreme Court in Albany before coming to Columbia as president in 1829. Prex's annual course of lectures to the Seniors on the Constitutional Jurisprudence of the United States bored Strong, and the lad was wrathful and flippant at times over Duer's weaknesses, but respected him and never wrote him off with the dreadful finality of which he was capable.

GEORGE GRIFFIN (*Griff, Counselor Griffin*) was an excessively pompous, correct and boring character whom Strong regularly deflated in his diary. A Yale man (1797), he had begun the practice of law in Wilkes-Barre, but left town when the citizens perpetrated a practical joke on him by electing him high constable of the borough. He went into partnership with the elder Strong in New York, and by his eloquence and learning soon attained prominence and wealth. In 1838 he retired from the firm to write treatises on theology.

THOMAS STRONG GRIFFING (*Tom*), Columbia 1841, a first cousin once-removed of Strong, was a lieutenant in the Mexican War; in the Civil War he was assistant adjutant general with the rank of captain under General McClellan in the Peninsular campaign; at other times he was a farmer at Setauket, Long Island.

The Reverend EDWARD YOUNG HIGBEE (1801–1871) was a clergyman much to Strong's taste, viz., High Church and "un-humbug-gical." A graduate of General Theological Seminary, he became assistant minister of Trinity Church in 1836, serving at St. Paul's Chapel and later at Trinity Chapel in Twenty-fifth Street.

WILLIAM TEMPLETON JOHNSON (*Templeton*) was Strong's cousin, son of William Johnson (Yale 1788), Reporter of the Supreme Court in New York, and Maria Templeton ("Aunt Johnson"); he was a Columbia graduate (1832) and lawyer in New York and went to concerts and fires with Strong. At his marriage to Miss Laura Winthrop in New Haven, June 10, 1846, Strong was groomsman.

The Reverend JOHN McVICKAR (*Mack*), Columbia 1804, son of a wealthy New York merchant of Irish birth, had married the daughter of Dr. Samuel Bard of New York and Hyde Park. McVickar was made Professor of Moral Philosophy at Columbia in 1817, and for nearly half a century he taught each class an hour a day, carrying them during their four years through English grammar, rhetoric and oratory, outlines of modern history, taste and criticism, logic, history of philosophy, and political economy, ending up with the evidences of natural and revealed religion. He also found time to serve as chaplain for the military post on Governor's Island, to write a dozen books, to preach in Episcopal pulpits and to keep an eye on his New York real estate. McVickar influenced Strong more than any of his other teachers or associates at college and was undoubtedly responsible for his defection from the Presbyterianism of his father to High Church Anglicanism.

The Right Reverend BENJAMIN TREDWELL ONDERDONK (1791–1861), fourth Protestant Episcopal Bishop of New York, Columbia graduate (1809) and trustee, was the son of Dr. John Onderdonk, physician of New York. His brother, Henry Ustick Onderdonk (Columbia 1805), was Bishop of Pennsylvania. Within one year both brothers were suspended from their high office, the elder for excessive drinking, the younger after a trumped-up church trial in which he was convicted of unepiscopal laying on of hands with certain women of his diocese. It seems apparent, from a voluminous literature, and from Strong's entries, that the Bishop's chief crime was being a High Churchman. In the Cathedral of St. John the Divine is a recumbent marble effigy of the old gentleman, and at his feet is coiled the serpent of slander.

JEHIEL JAGGAR POST (*Jehaggar*), Princeton 1837, was Strong's crony when they were studying law together and building organs. At his death in 1874, Strong wrote that it was a great while since he had seen or heard from him, though he lived only a couple of blocks away: "He was a most singular fellow, with an intellect vigorous and acute far above the average, but always subject to paralysis from indecision."

JAMES RENWICK (*Jemmy, Dr. Blowpipe*, etc.), Professor of Natural and Experimental Philosophy at Columbia from 1820 to 1853, son of a wealthy Scottish merchant of New York, Columbia graduate of 1807, was a man of distinction and varied talents whom Strong inveterately underestimated. A recognized authority in every branch of engineering of his day, he was constantly employed in public service. He invented the famous inclined planes employed on the Morris Canal to carry the canal boats over the elevations on the route, and in 1840 was one of the three United States commissioners who surveyed the North East Boundary, their data being used in concluding the Webster-Ashburton treaty. Renwick was a prolific writer in his own field, and also in politics, belles-lettres, and biography; he was a talented amateur of architecture, a skilled water-colorist, and a close friend of Washington Irving.

JAMES RENWICK, Jr. (1818–1895), Columbia 1836, like his father, could do no right, according to Strong; but the prevailing opinion was otherwise. Employed at first as a civil engineer on the Erie Railroad and the Croton Reservoir at Forty-second Street, he was self-trained in architecture and in 1843 at twenty-five won the competition for Grace Church in New York, one of the best examples of the Gothic Revival in the

United States; he followed with Calvary Church, the Church of the Puritans on Union Square, the Smithsonian Institution and the old Corcoran Gallery in Washington, the Free Academy (City College) on Twenty-third Street, St. Patrick's Cathedral on Fifth Avenue, Main Hall at Vassar College, and numerous hotels, theatres, city houses, and "cottages" at Newport and Lenox. He was one of the most successful architects of his day, and at one time owned two yachts. Most of his work is out of fashion now, but an unusual number of his buildings have survived.

WILLIAM COLFORD SCHERMERHORN (1821–1903), Columbia 1840, studied law with the Strongs and played the organ and chess with young George. An admirable representative of the best of old New York, he devoted a long life to the family estates, to music and the church, and to quiet public service and benevolence. A tower of strength to Columbia in its development into a university, he served forty-three years as a trustee, ten years as chairman of the board, and was the donor of the natural science building at Morningside which, along with a half-million-dollar endowment for religion given by his daughter, Mrs. John Innes Kane, perpetuates his name.

CHARLES EDWARD STRONG (*Charley*), 1824–1897, George's first cousin once-removed, had two years at Yale and was graduated from Amherst in 1843, immediately entering the Strong office; from this time the cousins were in intimate association, socially and in business, until parted by death.

PETER REMSEN STRONG (*Pete, Pedrillo*), third cousin of the diarist, was a B.A. of Columbia at seventeen (1840) and a naïve and gullible lad when he was thrown among the sophisticates of the Strong office. He was admitted to the New York bar, but never practised law, residing on the old Remsen place in Newtown, Long Island, until his death in 1878. In 1853 he married Mary Emmeline Stevens, daughter of John Austin Stevens (Yale 1813), president of the Bank of Commerce; the details of their divorce proceedings were painfully chronicled by G.T.S. in late 1865 and 1866.

THEODORE WINTHROP (Yale 1848) was a person of much the same temperament, whom Strong met at the Johnson-Winthrop wedding in 1846. They took to each other at once. A brave, sensitive, talented, mercurial fellow, Winthrop had a varied career; he worked in New York and Panama for the Pacific Mail Steamship Company, sailed up the coast to San Francisco, Oregon, and Washington, crossed the continent on horseback to St. Louis, then lived on Staten Island, studied law, and opened an office in New York. At the beginning of the Civil War he went to Washington with the Seventh Regiment; no summer soldier, he stayed on when they returned home, and obtained a post with General Benjamin F. Butler of Massachusetts. At Little Bethel on June 10, 1861, he died gallantly with a bullet through his heart.

1835

RETURNS TO COLLEGE · SCIENTIFIC INTERESTS ·
A STUDENT ROW · JOINS PHILOLEXIAN ·
GREAT FIRE OF 1835

———❦———

*S*trong's diary begins the day he returned for his second year as a member
of the class of 1838 at Columbia College. For the next three years college
was all-important, and beginning with brief jottings he developed into so
eager a diarist that he left one of the most extensive, honest, and amusing
records ever written by an undergraduate.

Columbia, beginning its eighty-first year in 1835, was situated in the
residential section of New York on College Green, a quiet two-block fenced
area shaded with sycamores and bounded by Murray and Barclay Streets,
College Place (West Broadway) and Church Street. Park Place led eastward
one block to "The Park," now City Hall Park. The college edifice, a long,
narrow building facing south, three and a half stories in height and surmounted
by a small astronomical observatory, had been built in 1756–60. King's College and its student body, never numbering over thirty, had been housed in it;
the Revolution halted instruction, and during the British occupation the building was used as a military hospital. The college, revived and renamed Columbia after the war, had enlarged the structure to provide residences for the
faculty, but for more than a century, beginning about 1800, furnished no
dormitory accommodations for students, a fact which largely restricted enroll-
ment to residents of New York City.

Although King's College had graduated men who played important parts
in the Revolution and the establishment of the new republic, the school had been
preponderantly Anglican, and therefore Tory. After the war the people to
whom it would have looked for support had had their property expropriated and

[1]

were in exile in Canada and England. Although President Washington had given his blessing to Columbia by attending the commencement of 1789 a few days after his inauguration, and the new corporation included Hamilton and other Revolutionary patriots, the new wealthy and ruling classes of New York did not show any haste in coming to its support, and for well over half a century Columbia remained relatively poor. The student body, homogeneous during this period, was drawn largely from the homes of the wealthier professional and commercial citizens.

The faculty in Strong's time consisted of five men of marked individuality who taught a fixed course of study heavily weighted with the classical disciplines: William Alexander Duer, president, who lectured to Seniors on constitutional jurisprudence, and Professors Charles Anthon, James Renwick, Henry James Anderson, and John McVickar. Various other men held the title of professor in Columbia College in these years, but their position was actually that of privat-dozent; they were principally employed elsewhere and were available to students for instruction in subjects outside the regular curriculum at extra fees. We need not accept all Strong's adolescent judgments of the stern gentlemen composing the faculty; in later years he revised many of these estimates himself.

Matriculation was conducted by the president himself; each student signed his name in the order of his scholastic rank in a large folio volume, promising to abide by the statutes of the college. At the beginning of the term in 1835, President Duer admitted one hundred students: twenty-two Seniors, twenty-three Juniors, twenty-nine Sophomores, and twenty-six Freshmen. The annual tuition fee was $90.

October 5, MONDAY.   108 Greenwich Street, New York. Went to college at half-past seven and had the pleasure of remaining there *solus* till half-past nine. Matriculated for the Sophomore year, and had the most atrocious pen to write my name with that mortal ever beheld. *Afternoon*, cloudy again, and rainy tomorrow, I suppose. Purchased some jars for an electrical battery.

October 6.   As I anticipated, raining most diabolically. How on earth we shall get to the church I can't imagine, for it blows and rains tremendously, and no signs of clearing, either. I suppose we shall have to go in funereal style—in carriages—and the faculty in a hearse.

Afternoon. We went in omnibuses. In spite of the weather, the church was very crowded and very hot. The speaking was better than usual, far better than at the [New York] University last July. The music was capital. I took the first classical medal. Got home at half-past three.

Columbia at this time held its commencement at the beginning of the academic year. The exercises described above were in St. John's Chapel on Varick Street, and twenty-three were graduated. Top man was Orlando Harriman, Jr., afterwards an Episcopal clergyman and the father of Edward Henry Harriman (1848–1900), railroad executive, whose great estate, Arden, at Harriman, New York, was given to Columbia in 1950. The best-remembered graduate of 1835 was the literary scholar, Evert Augustus Duyckinck.

October 10, SATURDAY. Went to college and entered the library and took out a book, as the statutes allow. Came home and struck off for Staten Island; went on top of the pavilion and was back by half-past one. *Afternoon*—fixed jars for battery.

October 12. Taking notes with Renwick. His room puts one in mind of Virgil's vision of Tartarus, and it smells like everything horrible.

October 13. Recited Aristophanes for the first time; very amusing when read as it ought to be. Purchased an electrometer for my machine.

October 14. Recited Plautus this morning for the first time. My Delphini edition helps me along gloriously and the variorum notes are well worth examining.

October 16. Geographical lecture with Anthon. Renwick gave us a lecture today in a voice like the wheezings of a broken-winded bellows.

October 17, SATURDAY. Out all the morning. Made a good haul in the numismatological line. *Afternoon*—coated the rest of the jars. I suppose, though, that this battery is destined to turn out like the generality of my other attempts, and that is, not amounting to much. My electrical machine is out of order too, so I don't see how I am to charge the battery if I should finish it.

October 21. . . . An idea has entered into my mind, viz., to make a plate electrical machine, for my own is as much out of health as ever. Plate glass is most atrociously dear, though. Looking at my *Scriptores Græci Minores* which arrived yesterday; beautifully printed, but Gaisford might have raised a little more commentary while he was about it.

October 27, Afternoon. Went out after a turner to make the frame of my machine—31 Greene Street up an alley five feet high and one broad—and of a most unchristianlike dirtiness; the man has an unpronounceable Dutch name which I forget. They have just come from Germany and can neither speak English nor understand it decently. As to the frame, if it gets done at all, I fancy it will be fit for nothing but firewood, for I couldn't get the man to understand me, though I preached for half an hour.

October 29. Made a cruise up to Greene Street. Frame "ees noot feeneeshed yet, sare." McVickar in the course of his lectures said that he had a work bearing the date 1473, the oldest in the country. *Quære de hoc:* I have one of 1470.

November 3, TUESDAY. The frame of my machine finished at last; answers pretty well. We have been recording all this week. Tomorrow Herodotus.

November 5, THURSDAY. Went to college; got there at half-past eight. At about quarter of nine, nearly all the Freshmen and Sophomores being assembled, a party of the former posted themselves near the chapel gallery door and commenced a racket: two benches kicked downstairs, hats, books, shot and slates with a variety of missiles flying in every direction. Enter the worthy Mr. Dugan,[1] with his usual "less noise, gentlemen," but in two minutes more the hubbub was recommenced in a sort of treble note that sounded like the yells of a strangled cat. Thirty boys (young gentlemen, I mean) with vigorous lungs, screaming in chorus, is no joke, and when some of the Sophomores joined, the noise was "prodi-gi-ous." Re-enter Dugan, and exit again with the same effect as before; then comes a noise of something advancing upstairs like distant thunder, and the Praeses himself makes his appearance, like a porpoise in a gale of wind. "All attend me in my room, if you please, gentlemen"—and exit the Prex leaving all of us, and especially the Freshmen, in a state of considerable bother. In two minutes, behold us all comfortably seated in the President's room, which has at least one advantage over the outside of the chapel door, and that is a good fire. Then comes a preachment from the Prex which I shall not take the trouble of writing down, but as the essence of a letter usually lies in the postscript, so the substance of his speech lay in the end thereof, which was as follows: "I shall therefore

---

[1] Thomas Dugan had been janitor of the college since 1825; he was also sexton of Trinity Church and an undertaker.

expect to see you all before the Board[2] tomorrow morning at ten." Very agreeable prospect this. However, the Prex said that there were some amongst us that he couldn't, wouldn't, shouldn't and didn't suspect of being such spooneys as to make a noise for nothing at all, but still he wanted to investigate the matter and so we must come. I was certainly quiet enough at the time and I guess I can prove it. I suppose a majority of the others will scrape off by lying; it's human nature. I thought that I should be in a predicament, while in the Prex's room, if he attempted to decimate us, for I found that as we sat I was precisely the tenth from the end. It's an unpleasant business altogether, for though I don't see what they can prove against me or what they can accuse me of, unless of having been in the second story when some fools were making a noise in the third, I suppose I shall get into a scrape; it's just my luck.

November 7, SATURDAY.   Went to college, and after trotting up there in the rain and hearing some absurd attempts at speechification in the chapel, went downstairs, and after a while we were summoned into the Sanctum Sanctorum. Present besides the Praeses, Anthon, Renwick, McVickar and Anderson. Roll called—there being forty-five of us—then the venerable Prex proceeded to make a speech at us in which he told the learned Board what naughty boys some of us had been, and then asked us separately whether we had any hand in it, to which question about half, and myself, of course, among the number said No, and the other half made some very wry faces and said Yes. Then the Praeses wiped his spectacles and blew his nose and told us that he shouldn't say anything more about it and we might be off, concluding with "I presume, gentlemen, that you are satisfied?" addressed to the Honorable Board, to which weighty question McVickar replied "Yessar," Renwick gave his head a jerk sideways, Anthon gave his ineffable skull a movement of six inches from the perpendicular, and Anderson, who had nearly fallen asleep during the Prex's harangue, replied by an inarticulate grunt. We cleared out as fast as possible and went down into Renwick's room to see some experiments on combustion with chlorate of potassium, in oxygen, chlorine, etc. We had not oxygen enough, so Douglass and myself stayed to make some. Remained there till two o'clock and then came off. *Afternoon.* Went to college again. Got there before Douglass, and burned my fingers with some phosphorus like a fool and stained my clothes with sulphuric acid like a spooney. Got home at six.

[2] "The Board" was the Columbia term for the full-time members of the faculty assembled as a body.

November 21, SATURDAY. Was voted in unanimously last night at the Philolexian. Walked up after college with John Hone[3] and made a splendid haul of antique coins in exchange for minerals, thirty specimens, including one of the Ptolemies. On my way home encountered Chittenden, brought him home, and fired off some more of the phosphuret of lime, thereby scenting the house from top to bottom. At college Spear engaged to come down this afternoon, and as he invited himself, I thought it only fair to direct him to *180 Greenwich*. He found the place notwithstanding, and when he came I saluted him with the remainder of my phosphuret of lime, thereby increasing the stench to infinity, so that when my honored parents entered the house they were nearly knocked down backwards.

November 25. The glorious Evacuation Day,[4] glorious in one point, at least, and that is that it allows us to kick up our heels all day at our leisure. Douglass came down in the course of the morning and we posted up to college together to try some chemicals. The laboratory was locked up, so we got in the window and spent three hours there making musses and stenches without number.

November 26. Exactly a year ago today that I commenced my gymnastic operations. This is first-rate weather for exercising. I wish the establishment was downtown.

November 27. FRIDAY. At about six it began to snow and I took up my march for the Philolexian. I found nobody there, everything dark and locked up, and I was anticipating a comfortable sojourn in the snow for an hour or so, when Dugan's little imp came to light the fire and dust the room, and it was soon quite respectable. They soon collected and at about seven the meeting was called to order by the worthy Mr. [Russell] Trevett, the vice-president, the president himself being absent. Then I made myself scarce, and was summoned into the room again soon after to witness the sublime ceremony of initiation into the occult mysteries of Philolexianity. I thought I should have had the impoliteness to laugh in the face of the august officers while the "ceremony" was going on . . . and no wonder, the vice-president staring in my face like a bullfrog in spectacles and Mr. Secretary fumbling about for a pen, and at last finding one

[3] John Hone and Charles Spear were classmates of Strong. Hone, the son of Isaac S. Hone, who lived on Bond Street, was a younger contemporary of Mayor Philip Hone's son John. Philip Hone, Jr., son of the mayor and diarist, was a member of the class of 1838.

[4] New York was still celebrating the anniversary of that great day in 1783 when General Washington rode into the city from Harlem at the head of the American troops as the last remnants of the British occupation force were embarking.

that wrote like a poker. Then began the other matters; the subject for debate was: "Are literary reviews advantageous to literature?"—decided affirmatively. The debate was a very good one and the *Observer* was read; a composition (absurd) followed, and then a miscellaneous discussion.

Few American colleges of the nineteenth century were without a pair of literary societies with Greek names. Columbia's, called Philolexian and Pei-thologian (established in 1802 and 1806 respectively), had meeting rooms in the college building, and each boasted a library of some two thousand volumes of current fiction and belles-lettres, fields entirely unrepresented in the college library. The Philolexian Observer *was a manuscript magazine read at meetings. Strong wrote for it constantly, frequently making use of articles in the obscure journals and books to which his insatiable reading led him. He was an enthusiastic member of the society, and rarely missed a meeting.*

December 4, FRIDAY.   Anthon has been highly savage all week, but today he was absolutely ferocious; the geographical lecture was highly edifying. *Evening.* Went off to the society in company with Papa, who was condemned to be vice-president of the Webster meeting. As it rained, our meeting was rather thin. The debate was rather dry: "Ought this country to aid Texas?"—decided in the negative. Afterwards some young scamps thought proper to vote in Mr. Satan as president of the anniversary committee. Rejected on the ground that he did not belong to the society. *Quære de hoc*: I am inclined to judge that he does.

December 10, THANKSGIVING DAY.   Went to church; after church went up to the Bowery to see the "splendid collection of wild Hanimals" which arrived there. I do not think that it is quite as well attended as it was last year. Otherwise it is precisely the same old thing over again.

December 12.   Diabolical weather, snowing and rainy. Woke up as stupid as possible. Rode to college and began arranging for the experiments. Renwick came in soon after. The experiments began as soon as the class came. All that we did was to make some most atrocious stenches with olefiant gas and phosphoretted hydrogen. A carriage was sent for me about one, and I came home. *Evening.* Sufficient for the day is the evil thereof, and on this principle I did not look at a lesson as I felt too stupid for studying. Took up the *Mysteries of Udolpho* instead and fell asleep in the midst of winding passages, unearthly sounds, ghosts, devils, distressed maidens and tyrannical ruffians—no great compliment to Mrs. Radcliffe's powers to entertain.

December 16.   Went to college and bargained with [Richard Henry] Douglass for a gold Arabic coin of his. *Evening.* At about nine o'clock there was an alarm of fire. Papa went to bed notwithstanding it looked near the office. The fire is evidently an extensive one and shines splendidly on the shipping and houses in the rear. Mr. [Rensselaer] Havens has just come to call Papa up, as the office is in danger. It is a tremendous fire, by his account. They have just left. *Eleven o'clock.* Mr. Lambert has just come in. He thinks the office out of danger, but the fire is still raging in Exchange, Pearl, Front Streets, etc. It is very cold—mercury at zero—and by his account the fire is yet unchecked. *Twelve o'clock.* The fire as we can see from the front windows is still raging, and Papa has not returned. I would give a good deal to be there. I shall turn in, notwithstanding, as my anxiety for the office cannot prevent me from feeling very sleepy.

December 17.   Very bad news. Papa came in this morning at five and his return woke me up. The Exchange, the office, everything in that quarter is going, and by his account we are in some danger, as the fire is unchecked. I went to college at eight. The smoke is hanging over all that part of the city, and from what I could learn, the fire is unchecked. At half-past eleven I left the college and walked down with Douglass, whose father's store is burnt. Such a scene of confusion I never witnessed. The fire is still raging in South Street. Papa has got a new office at 12 Wall Street. Brought Douglass home with me. *Afternoon.* Went up to the region of the fire, which is not yet got under. It presents a splendid spectacle.

December 18.   Everybody is talking of the fire, which is now got quite under. The citizens have turned out as patrols. The loss is estimated at thirty million dollars. Went to the society in the evening.

Strong's account of the Great Fire of 1835 is somewhat disappointing in the light of his later interest in such spectacles. He soon became an enthusiastic fire-goer and in time developed a real connoisseurship, disdaining mean and uninteresting fires and taking a great interest in the really spectacular ones, of which he wrote as careful a review as he would of a stage performance. In common with most enthusiasts, he was usually on the side of the fire, but when the big store directly at the rear of his home burned on the night of May 30, 1837, he worked valiantly, and wrote a fine tribute to the firemen.

December 22.   A considerable number of the students missing, having taken the holidays into their own hands. After the third hour, I asked

McVickar, the "extempore Prex," to let the upper classes have the use of the chapel for a class meeting (to draw up a petition and have a little sport). He enquired "What was the object?" and then observed that "we might have it, but that he could grant nothing contrary to the letter of the statutes." It seems that he gave different directions to Cerberus, for after the fourth hour when we went upstairs we found ourselves locked out, and a row ensued. Mr. Dugan in vain endeavored to keep the peace and the rebels were only dispersed by the appearance of McVickar himself, who was coming in a great hurry, looking like a turkey cock in a gale of wind. He was evidently resolved to inflict a speech upon us, but on reaching the scene of action he found that all had vanished and that he had nothing but Dugan and Dugan's black dog on whom to expend his oratory, quite a disappointment.

December 23.   Went to college. On entering the chapel we found Mack's audience to consist of *no* Seniors, two Juniors, five Sophomores and thirteen Freshmen. He waited as long as he decently could in hopes of a fresh supply, but in vain, until in the midst of the prayer three Sophomores walked in one after another, each accompanying his entrance with a tremendous slam of the door. No objection was made; he was glad enough to get an audience on any terms. Went into Anthon's room. He looked round the room—evidently in a considerable degree of wonder— "No more students in the chapel, Mr. Strong?" "No, sir," said I. "Well, gentlemen," was the reply, "of course, as a professor I can't give you such a piece of advice—altogether contrary to my principles—but nevertheless, if I was in your place, I rather think I should vanish out of the back door." We took his advice, of course.

1836

THE LEARNED MR. WELFORD · MURDER OF HELEN JEWETT ·
BOOK AUCTIONS · GENERAL BERTHEMY · NEW HAMPSHIRE
TRIP · JOINS ΑΔΦ · VISIT TO PHRENOLOGIST

The studious youth took part in more campus activities this year, though his adult disdain of prankishness kept him out of most of the juvenile scrapes of his classmates. The maturity of his taste and interest is shown especially in the additions made to his personal library. Book-collecting was to be one of the continuing satisfactions of his life, and it is clear that the books were bought to be read, not merely to adorn his shelves. The sale-catalog of his library (Bangs & Co., November, 1878; 1763 lots) shows that Strong's tastes changed little in later years.

February 29, MONDAY. I have taken up my pen again after an interval of two months, caused partly by my ardor for laziness and partly by my ardor for science, exemplified in blowing up my hand. *Memorandum.* Never to pound chlorate of potassium and sulphur together again without thick gloves and never to pound them at all when I can help it. . . .

March 2, WEDNESDAY. . . . In chapel some wretch crammed a pair of immense woollen gloves into the stove, where they could not be got out again, and such a stench I never smelt. Anthon gave us a long talk about dialects, Sanskrit roots, "chain of languages," and everything else of which the mind of man can conceive. Stayed after college to see two Freshmen attempt to manufacture some of Renwick's "soluble glass"— such a piece of absurdity I never witnessed.

March 3. On leaving for college I heard the cry of fire, and as I saw smoke in the direction of Trinity Church, I turned up Thames Street as

GEORGE TEMPLETON STRONG
ABOUT 1838

THE STRONG RESIDENCE, 108 GREENWICH STREET
NOS. 110 AND 112 AND CARLISLE STREET BEYOND

fast as I could. On reaching Broadway I saw that the fire was in [Charles]
de Behr's book store—the lower story was in a complete blaze and in a
very few minutes the upper story was in a similar condition. I met Fowler
among the crowd and we walked in front of the fire. The whole inside
of the building was like a furnace and no engines arrived yet, though the
buildings on each side were in great danger. At last the engines began
to come up, and they began to work, though not till the fire had extended
upon the roof and garret of the building on the side nearest Pine Street.
Ladders were raised and a party soon established themselves on the roof,
the garret windows were dashed in and the hose introduced. At last,
down went the roof of de Behr with a considerable crash and at the same
time down went the chimney of the building next door, right among the
party on the roof. "No one killed—play away No. 13" was the only
notice taken of it. I left soon after, as the fire was pretty much got under.
Mentioned it to [Professor] Anthon; he was horrified at the news.

Evening.   I see by the paper that de Behr has lost $30,000. He did
not save a single book nor any thing else; the alarm was so sudden that
he had to jump out of the window only half dressed. He had a superb
collection of books when I was in his store last, some very splendid
works of DaPonte's,[1] classics *ad infinitum* (by the by, he asked a scandalous
price for some of them) and I believe the largest collection of French,
Spanish, and German works in the country. The fire arose from the carelessness of a boy lighting a fire next door; the little reptile ought to be
tarred and feathered.

*Early in March, Strong learned that the examinations were to be held in
a fortnight and lamented: "The deuce take all examinations—they are the
most bothersome, confounded things that the genius of a professor ever invented.
If it be true that a man's life is in proportion to the amount of trouble he experiences, and that quiet people live much the longest, I am sure every examination
must shorten one's life a year at least." Nevertheless, he studied diligently—
and worried excessively—until the week arrived.*

March 7. . . . Set out on a cruise after a pair of India rubber shoes.
They are in great demand just now, and well they may be, for the streets

[1] Lorenzo DaPonte (1749–1838), son of a Venetian Jewish tanner, teacher,
Catholic priest, rake, exile, librettist for Mozart, printer, grocer in Elizabethtown,
New Jersey, and professor of Italian at Columbia from 1826 to 1838, supplemented
his income in his later years by importing Italian books to New York; two English
translations of his *Memoirs* were published in 1929.

of New York look like those of Venice or Amsterdam, or any other aquatic city, only the water that fills them is as dirty as it well can be, and thickened with mud to the consistence of molasses.

March 8. . . . Went out on another India rubber crusade; got a pair for $3, two inches thick and so wide that I can almost get them on either way. Stopped at Appleton's to see some coins that Mr. [Charles] Welford[2] was to bring there to show me. My mouth watered at the sight. I would give any thing to get them, and so I hinted to him, but he does not seem willing to part with them, and there seems little chance of my ever getting them, so I may as well give up all thoughts of it, but coins of Alexander the Great, Philip, Cassander, Hiero, Abgarus, and of Etruria, Carthage, Phoenicia, the Mamertines, Libya, Syracuse and Messana, &c., &c., are not to be met with every day. I would give my ears for them (almost), but I don't see any prospect of my ever having a chance. I can't conceive what this Mr. Welford is doing as clerk in a book store. He seems to know something about everything—talks about Sanskrit roots, Polyglots, scarce editions, boustrophedon inscriptions, and everything of the sort, like a second Anthon—and seems moreover perfectly well acquainted with the works of many authors not often read, and well versed in all sorts of literature. I should think he might find a better situation than that of a clerk. . . . Met Mr. John Jay[3] and his intended walking up Broadway. She's as ugly as sin; I think he's made a bad bargain.

March 12, SATURDAY. . . . As I was going up Broadway, I met that little blockhead young [James] Renwick, who was going to see the end of Capt. Harvey's trial. We walked across the park to the building where the United States Court is held and found a crowd round the door which was not yet opened for admission. . . . After some time we got in, and then after a considerable of a sojourn in the hall, the gallery door was opened and we crowded upstairs. I don't think I was ever squeezed quite

[2] Charles Welford was later in business with John Russell Bartlett as Bartlett & Welford, booksellers and importers; in 1857 he formed a partnership with the first Charles Scribner as Scribner & Welford, to import foreign books; he died in March 1885.

[3] The grandson of the statesman of that name; he was a Senior at Columbia, and was married June 23, 1837, to Miss Eleanor Kingsland Field of New York. That day Strong wrote: "John Jay is married this evening. Poor devil! I saw him this morning; he looked as weak as a lamb and perfectly resigned to his fate. Alas!" Jay was, like his father, William Jay, an ardent anti-slavery man, and interested himself in many humanitarian causes; he was U.S. minister to Austria 1869 to 1874 and president of the American Historical Association in 1890.

so thoroughly as in the crowd, but at last we got seats. The gallery was quite full. No one below but Judge [Samuel Rosseter] Betts, a half-dozen lawyers, &c., and the prisoner who stood wrapped in his cloak, looking sober and anxious enough—and no wonder. After a time Mr. Maxwell came in and told the constables "that there were about half a dozen gentlemen down at the door and they'd better admit them." It was done, but the half-dozen gentlemen amounted to about sixty ragamuffins of all sorts and sizes who came pouring in, to the great amazement of all. After this, the whole court became pretty thoroughly crowded and at about five o'clock the jurors began to appear. The prisoner took his seat with his back toward me (I wish I could have seen his face at that moment), the roll was called and the questions put: "Are you agreed upon your verdict?" and "What is it?" At the answer "Not guilty," several voices exclaimed "Good!" and the gallery, and indeed the lower part too, began to clap and then most obstreperously. Half a dozen constables screamed for silence and orders were instantly given to clear the galleries; it was obeyed, but we lost nothing, for by the time we got downstairs the court was adjourned. Stopped at Appleton's. Saw those coins again—if I could only get them!

Evening. Studied myself stupid over Legendre and then took up Priest's *Antiquities*; it contains, I think, more absurdity than one would imagine could be crammed into the compass of an octavo.

March 14, MONDAY. . . . Stopped at Chilton's to subscribe to Silliman's[4] lectures; there are to be 1000 tickets only. Went up to the stable and saw the puppies of which Elbert[5] spoke—very pretty and prodigiously fat. If I can keep one I will; they are English fox hounds.

Afternoon. Went up to Appleton's and saw a copy of Evelyn's *Diary*, which has struck my fancy exceedingly. . . .

March 15. Knox came down as usual. Worked at mathematics till eleven, when Mr. [Frederic] Anthon came in. He came to borrow my chemistry notes and brought with him some ridiculous anecdotes which kept us in a roar till it was too late to do anything more; by his account the examination is going to prove a mere farce. I hope it may do so, but I fancy he'll find himself mistaken. According to his account, McVickar asked a Senior "Who was Confucius?" and the answer was "A German

---

[4] Professor Benjamin Silliman, the elder, of Yale.
[5] Elbert was the family coachman. In May, Strong recorded with regret that he was going to leave: "He has been with us since some time in March, 1829, and there could not be a better coachman in every respect—he is going to be a *cartman!*"

chemist," to which the worthy Professor replied "Yessar—he was rather a Chinese philosopher."

Walked up to the stable with him, and thence to his house where we concocted some of the most atrocious stenches conceivable. Indeed my acquaintance with chemistry is chiefly in the art of making stenches, and in that I must confess that I am an adept. Worked at my Virgil and at eight in the evening got through the first book, of which 300 lines were new. Thirty more pages in history and then turned in.

March 16. . . . Spent the afternoon at Appleton's. Saw the cheapest book that ever came within my reach. Robertson's works—in seven superb quarto volumes for $12!!! I must have it by all means. . . .

March 18. . . . Took a walk around the burnt district [of the Great Fire of 1835]; there is enough mud there to put out the fire if the whole city were burning. A very great many stores going up—some have reached their second story and scarcely a single lot that has not some laborers upon it. . . .

I have not had time to learn my piece for [which] I was appointed to display my oratorical abilities [at the society] tonight, so I took up the debate instead. Question was whether trade unions are beneficial or not. Every one took the negative, so I volunteered on the affirmative, though utterly against my conscience. I was supported by Waters and [John] Mc-Mullen, but of course carried against me, and very properly. . . .

The semi-annual examinations began March 21, five days of public oral examinations of each class, and Strong reported them and recorded his feelings in detail. Each day it was the same: much apprehension in advance—satisfaction with his performance when it was over.

March 28. . . . Went to Appleton's and bought Bayle's *Dictionary*—$35. . . .

March 30. Absolutely *snowing*. Stayed at home all the morning putting my library in order and reading Bayle.

Afternoon. Went to Appleton's, and to my no small delight and surprise received an offer from Mr. Welford to dispose of his coins at fifty cents each; in fact he had given me a hint of it the day before. I jumped at the offer of course and brought them home at once, in number thirty-seven, viz., Roman silver, six; Roman copper, eight; Greek, Italian, Sicilian, Russian, etc., fifteen; English, etc., seven. Spent the evening in studying them out and reading Bayle.

April 2. Went up to the society rooms and took out some more volumes of Miss Edgeworth . . . came home and read Miss Edgeworth, finished *Patronage* to my own surprise. The end is rather more interesting than the beginning, but it is a great pity that her novels could not be compressed into one-third of their compass. It would be a decided advantage. . . .

After dinner went down to the foot of Murray Street to see the new Providence boat, the *Massachusetts*, perhaps the largest, certainly one of the largest steamboats in the world. On my way home stopped at Appleton's to look at his seventeen cases of old books just arrived. They are very handsome, but very few among them that I care for possessing. Stopped at Colman's. He began to puff his books of course, "curious," "rare," "valuable," "only one-tenth original cost," etc., but his books, as far as I could judge, amounted to nothing at all. What an inveterate puffer that Colman is; he'll lie in defense of his own books till he's black in the face. The only handsome thing I saw there was a really lovely engraving, for which he asked, of course, three times its value. Came home and read Miss Edgeworth till ten, devouring some half-dozen of her tales, pretty good appetite for one evening. . . .

April 12, TUESDAY. . . . Every one talking about the murder committed on Saturday night.[6] Went out in the afternoon with Chittenden, past the house, No. 41 Thomas Street. A very splendid barouche before the door, and as we passed it we saw in the entry an old lady, dressed in black, with a very good-natured, mild countenance whom I should never have suspected of being such a character as she is. The *Herald* of this morning says that Miss Helen was possessed of first-rate talents and was seduced under promise of marriage by a rascal in Maine. He deserves hanging as much or more than her murderer. . . .

April 15. . . . Old Stick-in-the-Mud, *alias* Dr. Blowpipe, *alias* Prof. Renwick, has returned from his peregrinations and seems to amount to as little as ever. After college went into Prof. McVickar's; showed him my 1470 Justin and saw some superb books of his—one in particular, a MS. Bible on vellum of about 1300, was the most beautiful thing I ever saw. . . .

[6] Helen Jewett, "a girl of the town," as Philip Hone calls her, was brutally murdered, apparently by Richard P. Robinson, "her paramour," in the house of Rosina Townsend, the woman Strong describes. Although the evidence against Robinson seems overwhelming, he was acquitted on June 8, greatly to the disgust of the community; nothing seems to have come of the charges that Joseph Hoxie, Robinson's employer, had bribed the jury. A fictionalized account of the affair appears in Manuel Komroff's *A New York Tempest* (1932).

April 18. . . . Set off in the evening for Clinton Hall to hear Prof. Silliman. He lectures admirably; what a contrast in manner between him and Prof. Stick-in-the-Mud. . . .

Half-past 11. Got home from a very pleasant lecture of Prof. Silliman's at half-past nine, one of the most interesting things I ever heard. I must get some work on geology; it is a much more interesting and simple study than I imagined, but Prof. Silliman popularizes and simplifies everything admirably. The place was tremendously crowded and dreadfully hot, and in spite of India rubbers, buttoned-up coats, and all other laudable and proper precautions, I have caught a bad cold, I suppose in coming out into the damp air. However, his lectures are worth a little inconvenience. . . .

April 22. . . . Commenced spherical trigonometry; judging from appearances it is still worse than plane, and that was bad enough. . . . After college went to Appleton's; saw a set of Rees's *Cyclopædia* on which I set my affections—only $123![7]

Evening. Went to the society debate on the subject of circumstantial evidence; it was decided to be insufficient for conviction. . . .

April 23. Cloudy. Went to college. Heard a famous Greek oration from Evangeles,[8] which was loudly clapped and expressly without the president's disapprobation. I must try to get some of his Greek poetry, which I understand he writes very well. . . .

April 24, SUNDAY. Went to St. Paul's in the morning and again in the afternoon. . . . Tomorrow morning, a public reprimand is to be delivered in the chapel to the unhappy billiard players—at least so report

---

[7] This great *Cyclopædia*, edited in England by Abraham Rees, had just been reprinted in Philadelphia, and was one of the wonders of the time. Nevertheless, at the auction sale of Strong's library in November, 1878, his copy in forty-eight volumes, half-russia leather, brought twenty-five cents.

[8] Christodoulos Leonidas Miltiades Evangeles, a Thessalonian, was rescued from the Turks in 1828 and brought to this country; he was first sent to Mount Pleasant Classical Institute at Amherst, Massachusetts, then to New York University, where he became somewhat soured on his benefactors, Rev. James M. Mathews, the "Evangeles Society," and the South Dutch Church; Samuel Ward, the banker, offered to send him to Columbia, and he spent his senior year there, graduating in 1836. He was much fussed over and lionized. R. W. Weir painted his portrait as "The Greek Boy" for Ward, and he made appearances in Greek costume and eloquent orations in Greek or English. He left America in 1837, established a school in Greece, published an edition of Byron's *Giaour* for school use in Greece in 1842, visited America in 1854–55, and returned to Athens where he was a college president until his death in 1881. A diary kept by him for the years 1835–40 is at the New-York Historical Society.

says. Horace with Anthon tomorrow. I hope he will not be as fierce as
he usually is when lecturing from his favorite author.

Have been prosecuting my attack in behalf of Rees most vigorously at
intervals throughout the day. Hope I will be successful, but I fear it is
too high. . . .

April 26. After college stopped at Appleton's and ordered Rees. It
arrived after dinner in two cartloads, but there was one volume wanting,
so I had to walk up again to Appleton's, and found out that in the meantime it had been sent down. . . .

May 5, THURSDAY. . . . Berths were taken this morning in the *Massachusetts* for our passage to Boston. . . . Took a walk uptown; as I was
coming down, met Travers[9] and we took a walk to St. John's Park, went
in, met [William] Green of the Freshman Class there, and we spent a
very comfortable half hour on the grass. I envy those who live in the
neighborhood. Came down again and met something like half the college
promenading Broadway.

May 6. . . . Went to college as usual. Came off after Anderson's
hour, and at four we left the door and at five, the wharf, with about a
hundred passengers. We could not have had a better time in every
respect. Off Whitestone, we came up with the *President* lying to; she had
broken her starboard paddles and was unable to proceed. We hauled
along side of her and took her passengers off, fifty-eight in number; this
detained us something like an hour. After tea, at which I laid in as much
coffee as I usually do on board a steamboat, I went forward and remained
there till eight, and then adjourned below to read *Japhet in Search of a
Father*, which I read till nine and then took myself to my berth—which,
by the by, was hardly a foot wide—but at any rate it was better than the
mattresses and settees that were crowded into the cabin for the *President's* passengers. As to going to sleep, it was out of the question; the
jar of the boat and the amount of coffee I had swallowed, combined with
the serenade of snoring around, kept me wide awake till about two.

May 7. Woke at five and was summoned on deck by my father at
once to see that awful spot, Point Judith; we were just abreast of it as I

---

[9] William Riggin Travers (1819–1887), classmate of Strong, was later a shipping
merchant in Baltimore, married the daughter of Reverdy Johnson, returned to New
York as a stock broker and made a fortune in partnership with Leonard Jerome
(Union 1840), the grandfather of Winston Churchill. A great sportsman, he was first
president of the N. Y. Athletic Club and one of the founders of the Jerome Park race
course; Travers Island, in Long Island Sound, was named in his honor.

got on deck and there was nothing extraordinary about it that I could see; the water was smooth enough—no agitation at all. . . . Passed Newport, a mean, wooden, contemptible-looking place, and were soon going up the Providence River at no small rate. Reached Providence a little after eight —from the river it looks still worse than Newport—I don't admire either of the places. We got into the cars at once and I was soon, for the first time in my life, traveling at the rate of a mile in 2 min. 35 sec., the first time I ever was on a decent railroad. In spite of the "great danger," "terrible accidents," "upsettings," and so on, as Mr. Cophagus hath it, we stopped at the depot in Boston at a quarter-past ten in perfect preservation, except that we were most copiously sprinkled with dust. In five minutes more we found ourselves how d'ye doing and shaking hands in No. 56 Boylston Street. . . . Was soon comfortably established in my room, and I wish I was to occupy it for three months instead of three days, for it commands a delightful view of the whole Common and is, I think, the pleasantest room in the house, which is in my opinion situated in by far the pleasantest street in Boston. After a little talking and looking about, went out with my father to take a walk up Tremont Street, and just as we got opposite the Tremont House, whom should I see sailing along just as usual, with his daughter on his arm, but—McVickar himself! There was no mistaking him—and he has gone to Boston *for his health* forsooth. He looks as well as ever, but did not see me. Went to my old haunt, the Antiquarian Boke Store, but saw nothing there worth much—papa bought a copy of Pasor's *Lexicon* and I got a couple of coins, one Spanish, the other of Queen Elizabeth, 1563. . . .

May 8, SUNDAY.   Went to Trinity Church and heard Dr. Wainwright[10]—and a very good sermon he gave us. Took another walk after church, and after dinner Mr. Derby very kindly volunteered to show me round Boston and Charlestown a little. We set out accordingly, and after something of a walk through Boston, crossed one of the bridges into Charlestown, which place by the by, looks very nice, and then turning off, went up Bunker Hill. The entrenchments still remain, but I believe they are not the original American ones, but entrenchments thrown up by the British immediately after the action. The ground being elevated, the whole scene of action lies before you like a map, and it is easy to fancy the aspect it must have presented on the morning of the action. The

[10] The Rev. Jonathan Mayhew Wainwright (1792–1854), Harvard 1812, later incumbent of St. John's Chapel, New York, provisional bishop of New York, and Columbia trustee, was to cross Strong's path many times in the future.

monument in the middle of the entrenchments will be a superb thing, when it is finished. It is formed of immense masses of granite with a spiral staircase in the center and is to be 180 feet high, about 80 feet of which are now completed, but unfortunately it is begun on so superb and grand a scale that like many other notions, it will cost too much to finish.[11] The Hill is a most interesting place to stand upon and I could have spent an hour there gladly. We then crossed to Copp's Hill on the other side, the place from which the Bostonians viewed the battle. It contains the oldest graveyard in Boston and I found many very curious old monuments of the early settlers. . . . We then went down to see the *Portland* steamboat, in which line Mr. D[erby] is concerned, come in. She came in at last, and we went on board. She is a first-rate boat, equal, if not superior to any on the Sound. . . .

May 9. The weather still delightful. Went out after breakfast and stopped at a store in Tremont Street which advertises "books, objects of natural history, prints and antiquities." Found very few valuable books, but quite a lot of modern coins, which I bought at two cents a piece. . . . Set out as soon as I got back to take a ride to Mt. Auburn [Cemetery]. We had an excellent barouche and a good driver—a regular intelligent, shrewd, guessing, calculating Yankee—drove to Mt. Auburn and spent an hour or two in walking about in it. It is really worth going to Boston to see. It is as fine a piece of ground as could have been selected for the purpose—very uneven, covered with woods, and containing several fine sheets of water. As yet there are not very many monuments erected, but those that there are, are generally beautiful, especially Mr. [William] Appleton's, which is the most magnificent thing of the kind that I ever saw, Spurzheim's,[12] two or three on the side of a hill in imitation of the Egyptian Tombs of the Kings, one or two very handsome obelisks and several others. Mrs. Richard Derby's is almost exactly like Spurzheim's —handsomer, if anything. Altogether it is a most lovely place, but there is one fault about it, and that is [that] the superb, massive gateway, with the winged globe, etc., is nothing but a paltry *imitation* of granite!

[11] The Bunker Hill Monument was finished by 1843 and was dedicated on June 17 of that year; President Tyler and his whole cabinet were present, and Daniel Webster was the orator.

[12] Caspar Spurzheim, Prussian phrenologist and disciple of Dr. Franz Joseph Gall, originator of the theory, had come to the United States in 1832 after a widely popular career in Germany, France, and England, to spread the "science" of reading character and mental faculty from the shape and contours of the skull. He died the same year in Boston.

Better have none at all. If imitation is out of place anywhere, it is out of place there. Stopped at Bunker's Hill on our way back and got home at half-past one.

Afternoon. Went to Mrs. Derby's and thence to the Antiquarian Boke Store again. I thought that I could find nothing at all there worth buying, and was just going, when I lit upon some fine old specimens of early Boston printing which I seized at once, and made the following purchases—1. Increase Mather's sermons (12mo. 1686)—I bought it for its rarity, but I believe that the sermons are very good ones; 2. How's *Narrative* (1756), a small tract; 3. Dudley's *Letter*, another small tract (written 1630), probably printed a few years later, which Drake says is very scarce indeed; and 4. a little reprint of some early tracts relative to the Indians.

May 10. Went up to Mr. Drake's[13] again and got two other works relative to early American history, *New England's Memorial* and the *editio princeps* of Hubbard's *Indian Warres*, which on Drake's authority is a very great rarity, and I myself can bear witness to its being a very interesting book. Came back to Boylston Street and then accompanied the folks to the top of the State House. The view is superb. . . . Got home, took dinner at twelve and started at half after for the cars. Left at a quarter-past one—and so ends my visit to Boston, the pleasantest visit I ever made. Everything has gone well; nothing at all occurred to render it at all unpleasant. And apart from Boston's being the pleasantest city I ever saw, and No. 56 Boylston Street the pleasantest house in that city, Eloise has been so anxious and exerted herself so much to make us comfortable and render our visit a pleasant one, that we could not help having a delightful time. We had a very comfortable ride to Providence, though with not a very good engine—and we met with several obstructions—so that we did not reach Providence till near four. On board the *Providence*. The boat was terribly crowded, owing to the *President*'s misfortune on Friday which prevented her running, and it was crowded with vulgar, low, people, with scarcely a single exception. Over three hundred passengers! After tea went on deck, passed Newport and got into the harbor—

[13] Samuel Gardner Drake (1798–1875), self-educated Yankee scholar and honorary M.A. of Union College, established the Antiquarian Bookstore on Cornhill in Boston in 1828, the first of its kind in the country; he was one of the founders of the New England Historic Genealogical Society and for a dozen years editor and publisher of its quarterly *Register*; an opinionated and quarrelsome historian, he nevertheless wrote or edited more than a score of important works on American Indian and colonial history.

wind strong at south-west and though the boat was but little agitated, I preferred going to bed to staying on deck among such a rabble, so I turned in before eight and got to sleep by four the next morning.

May 11. Got up at half-past six and got on deck without delay, for the cabin was too full of settees and too hot to contain any comfort. Found that we were just off Lloyd's Neck. . . . With the wind ahead and the tide against us, we did not reach the wharf till half-past nine. . . .

May 24. TUESDAY. . . . Went to Clinton Hall to hear Silliman's last lecture. He began with volcanoes, internal heat, etc., and ended with a splendid series of arguments from geology in favor of the Scripture account of the Creation. It was really admirable. The place was very crowded and though I got there by five minutes past seven, the room was so crowded that I had to take a bench in one of the passages.

May 25. Jemmy Renwick [Jr.] (*"spooniorum maximus"*) turned to this morning to bore me with some more of his doggerel—he may dispute the prize for *boring* with [Charles] Seymour himself. I escaped, however, with only the end of one poem, a "travesty" as he was pleased to call it, of Homer! and a "travesty" at the same time of common sense and everything else. . . .

May 26. . . . Stopped at Appleton's this afternoon and saw something worth seeing, the Second Folio Edition of Shakespeare. If it were only perfect, and a little cheaper than $12, I would jump at it—as it is, I rather think I shall let it alone.

May 27. . . . Went to college prepared to astonish the natives by my oratory, but was prevented (to my great joy) by Chittenden's giving us a speech of fifteen minutes long. . . .

Chittenden came down at five, and at seven adjourned to the Society. Found [George Gilfert] Waters and [Giles Mumford] Hillyer and one or two others reading Halleck's *Fanny*. The only other copy of it in town may *possibly* be got at Bancroft's for something over $5, which is a little too much for a pamphlet of twenty or thirty pages. Waters has promised me the pamphlet—and I shall certainly copy it if I ever get it. . . .

May 28. . . . Went to college—we had our society meeting, which lasted just seven minutes. . . . Came home with five octavos: Percy's *Ancient Minstrelsy* and Sale's Koran. Spent an hour or two with Trevett in the library talking over all sorts of subjects. He is, it seems, quite a theological student, and talked away on the subject quite well. He is fierce in the defence of High Church and takes Archbishop Laud (!) for his model, and is moreover something of a Universalist. On this latter subject he tried desperately to convince me—God knows I would give the world to *be able* to believe it, but I *cannot.* . . .

May 29. And one of those incarnations of woe, misery and blue devils—a rainy Sunday. Went to Dr. McElroy's[14] in the morning and in the afternoon tried to go to sleep and could not, and finally went in next door.

May 30. . . . Walked up to Fuller's and exercised a little—saw nobody there, so came off. Met Mr. Richards and stopped in at Appleton's. Examined that Shakespeare of 1632. There are apparently two leaves wanting at the end and the title page in the beginning, so it is hardly worth $12. . . .

May 31. . . . Spoke to J. Renwick [Jr.] about his *poetry* (as *he* calls it)—recommended him to publish it in an appendix to his father's *Rudiments of the Steam Engine*, or else to publish it by subscription. I told him it would create "quite a sensation"—and so it would I'm sure. . . .

June 2. Raining like another deluge. Walked to college—was called up in Anthon's and McVickar's rooms. We had a grand crash in Renwick's. Some worthies tied one end of a string to the knob of the door, carried it out through the laboratory window and tied it to a large box containing nearly a bushel of glass bottles, cracked retorts, etc., and when the door opened, crash it went like a volley of artillery. Renwick is in fidgets to find who did it—I had no hand in it. . . .

June 3. . . . In Renwick's room a gunpowder plot with a pack of crackers was attempted but did not succeed. . . .

June 4, SATURDAY. . . . Had an invitation to attend Robinson's trial which I declined, not caring particularly about being squeezed to death. . . .

June 5. Another rainy Sunday, and a pouring forth of dullness and ennui as well as rain. Lounged about the house all day dubitating on the propriety of suicide—for really this weather makes one feel decidedly like it. . .

I have concocted an idea today—and that is to take up as a project for vacation the formation of a dictionary—English into Greek. I don't know that there is any such article and it would be a convenient thing for me to refer to. Mentioned the idea to father, who laughed at the possibility of my doing anything in the country. By the ghost of Stephanus! I'll do it, if only to show him he's mistaken.

---

[14] The Rev. Joseph McElroy was minister of the Scotch Presbyterian (or Associate Reformed) Church in Cedar Street, later at the corner of Grand and Crosby Streets. This is the church the elder Strong and Mary attended regularly.

June 6. . . . The powder plot today was carried into effect finely. A tremendous howling was begun round [Renwick's] door when the class came in, and the moment his back was turned to find out the authors of it, the slowmatches were fired and a general *feu de joie* commenced—double headers—squibs and spiders—in sublime confusion. Renwick attempted to put them out, but some must have been left, and they kept popping off during the whole hour at the rate of one every five minutes. When the class went out, the grand finale was played, consisting of a large box containing perhaps thirty pounds of glass retorts and all sorts of articles, which was hauled down from the top of the highest shelves by a string through one of the windows. Poor Jemmy! They'll tease him out of his senses! He has been as busy as possible ever since to try to find out the contriver of the plot. He won't succeed, but it is too bad to tease him this way, for he behaves very civilly to anyone who behaves so to him.

June 7. . . . Renwick has taken the most excellent plan in the world with regard to [Wilmot] Johnson, who was discovered by Mrs. Renwick pulling down the box through the window. He says he'll send in a bill of $25 to his father! Poor "pyrints"—this is attacking him in his tenderest part.

June 8. . . . The first piece of news I heard this morning on coming down stairs was that Robinson has been acquitted! Chiefly, I suppose, through Furlong's evidence. He don't deserve it. I have no doubt whatever that Furlong is a perjured man, and a man who has perjured himself for the sake of some of Mr. [Joseph] Hoxie's cash. No matter—time will show—and if it should not, that will make no difference in the final punishment of either perjury or murder. . . .

June 9, THURSDAY.   Clear warm and delightful, the more so from the force of contrast, and for that very reason I never enjoyed the bright sun and the fresh air more than this day, even though attended by the drawbacks of a city. O for the 25th of July, when I shall be at last at liberty—free from the bore of mathematics, the prosing of composition, and that greatest of all farces, the chemical room—in short when Castle Humbug will be for a short time "laid upon the shelf."

Went to Fuller's in the afternoon and mentioned to [Professor] Anthon that curious scene that took place in Renwick's room. Nothing gives him such delight as to hear of these matters—it recalls to mind his school and college pranks, and gives him a chance of glorifying himself with the idea that he has subdued and disciplined these disorderly scamps —that his room is the best room in College, and nothing can give him greater pleasure than such an idea as that. Renwick has actually told Johnson that he will take no further steps in his case! How *can* they behave as they do,"after being treated with such mildness, such undeserved —unexpected—such positively improper, indulgence"? Though I'm a student myself, I cannot help thinking so and despising most heartily the conduct of sundry of my associates.

June 10. . . . Read a composition I wrote last night and after dinner went to Fuller's. Took a good deal of exercise—and came home again. Appleton has sent a lot of old books to R[oyal] Gurley's to be sold on Saturday night, theological trash principally, that I would not lumber my shelves with. The best thing there is a copy of Koberger's Boethius, 1476. I think I shall go to the auction, and take it, if it goes cheap. . . .

June 11. . . . Bought a copy of "Robinson's Life, with Extracts from his Diary" which the loafers are hawking about the streets. No more his diary than it is mine. By the by, I wonder if ever I shall be placed in a predicament of the same sort—and shall have this scrawl brought up to be argued on by lawyers and commented on and explained by that glorious trio, the *Sun, Transcript* and *Herald*? At all events it would puzzle the judge considerably to decypher it.

Afternoon. Saw [Professor] Anthon at Fuller's. He says those unfortunates who were brought up on account of the gunpowder plot, with the grand Guy Fawkes, Dick Douglass, at their head, are laid over till Saturday next. "The discipline of the college is shameful," as he says.

Evening. Went to Gurley's—the books all going "dirt cheap"— bought a very good old Cornelius Agrippa, with a piece of Erasmus bound up with it, for 75 cents. . . .

What ridiculous fools the New York literati are as regards books! There was an old copy of some trashy old work on animals, which I would not have taken as a gift, but which was adorned with a few wretched engravings which some aspiring young artist had daubed over with red, blue and green ink. It was put up at $2 and was run up to $5; the auctioneer was just going to knock it down at that price when he chanced to turn to a picture of a goose, colored green, sailing on an ocean colored red, and at this delectable sight half a dozen voices screamed $6! $6½! $7!! at which last price it was knocked down to a Mr. Darling. Verily, Mr. Darling, Thou art a sap, and if thou had'st only looked hard at the engravings, thou mightest well have found thy prototype in the goose— on an ocean made not of red ink, but of Humbug. It is a pity we have no Lucian here to ridicule such animals. . . .

June 13, MONDAY. . . . On my way to college stopped at Gurley's to get the Cornelius Agrippa I bought on Saturday. Found the bookkeeper lamenting pathetically that the books had not brought sufficient to pay their freight. I suppose that generally they did not. It was a wretched blunder to send such books to this country. . . .

Afternoon.   Went down to the *Massachusetts* to see the Lloyds off; spent half an hour in the lady's cabin and was nearly stewed. I compassionate those who are to pass the night there. . . . A steamboat is an unromantic thing, but it makes a superb appearance when in rapid motion and at sufficient distance to put all the prosaic paraphernalia of the machinery out of sight. Halleck's Ode to the Horse Boat in *Fanny* is something to the purpose.

Went up to Fuller's and took a good deal of exercise.

June 15. . . . Bought a copy of Burton's *Anatomy of Melancholy* [at Appleton's], $3.75.

June 16. . . . Went to Gurley's to see the end of the "rare and valuable" old book sale. Got the only two books I cared a straw for—the Boethius of 1476 for $2 and Vincent of Beauvais, *Speculum Historiale*—$1.75—a goodly folio, worth the money if only for shaving paper. Came off at nine, and then took to studying Horace for tomorrow. I have been reading a good deal in Burton today, and don't know when I have made a purchase I like so well. In spite of the author's rough, complicated style, pedantic display and far-fetched wit, there is so much originality, so many good ideas, and such a mass of rare and out of the way information in it that the book is well worth twice the money. . . .

Chittenden spoke to me today about joining that mysterious fraternity the ΦBK. He was to have been initiated this morning, and wants me to follow his steps. As no information about the society can be gained before you are tied fast to it, it is something like a leap in the dark, or a Turkish marriage, but still I'd like to join, though it is so exclusive I have not much chance of succeeding.

June 17. . . . Chittenden has joined the "Fraternity," not of ΦBKians, but of AΔΦians. . . . After dinner went up to Gurley's to get my purchases. Brought down the *Speculum.* If I had known how ponderous it was, I would have hired a cart, but as it was, I brought it home myself and was nearly roasted for my pains. Went to the Academy of Design; met Chittenden there and spent an hour in looking over the pictures. Generally they do not amount to a great deal, but there is a most superb one, a *portrait* (fancy) of a lady sitting; it is really magnificent. What a pity that such as could have sat for this portrait are so rare in Real Life and that it is only a creation of fancy.

Took a walk on the Battery. [Charles] Seymour met us and fastened upon us. I have been as cool as possible to that puppy for some time past, but it won't do; I must try what insulting him will do—though it's a disagreeable remedy, it must come to that at last. I understand, by the by, he never takes an insult. As Burton says, to make fools of such creatures is no sin.

Went to the society. Debate on the subject of capital punishment. Volunteered in favor of its abolition. We had a pack of crackers thrown in the windows by the rascally Peithologians.

June 18. As hot as if the whole sky had been transformed into one immense burning glass of which New York was the focus. Had quite a fracas this morning with that little reptile [Henry Feltus] Quackenbos. He had been in the habit for several days past of attacking me in chapel, trying to steal my books and tormenting me in every possible way, being perfectly aware that in chapel he is safe. Today the little rascal absolutely struck me as I was going down into the society room, whereupon I knocked him down, and he jumped up fairly sputtering with rage, with the evident intention of annihilating me. I quietly took hold of his hands and held him, as I did not care to do him any harm, while he was dancing with fury and invoking His Satanic Majesty and all the d——ls in the calendar to come to his aid. Just then Renwick came up and ordered him before the board. He sneaked off, however. It won't do. I must speak to the president or get ordered myself, or else he will take the chance to tell all kinds of lies on the subject.

Came off. Got my Boethius from Gurley's. . . .

June 20, MONDAY. . . . [Quackenbos] was at college but his black eye made him tolerably civil—or rather tolerably quiet. Went in to have a talk with Prex after the fourth hour and explained matters to him. He was very civil and promised that I should have an opportunity of defending myself if Quack was hauled up. So far so good.

It was raining dismally. A company of troops just went by— splashing through mud with their plumes all wet and destitute of every appearance of form and comeliness. Our military don't generally amount to much in my opinion. . . .

June 21. . . . Prex called me in this morning to ask whether I had anything to do with the torpedo affair yesterday. It seems that one was thrown downstairs, hit him on the head and exploded. So report says, but I doubt it.

The president merely asked me the question, which I answered in the negative, of course. . . .

June 23. . . . Looked over Audubon today with Cooper in Prex's private library. . . .

June 25, SATURDAY. . . . Spent the morning in looking over five hundred old *Mirrors* upstairs—and found several pieces which, fresh cooked and warmed up a little, will do very well to serve before our "fraternity."

Afternoon. Took a dismal walk up to the Academy of Design with my mother. Caught in the rain on our way back; very pleasant indeed.

Strong's preparation for the final examinations took most of his time and clouded his spirits in the next weeks, though life did go on: he made further visits to the annual exhibition at the Academy of Design: "I'm pretty well tired of it, but I'll have the worth of my season ticket, I'm resolved"; there were week-ends at Whitestone, games of chess, visits to Castle Garden to listen to the band, and faithful attendance at the meetings of Philolexian, of which he was now secretary. On top of all, there was a spell of hot weather.

July 3, SUNDAY. . . . *Evening.* As I did not care particularly about lounging away my time at home over [Rev. Gregory Townsend] Bedell's *Sermons,* or some other equally interesting work, I went to St. John's to hear Bishop [Jackson] Kemper preach on the subject of Western Missions. Found the doors not yet open and a good many people in the porch—the ladies all squatting (the only word I can think of) on the bases of the columns like so many bull frogs in a swamp. I was turned out of several pews, but at last got established in a very comfortable one, but it unfortunately contained six or seven ladies and one gentleman besides myself. Got along, however, very well considering, and heard a very interesting sermon; it could not well be otherwise than interesting. . . .

The [City Hall] Park presented a shameful spectacle: the booths lighted up, the people as drunk as dogs, and such a popping of squibs, rockets, pistols, etc., as I never heard. I'm not much given to moralizing, but it did not look much like Sunday evening in a Christian country.

July 4. Waked up at five by a terrible noise and jumped out of bed thinking of an earthquake or a bombardment, but it was only a patriotic effusion of gunpowder on the part of our "soldiers in peace, citizens in war," so I went to bed and to sleep and did not wake till nearly breakfast time. How I slept through the hubbub is a mystery. At twelve we had a shower which cooled the air a little, and soon after, the guardians of our country, as the Fourth of July orators call them, came past, to all appearance in a state of melting away. Studied my chemistry, read some in Robertson, Sir Walter, etc. Stayed at home all day, having no ambition to have my name enrolled in the records of newspaper immortality as a victim to the "pyrotechnic propensities of our youthful citizens." I fancy more gunpowder has been burned today than was spent in any three of the Revolutionary actions.

July 6. . . . Went over all the Plautus; we have got a scandalous amount to go over for this—I had got as far as "this" when I was aroused by a fearful yelling, which I took at first for a cry of murder, and then for the last "dying speech and confession" of some hapless cat in the agonies of strangulation, but on going to the window I found that the unearthly noises in question proceeded from a "feminine," or as Tom Cringle called it, a "young female lady," at a house a considerable way off, yelling forth . . . at the top of her voice, with a running accompaniment of what had once been (probably) a piano, but now sounded more like a band of marrow bones and cleavers, or Oky's "Chorus of Coffee Mills and Scissors Grinders," some boarding-school miss, probably. She's at it still, and some one of her beaux has just joined in the second verse, at the full stretch of his lungs, like a chimney sweeper, or Stentor himself. Horrible!

July 8. Chittenden [Nathaniel William Chittenden, '37] is without exception the best fellow I ever met with. I don't know that he has a single fault; I never saw any in him, unless perhaps his Democraticmania, but that's no fault, after all, and I had much rather be an enthusiast in the cause of freedom of any sort than an ultra in the cause of oppression, for it must come to that at last. . . . There's no mistake in Chittenden. He's sound in head and heart, both. . . .

July 15. We begin [final examinations] at nine—the first one examined was Hone, who made out rather shabbily, and I was the ninth called up. I got along perfectly to my own satisfaction; McVickar examined pretty severely too, on Louis XIV's period. I got through, though, without one mistake. We had some most original compositions read, and among them was *not* F. Anthon's; it has been very much admired, but I'm surprised he could raise brass enough to read it. I do not, candidly, believe that there was *one* original sentence in it—a splendid comparison between Napoleon's retreat from Moscow and the retreat of the ten thousand. To think of *his* writing such a thing! John Duer read one that he's read twice before and [Benjamin Tredwell] Kissam read a six decker or rather a six pager about Mary Queen of Scots. We had no lack of specta-

tors. There were my father, Dr. [John] Knox, John Anthon, Clement C.
Moore, R[obert G.] Vermilye, both the Mr. Wards [Henry and Samuel,
the Columbia trustee], and one or two others with whom I was not acquainted. It was a sight worth seeing, the *bow* that that most perfect of
asses H[enry] H[all] Ward made when his father and uncle came in. It
consisted in a convulsive spasm of the whole body accompanied by a jerk
of the spine—as if actuated by machinery or an *emprosthotonos*—and at the
same time displaying a grin just like that of one of his brother monkeys,
on his countenance: but to see the manoeuvre repeated twice nearly choked
me—it was too ridiculous.

It was horridly somniferous. How the conscientious Mr. Moore endured it I know not; he stuck by for three mortal hours. But as to the
faculty: the Prex was writing a letter, Anthon reading the *Herald*, Renwick
drawing pictures, and Anderson gaping and rubbing his eyes, evidently
half asleep. In fact F[red] Anthon did actually and *bona fide* enjoy a nap
of nearly an hour in one of the window seats much to the edification of the
class, who preserved themselves from following his example by firing
paper balls at his nose. I was half dead when we came out and did nothing
at all of any importance in the afternoon, but after refreshing myself with
seven or eight good cups of strong coffee in the evening I succeeded in
bringing myself up to par, and went over all the Herodotus. . . .

*Examinations over, Strong set about preparing for a New England trip
with his family. On the 21st all the clerks in his father's office took a holiday,
and he was pressed into service; Pierre-Augustin Berthemy (1778–1855),
one of Napoleon's generals, turned up at the office and Strong was introduced
to him: "Really a superb looking man; he made me three bows one after another, accompanied by a variety of polite speech."*

July 22.   Walked up to college in the morning, thence to Appleton's
to purchase Clarendon—spent the morning very agreeably in reading it.
I like Clarendon as well as any historian I ever read. He takes about the
right view of the state of things in England, and is more impartial in his
descriptions of characters of the day than I expected, though of course
strongly biased in favor of the Royal party.

July 23, SATURDAY. . . . General Berthemy took tea with us—and we
got along, per interpreter, better than I expected. After some time spent
in talking about nothing (or its equivalent) we got him on the Russian
expedition, and I never had a more interesting conversation. I should like

nothing better than to spend a week or so in traveling with him, to have an
opportunity of talking over all these matters.

His life must have been a most interesting one. To have been the
companion of Napoleon, from his rising almost to his setting, from the
Pyramids to Borodino and Moscow, is enough to make it so. What scenes
he must have passed through! The horrid retreat through Russia for
instance—Leipsic—Marengo—and the countless other bloody dramas
into which Napoleon's *aide de camp* must have been led. He gave a fearful
description of the Russian retreat—five hundred leagues through a desert,
the Cossacks on every side, the cold intense, all the officers—Berthemy
himself—on foot all the time to keep themselves from freezing—famine,
too. I had heard all this before, but I never heard it from an eye witness
before tonight, and it never seemed quite so dreadful before, perhaps on
that very account. He differs from Scott in two or three points; he says that
the French victory at Borodino was *decided*, and that the Russians were
superior by about fifty thousand men, that Napoleon never entertained the
least idea of making a push for St. Petersburg after the fall of Moscow, and
that during the whole expedition, to the very last, *Vive l'Empereur* was
the word throughout the army. He speaks of Napoleon as almost if not
quite the greatest man that ever lived, but spoiled by ambition—"Too
headstrong, willing to risk what he had already acquired to gain more"—
which is more than I thought any Frenchman would acknowledge. He says
"he considered men as mere machines to do his pleasure."

*General Berthemy was apparently a legatee of an American will, but
Strong does not inform us on this point. He spent the evening of the 25th at the
Strong home: "Curtis, one of the executors, is acting like a great scamp and
the general is in a bother about it. We had an awkward time of it, for the interpreter was obliged to leave a few minutes, and without some books of engravings
which I brought down, we could not have got along at all." Two days later
the family embarked for Boston:*

July 27. We were in the boat by a quarter-past five and at six precise
we left the wharf. The boat was nearly empty—only about sixty passengers
on board. There was a Judge Clapp with a large party, an old acquaintance
of my father's. I had a good deal of talk with him and had the felicity of
being introduced to three ladies from the backwoods who were traveling
with him, besides a brandy-faced colonel and a pug-nosed lieutenant from
the same part of the world. I had a terrible itching to enquire what they

were doing here, for it strikes me that Scott, Gaines & Co. are in need of all the forces they can muster down south. I put a few enquiries to the lieutenant about the Florida Indians. He pulled up his shirt collar and cocked up his nose and said that they were "miserable soldiers, wretched marksmen," etc. I felt inclined to suggest that he had best turn his steps south instead of north and win some laurels from these paltry antagonists; they seem to bother his "brother officers" considerably. . . .

In Boston by ten. Mr. Derby and Eloise were at the depot and we proceeded at once to 56 Boylston Street, and thence to sleep, as expeditiously as possible.

July 28, THURSDAY. *Boston.* . . . *Afternoon.* We started in the *Mount Pleasant* for Nahant, accompanied by little Hasket,[15] alias Totty, and his nurse. We rode to the boat and had a very pleasant sail down the Bay. I saw one thing that quite surprised me—and that was a number of seals sporting on a reef just off Fort Independence. I had no idea that they were found so far south and especially so near the habitation of man.

Nahant is a beautiful place, the shore one pile of rocks and crags of every shape, which must present a superb appearance during a north-east gale. We spent a couple of hours walking in every direction and I amused myself by scrambling hither and thither over the rocks, greatly to the dismay of my "governor." . . .

July 29. We took an early breakfast and got into the stage (an extra) at seven o'clock; we had four good horses and a steady, intelligent driver—a genuine Yankee—and away we went. . . . I established myself on the outside, for a ride of seventy miles inside would have utterly annihilated me—turned me inside out, at least. We passed through Charlestown and the cobbling city of Lynn and reached Salem (fourteen miles) by a little before nine. The great lion of Salem is the museum of its Marine Society, and thither we went. Mr. Pickman[16] is one of the directors and he, of course, procured us admission. . . . Ipswich next, and Newburyport— to dinner—and here to my dismay it began to rain. I got inside and resigned myself to my fate, but got through better than I expected. We passed through Hampton and Portsmouth and reached Dover at last after a day's ride of seventy-two miles. We took a walk through Dover after tea; the factories are immense eight-story buildings, and in my opinion,

---

[15] Hasket Derby (1835–1914), Amherst 1855 and Harvard Medical School 1858, spent three years of study in Europe, and was for half a century a famous oculist and ophthalmologist in Boston.

[16] Benjamin Pickman, Jr. (1763–1843), Harvard 1784, lawyer, merchant of Salem and Congressman, was an uncle of Elias Hasket Derby.

built altogether too close to one another to be safe from fire; if one of them should take fire during a high wind, nothing but a miracle could save the rest.

The next day the party continued their journey by stage to Alton, where they dined, then drove a mile and half to the shore of Lake Winnepesaukee to board the steamer Belknap *for Mr. Derby's Cow Island. Strong noted the singular construction of the vessel, "with a horizontal cylinder and discharging steam at every stroke under her side," which "does not seem very effectual, for the boat rarely exceeds five miles an hour." He wrote at length of the beauty of the lake, of its many islands of every size and shape, of the surrounding wooded hills and the White Mountains visible in the distance, of Cow Island with its three hills and belt of woods, of fishing with his brother-in-law. After two days on the island the family group left for Center Harbor, "finely situated at the foot of the Red Mountains." They climbed the Ossipee Hills, fished for trout, stayed over night at the Mountain House, returned and climbed Red Mountain—"the view was really magnificent; it is said to be the finest in the country and I think that it probably is"—then left by stage for Concord, where they spent the night of August 4. Another stage journey brought them to Nashua; then by boat they travelled down the Merrimack to Chelmsford and by omnibus to Lowell, of which Strong wrote that it was "nothing but manu-factories, brick houses, and all the dust and dirt of New York without half its conveniences and good looks." Thence they went by train to Boston, which by this time seemed almost like home to young Strong.*

On August 6 Strong had time for some purchases of books and old coins before the family, including Eloise and Mr. Derby, embarked for the return to New York. Much of the voyage was made uncomfortable by a large crowd of soldiers and others returning from the celebration of the second centenary of the founding of Providence. The Strongs and Derbys arrived in New York at half-past nine on the morning of Sunday, August 7.

August 8.   Went up to the office in the morning and trotted about as usual. After dinner as I was reading some of the old newspapers that have come during our absence, I was startled by a report seemingly of a cannon, which jarred the windows and jingled the glasses tremendously. The next minute the bells struck up and the engines rattled down Greenwich Street and I started off to see where the fire was. It was in Castle Garden—some of the fireworks had exploded and set fire to the little wooden buildings round the fort.

August 10. Accompanied Mr. Derby on board the *Rhode Island.* She is a superb boat and has *baths* on board, which is quite a novel arrangement. . . .

On the twelfth the family took the little steamboat Star, and after a three-hour journey reached Whitestone, Long Island, where they were to board for the remainder of the summer with a Mrs. Whitney. Strong reported that the place looked the same as it always did, and seemed flat, stale, and unprofitable after the scenery of New Hampshire. He expected to have a dull time. This was prevented by the arrival of additional boarders with "a brat (female) of eight or nine . . . [and] a dirty little abomination of three years old with a face like a brick wall and as much impudence, crossness, and strength of lungs [sic]." On September 2 he took his horse and

Rode out this morning for a little quiet. Went to Success Pond.[17] There is a hill there that commands a very excellent prospect, which I never saw, and I went to the top of it. The view is certainly very extensive: on the north and northeast you look over the pond to Long Island Sound, and on the south over Hempstead Plains to the ocean. Jamaica and New York bays are visible to those who have good eyes, but not to such short-sighted mortals as I am. There was a pear tree on the hill which attracted my attention considerably, and my devotions to it were evidently too fervent to please the keeper of the inn at the foot of the hill. However, his wrath met with very little attention from us and we left it to evaporate as soon as it liked. . . .

September 11. It rained all the morning, much to my annoyance; a rainy Sunday in the city is bad enough, but in the country it is dreadful. Nearly gave up the ghost in trying to find something to do. Walter Scott, the accordion, and Greek are proscribed, of course, but they were reading something edifying in the next room, so I went and joined the congregation. Was slightly benefited thereby, that is, it put me to sleep, a consummation most devoutly to be wished for and which I had been endeavoring to accomplish unaided.

September 15. . . . Rode out before breakfast in spite of the fog and traveled by the back roads to Jamaica. The roads here are about as crooked

[17] Of recent world fame as Lake Success, temporary home of the United Nations.

as I ever beheld, as if (according to what Elbert used to say) the d——l had chased an eel along them. . . .

September 23. Took another bathe. I have been bug-hunting with great success of late; I like to have some object of this kind in view in my walks. The only drawback is that I get stung about twice a day by the wasps, bees, and hornets who have not spirit enough to accept of the immortality I offer them, viz., the privilege of being attached by a pin to the cover of an old fig box which at present forms my entomological cabinet. . . .

September 25, SUNDAY. . . . After dinner we went up with my father on Mr. Howland's Observatory. . . . New York steeples were visible plain enough, and all distinguishable—St. John's, Trinity, St. Paul's, and all the rest of them— and in the opposite direction, the little white steeple of Van Zandt's Church. . . .

September 26. Started for *home.* We had rather a cool passage, and a very long one. In Hellgate we passed a schooner on fire; she had been loaded with lime, sprung a leak, caught fire, and drifted on one of the rocks. There was a vessel along side, and the crew seemed to be all saved. The fire seemed to be chiefly forward, and not much of it anywhere, but there was no attempt to check it, and she probably burned to the water's edge.

Got home safely, and so ends my summer's work. Went to the office, thence to Appleton's, to Arnoux's for some more outward habiliments, to George Anthon's—he was out—and then home. . . .

October 3. Walked up to college at half-past eight, and it was not long before nearly all "our set" were assembled, and the business of shaking hands and how d'ye doing was going on with great energy. The college gains a very large number of students this fall. In the Senior Class, a Mr. [Stephen] Douglass and another by the name of [Anthony] Halsey. . . . Our class loses in point of number—but in my opinion actually gains in other respects: [Wilmot] Johnson, Theodore Gordon, John [King] Duer and [Henry Feltus] Quackenbos leave us; whether we have any additions, I don't know. The Freshman Class (with the Literary and Scientific) amounts to forty-three! Glory to Old Columbia! We matriculated, and then I traveled off with Chittenden, Backus, Spencer and Knox to see about some badges for the Philolexian. . . .

October 4. . . . I was at college bright and early, and had to wait there some time before any one came. At a quarter-past eight, however, C[hittenden] and Backus arrived, and we went down to the Philolexian Room. By nine, the front of the college was quite crowded with students, trustees, etc. Among the rest were the members of the University "Chapter" of the ΑΔΦ Society (as a notice signed by Cox,[18] "Lord Privy Seal," called them) with their breastpins and red ribbons.

We got into motion in our usual *orderly* manner—and moved off. The procession was very long and we made quite a display with our Philolexian and Peithologian badges—the ineffable ΑΔΦ—and the graduating and committee insignia, not to mention the president, who was bedizened and adorned most sublimely. We moved quite rapidly, but it was after ten when we reached the church [St. John's Chapel]. After a good deal of crowding and squeezing we established ourselves quite comfortably and then the Prex proceeded to "open with a prayer," very much in his usual style, and then made his usual speech, nearly inaudible and quite unintelligible, except the last two words, which instead of *"ascendat* Orator" were *"ascendat* Hillyer." So up walked the immortal Giles Mumford in all his glory. His poem was well delivered and no doubt very edifying to the audience. Then came [John] Graham with the Latin Salutatory, also quite good, much better than I expected from him. Both these were in hexameters and not very well adapted for speaking, in my humble opinion. Next came the super-super-fine Mr. John Jay with an English Salutatory remarkable only for the quantity of blarney it contained, and then Mr. Christodoulos Leonidas Miltiades Evangeles "on the Greek Revolution." He was rather more moderate than I expected, but as it was, he cut quite a conspicuous figure. When his was finished I walked into the refreshment room, but soon walked out again. There had been an irruption of Freshmen and the whole place was one scene of kicking, gourmandizing, swilling, fighting, swearing, and crowding. I made myself scarce extemporaneously. In consequence I did not hear [Daniel McLaren] Quackenbush's speech, but it was said to be very good for him. Then came [George Gilfert] Waters "on the influence of the Gothic race." It was one of the best speeches delivered. Then [Edward] Hoffman—nothing remarkable—and then [Charles] Seymour on "Political Innovation"—quite decent. Last of this batch was J[ames] W[illis] Wilson, who spoke really very well indeed. I was quite surprised to hear him.

By way of interlude, we now had another performance from the band (Kendall's), and Ed[ward Huger] Laight next showed himself and talked away very lucidly about "The Pleasures of Hope." He was followed by [John Henry] Hobart, who did admirably, and then by way of contrast came Newbold Edgar on "Association"—quite somniferous. Harrison

---

[18] Arthur Cleveland Coxe (New York University 1838), afterward Bishop of Western New York.

Lynch on "Popular Education" did decently enough—and passing over H[enry] McVickar, the next was H[enry] Ward on the poetry of Greece. He sputtered and flourished and produced quite a sensation. His speech was about as fine a specimen of flowery, inflated humbug as I ever heard.

The next was an Italian speech, by [William] Thompson, and lastly James P[hillips] Lake on "Love of Praise." His speech was extremely shallow. He was hissed by the Freshmen, chiefly I suppose, because he used to teach, a short time since, in the Grammar School.

Then the Praeses descended from the pulpit and enthroned his sublime *corpus* in his chair of state and placed on his head a black velvet cap, very like a fool's cap, and then he proceeded to the distribution of the Honorary Testimonials. I felt as if I were sitting on pins—there was a sensation of something in my left side pounding and pounding, for all the world like the piston of a steam engine. In short (my indifference and independence of last night to the contrary notwithstanding), I felt as if the next ten minutes were to settle my fate—life or death. I hardly know what medals were given out in the other classes. [Giles Mumford] Hillyer and [Samuel] Blatchford each took the head in his class and I was glad to see that Chittenden and Waters took a good many medals also. Then came the Sophomore Class and I felt "queerer" than ever. First came Backus, and then—in Latin—George Templeton Strong. I walked up, feeling rather in doubt whether walking on my head or my heels. I took them also in Greek and chemistry, and then came the distribution of diplomas with all the usual formalities, and lastly, Harvey A[ugustus] Weed with the Valedictory, one of the best things I ever heard, certainly the best today. It has been very much admired.

I did not get home till half-past four. I was wretchedly tired—fairly exhausted. I had been in a state of excitement all the morning and felt, I suppose, very much as the opium eater or wine drinker does when the effects of the stimulant are over. My father is satisfied, that's one comfort. . . .

October 5. . . . We went into the chapel to get directions about books. I am glad to see that Barber[19] is to attend, for the purpose of teaching elocution. It is very much needed. He gives lectures to the Seniors and I think to us also—I hope so—for though speechifying will be a horrid bore, it will be a great advantage to all of us, myself most especially. With Anthon we are to read Longinus, Aeschylus, Terence, and Cicero

---

[19] Dr. John Barber taught elocution in the college in 1836–37, but his appointment was not renewed; see the entry of January 20, 1837.

*de Officiis.*With Anderson we take up astronomy (*eheu me miserum*), with Renwick, optics, and I don't know what else, and with McVickar, history of literature, composition, and I suppose all the other humbugs that appertain to his most humbuggical department. . . .

Read eight or ten pages in the astronomy. Let me try this year whether I cannot do something in Anderson's room. The way it has been hitherto is somewhat thus: during the session I have postponed thorough study of the subject till revision, and during revision have postponed it till just before examinations, and then have been obliged to work like a dragon and cram the business of three months into two weeks. I'll not do so this year if I can help it. . . .

Just one year today since I began this journal. What a mass of nonsensical shallowness I have put on paper since then! No matter—I hope I shall improve as I go on.

October 6. . . . Walked up to college. After prayers the president distributed, or rather caused to be distributed, a lot of "Regulations of the Board"—printed, I suppose, for our especial benefit. They are very edifying. . . .

Walked down with G[eorge] Anthon, and after dinner went up to his house where in consideration of the loan of my last year's notes, he made over to me the fee simple of his coins, or rather the remnant of them, consisting of one gold and a dozen or fifteen silver pieces, chiefly Eastern, with one or two coins of Charles and James II. Quite a snug little haul, and the best bargain I have made this long time. . . .

October 7. . . . After Society adjourned, Chittenden, Trevett, McMullen and myself got together in a corner and enjoyed a long talk on a great variety of subjects, till something like ten o'clock. Trevett at last got the conversation on episcopacy and church government, his favorite topic, and grew quite eloquent on the subject. Chittenden's ideas are diametrically the reverse of Trevett's. They are both, I think, rather too *ultra*, but T's ultraism is, I think, rather preferable, though Chittenden stands up for his side of the question most valiantly.

By the way, speaking of *ultraism*, who, in the name of wonder, would have suspected Henry J. Anderson, the upright, steady, stiff, immutable, cool, cautious, rational, judgmatical, reasoning, accurate, mathematical, matter-of-fact, sober, anti-enthusiastic, clear-headed, moneymaking, real-estate-buying, demonstrating Prof. Harry—that incarnation of a right angle—*who* would ever have suspected him of being a furiously enthusiastic Democrat? No—not a Democrat, the expression's certainly too tame, but a *"Pas eauto-*crat" (the word's coined for the occasion), an "every man himself-ocrat"—a man who believes in the utter perfectibility of the human race, and regards all law as an encumbrance, a shackle on that freedom which is the birthright of all mankind? Yet such he is—on the very best authority. Trevett has heard him argue on it; he grows perfectly rabid the moment he gets into the subject, e.g., "The fire laws are nuisances—every man has a right to have his house burnt down, and himself in it, if he likes"; "The laws prohibiting omnibusses from Wall Street are atrocious—shameful—*infernal*—" (on this topic he was particularly indignant, and in Trevett's hearing) "a shameful infringement on our liberties." Agrarianism, too, he supports. In religion no one knows his sentiments—they are not far from Deism—though he always speaks with respect of the Bible, and lives a moral life. Who would have thought it of Harry Anderson!!

October 8, SATURDAY. Walked to the office to get the cash for my matriculation fee, and then up to the College. "Forked out the ready." The president drove a pretty poor business this morning. Not more than one-third had brought the needful and I thought he looked bluer than I ever saw him look before. The new books have arrived at college but I had no time to inspect them. Took out one—Ackerman's *Roman Coins*. It is a splendid work and I have got a good deal out of it. I find several of my coins described there. . . .

By the by, Waters lent me *Fanny* this morning; I intend to copy it. . . .

October 10. College as usual. . . . Jemmy gave us a lecture on the microscope and showed us a compound one—the finest by far, I ever saw. . . .

October 11. . . . Handed in my name to the president to join the French class—after the fourth hour. Went upstairs to attend [Rev. Antoine] Verren.[20] There has only been one class formed and they are advanced in the language and were translating away with great activity; astonishing "translating" it was, judging from the style of their English, which was barbarous, Doric, and diabolical. Sat there an hour inwardly strengthening myself in the resolution of cutting the whole concern, which I shall do by withdrawing my name. I suppose the president will not make much objection.

I must study French, though, in some way or other—by myself if I

---

[20] The Rev. Antoine Verren (1801–1874), native of Marseilles, was rector of L'Eglise du Saint-Esprit in New York from 1827 till his death and professor of French at Columbia from 1828 to 1839; Columbia made him an honorary A.B. in 1831.

can't do better. Mary has grammars and everything of the sort by bushels, and if I can't make it out, I deserve a hiding. At all events, I must study it.

October 12.   Blowing and raining. . . . Walked to college. Got along quietly till I got to Dey Street when there came a puff that caught my umbrella and fairly lifted me off my feet. I thought at first I was going to astonish the city by an extempore aeronautic expedition. But I found my feet again at last, and reached college alive.

Anthon was, as I expected, very fierce on the Longinus. I believe I was the only individual who got off without a share of his ferocity. He said "the ghost of Longinus must be out on the Green raising the storm, in his wrath at the classical murders going on in the college." . . .

October 13.   Very clear and pleasant. Renwick invited me this morning to come into his room whenever I liked. He has been exceedingly civil of late, probably because the class behaves rather more decently than they did. No wonder; we have lost Duer, Gordon, and Johnson—three of the greatest d——ls among us. Fish and Douglass are the worst who now remain. . . .

At four, walked down to Castle Garden to see Lauriat make another ascension. Found very few inside, and the balloon not more than half inflated. I went inside the railing; I don't think I ever had an opportunity before of examining a balloon close by. It has a very fragile appearance—rather a slippery concern to trust one's self in at the height of a couple of miles or so. The transparent silk, I should imagine, would make the ascender ticklish, and the cords of the netting, which were not thicker than the cord in dresses, looked quite suspicious. However, I think I would run the risk for the delight of the ascension—for I certainly think it must be the most delightful sail one can possibly enjoy. It must be glorious. One might almost fancy himself moving self-sustained, like an eagle, through the air—nothing but the little basket in which he rests to break the illusion, and the immense globe floating like a cloud just above him, and below, earth and sea, hills, rivers, plains, forest, and field all spread out; it must be a magnificent scene. I think that one could not help forgetting the danger in the sublime feeling it might excite. I would give much to make the experiment.

It was a very fine afternoon—not a cloud to be seen—and wind about southwest. Lauriat seemed as cool and composed as possible. He jumped into the car at length, the music sounded, artillery thundered, and the mob hurrahed—and he shot off like an arrow. He said he meant to go to Boston, and by the way he traveled off I should judge he would not be very long in getting there. The balloon did not rise very high, but moved at such a rate as very soon to be out of sight, I should think fifty miles an hour at least. . . .

October 15. . . . It is in contemplation to have a meeting of the students about a semi-centennial anniversary of the college. It will be fifty years next 13th April since this college became Columbia College, and there is some idea of a little splutter on the occasion. Very good. The more fun the better. . . .

October 16, SUNDAY. . . . Went to Cedar Street Church morning and afternoon. . . . After tea, took a walk around the Battery. By the by, I've heard nothing of Mr. Lauriat. Has he been blown away entirely—or what has become of him?

October 17. Spoke to Renwick this morning about the Semi-Centennial project. He expressed himself highly pleased with it and told me some curious anecdotes about the troubles of the college during the Revolution. Its president at that time was Dr. Myles Cooper, a furious Tory, and oddly enough his favorite pupil was Alexander Hamilton, who was an equally furious Whig, and they wrote against each other for a long time on the politics of the day—each a leading man on his own side —and each ignorant of the real name of his opponent. At last the mob got very ferocious against Cooper and a large body moved at a late hour in the night [10 May 1775] towards the college with the intention of murdering or at least tarring and feathering its unlucky *Praeses.* Hamilton got scent of it, and at the corner of what is now Park Place and Broadway he made them a furious Whig address, and in this way kept them off till Cooper got intelligence of the state of affairs. He got out of bed, and without his breeches managed to get out of the back gate on Chapel Street and to scramble down the steep bank between the College and the river, and then proceeded along shore as far as Greenwich, where he stole a boat and paddled himself off to one of the frigates in the bay. Meantime the mob attacked his house, smashed the furniture, ran swords through his bed, in hopes of finding him there, and at last cleared out in disappointment. The first act of the Committee of Safety, it seems, was to displace the students and make a hospital for the Continentals out of the building. The library—then the finest in the country—was destroyed. The soldiers disposed of the books about the streets for grog. The apparatus went in like manner, except two or three articles which, with the remnant of the books, were saved and placed in St. Paul's Church steeple; there they were left and forgotten, till in 1804 or 1805 someone noticed a door in the steeple and had it opened—and here the books and apparatus were found, together with some other matters that had been long missing; an old theodolite was among the number, that now stands in one of the closets in the upper apparatus room. . . .

October 20. . . . Afternoon, stayed at home, studying like a dragon, and kept at it until half-past twelve, writing a composition, "Taste" No. 2. I have taken scarcely a bit of exercise of late—I must take more—for stooping over the desk from three till twelve steadily, as I have done the greater part of this session, short as it has been, doesn't seem to agree with me at all.

October 28. . . . Chittenden gave me a curious hint, just after college today, viz., "I might be an ΑΔΦ before long." *Quære de hoc.* . . .

Evening. Debate at the Society, on Universal Suffrage. Spoke against it. I would give a good deal for the fluency with which Hillyer, Chittenden, and one or two others can speak extempore. I may have ideas enough in my head, but the minute I am on my feet and have got past the words "Mr. President" I am sure to find all my ideas have departed—quite entirely out of my reach. . . .

October 30, SUNDAY. Went to St. Paul's *solus* in the morning and to Dr. McElroy's in the afternoon. Took a walk after church, and went to sleep over Dwight's *Theology* in the evening.

November 3. . . . Stayed after college till after three o'clock in the Philolexian Room with Chittenden and [Samuel] Blatchford, seeing about the Anniversary business, writing up the statement of proceedings, and so on. We sent out, got a lot of cake and some apples and made ourselves comfortable. Did not eat any dinner.

Went up to Appleton's. He has had his store expanded so that the Old Books, instead of being literally crammed upstairs, will be provided with some sort of decent accommodations below. It is a very good plan, for they were afraid the floor would break through, and moreover it was scarcely possible to navigate upstairs for the folios that were heaped up in piles six or eight feet high. I saw some glorious works there, a Montfaucon (English translation) in particular that I would like to have considerably, though I suppose it is out of my reach.

Went to Barber's lecture after tea. Besides about twenty students, there were not more than thirty people there. It was a first-rate lecture.

November 5. A delightful day. College as usual. Wrote up [Philolexian] minutes. Brought home with me the old minute book of 1816. They did things on quite an extensive scale in those days.

Took a walk on the Battery, and then went up to Appleton's to direct him to send down some Annuals and so forth, for inspection. He sent down quite a lot of them and one volume of Montfaucon besides. Gained the day—and got Montfaucon—$40. Paid for it in the afternoon and at six went with all the solemn feelings of awe which the occasion demanded (*vide* Fogruni's disclosures) up to the College Green to meet Chittenden for a ΑΔΦ initiation. . . .

Tucker and a lot of others walked down with us to Hillyer's—but here I must stop—it won't do to put all these terrible arcana on paper. Passed a very pleasant evening.

November 16. . . . Read a little in Boswell's *Johnson*; it is a very entertaining book, but neither of the two characters appears to me particularly amiable. Johnson is the great Bear of English Literature, and Boswell—I don't know what to call him—if his mighty patron were the Lion I should call him the Jackal; as it is, I don't know what name to give him—certain it is he's the prince and *beau idéal* of Toad Eaters. I should fancy him to have looked a good deal like McVickar, and Johnson must have resembled Charles Anthon I think, only with far more firmness and infinitely more common sense.

November 23. Diabolical outrage! They are not going to give us "Evacuation Day"—horrible! We shall have to *take it*.

November 25. Thought proper to absent myself from college, the first time I ever attempted anything of the kind, but this is a special occasion; I wonder what the result will be. Walked up to Chittenden's; stopped on the way to see how things looked at college. Encountered Prof. Renwick. Asked him whether there were any lectures. He said that the president had directed that there should be, but there was nobody to lecture. If I wanted one, he said, he'd be very happy to give it to me if I walked in with him. Told him I believed I wouldn't trouble him *today*—and took my departure. . . .

November 28. Evening. Studied Cicero and wrote some Observeriana—Percy Bysshe Shelley. I have been reading some of his poetry of late. Very "deep" they say it is. For my part it reminds me of the old story of "Did ye ever see a puddle in the middle of the road? Vara well. Ye canna see the bottom of it, not because it's deep, but because it's muddy." . . .

November 29. Went up to college. Great excitement about the affair of the 25th. . . .

COLUMBIA COLLEGE

CITY HALL PARK AND THE CROTON WATER FOUNTAIN

The good folks returned from Boston today, and my father brought with him a book I have long wanted to have, viz., Mather's *Magnalia*— the reprint [Hartford, 1820]. . . .

The college was considerably stirred up for several days and Strong and some of his conscientious friends were apprehensive of the measures it was feared the Board might take to punish the students who absented themselves on Evacuation Day. It had been a concerted move, and there was a suspicion that John King Duer "had been playing the part of a spy and carrying intelligence of everything to his father [the president]," which young Duer indignantly denied in a published "Manifesto." President Duer felt that the affair bespoke a lack of confidence of the students in him, and in chapel on December 5 announced with some emotion that no action would be taken. Strong's comment: "Depend on it, he would have taken severe measures if he could, but he was voted down in the Board."

December 6. Old General [Jacob] Morton's funeral took place today. Blatchford and myself walked down to the Battery and after waiting nearly an hour, it came past. The Military were out in force, there were the "Masons" with all their solemn humbugs, and a large number of citizens, Prof. Renwick among them. . . .

December 15, THURSDAY. Thanksgiving Day, and no college, of course. . . . Having a curiosity today to witness the Catholic services, I determined to go up to St. Patrick's to see High Mass performed by Bishop [John] Dubois. On my way up I met Blatchford; he turned round and we walked to the Cathedral together. After standing for some time near the door, little Shea[21] came in and offered us a seat in his pew, which we were very glad to accept. At a little before eleven, the services began. The high altar was very magnificently arrayed with three immense wax candles some six feet high and a great deal of tinsel and frippery besides. At last, in came the bishop, six or seven priests, and as many of the little boys in surplices, one of them with a censer. The bishop was very splendidly arrayed; he had his crosier in his hand, very richly gilt, and his hat—I forget the name—on his head; he is a very venerable looking old man, but was ornamented in rather a ridiculous manner. The priests were very richly dressed also.

[21] Charles Edward Shea, Columbia '37, son of James Shea, one of the teachers in the Grammar School.

The services began by a sort of recitative from the bishop, with responses from the choir. Every time they passed in front of the altar they kneeled or rather performed a sort of genuflexion, not quite kneeling. There was a good deal of incense burning and the whole scene was soon wrapped in *smoke*, very expressive of its real nature. At last Dr. [John] Powers ascended the pulpit and proceeded to give a sermon. He spoke very loud and with a great deal of gesture, and withal rather indistinctly. It was a strange sort of political, metaphysical, doctrinal, begging affair. He talked about the advance of mind and the progress of free principle, the beauties of "our adopted country" and the sweets of liberty, the tender mercies of Mother Church and the lies of the heretics concerning her doctrines. The Roman Church, he said, was not a persecuting church; the heretics advocated destructive principles—and the civil authority condemned them to be burned. Holy Mother Church was very sorry to burn them, but still she was *compelled* to burn them, and so did it, though most reluctantly—such seemed to be the main body of his discourse. He concluded with an appeal to the pockets of his auditors, in behalf of the Orphan Asylum. Then came the ceremonies of Mass—a great deal of chanting, genuflexion, etc. There was a crazy, or tipsy, Irishwoman in front of us who created quite a sensation while the bishop was busy with the chalice. She sung out at the top of her voice: "Jest pass the brandy and water along here, will you?"

December 16. . . . Shea told me today that the collection taken up yesterday at St. Patrick's amounted to $456, which he thought very large. I should think it rather small.

This is the anniversary of the Great Fire—what a terrible night that was!—and yet the excitement of it seems almost pleasing in the retrospect.

December 23. . . . The death of Charles C. Lee, one of our honoraries, was announced to the Society, and the usual humbug resolutions passed.[22] He died of a brain fever, the immediate cause being the excitement attendant on these medical squabbles, but the remoter, his tremendous, systematic dissipation. He was raving from his first attack, and I understand chiefly about a monkey he had recently dissected. He swore at his physicians—said they had murdered him—and fairly drove them out of the room.

[22] After the members of the literary societies had been graduated they were usually voted honorary memberships, and the president was chosen from their number. Lee '35 had entered the College of Physicians and Surgeons in the fall of 1836.

December 24. Today President Duer announced to us *pro forma*, the Christmas holidays, concluding with a merry Christmas and happy New Year to all; he was loudly applauded. Waited some time for the library to open, and in the meantime a good many delinquents were hauled up before the solemn tribunal of the Board—Cooper and Douglass of our class among the rest. Both received the same sentence, viz., to study four hours a day during the vacation and bring a certificate to that effect from their folks at home. They were both a good deal excited about it: Cooper, of course, cannot stand any thing of the kind, and Douglass said "his old man would blow him up terribly for it"; they both concluded to apply for a reconsideration—Douglass on the ground of the sickness of his brother and the consequent excitement of his father's feelings. His brother is quite ill with scarlet fever and Douglass displays a philosophic coolness on the subject not remarkably creditable to him. Both were unsuccessful, and both departed in wrath. Lucky for the faculty that curses do not kill —or else the faculty of Columbia College would have been swept from the earth. Went into the library at last, took out Dibdin's *Library Companion* and a couple of geological works. The first I have found very interesting; Dibdin is such an enthusiastic bibliomaniac that it is impossible to help feeling an interest in what he says, and sometimes equally so to help laughing at it. . . .

December 25, SUNDAY. CHRISTMAS—and the best day in the year, but its cheerfulness rather damped by a constant drizzle of rain with an accompaniment of fog. Went to St. Paul's in the morning and stayed home in the afternoon.

December 26. . . . I see by this morning's paper that Douglass's little brother, Brainard, died yesterday. He was a fine bright little fellow, and very mischievous withal.

Poor Douglass; he is in a bad way, I am afraid. Between [John Beekman] Fish, Roosevelt,[23] [R. M.] Vandenheuvel, and one or two dissipated characters of their stamp, he is going to the devil as fast as possible. He is naturally a good-hearted, fine fellow, and so is Benjamin Romaine, who is following his example, but he is captivated by their blackguardism, which he takes for wit—ruins, murders his talents, because he sees them doing the same with what little they have got. He lives at the billiard table and considers a spree as the height of human felicity. He has command of nearly unlimited means (I speak comparatively) from his

[23] There were no Roosevelts in Columbia at this time; the others were undergraduates there.

father, but he applies them to purposes that a sensible dog would be ashamed of, but which are sanctioned by his great model Fish and his other friends. Poor fellow, I prophesy that he will never amount to much if he goes on in this way.

December 27.   Called on George Anthon, and was sorry to find him really *bona fide* sick—laid up for a month with congestion of the liver, and starved, blistered, and physicked out of all sort of decency. And in Christmas Week, too! . . . Met Backus and went down with him to Appleton's to inspect his old books. Ordered a copy of Evelyn's *Diary*, $9. . . .

Evelyn arrived, and I spent the evening over him. His *Diary* is one of those books I have long wanted to read—the other two are Clarendon and Froissart.

December 28. . . . Went to Appleton's after breakfast, with my sister, who made some purchases in the Annual line. Took a walk on the Battery. . . .

December 29.   Went this morning to the Zoological Institute in the Bowery—much the same as last year, except that they have a band of music there, and atrocious music it is. I looked carefully to see whether the different animals were affected by it, but generally they were not at all—but perhaps this arose from their hearing it every day. None of the feline kind took the slightest notice of it except a superb royal tiger and a pair of hunting leopards—these seemed to rouse up a little on hearing it. A couple of kangaroos paid as much attention to it as any of the animals. I noticed in regard to them, by the by, that for short jumps at least, they do not use the tail as a spring to aid them as I recently saw somewheres, but spring entirely by the muscles of the leg. Perhaps, however, in longer leaps it is different.

Afternoon.   Called on Chittenden. Found him and Spencer vocalizing and fluting. Walked down to college with Chittenden and then to Clinton Hall, to see Mr. Fowler the phrenologist there and have my bumps examined. Bought a kind of chart with all the bumps registered. On the whole, impressed in favor of phrenological science by Mr. Fowler's statements; indeed I have always believed in it, in some degree. He gave me amativeness very strong—correct; fondness for music very strong— also correct; strong imagination and great benevolence—neither I think correct, especially the latter; firmness very strong indeed—in which he is decidedly wrong; conscientiousness, strong; mathematical talent, strong—in this he is mistaken; no memory of localities—right; good

memory of features—wrong, tho' this may be partly owing to my shortsightedness; ingenuity, very strong—in which he is, I think, quite out,
though he persisted that it was so; so I must take it for granted it is not
yet developed; fondness for good eating—there he's right; sensitiveness—
right again; desire for approbation, right again—perhaps he did not rate
it quite high enough. This, combined with my want of firmness, is I
think a very bad point; memory of fact, poor—there he is wrong—my
memory is better of facts than anything else; veneration low, that is, as
he explains it, no fondness for formalities in religion—correct; self-
esteem, high, there I certainly think he is wrong. And so on through the
whole catalogue of phrenology. He has been wrong in several instances,
but on the whole he gave a true account of what I believe to be my real
character—and that without any previous knowledge of me and without
any information gained by "pumping." In one or two minor points, he
hit it exactly.

*Phrenology, introduced into America by Spurzheim a few years before, was
sweeping the country at this time, and a vast part of the population, including
even such men as Emerson, had the bumps on their heads read. Orson Squire
Fowler, Amherst 1834, whose interest in the subject had been aroused by his
classmate Henry Ward Beecher, opened an establishment in New York with
his brother, and for years they gave "readings" and lectures and flooded the
country with pseudo-scientific journals and books on phrenology and eugenics;
their fame was enormous. Some of the octagon-shaped houses which they devised
and advocated can still be seen in the Hudson Valley.*

1837

PERSECUTION OF DR. BARBER · SAMUEL WARD'S LIBRARY · COLUMBIA SEMI-CENTENNIAL · PANIC IN WALL STREET · BOSTON TRIP · QUEEN VICTORIA BEGINS HER REIGN · SUMMER AT WHITESTONE

*S*trong bought a new blank book for his journal of 1837, and his daily entries grew markedly in length. He recorded briefly that his father escaped the traditional New Year's call-making by having "a very convenient 'bad cold' " and staying at his office all the morning of Monday, January 2. George himself "prudently and wisely made no visits at all." He wrote on January 4 that he was not sorry to see the last of the holidays, for "a period of leisure is pleasant only as a change, and . . . we soon feel inclined to desire another change, that is, back to studying again." College events thereafter occupied most of the diary. On the night of January 25 a magnificent display of aurora borealis was visible in the city, and next day a time-honored trick was played in the astronomy class: "We got Professor Anderson astraddle of one of last night's columns of light, and he shot off into infinite space; of course we heard no more of the appointed recitation." The semi-annual examinations occasioned the usual bouts of studying and apprehensions of failure, but when the medals were awarded, Strong stood at the head of his class. Preparations continued actively for the semi-centennial anniversary of the college in April. This celebration commemorated the charter of 1787, which had restored Columbia as an independent successor to King's College after three unsuccessful years as part of the University of the State of New York. The students had originated the idea of a celebration and had interested the alumni association, a casual organization headed by old General Edward W. Laight of the class of 1793.

When the year opened, the country seemed prosperous, and speculation and commercial expansion were giving multitudes an illusion of wealth. But

[48]

astute men saw trouble on the horizon. Jackson's Specie Circular of the previous summer, requiring that all payments on public lands be made in hard money, had distressed the banks which were financing Western land speculation; a financial crisis in England caused British creditors to call in their American loans; and poor crops had lowered the purchasing power of many farmers. Late in March, the failure of a large cotton firm in New Orleans involved other houses. Panic overspread the South and West, and debts there became uncollectible. Frantic efforts by Philadelphia and New York banks to stem the tide were fruitless. Merchandise fell thirty per cent in a few weeks; stocks dropped in even greater degree; and on May 10 the New York banks suspended, those of other Eastern cities at once following the example. Anxiety, bankruptcy, and want overspread the whole land.

January 7. . . . Went to the library and returned the books I took out a fortnight ago. I have only read Dibdin through, and some parts of the others. Dibdin is very interesting, full of anecdote and information, but the author is perfectly crazy, mad, on the subject of "large paper" and "tall copies," and insane about "fine old Morocco bindings," etc. I took out three volumes of the *Harleian Miscellany.* . . . Up to Appleton's for a copy of Southey's poems. Not to be had. Hunted about a good while and as a last resort went into that rascally citadel of humbug, [W. A.] Colman's, though I had made up my mind not to enter the place again. Succeeded in catching a copy at the moderate price of $6.50. . . . Spent the evening on Southey and Aeschylus.

January 13. . . . Stopped in Appleton's on my way from college and ordered a copy of Bacon's works in four volumes folio and a very handsome edition indeed, price $20. . . .

January 15, SUNDAY. I have been thinking today about taking Italian lessons of Signor Foresti,[1] one of the Italian exiles just arrived here, after eighteen years' imprisonment in Spielberg for republicanism and patriotism. If it were any other time of the year I would, but now with revision just about beginning and the examination at no very great distance, I don't see how I can spare the time.

[1] Eleuterio Felice Foresti, LL.D. Bologna 1809, had the misfortune to be an ardent liberal in a most reactionary period of his country's—and Europe's—history; nevertheless, during his exile here he continued his leadership in Italian movements and was finally welcomed back in 1858 as U.S. consul at Genoa, where he died the same year; he was professor of Italian at Columbia from 1839 to 1856.

January 20. . . . Came home with [Henry Partridge] Fessenden. He mentioned to me a piece of business which has lately been going on among the Seniors which surprised me not a little. The night before last, eight or nine of the class went to Barber's residence in Greenwich Street to serenade him. They sang a song composed for the occasion, each verse ending with Fia-a-a-a-a-*ay*! thereby giving the professor a practical demonstration of their progress in elocution. They then proceeded to the nearest druggist's and purchased a delectable compound of ipecac, castor oil, salts, and all conceivable nastiness, adding to it a quantum of a solution of tincture of asafoetida, so as to make the whole of the consistence of mud. Three times did Fessenden ring the bell to leave this diabolical compound for the professor, and each time he saw the professor himself coming with a stick to open the door, and he therefore beat a retreat. At last they gave a black boy sixpence to give the parcel to the professor; it was wrapped in two or three papers and formally directed to the professor as a "donation from the Senior class." The unfortunate black boy took it to the door, the professor nabbed him, and applied the cudgel lustily. The boy yelled "Help! Murder!" and so on, the students ran, the watchman gave chase, and there was quite a combobbolation. The president begs that they will desist from their persecution of the poor man.

January 21. Splashed, slid, and stumbled to college, and on my way home stopped at Wiley & Long's to purchase what I have long been most anxious to read, a translation of *Faust.* I have been nearly all day at it and hardly know whether to like it or not. It is not quite equal to my expectations, but has some splendid passages in it.

January 31. . . . Dr. [John] Neilson gave me this morning a regular exhortation. He tells me I don't take enough exercise, stoop too much in writing, sit still too much, and so on. He is right. If I go on as I have for the last three months, I verily believe it will put a very peremptory stop to my studying. I have taken little or no exercise and have often, after sitting the whole afternoon, sat at the desk, without ten minutes intermission, from 6:30 to 12. He says I must have a standing desk made.

Great news from Boston. "Totty" No. 2, Master George Strong Derby, made his entree into the light of heaven on Sunday at four A.M., in fine health and spirits. Eloise is well. . . .

February 10, FRIDAY. . . . Some rascal has put into the papers a notice of the death of Prof. Renwick, "after an excruciating illness, which he bore with Christian fortitude." I have no doubt that Douglass is at the bottom of it. Renwick stands it very well, more good humoredly than was to have been expected. Our class entered the room to the Dead March, and [Edward] Anthony asked him whether we were to attend the funeral or not. It has made quite a talk.

February 13. . . . They say that [John Beekman] Fish is the author of the notice of Prof. Renwick's death. He has applied for a dismissal, which has been refused. . . .

February 14. We had a row last night. A mob, with the usual discretion of all mobs, attacked Mr. Eli Hart's store in Washington Street and destroyed three hundred barrels of flour, because flour is high, and they wish to lower its price.

February 16. . . . I had a long talk with Fish today. He has got both [James Gordon] Bennett and one of [James Watson] Webb's clerks to declare that he was not the person who brought the notice. Their description of the person who brought the notice answered very well to Douglass, and in spite of Douglass's asseveration, I fancy he is at the bottom of the business after all. . . .

February 20. . . . My standing desk arrived today. It is an excellent article, no doubt, but it maketh the bones ache to study at it.

March 12, SUNDAY. Went to Cedar Street Church in the afternoon, for the last time, as it is to be begun to be pulled down this week.

March 17. . . . Went over to Chittenden's. Started off with him for a walk. We traveled up Broadway and along the railroad, some distance beyond that abode of sweet savors, the big glue factory on the Middle Road [Fifth Avenue]. Came home through the Bowery, a little tired.

We don't take near exercise enough generally; this week I mean to do a month's walking. To do anything in the world, we don't want mental strength merely, but physical abilities also; an educated mind in a weak carcass is like a powerful engine on board a leaky steamboat. Our walk was a very pleasant one. Chittenden has not lost one jot or tittle of his propensity for political life, and it was of that we talked. And we built castles in the air, of such architecture as has rarely been equalled. But who can tell? May not their substratum be a little more solid than it seems just now? Chittenden has energy and independence; I have perseverance; and who knows but twenty years hence we may amuse ourselves by talking over our daydreams of eminence and fame? I myself have but few political ingredients in me. I want decision and resolution. Chittenden has them both; he is a good speaker and I am not, and he, if he enters on public life, will not long remain unnoticed. I find that Chittenden is rather vacillating between two courses of life, one to remain here and the other to move westward. There he would find it easier to gain distinction than here, but when gained it is a far less valuable acquisition. Most sincerely do I hope that he'll do no such thing. We have been so much together for the last few years that if he were to leave the city I should find the change most disagreeable; for his own sake, too, I hope he'll stay, for I have no great opinion of the West, taken as a whole. He's a fellow whose equal I have never met with yet, sound minded and warm hearted, and afflicted neither with puppyism nor any of the absurdities of which nine-tenths of the youths of Gotham are so deeply enamored. He has been a fine friend to me through college and I shall fight for him tooth and nail wherever I can find a chance to do it.

Evening. . . . The books I bought this morning at Wiley & Putnam's arrived in good order, *videlicet,* a set of Sismondi, four volumes, and Sidney's works, one volume, both fine copies and both very valuable, especially the former.

March 20. In the afternoon went to Pike's and got one of those camera lucidas for taking views, a good purchase but a horribly dear one. . . .

March 23. Shelley in the afternoon. Rather humbuggical, I think. I agree with Backus about his poetry; it passes for more than it is worth, especially his "Cenci," which is great stuff, and his "Queen Mab," which is as flimsy and hyperbolical in composition as it is detestable in sentiment. Setting its sentiments aside, it does not compare in point of poetic fancy with "The Culprit Fay" or half a dozen other pieces which are not generally half so much read. Shelley in fact, like Byron, is rather a proscribed author; he is read by stealth and hence is read with more pleasure. Strike out from Byron's works those sentiments which make them in many cases forbidden fruit, and the fact that they are now open to all, free from censure, would deprive them of half their charm. At present it is fashionable, manly, to admire Byron and Shelley, and therefore they are admired by those who have no more poetic feeling than a horse, and five out of ten have not read the very author whom they glorify. . . . It is amazing to read the life of Shelley prefixed to any edition of his works and generally to read all the laudatory articles on him and Byron. To be sure he seduced women without number, to be sure the atheism and profligacy in his works has been a fountain of destruction to hundreds and so will continue to be; to be sure he displayed depravity in every shape conceivable, and no one can deny that he was a curse to the world while he lived and that his writings still propagate the infection after his death and go on raising up other Byrons and other Shelleys to do the same good office by mankind, but still "He had a good heart." What utter humbug! It reminds me of the fellow in the Pickwick Club who was tried for pummeling his wife when he was tipsy, and whose counsel said "it was only an amiable weakness." Shelley and Byron no doubt had some good qualities—they would be strange beings if they had not—but the tree is known by its fruit, and on these trees the rotten fruit predominated.

March 24.   Occupied myself after breakfast in arranging my books, which require an overhauling about twice a year, and then went to church, it being Good Friday. Heard a doleful sermon from a dolorous-looking parson. . . .

March 25, SATURDAY. . . . Crossed over to Jersey City with Chittenden for a ramble, and after roaming about a little while over that doleful region, where they are making the site of a future metropolis, we at last found a more civilized road running north, and on this we entered. Vacant building lots—everything of that kind which forms the outskirts of a city —are dreary, desolate, and dolorous to a very great degree, neither city nor country, but a detestable approximation to both. But ten times more so is a recently manufactured district elevated from a salt water bog into a collection of building lots, public squares and so on, and of that nature is two-thirds of the country around Jersey City. . . .

Read [John] Todd's *Student's Manual* this morning, or rather looked over it. Very utopian, I think. This evening read *The Pilot*, which I like, though it has the same fault with all Cooper's novels that I ever read, viz., not quite attention enough to probability.

March 27. . . . Read Cooper's *Prairie*, which is still more improbable than the *Pilot*, though interesting and spirited.

March 29. . . . In the afternoon attended an ΑΔΦ meeting at Columbia and in the evening read *Frankenstein* and Observerized. *Frankenstein* I have tried vainly to get hold of for the last two years, till Chittenden got it out of the Mercantile Society Library for me. It is a genuine production of the German school, the material well selected and well wrought up into one of the most unearthly and ghastly pieces of *diablesse* I ever heard of. But it is woefully deficient in probability. Matter of fact, real probability is not to be looked for, the very design of the book precluded it, "Dr. Darwin and the German Physiologists" to the contrary notwithstanding, but the book wants poetic probability also; it has not the truth of fiction. How does this monster acquire in a couple of years an elegant English style, considerable skill in logic, and sufficient acquaintance with the history and manners of mankind to enable him to converse and reason at least as well as his sapient creator Frankenstein? Where does the soul come from that enables the master to do this under any circumstances, or after any time for study? Does the "Modern Prometheus" create spirit as well as matter, or does the authoress mean to imply that the soul is matter, or that it is a nonentity? There the daughter of Mary Wollstone-craft and the wife of Percy B. Shelley shows herself. Again the hero is a fool. Why doesn't he shoot the monster in some of their tête-à-têtes? Nothing could be easier. Why does he not take measures to give him his quietus when followed through England by him? (There, by the way, is another piece of improbability.) Why does he not comply with his wishes and save himself and his family from destruction by giving the monster a mate, and thus producing a race of high-souled, generous devils who, if we may judge from the specimen shown us, are very glorious fellows indeed? And finally, why is Frankenstein such an infernal, cold-blooded, cowardly villain as to suffer Justine to be executed for a murder of which he knows her to be innocent?

What is the object of the book? The obvious "moral," I think, is a warning against a thirst for knowledge carried to excess. But that is not Shelleyish enough. The object of the authoress seems to have been to show what the soul becomes when deprived of all communication with other human beings. To show that all men if isolated like Frankenstein's devil would become as high-minded and noble as the conclusion of the book shows him to be. "Vain wisdom all, and feeble philosophy." In plainer language—all humbug. . . .

March 30. . . . Called at George Anthon's. Found him hard at work making out the catalogue of [Professor] Anthon's library[2] (some five thousand volumes!). George is a little too much awed by the mighty Taurus, who I fancy finds him a very convenient worker now and then. . . .

Afternoon.   Went up to Chittenden's and enjoyed a good laugh with him and Backus. Cut up *Lalla Rookh* in a very bloodthirsty manner and gave Backus a fair field for once. He never enjoys himself quite so much as when massacring a modern poet or a lovelorn novel writer. . . .

Heard a capital story today about Philip Hone (Senior). He was show-

[2] This fine classical library, numbering 6,500 volumes at Anthon's death in 1867, was sold to Cornell University, which opened the following year.

ing his library to some foreign gentleman and wanted to find some book, but could not succeed. At last he gave it up in despair and turned to the foreigner who was assisting his search. "Don't trouble yourself, sir," said he. "It's not to be found—never mind—*nunquam animus.*"

April 7. College. . . . Got off at the second hour. Walked up with the two Wards to see the library Samuel Ward[3] has brought out from Germany with him. Looked over Mr. Ward's picture gallery and then went into the library. In point of show it is certainly the finest I ever saw, a great majority of the books being in the finest possible condition as to binding and typography. Indeed I never saw anything comparable in the way of binding to many of the books there. It is certainly a superb and valuable library. In point of mathematical works, one of the finest in the country, I suspect, Mr. Ward having bought up all Lagrange's library. I noticed a superb Baskerville Bible, a complete set of the *Gentleman's Magazine*, sets of many reviews, magazines, etc., transactions, without number, of societies in England, France, Italy, and Russia. It is particularly rich in German literature, and almost equally so in French and Spanish. It is a splendid collection though I fancy more for show than use.

Afternoon. Bought the first volume of Capt. Marryat's *Snarleyyow*, not quite up to his former books, though amusing. . . .

Terrible state of things out of doors. Merchants failing by the dozen. Some fear that all the banks will stop payment. We are on the eve of a

---

[3] Sam Ward, Columbia 1831, brother of one of Strong's Ward classmates and cousin of the other, was a fabulous nineteenth century character. His father was a banker and Columbia trustee, and one of his sisters was Julia Ward Howe; the family lived in a mansion at the corner of Bond Street and Broadway. Sam was prepared at the Round Hill School at Northampton, and after graduating from college spent several years in a Grand Tour of Europe, on which he paused long enough at Tübingen to write a dissertation on higher mathematics in Latin which brought him a Ph.D. At this time he was having a gay whirl in New York society, writing for magazines and acting as literary broker for his friend Longfellow; in 1838 he married the daughter of William Backhouse Astor (Columbia 1811), the richest man in the United States. Before long misfortune crowded upon him: his father died and the firm of Prime, Ward & Co. failed; his wife died and a second marriage resulted in estrangement from the Astors; his second wife tired of his financial reverses and left him. In 1849 Sam joined the gold rush to California and is said to have made and lost a fortune there; by the middle fifties he was back in New York in the brokerage business, and just before the war accompanied William H. Russell, correspondent of the London *Times*, on his famous tour of the Confederacy. After the war he found his real vocation—as a lobbyist in Washington in which he was a tremendous success; he was called "The King of the Lobby" and Lord Rosebery extended his title of "Uncle Sam" to "the uncle of the human race." After losing his money again, he went to England to live with the Roseberys, and died on a visit to Italy in 1884.

change, a revolution in business matters, but it is a change that cannot be effected without shaking the whole fabric to the very foundation. I trust it will stand, but——

April 10. Met Charley ⌈Anthon⌉, who talked very fiercely about the Semi-Centennial, being, I take it, somewhat huffed about the lamentable and untimely death of his Greek ode. His nephew ⌈George⌉ tells me that he had avenged the ode by perpetrating a poem on the Semi-Centennial of six hundred lines, cutting up president and professors, making them sing songs and do no pretty conduct for a professor!

Professor Anthon had taken a dim view of the celebration from the start— Strong felt that it was because he had not been permitted to run it—and when his plan for a Latin play to be given at the Park Theatre under his direction was turned down, he was wrathful indeed. The Greek ode he wrote for the occasion went unread; he was sulking in his rooms.

Took a long rambling walk nearly out to the Shot Tower. Being two-thirds famished, we stopped to get some grub in the Bowery. Found it to be a very loaferish place—pie tasted of potato peelings and coffee was a dirty infusion of tobacco—accommodations to correspond. Cleared out in a hurry, leaving pie and coffee to take care of themselves. Minus eighteen pence for this speculation.

April 12. Another luxurious, warm, delicious, glorious day. Hurrah for the Constitution! Hurrah for the Semi-Centennial!!! and hurrah most especially for the clear weather I trust we shall have on the truly tremendous occasion. Went up to college as usual. The business of decorating the chapel doth verily flourish like a green bay tree. There are busts and statues ad infinitum, the only fault that can be found with them is the overwhelming majority of plaster over marble. Then there are portraits of all the great men and all the little men that can be scraped together, from Washington to McVickar. Then there are paper flowers by the shipload and a big pasteboard column extending through the staircase, from the first floor even to the garret. . . . Moreover, by the spirit of humbug! I must not forget the gilded chandeliers nor the portrait of Bishop Onderdonk, nor must I pass over a really admirable portrait of Prex in commencement robes (there shines forth the spirit of William Alexander Duer, LL.D.!), nor a representation of McVickar which may lay first claim to the title of "admirable" since it has made him look like a decent, sensible man. Then there's a whole forest of greenhouse plants . . . red and blue curtains alternately all round the chapel. Mirrors in each pier! The chapel looks for all the world like an old dame of sixty dressed in her granddaughter's French finery. Really I question whether the venerable dust hole was ever so thoroughly aroused before. . . .

After college went over to Brooklyn and enjoyed a very pleasant amble. Came back by a delightful back road which I never traveled before. Very warm, grass green and birds singing. . . . Came home and read Charles Lamb, which is a genuine and real acquisition to my library. . . .

Terrible lot of failures today, Mr. Hull and Abraham Ogden among them. Awful bad times. The merchants going to the devil *en masse*. Hope they'll carry nobody else after them. They say the Locofocos are going to come down on the Bank for specie, but that's no go, for the whole party (taking out some half dozen men) can't raise $1000 among them. Their strength lies in dock loafers and scavengers to whom bankbills are a rarity and whose circulating medium consists of coppers and sixpences and "such small beer." No bills to claim specie with are to be found in their pockets, even if they have any pockets to put them in. . . .

April 13. Got up with a dreadful headache and sickness in the stomach. Felt more like going to bed again than dressing and going to the Anniversary. . . . Conquered the feeling, though with difficulty, and started for college. The weather, which had been miserably cloudy and with every prospect of rain, cleared off bright and pleasant by half-past eight. Very warm and a finer day we could not have had.

Found Chittenden in the Prex's room and Prex himself in silk tights and a new coat, looking very tremendous. Got my secretary badge which we officers (whew!) of the Philolexian are to wear on this terrific occasion. . . . The AΔΦs met in Vermilye's lecture room. . . . The students kept pouring in meantime and so did the alumni, etc., in great abundance; the Green soon presented a very animated appearance. The [New York] University AΔΦs soon made their appearance in full force, and I must not forget the Grand Order of Digamma, a new special society manufactured expressly for the occasion by Messrs. Cooper and Douglass. Cooper is of course piqued at not having sufficient deference paid to his immense talents and at not being respectfully solicited to favor the AΔΦ by becoming one of its members. . . .

At ten o'clock the bell tolled and the procession began to form, a task of no small difficulty. At length we succeeded in getting into an approximation to decent order and moved off at twenty minutes past ten precise . . . the whole procession occupying something like five blocks. . . . We moved slowly, through Park Place, Broadway, Chambers, and Hudson

Streets to St. John's Park, and then through the park to the church. . . . I never saw a church so full, the aisles crowded, the very windows over-flowing, and as hot as the inside of Tartarus in July. . . .

Eastburn's speech was glorious, both in matter and manner. I had expected something good, but nothing equal to this. He handled the sub-ject in the right way. He avoided all the cock and a-bullical stuff that some men would have delighted in, about the "glories of Alma Mater" and so on, but he struck a happy mean between the depths of Prose and and the heights of Poetry, i.e., the heights of humbug. . . . Then came the "Rex tremendae majestatis et Benedictus" by Mozart, which made a terrible noise, and then came Mr. [William] Betts with his poem. I have no doubt that it was very good, but I could not hear it, nor could anyone else. The poor man was dreadfully scared, too, and his hand trembled and his voice faltered and altogether everyone said it was a flunk. This was followed by the *Te Deum* [of Haydn] which I never heard more agreeably performed. . . . Prex then proceeded to utter the honorary degrees. I don't recall all the names, but there were [Fitz Greene] Halleck, [William Cullen] Bryant, and George Griffin!!!![4]

Renwick then appeared on the stage and ejaculated that the students were to form a procession and return to the college, so we made our way out of the church and assembled in St. John's Park, where after a great deal of fun and hurrahing for Giles M. [Hillyer, student marshal] and so on, we succeeded in forming a sort of half-procession, half-mob and marched toward the college. The students were all glorious and more than one potato and apple was cabbaged from the barrels in front of the groceries we passed, to pelt with, so that our whole line of march pre-sented quite an uproarious appearance. . . .

Read Charles Lamb all afternoon. I never got hold of a style which I think is quite equal to it, and it is truly, as they call it, "inimitable."

Started after tea for college. . . . About eight o'clock, at which time I succeeded in forcing my way through the crowd into the chapel, to half-past nine all the rooms were perfectly jammed; a single small ring around the president for introductions was the only space that could be found. At ten it was just possible to move about.

[4] Fourteen honorary degrees in all were conferred, mainly on clergymen and lawyers; George Griffin was the godly partner of Strong's father. A third Knicker-bocker author, whom Strong does not mention, received the A.M. with Halleck and Bryant: Charles Fenno Hoffman, a non-graduate of the class of 1825.

I must not forget that the Sophomore Class had their dinner today and that four of them got most magnificently drunk, [Richard Stockton] Emmet, [Edward Rogers] Bell, [James William] Walsh and Charles E. Anthon; the former pugnaciously cocked, fought everyone, swore like a trooper, and ended at last by tumbling down and breaking his head. Bell was loafing about all evening, most delightfully cocked, until Dugan kicked him out of the college for calling him a —— liar. Walsh was philanthropically cocked and went about hiccuping and running over with the milk of human kindness and declaring his love, affection, and esteem for everybody he met.

But the music was magnificent and the feminines were enchanting and I felt altogether altitudinarious, especially the "Marche Moses" and "La Bayadère." They played delightfully, the finest music I ever heard by all odds, and I thought at one time there seemed strong symptoms of a cotillion in the chapel. Praeses was in such a supremely good humor that I don't think he would have thought of objecting. If he don't get an affection of the spine from excess of bowing he will be fortunate. Renwick, too! his mouth was not straight once during the evening. It was a gay scene. One of Frederic Anthon's bean-pole sisters stuck the Philolexian society badge in her hair for a headdress and one of the McVickars' thousand and one daughters or nieces mounted the Alpha Delta Phi collar round her neck. Mac himself was likewise exceeding glorious.

Refreshments I did not try for. They say that the Freshmen monopolized them, the little cormorants! They deserve the horsepond.

The AΔΦ paid their respects to the president as a society in the course of the evening. At about eleven the students began moving around the chapel in a circle, to the tune of *Hail, Columbia* by the band (I wish that I could hear such music every evening), and we soon took our leave. The students were tremendously uproarious as soon as they got on the Green, and as for myself I was very festive, too, and joined in their three cheers with all my heart and headed for home where I arrived safe a little before twelve. . . .

April 14. . . . Afternoon. . . . Junior dinner. Walked up with Frederic Anthon to the Athenaeum Hotel. . . . Had a royal time. Cooper was tremendously drunk and smashed the glasses, had a row with the waiter, got on the table and delivered an oration, and so on. . . . Drank but little myself. I was cautious, for I scarcely know how much wine I can swallow without making a fool of myself, and moreover I have not acquired much taste for it, nor do I care to. Expected to sit till eleven, but came off at eight and walked home with Backus, who was very tipsy. . . .

April 15. Spent a couple of hours in the college library. Fixed up some portraits under the direction of the Praeses. Came home. Journalized. Read *Pickwick Club.* Capital. All Smollett's humor and none of his vulgarity.

April 17, MONDAY. College. Everything much as usual. Philology with the Philologian. R. H. Douglass and Daniel Lord of the sophs called this afternoon; Lord appears to be a fine gentlemanly fellow.

Had learned some of Horace this afternoon, imagining that that was the lesson for tomorrow. By the way, we're to read Aeschylus and that detestable Horace this session. . . . Found myself mistaken, so all that I had spent on the Horace was lost time. Had an immense deal to do this evening but everything went so contrary I was constantly tempted to give it up in utter desperation. First there was the mistake about Horace, then before I got fairly under way on Aeschylus, who should make his appearance but that good-natured old proser, Dr. McElroy, who favored us with a sitting of three mortal hours. Endured it for a season and then went downstairs to find some place to study. Out of the frying pan into the fire. David Lambert and his brother Henry from the West were downstairs. I was in the room before I saw them and was fairly nabbed. Cleared out at last.

Got through my Aeschylus and wrote a composition which kept me till one o'clock. On Southey, and containing a rowing up on the subject of his political tractorism that would have made Byron look tickled. . . .

April 18. . . . Bought a copy of Byron this afternoon. Byron, from what I've seen of his poetry, is not such an incarnate Satan as he's cracked up to be. I don't think his wit is generally enough appreciated. One scene in the beginning of "Don Juan" is glorious, and Donna Julia's scolding oratory brought tears of laughter out of my eyes. Pity that poem is contraband. Cut out a few "improprieties" and it's glorious.

April 19. Recited in Horace. State of things in Wall Street worse than ever. The whole city going to the devil in a pecuniary point of view.

April 21. . . . *Afternoon.* Wall Street. The blackness of darkness still hangeth over it. Failure on failure. . . .

April 22, SATURDAY. . . . Went up to Chittenden's . . . and with him to the Academy of Design. . . . There are two rooms open and the exhibition is infinitely superior to what it was last year. [Daniel] Huntington of the University has several good pictures there and so has [Cornelius] Ver Bryck. . . .[5]

Philip Hone has gone to the d—l, figuratively speaking, having lost pretty much everything by his son, by Schenck & Co. (of Matteawan factory) and by some speculation moreover, all of which have eased him out of not much below $200,000. What will become of his sons now? for they have nothing to prop their conceit but their father's cash, and now that that is gone, what will become of them?

April 25. . . . *Evening*, AΔΦ. Some of the best singing that an AΔΦ meeting ever heard. . . . Had no idea of the beauty of German songs. Heard one or two from the Wards, who are very Germanic in their tastes. They were really beautiful—have more of the "real gift" of music about them than a dozen appoggiaturing Italian airs. Italian music is like filagree work compared with them, to my ear at least.

April 26. . . . Went to the Academy of Design. Saw Chittenden by appointment, and Ver Bryck of the University. Some deuced good pictures there. There's a portrait of the daughter of Morse of New Haven, a splendid painting, and according to Chittenden, a good likeness. There's a portrait of [Arthur] Cleveland Coxe, full length, tolerable. A couple of Yankee pictures by [William Sidney] Mount,[6] perfect, expression and everything true to life; they are "Farmers Nooning," half asleep under a haystack, one kicking his heels, and one boy half asleep himself tickling a nigger with a straw, the nigger being sound asleep. It is insurpassable.

There is Prex's portrait [by Henry Inman] in all its glory, and a portrait of Mrs. Duer just above it and two very handsome Spanish-looking female portraits one on each side. Huntington's paintings are both very good indeed. I like them as well as any there. There are some

[5] Daniel Huntington was just at the beginning of his long career as a painter of portraits, landscapes, genre and historical pieces, which was to bring him to the presidency of the National Academy of Design. Ver Bryck, Huntington's brother-in-law, was an esteemed young painter of landscapes and allegories who died at the age of thirty. They were residents, but not members, of New York University. The first chancellor of that institution, Rev. James M. Mathews, having sunk all their funds in an imposing marble Gothic building on Washington Square, the university was obliged to turn most of it into a rooming-house, and Professor S. F. B. Morse was the nucleus of a famous colony of artists and bohemians. A vivid picture of this group is to be found in Theodore Winthrop's novel, *Cecil Dreeme* (1861).

[6] William Sidney Mount (1807–1868) of Setauket and Stony Brook, Long Island, had progressed from sign-painting to portrait-painting and delightful scenes of American genre, and became National Academician in 1832.

(and not a few) of the most abominable daubs that ever were hung at a tavern door. I'm surprised they should have ever got into the Academy.

April 27. . . . Matters very bad out of doors. Confidence annihilated, the whole community, big and little, traveling to ruin in a body. Strong fears entertained for the banks, and if they go, God only knows what the consequences will be. Ruin here, and on the other side of the Atlantic, and not only private ruin but political convulsion and revolution, I think, would follow such an event. My father looks and talks and evidently feels very gloomily on the subject. For myself, I feel very philosophic, on my own account. I firmly believe that in a moral point of view it would be all for my good to have to push my own way, entirely unsupported, and I think I am competent to do it. I have no very extravagant tastes that I know of, unless perhaps in the way of books, but I can't accuse myself of wasting money on dress or billiards, or horses or on sprees, or any other follies of that nature. . . .

As for the banks, they are losing from five to fifty thousand dollars daily in the way of specie and everyone seems to have the same fears, though almost everyone is afraid (and I'm glad to see it) to give them utterance. Where in the name of wonder is this all to end?

May 1, MONDAY. . . . Arthur Tappan has failed! Help him, ye niggers![7]

May 2. . . . Matters worse and worse in Wall Street as far as I can learn; everyone discouraged; prospect of universal ruin and general insolvency of the banks, which will be terrible indeed if it takes place. Workmen thrown out of employ by the hundred daily. Business at a stand; the coal mines in Pennsylvania stopped and no fuel in prospect for next winter—delightful prospects, these.

May 3. . . . Went up to the office at six. Fresh failures, Talbot Oly-phant & Co., among them. So they go—smash, crash. Where in the name of wonder is there to be an end of it? Near two hundred and fifty failures thus far! Bush & Hillyer have stopped, but Giles [Hillyer] is as extensive as ever.

Locofoco meeting in the Park this morning—and such a meeting! It looked like a convention of loafers from all quarters of the world.

May 4. . . . Terrible news in Wall Street. [John] Fleming, late president of the Mechanics Bank, found dead in his bed this morning. Some say prussic acid; others (and the coroner's jury) say "mental excitement"

---

[7] Tappan was the great abolitionist and philanthropist, a founder of Oberlin College and lavish donor to Lane Theological Seminary, the American Tract Society, and anti-slavery causes.

and apoplexy. Anyhow there's a run on the bank—street crowded—
more feeling of alarm and despondency in Wall Street than has appeared
yet. The bank is to be kept open till five o'clock; politic move, that.
Fears entertained that tomorrow the attack will be general on all the
banks; if so they'll go down and then all the banks from Maine to Louisiana must follow—universal ruin. People talk ominously about rebellions
and revolutions on this side of the Atlantic, and if they come on this side,
political disturbances will soon break out on the other.

There are matters of no little weight depending on the doings of Wall
Street for the next four or five days. I wish I were ten or fifteen years
older.

Afternoon. Studied till five. Went to the office. Things look no better.
If my father would only bear up a little under this state of things, it would
be better for him. But he's not calculated for such times. They oppress his
spirits and weaken his nerves.

May 5. . . . Something like twenty failures yesterday! . . .

May 6. . . . There's a run on the Dry Dock Bank and the other banks
have refused to sustain it! At least they are to have a meeting this night
to decide definitely on the subject and there's scarcely a chance of their
decision being favorable. Uncle Benjamin [Strong], the president, is
almost dead with excitement and misery. He is personally involved to his
utter ruin, so at least my father fears. He called this evening and had a
kind of private consultation with my father. There's scarce a chance of the
bank's going on.

May 7, SUNDAY. St. Paul's this morning and afternoon. Regular
tirade against the ladies from [the Rev. John Frederic] Schroeder this
morning, very tremendous indeed, how their extravagance was ruinous
and their frivolity detestable, and so forth. My father was at Uncle
Benjamin's all the afternoon and evening. The bank will not open tomorrow morning. It is very hard for him, in his old age, and he feels it
deeply.

May 8. Not feeling very thorough on Anthon's stuff, I got leave of
absence from the president and went down to Wall Street. There was a
crowd round the bank ready to recommence the run on it, eagerly waiting
for ten o'clock to begin it. But the only notice the bank took of ten o'clock
was to close its windows also, much to the consternation of the multitude.
The crowd increased rapidly and I expected a fight, but they were at last
dispersed by the Mayor [Aaron Clark], who made them a speech and
told them that the other banks would redeem the Dry Dock bills. The

mob dispersed incontinently for their cash; it was the best means that could have been thought of for scattering them. . . .

This affair of the Dry Dock Bank has gone better than I expected, but I fear it will prove the entering wedge to split up all Wall Street. The other banks are generally blamed for not sustaining it, and justly so.

Only imagine that [Uncle Benjamin] should actually have come to such a situation as to be afraid of personal insult if he go into the street! Yet so it is. What can be more dreadful? I can scarcely realize it—as kind and good-hearted and benevolent a man as ever breathed, his character unimpeached and unimpeachable, yet obliged to secure his house from attack and afraid of showing himself. These wretched banks and credit systems and paper wealth; they have done all this.

May 9. . . . As I expected, there's a run on all the banks, the depositors drawing out the specie as fast as the tellers can count it. They are in a dangerous situation most certainly, and if they break we shall have a revolution here. I don't see how they can help breaking; this run must increase every day and they can't possibly stand it more than three or four days longer.

Studied hard all afternoon. George Anthon called at seven and then I went up to Gurley's where those books are to be sold. Never saw books go so low. Bought about $25 worth of them for which I paid between $9 and $10. They sold for nothing, in fact.

Let me see what were my purchases. Browne's *Vulgar Errors*, a very fine folio edition; Hobbes, *Leviathan*, ditto, and moreover the *editio princeps*; and Camden's *Annals*, also folio and all three in the very best of strong solid old binding I bought for $4 and one or two shillings. I have been asked $6 for a very inferior copy of the first alone! Quevedo, translated by l'Estrange, I got for twenty-five cents, a little collection of Greek Epigrams for six cents! Prior's *Poems*, the earliest edition, a very magnificent folio, I got for $1.50! I had not the remotest idea of getting it, for I took it for granted it would bring $6 or $7, and even then very cheap. A very handsome quarto Catullus in fine binding and excellent type and paper I got for 95 cents, and lastly a folio Philostratus, Greek and Latin, for $3. Many other books that I would have given a good deal to have went in the same style and I could have laid out fifty dollars easily and got ten times the worth of my money, but I was afraid that in these hard times I should find it difficult to raise the wind for what I did get.

I understand that the banks are now in session to devise means of support. It will be of no use.

May 10. Extensive news in this morning's paper. The banks (except three) have concluded to stop specie payment! ! ! Glory to the Old General! Glory to little Matty, second fiddler to the great Magician! Glory—ay, and double patent glory—to the experiment, the specie currency, and all the glorious humbugs who have inflicted them on us.

Commerce and speculation here have been spreading of late like a card house, story after story and ramification after ramification till the building towered up to the sky and people rolled up their eyes in amazement, but at last one corner gave way and every card that dropped brought down a dozen with it, and *sic transit gloria mundi*! How people have grown rich of late! I often wondered when I heard how Messrs. A. B. C. and D. were worth a million apiece and how people were now worth half a million at least before they could be called more than paupers. I often wondered where all the money had come from and how such a quantity of wealth had found its way into the country. But here's the result of it. No matter.

Went to college. The military out, in Park Place and in front of the City Hall. Wise precaution, that. McVickar losing terribly. Saw him this morning coming up from Wall Street. He looked half dead. . . .

Afternoon. The Bank of America, Merchants, and Manhattan, which had resolved to try and hold out a little longer, have closed. Immense crowd and excitement in Wall Street, but the military prevent any disturbance.

Went to the Long Room for my purchases of last night. Glorious haul. George Anthon called this afternoon. Walked up a little way with him. Had a $3 bill in my pocket, paper money and a drug now, so went up to Appleton's and laid it out on an edition of Wordsworth.

May 11, THURSDAY. . . . Went to Cooley's where the library of [President] Edward Dorr Griffin of Williamstown College was selling. Great many clergymen there, this being the season of anniversaries, and therefore probably selected for the sale. Books brought their full value. Bought nothing of any importance but a copy of Roscoe's *Lorenzo de Medici*.

May 23. . . . Went with Backus to Stebbins's where I saw an eyeglass that fit my eye exactly; must have it, foppish and baboonish though it looks. . . .

We had our foot ball on the Green today and were just beginning to enjoy some good sport with it, when the old Praeses put his veto on it and knocked up our sport tetotaciously. Deuce take him.

May 24. . . . Got the eyeglass I saw at Stebbins's. Capital thing.

May 26. . . . The students very savage because Prex has prohibited the foot ball—the old sap-head. General feeling of rebellion and contumaciousness prevailing among them.

May 30, TUESDAY. . . . Made a valuable and beautiful purchase today. A vellum MS., very splendidly and elaborately illuminated, and several large pictures of the Crucifixion, etc. I had to pay pretty heavily for it. But it is a curiosity worth possessing. . . .

Have read the *Areopagitica* and mean to read it two or three times more. It is excellent; in sentiment it is clear, energetic, decided, and republican, but in style it is labyrinthine and rather obscure, to me at least, though it may be heresy to say so. . . .

June 2. . . . *Evening*. Went with Chittenden and Backus up to [New York] University, to the anniversary of the Philomathean Society. It was very crowded; so much so that we found very great difficulty in getting in at all, and as to finding a seat, it was not to be thought of. The speaking was moderate; the music quite good. One of the speakers on the debate was Charles H. A. Bulkley, who, if I am not mistaken, was an old enemy of mine at Holbrook's in '28 or '29. . . . The chapel, about which I've heard so much, I'm rather disappointed in, though it certainly has a fine effect on the whole. But if I know anything about architecture, I should say that a bright blue ceiling with big gold stars and with the arms of the U. S. and likewise those of the university is rather out of place in a room that calls itself Gothic. . . .

Chittenden and I nearly perished on our way home; the walk and the heat of the chapel had made us very thirsty and we were both out of funds. At last we succeeded in mustering a shilling between us and I never enjoyed a glass of soda water so thoroughly in my life. Came down to college where we made amends by inundating our insides with cold water. It was a real luxury.

I went to bed rather early, and at about one o'clock was waked up by the information that the store back of us was on fire. The way I hurried on my clothes was a caution, and on going to the back windows I saw that the building (a public store very full of goods, and in point of size, three times as bulky as ordinary sized stores) was so enveloped in smoke as to be nearly invisible; there was as yet no appearance of fire and no alarm, but the smoke was such one could scarcely see anything. My father had dressed himself and gone round there. He found about a dozen people round the door deliberating whether to open it or not. He told them to open it at once in the hope that the papers and so on might be got out, but the moment the door was opened the fire flashed out upon them, and they were forced to close it as fast as possible. Mr. Derby and myself now got out a step ladder and posted ourselves by the fence. The smoke was the most acrid I ever smelt; we could scarcely breathe and our eyes smarted terribly. We looked out anxiously for the result, the store being so close to us that its destruction might very possibly carry our house along with it. Engines were now beginning to appear but without producing any effect. The firemen smashed a partition and got into Mr. Lockwood's, next door, and began playing on the rear. We noticed that the iron window shutters of the first story were quite red hot and had cracked and started so much that the smoke was pouring out in dense streams. At last the fire found a passage way and the flames flashed up beautifully through the dark smoke. It was thus far confined to the first story, and from the great quantity of goods in the store, it took some time to penetrate to the others, but at last it was successful and the fire appeared in the second, first in the rear and very soon after in the front. Matters now looked serious. . . .

At last the flames broke furiously out of the farthest third story window, and now began the real combustion: what we had seen thus far was a mere preliminary. The flames poured steadily out in a torrent on which the operations of three or four jets had no effect at all. At last it burst out fiercely on the third story on Washington Street, caught the roof like tinder, and in an incredibly short time the whole roof was a mass of flame—the scene was the most terrible one I ever saw. Our danger was now imminent; it was scarcely possible to stand on the stoop or in the yard without being scorched and blinded; the shed smoked and the windows and window frames and every thing else that was at all exposed were almost too hot for the hand to bear. Had there been a breath of air, our case would have been hopeless; as it was, I expected every moment that some of the flakes of fire that were flying about would communicate with the roof and set us in a blaze; it would not have taken much to set the old house a-going.

Down came the gable end at last into the lumber yard with a most tremendous crash, killing two men and injuring a boy very badly. Another crash followed, the roof fell in, and the fire raged fiercer than before. I never saw a fire on which water made so little impression; the harder they worked, the hotter it burned.

At about daylight it seemed the danger was pretty much over; the firemen of No. 17 who were posted in the yard now eased off a little and attacked some provender, eatable and drinkable, ravenously and no wonder; they had worked desperately and they drank water by the gallon. Some of them refused to drink anything else. After using up several bottles of wine, some ale was sent for, on which they got somewhat cocked, and rather obstreperous, but I'm sure they were excusable after such a night's work, and a more orderly, considerate, well-bred set of fellows no one could desire.

June 5. . . . I'm deuced lame and sore and stiff just from taking hold of an engine a little on Friday night. It's grand exercise.

June 7. . . . How everlastingly tedious some of the *Faerie Queene* is; it's the first time I ever fairly tried to read it through, and if I succeed, verily 'twill be an achievement. Yet it grows better as I go on, or rather I get more used to it. I have mastered two books and a half.

June 8. . . . Bought a copy of Lyell's *Geology* this afternoon. It's very agreeable and refreshing after that bore De La Bèche. Geology and German literature and the Sanskrit are new things, as yet mere infants, but they've a vital principle in them and they'll progress faster and faster and in fifty years they'll be $x+y$ miles ahead of the station they're in now. . . .

German I've a kind of sneaking kindness for. I mean to study it. Had a good subject for an essay suggested tonight, viz., a degladiatorial and incisory attack on classic authors. Well managed, it would be primordial, and my first leisure day shall be devoted to it. And what's more, there's some foundation for such a position; it might be defended seriously. We are brought up to admire them as things of course. Aeschylus is jaw-breaking, hyperbolical and humbuggical. Euripides is dreadfully hum-buggical though comparatively underrated. Sophocles might be cut up on the ground of the inherent defects of his rules and regulations, for there's no mistake in this, the classic drama, however we may glorify it in a composition or magnify it in a commencement speech notwithstanding, it amounteth to nothing but spouting, singing, and dancing, of which last majestic elements we modern *readers* are debarred the enjoyment. Aristophanes I couldn't cut up; he's a fine old fellow, but Virgil, and Plautus and Terence and all the rest of that mob have weak points *ad infinitum*, and a very good essay might be worked up at their expense.

June 11. . . . Evening. Studied away at John Milton's prose, which has afforded me more gratification than ever his poetics did. It is beautiful; he is the *beau idéal* of an English patriot, gentleman, and scholar. What a pity he ever came in contact with Salmasius and that he should have wasted so much wrath on such a trifle as he was. . . .

June 13. . . . Saw an amusing scene after college: two pugnacious Freshmen engaged in a duel on the terrace. The way they pulled hair and cuffed ears was a caution. Really, really, I did not imagine that any such sanguinary young heroes were to be found in old Columbia. . . .

Evening.   Attacked Horace. Went thirty lines and then my notes gave out. *Quid faciam?* Of all authors ancient or modern, pagan or Christian, that Horace is my detestation. He's an old enemy of mine. I've flunked oftener on his tarnation odes and satires than on all the rest of the Greek and Latin I've read since I was born. And I suppose I shall have either to flunk or sneak off or beg off or something of the kind tomorrow. The devil take Horace, that's all. Well, well—very little difference *arter all*—"all the same a hundred years hence, Samivel, my boy."

Positively the study of astronomy is making a philosopher of me, of a new sect, too, not the Stoic, nor the Epicurean, but the "don't care a straw" sect, a very comfortable sect to belong to, essentially philosophical in everything.

Only to think of it, seriously: the stellar system very possibly but a mere spot in infinite space, the solar system, certainly, a mere point in that stellar system and our earth one of the smallest bodies in that solar system. And we, all our concerns, so insignificant, so utterly insignificant, in our relations to what we think of as "the great globe," but which is really this atom of matter whose annihilation would as far as we can judge be hardly known save by its immediate neighbors. What is the summit of greatness, learning, the sovereignty of the whole earth itself? Why nothing at all, and what are these affairs about which we busy ourselves so much—Columbia College, its societies, the hard times, and so on and so forth? Why they are infinitely less than nothing. . . .

June 14, WEDNESDAY. . . . Recited in Horace and did very well moreover, having got hold of somebody else's notes in the meantime. . . .

June 15. . . . Took a wandering, loaferish walk round about. Lounged into the Academy of Design, this being the first time I have been there since I mounted a glass. I was able to see the upper pictures which have hitherto been pretty much invisible unto me. . . .

June 18, SUNDAY.   Clear and cool. St. Paul's. Schroeder preached as ridiculous a piece of conceited self-glorification as I ever heard from the pulpit. What a fool the man is! Surely he must know that whatever his merits may be, people will only value them the less for being put in mind of them. . . .

June 20. . . . Bought at Wiley's a very handsome copy of T. Browne's works in four volumes octavo, edited by Wilkins and with all the care and reserve of a classical edition. Good purchase, though a somewhat dear one. The book is splendidly bound; I was unable to resist the temptation of such an ornament to my shelves. Paid $5 additional, the first money I ever laid out on costly binding. However, the binding is cheap, for it's the best and richest kind, very strong and very handsome.

June 21. . . . Saw an extract from some foreign periodical ascribing this queerest, dampest, cloudiest of all springs and summers, to the influence of Halley's comet. It seems as if some extraordinary agent must be at work, for the clear days since the middle of March have scarcely numbered one in ten. . . .

June 22. . . . Sat down this afternoon again, to Browne, and kept at him steadily, at the *Religio Medici*, which for original, out of the way speculations and ideas is the greatest book I ever read—hard, too, almost obscure; but his style is ultra Johnsonian in point of Latinity and condensation. I can't *read* his writing; I have to study it. But the fact is I'm yet a novice in the art of reading. I have got myself into a sad habit of careless, desultory, hasty reading, running over the words but not the ideas, and I must work hard to break myself of it; in fact I cannot remember what I merely read, I have to learn it. . . .

June 29, THURSDAY. Last evening as I was exercising a little with a pair of dumbbells just before getting into bed and was employing them pugilist-wise, I brought one of them in some strange way in contact with one of my front teeth, and though the stroke was a very slight one, it knocked a piece off, laying bare the nerve, and disabling me from eating anything warm or cold—and using my front teeth at all. Moreover, so much enamel is detached that the tooth will inevitably decay, so now for toothaches, dentists, wrenches, files, saws, false teeth and so forth— comfortable prospect. Well, what's done can't be helped. . . .

Saw some magnetic operations, and capital ones too, with Renwick. The electro-magnet is tremendously powerful, supporting about 100 lbs. of iron and stone, myself on top of that, and how much more, I don't know.

July 5. There's a fire and that dolorous City Hall bell is banging away for the Fourth District. Really, I think Milton must have had a prophetic vision of that bell when he wrote about the "far-off curfew sound"; this has the "sullen roar" to perfection. To hear it in the middle of the night when everything else is utterly silent and it is pouring out its dismal, ominous peals is really the most lugubrious noise I know of, except perhaps the distant howling of a dog on a windy night, which is the perfection of all doleful sounds. But this bell isn't fit for New York; it ought to be trans-ferred to St. Sepulchre's or the Inquisition or to La Trappe—it would be an acquisition to any of them, to the former especially. . . .

July 6. . . . Amused myself with devising some ciphers; some of them I may find useful some day for this Diary. One in particular I made out on a system not referred to at all in Rees.

The following week came final examinations, and on the 13th he reported "Gloriously through!" Next day he and his family sailed for Boston on the Narragansett; *Saturday they were welcomed by the Derbys at 56 Boylston Street, "which looks as good as ever, which is optimum." Strong went around to the bookstores as usual, and Mr. Derby took him to an exhibition of paintings at the Boston Athenaeum, which he found "immeasurably superior in quality, though not in quantity, to our exhibitions." He was particularly interested in "Mrs. Richard Derby's portrait as St. Cecelia, by Copley and very splendid certainly, though I had heard too much about it not to be a little disappointed. By the by, why should the saint be represented as playing on a superb harp with pedals and everything according, and in the fashionable dress of a dozen years or so since?" There were visits to Jamaica Plain, to the StateHouse cupola, and rambles around the city: "This is the hardest city I ever was in to find one's way through. Even with a map, it's next to impossible, for half the streets have no name on them." On the 19th they started home on the* Lexington.

July 21, FRIDAY.   Clear and warm. Went down to Staten Island this morning at eleven with my mother and Mary. Saw Miss Lane. Did not see Mrs. [Charles Taylor] Catlin,[8] she being unwell, having I believe lately kittened. Spent a pleasant hour or so, then came off in the two o'clock boat. Got in a little before three. Staten Island is a beautiful place. I think the New Yorkers can fairly set it off against Nahant. . . .

July 25.   The King of England's dead, and so long live Queen Vic-toria! who will do quite as well, I dare say. She'll be a fool if she marries; let her think of Elizabeth. A mere nominal queenship—and actual cypher-ship—is a state she'll keep clear of, if she has the independent spirit of a cockroach.

Went to the office this morning. Spent the morning there reading Guizot on Civilization which Mr. Welford recommended very strongly to me, and rightly, for it's original and philosophical and altogether very good.

[8] Mrs. Catlin was Lucy Ann Derby, twin sister of E. H. Derby.

July 26. . . . Judging from what I've seen of the way law students in general go on, I shall think it hard if I can't cram what they accomplish in three years, into *one*. I mean to devote myself to that study, repulsive as it is, heart and soul. There's but one alternative: I must either neglect it entirely or else force myself to like it; there's no half way.

August 1.   Took a ramble over to Hoboken this morning. Saw a sort of Indian colony over there, consisting of a couple of Indians, a squaw and a lot of papooses, horrid little loafers in appearance. They carry on the trade of basket-making and look altogether philosophical and comfortable. . . . What fools! as if Hoboken could be to a true-blooded and true-hearted Indian any sort of approximative likeness to his woods and rocks and lakes at home. Hoboken! Where all sorts of cits and cockneys and pert nurses and perter misses and dirty loafers and Corinthians from Chapel Street and all things anti-Indian in every respect most do "go a-pleasuring." . . .

Strong continued to enjoy his vacation quietly in town, reading Scott, occasionally making himself useful to his father at the office, and spending the evening at Castle Garden enjoying the fireworks, the cool sea breezes, and some good music. Mr. Derby and Eloise came from Boston for a visit, bringing their children: "Hasket has improved greatly in speaking; he talks like a book. The other little animal [George Strong Derby] is as fat as ever; he looks like a gigantic oyster or a young squat puppy dog." Early in August the family went to Whitestone for the remainder of the summer.

August 10.   Clear and cool. Glorious, so mounted Charley and took a ride around Newtown. My pants too thin and my lower end dreadful sore in consequence.

August 25.   Took another ride around Little Neck. I must not forget to note that it is announced in the papers that G. W. Strong, Esq., is an LL.D. of Vermont University. Through Dr. [John] Wheeler [the president], I suppose.

August 28, MONDAY. . . . The *Lexington*, Mr. Derby on board, was run into at 3 A.M. Friday by a sloop off Milford. The sloop's bowsprit went through three of the staterooms, but what is wonderful, only one man was much hurt. Had it taken one of the berths sideways it would have crushed whoever was in it. The poor devil's name was Dow of Philadelphia.

September 1, FRIDAY.   Took a ride to Rockaway—about thirty-two miles coming and going—a pretty good day's ride. The musquitoes in that neighborhood are of a peculiarly fine breed, approximating in size to wild geese, and in ferocity to wild cats. . . .

On the 4th of September, Strong ran into the local militia:

Walked to Bay Side, along shore, and on coming back heard a drum, and found that there were very warlike doings going on at Cookie Hill. Found Edward and old Brickface there as spectators of the exhibition besides Admiral Powell, at present commandant of the dung sloop.

There were forty warriors, very miscellaneous indeed. Three of them were not serviceable, having sticks instead of guns, and several more were supremely drunk. The gallant captain wore a sword like a scythe blade, and his heroes looked like Sir J. Falstaff's ragged regiment. The line was very crooked; there was an astonishing curvature towards a certain beer room.

The artillery (one six-ouncer) was loaded with a teacup full of powder and a chap screwed up his courage and took a coal of fire at the end of a tongs, for a *feu de joie*. When lo! there appeared from a neighboring house two old ladies who swore by —— and —— that if they fired the gun there to break the windows, they'd throw a pail of water on them. So the artillery performed a retrograde movement.

September 12, TUESDAY. . . . They brought up the fourth number of Lockhart's *Scott* this evening. That's without exception the most interesting biography I ever got hold of. If I had my choice, I'd rather exchange places with Walter Scott than any author ancient or modern that I know of. There have been greater men, but I know of no one who ever combined so large a quantum of talent and genius with so much of personal lovability and happiness through life. Only his last misfortune! Take out that, and his history had very few sources of discomfort in it.

On the 16th the family went to Rockaway to spend the night: "We put up at the Pavilion, now almost deserted. Henry Hone [Columbia 1818] was there, whiskers and all, with the interesting Miss Haywood, his cara sposa, she seventeen, he a widower of fifty and a blackleg to boot. Charles Clinton, son of DeWitt Clinton—the best part of him is his father (if that isn't a bull)—like a turnip, his best part's underground. He loafs about, plays billiards, and shoots snipe. . . ." A week later Strong and his family returned to the city. George Anthon called, wearing a new long-tailed coat, and Chittenden turned up, after a trip to Indiana and Washington, sporting a pair of whiskers. Strong went to

Castle Garden on the 25th to see the Regatta: "It was a great crowd and rather uncomfortable, but it's a splendid sight to look down on the bay covered with boats and barges of all sorts and sizes, flags flying, steamboats black with gazers, sweeping majestically down, and the long graceful boat club barges shooting like arrows among the throng. The first race was won by the Yankee Doodle, *the second by the* Gazelle, *and the third I did not see finished, but the* Wave *took the lead at once and most probably kept it." Even before college opened the Philolexian society met and Strong was plunged into politics again; John Ireland Tucker '37 (later for over half a century the saintly rector of the Church of the Holy Cross in Troy) had made enemies in the society, which refused to vote him an honorary certificate, and there was also an unfulfilled threat to hiss his commencement oration. Commencement was held October 3 in St. John's Chapel. The Greek salutatory oration, which Strong thought "on the whole, good" was delivered by the top man of the class, Samuel Blatchford, later justice of the Federal Supreme Court. Chittenden's oration, "The Influence of Woman on the Destinies of a People," was a great success, and the Philolexian society had it printed as a pamphlet (at a cost of $22.65). Mancer Mark Backus took the gold medal as head of Strong's class where he was to remain. Strong was second, taking eight silver medals—in belles-lettres, Greek, philology, metallurgy, chemistry applied to the arts, geology, archaeology, and descriptive astronomy; he felt that it was "a pretty good haul and about as creditable,* me judice, *as the gold would have been."*

The senior year began quietly, but Strong thought that "we are going to have a tremendous session of it, judging from present portents."

October 6, FRIDAY. . . . The Praeses read us a lecture on the history of the origin of our Constitution—on the whole good—though each word contained six syllables and each sentence was at least a yard in longitude. But it was good, warm, patriotic and national, and ended with "the Union, it *must* be preserved." Hurrah for the Constitution! . . .

Evening. . . .Went to Delmonico's with Trevett and drank some of the only good chocolate I ever tasted, as much superior to the stuff that ordinarily goes under that name as champagne to small beer.

October 10. Recited in Lucretius, imbibed philosophy, sucked in some of that awful "Mechanics" and underwent some premonitory symptoms of the calculus. *Eheu nos miseros!* . . .

Evening. Sat down to Pindarus. His odes were probably written when

PARK PLACE FROM BROADWAY

COLMAN'S LITERARY ROOMS ON THE CORNER: COLUMBIA COLLEGE AND THE HUDSON IN THE DISTANCE

ST. JOHN'S CHAPEL AND PARK

VARICK STREET LOOKING SOUTH FROM LAIGHT

he was under a little "tremendous excitement" from a few glasses of whiskey, if he ever knew the delight of tasting it. His sentences read as if he had shaken the words in a bag and then dropped them on the page, and for the verse, I can cut an auctioneer's advertisement into as good any day.

October 14, SATURDAY. Got the fourth part of the *Pickwick Papers* and spent the morning in reading them. They do not, as I expected, come quite up to the previous numbers. So it always is with a series of that sort, or any sort. Either the writer falls off, or the public get tired, but the last never equal the first of them. . . .

Harry Ward has gone to Europe. His pedestrian tour knocked him up. No wonder. They averaged thirty miles a day, and one day they traveled forty-seven miles. [Francis Marion] Ward visited Lake Winnepesaukee in the course of the ramble. He gives an interpretation for the Indian name which is almost as beautiful as the lake itself: "the smile of the Great Spirit"; I never heard it before. . . .

October 16. . . . Went to college, and it was announced by Prex that McVickar was sick, whereat we sang *jubilate*. May he be sick for a month to come—that is, moderately, pleasantly, and comfortably sick, just enough to make him think himself better at home than in the lecture room. . . . I stayed to take a look at the drawing business. . . . I think I'll try my hand. It's a first-rate accomplishment to possess. The teacher (along with Renwick), [George C.] Schaeffer, seems to be a very good fellow—with a fearful pair of whiskers. Went and made some purchases of paper and pencils for the operation. . . .

Sophocles till 5 o'clock. . . . Sophocles is as much easier than Aeschylus as that is easier than Longinus. How perfectly I remember the first day I ever saw a Greek play, the 2d of November, 1833. I had read some few articles in Anthon's [edition of] Lemprière['s *Classical Dictionary*] which had set my head full of Greek tragedies as being something very splendid, but had not given me the remotest idea that they had any difference from our English ones. So I went to Colman's right after breakfast—it was a Saturday—paid 75 cents for my Sophocles, marched home and sat down to investigate the *Oedipus Tyrannus*. . . . No *Act I, Scene I*, nothing of that sort, no divisions, nothing but naked dialogue which for my life I could not manage. I bored at it a few hours and at last set it down in utter disgust. . . . By good luck I lit upon a poetical translation of Sophocles which indoctrinated me into Greek tragedy, and then set to work on writing a translation of the same. Between the middle of November and end of December I contrived to fight my way through *Oedipus Tyrannus* and *Antigone*. I have not looked at my translation since, but I remember that I used to write, *currente calamo,* with the translation in part, and the dictionary reposing somewhere out of sight, and I've no doubt that they're infamous trash, though probably not quite so bad as the *Agamemnon, Orestes* and *Eumenides,* which I translated with a hop, skip, and jump in no time at all chiefly during a Christmas vacation, leaving out most of the long speeches as tiresome. In the spring following I translated the *Clouds* with a little more care, really enjoying it as I went along, and then the *Wasps* in awful slip-slop style. In November and December of my freshman year, I went through the *Medea* quite carefully and then part of the *Iphigenia in Aulis* in the following March, finishing it at Whitestone the next summer—and that's the history of my doings in the Greek drama.

Aristophanes and Sophocles *alone* I have really enjoyed, except two scenes in Aeschylus, one in the *Agamemnon* between Cassandra and the chorus and the other in *Eumenides* where the ghost of Cassandra arouses the Furies—that always seemed to me to be fearfully sublime. . . . As to what I've read of Latin drama, it always seemed to me frigid, stale, low, dirty, flat, poor stuff. . . .

October 17, TUESDAY. . . . Terrible news. The *Home,* steam packet, Charleston, sprang a leak in a heavy gale near Ocracoke [North Carolina], became waterlogged and unmanageable and went ashore—95 passengers, of whom about 70 were lost, and of 45 crew, about 25 lost, and the captain escaped, of course. It is dreadful. This is just the time when the Southerners are returning from their northern tours, and no doubt many of the first of them were on board of her. There were about thirty lady passengers, of whom *two alone* escaped. It's a horrid affair altogether. So utterly unseaworthy was she, though only on her third trip, that at every swell the bow and stern were lifted three feet from their proper position, what they call hogging, I believe. Her fault was too great length in proportion to her width and her solidity. . . .

October 22, SUNDAY. Went to church. Heard Mr. Higbee in the afternoon; his preaching always attracts a goodly congregation and people certainly had a foreboding of his place this afternoon for I was ousted and obliged to take up my abode in Mr. Wolfe's pew.[9] I looked out in expecta-

⁹ This was John David Wolfe (1792–1872), the merchant and philanthropist, and a vestryman of Trinity Church. The "Wolfewhelps" included Catharine Lorillard Wolfe (1828–1887), at one time estimated to be the richest unmarried woman in the world. She continued the family philanthropies, and left her collection of paintings to the Metropolitan Museum of Art.

tion of seeing Mr. Wolfe, Miss Wolfe and all the little Wolfewhelps
enter, but I was agreeably disappointed. Mr. Wolfe was the only animal of
the species. . . .

November 3. . . . It seems there's a new project about the [college]
library, viz., that Moore[10] throw into it all his library and then be appointed
librarian with a salary of $1,000. Charley [Anthon] don't like it, of
course; but I don't see why it's not a very good plan. . . .

November 8, WEDNESDAY. Recited in differential calculus. We have
got through with that, and now take up the integral. What a farce it is!
I have not succeeded yet in comprehending what a Differentiation means,
and to whisk us off in this style is an unequivocal indication of lunacy in
Anderson. He's probably disordered in mind by the bad prospects of the
Locofocos—*quem deus perdere vult*, and so on. . . . *Evening.* Went out with
my father to find out election news. Went up to Tammany, where we were
informed by a miscellaneous looking loafer that "us Democrats licked the
Whigs like hell." . . .

November 9. Yes, by St. Matthias, whom I take to be the regularly
constituted saint of elections, the Whigs have carried all before them, all
the river counties changing. Newburgh gone. Albany—city and county—
tenues in auras; towns that gave three or four hundred to Van Buren last
year now giving a corresponding Whig majority; it's wonderful. The
Whigs don't quite know what to think of it themselves. The city is carried
by near three thousand. Van Buren must feel peculiarly capable of creeping
into a tobacco pipe. . . .

November 11. . . . Received a note from Mr. Welford that he had got
hold of Froissart and Percy for me. I went off in a tangent, of course, and
got them, though they came rather high. I've now got Froissart, Percy and
the fifth part of Lockhart's *Life of Scott* to read and I hardly know which
to take hold of first; the former I have had a longing after ever since I
heard of it, and this is exactly the copy I want.

November 14. Recited with Renwick. That old ass has absolutely
given us some problems to work out in gunnery, just as if we cared
a quarter of a continental for parabolas *de but en blanc*, howitzers, breeches,
chambers, and so forth. It's rascally. . . .

---

[10] Nathaniel Fish Moore (Columbia 1804) had been adjunct professor of Greek
and Latin from 1820 to 1835; in January 1838 he was appointed librarian, and his
library of about a thousand titles in the classics, philology, and theology was incorporated with the college collection, which he then classified and catalogued. He was
president of Columbia from 1842 to 1849.

November 15. . . . McVickar lectured on a Future State—all fished from that "physical theory"—but it's a grand subject to think about, and all this attempt to enter into it brings it home to us and does us good. Those lectures, though trashy, have done me much good; they have made me believe what before I only took for granted. . . .

November 20, MONDAY. "Poetry" with Anthon. Gained decidedly. Drew. Schaeffer seems to be quite a decent fellow. I have improved, I think, in drawing. It's a pleasant accomplishment. We must have some silk and velvet, though they are secondary or tertiary matters, and under that head I count drawing and similar elegancies. Music is far more than a second-rate matter; it's not a mere accomplishment. Dancing is below it; it's infinitely small, an nth rate accomplishment; indeed, I can't help thinking it rather a negative quantity. I don't mean that it's wrong morally, but it is foppery and foolishness, and I should feel peculiarly nasty if I ever did attempt it, as I never shall—at least I can't imagine it possible I ever can.

November 26, SUNDAY. . . . Thomas [Strong] Griffing called and took tea with us. College is rubbing off his greenness and he'll soon be a fine fellow. Walked uptown with him after tea to see the ruins of the Unitarian church in Mercer Street—Mr. [Orville] Dewey's—and one of the neatest in the city, which was burned this morning. . . .

November 28. . . . If I were obliged to attend the Prex every day instead of only two days in the week I should commit suicide or else emigrate uptown, settle in the "new country" and become a "University man." His lectures are the greatest bores conceivable—before I knew them I knew nothing of the perfection to which the science could be carried. What an acquisition the old gentleman will be to the Devil—in the art of torturing!

November 29, WEDNESDAY. . . . Prex made an Address to us this morning —worthy of its subject—*videlicet*, the Moral Turpitude of Snowballing. He talked about riots and riotous acts, and the civil magistrate, and all that sort of thing in ridiculous style, and said that he had received a formal complaint from somebody "of the highest respectability" whose carriage had been cannonaded. It was beautifully done. I saw the operation—the shot carried away the footman's gilt-banded hat into a very beautiful mud puddle in the neatest way imaginable. No practised artillerist could have done the thing in prettier style.

December 5, TUESDAY. . . . Anthon excessively facetious, gave Backus, [John Mason] Knox and G.T.S. some excruciating comicality for staying the differential of a second, after the roll was called, to confer with Prof.

Anderson. Backus, he said, he would report as *non paratus.* If ever a professor deserved an ablution under the college pump, Charley does.

Charley excessively comical likewise on Coleridge: "um—crazy Platonist—opium eater—crack-brained metaphysician—crazy man altogether." Well, after the lion's dead every ass may take a kick at him. However, there can't be two more directly opposed to each other—more completely antipodal in their ways of thinking and mental disposition than S.T.C. and Charles Anthon, LL.D., Professor Jaius, etc.

December 10.   Read Jeremy Taylor all the morning. He must have had an immensity of learning and at his fingers' ends, too, for he brings his erudition in so naturally and with so little pedantry that he is evidently no index-hunter. . . .

December 12. . . . Chittenden . . . got in town this morning. . . . He's brought a piece of news with him that I can hardly swallow: that the Canadian rebels (if the news be true, we must call 'em patriots) are in possession of Toronto! Hurrah for republican principles! In this case, though, it won't do to look at it anyhow but abstractly—for *de facto* the Torontonians are a paltry set of Scotch, English, and Irish radicals. They disgrace their business of patriotism.

During the autumn months, Strong was up to his ears in Philolexian politics. It is sufficient to record here that at the election of officers which took place December 15, Chittenden was unanimously elected president and Strong was elected vice-president with only three opposing votes. He, Chittenden, and Backus celebrated at Delmonico's.

Little George Strong Derby died of dropsy at Boston on the 17th, and when the news came on the 20th, Strong wrote: "I can scarcely realize that that fine, strong, hearty little fellow that they were all so proud of is dead—but so it is, and it has dulled me all day."

December 28, THURSDAY. Went to Professor Anthon's Grammar School exhibition. The Grammar School is in a palmy state as regards number of members; the parent school contains 290, the branch school uptown about 70. But the students are generally a poor-looking set of loafers. The chapel was very crowded, above and below. More so than it was of old, when we had our doings there, and we had those Latin colloquies with their nonsense and tomfoolery. But those exhibitions went off, I think, better than this, by a jugfull.

1838

JOINS SOCIETY LIBRARY · ARRIVAL OF *SIRIUS* AND *GREAT
WESTERN* · LOCKHART'S *SCOTT* · MR. BIDWELL ·
GRADUATED FROM COLUMBIA · BEGINS
STUDY OF LAW

*T*he country was still suffering heavily, as the year 1838 opened, from the
effects of the panic and depression. Many factories remained closed, merchants sought in vain for markets, the recently vigorous trade unions had col-
lapsed, and in New York thousands were utterly destitute. People talked of little
but the economic troubles and the question when confidence and prosperity would
revive. Some attention, however, was given to the battle over abolitionist peti-
tions which began to rage in the House of Representatives in late December and
January, with John Quincy Adams defending the right of petition; and the
aftermath of the Mackenzie-Papineau rebellion of 1837 in Canada aroused much
interest. Various leaders had fled to the United States, where they found border
elements ready to espouse their cause. Societies were formed from Vermont
to Michigan to assist in a reckless invasion of Canada, many calling themselves
Hunters' and Chasers' Lodges. During 1837–38 forays were made across the
boundary line. For the most part they were easily repelled, but they were accompanied by incidents that excited angry feeling. The worst of these incidents
was the burning of the steamer Caroline. Mackenzie had mustered a force on
Navy Island in the Niagara River at the end of 1837; the Caroline was hired to
carry food and munitions from the American side; a small Canadian force was
sent to destroy the ship; they found her moored to the American shore, killed an
American defender, and sent her blazing over the falls. A wave of indignation
swept across the United States, and reprisals followed, including the destruction
of the Canadian vessel Sir Robert Peel. A Canadian named Alexander
McLeod was arrested in Buffalo for the murder of the man killed on the Caro-

line, *and a difficult situation ensued when the British government demanded his release and the American government refused.*

The diarist was almost completely occupied with college affairs. The Philo-lexian Society, celebrating its anniversary on February 22, invited Rev. Edward Y. Higbee of Trinity Church to deliver the address, and Strong thought that "he acquitted himself most creditably." On February 25 he attended the conse-cration of the new Catholic church, St. Peter's, on Barclay Street, a stone Ionic temple, where he was impressed by the fine painting used as altarpiece, the excellent choir and organ, and the choice of music. "No wonder the Catholic Church has so many votaries—and so devoted," he exclaimed. When the semi-annual examinations came on, he "spent the day monastically—in studious seclusion"; he "felt dull, dispirited, and dismal"; and he conned Duer's outlines of the constitutional jurisprudence of the United States until they became "muddled and foggified beyond conception." But he came through, in his own phrase, as slick as a new-greased cartwheel. When the certificates were awarded, "Backus took No.1, and rightly, too," but Strong took six, while only one other student got as many as three.

January 3. . . . Went up to college to see the Sophomores inhale nitrous oxide. . . . I should have liked dearly to have tried it myself, but I didn't care to make a fool of myself before half the Freshmen and all the Sopho-mores.

January 4. . . . There's a great deal of excitement about this affair of the *Caroline,* and I don't wonder. It's infamous—forty unarmed American citizens butchered in cold blood, while sleeping, by a party of British assassins, and living and dead sent together over Niagara; it is one of the most high-handed outrages I ever heard of. I shan't be surprised if the feeling it gives rise to produces a war. I shall not be sorry if it does. . . .

January 9. I understand they have finally resolved on that arrange-ment about the library. N. F. Moore becomes librarian with the salary of $500. He throws in his private library (chiefly classical and worth six or eight thousand dollars) into that of the college. [Moore's salary was actually $300 a year; he was paid an annuity of $500 for life.] And now I do hope that the library will be so managed as to be of some use to the students. If we could get up a reading-room, for instance, it would be a first-rate thing, though it comes late for us.

January 11. . . . Subscribed at Dearborn's for the *New York Review* and got the back numbers. Read that famous article of [Rev. Francis

Lister] Hawks's on [Aaron] Burr. It's the most savage cutting up I ever read, almost unclerical. Moreover, it is richly deserved.

News from Navy Island. An attack has been made, result not known. A magnificent time they will have of it, though a fight near Niagara is almost a profanation. It is a night attack. I should think the shades of the murdered Carolinians would rise up from the falls, or hover in the mists, to watch the onset and call out for vengeance on their murderers, or to receive their corpses as they are carried down the current and over the cataract. A fearful idea for the assassins, if they happen to be in the attacking party. . . .

January 13. . . . Read the fifth and last part of the *Pickwick Papers.* It's far superior to the fourth part. It is evident, I think, that it has been written, as it came out, in parts. For there is a marked change in the tone of this last part; there's more of serious interest in it, and Mr. Pickwick, who is in the first parts an entirely quizzical personage, has his character further developed into something like Matthew Bramble, Esquire. It's very good, and I must get myself a good copy of it, for it's a book worth keeping.

January 14, SUNDAY. . . . Took a walk with my father up to Eighth Street. He tells me that Hawks's statement in the *New York Review* that Burr practised with a pistol some time before his duel with Hamilton is a fact. He went out once to Burr's place at Richmond Hill on business, and there he saw the board set up and perforated with pistol balls where the infernal cold-blooded scoundrel had been practising.

January 20. . . . Went into the library, which is making headway in glorious style. Moore is there, and the floors and tables are heaped up with his books. This library is certainly a glorious one, more splendid and more general than Anthon's, though possibly not so large. . . .

January 27. . . . Went up into the library, now nearly arranged. Had some little conversation with Dr. Moore and was highly pleased with him; he seems a mild, gentlemanly, communicative, clever man. . . .

March 10, SATURDAY. . . . Went with Trevett after the Synagogue to see the ceremonies. We stopped first at the one in Elm Street, which is a shabby place with a loaferish congregation. We then went to the establishment on Crosby Street, which is in every way more decent. The services I was much disappointed in, for though interesting, they grew tedious. The chanting of the reader is less monotonous than the Catholic, but more rapid and far less respectable in sound. Then the demeanor of the officiating gentlemen and of the congregation is very different from the superstitious and reverential devotion I expected. The hats worn by all without exception, even by the reader, had a singular effect, and so had the shawls worn by the congregation. But the congregation took a hearty and zealous part in the services and roared out their unintelligible responses with good will and strength of lungs. I like that. In our church it looks too much like going to heaven by proxy. The Rolls, of which there are six or seven in the holy of holies, must be curious things. . . .

This month Strong's father took him to the New York Society Library on Chambers Street to see about purchasing a share which had belonged to "old Mr. Griswold"; and within a few weeks the youth was in full enjoyment of this excellent collection of books. Meanwhile, curiosity drew him to the Chatham Street chapel to hear Jedediah Burchard, an evangelist:

March 14.   His style is very conversational and he speaks fluently— and to all appearance naturally—and on that, and on his very impressive manner, his success has been founded. He has great command over his voice, and when this evening, after a passage of rant and hyperbolical stuff delivered in an elevated voice and tone, he suddenly sank his voice to a whisper almost, and proclaimed the "everlasting damnation in the fires of hell" of all who didn't become Christians on the spot, the effect was startling and the congregation seemed to shrink and shiver, as it were, and then everything was still again. . . .

March 16, FRIDAY. . . . At Prescott and Philip de Comines. I'm beginning to feel *operative* once more after a pretty good spell of laziness.

March 17, SATURDAY. . . . With Chittenden up to St. Patrick's, this being St. Patrick's day, to hear and see the services in his honor. The Cathedral was crowded, the aisles jammed, but we had a pew (locked) nearly to ourselves and got along right comfortably. Mass by Bishop Hughes and clergy. . . . Music tolerable. . . . The sermon was immensely absurd—outpowered Powers himself. I never heard a comparable farrago of nonsense, falsehood, blunder, hibernicism, bombast, nonsense, fun, flummery, bad grammar, false logic and stuff. The preacher was a raw Paddy apparently, named Byrnes. . . .

March 18. . . . Catarrh no better. Weather unutterable. . . . Read Bishop Berkeley and the lives of the saints. Berkeley indeed! I'm growing etherial decidedly. Read *Vivian Grey* also, which rather partly restored my corporeality and brought me down to this world again. . . . *Evening.* Gormandized pickled oysters. Degenerate Berkeleian! Fallen star!!

March 30. . . . Evening. No meeting at the Philolexian, of which I'm not sorry, for the Freshmen were raising a most infernal row on the Green. That's the hardest class in college. They are all up before the Board tomorrow for knocking in a panel of the chapel door, spiking the keyhole, and throwing the knobs into the temple of cloacina. . . .

April 3, TUESDAY. . . . Got some notebooks and went to college. Mack began his Political Economy, "a solemn humbug" according to Coleridge, and according to Mack a very ridiculous humbug, but he imparteth his own spirit to everything he touches. Anthon gave us Numismatics. Very pleasant, and infinitely better than that horrible biographical Greek literature. . . . Went to that establishment in Chatham Street and enthusiastically made some more numismatological purchases. Charley may make that course delightful if he chooses. . . .

April 6. . . . Went and got some coins at that Chatham Street establishment. Got some decent ones cheap, and then as I was turning over a box of dirty half-pennies and tradesmen's tokens and other trash, I noticed a coin which I soon discovered to be the Rosa Americana half-penny of 1722, a coin that I've hunted for this great while without success. I never saw it for sale before and I secured it and cleared out triumphantly. . . .

April 7, SATURDAY. . . . Went to an auction of Gowans' this evening. Bought nothing of much importance. The only books I really cared for, viz., an old missal, and Reginald Scot, Gowans had orders to bid in "regardless of expense for Judge Firman." And I ran them up to about five times their value and then left the judge in peaceable possession. I fancy he'll curse me when he sees the bill. And now it's a consolation to consider that the missal was vilely printed and that Scot wanted the title page and would have required new binding. But confound the old judge—what business has he to be sweeping up books that he'll never look into?

April 23, MONDAY. . . . The *Sirius* steamship got in this morning: the first steam vessel that ever crossed the Atlantic. Hurrah for the Advance of Mind!

I went down on the Battery with my father to see the *Great Western*, which has just made a three days shorter passage than the *Sirius* and was just rounding to when we reached the Battery. She's a great concern— four masts and 1300 tons. The two strangers have created quite a sensation and the Bay is all alive. . . .

April 24. . . . My father went aboard the *Sirius* today. There was a "cold collation" there, but the small cabin was monopolized by the porcine corporation and he got no dinner and was half-frozen besides.

April 30. . . . Afternoon. Called on Templeton [Johnson]. Went with him to the Academy of Design. I think the exhibition inferior to last year's; there are but few that amount to much. [Thomas] Cole's two paintings, "The Departure" and "The Return," are noble—worth all the rest. They are the best paintings I ever saw at this exhibition, especially the former. I guess he's the most talented of our painters. Those "Course of Empire" pictures and these ought to immortalize him. . . .

May 1, TUESDAY. . . . All our class wanted to go down to the *Siddons* and see John Hone off, so one or two of us went in and got leave of absence for the class after the first hour. But Jemmy let us off at a little past ten, so Backus and I posted downtown, and then went to Whitehall. The crowd was outrageous, for there were three packets to go and the *Sirius* besides, and there were lots of passengers, tearful friends, spectators, and loafers. Two-thirds of Columbia College were on the wharf amid the jam, besides many of the last Senior class to see [John Ireland] Tucker and [Samuel H.] Whitlock take their departure. Only a few got on board the steamboat (the *O. Ellsworth*); there were Backus, [Isaac Vanderbeck] Fowler, [Edward] Anthony, the Wards and Phil Hone, Jr., of our class. We got off at eleven and went down the Bay in great style. The idea was that we should find the *Siddons* just off Staten Island and should be back by one or two o'clock. But we went down the Narrows and past Fort Diamond and saw nothing of her, and the impression began to prevail that she had cleared out and left us. At last, though, we caught her, laying to just off Sandy Hook and came alongside at two. We went aboard and the steamboat took her in tow.

Magnificent cold collation in the cabin, but after hard fighting I couldn't get a seat. There must have been two hundred aboard. Contented myself with what I could get and enjoyed the fun. Prex, whose daughter Frances, Mrs. [Henry S.] Hoyt, was going out, enjoyed himself magnificently with the champagne and cold turkey. We kept her in tow till three o'clock, when goodbyes were exchanged, and with "three cheers," "three more" and so on *ad infinitum*, we cast her loose—and never did I see a more beautiful sight than she presented under a press of canvas, careering gracefully over, and sweeping off, faster than we left her. We cheered and cheered, as long as our voices were hearable on board, then Backus and Fowler and I went and talked matters over a little. Here we were, seven miles outside the Hook, half-starved, all of us, but by special good luck there had been some cold turkey, roast beef, champagne, etcetera, smuggled on board from the *Siddons*, so downstairs we went. It was a sort of private concern, about a dozen enjoying it. But to work we went, though it was rather a rowdy concern, and I ate like a hog, and drank some champagne and other matters that nearly set my throat on fire, and when I went on deck I was quite warm and comfortable and we had a very pleasant return voyage. Got home at six.

May 7, MONDAY. . . . *Afternoon*. . . . Proceeded with Backus up the Bowery to get an alarm clock. I got one very convenient in size and so on, for $5, but now it's come home I can't make it go, which is rather a bore. . . .

I saw the *Great Western* off today. She was escorted down the bay by seventeen steamboats with music, flags, and any quantity of men and women. They were all absolutely crowded, so were the Battery, wharves, woodpiles, Castle Garden, all the streets, and every point from which a glimpse could be got. Col. James Watson Webb goes out in her with some sixty fellow passengers, of which very few are female. They're shy of steampackets as yet.

May 14. . . . On going to college, received the not very painful intelligence that our revered Praeses has absconded to Charleston—for what object, authorities disagree. Some say on Colonization Society business, some say to found a branch of Columbia College, some say on account of the urgency of his tailor, and G. C. Anthon is positive he is gone to grub up some old lion from the ruins at Charleston and so to make a spectacle of it. It's consolatory, though, to escape an hour of International Law.

May 16, WEDNESDAY. Very lazy this morning. Did not get out till near six o'clock. However, the Battery is very pleasant at that hour. . . . Went to the Society Library in the afternoon. And in the evening I set to work to clearing out that Augean stable, my writing desk.

I've finished Lockhart's *Scott* with the conviction that Scott is Britain's *optimus maximusque* in the ranks of literature. Take up any biography of her great men, and it soon appears that their works are *all* their claims on our admiration. Not so with Walter Scott, and taking all in view, his character (and let his diary speak if his biography be accused of partiality), his writings, his rare combination of genius and learning, the richest imagination and the profoundest and mustiest antiquarian research— what can we say of him but that his is the most lovable name in the annals of authorship? Lockhart may very likely be partial—he would be a cold-blooded thing if he were not so—but the diary shows that his partiality has not made him exceed truth in his estimate of character. . . .

May 23.   Prex's daughter Ellen has been *gittin' married* to George T. Wilson, our next-door neighbor! This accounts for the marvelous hurry of the old gentleman. It's rather undignified, to be sure, for the lady to be absconding to Augusta after her lover, but then it's another item off the old gentleman's hands, and if the mountain won't come to Mahomet, why Mahomet must go to the mountain. The match was very romantic. Miss Duer heard that Mr. Wilson was sick, and thereupon asseverated hysterically that she must go and nurse him—and if nobody would go with her she'd go *solus.* So the old gentleman, though at first greatly opposed to the match, finally gave in. So Professor Renwick tells us. Prex's progeny can't do anything in the ordinary and commonplace way.

Strong's last weeks in college were full of furious activity: meetings of '38 to elect class officers, accompanied as usual by electioneering and log-rolling; fierce meetings of Philolexian; week-ends at Whitestone; a sudden interest in English drama which kept him immersed for days in Beaumont and Fletcher, the Duke of Buckingham, Ford and Webster; housecleaning and painting at home which compelled the family to take over his study as a dining room: "So the population has emigrated hitherward and this retreat of deep science and all ethereal and elevating pursuits is converted into a piggery where human biped animals come to satisfy their vulgar appetites by eating and drinking. Yes, by the bones of the ejected saints of Henry VIII's days, this place consecrated to learning, Latin, and similar glorious themes is now a place for gormandizing aliment. . . ."—and in the midst of all his studying, a heat wave.

Examinations finally came, and he slipped forever from the clutches of his professors, one by one: Charley, Mack, Jemmy, Harry. On July 6 he wrote: "Blow ye the trumpet. I add no more glorification. I'm through!" After the final examination: "Prex made us a speech and we took off our hats as he swept out of the venerable hall and gave him three screamers that all but carried away the roof thereof. Then Backus and I marched down into his room and got a couple of certificates enabling us to enter our names as students of LAW." The following day he learned that he was to be graduated second in his class (Backus was first) and was to give the Latin Salutatory. Anthon recommended "Alaricus" as a subject, and Strong started "manufacturing hexameters." After three weeks of steady work, interrupted only by occasional evenings at Castle Garden, he spent morning and afternoon of the 27th with Anthon, "and praised be the nine forever and ever amen, finished the whole concern."

Early in August the family went to Whitestone for the summer, where they boarded with the Scott family; "the old gentleman" commuted to his office in the city daily on the little steamboats Star and Comet. Strong took a greatly needed rest, vegetated and perspired, took moonlight rambles, went bathing, and rode horseback. "I've been enjoying a select company, viz., Homer, Plato, Shakespeare, Spenser, and Walter Scott, and considering the heat, I've done well in the way of reading, specially in Plato (I wish his Greek were a little plainer)." Word reached the family that his cousin, Eliza Johnson, was going to marry Horace Binney, Jr. (Yale 1828), the son of the distinguished Philadelphia lawyer. His mother talked off and on of buying the Scott place—"a glorious conception!"—but the idea had to be given up: "Those aunts of mine don't know their own minds two hours at a time. It's very vexatious."

One unexpected result of the Upper Canada insurrection was the appearance in New York of Marshall Spring Bidwell, a political exile from that fracas, whom the elder Strong took into partnership in his law firm in September. He was admitted to practice in the New York courts by special orders and had a successful and distinguished career there. On October 15 Strong "Got Mr. Bidwell talking Canadian politics. He lays down republicanism with all his soul, and thanks God for the existence of one country where proscription for opinion's sake is unknown. He says he believes the discovery of this country was reserved till late by the especial design of Providence that it might be a field for the exercise of self-government and the political regeneration of the world, because unshackled by the relics of barbarous and feudal institutions. Good."

Strong was on the commencement committee, and as soon as he reached the city after his vacation he found himself in the midst of plans and arrangements for the various events. St. John's Chapel could not be had, so the public exercises were to be in Trinity Church. The class spread was to be in a building on Lumber Street, and when Dugan took him there to see the room, it turned out to be Holbrook's schoolroom "where eight years ago I spent so many dreary hours." There were rehearsals of the orchestra at the Park Theatre. A couple of times Professor Anthon took him and Backus down to Trinity and they rehearsed their parts in the empty church "greatly to the admiration of two upholsterers' *boys at work in the gallery." One morning he went to the college chapel to hear the re-examination of "the Flunkies of July." "It was highly edifying. Cooper barely scraped through, and Douglass was, if possible, worse. Both had to draw* [*questions*] *more than once. But the asininity of poor Phil Hone was utterly indescribable." The weather for several days was execrable.*

October 1, MONDAY. . . . How could the malice of Satan himself have devised anything so outrageously unpropitious, so exquisitely mala-propos, so infernally vexatious, as that I should at this moment be enjoy-ing one of the most horrible colds that ever I sniffled under? How I'm to speak tomorrow, heaven only knows; I fear I shall make an ass of myself at any rate, but if things go on at this rate I shall be a most edifying spectacle. I have smoked cigars, I have swallowed liquor, I have rubbed my nose with mustard (that's original), I have put on flannel, I have worn nightcaps, I have starved myself—but it's hopeless—and tonight as a desperate resort I am going to try a regular sweatation, with cayenne pepper and catnip tea, which will like enough make things worse. At all events, I'm going to make a real failure of tomorrow's business—between stoppage in the head, hoarseness and embarrassment I stand no chance. Well, it can't be helped, and it's not much matter after all. Who'll remem-ber it a week hence?

October 2, TUESDAY. Got up in a state of stupefaction, which was increased by the state of the weather, a delightfully dense fog. Went up to the college and then down to the church to dispose of some programmes. Though it was only a quarter of nine, we found the people streaming in. Came back to college. The fog cleared off rapidly and the sun broke forth most gloriously.

We soon got into line and marched down to the church, greatly to the admiration of the loafers, and greatly to our own discomfort, for the weather was fearfully hot and I sweated as if under the operation of a sudorific of fifty horsepower. Reached the church and marched in, to the tune of some scientific twistification of "Hail, Columbia" which was the first thing to put any feeling of life into me. Prex prayed, and said *"Ex-pectata,* etc. etc. . . . *ascendat Backus!"* Up went Backus, I following as prompter. He went through [the Greek salutatory] well, and there fol-lowed an awful pause while the band played Weber's L. waltz. I sat in a state of tremulousness which reached its maximum when the concluding notes of the magnificent waltz were sent forth by the band, and the Prex said, *"Nunc* bow wow wow, *ascendat Strong!"* Up I went, and by the time I got to "Doctrinam . . ." I was as cool as a cucumber; and when I came to the blarneyation of Prex I had a marvelous difficulty in keeping my face at the proper degree of gravity. To my surprise, I felt not the least embarrassment, but actually entered more into the spirit of the speech than I had done before. I was fearfully hot, and just as I began, an ambitious fly established himself on my nose and made the grand tour of my physiognomy. I hadn't got cool enough yet to crash him off, but at last he got tired of hearing Latin, and retired. I found my cold somewhat bothersome, but less so than might have been expected.

Then came a march—I don't know the name of it, but never did music sound so comforting—and next up went [John Mason] Knox, whose oration "on the Progress of Political Liberty" was fairly written and quite well delivered, though with more embarrassment than I expected. But towards the end he became more spirited and did well. He praised Oliver Cromwell and the Scotch fanatics, though, which was a great blot on his speech.

Then I went out with Backus, Chittenden, Fowler, and George Anthon to the refreshment room, where matters were as yet orderly and respectable. It was not until two or three o'clock that they became rowdyish and disgraceful, through the agency of such characters as Travers, [Philip Kemble] Paulding, Fish, the Duers, and the clique to which Cooper and Douglass belong, which last were riotous, obstreperous, and over-whelming.

While I was out [Benjamin Tredwell] Kissam spoke, and H. H. Ward, the former, it is said, well; the latter absurdly awkwardly and ridiculously. I heard the conclusion of [Alfred Mersan] Loutrel's speech. It was very well done, clearly and distinctly delivered. So was [Edward] Anthony's, though it was not quite so spirited and was too full of names. Phil Hone spoke pretty well, but was embarrassed and hurried; and as to his speech, it was a piece of patchwork—in one place half a dozen sentences entirely *sui generis* and attributable to none but himself—then half a dozen more that were rational and well-written, and so on alternately. F. Anthon did decidedly well; his speech was less cock'n'abullical than I expected, and some portions of it were well done, almost too good for the credibility of its authorship. Little [Jeremiah] LaRocque, I'm sorry to say, was rather flat and spiritless. Douglass did tolerably. His (!) poem, however, betrayed its paternity; it was rather cold and stiff, though smoothly written. Then came [Benjamin] Romaine, who made a most unmitigated ass of himself with affectation and theatricalism. He apostrophized Bishop Hobart's monument, and growled, started, and sputtered in a way that was truly comical to hear.

Medals were distributed next. I took six silver. Knox, who was third, took two silver and two bronze, and though I was notoriously swindled out of three or four, this was doing decently enough. . . . Next degrees were conferred. . . .

Then Overture to *Masaniello* was played, which sounded good, especially as it's six years since I've heard it, and Fowler came last. His valedictory to the class was especially liked—"the best valedictory," some call it, "that they've ever heard"—so much the better. Charley Anthon didn't like it much; he complains of its likeness to the Carlyle school and with a degree of acuteness which does him great credit; he has smelt out the secret, though of course only conjecturally. Sly dog, that Chas. Anthon.

The whole affair went off well.

After stepping down home for a few minutes, I came up to the room again and found about a dozen of our fellows over some oysters and champagne. I joined them and we were soon in very high glee. I never felt more glorious than I did at the thought that the job was over, and what with the songs of Ward and Fred Anthon and Romaine, and the general good humor, we all forgot what we were doing, and when Fowler got up and said he must be off for the Newburgh boat and we dispersed, I found that I had as much champagne on board as I could stagger under. I had poured it down, like the rest, pretty freely, to be sure. We were all quite high, and I knew very well it wouldn't do, so having found on trial that I could walk a crack without difficulty, I got some soda water and then started to walk myself sober. I walked up Front and Water Street to the other side of Corlears Hook, and then walked back all the way to test my sobriety and rationality. Came back and got some of Delmonico's coffee and then went home, quite cool, though tired. That was (correctly) attributed to the "excitement." . . .

October 4, THURSDAY. Clear and very glorious. Walked into the office. A new act of my life is just beginning. God grant I may so bear myself that the next three years may be years of success and improvement. I must begin by forming a *plan*, and then act up to it steadily and firmly. This I can't do, of course, till I can see my way. At present everything is in confusion, and the Law looks like an infinite wilderness, and not a very interesting one. But I had made up my mind to be disgusted with its commencement. . . .

Strong now settled down to become a lawyer in traditional fashion, by a three-year clerkship in the office of a practising lawyer (in this case, his father) with three years of reading for the bar examinations; seven years were required of men who did not hold the A.B. degree. There were law schools at Harvard, Yale, and New York University, but it does not appear from his diary that these were ever considered. Of his office companions, he writes October 9, "M. S. Bidwell is a first-rate man, very good natured and very ready to communicate information. [Richard] Varick seems to be a good sort of fellow, not very luminous, and too rich ever to be a lawyer. Seymour is Seymour [this was Charles Seymour, Columbia '36, who later became a clergyman]. [David Smith] Coddington is Mr. Nathaniel Winkle over again. Mr. [William] Deane is a very well-regulated piece of copying machinery." Chittenden was about to join them. Mr. Strong immediately set his students to work mastering Graham, and there are daily lamentations from the son ("I wish that man no worse punishment than to be condemned to read his own book, which casts all other bores utterly into the shade"); the offending volume was the second edition of Practice of the Supreme Court of the State of New York *(1836) by David Graham.*

On October 19, a letter was received from Mr. Derby "announcing the appearance of George the 2nd. God save his Majesty. May he prosper better than the first of that name." This was a second son named George Strong Derby born to his half-sister Eloise; he prospered, was graduated from Harvard Law School in 1861, and lived until 1875.

October 20. . . . Got *Rubeta*, which as a poem is worthless, though many of the notes are very good. But it is breaking a butterfly on the wheel. Some of it is dirty and some smutty and some dull. I am tolerably sure that J. F. Cooper is the man; that review in the *Knickerbocker* proves him to be meanly malignant enough for anything, and all *Rubeta* is a concentration of the bitterest malignity against those two poor devils, Stone and [Charles] King.[1]

[1] *The Vision of Rubeta, an Epic Story of the Island of Manhattan,* with illustrations, done on *stone* (Boston, 1838), is a long, raffish poem with exhaustive scholarly notes and *apparatus criticus* and several amusing lithographs in the style of Phiz. The poem itself is a take-off on *The Awful Disclosures of Maria Monk* (1836), the supposed revelations of an ex-nun from Montreal, and the notes give the contemporary celebrities of New York quite a going-over, particularly William Leete Stone, the editor of the *Commercial Advertiser,* who is accounted for in the pun on the title page. Strong was way off in attributing the book to Fenimore Cooper, who was no classicist; the

October 29. Worked faithfully today. Nine hours, or rather eight and a half, of steady writing, and three devoted to Blackstone and Lord Brougham's Defence of Queen Caroline, sent me to bed at twelve quite tired. I don't care how much writing I do, for it clinches matters in the memory more effectually than twice the time spent in studying would for them.

I'm bent on making myself thorough in the law. But really and truly, I don't think I've got one lawyerlike faculty. My memory is vile, though I rather hope it's improving, my reasoning and logical powers are slim enough, and I don't believe that reading such stuff as Graham's *Practice* and copying the verbiage and repetition of legal forms is any ways calculated to improve them. But Chillingworth and Locke, I think, will put them in good training, especially the former. My memory I'm in despair about. I don't know anything more vexatious than its failing as it does. The source of all the difficulty is the infamous habit of careless slip-slop reading which I suffered myself to get into.

November 2. . . . Great Whig meeting in front of the Exchange. Uncle Benjamin [Strong] in the chair. Speech from Philip Hone and another from Reynolds. Neither were much more than sufficient to set the North River on fire. But matters seem to go off with spirit, so hurrah for the Whigs and down with the Sub Treasury. . . .

November 4. A deplorable rainy Sunday. But I saved myself from a fit of the blues by spending most of the day on [William] Chillingworth, the prince of logicians. I am making out an analysis of that most masterly piece of argument, the second chapter. It is convincing, unanswerable; in short, a mathematical demonstration of the weakness of the foundation stone of Papal error. No man can read it and remain a Papist unless he be one of those who "pray, but that they may be confirmed in their faith, not that they may be led to the truth."

November 5, MONDAY. . . . The election has begun warmly enough, though as today is rainy it has rather abated the fury of the belligerents,

---

Anthonian footnotes should have pointed inevitably to a Columbia man. The author, Laughton Osborn of the class of 1827, son of Dr. Samuel Osborn, was a well-to-do dilettante who lived in retirement in New York; embittered by the harsh reviews of his first novel, he waged endless warfare against the press and his critics. He published novels and poetry at his own expense and printed several plays which were never produced. Cooper's review of Lockhart's *Scott* in the *Knickerbocker* for October 1838 was a savage one and outraged the Scott-worshipers, but Cooper was a man of extremely high principles, and from his Olympian position the criticism was not unjust.

even as a pail of water well bestowed cools the ferocity of two contending tomcats. The general impression is rather against the success of the Whigs. At all events, there will be a very close run.

Two things I'm sorry to see in this election: one, the introduction of abolitionism into politics, which may play the devil with our institutions and which is at any rate a new force brought into the system, with an influence now almost inappreciable, but which may grow greater and greater till it brings the whole system into a state of discord and dissension, from which heaven preserve it! The other is the increasing tendency of the Whig party to absorb all the wealth and respectability, and of the Democratic (so called) to take in all the loaferism of the nation, a tendency which may bring us finally to be divided into two great factions, the rich and the poor; and then for another French Revolution, so far as American steadiness and good sense can imitate French folly and blood-thirstiness.

November 6. . . . The prospects of the Whigs seem to be encouraging. But it is impossible to say anything about the result with any sort of certainty. It was enough to turn a man's stomach—to make a man adjure republicanism forever—to see the way they were naturalizing this morning at the Hall. Wretched, filthy, bestial-looking Italians and Irish, and creations that looked as if they had risen from the lazarettos of Naples for this especial object; in short, the very scum and dregs of human nature filled the clerk of C[ommon] P[leas] office so completely that I was almost afraid of being poisoned by going in. A dirty Irishman is bad enough, but he's nothing comparable to a nasty French or Italian loafer.

November 9. . . . Hurrah for the Whigs! George W. Bruen says they have carried the state by 10,000, which I can't quite believe. However, the *Evening Post* gives it up as a gone case. . . .

November 19. . . . There is a curious story about the Rev. Church Historian, Anti-Jeffersonite, Professor of Rhetoric, D.D., and great man altogether—Francis L. Hawks, the all-but Bishop of the Western Diocese, viz., that he has got himself into a snarl with an amiable young sister of his congregation. He goes too far in comforting the widows. Bennett serves him up [in the *Herald*], though without names, but the scandal is current everywhere, and if it is anything but scandal, will raise a tempest. I never thought him anything more than a man of talents. Those two *New York Review* articles of his showed him to be no true Christian minister, though I liked their principles. His wife is at New Haven. . . .

November 20. . . . Started at one for White Plains, where the old gentleman has some business with reference to Mr. Schermerhorn's Yonkers property. Found the Harlem Bridge up, and we had to wait half an hour before the clumsy draw could be let down. I thought it was a judgment on my professional parent for defending Mr. Coles's cause [the Harlem Bridge case], which I'm now firmly convinced was an unrighteous one. And as to the road, I really wonder how any witnesses could have been got to defend its character. The Westchestrians are not to be blamed for grumbling at such a slough, for it certainly surpasses all roads I ever saw or heard of save the unsurpassable New Jersey turnpike whereon a traveler saw a hat reposing, and on attempting to pick it up, was hailed by the owner beneath it, who said he had a good horse under him, and was getting on very well considering. . . .

Went over to the clerk's office after tea, and while my father was busy in verifying searches, I overhauled sundry old records. The earliest are recorded in 1684, and one of these is a singular affair, a kind of ac-knowledgement (all papers seem to have been recorded promiscuously) by one Edward Hornett stating that he had formerly brought scandal on his wife's reputation by his ill treatment of her by "leaving her to her shiftes" on divers occasions at New York and Oyster Bay, etc., and that he was now moved to do justice to her and to acknowledge that his ill treatment of her was caused by no fault of hers, but by a quarrel between them, because he had twice committed "carnell coppellation" with Mr. Archer's negroe womann, on one of which occasions his wife, being present, was greatly moved thereby. But to save his own character said that this proceeding of his was caused by no carnell lust, but that he had been injured by working in the sun on Long Island and was told that this was good for his health.

December 1, SATURDAY. . . . Astonished Chittenden in the afternoon by talking High Church, episcopal ordination and a chain of ministry from the Apostles down. He can't swallow those doctrines. The fact is that for the last six months I have been trying to make up my mind as to *what I believe* and *wherefore.* I prefer doing it coolly and leisurely, to setting down and making a job of it, because these matters wherein I'm unsettled are after all of but secondary or tertiary importance, and be-cause, moreover, it can't be done in a hurry. At present I find myself with a strong prejudice against Low Church and "Presbyterian" doc-trines, though whether that's founded on feeling, or on right reason, *non constat.* . . .

*Strong had been president of Philolexian this fall, but he lost interest in its
constant teapot-tempests—"It makes one so riley to have to sit as president over
such a pack of small animals"—and on December 14 he resigned the office. He
now plunged into the squabbles of the Law Association.*

December 19. . . . Looked into Coke upon Littleton. I must read that
book, but gods! what an undertaking it is! And I am not sure but time
might be more profitably spent than in attacking such antiquated learning.
But *credo expertis*. At all events, Littleton will teach me Norman French
and Coke will teach me patience and perseverance. I am almost dismayed
at the wilderness I'm entering on, a wilderness of which these confounded and corpulent "law calves" are but a section, and a very small one.
However, I'll try what scrambling can accomplish.

December 23, SUNDAY. . . . The wind is moaning and howling outside,
fitfully and with a melancholy sound enough. It is the saddest note of
nature's music, especially in such slaughterously cold weather. If my
head didn't feel as if all the brains had been scooped out and the vacuum
filled up with warm pudding, I should enjoy Fuller's *Holy Warre*, over
this glorious fire. That's the best of his books, I do think, and it is outrageous injustice in me to be dozing and winking in utter stupidness
over its pages, as I have been tonight. This comfortable fire has a tendency to encourage somnolency, and the wailing of the cold wind on the
other side of the windows gives me a sort of physical self-congratulation
on being on this side. It must sound like a death march to some—the
destitute, houseless, and fireless. This is a night to teach one charity.

December 26, WEDNESDAY. . . . John [*sic*] Osborn is rumored to be
the author of *Rubeta*. That accounts for his ravenous onset upon Alma
Mater in general, and her "vain head" in particular. The poem has
proved rather a failure, though it has certainly marks of talent. It's a
decided attempt to follow up the career of Byron. Probably some tender
bud of Mr. Osborn's genius has been nipped by the winter's breath of
King and Stone, and so as Byron's poetry was damned and Byron got
glory by slaughtering the critics, so Mr. O.'s poetry is damned, and Mr.
O., etc. It's a branch of the Rule of Three—practical mathematics.

1839

WAR TALK · OXFORD TRACTS · J. Q. ADAMS'S SPEECH ·
NAHANT TRIP · REBUILDING OF TRINITY · JOHN
MASON'S WILL · ANTI-RENT TROUBLES

*T*he domestic scene was growing somewhat brighter as the effects of the panic of 1837 continued to wear off. Whigs in particular were in a happy state of mind as the new year began, for a Whig governor, William H. Seward, was just taking power in Albany, and the party would easily control the House in the next Congress. All omens pointed to a Whig victory in the coming presidential contest. In the international sphere, however, the heavens were gloomy. Relations between Britain and the United States were threatening. "Hunters' Lodges" all along the Canadian border were sworn to end British power in North America, and were making as much trouble as they could for the Van Buren Administration, which had sent General Winfield Scott to the area to maintain American neutrality. New forays were made into Canadian territory in the last weeks of 1838. The Maine boundary, meanwhile, was in dispute, and a source of inflammation. The British, anxious to build a military road over practicable ground from Halifax to Quebec, insisted on holding much territory claimed by Yankees. When in February, 1839, a body of Canadians began cutting timber on the Aroostook River in the unsettled district, American lumberjacks moved in to stop their operations. Both Maine and New Brunswick called out their militia. The bloodless "Aroostook War" was under way. While the American, Canadian, and British press fulminated angrily, Congress voted ten millions and gave President Van Buren authority to enlist fifty thousand volunteers. However, the stage was being set not for a bloody Anglo-American conflict, but for the compromises of the Webster-Ashburton Treaty.

*Strong began the year with a fit of the blues which lasted well into April,
and which had its foundation in some obscure and baseless fears of a personal
disaster.*

January 27, SUNDAY.   Colder and windy. One of those execrable raw,
chilly, murderous days that we have been cursed with such a super-
abundance of for the last two months. . . . Went to church twice. Heard
Mr. Higbee in the afternoon, and a strange-looking being in the forenoon
who resembled in appearance a boiled chicken a good deal overdone, and
whose apology for a sermon might have been composed by an animal so
circumstanced without any necessity for supporting a miracle.

January 31.   Old Lady Hamilton[1] was in the office this morning;
she's as spry as usual. She had walked down from St. Mark's Place and
was going to walk back, which is certainly doing very well for an old
lady of her degree of antiquity. . . .

February 28. . . . Eloise wants me to go on to Boston and attend Mrs.
Richard Derby's fancy dress ball. *Quaere:* does she see anything GREEN?
Fancy balls I opine in abstract reasoning to be great humbugs. The
proper way to conduct a thing of that sort would be to confine it to some
forty or fifty and to have the characters managed systematically; for
example, let the Court of Elizabeth or Henry VIII or Charles I be represented. . . .

March 1, FRIDAY.   We've a new individual in the office, Walter
Livingston Cutting, a brother of Francis Brockholst. I have had no chance
yet to form an opinion of him on good and substantial grounds, but I
predict that he's a smart and rather industrious conceited ass. He's lived
near all his life—in France, poor devil!

March 4, MONDAY. . . . Read through the evening, but for some reason
or other felt as stupid as a dog—by the way, that's a queer comparison
we hear often used. Dogs are the most sagacious and the noblest of the
four-legged vassals of man, but we make them standards of stupidity,
and their names—dog—hound—whelp—puppy—are most significant and
outrageous expressions of contempt when applied to a biped. So we say
"as sick as a dog," but are dogs peculiarly subject to nausea?

March 5, TUESDAY.   My father got in town this morning after a most
fatiguing time, for the roads were as bad as anticipated, or if possible

[1] Elizabeth Schuyler, daughter of General Philip Schuyler of Albany, was married
to Alexander Hamilton in 1780; she survived her husband fifty years and died in
Washington in 1854 at the age of ninety-seven.

worse; going, it was traversing one slough from Hicksville to Mt. Misery, and coming back the roads were frozen, and of course about as pleasant to travel on as the treadmill may be supposed to be.

. . . Uncle Thomas [Strong] is in a wretched state—bad enough it has been ever since I remember, but now his nervous system is said to be completely shattered; and though his bodily health holds out wonderfully considering the wear and tear from within, though he has every element of happiness that a man can have at his command, I'd rather stand in the shoes of the poorest Negro on his place than in his. Poor man, he deserves pity if ever man did. I think that all our people (on my father's side, I mean) possess to some extent the faculty of being miserable about trifles and inordinately anxious about nothing at all. My father certainly does—and so do I. But with him the disease has reached a fearful height, and by all account he is positively in a state of monomania on some subjects. Uncle Thomas was for many years a martyr to *tic douloureux.* Dr. [Valentine] Mott, I think it was, in January of '30 or '31 performed a very severe operation for it, but with only temporary success. How perfectly I recollect that 15th of January (I think that was the date) when, after expectation and hope for an indefinite period, I first went to the Park Theatre with our people and Edward Weeks. It was a great night entirely, and I mention it here because that very night Uncle Thomas arrived from Long Island almost frantic with the agony of that disease—driven to capitulate and consent to an operation. . . . The Hercules that finally vanquished the Hydra—that all Dr. Mott's science wasn't up to—which cured the *tic douloureux*—was a preparation of rather quackish origin, an ointment prepared by rubbing down five grains of aconitine with five drachms of chate, and applying it twice a day on the end of the finger along the track of the diseased nerve and rubbing the surface slightly with it. It effected an immediate cure—after one hundred and fifty other expedients had failed. The pain now and then recurs slightly, but a slight application instantly destroys it. . . .

March 9, SATURDAY.   Everybody is talking *War.* I don't know what to think about the state of things and I don't know that my opinion would be worth much if I did. There seem to be strong reasons pro and con of its probability. The pecuniary and commercial connections are the strongest arguments against it; there's a powerful interest in both countries that will struggle against a war, as certain ruin to themselves. But the aspect of things in Maine and New Brunswick is bad. There may be a collision, and if either party taste blood it will be like rousing two tigers.

If there were to be war, what would the end be? God knows. But we should go into it with "the Law on our side," and that is as essential a point to a belligerent nation as it was to the pugnacious follower of the Montagues. The right is on our side most certainly. And we should go into it with an unanimity and a wholesomeness that hasn't been seen since '76. It does one good to look around—the general feeling on the subject even now. The Canadas would rise, and they'd be free, too, in six months, or I'm mistaken. Russia would come down on England "like a herd of buffaloes" and the two St. Georges would be well matched. But there are sixty thousand Indians on the Western frontier that England would bring about our ears and there are Heaven knows how many niggers in the South, and England could land a woolly-headed and flat-nosed regiment on the shores of South Carolina from the West Indies, with a respectable force to back them, and proclaim emancipation, and the South would swim in blood. And how popular this would be in England! It makes one's blood boil to think such a thing. It would be a war of extermination on both sides—and it should be so far as the Negroes are concerned—and the only good that could follow would be the extermination of that race. But all this, if it should take place—and I do believe something of the kind could take place—would bring back the days of the Revolution, turn the war into a national struggle—whew! Hurrah!

March 11.   Much the same sort of day as yesterday. The papers this morning look very bellicose indeed, and the *New Era* is as savage as a hornet in July; it will soon be recommending the extension of every Englishman from Bangor to New Orleans. . . .

Mr. [Isaac H.] Bronson, a M.C. who was in the office today, seemed to favor the idea that the great Dan Webster was slightly "O be joyful" when he made his war speech in the Senate. . . .

March 15, FRIDAY.   Went this evening to the sale of Major Douglass's very splendid library. New York is certainly infected with the Bibliomania. I never saw anything like the eagerness to buy, and the prices given, at any book auction before. Many books went for more—twice as much—as I could go to Wiley & Putnam's and get better copies for. The sale was kept up, to an intense crowd, till half-past twelve. I left at eleven, giving Carey instructions to secure for me that copy of Dibdin. I bid on Burney, Walton, and one or two more, but they all ran up so high that I got frightened and gave it up.

April 9, TUESDAY. . . . Went up to church at McElroy's with Mary. . . . I never leave a Presbyterian church without being a warmer advocate for Episcopal forms and the Episcopal liturgy and Episcopacy in general, than when I went in. All the routine of their doings (unless when extraordinary talents and eloquence and so on alter the case) seem to be flat, stale, and unprofitable, without form and comeliness, and greatly wanting in decency and order. . . .

Hurrah for the Oxford Tracts! Glorious be the memory of Archbishop Laud—and may the nineteenth century be sufficiently thankful for Keble and Froude and Palmer and Pusey, I having been sent down on Earth during its continuance.

April 10, WEDNESDAY. . . . Rambled about to sundry of the polls with Chittenden in the afternoon. There is generally a great tendency to rowdyism at those palladiums of our freedom. The Whigs are going to be "regularly flummoxed," to use a Wellerian expression. But they'll be great fools if they are. They are the Ins, and the Ins need never be beaten by the Outs, unless there's treachery in the camp, or disaffection or disunion or something of that sort. . . .

April 12. The elements are sympathizing with the Whigs; storm and tempest mark the downfall of the Whig dynasty as they did the murder of the righteous Duncan. "How short the race our friends have run." Verily they are "cut down in all their bloom." The grass withereth, the flower fadeth—and Isaac L. Varian is mayor by a one-thousand majority. . . .

April 13. . . . Have been engaged nearly all day in making out the title to the Pearsall property. A queer rigmarole my abstract will be. It has gone from father to son since Governor Dongan's patent in 1685, and now the dissipation of that worthless scamp Tom Pearsall sends it under the hammer—to pay debts that he has (*de facto*) contracted for tippling expenses. . . .

April 16. The *Great Western* is in, and to my surprise she brings no news of mustering squadrons and coming foes, of rolled-up coat sleeves and flourished cudgels, from the other side. But they're in great trouble in England—a change of ministry seems to be looked for. If so, I suppose the Tories go in, and I verily believe that of the two they're the better. This ministry seems to me to be a weak and selfish set, no more governed by the principles they profess than they are by the Prince of Patagonia, if any such there are. The great gravitating law—or rather law of gravitation—*pro me*, the great doctrine of "I myself I," a sort of practical Fichteism, the all-pervading power of unadulterated selfishness, governs all their doings. If there's any difference, which is a doubtful question, I believe the Tories have more principle, more energy and patriotism—not than the Whigs—but than the Whig ministry. . . .

April 17.   Saw a copy of Sir Francis Bond Head's *Narrative.* Bidwell was reading it, and from some manifold blunders that he pointed out, I suspect the veracity of the book isn't much. It's full to the brim of vanity, pomposity, and the absurdest egotism conceivable. It's nothing but Bidwell, Rolph, and Mackenzie and Sir F.B.H. from beginning to end— Bidwell—Bidwell—Bidwell—from the title page to Finis. Mr. Bidwell says he never knew his own importance before; he's discovered that all the Canadian controversy has been simply Head *vs.* Bidwell. . . .

April 23, TUESDAY. . . . Laid out eight dollars of my capital on Ben Jonson, with which investment I am well pleased—but economy must be my rule of life for a little while.

Went up to church with Mary in the evening. Shan't go there any more—it's a great humbug. . . .

April 25. . . . My father has been all day engaged in the duties of that high and responsible office of public trust, a commissioner of schools, or whatever it is, and traveling all over the island with his compeers, examining, admonishing, and inspecting its various nurseries of the tree of knowledge. So we've had the office pretty much to ourselves. . . .

April 26, FRIDAY.   Splendid weather. Went up to St. Peter's bright and early expecting to see a tremendous jam and to undergo all the discomforts naturally resulting therefrom. To my great surprise the church was not more than two-thirds full, so that we got along very comfortably. . . .

They had a very full band and choir and any quantity of bassoons and trumpets and several immense articles which I take to be kettle drums, and which added greatly to the effect of some parts of the performance. I am not scientific enough to appreciate this *Mass of Requiem.* Some parts of the "Dies Irae" are certainly very splendid indeed, but I think on the whole I'd rather hear the *Twelfth Mass.* The whole affair today was first rate, but if it had not been for the splendid style in which it was got up, I should not have thought much of it. I never heard anything equal for richness and softness and grandeur the magnificent body of sound that the full band with the kettle drums or the sub-bass of the organ produced. The only fault was that it was too powerful for the size of the church.

Bishop Hughes preached a very good sermon, decidedly the best, indeed the only rational and decent one, I ever heard from a Catholic.

His manner is very good—plain, candid, and serious. He's no hypocrite, I think.

They'll have to get up another requiem before long for old Bishop Dubois; he's very infirm indeed—scarcely able to go up the steps even with assistance. . . .

April 27. . . . They are going on gloriously in the upturning of the City Bank, and we shall have a second edition of the Griswold Quagmire as soon as a rainy day comes. The Merchants Exchange makes a bog of the other side of the street, so there's nothing to be gained by crossing. Then the Merchants and Union and Manhattan! Heaven help the Wall Streeters.

April 28, SUNDAY. . . . Heard a sappy sermon from Berrian[2]—about angelic wives and cross husbands. That was the view he took of unequal marriage. I trust in his next sermon he'll show us the other side of the picture. . . .

April 29, MONDAY. . . . Drew orders from bills of particular and got them signed by Judge [Thomas Jackson] Oakley. He sits in his "chambers" there like some huge owl in an ivy bush, goggling and winking and staring in a strange and uncouth manner at all the birds of light (i.e., lawyer's clerks and similar sprigs of the profession) who come to visit his abode. . . .

Twenty-five hundred tickets have been issued for John Quincy Adams's great speech tomorrow. If it's a decent day, the jam will be intense. . . .

April 30. A cloudy morning followed by rain. Dirty and execrable.

Went up to the Hall and then with Chittenden and [George] Anthon to the Middle Dutch Church to hear John Quincy Adams's oration before the [New-York] Historical Society. Got a first-rate seat in the gallery, and by great good luck the pew filled up with *men*, and the access to it was speedily obstructed by the same, for it was an immensely crowded affair, so we escaped the bore of being ejected by the womankind and could look down and philosophically enjoy the sight of the crowding, squeezing, and elbowing below.

The church was very full and the stage was occupied by such big bugs as Winfield Scott (the Praeses that is to be), by William A. Duer (the Prex that is), Philip Hone, Peter Stuyvesant, and others. . . .

The operations were opened by the Rev. Dr. [John] Knox in a sort

---

[2] William Berrian (Columbia 1808) was a quiet man who became assistant minister of Trinity Church in 1811, and rector in 1832, serving until his death thirty years later.

of modulated whine—worse than Bishop Dubois's *vere dignum et justum est aequum et salutare* etc.—in which voice he poured forth thanksgiving for everything and a prayer for everything else and a good deal that was neither prayer nor thanksgiving, but an indefinable *tertium quid* perhaps most aptly called twaddling. Wainwright's concluding prayer was very much better—short and sweet.

An "ode" (!!!!!!) of sixteen lines was sung to the tune of Old Hundred and then old J. Q. A. let slap. His hand trembled and he seemed agitated and embarrassed at the beginning, but that soon passed off and he went ahead and gave us a speech of one hour and forty minutes' duration. It wasn't too long. His delivery is not bad, especially when he says anything that's meant to be forcible, and he sat down at last in a perfect hurricane of applause.

Backus called this morning and again this afternoon, having arrived in the city today. He looks much better than he did in October and seems to be highly comfortable. He has come to town to purchase books for the formation of a library for the Utica Academy, I believe, but whatever has brought him here, I am exceedingly glad to see him again.

May 5, SUNDAY. Mr. Derby arrived from Down East. He comes to the city with reference to the projected establishment of a line of steam packets between Boston and Liverpool, in which enterprise he takes considerable interest, apparently. Went to St. Paul's with him in the morning and heard that amiable successor of the apostles, Berrian. Went with him after dinner uptown to Dewey's new church, understanding that there was to be service there, but found it hermetically sealed, so walked around a little to look at the various edifices adjacent thereto and came home, taking the Egyptian Tombs in our way.

Boston is looking up. After some twenty years of inaction, the city has waked up and all its energies are now directed to commerce. With all its advantages, with the past strength given by its manufacturers, and with its countless railroads like the hundred arms of Berarens of old, it bids fair to grasp and to sweep away its full share of the commerce of the country. So be it. None the better is it for the happiness, peace, and morality of any city to expand and "improve" and grow rich and have its merchant princes. Cities are bad enough at the best, but a rich commercial city (like this) I regard as a *hell*—a sink of vice and corruption and misery—lightened on the surface by the false glare of unhealthy exhalations. . . .

May 7. . . . Mr. Derby went down to Staten Island this afternoon and spends the night there. Meantime the *Liverpool* has come in and Mr. [Samuel] Cunard on board of her. It would be funny enough if some of the New Yorkers should get around him in the meantime.

Went to the office after tea and read Mr. William Lyon Mackenzie's Grievance Report and his *Sketches of Canada*. Queer medleys they are. He seems to be a remarkable instance of a man of considerable industry and activity, and with a great deal of acuteness and talent in getting up anything, and altogether of no despicable abilities, failing utterly to do anything and produce any results, by reason of his total want of arrangement of ideas and steadiness of purpose.

May 8. Mr. Cunard has not arrived, so Mr. E. H. Derby will have to go home with a prodigious flea in his ear. . . .

May 9. Hot—positively stifling. Wall Street, always a Purgatory, has this day become a Pandemonium: clouds of dust flying, chippings of granite whizzing in volleys like grapeshot, the street encumbered with brick, blocks of stone, and huge Irishmen; the National Bank nearly inaccessible from the fact that on each side of it a big house is being pitched into the street; brokers, bank directors, and merchants' clerks dodging in and out as soldiers enter a town through the crossfire of the besiegers; Bob White's big dog walking disconsolately about the streets and gazing with a melancholy air at the progress of ruin; striking resemblance of the south side of the street to the passes of the Cordilleras. . . .

May 14, TUESDAY. . . . Went to the wedding [of Eliza Johnson and Horace Binney, Jr.]; Mr. Higbee was the operator. Julia and one of the Miss Binneys bridesmaids, and Templeton Johnson and Mr. B's cousin [Horace Binney] Wallace of Philadelphia groomsmen. There was quite a multifarious assemblage, and the affair seemed to go off very well, though it was outrageously hot. I found it a great bore. Had the honor of an introduction to the illustrious Chancellor Kent, who looks more like an antique baboon than the Lord Mansfield of America. . . .

On the 24th, the Strongs went to Boston for the week-end for the christening of George Strong Derby; as usual, the diarist enjoyed himself and greatly regretted leaving: "Boston is an exceedingly glorious place. I wish my lot had been cast there instead of in this pestilential hogsty, New York."

June 2, SUNDAY. . . . Trinity Church is at present sharing the prevailing epidemic, i.e., it is being pulled down; or at least being overhauled generally. They ought to pull it down and build a big cathedral in its place, if only to sanctify Wall Street; a fine building on that situation would show to very great advantage. . . .

June 3. . . . Went up to Richard & Platt's to look at the material of their next auction. Don't see much that's worth purchasing except perhaps Horne Tooke's *Diversions of Purley* and a respectable copy of Ludolfus's *History of Ethiopia,* which seems to contain some particulars of Prester John, doubtless very satisfactory. That is one of these out-of-the-way subjects that it is impossible to find on an emergency in the general run of books, and it is as well to secure the books that refer to them whenever they can be found. . . .

June 5. . . . After dinner went round to Mr. Bartlett's and got Malcolm's *History of Persia,* a very interesting book apparently, and a magnificent copy. Handed Mr. B. a list of books which he has very obligingly offered to import for me. I almost hope he mayn't succeed in getting them all, for pounds sterling do contrive to run up into an amazing quantity of dollars. . . .

June 6. . . . Spent most of the morning at the Register's office in tracing the title to a valuable piece of ground on Tenth Street, which I finally traced into the hands of my respected great-grandfather, William Brownejohn, *Physitian.* He appears to have owned acres of real estate in the city, from Hanover Square to low-water mark, and a great deal of land besides in that quarter—property that is now worth hundreds of thousands, aye millions. And when he died, it was partitioned, and every foot of it sold in Chancery pursuant to the directions of his will. Confound the old doctor's shortsightedness! I must set to work to look for flaws in the proceedings. . . .

June 13. . . . Spent most of the morning on Graham. Went once or twice up to the Hall. Spent a little time in the Court of Chancery—to see the lawyers tortured by the Chancellor. Walworth[3] is, I believe, a smart man, certainly smart in the New England sense, and he exhibits his smartness by snubbing the lawyers most outrageously. He anticipates

[3] Reuben Hyde Walworth, LL.D., who succeeded James Kent as Chancellor of New York in 1828, was famous for his outrageous treatment of counsel from the bench, and various efforts were made to kick him upstairs or get him out of office. A nomination by President Tyler to the Supreme Court failed of confirmation when Thurlow Weed made known the real reasons for the high recommendation of Walworth by the bar of the state. His retirement was finally achieved by the abolition of the Court of Chancery when New York adopted a new constitution in 1846. Walworth spent his later years compiling a monumental history of his mother's family, the *Hyde Genealogy* (2 vols., 1864).

JOHN McVICKAR

WILLIAM ALEXANDER DUER

JAMES RENWICK

CHARLES ANTHON

their conclusions, mangles their speeches, interrupts their arguments, and annoys them in every way, so that an argument before him becomes merely a conversation between chancellor and lawyer. Poor George Griffin was holding forth, and of course he was soon worked up into a perfect fever—and of all queer figures, Mr. G. G. in a flurry is the queerest. His very boots, each two feet long, vibrated galvanically. . . .

June 14, FRIDAY. . . . Went into the Superior Court and listened to an exceedingly funny suit: an action for assault and battery committed on the distinguished Mr. [Joseph] Palmieri of the Astor [House].

It seems that the defendant had called Mr. Palmieri the first cousin to an ourang-outang and had cracked sundry other equally classical jokes on his personal appearance, which is remarkable for an unsurpassable pair of black whiskers, which finally led to a quarrel which resulted in a row which terminated in Mr. Palmieri's being knocked down and dragged out, to his great damage and detriment. Prescott Hall for the defendant made the funniest speech I've heard yet, and then Buffalow Sedgwick[4] attempted to raise a little sympathy for his maltreated client. But it wasn't of any use; the whole affair had been put in such a ludicrous light by Hall that all his indignant denunciations went for nothing at all; and instead of $3,000, the jury gave the much-injured dresser of hair only $150. I suspect Palmieri's whiskers had an unfavorable effect on the jury. He looked very grizzly-bearish, not at all like a safe subject for an assault and battery. . . .

June 18. . . . Went to the office in the afternoon and read Thompson's (of Hempstead) new *History of Long Island* with a good deal of interest. It contains much that is curious. The author is evidently green in the art of book-writing, but he seems to have bestowed much labor on this work and if he didn't use so many big words without apparently a very clear idea of their meaning, I would think him quite a sensible character.

June 19. . . . Looked into Appleton's new assortment of old books— sad trash they are, generally speaking. I noticed a gigantic basket full of them, and it turned out to be an assortment selected last night by the distinguished Mr. Nick Biddle—about as trashy as the rest, a fine set of the *Harleian Miscellany* excepted. If Mr. B. has no more skill as a financier than as a collector of books, he's very little of a loss to the U.S. Bank. . . .

[4] The attorneys in this cause were Jonathan Prescott Hall (Yale 1817) and Theodore Sedgwick, Jr. (Columbia 1829); both men later held the office of U.S. District Attorney for the Southern District of New York.

June 29, SATURDAY.   Spent the morning miscellaneously. Old Gallatin was in the office to see if anything could be done for his unlucky
nephew A[lbert] C[hrystie]—poor fellow. His operation in 1837 not only
cleared him out, but left him minus some six or seven thousand dollars.

Left at five in the *Narragansett*. We had as beautiful an evening as
mortal could wish, and sat on the upper deck looking at the Long Island
shore and enjoying ourselves very pleasantly till eight or nine o'clock. . . .

June 30.   Got into Stonington bright and early—and whizzed off in
style. . . . It wasn't altogether pleasant, though, for I contrived to get my
eyes full of sparks from the engine and I never suffered more in that way
in my life. Didn't get rid of the trespassers till after dinner, just as I had
made up my mind to go to Dr. Somebody—and recover his fee by a suit
against the company. It's wonderful that such a nuisance isn't stopped.
It really is a serious objection to the route, for I wasn't by any means the
only victim. Why have they taken off the sparkers?

We came into Boston in fine style. All well in Boylston Street. . . .

July 1. . . . Mary and *pater meus* left [for New York] this afternoon.
Saw 'em comfortably off. It's a great sight to see a large train get under
way. I know of nothing that would more strongly impress our great-great-
grandfathers with an idea of their descendants' progress in science. As to
the engine, the most pithy and expressive epithet I ever heard applied to
it is "Hell-in-Harness." Just imagine such a concern rushing unexpectedly
by a stranger to the invention on a dark night, whizzing and rattling and
panting, with its fiery furnace gleaming in front, its chimney vomiting
fiery smoke above, and its long train of cars rushing along behind like
the body and tail of a gigantic dragon—or like the d——l himself—and all
darting forward at the rate of twenty miles an hour. Whew!

July 3. . . . It was so obliging as to clear in the afternoon, so we got
into the *Thorn*, bag and baggage, and came off. Very pleasant passage
down the bay, only after we got through the Gut, as I believe they call
the passage between Deer Island and the mainland, we found ourselves
in a heavy ground swell, that is, heavy enough to give the boat a highly
pleasing oscillatory, undulatory, or see-saw-atory motion which made
poor Eloise dreadful sick. Otherwise we got to Nahant in a very comfortable way. . . . Went forthwith to the Pulpit Rock with E. H. Derby, Esq.,
to let the perch know we'd come. They called on us in numbers and we
pressed 'em to stay so that they really couldn't say no. We hauled in
some noble fellows and then came home and went to tea. . . . Walked
about; Nahant is a fine place and no mistake.

July 4, THURSDAY. . . . We drove down to Lynn at ten o'clock and put Mr. Derby on board the Salem train for Boston. Got myself a new pair of boots—for the rocks of Nahant try men's soles terribly. The afternoon was rather showery. Saw Lauriat's balloon—and after tea saw the rocks illuminated with tar barrels and blue lights, rockets and crackers and whizzers of all sorts in great style. It was as brilliant a 4th of July celebration as I ever saw.

July 6. Nahant. Cloudy morning. We took a barouche and good pair of horses and drove over to Marblehead with Master George Strong Derby. The road thereunto is rather pretty, but of all strange, antiquated, unchristian-looking places that I ever saw, none come within a mile of this. We had to drive hither and thither through the convoluted alleys that the natives call streets and troops of young aborigines staring at the unusual apparition, before we could find any place to put up at. And such streets, such houses, such a smell of rotten fish, such a primitive-looking race of beings I never saw. There are a few modern houses with paint on them that shine out from the *vulgus,* but generally the places where the people live are as guiltless of paint as the wood that composes them was before it was cut. But this don't look so bad after all, for the houses have a staid and respectable dinginess that harmonizes very well with their antique structure, and as fast as the houses become in the course of human events untenantable by humanity, they turn them over to the pigs and emigrate to other quarters. It's completely at the Land's End. Nobody ever goes there, and it's consequently just a century and a half behindhand. Moreover, it's just like a rat trap; when once you're in it, it's next to impossible to find your way out. We drove a couple of miles out of our way in trying to get out, for the streets don't carry you to the end of the town, but round and round it. . . .

July 10, WEDNESDAY. Goodbye to Nahant. Omnibus at quarter past ten. Hot ride over the beach—slow going—omnibus full of Yankee servant girls, apparently, queer-looking beings (yet, saith patriotism, compare them with the servant girls of other lands). Lynn. Railroad—decidedly the best thing of the sort I ever patronized—comfortable cars and few passengers, and quick going. East Boston. Ferry boat. (N.B. They can't understand steamboats in Boston.) "Stage" to 56 Boylston Street—detestable.

In the afternoon Strong and his mother left for Stonington, took the Rhode Island, *and were in New York the next morning by seven: "Alas for the* bracing air of Nahant. *This infernal atmosphere makes one feel like a wet shirt collar. It's almost too much trouble to breathe such an air at such a temperature.*"

July 13. . . . *Inter alia*, read a little of Carlyle's *French Revolution*. I don't agree with his worshippers in thinking these phantasmagoric scenes of his models of history. Everything is indistinct and misty, yet his phantoms have *life* in them, and sometimes they become clothed with reality and distinctness enough. . . .

July 15, MONDAY. . . . Called on Mrs. Cave Jones about that bothersome chancery business of hers. Never heard such a rattle rattle rattle of words in all my life. Mrs. J. and her respectable old daughter (who's affected with strabismus) talked both at the same time, like two several steam engines. They both know what they're about—pretty particularly well.

Three days later: "Had to go over to Park Place this morning and read that answer in chancery to Mrs. Jones & Co. They're as sharp as steel traps— capital men of business they would make."

July 17. . . . Not much of importance. The alarm about the importation of yellow fever seems to have died away, but if this warm showery weather holds on, we shall have it originally and spontaneously. The streets are very dirty and pestiferous, and a few days since I passed Coenties Slip, and from the state it was in, I should suppose it was competent to inflict the whole city. The water was saturated with filth and where the sun fell on it, it was literally effervescing—actually sending up streams of large bubbles from the putrifying corruption at the bottom. There might have been half a dozen of these bubble streams in a square foot, in some places more. And the stench of sulphuretted hydrogen was enough to poison one. . . . Venus Cloacina and her train of handmaidens, "the Nymphs who reign o'er sewers and sinks," is indisputably tutelary goddess or patron saint of this, our Athens. We are worse than the men of Marblehead; they're neat and decent enough to abandon their dwellings before making pigstyes of them, but we live in pigstyes. The whole city's one huge pigstye, only it would have to be cleaned before a prudent farmer would let his pigs into it for fear of their catching the plague.

George Anthon finished his work at Columbia this month, and Strong went with him and his "reverend papa" (Henry Anthon of St. Mark's Church) to enter his name as a student of law; he was to be one of the group in the Strong office. John Weeks entered a few days later.

July 27, SATURDAY. . . . After dinner, took the carriage and went with Mr. Bidwell over to the "Greenwood" Cemetery—a most exceedingly beautiful place it is, and I sincerely hope it won't turn out a bubble, for in this city of all cities some place is needed where a man may lay down to his last nap without the anticipation of being turned out of his bed in the course of a year or so to make way for a street or a big store or something of that kind, and this place, when it is a little improved and cleared up, will exceed Mt. Auburn. . . .

Strong spent nearly all of August and September at Whitestone. The 9th of August, he set down a complaint of the Long Island Railroad, the same complaint that was heard a century later: "That railroad is about as poor an affair as bad tracks, slow engines, and frequent stoppages can make it." Strong took it easy at Whitestone, fished a great deal, and read with enthusiasm the Oxford Tracts—*"the greatest theological productions since the days of Hooker."*

September 24, TUESDAY.   Left this morning. . . . Nothing new in town, except that poor old Trinity is in the last stages, and that there was a great fire last evening destroying the National, the French Church, the nigger meeting house, and the Dutch Church below Verren's, besides several houses. . . .

September 25.   Saw the plan of the Trinity Church that is to be—a most magnificent edifice if carried out. The larger the better; I hope they'll carry it back to Lumber Street. It should be a kind of cathedral— the St. Peter's of the Church in America. A bishop's chapel for consecrations is talked of, but I think it very doubtful if it is erected. If it is, it will disturb our vault—I mean the vault of my mother's family—the Brownejohn vault. . . .

September 26.   Up very early—breakfasted at half-past six—to enable my father to go on with [John] Mason's will. His death may take place at any moment, and he has scarcely a hope of living through the week. A large estate and profligate children to spend it, and I believe that the fatal system of trusts is to be resorted to—and in these times a trust is enough to sink any will if anything of a storm rises up among the heirs. . . .

It is said that old Mason died this afternoon; if so it must have been but a few hours after executing his will, which he did at twelve or one o'clock. The report was current at three. If his disease was an affection of the heart, it is not unlikely that the agitation of executing the will hastened his death.

Mr. Mason died within fifteen minutes after the signing of his will, and the expected contest took place; the great Mason Will Case dragged on through the courts until 1855 and was one of the most famous legal battles of its time. Strong's comments on the case have been included in Mr. Henry W. Taft's extensive accounts of the litigation in his book, A Century and a Half at the New York Bar (*New York, 1938*).

Strong went to the Columbia commencement on October 8 at the Middle Dutch Church and watched and commented on the proceedings with as much interest as he had shown when he was himself involved. The following day he went up to the college to attend the meeting of the alumni. Judge William Inglis's address he thought "no great affair; it was evidently the result of much labor— and very little thought." Strong was elected treasurer of the Alumni Association: "My election (like all the rest) was most flatteringly unanimous, the nomination being followed by three or four grunts which were interpreted as signs of the meeting's approval." "Alma Mater," he concluded that night, "reminds me of the 'long-armed baboon' to which (vide *Hood's* Zoological Report) *'the young kangaroos were put to dry nurse'; she's about as hopeful a parent."*

October 11. . . . The Whigs have nominated Philip Hone for senator. *Quem deus perdere vult,* etc. We're going to be most overwhelmingly used up at this election. The only case in which Mr. Hone would fill that place well would be if a view of the interior of the Senate Chamber had to be taken, in which event he would be highly ornamental. But he'll never have the chance. . . .

October 13, SUNDAY. . . . Heard Higbee preach an admirable High Church sermon this morning. Why can't some better name be found for the principles of the Oxford Tracts and of the First Founders of the Reformed Religion, say rather—of the Restorers of Apostolic Usage, than "High Churchism"? I don't like the name. "Churchmen" is indefinite as applied to the maintainers of those principles. "Catholicism" is pre-engaged by pseudo-Catholics who maintain a sort of negative universality by denying the existence of any but themselves—calling the narrowest sectarianism "Catholicity." . . .

October 14. . . . At the office after tea. Read Graham. I am beginning to comprehend the subject of bail at last—*at last*—and I've been studying (?) for a year! *Ars longa, vita brevis.* I'm beginning to despair of ever making a lawyer, unless I outlive Methusaleh.

October 16. Glorious change of weather. Clear and warm; genuine

Indian summer. Talk of spring! October is the loveliest month of the twelve, and shameful it is—"sorrow and shame"—to spend it among brick walls and bills in chancery. . . .

Governor Seward is to review the militia tomorrow; a token fifteen thousand of those unhappy scarecrows are to exhibit themselves to his excellency. I have been warned out; how they caught me I don't know, but I am caught. However, the note was addressed to me as George D. Strong Jr., so when it comes to the court martial I shall plead misnomer in abatement, and if that fails, try another tack and plead nearsightedness in bar. If nothing else will do, I must get some nominal office for economy's sake. Templeton Johnson offered to get me a *chaplaincy*, for it seems the militia chaplains are all laymen, something like Friar Tuck, I suppose, or any other "hedge priest." Their duties I can't ascertain; probably they embrace offering ghostly consolation to the wounded and soda water to the cocked and saying grace at militia suppers. But I haven't a call that way.

November 7, THURSDAY. The Whigs are woefully beaten—another Waterloo. Minority from 1700 to 2000! perfectly overwhelming and astounding to the victors themselves. . . .

November 9, SATURDAY. . . . Did some writing and some trotting, and in the afternoon enjoyed the melancholy pleasure of reading the last number of *Nicholas Nickleby*. I never enjoyed a work of fiction as I have enjoyed that. It has been drop by drop, and each drop glorious. It is Boz's masterpiece. The plot is altogether better than *Oliver Twist*, and altogether I don't think there's any one of Scott's novels that equals it; Mrs. Nickleby, Ralph, Tim Linkenwater Noggs, Squeers, Miss LaCreevy and so forth—what a portrait gallery they form! To read the book seems to enlarge one's circle of acquaintance most wonderfully.

Old Verren has been getting into a scrape with those unfortunate people the Heywards—marrying another of the daughters to a man who is generally believed to be a French blackleg, worse if possible than Henry Hone. The match was clandestine and the old sinner knew it—and Francis B. Cutting and the Heywards are in great wrath and shook their fists at Saint Antoine and Saint Antoine has sued them for it, and held them to bail. . . .

November 12. . . . Professor H. W. Longfellow is a great man. I read *Hyperion* this summer and it led me to think highly of his taste and abilities, though there's some *smoke* in it. But a little poem of his that I saw in a newspaper, taken from the *Southern Literary Messenger*, is really *great*, worthy of the author of *The Ancient Mariner*. It is called *The Beleaguered City*. . . . Glorious. I don't know of a more beautiful and forcible comparison anywheres, nor of one more admirably carried out with all its details, yet perfectly free from strain or unnatural similitude. . . .

November 15. . . . Have been looking this evening into Luther's *Table Talk* which John Weeks got for me last evening at the sale of the second part of Douglass's library. It confirms the idea I had formed of the rugged old Reformer. It would seem to have been a special design of Providence that the apostle of Protestantism should not be an absolutely perfect character, lest those who followed him should become worshipers of the man as well as believers in his doctrines. But let Oxford say what she will, I believe him to have been one of the greatest men the world ever saw, in strength of mind and real living energy of character. It is remarkable, too, what a vein of sound homely good sense seems to have run through his character, judging from this book.

Talking of man-worship, I am persuaded that it exists in the Protestant world, on this side of the water at least, at present to a sufficient extent almost to be set off against the saint-worship of Romanism. To anyone who has a taste for being a Triton among the minnows and enjoying a Grand Lama adoration on a small scale, I should recommend setting up as an unmarried "pastor" in some Dissenting church. That those people don't have altars erected to them and honors paid to them as do their wooden analogies in Spain isn't from any less exalted reverence or less profound veneration belonging to them. This applies chiefly to the womankind, and to be sure, it is an amiable weakness. But all share it. The eloquence, the "delivery," the fervor of a man, or of the men who preach in any church generally, constitute the sole inducement to adopt that church, or to go to any at all. Therein consists the great merit of the Anglo-American Catholic Church; it keeps the person of the minister out of sight; in prayer he is the mouthpiece or personified voice of the Church Universal; in the sacraments he is her representative and instrument— and whatever respect he claims is in virtue of the sacred office which the church has invested him with. . . .

November 16, SATURDAY. . . . Thomas H. Smith is actually married— I did not believe the rumor before—and his blushing bride is a protégé of that respected female, Mrs. Miller of Duane Street, a damsel who has been on the town for twenty years. I never heard of such a case of deliberate infatuation. He urged and implored her to marry him for a long time, and she wrote a Southern friend to know whether he'd keep her or not if she didn't. He declined and she thereupon consented. Very pleasant, this, for Bruen and Waddell. I should be sorely tempted to shoot a brother of mine who should perform such an operation—or rather I'd kidnap him and send him off in a quiet way to Tierra del Fuego or the northern coast of Kamchatka or the southern extremity of California or dispatch him overland to the center of Mongol Tartary and leave him to find his way home and cool off during the journey. Poor devil, he's to be pitied, after all. . . .

Went to the Law Association this evening, or more properly the 'Sociation of Law Asses. Found a dozen or two dingy specimens sprawling about the room and trying to look professional, but no sign of a meeting, so I incontinently cleared out, took a walk, and came home. . . .

November 17. . . . Welford tells me that while at Oxford he heard Newman preach, and described his style as very peculiar, rigidly rejecting all appeal to the feelings or senses, I suppose because they savor of dissent and Methodism. I think he errs in the opposite extreme. Such things are well if not carried too far, and no one can read a page of the sermons of the old High Church standards without seeing that they sought to work on their auditors in that way. . . .

November 19. . . . I don't know why it is, but the antiquities of the Middle Ages interest and attract me far more than those of classic times. It's a barbarous taste, I must confess, but I look with more reverence on an old missal than I should on the finest monument of Grecian art. I'd rather see York Minster than the Parthenon, and I take much more delight in the barbarous black-letter legends of those rude times than in all the graceful mythologies of the South. Perhaps it is because those mysteries were stuffed into us *usque ad nauseam* by Professor Anthon that I'm now disposed to undervalue them, but I don't think that's the reason. . . .

November 20. . . . Drank a glass of absinthe this morning which nearly poisoned me; if the homely epithet of "rotgut" is applicable to any kind of vinous fluid, it certainly is to that. . . .

Went to the office in the evening. Did an affidavit and then took a very comfortable walk up to Union Square, a walk of four cigars. I measure time and distance by those articles now as Dutch express riders and Canadian *habitants* do by pipes. Post has got back from Flushing and tells me that Hawks's school building is going up—a single Gothic quadrangle—and that Schroeder's Labyrinth is in progress. He intends it for the exercise of his young lady pupils who are to ride about therein on donkeys, whereupon John Weeks says he ought to go down on all fours himself and make one, a very good suggestion. It is also reported that he's to take the first class out in a steamship every year and present them to the Queen; but that's said to be unfounded.

November 21. . . . Fanning C. Tucker is going to be married. . . . What gives me a peculiar interest in the major's connubial intentions is that I am forewarned that I am marked out by destiny—little Thalaba— to copy his antenuptial settlement. Very delightful prospect. I wonder if I shall ever do a thing of that sort. It seems to be the common lot of humanity. Who can tell? Only this much I know, that I've never seen the woman yet that I'd dream of making up to. It must be a very awkward business. But if I am so destined, I wonder where the distinguished *she* is at this present moment—what's she doing? What's she thinking about (dreaming about more properly, for it's eleven o'clock and she ought to be in bed by this time)? I wish somebody would tell me which of Burns's charms is operative on this side of the water, for, absurd as it sounds now, I suppose I shall be hooked some of these days, and I'd like to have some foreknowledge of the where and the when. . . .

November 25, MONDAY. . . . Went to the office after tea and sat down steadily and resolutely to a cigar and Graham when—Enter the Tempter in the shape of Post, and as human nature is weak and Graham is dull, I yielded to his insinuations at length and went to Miss Shirreff's concert at Niblo's. On the whole, very well pleased. Much of the music was good, substantial, old-fashioned and Scotch, and some of it was spoiled by too much execution and the asinine airs of the performers. Wilson's ears lengthened visibly during that "scena" from *Fra Diavolo.* He must be obliged to cut them every week or so, like his nails. . . .

November 28. . . . Old Samuel Ward is said to be dead; so they go. His benevolence and other virtues innumerable are greatly lauded now; I never heard anything about them before. . . .

December 2. . . . I must get Jonathan Edwards's book[5] and read it carefully. I detest those doctrines most cordially, yet I should like to see what can be said in their favor. His doctrine I understand to be that the will is governed by the same laws of cause and effect as operate in the material world, and that we have, therefore, no power to determine our

---

[5] Jonathan Edwards's great treatise, *A Careful and Strict Enquiry into the Modern Prevailing Notions of that Freedom of Will which is Supposed to be Essential to Moral Agency, Vertue and Vice, Reward and Punishment, Praise and Blame,* was first published in Boston in 1754.

own actions. Admit this, and of course all the high Calvinistic doctrines of predestation are undeniable. But how any man can believe what his own heart and the spirit of truth and reason which God has implanted in every mind must every moment testify to be a lie, and to be downright blasphemy against the Being he reveres, I cannot imagine. Indeed, those decrees of the Synod of Dort seem to me not to deserve those epithets only because they are pure nonsense—words without meaning. Reflect on the meaning of the words God, man, eternal misery, and put them together in the order in which a Calvinist would put them in declaring his creed, and they are absolutely meaningless.

That serious, reflecting, educated men, good Christians many of them, and untrammeled by any authority of any supposed infallible church, should be able to believe that a God of Goodness has created millions of men and women whom, by a previous decree, he has cut off from all power, all ability to do good, who, by the law of their existence, are not *able* to will anything which may lead them to happiness—not able even to feel a wish for truth and right or to utter a solitary prevailing prayer for divine assistance to lead them to it—men, in short, created only to be damned—is inexplicable. . . .

December 4, WEDNESDAY. . . . Washington Coster's assignment is to be executed tomorrow! [Henry] Wallack, I imagine, has plucked him about as successfully as ever a greenhorn was fleeced by the rowdies of the Five Points; he has fairly gammoned him out of probably the larger half of an estate of $200,000, and his other debts are more than sufficient to swallow up the balance of it. I don't pity the man a great deal; in fact he has made himself so notoriously asinine of late by his personal appearance that his collapse will be regarded by nine-tenths of the community as a good joke rather than otherwise. . . .

December 10, TUESDAY. . . . All the mighty Men of War of the city of Gotham—all our little great men—are in a state of turmoil, bustle, excitement, fuss, and fury unparalleled. Little Jemmy Graham, Colonel—no, General—Sandford and ditto Morris are running about the city cackling like so many old hens. The minor officers and the rowdy privates are bustling about by twos or threes with all the impressive dignity of actual service. They were to leave tonight for the scene of war—the Van Rensselaer estates—and though it would be too bad, after all, it would really be highly laughable if the refractory tenants were to give them a drubbing. If they can be brought up to the scratch at all, and the tenants show the spirit they've hitherto manifested, I think it highly probable that they will be magnificently licked, for neither the officers nor the men have got the necessary pluck for anything but marching round a puddle. It's very amusing, though, to see the mighty affair that the officers are trying to make out of this little piece of contumaciousness. But I'm told —I hope it isn't so—that the Tammanyites are to hold a grand sympathetic meeting tomorrow night to denounce Seward and all connected with him for their blood-thirsty conduct in calling out troops to shoot down our fellow citizens. I haven't much respect for either of the political parties, and value them both about alike, but I do not think the Whigs would be guilty of such a shameful and flagitious procedure as this. Any man who presumes to take part in such a meeting, who dares in order to gratify his own party ambition, to make political capital out of this business, to oppose the execution of the law and the protection of private property for the sake of promoting the success of a party, ought to be unanimously kicked out of the country. This is the worst thing I've heard of The Democracy yet, and if it be an act of the party, it fully justifies all that has been said of their agrarian, disorganizing, law-defying character. To sympathize with "a set of rebels" for whose conduct there isn't the slightest excuse except that they think they have paid rent long enough, to support and encourage such men in withstanding the laws of the land solely because this gives an opportunity of introducing big words—"murder," "tyranny," "military despotism," etc.—into their abuse of the Whig administration and so tickling the ears of the mob and producing an effect, is a degree of infamy below what I supposed any political party on earth would be guilty of.

December 11. . . . The state of martial enthusiasm pervading the Park was truly soul-stirring to behold. Rumor says that the militia officers have taken the responsibility of hiring their horses for two weeks! . . .

December 17, TUESDAY. . . . Rather an amusingly lugubrious, or melancholy, laughable affair this afternoon at the office. Enter John C[lark] Derby with a burly loafer in a shaggy great coat for a walking companion, who seated himself deliberately in the outer office while Master John went in to have a private talk with the old gentleman. I thought he had a singular taste in the selection of his friends, but the whole mystery was solved when I learned that the rowdy was a turnkey from the granite edifice in Centre Street and that our friend is in the Tombs! ! ! !—on an attachment for not answering a creditor's bill filed by those good-humored little fractions the Arnoux in Fulton Street for a debt of $220. Poor Mr. Derby gave a moving description of the uncomfortablenesses of the various stone jugs, to one of

which he was to be confined, and my father gave him no consolation whatever, on the principle of letting him "suffer some," in the way of fright at
least, for the idleness and inefficiency that have brought him into the scrape,
and the unfortunate individual walked out with his tail between his legs
and his amiable friend at his heels. But after tea the old gentleman went
up to Arnoux's, advanced a good slice of the debt, and sent up to the Tombs
to discharge him, with strict instructions, too, to keep his agency *sub rosa*,
so that probably Mr. Derby will look sour at us forever after on the strength
of his cool reception and unanswered hints for aid this afternoon. Poor
fellow—he is to be pitied, to be sure, for he's a good-hearted man enough,
though in everything else so wonderfully different from his brother [E. H.
Derby]! But I don't know when or how he can hope for better success in
the world so long as he continues his indolent habits . . .

December 31, TUESDAY.   Half-past eleven o'clock. "I've been savagely
busy all day and took a walk uptown after tea." That's the sum and substance of most of my memoranda, of late. Tomorrow I suppose there will be
something else to write about, for I'm condemned to make a whole lot of
calls, though the weather just now don't look particularly auspicious.
No matter—we must grin and bear it. It'll do very well, provided I get
along without making an ass of myself by some blunder or contretemps,
my custom always in scrapes of this sort. Well, it's got to be undergone
anyhow. There are some places that I don't want to go to a bit, where I
just know the people sufficiently to make it a bore. However, *che sarà*,
sarà, as somebody says somewhere. That'll do to gain me the reputation
of an Italian (isn't that the language?) scholar . . . three centuries hence
when these hieroglyphics will be discovered in an obscure garret and
added to the curiosities in the American Museum for the time being as the
productions *anonymi cujusdam scriptores*, or perhaps sold at auction in somebody's library, "Lot No. 3918726: Curious old MS. partly undecipherable,
apparently the 'Diary' or 'Journal' (*vide* Klootzenberg's *Dict: Antiq*: for
explanation of Old English Terms) of an inhabitant of the ancient city of
New Amsterdam during the XIX century. It is remarkable not only as
exhibiting many singular details of the manners and customs of our fore-
fathers, but also as developing the unsophisticated greenness of the author
and his times. Sold at the Fitzflamberg sale for $500.06 1/4."

Looked into the January number of the *New York Review*. Rather good
—a very spirited straightforward article on Oxford Theology and another
very sensible one on the stern virtues of those great humbugs, the "Pilgrim
Fathers." I'm glad to see that one reviewer has at last had the moral cour-

age to apply to those men the epithets they deserve, and this article does
it well and explodes the notion that they were exiles for the sake of
"Liberty of Conscience" to the four winds of heaven. A more detestable
set of men never existed, with all the bigotry of the worst times of Romanism and without its splendors and its glorious externals to mitigate their
internal corruption—persecuted, themselves, without having learned, as
Christians should have done, lessons of tolerance, they preached and
practised the doctrines of the Inquisition in all their literal atrocity. . . .

1840

LEXINGTON DISASTER · FIRE IN STRONG HOME ·
UNITARIANISM · QUEEN VICTORIA'S WEDDING ·
HARRISON CAMPAIGN · ARRIVAL OF
THE *BRITANNIA* · ELECTION

*When the year began the stirring Tippecanoe campaign had already com-
menced. A Whig convention meeting at Harrisburg early in December
had passed over the two great men of the party, Clay and Webster, and selected a
more "available" candidate, the venerable William Henry Harrison, victor over
Tecumseh. Log cabins, coonskins, and mugs of hard cider were soon the staple of
Whig electioneering. It was certain that the Democrats would renominate Van
Buren, and all but certain that the enthusiastic Whigs, rolling great balls from
town to town, would prove that "Little Van is a used-up man."*

*Strong was now working like a galley-slave in the law office, and occa-
sionally bemoaning his hard application. At the close of the first Saturday of
the new year, spent crouched over his desk, he set down a morose record: "I've
manufactured more deeds and bonds and mortgages this week than I ever did
before. If law fails, I shall be able to set up as a scrivener. Today I've done
nothing but write from nine A.M. till eight, when I took a walk on the principle
of counter-irritation, to reinvigorate my fingers by exercising my legs."*

January 1, WEDNESDAY. . . . Started for our yearly campaign at eleven
and paid some forty visits, including card visits. It was savagely cold, and
the only consolation we got in our progress was from Mrs. [Alexander]
Hamilton, who said it was a mere trifle, nothing at all to the winter of
1780. The Lawrences didn't see company, on account, I suppose, of the
late death of old Mrs. L. Saw Mrs. Bidwell for the first time; she was in
the West Indies last year. She seemed a ladylike person. Went to Mrs.

[Henry Augustus] Coit's; Mrs. [John] Borland and the amiable Miss Martha Derby are staying there. Spent an agreeable minute and a quarter at Mrs. James Strong's, and had another comfortable visit at the Wellses'. Heard there that it's all true about Chief Justice [Samuel] Jones; his property, furniture, and so on, have been sold at an immense sacrifice under divers executions, and from a reputed estate of $900,000 he'll probably have nothing left, or still more probably he'll be extensively minus. It's a great pity not only for himself, now near seventy years old, to be beggared in this way, but it's bad for a judicial officer holding such a respectable station to be put in the same category with so many blacklegs. . . .

Saw Professor McVickar and Argenti and Henry Winthrop at 75 Murray Street; the first was even uncommonly saponaceous, probably in good humor because of his clean shirt, the strangest phenomenon of this day.

January 8. Chancellor Kent paid us a visit this morning. He's going to get out another edition of the *Commentaries*, and to do it on his own hook without the help of the rascally booksellers, as he calls them. . . .

January 11, SATURDAY. Damp, drizzly and diabolical—very exceeding stupid all day long—diddled and dawdled about all morning—snarled and swore inwardly all the afternoon—and smoked two dozen paper cigars, and made out a lot of subpoenas, in the evening. It has grown much colder and consequently the walking is shocking, "sliding on the ice" all the way home. Life insurance offices should put a clause in their policies prohibiting the insured from walking down Rector Street when the thermometer's below 32°, for if the pavements are clear everywhere else, the frozen deposits of those who *mingunt in patrios ceneres* along Trinity Church embankment make that street very dangersome. Came home and read Southey. He may be despicable as a politician and a man (though from his writings I believe he is not), but as a poet, there are few English names since Milton that I would put on a level with him. Wordsworth is a deeper philosopher. Scott has more of the glow and fervor of genius. Coleridge has accomplished little (of poetry) that will live, though the gems that he has left for posterity—to wit, *The Ancient Mariner* and *Wallenstein*—are unsurpassable. Byron I suppose must be a greater poet, though he don't suit me so well, and Shelley, if I'm not mistaken, had a more glorious mind than any of them, only he wasted its energies and threw himself away. . . .

January 14. . . . Peter G. Stuyvesant—if the stories be true that I've heard today of his merciless treatment of poor Chief Justice Jones, insisting on the payment *ad diem* of a balance due him, refusing a moment's extension, and on his default proceeding against him forthwith and selling everything under execution at an enormous sacrifice—is a veritable Shylock, a native American Ralph Nickleby, a cold-blooded disgrace to human nature. I always disliked the man's looks and ways, but I didn't suppose him such an unfeeling brute as he must be, to have acted as he has done—a great fat foreclosing spider. When such men live and think, I don't wonder that theorists begin to dream of Agrarian Laws and Locofocos to talk of "the rich against the poor." It is a pity we have no Areopagus here, no Court of Conscience to punish such sharks.

January 15, WEDNESDAY. I confess I feel altogether blue and dispirited. *Inter alia*, and most prominent of the causes, is this terrible disaster on the Sound, the loss of the *Lexington* on Monday night, the news of which arrived here today. She took fire off Eaton's Neck with a hundred and fifty souls on board (some say two hundred), and all but three have perished. A more horrible business I never heard of, nor of any disaster in which the ruinous effects of terror and confusion, the importance of presence of mind are so clearly marked. The boats were got out while she was under full headway, and of course swamped when they touched the water; the life boat was knocked under by the waterwheel. I suppose at least a hundred and twenty might have got off at the first trip, and then the rest saved, for they were close in shore when the engine stopped. The fire engine had "to be rigged," and in the confusion they could not do it. The tiller ropes were burnt—and for the illegal use of ropes, I hope someone is answerable—for had chains been used, they could have run her ashore. The captain has gone to his account; but are not the inspectors liable? Under a despotism they would be hanged. George Woolsey was on board (William Woolsey's nephew), Brown, one of the members of that refining establishment in Boston, Richard W. Dow of Dow & Co. in Pearl Street—I knew him slightly—and Captain Vanderbilt. It is most fortunate that Mrs. Borland and Martha Derby were not on board. But it's wonderful to me that under all the circumstances more did not escape. It was a still night, and surely they might have sustained themselves on timbers or with life preservers, for every one carries them now. The coldness of the water, however, must be taken into account. It's the merest chance that poor John Derby wasn't in her; he left for Albany today, instead of going to Boston as he first proposed. Well, everybody is talking of it now and so it will be for a week, and then it will be forgotten, by all but those whose friends or brothers or fathers were on board and every tear they shed will call for vengeance on those whose murderous carelessness has caused this. . . .

January 16.   Bitter cold. No further news from the *Lexington* except that Dr. [Charles] Follen[1] and his wife were among the passengers. My father has written to Lloyd's Neck with a description of the persons of Charles W. Woolsey and another man just from England—a particular friend of Mrs. Pickersgill's—and a reward of $100 for the recovery of the body of the latter. It is rumored that Professor Longfellow was on board: I hope not.

Looked into the second part of Marryat's *Diary;* the first was sportively slanderous, but this is stupidly malignant. Mrs. Trollope can't hold a candle to the captain in fertility of invention. I never read such a farrago of lies. He don't lie like a gentleman, either (literary lies being gentlemanly by usage, when genteelly done), but rampages in his mendacity like any loafer.

January 17.   Grahamized comfortably in the afternoon, and proceeded to be examined thereon after tea with only little Pat for a companion in misfortune. Hadn't got very far when an express came up from No. 108 to say that the house was on fire, so away I went in double-quick time leaving *meum patrem* to follow after. The simple fact was that the kitchen range recently erected at No. 106 had communicated with the wall of our kitchen entry by a beam passing through, or partly through, the wall, which had gradually burned away till it set fire to the woodwork of the surbase. The house was so full of smoke that one could hardly breathe in it, and the combustion was just bursting into flame when it was discovered. Two men had come in from next door; the woodwork was soon demolished with a hatchet, and a few pails of water settled the incipient conflagration without much difficulty. But if it had happened six hours later when we were all asleep, I suppose it would have made matter for a paragraph, for it would soon have burned the kitchen stairs and then our domestic resources would have been quite inefficient.

[1] Charles Theodore Christian Follen, J.U.D. Giessen 1817, a liberal for whom life had been made dangerous successively in Germany, France, and Switzerland, fled to America in 1824 and was instructor and later professor of German at Harvard. In 1828 he married Eliza Lee Cabot of Boston. A friend and disciple of Dr. Channing, he also taught at Harvard Divinity School and was later ordained to the Unitarian ministry. Follen became prominent in the anti-slavery movement, then unpopular at Harvard, and the corporation refused to continue his professorship after 1835; he kept on as a zealous abolitionist, preached, taught, and wrote, and was on his way to a ministerial post at East Lexington, Massachusetts, when he lost his life.

January 18. The story of a survivor from the *Lexington* having drifted ashore at Riverhead on a bale of cotton, after a voyage of forty-eight hours, is confirmed, marvelous as it sounds. I thought Captain Hilliard's escape sufficiently astonishing, but this out-hilliards it.

January 23. . . . The late disaster on the Sound continues the subject of general interest—positively wonderful that people should remember for *ten whole days* that a hundred and fifty of their fellows perished miserably in a single night, within forty miles of this city and no one to aid them! There don't seem any reason for blaming the company after all, except for loading the *Lexington* with such a cargo (and that is sanctioned by usage). Every precaution seems to have been taken, every means of opposing the fire at hand, ample means of escape within reach, yet all rendered useless by the want of reflection and the universal panic of those on board. I don't believe the whole black catalogue of maritime disasters contains an instance of so fearful a loss of life under circumstances so favorable. Had they been fifty miles from land in a violent gale, without boats, without buckets or engines, or in intensely cold weather, I could have understood it. If blame can be imputed to anyone, it is to the unfortunate captain. Had he been possessor of coolness and energy, as every man should be who is chosen to perform such duties, all might have been saved. . . .

January 26, SUNDAY. I hear that our people at Setauket have picked up, among other matters, a paper containing sundry memoranda or something of that sort, written after the fire in the *Lexington* had broken out. Particulars of its contents not stated. It must be an interesting relic.

Orville Dewey's sermon on the disaster is published in the *New World* of yesterday. It's a rather ably-written and somewhat prosy moral essay on the shortness of life, the valuableness of fortune, the propriety of being duly shocked on so melancholy an occasion, the importance of presence of mind, and the virtues of Dr. Follen, together with certain consolatory remarks, intended I suppose for the friends and relatives of the victims of the disaster, that after all, sudden death isn't such an unpleasant affair as people think; they and their friends are saved the pain of parting and the disagreeablenesses of anticipation (he should have added doctor's bills and funeral expenses).

People may say what they like about the spread of Unitarianism. It never can be general. In wealthy cities, it will be the fashionable and aristocratic faith (if that term can be applied to a system which is the negation of all faith). Imposing no unpleasant restraints, requiring nothing but what decency and regard for the opinion of others also demand, involving no points of belief above the reach of common sense, it will be very likely to become the favorite creed of those who want a religion at once convenient, compressible, and fashionable, for show—not use. But with the great mass of people, this cold-blooded system of combining the minimum of belief with the maximum of license will not *take*. It never can be a popular religion. Men are carried into it by the impulse that takes them out of the church into dissent in general, though with by far the greater number the impulse is not strong enough to carry them beyond the first stage....

January 27. This has been an igneous evening. When I left the office at half-past seven, there was a fire in Broad Street, or rather in Water near Broad. . . . I didn't stay to see the end of the combustion, for there were so many "soap locks" and "round rimmers" and other amiable persons there congregated, and so much hustling and swearing and rowdying going forward, that I concluded to clear out—and walked off for a ramble uptown. Got a little way up when I saw that another fire which had broken out an hour or so before in South Street was making quite a show and the temptation was irresistible so I made for the scene of action, the corner of Dover Street. I couldn't get in front of the fire and was unable to make out whether two or three stores were burning, but it was quite a showy affair: the fire reflected on the snow and lighted up the masts and rigging of the ships, the groups of firemen on the docks with their engine and lamps, the crowd and bustle in front of the buildings, the raging fire, and just above it the cupola of Thomas H. Smith's big store blazing away and half-hidden by the eddying smoke—altogether made quite a display. Thomas H.'s store I think must have been saved; I didn't stay to see the finale, being rather tired of wet feet and obstreperous rowdies. . . .

At three o'clock [this morning] I was waked by a furious alarm of fire which seemed so near and so terrible that I roused the old gentleman and we bundled on our clothes and made streaks. On reaching Wall Street we saw it wasn't there, but the cinders were showering down like a snow-storm in Pandemonium or a "sulphur shower" in Padalon, and the fire shown as brightly on top of the Exchange and other elevated buildings as if it were only one block off. It *was* the Thomas H. Smith store, probably the finest and largest, twice over, in the city, and I never saw such a scene as Peck Slip presented: the store extending from South to Front Streets was burning like a volcano, one body of fire from top to bottom. It was crammed with hemp, cotton, and tea, and the fire was so intense it was impossible to come near it. There were only two engines and perhaps a couple of hundred men. Several other stores had caught and were burning fiercely;

in fact the whole block was on fire from Smith's store to Dover Street, but everything else sank into insignificance before the big store. It seemed as if the whole area, where the roof had been, 50 feet by 200, wasn't wide enough for the flames to get out . . . .

The fire was wholly unchecked when I left. Lucky for old Bruen that he sold out not long ago. The loss must have been immense.

January 28. The loss last night is estimated at about $1,500,000. Everything from Smith's store to Dover Street on South and Front Streets has gone *in fumo.* Went down to the scene of action with George Anthon; they were demolishing walls, etc., and I noticed in pulling down a five-story brick front, entirely supported by side walls, that a rope passed in at the fourth story window and out at the third so as to form a noose, when pulled, though the wall shook and tottered and cracked in every direction, actually *tore* through the wall intermediate the windows, as if it had been made of wet paper, bringing out just bricks enough to come through—a pretty specimen certainly of modern masonry. Smith's store still burning fiercely. Two whole cargoes of tea in it just from Canton, and I noticed the melted lead of the chests streaming down from the piles of ignited matter that are piled within the ruins. It is most fortunate that there was no wind when this fire took place. Had there been any, half the city might have been used up, for the firemen were exhausted and totally inefficient. As it is, the shipping seems to have escaped by miracle; they were mostly frozen in and couldn't be hauled out of the docks.

Spent the rest of the day promiscuously. After tea Walter Cutting and I underwent Graham *soli.* . . . Came home and at a little after ten had the pleasure of drumming my father out of bed again to announce another big fire. Didn't wait for him to dress, but made off as fast as possible in search of the *locale.* It was in Pearl Street and Stone Street (i.e., stores extending through from one street to the other), and a very splendid fire it was. It spread furiously for a short time and was not checked until four stores were thoroughly on fire and past salvation, and they didn't get the fire under till near one o'clock.

January 29. The fire last night was a small affair, as fires burn nowadays, only about $200,000. Rumor saith that Hayden, the occupant in the part of the store wherein it originated, is the incendiary. Really it's hard to tell exactly what we're coming to. If he is, I hope he'll meet his reward, for this practice of merchants setting their stores on fire to get the insurance on an unsaleable stock is prevailing to such an extent in this community, and carries so small risk of detection, that if anybody is caught he ought

to be operated on without benefit of clergy, *in terrorem.* Or if anybody is
suspected there should be "some fuss made about it" just to remind others
that it is a rather hazardous amusement, a speculation which the policy of
the law does not countenance. . . .

February 3, MONDAY. . . . After tea went to the office and began to dip
into Graham. Another alarm of fire, and as it seemed rather long and loud,
I shut Graham and cleared out. Fire in Gold Street from Ann to Beekman,
in a large six-story cabinet warehouse and manufactory extending from one
street to the other. It had caught in the upper story and from the nature of
its contents burned furiously, but the firemen ought to have been able to
save the building. However, it burned gradually down and when I cleared
out there wasn't much of it left unburned that was worth saving. This was
not one of the gunpowdery, irregular, flashy fires that have been so common
of late, governed by none of the acknowledged rules of the art, but a good,
steady, old-fashioned conflagration, in which the dramatic interest was well
sustained throughout, and fire and water were "head and head" till the
grand finale when the walls tumbled down in various directions with a
great crash, and then fire triumphed, which as the hero of the piece it was
very proper and perfectly regular that it should do. On the whole, this was
a very fair fire. I'm getting quite a connoisseur.

It's very amusing to notice the view the loaferage (i.e., the majority
of the lookers-on at fires) take of the subject. They consider it a sort of
grand exhibition (admission gratis) which they have a perfect right to
look at from any point they like and to choose the best seats to see the
performance; the interests of the owners never seem to enter their heads,
and any attempt to keep them back, or to keep a passage open, or any
other effort to save property by which their freedom of locality or locomotion is impaired, they consider an unwarrantable interference, of
course. . . .

But the state of things is really too bad. Here, in the two first days
of last week $2,500,000 of property were destroyed by fire. Now comes
another, the loss of which can't be under $80,000, and as to the little fires
that have taken place during the interval, I don't take count of them. One
committee, appointed by the merchants on Saturday, at heir meeting,
to devise means for stopping this extraordinary inflammability, don't seem
yet to have done much. From all I've seen of fires of late, I'm fully convinced that our fire department is utterly and shamefully incompetent.
The engines are not powerful enough to throw water to any considerable
height, the hose are so full of rips and holes that a third of the water must

be lost, the hydrants never seem to have any water in them, a large part of the firemen do nothing but bustle about in their caps, swear at everybody and try to look tremendous, the engines are never worked for five minutes in succession, and everything in short is as badly conducted as possible. It's a wonder to me at every large fire that half the city don't burn up; some night it will, and then they'll get to work to reform in earnest.

February 6. Be it remembered that Mrs. Elias Hasket Derby, our affectionate sister, hath transmitted to us, in the fullness of her benevolence, a goodly specimen of that unctuous and appetizing conglomeration, that flower of porkdom, that noblest result of slaughtered porcinity—*quem ambrosiam Dii vocant, mortales* "headcheese."

Very nice it was to be sure, and in our innocence we partook of it liberally. Fortunately, there were other good things on the table so my paternal relative and I were comparatively moderate in our devotions thereto, but Mamma dined off it almost entirely—Mary ate very little— and a supply was sent in next door; this is a "matter of induction to the action," though in fact it amounts to the cause of action itself.

I felt queer all the afternoon; tried a cigar, but it didn't seem to work right, and I walked home at six o'clock feeling rather sick, comforting myself with a prospective cup of coffee, and thinking how nice I should feel thereafter. Got home: general confusion and dismay. Mrs. Strong had been taken sick immediately after dinner, Dr. [John] Neilson sent for express; he was upstairs, and when he came down reported a serious attack of cholera, or something like it, he couldn't tell what. I continued to feel more and more unwell and in ten minutes I was deadly sick—*cor eructavit meum*—and when Dr. Neilson made his second visit half an hour after, he found my father and myself undergoing the same unpleasant symptoms, though not so bad in degree as his original patient. I never suffered more from sickness in my life. . . . *Pater meus* suffered still more. Mary was slightly unwell. Two aunts fearfully sick. Peter half dead (he was the only one of the servants who had touched the delicacy; he had contrived to get it all for himself). In short the house was a complete cholera hospital.

February 7. Gloriously warm weather, but we're all under a positive *ne exeat*, though decidedly better than yesterday. Two more visits from Esculapius, two from Hon. Marshall S. [Bidwell] and sundry others from divers anxious friends, Walter Cutting and George Anthon among the number. . . .

Dr. Neilson says there was arsenic in the cheese. I don't believe it. I don't believe the primitive Pillsburies on Cow Island know what arsenic means, nor is it likely they ever have occasion to use any mineral poison whatever. There can't be any rats on the island. If this has been caused by anything other than some unhealthiness in the pork, or some vegetable put in by mistake, I'm inclined to think a badly tinned copper boiler has been the discomforter of our stomachs. I couldn't get my old chemical gim-cracks together to test the stuff in a scientific way, so I applied a spirit blowpipe, without producing any of the fumes of arsenic. But the cinder that resulted tinged the flame green and therefrom I infer copper. . . . I'm anxious to hear from Boston, whether they've been poisoned or not, and if not, what poor Eloise will say when she hears of this unlucky result from her present.

February 9, SUNDAY. . . . Read, among other things, some of Cranmer's book against Transubstantiation which I picked up yesterday at Wiley's. I don't think it amounts to much. The old archbishop knew better how to suffer and die for the truth than how to write for it. . . .

February 13. . . . There has been some talk about our changing offices—emigrating into the rooms now occupied by Palmer—a splendid plan, for these offices are quite too small for eight, especially when five of us are such an aspiring set of law students. But it seems to have all died away and I suppose we shall have to be cabined, cribbed, and confined for a little longer.

February 14. . . . Letters from Boston this morning from Eloise and from Mr. Derby, both of whom write in terrible distress at the dire effects of Yankee headcheese. Never did pork raise such a hubbub before. . . .

February 16. . . . What a ridiculous book that Rabelais is, certainly quite *sui generis* as far as my experience goeth. But I think that its out-rageous coarseness is not calculated to hurt anybody: certainly not to do half the injury that the refined and elegant and stimulative *suggestiveness* of [Thomas] Moore and many others is daily effecting. Its tendency is to disgust more than to allure, and I think a man's mind must be in a beastly state if reading Rabelais can corrupt it.

February 19, WEDNESDAY. . . . I have felt in a state of blue devilism all day long chiefly because of a piece of news which it's very selfish of me to be sorry for, to be sure; a petition has been presented to Poulett Thomson by a majority of the Upper Canada Bar that the agreement extorted from Bidwell by Sir Francis Bond Head be canceled, that he be invited to return and be appointed to the vacant attorney-generalship. To this the governor cheer-fully assents, or rather declares that he will cordially recommend it to the

Colonial Office, which amounts to the same thing. Along with the other papers was a highly eulogistic letter from Col. John Prince, of all people (by all that's decent, I should be afraid of myself if I were praised by such a cold-blooded disgrace to manhood as that man). I didn't have a chance to speak to Mr. Bidwell, except in court where we couldn't speak with freedom about it, but I understood him to intimate decidedly that he'd have nothing to do with their offers. However, I can't entertain a doubt that he'll finally accept the offer, and I don't know of any acquaintance whom I should be so sorry to lose. And it would knock me up completely, too—disconcert everything—but *quod non est curandum*, etc. . . .

February 21. . . . Heard three startling pieces of news today. First, that Crumby & Draper have exploded and gone utterly to pot; Bennett's friend "O'Haggerty's" name is on the paper to a considerable amount. Second, that Sam Ward's estate is going to turn out absolutely *minus*, and that proceedings have been instituted against the property settled on Sam Junior by prior creditors—absolutely incredible and astonishing, though stated on good authority. And thirdly, that Isaac Lawrence and his son are going the way of all flesh, i.e., going to break—notes protested and all that sort of thing—pro–di–gious. As to the last, the opinion of their impregnable strength and unimpeachable credit was such that I believe my father, as wary in these matters as any man in the world, absolutely thought himself lucky in getting such excellent security for a loan as Isaac's note. I wish, though, for his sake that the story may be unfounded, but as matters go in these times, I'd hardly trust John Jacob Astor with twenty dollars unless secured with real estate worth a hundred. Manhattan Bank stock is at seventy—all glory to Bob White—and Arthur Tappan has exploded, and everybody and everything is going—going—going—to the devil.

The history of New York for the last three years is comparable to nothing but the explosion of a pack of crackers—pop—pop—pop—one after another they go off and all their substance vanishes in fumes.

February 22. . . . Went up to the Hall after tea with George Anthon to hear Bidwell's lecture before the Law Association on "Marriage." Very unusually decent audience; the room was, in fact, full beyond all precedent—"great bespeak for Mr. Bidwell"—and everything went off very comfortably, except that one man got asleep and snored obstreperously. The lecture was good, emphatically, as I supposed it would be, for Mr. Bidwell has all the qualities of voice, person, manner, and style essential to a first-rate lecturer. Its length was the only objection—indeed, delivered by anybody else, almost, it would have been intolerable—near two hours. But he continued to keep the audience attentive to the end. He recommended all the association to try it for themselves: "the most interesting trial in which they would probably ever be engaged." Hum. Doubtless to get a first-rate wife must be a very fine thing, but the chances are rather against such a desirable result, and what a horrible business it must be to find oneself mistaken. . . .

February 23, SUNDAY. . . . Rumor says that Professor Mack [McVickar] has gone to pot. Don't pity him much. Clergymen have no business to speculate and shave notes. It's unclerical if not unchristian—certainly it's not at all harmonious with Christian principle.

When lands and livings are all spent
Then learning is most excellent.

But I fear the professor's brain is nearly as empty as his pockets. Poor Mack. However, he always was good to me and I oughtn't to laugh at his mishap on account of his doing what there has been for the last eight years so strong a temptation to do.

March 7, SATURDAY. . . . The *Great Western* is in. Cotton is down and her Majesty is married, and so farewell to all the romantic slops about the maiden queen with which we've been pestered. She'll die away now into a humdrum, commonplace woman, until the "natural and common place consequences" follow her nuptials, and then whe—e—ew what a fuss and cackle there will be. . . .

March 9. . . . All the papers are running over with stuff about Her Sacred Majesty's nuptials. Whole columns devoted to accounts from different sources (so to give us Americans better opportunities of making up our minds on the momentous subject) of her Majesty's demeanor on the interesting occasion: how her Majesty ogled his Royal Highness during the ceremony, and how the Duke of Sussex shook hands with her Majesty, and how his Royal Highness seemed in very good spirits, and how her Majesty's deportment was "marked by all that dignity" etc., all which is doubtless very interesting and important to her Majesty's loyal subjects, but which to us republicans is, or ought to be, rather dull and profitless. His Royal Highness must have chuckled internally with great satisfaction when he came to "with all my worldly goods I thee endow," and his princely sire ought to have placed his august thumb against the tip of his serene nose and imparted a fluctuating motion of his four illustrious fingers.

April 6. . . . Read Carlyle after dinner, *Sartor Resartus*. A second look threat confirms my first impressions of the book: that with all its wildness and all its humbug, there is a good deal in it worth reading and that it fulfils the highest object of book-making, to set the reader thinking and to open his eyes to what is around him. . . .

To change the subject: Thomas H. Smith's amiable bride has left him, having cleared out across the Atlantic with a young gentleman of nineteen (we are growing precocious), Goodwin, by name, a clerk of Wyeth, Cripps & Co., who carried off at the same time the snug amount of $6,000 from his employers. Smith will have to bring an action against him for *crim. con.* What a mighty flourish his counsel could make about the lacerated feeling of the injured husband, and the satanic arts by which the vestal purity of his bride was contaminated and corrupted, à la Massy *v.* Headfort. . . .

Strong became restive and bored with the law at times, felt that he was in "a hopeless state of muddiness," that his brains were "in progress of transubstantiation into hasty pudding," and wished for something he could really and heartily bend himself down to, "something more than debtor costs and lis pendens"; but these complaints do not occur too often. He took up chess again, managed to put aside Graham occasionally of an evening to go to a concert, and took great pleasure in a new meerschaum pipe. A new interest, which was to absorb him deeply for the rest of the year, begins innocently in the next entry.

April 13, MONDAY. . . . Went up to Erben's[2] after dinner. If he will do so, and won't be too exorbitant, I want him to take our organ off our hands and give us a better. Ours is well enough as far as it goes, but its range of stops is limited, it has no sub-base, and what's more important, no swell. One that I examined there I rather liked the arrangements of, though as intended for a church, it was too powerful for us. I think the fifteenth [stop] should be left out. The stops I should want are the diapasons: principal trumpet (?), flute and hautboy in all; as to the trumpet I'm doubtful whether the last wouldn't supply its place, especially as I never heard a trumpet stop from Erben yet that didn't sound like a tin horn. It's all nonsense to have those thundering crashing roaring stops in a parlor organ and if we do order one, I'll have the swell made as deadening as pasteboard and flannel and all the other sound barriers can make it. But I'm afraid we shan't be able to accomplish it.

[2] Henry Erben (1801–1888) was a famous New York builder of organs; he had been apprenticed to Thomas Hall in 1818, and after 1822 was his partner.

April 16. . . . Quite a respectable fire in Water Street near Old Slip at five o'clock. Saw the new Philadelphia engines in action. They are cumbrous, unwieldy things with their two ranks of pumpers (like a double-banked galley), but they throw glorious streams of water, and throw them with ease, over the roofs of the highest stores. I suppose they require each about thirty men, and probably two ordinary engines to keep them full. This was a dry-goods store, and all of it that wasn't burnt must have been soaked by the Philadelphia deluge. . . .

April 17. Warm and pleasant. Went to church this morning, this being Good Friday, and heard a first-rate sermon from little Higbee. I believe the impressiveness of his preaching is chiefly due to the simple earnestness of his style and manner of delivery. In enforcing religion I think he keeps Coleridge in view and instead of appealing to people's fears, addresses their sense of duty and shows the consistency or the identity of religion with all that is true and noble and honorable in man. This is very different from the Kirk and Knapp school of pulpit eloquence. Those people produce effect by working on peoples' fears and nerves, with threatenings of hell-fire and damnation, by simply endeavoring to excite the selfish feelings of desire of pleasure and dislike of pain into irritability sufficient to make them forego present gratification for the sake of a future reward. Now this is not only degrading preacher and congregation (for how does it differ *in kind* from the nursery logic with which a child is led to give up its stick of candy today by the promise of two tomorrow?); but it seems to me that (humanly speaking, and setting other influences out of the question) it is impossible to lead a man to the Truth by such means. Happiness as an end is unknown to Christianity— nay, its most deadly opponent is the desire of happiness for itself. To set self out of the question is its fundamental principle, and why doing good from the fear of future punishment is not identical with doing good for the sake of popular applause or through any other selfish motive, I'm really unable to see. . . .

April 19. Was utterly astonished this morning by the news from Setauket that Uncle Thomas [Strong] died yesterday morning at seven o'clock, very unexpectedly to everyone. . . .

April 20, MONDAY. . . . Had to go to Brooklyn, and took the opportunity of going through the Navy Yard with George Anthon. The din of warlike preparation is going on there ominously—perhaps four hundred men hard at work getting ready the different vessels there—several on the stocks are just ready to launch; in short they are all as busy as bees.

The new steam frigate and a corvette are just ready, and one or two line-of-battle ships that are laid up, and I should think almost rotten, are in process of brushing up. All this is ominous of war, and war we are to have in less than a year's time unless I am very much mistaken; sooner or later it must come unless Uncle Sam backs out, as he won't. . . .

April 21. . . . Went to Erben's with little Post. Saw Hall and got along very well with him; the only difficulty now visible is that the case may be too big. He's building a magnificent instrument for some schismatic church in Ithaca; it looks like a forest of pipes, or an immense jungle of reeds and rushes all standing up stiff. What business have Presbyterians with such a glorious "chest full of whistles"? . . . I'm insane on this topic just now. My head's full of diapasons, trumpets and vox humanas. . . .

April 22. . . . Made another pilgrimage to Erben's. . . . The organ is certainly a glorious instrument. If I were worth a few hundred thousands, I'd certainly lay out $30,000 on a regular three-decker with a hundred stops, a small steam engine to work the bellows, and a large barn to contain it all. . . . How the old Byzantine who first stumbled on the idea of a row of shrill pipes, a bellows to blow them, and some clumsy contrivance to open them successively, would stare if he could hear one of the great cathedral organs of England, into which his awkward improvement of the Pandean pipes has been developed.

April 24. Very busy all day, though I found time for a tramp up to Erben's with Post. I have settled the plan of the proposed instrument much to my own satisfaction, thanks to the warm weather which has prevented anyone else from going up there to hum and haw about the expense. I fancy there will be some long faces when the bill comes in, but no matter for that.

Took a walk uptown with George Anthon. He's anxious that I should visit his Fourteenth Street friends with him some evening. I have no doubt that they are people worth visiting and that by my indolence and loutishness in not going a little into that line of business, I deprive myself of much enjoyment and some improvement. But I cannot make the effort and subject myself to the annoyance and risk of making a fool of myself by so doing, for until I am used to such matters and acquire the brass, it would be a terrible bore. I should have begun earlier when there would have been some excuse for playing Dumbiedikes. As it is, I must e'en content myself with looking on that class of animated nature as invested with a sort of theatric ethereality, and preserve the charm by avoiding a nearer approach or a more intimate acquaintance. Doubtless the society of sensible womankind must be an enjoyment worth possessing, but it's what there's not much prospect of my enjoying in a hurry.

April 25, SATURDAY. Went to Erben's and gave an order. The instrument will be done in two months, they say; probably in four. . . .

April 28. Nothing very special going forward. I think we're all improving at the office in the way of chess, Cutting especially. He has been a good player, I think, but when we began playing was rusty for want of practice and is now recovering his former skill. He's at least a match for me. . . . George Anthon is too hasty to make a decent player, though so long as he attends to what he's about, he gives one some trouble. I think the practice of playing one or two games every day will be of service to all of us. It teaches one to look before he leaps; and to study out all the bearings of a complicated arrangement is really no contemptible exertion of mind, and must contribute a good deal towards strengthening one's powers of combination and analysis. The secret of successful playing is, I believe, concentration on a well-selected point in the opposite game. . . .

April 29. The first number of Boz's new work has appeared in the shape of a *New World Extra,* and the author would certainly be flattered to hear the number of voices and the variety of tones—squeak, bellow, and howl—in which the name of his offspring is proclaimed through Wall Street and the parts adjacent.

> "He-e-ere's the *New World Extra*—get *Master Humphrey's Clock* here they are"—
>
> "He-e-ere's the *New World*—Dick's new work"
>
> "Here's the *New World*—buy *Master Humphrey*, sir?"

He creates as great a sensation in the street of Mammon as the arrival of the *British Queen* with "cotton down" possibly could do.

I have read the first number. I think Boz is going out of his element. This is excellently well done, but his power is not so marked in the "Old English" department: "pretty mistress Alice," "Old Simon the Lawyer," "gallants," " 'prentices," and all that sort of thing, as in the times and manners he has hitherto chosen, things as they *are*. I suppose the work is to be a collection of stories—perhaps he thinks he isn't able to manage a long and connected plot with success; certainly he is not very skillful in that, and so far he has done well in altering. But if this be a fair specimen of the book, I think it will be far less popular and successful than its elder brethren.

May 1. . . . Examination this evening, rather brilliant than otherwise, I thought. But the old gentleman told us solemnly that "there was a good deal for us to learn yet"—which is a novel and important piece of intelligence, certainly. But we'll be O.K. by and by, perhaps according to the new Whig interpretation: out of kash, out of kredit, out of karacter and out of klothes; perhaps out of klients may be added, including out of kansas and out of kosts. . . .

May 2. . . . Not much of importance going on today. Went to the Hall and thence to Erben's. I'm itching to have more stops in that organ of ours, but it won't do—I can't overleap the bounds of space. No matter, it will be almost powerful enough to blow the house up, as it is.

May 6. Clear and cool. Nothing new today. Harrison is going ahead. How little one can calculate on political events. When he was nominated, I thought it the most ridiculously ruinous act that the party could possibly have stumbled upon, and now if he isn't elected, at least he's going ahead, far beyond the possible success of Clay or Webster and probably of Scott. It's a pretty commentary, though, on the wisdom of His Majesty the People that he can be so bamboozled by the slang of "hard cider," "log cabins," and "Tippecanoe."

Van Wagenen, I understand, is going to be married to the Miss Livingston, Robert Swift Livingston's beautiful, sensible, and illegitimate daughter. It's hard, after all, that such a prejudice should exist, but still it does exist, against persons of that description, and I think it would require very powerful reasons to overcome it in me, so far as to seduce me into a match of that kind.

May 8. Pleasant weather. Had our professional cousin from St. George's Manor to take tea with us this evening, and with him Tom Griffing, with the latter of whom I went to the office, and there met George Anthon for a Tippecanoe pilgrimage. Tonight is the anniversary of that greatest military operation of the present age, that most heroic achievement of ancient or modern warfare—surpassing all "affairs" on record from the siege of Troy down to the Battle of Brokow—to wit, the raising of the siege of Fort Meigs, when the Britishers were smitten hip and thigh by the immortal Harrison. Candidly, I never heard of the affair till the last three months. But that only shows what ignoramuses we are. Just to think of the besieging army's firing some two hundred and fifty shot in one day—and actually killing one man and wounding ten! What a regular fire-eater the old Hero must be!

However, the loaferage of New York not being particularly well versed in the history of this or any other age, the Battle of Fort Meigs does as well to tickle them with as anything else, and to be sure the procession and fuss tonight surpassed in spirit and numbers anything of the sort that I ever saw here—except during the excitement of election. The procession seemed interminable. I thought as the Irishman did that somebody must have cut off the other end of it. Banners, log cabins on wheels, barrels supposed to be full of hard cider, and all sorts of glories adorned its march. Getting into Niblo's wasn't to be thought of; not more than a third of the procession accomplished it. The Locos, of course, disgraced themselves as usual, by a fierce attack on one banner in par-ticular—representing Matty shinning away from the White House with O. K. under it, i.e., "Off to Kinderhook." Brick bats were thrown and heads broken and an attack was made on the Garden (subsequently), but the siege was raised by a few sticks and stones dropped on the heads of the assailants from above. Altogether it was a grand affair—Harrison forever!

May 12, TUESDAY. . . . I wrote my last night's journal in such a hurry that I forgot to record the important fact that our emigration into the new offices took place at half-past five yesterday morning. The new establishment is as much better than the old as Kanaster [tobacco] is better than pigtail. Altogether it is like getting two half-dollars for a wildcat shinplaster, decidedly a change for the better. We couldn't be in a more comfortable establishment, and I think we shall find the rooms exceedingly cool and pleasant during the roasting season, of the advent whereof these warm sunny days are giving most emphatic hints. . . .

May 18, MONDAY. . . . After tea entered the Halls of Alma Mater to hear [Rev. Benjamin Isaacs] Haight's anniversary address before the [Philolexian] Society. It was good; that is, it didn't amount to a great deal, but it was unpretending, rather spirited, and uncommonly free from foppery and affectation. I wonder if squaring the circle can be much harder than writing a college address of any sort without introducing some stuff about early recollections, venerated instructors, etc. Very fair audience assembled. John L. Lawrence presided. . . .

May 26. . . . Spent the afternoon at Post's over sundry cigars accom-panied by divers refreshing and satisfactory edibles and potables. Then went with him to Erben's. We shan't see our organ till next fall. . . .

June 7, SUNDAY. I have rather let this fertile field, my Diary, lie fallow for the past week—chiefly for want of good seed wherewith to sow the same. Let me think whether there's any event to be preserved

for posterity—I can think of none. The rain hath rained every day with
one or two slight exceptions and I have smoked, lounged, loafed, chessed,
grumbled, groaned, gaped, looked at the clouds and wondered whether it
would clear—much as might be expected in such lugubrious weather. *Inter
alia*, I heard part of Bidwell's argument in that copyright case of Hiram
P. Hastings, and a very able speech it seemed to be. . . .

Well, this state of things has got to be altered. I must and will *Reform*. I don't want to draggle through life a slipshod, fifteenth-rate
lawyer—and I must make an effort to study (*Flourish of Trumpets*).

June 9. . . . We're to have a new "student" (in the technical sense of
the term), that distinguished individual Mr. [Henry] Augustus Cram:
son of that respectable boiler of the devil's teapot, old [Jacob] Cram the
distiller. He's going to be a great bore, I'm afraid; however, he has
probably addicted himself to the law merely as a gentlemanly way of
doing nothing, and we probably shan't be troubled with him for more
than half an hour *per diem* after the first fortnight. He's a graduate of
Princeton [1837], and the reputation he bore there was that of a very
talented, lazy, conceited, overbearing puppy. I presume that he'll turn
out to be Thomas C. Cooper with a slight twinge of extra Cooper folly
and foppery. He's a traveled gentleman withal—recently returned from
the grand tour of Constantinople, Mesopotamia, and Chinese Tartary
besides, for ought I know; and when he got back, he said he thought
New York "quite too contracted." The infatuated youth seems to be
making desperate efforts to raise a moustache, but I doubt the ultimate
success of the project. . . .

June 12. . . . [Samuel H.] Whitlock is going to enter the office!
He'll do very well if he isn't spoiled by his travels.

June 15. . . . Old Kermit in the office in great dismay about his very
amiable niece, who was married last Thursday and whose post-nuptial
settlement has just been prepared. She will probably become a happy
mother in the course of the next week. Well, people do everything by
steam these days, but this really passeth all understanding. As to the
settlement, "I guessed," as Coleridge and Mr. Cox say, that her husband
will be in no hurry to sign it. I hardly see why he should divest himself
of his rights, settle his wife's property on herself unless she wishes it, or
unless he is engaged in mercantile business or in speculation, in which
case it would be well enough to provide for the event of loss, and to have
some $200,000 to fall back upon beyond the reach of creditors. He should
have a talk with Coster on the subject.

June 24, WEDNESDAY. If the d——l comes on earth about these times to cool himself, as Southey says he used to do, because "the weather was close below," he certainly won't choose New York for his visit, though it is undoubtedly a favorite resort of his. The weather is outrageous, hot, heavy, and close, a regular dead set of caloric "from morn till noon, from noon till sweaty eve," as Milton would have said if he'd been a New Yorker and written on or about this blessed 24th of June in the year of grace 1840.

Up early and promenaded the Battery. I spent the rest of the day much as usual. Bathed; the Globe is a nice place, much less nasty than Stoppan's, but I never get into a public bath without sundry qualms. Sundry diseases, I've no doubt, may be communicated from them. Dr. Smith says so, but adds that the only cases he ever met of delicate disorders so contracted were clergymen.

Henry Rogers [Columbia 1827] is dead, poor fellow. Died of delirium tremens. He used to drink like a fish for the last four or five years, only he took brandy instead of water. . . .

June 27, SATURDAY. Hot. Today has been spent much as usual: by the aid of bath and soda water and ice cream I now survive. I have bathed of late nearly every day, and find it is a very good plan. . . .

June 28, SUNDAY. Enormously hot. Nevertheless, I walked resolutely out to St. Peter's [in Chelsea], calling on Chittenden by the way, to see Jesse [Ames] Spencer ordained. It was no small job, but I achieved it and reached the church without sweating away more than two pounds of flesh. It was tolerably full and intolerably hot. Music poor, for though their organ seems a very fine affair, with some twenty-five or thirty stops, much can't be expected from it when operated on by Clement C. Moore. I do believe I could play better myself. He may be a very scientific musician, but he's sadly lacking in the mechanical department. The Bishop preached a very fair slap-dash sermon on the proper subject: the Church as distinguished from sects and schisms, and went through the ordination with his usual dignity and grandiloquence. Jesse was selected from the candidates (ten in number) to read the Gospel for the day, which he did very well, though his voice sounded like a penny whistle after Onderdonk's thundering diapason.

I'm not insane, but after dinner I walked uptown to St. Peter's to hear Jesse preach his first sermon, which was just what I expected: good, sound sense and simplicity without any attempt at humbug or affectation. . . .

July 3, FRIDAY. Hot, close, and damp, occasionally drizzling a little. I hope it'll rain cataracts tomorrow, to save me the bore of a projected excursion to Setauket in the *Sun*. I presume she'll be crowded, and as they are pretty well crowded with cousins and nieces at Mt. Misery, we are going to stay at the Hotel at Drowned Meadow, and that'll be a bore. Saw Thomas Griffing this evening, who increased the delightful prospects of tomorrow's excursion by announcing that there's to be a "cotillion band" on board according to the advertisement, *ac etiam* a ball at the hotel, all of which is eminently agreeable to anticipate.

July 4.   The immortal Fourth. Couldn't sleep all last night for the infernal noise of the wretches who were popping off squibs and other small artillery in the streets. . . .

Left in the *Sun* at eight o'clock with about a hundred passengers and a fine clear day. On the whole, we had a comfortable voyage. Among other matters, the "cotillion band" must not be forgotten, to wit: two amateur fiddles, of which the captain was one, and a young gentleman— by profession a tailor—another, and one very dirty professional clarionet, whose movements reminded me of the Pandea Tympanist in *Little Pedlington*, and two dingy guitars, one of them of mulatto origin apparently. And the perseverance with which they played about four varieties of jigs on their way up was truly worthy of a better cause, and only equaled by the energy and ferocity with which they squeaked, twanged, and tooted *Hail Columbia* to give dignity, effect, and éclat to our entrée into Northport Bay, otherwise late known as Cow Harbor (and by the way a very beautiful place indeed). It consisted of three scattered houses with a distant prospect of two more, also of one tavern and one "steamboat hotel" about as large as a small necessary.

Still greater effect was given to one entrance aforesaid by a salute of two percussion caps and one fowling piece from the dock, which was replied to according to naval etiquette by our artillery, to wit, one one-pounder, borrowed for the occasion from Captain Pennoyer, and a curious thing, too, brass richly carved and bearing date 1668, the maker's name Gerard Koster, and the arms I think those of Antwerp.

Reached Drowned Meadow at half-past two. The hotel is a tolerably decent place ordinarily, but all today it has been a perfect Pandemonium, the bar room full of drunken rowdies making desperate efforts to sing each a different tune, and all grunting, roaring, and swearing without effort and very naturally, indeed.

Rode over to Mt. Misery when I had got partly rested. Found them all pretty well and spent the evening there comfortably enough. Had a grand Indian clam roast and took tea under the shade of the umbrageous specimens which tower aloft in all their native efflorescence. . . .

July 5, SUNDAY.   Warm and pleasant enough after the bustle and racket of yesterday. Went to church, or rather to meetin', and heard Dominie Green, who was about as eloquent and spirit-stirring as usual. They do things in great style. The psalm was given out, and the chorister got on his legs and gave the first two lines, as of old, with the mellow tones of his nasal organ and then stopped short, shut his book and bolted out at the top of his lungs: "There," says he, "I knowed I couldn't sing— I told you so afore I came—I've got a hoarse cold," and down he sat, looking as if he thought he'd done something rather clever and credit-able.

Dined at Mt. Misery and then Tom and I bolted for the shore and reached the same after a pretty hot walk, stripped, and took a highly comfortable bath—water rather cool, but on the whole very comfort-able, indeed.

At five o'clock we bade them good evening and drove over to St. George's Manor where we took tea. It's the first time that I saw the place and it certainly is a beautiful estate, though it don't seem to have so many fine views of the Sound as the Mt. Misery property.

July 6.   Woke with a terrible sore throat, the invariable precursor of a cold, confound it; the result, I suppose, of my yesterday's cold bath and of my ride home from Selah's last night when I found it, I remember, rather chilly.

Came on board the *Sun* at eight. . . . The Russells were on board and Uncle Benjamin, etc. Got down comfortably enough, though when we reached New York the weather had changed from cloudy to rainy. In the meantime my cold had developed itself into full bloom and I felt like a gib cat or a lugged bear.

July 7.   Half dead. Weather drizzling. Went to the office. Found a new student there, cognominated Howard, a decent fellow enough, seemingly. Couldn't do anything, so came off and spent the rest of the morning at home with George Anthon. Couldn't even read *Ivanhoe*.

Strong managed to get over his cold and to survive a week of extremely hot weather; on the 14th he left with his mother on the Massachusetts *for Nahant, where they joined the Derbys. The hotel was well populated, too well populated for Strong, and when Counselor Griffin and his party spotted him, his fate was sealed; George Griffin, his father's former partner, a garrulous and condescending old man, immediately nabbed him for "walks with the ladies," bowling, and other distasteful activities, which Strong nevertheless underwent with "Christian fortitude and resignation."*

July 17. . . . Evening. Bored by the Counselor again and his confounded stupid "twenty questions" game. N.B. if anybody ever asks me to play an "intellectual game" of that kind again I'll take it as a personal insult.

Everybody's agog for Cunard's steamer, the *Britannia*. She's hourly expected, and the slightest semblance of smoke along the horizon sends everybody in a state of frantic excitement to the rocks to look out for the steamer.

July 18. . . . Evening. The *Britannia* makes her appearance at last, or rather goes into Boston Harbor without being able to make any appearance through the fog, which was as thick as hasty pudding, her course being indicated only by the line of smoke and an occasional rocket, much to the indignation of those who had calculated on a full view of her. . . .

July 21, TUESDAY. Spent the day in East Boston at the Cunard dinner. Went down at eight o'clock with Eloise and Miss Story, and after waiting some time at the Maverick [House] I finally left Eloise with Mrs. Grattan and went to the wharf and looked through the *Britannia*. Then I joined the rest and marched up to the festal hall feeling mighty like a fish out of water, for there wasn't a soul in my part of the procession that I'd ever seen before. The dinner (or rather, cold collation) was given under a sort of temporary pavilion or awning erected against the side of the Maverick, the windows and piazzas whereof were occupied by female lookers-on and otherwise very finely tidivated and adorned. I went for the sake of the speakers. Heard Daniel Webster, Judge Story, [Edward] Grattan [the British Consul], President Quincy [of Harvard], my well beloved *frater-in-lege* Counselor Griff, *et al*. Webster was great. His speech was substantial and worth hearing. Grattan was funny and very successful, and the Counselor spoke on the many excellencies and glories of steam, from which he somehow or other jumped into an eulogy upon the Common Law of England, wherewith he concluded. The Counselor left Nahant yesterday and I humbly hope we've seen the last of him for some time to come. We broke up at about eight o'clock and altogether the affair went off in very good style. The eatables were decent, the wine very tolerable. I took possession of a bottle of sherry, ditto of claret and ditto of champagne and soaked and sippled and listened in very comfortable style—drank enough to give me a sort of fever all night. Came home at nine o'clock.

Strong greatly enjoyed his fishing and rock-scrambling expeditions with Mr. Derby, Joseph Anthon, Thomas H. Perkins, Horace and Frank Story, and George Upham. Sunday the 26th he wrote: "Some Unitarian preached today and of course my principles of orthodoxy wouldn't allow me to hear him.... Singular phenomenon visible this afternoon, what they call here (not very correctly perhaps) a mirage. It was chiefly visible towards Marblehead and so along the coast to Cape Ann, the lighthouse whereon was visible with the naked eye. Marblehead was brought within a couple of miles and all the coast north-eastward was raised up from its native flatness into the semblance of high banks, long ranges of steep woody hills, now even and uniform and now refracted into all kinds of fantastic forms. One hill was suspended in the air like Gulliver's floating island and then connected with the terra firma *by a stem like a huge pumpkin. It lasted several hours." Strong's father came up on the 29th: "He looks on Nahant with perfect contempt, I'm sorry to say."*

July 30, THURSDAY. Left in the steamboat and came to town. Dined at Eloise's and after dinner left in the Springfield train and reached Springfield before dark. The road certainly passes through a beautiful country, far different from the howling wilderness that lies between Providence and Boston.

This is beautifully undulating, thickly wooded and richly cultivated, and bright with ponds and water courses; altogether the journey so far is exceedingly pleasant.

Springfield's a fine place, too, more like the abstract idea of an English village than any place I ever met with—a great many pleasant houses in it, all surrounded by noble old oaks and chestnuts; in short I was much pleased with the place, and the Hampden House is for comfort and good fare the very prince of hotels.

July 31. Leave at eight in the *Agawam,* a quaint little caricature of a steamboat, with a wheel in its tail, to go down the Connecticut. She makes about six or seven miles an hour with the current and lands passengers in the most offhand style by running ashore and putting out a plank, and then they shove her off with a brace of long poles. But it's really a very pretty voyage, and the way she goes through the rapids with one man at the bow steering her between the rocks with a long paddle is singular enough.

Reached Hartford and put up at the United States Hotel—decent place enough. Went to the top of the State House, where there's a fine view of an endless expanse of flat with the Connecticut winding from one side of the horizon to the other. Introduced to Mr. [Royal R.] Hinman, the Secretary of State. Saw the far-famed Charter, the most remarkable thing about which is the portrait of Charles II in the initial letter, most admirably executed. Saw a very handsome original of Washington by somebody or other [Gilbert Stuart], which stands in the Senate Chamber, the very room occupied by the famous Hartford Convention, of which portrait some Southerner said that "by G—d, the old man hadn't got the blush off his cheeks yet."

Left after dinner for New Haven by the cars. The railroad don't amount to a great deal. Put up at the Pavilion and walked and smoked a little after tea.

August 1.   Leave in the *New Haven* in the midst of a quiet comfortable rain, and never did I study the geographical features of the northern coast of Long Island with such an intensity of interest: Old Field, Eaton's Neck, Lloyd's Neck, Dosoris, Sands Point, Light, Cow Bay, Throg's Neck, Whitestone, we passed one after another and at last we got into this stinking metropolis, and right glad was I to see it again, for I was half tired to death. . . .

Within a week the family left the city for the customary summer sojourn on Long Island; this time they boarded with a family named Willetts on the Little Neck Turnpike. Strong evidently did not bring his diary with him.

September 21, MONDAY.   Hurra for Maine! She has gone for Harrison triumphantly and Locofocoism is routed there, horse, foot, and dragoons —*sic transit gloria Van Bureni.*

Got back to town this morning "for good," and right glad am I to see this city of abominations again, for the last three weeks or so have been as heavy and as dull as the *Statutes at Large* or Rollin's *Ancient History.* Between walking, reading, and smoking, I contrived to exist, and a toad of meditative habits and a turn for minute philosophy and geological pursuits on a small scale probably exists much after the same fashion in his rock parlor a hundred feet under ground. But here I am and now for the winter campaign and for work. I feel as if this were the last year that's left me to form myself and redeem the years and years that I've thrown away. I can't make myself a lawyer and a man in one winter, to be sure (for *"nemo repente fuit turpissimus"* hath been translated: it takes seven years to make an attorney), but I can do a good deal towards gaining habits that will carry me onward. . . .

September 25. . . . Tried to read Kent this morning, but his pages, which never were remarkable for order and perspicuity, seemed even more hazy than ever. It was a toss-up between the ex-Chancellor and the Boston transcendentalists. The latter gentry have rather the advantage, by the way, for whereas the Chancellor merely contradicts himself on alternate pages and writes a book as his wife would make a pudding, by taking care to mix the ingredients—eggs, butter and all—into undistinguishable homogeneity, the Eastern Magi take care to write so that it's impracticable to know what any one sentence means and no one can therefore safely assert that any two passages are irreconcilable or unconnected, which is very delightful to behold and shows a true Yankee ingenuity in dodging the shafts of criticism. They're safe behind the thick cotton of the infinite and The Incomprehensible.

As to their enunciation of the fact that "Matter is orbed and spirit is sphered" (or *vice versa*—I forget which and it don't much matter), I do not entirely agree with the pundits aforesaid. The thoughtful mind can never forget that in the polarization of the universal dual the essential idea is first individually evolved, and that from this purely spiritual genesis, extending as it does upwards into the profound and downwards into the exalted (and not according to Locke, *vice versa*), or in other words from the intensely spirituous, is first seen to emanate the dawnings of the Exotic. Strange, then, that any should be so utterly blind as not to deduce from these self-evident propositions the identity of the Ideal and the truncatedo-conical of the material and the right angulo-hexagonal triangular!

"Ho there, my friend," said Pantagruel fair and softly, "do not put yourself in a passion—I understand the case, go on."

September 26, SATURDAY. . . . Read some of [Samuel] Warren's new book *Ten Thousand a Year.* It's capital, but I don't agree with those who prefer him to Boz. I should have known the author from the peculiar style of his conversations, like those in the *Diary of a Late Physician,* abrupt and jerking and peppered with dashes and interjections. It makes them rather tiresome. It's an original idea, so far as I know, in these days to write the history of a supremely contemptible hero, for there seems no chance of Titmouse's being reformed into a decent person in the course of the story. . . .

September 27, SUNDAY. Cloudy morning. Went to church this morning and as it came on to rain after dinner, spent the afternoon in reading the *Magnalia*, which I haven't touched for three or four years, and in fact never read much of, but the Salem Witchcraft stories. I think Mather is a most favorable specimen of Puritanism, both learned and liberal beyond his tribe and with a good many points that remind one of old Fuller. Quakerism and the Church of England seem his only abominations. It's amusing, the simplicity with which he speaks of the refusal of the devils to let the bewitched damsel enter "the study of one of the family . . . assigning a reason which its owner thought more kind than true," and the comfortable chuckle with which he intimates that she could read the Prayer Book and the Scriptures contained in it without hindrance from the d——l, but went off into blue convulsions when they gave her the Bible itself. But the Salem witches must have been very paltry and miserable devils indeed, judging from the style of their pranks, more like the devils of *Woodstock* than any others. . . .

September 28. . . . Commenced reading Reeves' *History of the Law*, which I like, though he hasn't Blackstone's easy and graceful way of handling those subjects. . . .

Today has been great in the annals of stump oratory. The Park has been disgraced by the herding together of the unshorn, unwashed, and indecent heathenness of Locofocoism, while at the Exchange has been a grand gathering of the merchants of New York to hear the Almighty Daniel Webster discourse of the Militia Law, the Subtreasury and General Harrison. The crowd and jam was marvelous to behold. Webster spoke about two and a half hours; I heard part of it, but the squeeze tightened every minute, and I eloped, out of regard to my ribs. Webster certainly has intellect stamped on his face in clearer characters than any man I ever saw. . . .

September 29. Haskey came screaming in from the Common one morning in horrible consternation: "Mamma! Mamma! there's a little busy bee in the Common!!!" I've been a busy bee in the City Hall, or to speak more properly, like a sort of great ugly wasp of active business habits, for I was savage enough part of the day. Those causes (*pereant isti*) didn't come on, of course, and then as if that wasn't aggravation enough, after two or three hours of stew and fidgit to assemble witnesses, some rascal (may Shitan be his resting-place and may all his buckwheat cakes this winter be sour, heavy and indigestible) had the audacity feloniously to abstract my hat in the very face of the awful tribunal of justice then and there sitting. After a sufficient amount of bother and fuss in a fruitless search, after I'd made up my mind to wait till the Court went to dinner and then take the *left* hat, and after going into two or three cold perspirations in thinking of *what* that hat might be, by great good luck one was sent up from the house, Bidwell having informed the old gentleman of my distressing predicament. . . .

September 30, WEDNESDAY.   The hat abstractor turns out to be Mr. [Horace] Holden. Pretty well for one of Dr. [Gardiner] Spring's elders; but he's a schismatic, to be sure. . . .

October 1, THURSDAY.   Of all the shocks to which we are exposed in this vale of tears, the most agonizing to humanity, the most intensely "soul harrowing" is that which he feels who, when just sinking into repose, hears through the stillness of his cubiculum, far away, that low, delicate, wavering note, gradually swelling into distinctiveness, which marks the presence of the *Culex musketoensis,* or "domestic mosquitoe." The horror with which he starts into full and decisive wakefulness, as conviction flashes on his mind, the successive aggravation of that horror with which he hears the solo become a duo and finally perhaps a quartet, the tormenting uncertainty with which the various performers tantalize him before finally closing in, and the series of energetic cuffs bestowed on his own countenance, wherewith he maketh the fire to flash out of his eyes, in vain, from a series of awful "experiences" (to speak evangelically) wherewith the spirit of patience within me was last night sorely exercised. But the remembrance is too painful to be longer dwelt upon. . . .

October 2.   I see that poor Henry Ward [Columbia 1836] is dead . . . ; there were many good points about him and if he had not been born with a silver spoon in his mouth, there doubtless would have been more. . . .

Cram, I think, is not the despicable character I supposed him to be. Notwithstanding his moustache, his *distingué* air, and the exquisite cut of his coat, he is decidedly intelligent, very well informed in matters that can be drawn from books, and what is a rarer merit, he has gathered knowledge for himself by traveling with his eyes open. I think the character which he aims at is one which many young men affect at present, a sort of Pelhamism: a combination of ultra foppery in person and manner, with a cultivated intellect and a certain degree of manliness and decision to be displayed on great occasions. It is a higher standard than used to be fashionable, and a sort of reputation can be cheaply gained by it, for no one expects sense, knowledge, or literary taste in what seems an animated suit of clothes, and any indication of them is valued more highly than the same would be in a "mere plodder."

October's *New York Review* appears with a very indignant defense of Bull [Anthon] from the slanders of the *North American*. McVickar is the author, though doubtless Bull has had a finger in the pie. But he clearly wrote none of it (though he may have helped Mack in his Greek quotations) for it is expressed in good English, which Bull knows nothing about. His own Reply in the *Knickerbocker* of July or August is a curiosity, a triumphal vindication, to be sure; but written as none but he knows how to write. There's a short but severe article on that infamous apostle of Jacobinism, Mr. [Orestes Augustus] Brownson, to whom Jack Cade is an angel. He had much to rebel against, and came forth boldly to encounter all the perils of the storm he raised, while Mr. Brownson contents himself with talking suggestions about certain unutterable blessings only to be enjoyed by the poor when wrested by a long and bloody struggle from the rich, and then when every paper in Boston cries shame on the cold-blooded incendiary, he comes out in the *Post* with a Jesuitical letter, about his not advising such a war, but merely stating his convictions that human perfection is unattainable without it.

October 3. . . . Walked up to Erben's. The *novum organum* isn't yet on its legs though its viscera seem to be making rapid progress. . . .

October 5, MONDAY. . . . Went to the Franklin House after tea to see Post, who was anxious to talk over certain of Erben's vagaries, and had a confab of an hour or so and then came home. King tells me that that organ of ours is going to be the completest instrument of the kind (i.e., for a parlor organ) that he knows of. He might add: the biggest and the most absurd.

October 6. Fine weather. Fairly shirked the office and went to St. John's [Chapel] to attend Alma Mater's annual glorification. How astonishingly impressive, "solemn and splendid," did that august ceremonial seem some four or five years ago! With what veneration did we look on those over whom Prex performed his mysterious incantation of *baccalaureatibus in artibus,* and how remarkably flat it all seems after one has been inside the curtain! As when the traveler whose path has lain amid hills and glades which to his unpracticed eye seem great affairs suddenly reaches the lofty summit of some superior eminence, the objects which lately seemed very big now seem very little. (That's terribly bathetic. One gets grandiloquent after attending a commencement.) . . .

October 10, SATURDAY.   Went to the Hall after tea to attend a solemn convocation of the Law Association. Found it to be shut up, and concluded that as the concern is in debt for its candles they'd been unable to procure a local habitation for the evening. Walked uptown and down again and stopped a second time at the Temple of Justice, and with better success. Found a dozen or so lounging about the lobbies waiting the result of an attempt to mollify the sergeant at arms into trusting them a little longer. I suggested a mass meeting in the park, but at last the room was opened and we had quite a screed of doctrine from various members on the most feasible plan to pay off the debts and put the concern on its legs again. . . . Such was the fervor of the occasion and the inspiring character of the whole affair that even my tongue was loosened. The present plan is the delivery of a course of lectures on subjects not of a mere technical character, but such as may be generally interesting. It don't bear a very encouraging aspect, but a great deal may be made out of the sovereign Public by a combination of humbug and gumption.

October 11, SUNDAY. . . . I took a walk up to Eighth Street and down again. It's a pity we've no street but Broadway that's fit to walk in of an evening. The street is always crowded, and whores and blackguards make up about two-thirds of the throng. That's one of the advantages of uptown; the streets there are well paved, well lighted, and decently populated.

October 25, SUNDAY. . . . This evening saw Tom Griffing, who tells me that Professor Jeemes [Renwick] has got back from Maine without being scalped by the Indians or lynched by the inhabitants of the Debatable Land—and also that it's reported that one of the Freshmen has a servant to come to college with him at nine o'clock and after him at half-past one. The next step will be wet-nurses and diapers.

October 26, MONDAY.   Molloy missing [from the office] this morning, so we had quite an old-fashioned amount of writing among us. I met him in the street smoking a cigar and he said he was sick, but it struck me that he was cocked. Well, it's as natural for a Hibernian to tipple as for a pig to grunt, and you can hardly blame them for it. This Father Matthew, by the way, must be a great man. If his work stands the test of time, he ought to supersede St. Patrick as the tutelary saint of Ireland. One can hardly calculate the effects of such a revolution, but they must be good, and it may go far towards making the country the free and happy nation that it ought to be. Separation from England and national independence are brought far nearer to probability when the people have thrown off the chains of *one* tyrant and become thereby sober and capable of resolute, steady, prudent and united action. I'm told that many of the late emigrants have brought out Matthew's medals with them, and eschew even hard cider. So much the better.

Everyone was stirred up over the presidential election of 1840, and as early as the middle of October Strong began to write about results of the elections in the outlying states. On the 19th he recorded the chant: "Van Van Van Van Van is a used-up man man man man man man!!" Ohio had gone Whig and "the Locos look as if their under jaws were broken." On the 23rd he went to a great Whig meeting in Hudson Street. "There was an immense crowd and a vast deal of fun—banners, bonfires, the old Hero staring grimly in plaster of paris, and 'Tippecanoe and Tyler too' in grand chorus, given with more effect than any effort of the Sacred Music Society." By the 29th he was dubious about the election but wrote: "If I were a better, I'd take, I think, three to two on Harrison." On Sunday evening, November 1, he reported that he had never seen anything like the excitement of this election. "Nobody can talk or think of anything else. I suppose that money enough is staked on it to buy the consciences of nine-tenths of the politicians on both sides." The next day, "Fearful election excitement all day. . . . Went this evening to the great Whig mass-meeting in front of National Hall and heard a rather good speech from [Hugh] Maxwell. There was a vast deal of fun and a little fighting. On the whole, things looked well. The Whigs are in good spirits, better, I think, than their opponents. The only Loco procession I saw was the 'Albany Basin Rattlers'—a very rowdy gang of draggle-tailed blackguards."

November 3. Really, I'm beginning to wish this affair ended; the novelty of the thing is over and I'm tired of humbug, lying, spouting, swearing, O.K., and the Old Hero. Nothing but politics. The newspapers crowd out their advertisements for mendacious "returns" that nobody believes, the walls are papered three deep with humbug, banners and inscriptions dangle over every street, mass-meetings are held in every groggery from National Hall down. If the North River were actually on fire, or if a live kraken were to sail into the harbor, or if the continent of Europe were to sink in the sea, the papers wouldn't be able to find room for the news.

Before the returns were all filed and the election of Harrison settled, Strong was taken sick with what turned out to be a mild case of the smallpox. This kept him housed for a week, and stimulated him to a fierce bout of reading:

Vivian Grey, *Beckmann on inventions, Palgrave on the Anglo-Saxons,* Shirley, *Aubrey's* Miscellany, *Shakespeare, Matthew Paris, Sidney, Hone's* Every Day Book, Peter Wilkins, *the life of Benvenuto Cellini, and other volumes. Anticipation of the completion of the new organ cheered him. On November 14 he wrote: "I hear that Post has got his Goliath at last. Lucky dog. I wonder how long it will be before I can congratulate myself on the same score. I think on Monday I will go to work to learn the notes regularly. I have been accustomed to play by ear now almost ever since I can remember, though it's not till about two years since that I discovered that there was any way of playing except on the naturals alone. I don't know what the name of the key is. When I stumbled on the discovery it opened quite a new field, and since then I have made out some dozens of keys and devoted more time to the amusement than I ought."*

On November 16 the journalizing fever hit him: "I'll be hanged if I am not in a humor for shedding ink tonight—feel as if I could scribble, scribble, scribble to the extent of a quart bottle full"—and he suited the action to the word, writing quantities of fluff. Finally on the 17th he went to the office to resume his "immensely important duties. I don't find that it has gone to pot in consequence of my absence."

November 27. We heard today of a shocking affair indeed. Old Nathaniel Prime committed suicide yesterday by cutting his throat. William H. Aspinwall was on the coroner's jury and Edgar Howland told me that Prime went to his room at two o'clock and appears to have taken up and read his prayer book, then went before the glass, cut his throat coolly and steadily from ear to ear, replaced the razor in its case, and then walked into the next room, and there fell. The jury found "insanity." He had been dyspeptic and nervous for some time; he was retired from active life and his mind, I suppose, preyed on itself for want of occupation. . . .

December 2, WEDNESDAY. . . . Reasonably busy at the office, but I found time for a pilgrimage up Centre Street and to my delight and surprise I found Goliath established downstairs and Fawcett stuffing in pipes by the handful. . . .

December 9. . . . Went to Erben's. Looked in at the Tabernacle and heard a part of a lecture by that prince of stovemakers, Dr. Nott.[3] He was rather prosy and I adjourned to see [Thomas] Cole's paintings of the

[3] The Rev. Eliphalet Nott, president of Union College from 1804 to 1866, theologian, educator, financier, abolitionist, and temperance advocate, was also the holder of some thirty patents, and the inventor of the first base-burning stove for the use of anthracite coal.

Stream of Life.[4] They are very beautiful; the idea is a good one and well managed, though after all, the allegory merely serves to string together four beautiful landscapes. The first two are very good—I can't say which I like best. The third I don't think quite equal to them, and the fourth different from any of them, somewhat in Martin's style perhaps, and the grandest thing I ever saw of Cole's handiwork. Altogether they form a beautiful series and if I were a son of Croesus I'd have them, though they do say Samuel Ward was to have paid $12,000 for the set. . . .

December 15. . . . Went over Graham this afternoon in double quick time, for just after dinner there was a fire in Maiden Lane which of course I had to go and see, but it wasn't much of a fire after all—merely the upper stories of a large store, drugs I think, from the preternaturally hideous stench (like my old acquaintances in Jemmy's laboratory) that it diffused around.

Rumors of War!!! News from Maine of a British regiment marched *vi et armis et contra pacem Domini populi*—or *domini plebis*—into the Disputed Territory. Well, I do believe that wars of almost every sort—on almost any quarrel—are utterly wrong, unchristian, and unhuman, that in their effects they are most destructive to happiness, to the diffusion of truth and the general well-being of mankind, and that another century will not have elapsed before the progress of knowledge and the voice of mere common sense (in this case its jurisdiction is undisputable), not to speak of religion and philosophic "philanthropy," will have driven them from the earth as the bloodthirsty relics of barbarism, the instrument by which reckless tyranny forges its chains, and the greatest curse of man (as a political being) that the world ever knew. But a war on this quarrel would be as justifiable as war can be, and the deep load of guilt that must rest somewhere would lie with the aggressors. . . .

December 16. . . . Went to Erben's . . . and Post and I thumped and twanged on Goliath to our hearts' content. I'm pleased with it on the whole. The dulcinia and hautboy are unsurpassable, and the diapasons and flute are very good, quite good enough for me. . . .

December 19. . . . Looked a little into *The Vision of Rubeta* this afternoon. It's said that [A. Cleveland] Coxe is the author and I wished to see if there were any marks of his hand work about the book. There are some things in it unquestionably that he might have written—many others

---

[4] This famous series of allegorical paintings had been commissioned by Samuel Ward, the banker, who died before they were finished. They now hang in St. Luke's Hospital, New York City.

which, with his present sentiments, he could not. But as he is one of those who have no character, no opinions and no feelings save those which prejudice or the circumstances in which he may be placed lead him to assume, and (always excepting the permanent features of folly and conceit) in short as he is in my opinion always unconsciously performing a part, this isn't much of a reason why he shouldn't have the credit of the authorship. But on the whole I hardly think he can be entitled to it. Heaven forgive me if I estimate the man's character unjustly, but I verily believe he's a great bag of wind. . . .

December 21, MONDAY. . . . Quite busy all the morning between law and organ-building. Went to Erben's and found things going on very well. The concern can be all ready for Wednesday, but I found Hall would be very pleased if it could be left in the factory a day or two for some people to look at—Crosby, Lenox, Fanning C. Tucker, and others who may order similar instruments—and I thought, after the bother they'd had, it wasn't fair to object. . . .

December 24. Busy this morning—decidedly I had my hands full all day—between judgment records, Kent, organ-building, and High Church argumentation. Cram's decidedly a heathen and Peter Strong a schismatic; they're the black sheep of the flock. All the rest of us are ferocious churchmen except perhaps John Weeks, who I fear is a waverer, albeit one of Seabury's disciples. Went to Erben's. Goliath prospereth. . . .

December 25. Christmas. Hurrah for Christmas! . . . Alas for our schismatic city, but few among its churches were open today. One would think that even if the matter-of-fact dissenters did consider it not quite demonstrably certain that this is the anniversary it professes to be, and if the Papaphobic dissenters did esteem its celebration a relic of popery, they wouldn't be quite blind to all its glorious associations, quite oblivious that from all corners of Christendom, save those they occupy, the anthem of thanksgiving rises this day unanimously, and all mankind are happier under the influence, I believe, of better and kinder feelings from its recurrence. One would think that they couldn't find any great evil in setting apart one day even if not the *right one* for such an object. . . .

Saw some curious documents this evening relative to General Hamilton, left with my father by old Mrs. Hamilton, in particular the drafts of a letter written by him to [Henry] Laurens narrating Arnold's treason and the capture, death, and conduct of André. It is a very long affair, very interesting, very minute, and written in rather a labored style, too artificial; it would have been far more interesting in the offhand style of common friendly correspondence than in this dignified elegance with its moral reflections and philosophic remarks. The writer must have foreseen his letter's destiny. It's to be put into [the Reverend Francis Lister] Hawks's hands, with all the rest of the General's papers, for publication after the old lady's decease.[5]

December 28. . . . Rather busy all day. Went to Erben's, however, and found Goliath O.K. Dr. Wainwright was there, and several others, and Hall made the instrument speak to some purpose. It certainly surpasses my expectations. Brother Jonathan glorifies it exceedingly. But it is as big as a small house. . . .

December 29. Today has been generally devoted to organ-building. Went to the office and worked till eleven, and then came home, and finding all quiet and no Goliath yet, I adjourned incontinently to Erben's by the aid of the first omnibus I could get into. On my way up, however, I met the whole affair, i.e., instalment No. 1, sailing majestically down Broadway, the big cart piled ten feet deep with pipes and mahogany and cutting altogether a most terrible figure. They took off the little concern [the family's old organ], and I was really sorry to see the poor little instrument take its departure—I wish it may get a good master in its old age—and at about seven they had the case set up and absquatulated. It looks awful. My only sources of consolation are, first, that everybody in the house thinks it splendid and not a bit too large, and secondly that it looks much larger now than it will when all complete and set in its place.

December 30, WEDNESDAY. Goliath has made fair progress today. He's all up and all the pipes are in save the reed stops. It's a terrible job to set it up. On the whole, now it's in its place it don't look so preposterously big as it did last night, though to be sure, to any stranger entering the room it must seem gigantic. . . .

December 31. Variable weather. Well, the "long agony is going over." Goliath's all finished at last, and I'm far better satisfied than I supposed I should be. . . .

[5] This letter was published in the Lodge edition of *The Works of Alexander Hamilton*, VIII, 18–29.

1841

MR. LLOYD'S INSANITY · DEATH OF PRESIDENT HARRISON ·
BAR EXAMINATION · SARATOGA · ADMITTED SOLICITOR
IN CHANCERY · GENERAL CONVENTION

*T*he new year brought in fresh troubles with England, for Alexander
McLeod, the before-mentioned Canadian accused of murder in connection
with the Caroline raid, was—despite fervid British protests—being held in jail
preparatory to his trial before a Utica jury. It brought in new financial difficulties, for at the beginning of February the United States Bank in Philadelphia suspended payments, and as other banks followed, nearly all stocks dropped with a
crash. Early in the year General Harrison made a deliberate triumphal journey
from Ohio eastward for his inauguration, received everywhere with Whig processions and jubilant banquets. The first Whig President, alas! was not to hold
his seat long. A month after being sworn in he was dead, and that little-known
Virginian of aristocratic antecedents, John Tyler, who had a record of stubborn
opposition to nearly all the main Whig tenets—a protective tariff, a national
bank, internal improvements—took his place. The Whig garlands of victory
had turned to funeral wreaths indeed. But Webster remained Secretary of
State, and was to achieve a partial settlement of the difficulties with Britain.

January 11, MONDAY. . . . I got hold of a prize this morning—a sealed
book, to be sure, but some day I hope I shall be able to make something
out of it: the complete score, to wit, of Mozart's *Requiem*. It don't look
very difficult. . . .

January 17. . . . Read myself into a horrible rage over Southey's *Book
of the Church*. Those beastly Puritans! They're the men we glorify, the
pure-minded, patriotic, liberal "Pilgrim Fathers," those advocates for

liberty of conscience. Politically the party was bad enough, but as a religious body they were vile.

January 22. . . . The *Columbia* is in, but the extras contain nothing very exciting, save the details of the Royal Infant's health and position in society. The Royal Infant has been vaccinated; the Royal Mamma in the plenitude of her maternal affection (how beautiful in a Queen!) spends half an hour in the Royal Nursery every day directly after the Royal Breakfast; the Royal Cradle is very grand; and the Royal Diapers, I suppose, are white satin. . . .

January 26, TUESDAY. . . . *I'm twenty-one today.* . . .[1]

February 10. . . . Spent the morning variously and, among other things, looked in at Colman's with Post. He has some of the most distinct and perfect Daguerreotype pictures I ever saw, portraits especially. I think that invention succeeds best in buildings and statuary. I wonder if it can be employed to take facsimiles of paintings. . . .

March 5, FRIDAY. . . . The prospect of war with England seems to be in everybody's sight and the general opinion is that we shall be most lamentably used up for the first three years perhaps; after that, the public opinion is very strong that the British Empire would be wiped out from the face of the earth. If tall talking can do it, John Bull is a used-up man. . . .

March 11. . . . Mr. Derby astonished us by a sudden return instead of going on to Washington. He found the weather bad enough at Philadelphia and heard it was still worse farther south, and returned in desperation. He came on with Joseph Story, who says [Peter Vivian] Daniel, the new justice of the Supreme Court, is a man of prodigiously small calibre. Too bad.

March 14, SUNDAY. . . . The governor has gone to Mr. Lloyd's. He's in a fearful state of nervousness, hypochondria, and desperation, has made up his mind that it is to result in lunacy, and sent for my father this morning to express his dislike to the asylum and make arrangements to be placed in some private establishment when the event takes place! *Aegroto animo magis quam corpore,* I believe. He came to town three or four weeks since to consult Dr. [Alexander Hodgdon] Stevens about some real or supposed

[1] This entry places Strong's birth on the 26th of January, 1820. In the Strong genealogy, Benjamin Woodbridge Dwight's *History of the Descendants of Elder John Strong of Northampton, Mass.* (Albany, 1871), to which G.T.S. contributed the records of his own family, the date is twice given as 26 February, 1820, but we must accept his father's record, copied into Vol. IV of the Diary, which states with great exactitude that George Templeton Strong was born at 50 Franklin Street, New York, Wednesday, 26 January, 1820, at 7 o'clock in the morning.

ailments and by his advice engaged a passage for St. Croix, and then gave it up under the impression that he could not stand it—that he might lose his mind there—and fairly determined to die at home. Since then he has grown worse and worse in mind every day, and I suppose his condition is as pitiable as mortal's can be. . . .

John Nelson Lloyd, the wealthiest member of the Yale class of 1802, was the brother of the elder Strong's first wife. The melancholy progress of his disorder was chronicled at some length by the diarist. "His monomania is singular—a sort of Quixotic exaltation of principle. He thinks that there are two sums of about $1000 cash which he owed some thirty years since and never paid (though even this is questionable) and that he is bound now to pay both with compound interest, which runs it up to about $20,000. His last idea on the subject is that he is bound to pay one of them, due to the Phoenix Bank, twice over—first to the bank and secondly to the stockholders of thirty years since, or their representatives, each with compound interest. This would sweep away about one-half of his property." Religious despair later got hold of him, and he thought he had committed the unpardonable sin; various attacks of violence occurred which had to be physically suppressed. Death finally came on the 31st of May.

Peter Remsen Strong, a lad of seventeen with a Columbia A.B., and cousin to George, had joined the embryonic lawyers at the office; he was green and credulous, facts which were quickly seized on for some office fun: "Poor Pete Strong's powers of suction are certainly unrivalled. As if Anthon's story about Post's being the first cousin to the 'Earl of Derby', possessed of a splendidly emblazoned genealogical tree, excessively aristocratic in his notions, and very unwilling to speak first to commoners, wasn't gross enough to be difficult of digestion, he was told today, and swallowed it too, that one of Post's ancestors had a quarrel with Shakespeare and was immortalized by him under the name of Caliban."

March 23. Had to wait half an hour in the drizzle at the corner of Rector Street and Broadway while Matty's [Ex-President Van Buren's] triumphal procession was going up. A disgusting assemblage of the unwashed democracy they were, generally speaking, a more rowdy, draggletailed, jailbird-resembling gang of truculent loafers than the majority of them I never witnessed before. Considering the rain, they turned out in force—and the rain, by the by, was a blessing to some of them, for the ablution was badly needed. Butler boys on horseback—there was an unlimited number of them. Carts with twenty little blackguards sticking to each, a dozen grand marshals with chapeaux and swords galloping about and getting into everybody's way in the intensity of their excitement, several very formidable brass bands, divers gorgeous banners, and so forth, with a great predominance of pedestrians from the neighborhood of the Points apparently, passed one; and then came the triumphal car, to wit, a shabby barouche and four with Matty himself, hat in hand, looking as happy as a man could be expected to in the rain without hat or umbrella. He looks older than I supposed.

March 26. . . . Lit a pipe and read King James's *Counterblaste*.[2] His Majesty was a superlative ass. For pompous absurdity and solemn egotism I never read anything like the contents of that venerable folio of his. . . .

March 28, SUNDAY. Went to church. Heard [the Reverend John Murray] Forbes[3] this morning. Matty Van Buren was there, in the pew of his brother president, Duer of Columbia College, and by a curious coincidence the subject of the sermon was the spiritual blessings that flow from retiracy and seclusion for a season from the busy world and the cares of active life. If I wasn't nearsighted I've no doubt I should have observed Matty wince considerably.

April 5, MONDAY. Mournful news this morning. General Harrison died on Saturday night, a few hours less than one month from his inauguration. The news was most unexpected to me, for I didn't suppose him very seriously ill, and he was said on Saturday to be recovering. I confess I never was so sincerely sorry for the death of any one whom I knew of merely as a *public* character. Though not possessed of any great talent, I believe he was a good, honest, benevolent, right-minded man—qualities far more rare among our political people. It's a bad thing for the Whig party—for Tyler I imagine is half a Democrat—a bad thing for the country at this crisis, when the commercial interest is looking so anxiously to the

---

[2] James I's *Counterblaste to Tobacco* was published anonymously in London in 1604.

[3] The Rev. John Murray Forbes (1807–1885), Columbia 1827, was at this time rector of St. Luke's Church in Hudson Street; in 1849 he joined the Roman Catholic Church and two years later became pastor of St. Ann's Church in Eighth Street; he was made S.T.D. by a Vatican decree of Pius IX in 1854. Having undergone a change of heart, he withdrew from Catholicism in 1859 and three years later was restored to his Episcopal orders and went back to St. Luke's Church. From 1869 to 1872 he was dean of the General Theological Seminary. He should not be confused with two other John Murray Forbeses, all living at the same time, one a Hispanic-American diplomat (1771–1831; Harvard 1787), the other a great railroad man (1813–1898) whose son married Emerson's daughter.

movements of government, and when we may be on the eve of war and can ill afford any time to make new arrangements at home. The news by the *British Queen* looks black enough, certainly, and were it not for this calamity, would have put the city in a ferment. That despicable report of Pickens's has produced in England the surprise and indignation which such a piece of stuff ought.

Everything in the shape of a flag in the city is up today and at half mast, and I was heartily glad to see one flying on Tammany, and to see the *Standard* in mourning. All the papers except the *New Era*, the *Post* and the *Journal of Commerce*, have had decency enough to let party feelings drop. . . .

April 7. Cloudy and showery. Harrison's funeral was to take place today, and the city has therefore been in mourning pursuant to the notification of the Common Council, who have displayed a better feeling than I expected from such a partisan body. The shops were closed at twelve, bells tolled, minute guns fired, etc. A funeral procession takes place on Saturday. . . .

April 10, SATURDAY. Weather raw, cloudy and unpropitious. Went out at twelve o'clock to see the funeral procession. The whole population of the city in the street either as actors or spectators. Houses hung with black, particularly along the line of march. Chatham Street literally hid with lugubrious drapery. I established myself in Chatham Square, and a fine sight it was to look up the rising ground towards the Park, the houses on each side shrouded with black, the dense mass of people between, and in the centre the procession pouring down, a wide stream of plumes and bayonets and dark banners. It began to pass at a little before one, moving rapidly, headed by the military—about 6000—uniform companies and U.S. troops and Marines, then the urn, the General's horse (hypothetical), the "pall bearers," Martin Van Buren, and divers other great men, the civic dignitaries, all the fire companies, about 3000 men I presume— generally a rowdy set, though one or two companies looked decent, then Masons, etc. By that time it was half-past two and I was tired and it was beginning to snow, so I walked down Chatham Street to the Park, where at least one-third of the procession remained, filing slowly out—indeed, it was half-past three before they were all in motion. . . .

April 12, MONDAY. . . . Election going forward. Very apathetic. Exercised for the first time the great and glorious right of suffrage. Experienced the regular amount of sublime emotions and the proper quantum of "lofty consciousness of the exalted privilege of a freeman.". . .

May 5, WEDNESDAY. . . . Played a victorious game of chess after dinner and stayed at home tonight. I've been reading that notable production of Mr. [Johann Heinrich] Jung-Stilling's on Pneumatology. He's an extraordinary biped. I thought I was credulous enough on all these matters, but he's altogether beyond my powers of absorption. . . .

May 14, FRIDAY. Today's the general fast—humiliation and so on. *Peccavi, confiteor*—I didn't go to church; in fact I couldn't very well, but stayed at the office and did penance over some narratives and costs and so on. Worked hard, and on the whole consider myself to have anacenated and mortified the flesh enough to make up for my absence from church—especially as I kept a black fast from breakfast to dinner, and another from dinner to tea.

Today has been generally well observed. All the shops closed (their windows at least) and Wall Street in utter desolation and abandonment.

May 23, SUNDAY. . . . Lost my Third Eye—my *sine qua non* of vision—my *glass*, somewhere about Whitestone this morning, and search has proved unavailing. I'd got quite an attachment to the article—and I think that I'll try to get along without one in the hope of remedying the defect, which I'd gladly give a thousand dollars to be rid of. No one who's not nearsighted and who doesn't wear glasses constantly can think how serious an inconvenience it is.

May 25, TUESDAY. . . . Read miscellaneously this evening. Looked into the *Morte d'Arthur* again. I enjoy the book much. It seems to me that one may improve himself in composition by reading it; for the style, with all its uncouth spelling, is real, solid, nervous old Saxon English. There are some beautiful things in the book and all told with the unpretending, unconscious simplicity of scripture narrative. Perhaps the finest is the fatal war that ends King Arthur; there's a fine feeling of gloom somehow spread through the story, like the Twilight of the Gods in the Edda. . . .

May 26. Warm and showery. The Quakers are holding their yearly meeting, so we shall probably have a week of rain. . . .

Went to the Academy of Design with Anthon. A great crowd. Certainly the public can't be accused of neglecting the arts when they throng to such a collection of ugly faces. Scarce anything there but portraits—and one or two are rather pretty ones. Generally they're terrible; there's quite a collection of infants and they all look like foetuses—one would think hydrocephalus epidemic. One of Huntington's (*Mercy's Dream*) is really about the best in the collection, and that's not saying much. Cole and Mount have pictures there but they're below par.

I'd go on hands and knees out to Harlem to see the original of one portrait there—it is a most exquisite thing—but, alas, I never saw an original
yet half so good-looking as her likeness. The Daguerreotype is the only
limner that doesn't flatter.

But it's all folly to get enthusiastic over these things. I'm becoming
more and more of a misogynist every day. Anthon's just the reverse. He's
fiercely connubial at present—swears that marriage is the *summum bonum*
and that he'll provide himself with a discreet consort at the first opportunity. He may do as he likes. I had a tendency to the same disease some
two or three years since and thought it rather a clever thing than otherwise
to go into voluntary slavery, but the mists have been clearing away for
some time past, and I've now sobered myself into determined old bachelor-
dom.

May 29, SATURDAY. . . . The National Theatre was burnt up in about
twenty minutes this morning; set on fire, unquestionably. The walls have
mostly tumbled down, and from the way they tumbled, one would think
the builder had used gum arabic for mortar. One side pitched into Verren's
yard and did no other damage than smashing his necessary. Another tumbled on a new and very magnificent temple of Venus, kept, I believe, by that
respectable person Mrs. [Julia] Brown, and demolished one-half of it—
and one unfortunate young lady who had set up in business a day or two
before, and whose life fell a sacrifice to a modest reluctance to appear in
public in *deshabille*. It's said that the first individual who emerged from the
establishment when the alarm was given was that indefatigable pipelayer
Mr. [James B.] Glentworth. I don't believe they'll rebuild the theatre in a
hurry.

June 6, SUNDAY. . . . Read some of Newman's sermons. They're glorious—the only modern sermons I ever could read with satisfaction.

June 9. . . . Commenced studying for that beastly bore of July this morning, after gormandizing myself into comparative coolness with Roman
punch at Thompson's. . . .

July 13, TUESDAY.   Start in the *Albany* at seven. Boat tolerably full,
and as hot as a locomotive Dutch oven. I never suffered so much from heat
as this day—not a breath of air, and the glassy water reflecting back the
sun and putting us between two fires.

Haven't been up the river at all since '31, and not as far as Albany since
'29 or '30. I enjoyed the splendid scenery much till we reached Newburgh
and the shores sank into flatness, and then it was dull enough till we reached
the venerable Catskills, and then I exulted greatly over the progress we

were making, but it was premature. We kept in sight of them and couldn't get out of sight of them, till at last I began to think seriously of the diabolical influences that are said to endanger the neighborhood of the enchanted mountains of Hendrick Hudson.

At last the cool of the evening came on, and it was delicious enough, though at any other time I should have called it fearfully warm and close. Reached Albany and put up—literally *up,* heaven save us and confound State Street—at Congress Hall: Cortlandt Schermerhorn, John B. Lawrence, and old Brinckerhoff.

July 14. Weather still very intense. Off for Utica. Albany to Schenectady: disgusting railroad, endless detentions, great bore of an inclined plane, startling legend of certain cars that ran down the said inclined plane by mistake and into the woods and over the hills and far away and never were heard of more. Schenectady: dingy-looking collection of brick houses and Dutch aborigines. Didn't stop and didn't want to.

Schenectady to Utica: fine country, beautiful wooded hills sweeping off on each side of the road, approaching and receding, with the Mohawk between; two showers, weather cooler and sultrier after each, a third would have set the woods on fire; several palpable law-students in the cars, recognized by a certain hang-dog expression and the assiduity of their applications for brandy and water and other drinks at the various groggeries at which we stopped to wood, water, and liquor. Romaine and Kissam [classmates of Strong's] on board—bless 'em both. We did not recognize each other—poor fellows, I dare say they think me a very bitter enemy of theirs, but I should have been really and sincerely glad if they'd show any indications of a wish .to forget those old squabbles. But they didn't; and this is probably the last time we shall be thrown together, so let them pass and we'll henceforth move on in our separate orbits.

Reached Utica at two. Crowd, crush, and discomfort till the cars pushed on for the west after dinner and then trudged up that delightful promenade for a hot afternoon, Genesee Street, in quest of Mr. Clerk [Hiram] Denio. . . . Very civil and complimentary.

Comprehensive survey of Utica this afternoon—and another with Backus tonight. Queer place. Canal—not much doing. Mohawk—not much larger than the Norwalk River or the big gutter in Centre Street. Genesee bridge nice place for a smoke, at least so I found it, and smoked, and spit into the gentle river and thought of the coming terrors of the 2d Thursday, with great placidity and contentment, for I've grown courageous on seeing the gang of shakebags who are to pass the ordeal with me.

N.B. Bagg's Hotel reminds me of an Eastern caravanserai—incessant stream of passengers running through, dining and talking and not much else. What sustains this ambitious little city I can't conceive.

July 15. A little cooler than yesterday. After a slight walk with one or two rather sappy personages—fellow sufferers of mine—went to the Court Room, to wit, the cockloft of the Academy. Enter his honor the Chief Justice [Samuel Nelson]. Great buzz and excitement among the victims as his honor announces the names of Comstock, Hill, and Tracy as the Inquisitorial Committee. Neither note nor comment added by the oracular functionary aforesaid or his associates—no harangue—no *concio ad clerum* —much to the relief of the said victims. . . .

Now for the examination. Went up at four. About sixty-five in all— of which I knew [William Maxwell] Evarts, A[ugustus] F. Smith, Wickham (from Suffolk) and one or two more. After some bother the examiners "marshalled the asse(t)s" and went ahead.

Flourish of trumpets. Breathless expectation. Examiner Comstock *loquitur* (he looked like a half-way house between utter spooneydom and sharp practice, or rather a *tertium quid*, and examined as sharp as he knew how, which wasn't much): "Mr. A, what is an action, and into what are they divided?" This brought the first half-dozen hard up. One man said "civil and annual," next "legal and equitable," next "ex contracto," etc., and the examiner chuckled greatly, for he was evidently laboring under no plethora of ideas—and knew he'd run dry of questions to put before he got through—so every student that boggled at a question was rather conferring a favor on the examiner. At last one man quoted Blackstone and the Revised Statutes definition, and Comstock went ahead. At last he came round to me and propounded the following searching interrogatory: "Mr. Strong, how do you serve a decl[aration] in ej[ectment]?" which hideously entangling and horribly recondite query I thereupon made a great effort and answered.

Then came Tracy's turn at the thumbscrews. He didn't know much more than Comstock (I was fresh from Graham and I'm certain that all three made some surprising blunders), but then he examined in a very kind and gentlemanly way, evidently trying to help the poor devils and lead them right instead of endeavoring, like the others, to puzzle and bother them— a very unnecessary exertion, by the way. He put some two or three questions to me as to the pleadings in proceedings to settle claims to real property and I answered them, and that was the extent of my examination.

Then Hill took up some half-dozen of those who had flunked the most barefacedly on the preceding queries and put some dozen questions to each, and this was the richest part of the affair. . . .

Such a farce of an examination, such an asinine set of candidates, and such prodigiously uncomfortable timber benches I never met with before.

Got home before eight. Paid $1 for a license and went to bed.

July 16, FRIDAY. . . . Took a pleasant walk along the banks of the Mohawk with Backus and Backus's dog, and when we were a mile or two out, stripped and took a grand swim. Never enjoyed a bath so much before.

News from Court—"All passed!". . . . Went up to Court and signed the roll, and after dinner went up again and took the oath—imposing ceremony—cost $1.50 and cheap at that.

Start at nine for Albany. Ride all night. Got but precious little sleep. They stop every ten miles for "refreshers," and when they stopped somebody always got out for a drink and generally managed to wake me up out of an incipient doze.

July 17.   Reached Albany at six and went straight on board the *Troy*. She's a fine boat and brought us to New York at five-thirty in very comfortable style. . . .

July 26, MONDAY. . . . Well, tomorrow I must see that amiable old swine [Vice-Chancellor William T.] McCoun to arrange for examination. This is bore No. 2. I've got a tolerable idea of equity practice, and if McC. conducts himself in a decent way, I oughtn't to apprehend trouble. No matter.

July 27. . . . Went to the vice-chancellor's after dinner, at five, and spent half an hour with him. His examination was fair enough—little to it but what's to be found in the rules—and I went through without any mistakes and very comfortably, to my surprise, for except what I've picked up during the last week, my knowledge of chancery practice might be put into a pillbox without squeezing. . . .

July 28. . . . I've got to start for Saratoga tomorrow—to be manufactured into a solicitor. It's a horrid bore, which I'd give twenty dollars to dodge. It'll be hot and tiresome and I hate traveling even when there's some prospect of enjoyment, for I'm sure to get in trouble with my baggage or my breakfast or something else.

July 29, THURSDAY.   Left at seven in the *Albany*. It was a beautiful morning, clear and cool, with a bracing northwest breeze that drove some people into thin coats and cloaks, and to be sure it felt almost like an October day. The scenery on the river never looked so glorious before—even distant objects stood out sharp and distinct on the clear sky—and the green of the woody hills was as fresh and bright as in June. An American must "feel the prouder of his native land" as he sails up the Hudson. . . .

Nothing very notable occurred on the voyage. Reached Albany at six-thirty and got into the *John Mason* for Troy—I never traveled this part of the river by daylight before. It's exceedingly pretty; the banks are so varied and the channel runs sometimes so close into shore. I enjoy such navigation more than if it were on a broader and finer sheet of water, because I'm nearsighted, I suppose.

Put up at the Troy House. It's rather a decent place. Walked through the place a little. There's not much of interest in it. The Gothic church[4] is a more expensive and handsome building than one expects to see in a little place like Troy, and if they'd knock off the queer-looking battle-ments on it—which I think must be an originality of some Dutch (or Chinese) architect—it would be a very decent affair.

July 30. Walter Cutting made his appearance here before breakfast, having come up in the night boat. Made a very decent breakfast and left for Saratoga. The road runs through a beautiful country, particularly as far as Waterford. Poor Waterford, there's scarce anything left of it, the part destroyed seems to have been the best of the town. Strange that they couldn't have checked a fire burning in one direction only, and down a long narrow strip of buildings; surely a little gunpowder would have brought it up.[5]

Passed through that faded haunt of fashion, Ballston, and got into Saratoga at twelve. Went to the United States Hotel.

O Saratoga, Saratoga—if proof demonstrative be wanted of fashion's omnipotence, truly thou dost furnish some four thousand unanswerable arguments! It's my first visit, and I devoutly hope my last. A mean little country town, ambitious of looking as much like a city as it can, with its brick houses and paved sidewalks and immense wilderness of hotels—like stray cabbages in a potato patch, situated in the midst of an indeterminate sandy plain—is the place to which people go to be happy in hot weather, and in the midst, too, of such a crowd and such confusion as would be thought wholly unendurable in town. I never saw aught like the U.S. [Hotel]. Everybody was there. . . .

---

[4] St. Paul's Church, Protestant Episcopal, built in 1827–1828; the "battlements" disappeared many years ago.

[5] There had been a great conflagration in Waterford not many days previous to Strong's visit—on the 11th of July; a stiff breeze had hampered the work of the fire-men.

I rushed up to the Chancellor's[6] in sheer desperation. He was out. Walked round the environs. I supposed Hempstead Plains were the last place made—the fag end of creation—but they're only the last but one. Dust on an average two feet deep. Called again—*out*. . . . Went to the Pavilion Spring and gave the genius of the fountain a shilling, which unheard-of liberality put the dispenser of health aforesaid into a state of great anxiety as to my health and led him to insist on my swallowing some six consecutive glasses of killibeate—under various modifications. The killibeate isn't bad at all, even in its native simplicity—with gin and sugar it's really a very tolerable tipple. The other springs being potent cathartics, I kept shy of them.

Went back to his Honor's and found him at last, to my great relief, for I was beginning to be seriously alarmed as to the possibility of my having to spend a night at Saratoga. He was very civil and made a solicitor of me in no time.

Went back in time for dinner—fare bad and attendance worse. Cleared out as fast as possible and put myself on board the half-past three train for Schenectady. Passed through Schenectady and reached Albany just in time for the seven o'clock boat after a rather pleasant ride.

I calculated on a pleasant ride down the river, for there's a beautiful moon, and to be sure till ten o'clock it was extremely pleasant. Then I went downstairs and lay down for an hour or so, but it was hot and the churning of the engine would not let me sleep and I can't feel very safe on board these anthracite coal boats, so I went on deck and found the weather threatening. Still it was well enough till we were nearly down to Newburgh, and then the rain burst on us with a grand crash, and the bore was insufferable till we got into New York; it rained furiously, was pitch dark, and everything was gloomy and comfortless. Got in at six, and then after standing on the stoop of No. 108 in a nice little pelting rain for some half an hour I at last woke somebody up and got inside of the house and took half an hour's nap before breakfast, which rather refreshed me.

August 3, TUESDAY.   Nothing worthy of note going on. We were to have evacuated the city today, but we didn't. Spent the morning in the office and made out some lunacy papers. After dinner walked up to the [General] Theological Seminary to look for [Russell] Trevett, but with no success. I wish I were able to give a couple of hundred thousands to that concern—for enlarging the buildings and the library, increasing the faculty,

[6] Chancellor Walworth's home was in Saratoga.

setting up scholarships and fellowships, etc. It might be made a grand affair. . . .

September 30, THURSDAY. Home at last "for good." I haven't journalized since I've been gone; in fact I've not had time, oscillating like a particularly indefatigable pendulum between Flushing and New York. My regularity has been beyond all praise; I've only stayed three days out of the city (Sundays excepted), and as near as I can calculate I've traversed that delicious mud flat, Flushing Bay, about a hundred and twenty times.

However, there's been no lack of matter to journalize about: the two vetoes [of President Tyler], the [August] Belmont [–Edward Heyward] duel, the Mary C. Rogers murder, Mr. [Washington] I[rving]'s illness, Mr. [Samuel] Adams's assassination, etc. might each have been expatiated on at length had I been quietly domiciled in town, but the case being otherwise, those matters lose a great deal of light that might have been thrown on them by my profundity, sagacity and other luminous qualifications.[7]

October 4, MONDAY. . . . I haven't smoked a cigar nor a pipe, and have scarcely touched tobacco in any way since I came to town, and I do verily believe, though it may be a fancy, that I feel the better for it—especially in the mornings. The fact is that for three years I've been a perfect slave to the habit and it won't do to be so any longer. I won't say that I'll never touch another cigar, even in the city, but I shall adhere to total abstinence for some little time and after that indulge sparingly. . . .

October 5, TUESDAY. Spent the greater part of the day at St. George's Chapel where Alma Mater's "annual festival" came off—much to the indignation of its presiding luminary, for whose ambition it was quite too contracted and not sufficiently aristocratic. Prex, by the way, looks very poorly indeed; I'm afraid this is the last commencement he'll enjoy. . . . Saw some friends and acquaintances—indeed the main inducement to go to commencement is that one meets everybody there. . . .

For two weeks in October the General Convention of the Protestant Episcopal Church was in session in New York: "Bishops are as plentiful as black-berries just now—the market's overstocked." Strong attended a number of the meetings with great interest, but never failed to turn up his nose at "Low Churchism." On the 12th he went to St. Paul's Chapel to witness the consecration of Bishop Alfred Lee of Delaware. "The ceremony is a grand one,

[7] Others, however, handled these incidents very nicely. Philip Hone commented on all of them, and Edgar Allan Poe wrote of the murder of Mary Cecilia Rogers of New York in one of his best tales, "The Mystery of Marie Rogêt," changing the locale to Paris.

especially when there are twenty bishops behind the chancel rails, besides the whole convention to give the responses. I saw Dominie [John] Knox prowling about the church. I think the liturgy as read and responded this morning and the whole aspect of things inside the church must have put the doctor a little out of humor. I'm confident that many of the schismatic parsons (and especially the 'Dutch Deformed') among us, would be heartily glad to get into a church— *but for the fear of being charged with inconsistency and weakness."*

October 8. . . . Went to the Library this evening. . . . What a beastly concern that *Dial* is! I never saw a number of it till tonight, and from this specimen I should judge it to be the organ of the rankest kind of Deistical New England Socinianism.

October 31, SUNDAY. . . . Went to church as usual. Walked uptown tonight after going to Murray Street and back. Looked in at St. Thomas's and heard some admirable music.

Let the enemies of church music only mark the effect it has in soothing and quieting one when he's in a black rage at matters and things in general and feels disposed to be ugly and vicious and savage and selfish, and to bite his own nose off, and cut all his friends and acquaintances, and abandon everything, do nothing, say nothing to nobody and just vegetate venomously. Let them note how soon it will bring one who's in such a beastly temper back to healthy and natural feelings and I think they'll abandon their opposition.

November 2, TUESDAY. . . . Went to the Tabernacle tonight to hear *The Mount of Olives.* It is an extraordinary composition certainly; I understand now why Beethoven is spoken of as the Byron of Musicians; such strange, wild, terrible passages, such *speaking* choruses, such startling changes from the darkest and most savage discords to passages of sweetness and exquisite beauty I never heard. . . .

November 10, WEDNESDAY. Weather very disagreeable—chilly, damp, and I think premonitory of snow. I've been in a high state of excitement all day over a magnificent MS. Bible that old Appleton got for me of Payne & Foss pursuant to my letter of last September. It eclipses all my missals utterly, in every respect, and it seems to me remarkably cheap, considering its size and beauty and superb condition. The binding must have cost two or three guineas at least.

I can't conceive any higher physical enjoyment than traveling in Europe with thirty or forty thousand dollars to invest in old books and especially in old parchment.

This is of English manufacture and is of about 1320 probably. If one could only transfer himself for an hour or two to the cell of the monkish calligrapher who wrote it! How delightful it would be! I wonder how the Frater Nicholas or Ambrosius or Eustacius, or whatever his perished name may have been, felt when he got through, whether he snapped his fingers and left his cell and took a lunch in the refectory, or merely mended his pen and commenced another copy. I'd like to make a call at the convent and have a talk with the stately father abbot, or take a quiet ride with him over the convent demesnes. . . .

November 16. In a vehement state of activity all day. I do begin to hope that I may overcome my laziness some time or other. Post came down tonight and we considered our escrow case and devised ways and means of overruling Sheppard's *Touchstone*, Coke and Blackstone, all which are dead against us; but we didn't get far, for after examination down came Cram and George Anthon upon us and we had a rather rich time thereafter.

We've got a new "student"—Mr. Gus Jay, Peter Augustus Jay's hopeful progeny, whom I remember at college as a rampant rowdy. We've a very *rum* set there certainly. However, we couldn't well have a better. In spite of all the plagues I've been subjected to, I shall always think of my office companions and office days with much pleasanter feelings than of my delightful gang of college classmates. They do bore me awfully, though, now and then.

November 23, TUESDAY. . . . Went with the maternal relative and others to hear Braham at the Masonic Hall. He sang magnificently. Some of his crack songs, such as "The Bay of Biscay," though superbly sung, were spoiled by clap-trappery and gesticulation. A man of his reputation should scorn such humbug, and a man of his corpulence should be careful about attempting it. . . .

November 30. . . . It's said that there were divers very curious characters who contrived to find their way into Mrs. Mott's ballrooms at her late Joinville rout—among the rest the notable Miss or Mrs. or Madam Julia Brown with some of her sisterhood, sent there, 'tis said, by some malicious acquaintance of the Motts whom they had cut, in their magnificence, on returning from Paris, and who took this mode in revenge for not having been invited.[8]

[8] Lord Morpeth and the Prince de Joinville were visiting New York at this time and were being entertained lavishly. The ball to which Strong refers was given by Dr. and Mrs. Valentine Mott at their house in Bleecker Street—"in a style of magnificence," said Philip Hone, "which we have not witnessed for a long time."

December 8. . . . There's a Prince Royal born to the Throne of England and the Princess Royal's nose is decidedly out of joint—her sun is set—her popularity gone—her prospects blighted.

December 22.   Worked like a horse in a mill this morning. I'm getting to be a kind of professional steam engine. Or to speak more seriously on what's no fit subject for jest (indeed, how many things are there in the world that rightly considered *are* strictly and in every point of view fit subjects for jest?), I do humbly hope that I'm beginning in some remote degree to feel myself getting the better of the moral paralysis of the last three or four years. . . .

December 25.   Christmas, and the day has been verily well observed—that's encouraging. Wall Street looked like Sunday. The most notable indication I've observed today was a lachrymose paragraph in the *Presbyterian* headed "Times are Changed" and consisting of a sorrowful quoting of certain laws and regulations of those fathers of civil liberty, the Puritans, making the observance of Christmas a penal offence, for which golden age the amiable editor evidently intended to convey to the public his deep admiration, his regrets for its departure and his aspirations for its return. . . .

Went to St. Paul's. Rt. Rev. Bp. Onderdonk in the pulpit looking as Episcopal as ever. Then went to St. Peter's; church jammed, squeeze terrific. . . . They had a choir of fifty or sixty, were drilled, and the effect with which the choir and the full organ came out with the Hallelujah Chorus at the end of the services was great. . . . It's a shame that The Church can't or don't have such music as is thrown away on those rowdies at St. Peter's. . . .

December 26, SUNDAY. . . . Our Mt. Misery friends inundated us to-night. Certain of them are very nice people, i.e., they are simple country girls and they pretend to be nothing more than what they are—but certain others—

If there's anything that has a strong tendency to set one's teeth on edge it's to see womankind from the country whom nature and their habits of life tend to make so much more unaffected and every way respectable than the denizens of a city like this—to see them aping the frivolity and trying successfully to acquire the follies that by habit and education they're free from. . . .

December 28. . . . Looked into *Amadis de Gaule* this afternoon. It's pretty much what I expected—the same endless series of adventure growing out of adventure, like the successive leaves of a prickly pear—like *Morte d'Arthur.* It seems to have more unity than that book, but it wants its rugged primitive old English bad spelling: though Southey's translation is nervous and good—as good, I suppose, as any modern translation could make it. . . .

December 31, FRIDAY. . . . Poor Ben[jamin] Romaine [Columbia 1838] *died and was buried today*—died of the smallpox in its most terrible form: the most fearful case of that disease I ever heard of. He caught the disease at the Stuyvesant Institute, where the University Medical School is held. He passed through some part of the building, it seems, just as they were bringing in a subject that was afterwards ascertained to have died of small-pox in a milder form. It was very offensive and made Romaine sick at the moment. On last Tuesday night he was a little unwell and this Friday morning he died and was buried immediately. . . .

1842

MRS. STUART'S TRIAL · ERECTION OF TRINITY CHURCH ·
MESMERISM · FIRST APPEARANCE IN COURT · DORR'S
REBELLION · CROTON WATER CELEBRATION ·
COLT'S LAST DAYS · *SOMERS* MUTINY

*A*s Strong's diary indicates, the early books of Dickens—Pickwick Papers,
Oliver Twist, *and* Nicholas Nickleby—*had taken America by storm;
and the country vibrated with excitement when the first weeks of the new year
brought the celebrated "Boz" to its shores. Another storm over the right of
petition was raging in the House of Representatives, where John Quincy Adams
was withstanding the onslaught of a cohort of Southerners led by Henry A.
Wise of Virginia. But the event of January which chiefly agitated New
Yorkers was the trial of John C. Colt for the murder of one Samuel Adams.
The previous September the dissected body of Adams had been discovered in a
box placed aboard a vessel about to sail for New Orleans. When the police
investigated the matter, they fastened upon Colt as the apparent perpetrator of
the crime; and a man who occupied an office adjoining Colt's testified that
when he found Colt behaving very strangely, he had peeped through a keyhole
and seen Colt wiping a pool of blood from the floor. The trial took place under
Judge William Kent. Strong, who made no effort to attend it, expressed
great annoyance with the crowds which blocked up all the means of entering
and leaving City Hall, and so delayed him in his routine business. He saw
evidence in the demeanor of the crowds that if Colt was acquitted, mob action
might result. Indeed, the evidence seemed quite conclusive. The diarist was
both relieved and astonished when the jury, which might have found the man
guilty of manslaughter, brought in a verdict of wilful murder.*

January 1, SATURDAY. The finest New Year's Day in the memory of the oldest inhabitant, and such a universal turnout of the male part of the community I never witnessed before. Went out as usual with the paternal and made our usual tour. I don't remember anything very notable. The Lawrences were in as good spirits as usual. Old Mrs. Hamilton was in uncommonly high feather. Pete [Strong]'s people were patronizing and polite. The Aesculapids [Dr. John Neilson's family] were brilliant and talked organ assiduously. Called on Dr. Stevens. Saw Mrs. William M. Strong—prospects of an addition to the family. Visited various relatives— dull work.

January 6. . . . I was indefatigable this morning and tonight I stayed quietly at home, smoked volcanically, and read Burns, of whose writings I ought to know more than I do.

January 7. Burns's "Holy Willie's Prayer" is admirable—as burning a satire as I ever read. Its only fault is irreverence—a heavy fault, to be sure. But the opening verses are equal to any ten sermons against those doctrines that I believe constitute the sum and substance of Calvinism; indeed, no argument against that system can be stronger than a statement of the system itself in theory and practice, and the man who can listen to the creed of a Calvinist and hear a sincere and unflinching Calvinist state the opinions and feelings which such a creed must produce, as regards himself and others, and who does not instinctively shrink from such a creed and from its legitimate fruits, can't be likely to yield to any less direct and palpable arguments against it. . . .

January 8, SATURDAY. . . . I'm beginning to get a little into business habits. There are some bores connected with professional dignity, however, and one is the having to do with pecuniary concerns—receiving and paying out. I'm so unused to matters of this sort and have so little of the calculating, money-making spirit suitable to attorneyship in me, that I shall inevitably get myself in some botheration or other before I'm used to the novelties of a bank account and partnership duties. . . .

January 10. . . . Mr. Higbee called at the office and I went with him to the library of Alma Mater to inspect Audubon. It's a fine book; I wish I could afford to own a copy.[1] . . .

January 11. . . . Among other matters I attended a chancery sale of Aspinwall's and had the satisfaction of seeing him buy in for $10,000 prop-

[1] Columbia was one of the original subscribers to the folio edition of John James Audubon's great work, *The Birds of America*. Audubon paid a visit to Columbia in 1833 and a number of people were invited to the President's Room to inspect his drawings; a subscription of $800 was raised to purchase the work for the college.

erty mortgaged for $24,000. The store brings in $1,500 a year rent. I wish I could get hold of such investments. . . .

February 4. . . . The Bostonians are making horrid asses of themselves with Mr. Charles Dickens, poor man. He'll have his revenge, though, when he gets home and takes up his pen again. How people will study his next productions to see if they can find any portraits! However, we shall be fully as bad, with our Boz ball.

February 5. . . . News from Philadelphia tonight. Mr. Horace Binney's afflicted with another son—and I suppose he's very happy and thinks in his delusion that it's all very fine. Well, it should be a caution—*I'll* never marry—I've made up my mind to that.

No doubt a year before and after marriage are years of happiness. After that it may be a source of quiet comfort *or* of intense annoyance, anxiety, and misery. My nature teaches me to avoid risk and hazard and prefer a shilling in certainty to the chance of making two or losing both, and "he who has wife and children has given hostages to fortune."

February 21. . . . It's rumored that Orville Dewey is going to join the Church. I hope he may—provided he'll stay in it when he gets there.[2]

February 26, SATURDAY.   Horrid weather. The paternal has been off all day at Hempstead, so I've been compelled to mount guard *solus* at the office except when I was running about town through the cataract of rain, up to the Hall and down again, and so forth. Of course the genius of rowdyism ruled absolutely at the office and my subjects (I'd like them to see that appellation) played chess all the morning except while they were "matching pennies." My office is getting to be a regular *hell*, as bad as any in Barclay Street. I have known pennies to the amount of a shilling and upwards to change hands in the course of a single morning. . . .

March 7, MONDAY.   *Marco Polo* today. It's a scarce book and curious, and tolerably dear withal. I don't know whether I shall be able to keep it or not.

Bad news from the North by tonight's paper—another McLeod affair, another unlucky hero of the *Caroline* affair fallen into the hands of our beastly borderers, and with a stronger chance this time than last that we've waked up the right passenger. We're fated to have a war, I do believe, and if we do, and if a British fleet bombards this city, I fear my

[2] The Rev. Orville Dewey (Williams 1814), minister of the Church of the Messiah, was suffering from a breakdown of health at this time; he had become a Unitarian shortly after leaving Andover Seminary, and remained in that fold until his death in 1882.

library will stand a bad chance. We ought to move uptown, if for no other reasons but because No. 108 would be demolished in a twinkling by the very first broadside.

I see that McDonald Clarke has departed this life—poor man—the last few months of his life have been pretty hard. He has fallen victim to a practical joke.[3]

March 10. Actively engaged all this morning in this delightful job of Mrs. [Agnes] Stuart's[4] Commission of Lunacy, and spent the evening from four till eight in the Sheriff's office, taking notes of evidence and so forth. Griffin and Mr. Bidwell appear for Mrs. S. It's a very curious case of monomania and the evidence will bring out some curious details of family quarrels. . . .

Strong was fully occupied for nearly a month with Mrs. Stuart's case. He made out a batch of subpoenas, served them, and "discovered several old women who'll be only too happy for an opportunity of testifying their well-grounded conviction of the earth's opening some fine morning and swallowing Alexander and Robert L. We shall bring in some pretty strong evidence in the old lady's favor. . . . The issue to be tried is not insanity but incompetency." At the trial "Counsellor Griffin opened the defense briefly and well. He piled up the agony rather too high, though—went the pathetic rather too strong. But he drew tears from all the old women—there was a universal snivel." Strong complained bitterly of the manifest partiality of the judge, David Samuel Jones [Columbia 1796]: "Jones is dead against us. He's a horrid swine. I never saw such a brute, and such a silly brute, exercising judicial functions before." Later he wrote: "Jones is unspeakable; I never saw such deliberate, unblushing

[3] McDonald Clarke, the "Mad Poet," was a gay figure on Broadway for two decades; he had a vivid personality, a volatile temperament, and numerous eccentricities, was harmlessly insane, constantly penniless, and wrote poems about all the pretty girls he saw. He published *The Elixir of Moonshine* (1822), *The Belles of Broadway* (1833), and other volumes. Found one night destitute and apparently demented, he was lodged in the city jail by a policeman; the next morning he was discovered drowned in his cell by water from an open faucet.

[4] Mrs. Stuart was the widow of Kinloch Stuart, an Edinburgh confectioner who came to New York in 1805, prospered, and was succeeded by his sons Robert Leighton and Alexander, who made a large fortune as candy makers and sugar refiners. The sons made it a practice to devote a certain sum annually to Presbyterian benevolence, and the Presbyterian Hospital in New York, the Princeton Theological Seminary, and the College of New Jersey benefited handsomely from their largesse. R. L. Stuart's library and gallery of paintings were bequeathed by his widow to the Lenox Library, later incorporated into the New York Public Library; under the terms of the bequest they are forever to be withheld from public view on Sundays.

partiality in a judge before. He tries to fritter away our evidence, browbeats
our witnesses, and insults Griffin most outrageously. He's grown worse and
worse every day, and now he's as bad as possible, and indeed it is rather
better as it is, for his unfairness is now so palpable that it can't do much harm
with the jury." Medical witnesses were brought in who testified decidedly
and emphatically on the side of the defense. On April 8, Strong wrote in all
the excitement of victory: "Nine cheers for Agnes Stuart of the city of New
York, widow! . . . The jury were out near an hour and twenty minutes. . . .
Enter the jury. The whole fifteen for the defendant. It came on the commis-
sioners and on the opposite side like a clap of thunder. Schieffelin got into a
fearful rage and made an ass of himself. Jones looked aghast. . . . Robert L.
and Alexander grinned horribly and asseverated that they'd begin de novo
tomorrow. . . ."

Richard Upjohn's great Gothic masterpiece, Trinity Church, was now
actively going forward, and Strong followed its erection with intense interest.
There will be bulletins from time to time on the progress of the work.

March 24.   Looked in at Trinity Church this morning. They've
altered the design of the tower, and I don't know but they have improved
it. The side windows are to be omitted and their places supplied by
niches with statues, and a profusion of ornamental carving. I think they
must have the church under roof by the coming fall. . . .

April 13, WEDNESDAY.   Lugubrious weather, and not much going
forward that's worth the trouble of a memorandum. The Whigs did
better yesterday than I supposed. [Robert H.] Morris goes in, of course,
[as mayor] by near 2,000 majority, but they've carried the Common
Council through the beneficent aid of the Locofoco splits and squabbles
and intestine feuds in the ranks of Irishdom. Though by the way, it's a
little doubtful whether the said alleged majority won't turn out to be a
minority by one of those atrocious frauds, those infamous infringements
on the rights of the people, those appalling outrages on the indignant
community, which *the other* side, the losers in the game, are always so
fearfully eloquent about.

We had some hard fighting yesterday in the Bloody Sixth, and a
grand no-popery riot last night, including a vigorous attack on the
Roman Catholic Cathedral with brick bats and howls, and a hostile
demonstration on Hughes's episcopal palace, terminating in broken windows and damaged furniture. Also the Spartan Band got into the Sixth

Ward Hotel, as the no-popery rioters of old did into "the Maypole," and "made a noise and broke things" in great style. Well, this is the beginning of the end, the first fruits of that very abominable tree—the School Bill.

April 14. . . . Tolerably busy this morning. Went to Post's. But I am in a state of mystification and can write of nothing but animal magnetism. Went to Peale's Museum tonight with Anthon and Cutting and after the ridiculous "performances" were over, prevailed on old Peale to show us his blind patient. He "mesmerised her" in a very business-like way, and we spent perhaps an hour and a half in experimenting.

I don't know what to say of it. In the first place, I'm inclined to think favorably of the operator's honesty. But setting that out of view, some, perhaps the greater part of the experiments, *might* be accounted for by the increased sensitiveness of the hearing of the blind. Others *could not.* . . .

April 28, THURSDAY. Went to the Academy of Design last night. It's a queer collection. It forms a distinct and well-defined species of monomania, the insane longing that ugly people have to publish their ugliness at these exhibitions. There are not more than three or four decent portraits in the whole concern, but two of them are beautiful enough to redeem the rest, if that be possible. Should like to enjoy the pleasure of seeing the originals, as Sam Weller did the original that Dodson & Fogg sent him. One or two pretty landscapes. One grand historical piece—don't know what it is—but it's either Judith and Holofernes, Richard the first and Berengaria, Don Juan and Haidee, Sir Otto von Franksaugen and Bertha von Lichtenried, or Hagar and Ishmael, or Jael and Sisera, or Diana and Endymion, or Saul and the Witch of Endor, or a fancy family piece—Mr. and Mrs. Snooks, or something else. It's an extraordinary production. Then there's an attempt at an Ascension— all red draperies, light, and all quite uniform, except some dark indigo clouds—and one gamboge cherubim. Also the "Marriage of Pocahontas," very extraordinary; the bride's absolutely indecent, and the costumes of the civilized and the hides of the uncivilized are of a consistent, yellow-jaundiced, dirty orange color. Three great Sagamores roosting on a cross beam up in one corner have a grand effect; one's sympathies are so excited in thinking how they'll get down. . . .

May 3, TUESDAY. Made my debut in Court this morning before Judge Randall. "Great oaks from little acorns grow"—and possibly from a Marine Court practitioner I may emerge into the Court of Errors!

Opposite "counsel" named Jones, rather a decent sort of person seemingly. We had a two-and-a-half-hour fight, in the course of which I performed the duties of excepting and objecting or apprehending and submitting and suggesting and insisting, in a masterly manner, and at last I proceeded to "sum up" in a speech, Demosthenian as to eloquence, sledgehammer-like as to force, and twenty minutes as to length. Raised divers points of law, which the Court "took time" to consider, and came off highly pleased that I'd got through without any distinct flunk. . . .

May 5. . . . Went tonight to the Tabernacle, Timm's concert—Rossini's new *Stabat Mater.* Vocal part good decidedly, but no orchestra, nothing but Alpers at the organ, and that Tabernacle organ is no great thing. The finest thing I heard (they did not play the whole) was the aria and chorus—"in die judicii." They've made a great row of it. Walsh said it was equal to the best production of Pergolesi, Haydn, Mozart, and so forth—but it struck me as too operatic, just what one might expect from Rossini writing church music, or Tom Moore writing a tragedy. It's a very admirable performance no doubt, but I suspect when its novelty's gone it won't be so much thought of.

John Henry Hobart's going to be married—one of the Miss Riggses;[5] both were at the concert tonight. Why don't he go the clerical celibacy system? I don't hold him quite so high as I did before. Confound it, it lowers one's good opinion of the clergy as a body to see how they snap up wives as soon as they've the opportunity. I suppose there is some strong temptation when one falls in with a pretty and sensible woman that proves too much for one's prudence, philosophy, love of comfort, and self-respect, but I've made up my mind to be an unflinching misogamist and *misogynist,* too, in the abstract, till I meet with my *beau idéal* of femininity. I'll put down a slight schedule of necessary attractions:

(1) Piety—and of the right sort—including admiration for the Oxford Tracts
(2) Excellent sense—firmness—discretion—talent for obedience, and submission to conjugal authority
(3) Amiability—agreeableness—good humor
(4) Personal attractions—A. No. 1—(I haven't talent enough for nymphography to describe them in detail)
(5) Good education—some literary taste—but not an atom of blueness

[5] John Henry Hobart, Jr. (Columbia 1836) was the son of Bishop Hobart; he was married to Miss Elizabeth Riggs in 1844; from 1848 to 1863 he was assistant minister of Trinity Church in New York.

(6) Music
(7) From $50,000 to $100,000
(8) No relations to bore one
(9) The entire absence of fault in every department not above alluded to.

When I meet the original of the above portrait, I'll review my anti-conjugal decision and consider the matter anew.

May 9. . . . I may as well commemorate here, while I think of it, that his Honor Judge Randall decided our great Marine Court case on Saturday, for us, so that's disposed of. . . .

Nothing very important going on today. The great race comes off tomorrow—what a crash there will be among the green ones: how the *cognoscenti* will diddle people tomorrow at that same Union Course. I've been asked to go—but I'll do no such thing.

Rhode Island treason seems to be going down—democracy at a discount—rights of man below par. What a tempest in a teapot it has been! It's only a pity that things hadn't got a little hotter, that there hadn't been a little heading and hanging there among the apostles of liberty, a few Hampdens martyrized with a knot under the left ear—a pity because such a transaction would be good *per se*, and because it would add a certain romantic interest to our history which as yet it don't possess. It would create a few historical associations for the benefit of our natural scenery, which it wants badly.

Prex [President Duer of Columbia] has resigned, poor old soul. He never got over the effects of the severe illness that he was attacked by a year ago. It shattered him, body and mind, and he hasn't been able to fulfil any of the duties of his office for a long time. All sorts of ridiculous resolutions have been passed on the subject by the students, societies, and so on. Who'll be the successor? Mack? I thought he'd have it, of course, but I know that one of the strongest of the trustees has come out dead against him. Next to him, perhaps Verplanck stands best—if he'll take the place. Wainwright wants it—but he won't get it. Seabury is talked of by some. He stands no chance, I fear, but I wish I were a trustee that I could make fight for him. . . .[6]

[6] Professor McVickar was made acting president for the second time, and was again passed over when the election came. Gulian Crommelin Verplanck, grandson of a Columbia president and graduate of the college (1801) at fourteen, lawyer, litterateur, and Congressman, would have adorned the office. Dr. Wainwright was then incumbent of St. John's Chapel; he became provisional bishop in 1852. The Rev. Samuel Seabury was editor of *The Churchman* and rector of the Church of the Annunciation. Nathaniel Fish Moore, former professor and librarian, was elected president on August 1.

May 10, TUESDAY. All New York went to the Union Course this morning to see the great race between Boston and Fashion. People came on from the East and the West and from all quarters to see the fun—some came from New Orleans. I don't know whether Polynesia was represented or not. The North triumphed. Fashion was victorious. . . .

Saw little Charles Edward Strong this morning. He is at Amherst College. Rather pleased with him—though he has rather too much assurance in his composition and hasn't quite done sowing his wild oats yet. But I'm sorry for the poor fellow, for he labors under certain misfortunes and disadvantages which he had no share in bringing on himself.

I hear, by the way, to my great comfort, that Appleton's book buyer has picked up a copy of Chapman's Homer for me in London. I've sent for it near a dozen times without success. It'll be a month or two, though, before it comes.

May 11. . . . Played a game of chess with Walter Cutting (tonight was his and John Weeks's *last* exam) and then walked uptown. Alarm of fire. Being a donkey, I started in pursuit of the fire—being a donkey peculiarly and unprecedentedly deficient in common sense, I went off on a run. Of course I was sure it was on the *next street* all the way, and the result was that I found myself at last somewhere in Rivington Street in the midst of the largest swarm of soaplocks and rowdies that ever I witnessed. Couldn't get near enough to the fire to take in the "Coop de Eel" but it was rather a clever performance apparently, though being a chair manufactory, or some such flashy subject, the composition was rather too florid to suit my taste. . . .

May 17. Heard De Bonneville lecture on mesmerism tonight at the Society Library to a rather slim house. His lecture was fair, candid, and rational, but he labors under the difficulty of talking shocking bad English and is rather deficient in the bumps of perspicuity, connection, *lucidus ordo,* and so on.

After the lecture was over Post and Mead and I had some talk with him. Found him a pleasant, gentlemanly person, enthusiastic enough as to Animal Magnetism (and disinterestedly so, it would seem), and made an appointment for tomorrow to witness experiments on ourselves.

May 18. Quite summerish—ice cream and soda water looking up— sherry cobblers in great demand.

They are painting No. 56 [Wall Street] and I do believe that the owner of the fee had chosen the most *stinking* paint that he could find, either because it's the cheapest, or else to make it an object with the tenants to keep the walls as nice as possible and postpone a repetition of the nuisance. . . .

May 21, SATURDAY.   I was in an execrable state all yesterday—headache and "nausea," as Post says. I only wish I could put the woeful countenance with which he says it on paper. . . .

Felt somewhat better this morning, but the first breath of the paint shop set my head aching again. Went out in a hurry and didn't come back again. Went to Post's office and found that Lorton was going to operate on the juvenile patient who displayed such brilliant powers on Saturday. He did so with entire success, and the result is that I'm convinced from what I saw that mesmerism is no humbug. At least so far as this: that the power exists, by the will and the magnetic passes, of throwing people into an unusual and what may be called an unnatural state, different from any other that I'm acquainted with. The experiments we tried in clairvoyance were not perfectly satisfactory, though there were some answers given rather startling.

This was more satisfactory than Peale's exhibitions. There was nothing like collusion here, and there was always an unpleasant suspicion of some systematic humbug in Peale's performances. In short, as far as it went, it was to my mind conclusive. . . .

May 23, MONDAY. . . . Governor Dorr has absquatulated—and the Rhode Island Treason has busted its b'iler. That news is perfectly stale now—so there's no use in expatiating on it.

May 24.   Heard *David* tonight. I could hear some of those choruses twice a day for a month without tiring. It was pretty well performed, to a shocking slim house. The solo parts were vile. David was well enough, but his voice cracked whenever it reached a certain altitude; Goliath's voice was like that of a suffocating cow—such a voice as Goliath might have had if he'd stayed at home and lived to grow pursy and fat and rather asthmatic.

May 26.   Saw Post. He has several important doubts. Mount's boy has been magnetised again and is decidedly clairvoyant. Post thinks, but won't be positive, that the d——l's unchained and is at the bottom of the whole science.

Confound Appleton. I wish he'd make my Chapman arrive. I wish he'd get his old books out of the Custom House. I wish several other things: that they'd go ahead faster with Trinity Church (they're beginning to work on the *second* south wall now), that they'd make Seabury president of Columbia College, that I had ten millions to found a prodigious cathe-

dral in the city, and as much more to set up Columbia College and the
Theological Seminary and two or three minor colleges into a big university about fifteen miles out of town, with a senate house and a public
library—and proctors and fellows and a chancellor and head of houses
and all that sort of thing. Wouldn't it be grand!

Walked uptown with Anthon tonight. Stopped at Contoit's and
called for Roman punch. Was presented with a vast gallon tumbler half
full of frozen lemonade and half of Jamaica rum—such stuff I never put
into my mouth before. . . .

June 8, WEDNESDAY.   The paternal *hors du combat* today, and Esculapius called in to settle whether gout or tight boots were at the bottom
of the trouble. He pronounced it stomach, as he does everything. I believe
that if I were to tumble off St. Paul's steeple and be brought home in ten
pieces, he'd say "the stomach is at fault" and add that there was a little
febrile irritation. However, the event bore him out in this case, for an
emetic of ten horse power being administered, the pain in the foot disappeared. I believe I'll doctor my corns on analogous principles. . . .

June 10.   Well, there's nothing new except Contoit's strawberry
ices, which are superlative. How much I've lost in not having known
them before—and if ice cream were brandy and water, what a drunken
dog I should be! . . .

June 28, TUESDAY. . . . Rhode Island is in a state of ever-increasing
ebullition—martial law proclaimed, armies mustering, and all that sort
of thing going on faster and faster. There must be a speedy collision,
and like enough tomorrow will bring news of it. As to the rebels, not
even an abstract democrat of the most mobocratic views can sympathize
with them, for they're seeking not suffrage but plunder, they're literal
anarchists, acknowledged banditti, chiefly gathered from the bullenders
of this city of blackguards. The city ought to send on letters rogatory to
Governor King, praying that no quarter be given the scamps—they don't
deserve any better—and we should be rid of a few of our supernumerary
vagabonds. I don't believe they can do anything; yet the boldness of the
attempt makes one suspect that they've not shown their hand yet. If
there be *not* anything behind to better their prospects, they must be a
most reckless set.

Col. Webb's duel with the Hon. Tom Marshall[7] came off on Saturday;
the reg'lar army was bored through the calf of the leg. Pity they hadn't

[7] Thomas Francis Marshall, Representative from Kentucky, was the nephew of
Chief Justice Marshall.

made a Kilkenny cat affair of it and eaten each other up all but the whiskers. Each would have deserved a cenotaph at the public expense for ridding the public of a nuisance. Moreover, the Croton Water is slowly flowing towards the city, which at last will stand a chance of being cleaned —if water *can* clean it. . . .

June 29. . . . So Governor Dorr has run away again—fairly absquattled—sword and all. Well, if there ever was in the whole course of human events a transaction utterly and unutterably ridiculous and silly and despicable, it has been this same Rhode Island Rebellion. Such a pair of signal flunks never were known before. If I were a Rhode Islander, I'd expatriate myself in disgust, I wouldn't degrade myself by belonging to a state that can't get up better rebellions than that. After all the fuss and preparation, hourly bulletins and as much parade and row as there was in Paris when Napoleon was coming back from Elba—the hostile forces onset, and the rebels run away, killed, or wounded—one man in the cartridge box. I heard some story, however, of a citizen soldier among the constitutional forces, "when nearing the enemy," having, in a sudden fit of frenzy occasioned by the novelty and excitement of his situation, turned short round upon his lieutenant and, without provocation, from sheer nervousness and desperation, shot him in the rump. If so, there has been blood shed at Chepachet, and the affair rises a little in dignity. And what can be expected from such a little state? If it were all to sink in the earth, one would be puzzled to find the hole.

As to Dorr, I trust he'll be hanged up by the neck, though that isn't equal to his deserts. He ought to be put in a bag and carried around the country for exhibition first. I'd give a shilling myself to see the man. . . .

August 1, MONDAY. . . . There's nothing new in town, except the Croton Water, which is all full of tadpoles and animalculae, and which moreover flows through an aqueduct which I hear was used as a necessary by all the Hibernian vagabonds who worked upon it. I shall drink no Croton for some time to come. Post has drunk some of it and is in dreadful apprehensions of breeding bullfrogs inwardly.

Talking of Post, he and Anthon have formed a *copartnership*—a rum concern 'twill be. But it was very clever of Post to make the offer, for Anthon would have cut the law in a month if he'd set up alone.

As to other news—there's the death of the Prince Royal of France, a sad event for the nation. Louis Philippe can't probably stand the wear and tear of governing such a people much longer, and then will come a regency, and then a revolution—if for no other reason but because everybody expects one. . . .

August 10, WEDNESDAY. . . . I'm going off in the plenitude of my folly to Deal tomorrow. You don't know where Deal is? (This by way of parenthesis, to my literary executor.) I don't either. It's somewhere near the Atlantic Ocean, between this and Cape Sable. I'm to put myself on board some steamboat or other tomorrow morning, tho' I can't find out at what hour, and trust to good luck or to bad luck to bring me there. All I know is that Mr. Binney and Julia Johnson are staying there and that I've been fool enough to stipulate to go to the place. Well—that I shall find it a bore I'm sure. But if I do, I shall abbreviate my visit. . . .

Another veto message from the old veto-grinder Tyler the First. The Tylerites are firing guns in the park tonight and the Whigs say they'll do something dreadful. What—*non constat*. What can they do? It's of no use to legislate. After all, I believe Congress right in this matter. . . .

So Moore is President of Columbia College. Poor McVickar will cut his throat with that everlasting paper folder of his, and Bull will abdicate, or die a natural death by explosion most inevitably. I think it's a very fair appointment.

August 18, THURSDAY. . . . I went to Deal on the 11th and returned with Julia on Monday. On the whole I spent my time pleasantly, for I had pleasant company, to wit, Mr. and Mrs. Binney, Julia, and one of Mr. B's sisters whom I don't think I ever saw before—a very nice person. Then there was the beach and the surf and the bathing, which last was grand. . . .

September 17, SATURDAY. . . . Since my last journalizing I've been going up and down between Flushing and New York with exemplary precision, so there's not much to chronicle. There's been a most special piece of brutality just played off in Westchester County—that's the last piece of news—that somebody ought to swing for, though nobody will; to wit, a prize fight that terminated at the 120th round with the death of one of the parties, not by any chance blow, but by sheer exhaustion and suffocation. I only wish I'd had the old *Fulton*, with seven Paixhan guns mounted, loaded with a bushel of grape each, one to rake each steamer as it came up and then one hollow shot for each gun, to sink them one after another. It would have been a great public benefit.

I got into an awful scrape last Sunday—was seized upon with force and arms and violently abducted to Douglass's to dine with six young ladies. A capital dinner it was; the champagne was unimpeachable and everything was just right. But a dinner of live horse flesh with a club of Mant-chou Tartars would have been as much to my taste. One of them was a most particularly pretty girl, by the way, (not the Mant-chou Tartar, but the sixth young lady). But what's that to the purpose? I felt like a great he-bear. . . .

September 23, FRIDAY.   Settled down at last. Home for a season. Let me take a retrospective review of the events of the last few days:

Left for the Yankee Metropolis Saturday afternoon in the *Cleopatra*. Beautiful evening, and I smoked cigars on deck during the greater part of it. They burn anthracite coal on board that boat—it's dangerous but cheap, and that's the main point. I didn't like it a bit, for we went off at near twenty miles an hour (we were abreast of the *Oldfield* at eight o'clock), and with two great flickering, waving streams of pale yellow fire pouring out of flues it looked downright awful. One passenger, a fat man in a cloak, wanted me to join him in getting up a meeting of the passengers to expostulate with the captain and, I suppose, to depose him if he wouldn't accede to our views, but the plan didn't strike me favorably.

Into Norwich at half-past two, and at 56 Boylston Street at eight. Everything very comfortable. Haskey at boarding school; the others in great health and spirits, with a healthy appetite for mischief. *Monday*. Walked about Boston with Eloise. Went to the Athenaeum—some clever pictures there. *Evening*. Went to bed in a fearful rage with a sore throat coming on. *Tuesday*. Perfectly used up with a tremendous cold. Took a drive nevertheless, and a very pleasant one considering, with Eloise and James Lloyd and Master George, to see Haskey at school. He's improved. Went to Mt. Auburn. It's getting too full—looks cockneyish. Nearly all the monuments are in shocking bad taste. . . . Left on Wednesday and got in yesterday morning.

September 25, SUNDAY.   Took a walk uptown. Looked into Union Square. I find the fountain there is to be, as well as one can judge from its present appearance, just like that in the Park, viz., a circular basin with a squirt in the middle, and nothing more. A squirt of three or four inches in diameter and rising fifty or sixty feet will be a pretty thing, but we ought to have one or two fountains, at least, like those we commonly see in pictures, where the water is carried up nearly to its greatest height in a pipe and then falls from two or three basins successively. . . .

September 26. . . . Yankee Sullivan is arrested. They've got now several of the leaders in this beastly prize fight arrested, and there ought to be some examples made. . . .

September 30. . . . My new shelves were put up yesterday. They're not full yet by any means. But they'll fill soon enough, I dare say. Bibliomania is a kind of constitutional disease with me—I've been subject to it almost as long as I can remember. I should like to be able to bequeath a library of about 12,000 printed books and 1,000 MSS. to the Theological Seminary.

October 1. . . . I'm afraid they're going to make a couple of horrid monstrosities out of those two fountains. . . .

October 4, TUESDAY. [Columbia] Commencement at the Middle Dutch Church. Never saw such a crowd in the course of my life. Moore was inaugurated—i.e., Peter A. Jay made an inaudible address and Moore an inaudible reply. They might have sung a comic duet without the audience being aware of the fact. Then the ordinary exercises commenced and went forward much as usual. . . .

A chap named Hewit was Greek Salutatorian, an individual described as "Kernochan" Latin.[8] The speeches, so far as I heard them, were just as good as usual—and no better. . . .

October 5. . . . Went to Columbia College after tea to hear the address before the Alumni delivered by Hugh Smith; a frightful bore it was— horrid, long, and sensible, and prosy. If it had been any ways absurd it would have been most tolerable; but as it was, I never listened to such a monotonous string of stupid truisms in my life.

I resigned the treasurership, declined the flattering prospect held out to me of a reëlection, and maliciously suggested Chittenden to G. G. Waters. He was nominated and elected with the usual degree of enthusiastic unanimity.

Saw Jemmy Renwick. He says the two fountains are going to be no great shakes: "My son offered a plan which was declined."

October 6. Fine weather. Saw Chittenden this morning. He suggested the vast advantages that would accrue to me from Odd Fellowship, in which he's wrapt up heart and soul at present. I'll see him and the rest of the fraternity hanged before I'll dirty my fingers by any connexion with the concern. I don't like it on a great many accounts; and if there was no other objection to it, I don't choose to swear brotherhood and form some mysterious connexion or other with a gang, nine-tenths

[8] William Seymour Kernochan, Harvard Law School '44, became an attorney in New York and died in Paris in 1904. The "Hewit chap," Abram Stevens Hewitt (1822–1903), iron manufacturer, Congressman and mayor, was for many years one of New York's most distinguished citizens.

of whom are probably heretics and the other tenth infidels. The object is to form an union for assisting distressed brethren, educating their orphan children and doing all sorts of good among themselves. And the Church —if its principles be but carried out as they should be—is quite union enough for that or any other purpose. I'll have nothing to do with any of these self-created substitutes, whether they call themselves Temperance Societies or Odd Fellow lodges. What the present age seems to want is to get by voluntary societies and unauthorized and unchristian (if not anti-christian) means and devices at the temporal and visible benefits for which, among other things, the church was instituted—which she ought to be effecting now, and which in former days she did effect, and to do so without what their devisers call bigotry, priestcraft, and superstition. . . .

In short, I'm strongly inclined to think that the I.O. of O.F., with all its humbug and frippery, is intended to be—and seriously expected by many of its brethren to become—a sort of cheap substitute for Christianity, and I won't touch it.

October 7, FRIDAY.   Left this morning for Lloyd's Neck. Had a decent time enough, considering what a miserable affair the Long Island Railroad is. Dined at Huntington and reached the Neck at half-past three. Spent the afternoon in walking about, rambling in the direction of Underwood.

The country is very beautiful just now, as much in its way as later in the season, though the coloring is not so brilliant. All the woods are in full leaf yet, but there's a warm, mellow, golden tint upon them like the effect produced by a sunset just after a light summer shower—only here and there some tree about to yield before its brethren varies their foliage with crimson or deeper gold. The woods on West Neck with the afternoon sunlight streaming on them and their colors reflected in the still water, and all seen through the hazy quiet Indian summerish atmosphere, looked the perfection of autumn scenery—more to my taste than the splendors that will take them a fortnight hence. . . .

October 11, TUESDAY. . . . Went away up into the Sixth Avenue this afternoon and made some enquiries successfully, and thence walked up to Union Square where the new fountain was playing. I saw that in the Park in full blast this morning. They're splendid, both, the latter looked magnificent with the sun streaming on it. I hope they'll play permanently. . . .

October 14.   The great day of the Croton Celebration. Not much done in Wall Street, of course; all the population of the city, and of the

surrounding country too, I believe, seemed to have precipitated itself
bodily into Broadway at about ten o'clock. Never saw the street so
crowded.

The procession was mighty fine. There was no end to the military
men, including Giles Hillyer and the Wards, so stuffed up that their arms
looked like the inverted antennae of some strange insect—no end to the
firemen and their red shirts, nor the Temperance Societies. On the whole
it was much like the generality of these great civic processions; just the
usual amount of clap-trappery and stuff and humbug and rowdyism.
Rowdyism dressed up and exhibiting its grandeur to the public is very
amusing.

October 15. That fountain in the park is beautiful—I've changed
my mind now, and hope most sincerely that they'll not interfere with its
simplicity by any additions, statuary or otherwise. If they try to improve
it they'll be sure to spoil its effect as far as they can by some monstrosity
or other. A simple basin of marble only just high enough above the water
to conceal the iron work might be well enough, but tritons or neptunes
(in fresh water) or "Knickerbockers" (in a shower bath) or sea nymphs
(in the Park) or any such stuff will be calamitous.

November 8. . . . Been reading Dickens's *American Notes* today: clever,
light stuff, with some good things in it, in his best style.

November 14. . . . So the Governor has refused to pardon Colt or
commute his punishment. Rightly I think; but it's a horrid thing to hang
a man. His friends are getting up another petition, but I greatly doubt its
success, after Seward has so far committed himself by his opinion to
reply to the former petition. So if Colt don't commit suicide somehow or
become insane (as Jemmy Graham, our immortal postmaster who delivered him the despatch, thought he would) or get a reprieve, he'll be
hanged on the 18th. At Graham's suggestion, he has sent for Henry
Anthon, to that reverend gentleman's great dismay. He said he'd have
nothing to do with Presbyterians, Methodists, and Baptists, and all that
tribe—that they'd nearly pestered him to death. . . .

November 15. . . . Saw George Anthon tonight. His father has hopes
of getting a confession from Colt, and a public one, too, but if one may
judge of the man's character from his conduct and his published letters, it's
a fruitless attempt. His friends are still moving heaven and earth to save
him and I don't think his case hopeless yet, though he himself seems to
have given up all hope.

November 17. . . . Colt is the all-engrossing topic. First there was a rumor, confidently repeated and believed by everyone, that he was reprieved till January, but it was unfounded; the Governor sent down another message which appears in the evening papers, returning a positive refusal to the request of that ridiculous self-constituted "meeting of the bar"—i.e., of thirty-six of them—that he be respited till the Court of Errors could pass on the question of the right of the aldermen to sit as judges.

The sheriff has abandoned the idea that he is not justified in executing the sentence, and as a last resource a special messenger has been sent to the Chancellor with a written statement from Colt's counsel, backed by a letter from Benjamin F. Butler and praying that the Chancellor will reconsider his refusal to allow a writ of error.

Poor creature. He's to be pitied, and if he knows of this last effort, doubly to be pitied, for the agony of suspense, of a faint, an almost desperate hope, a shadow of uncertainty, is added to his miseries. Yet he has indefatigable friends, and it remains to be seen yet whether the law can triumph over an array of persevering pleaders for mitigation of its penalties. I think it still almost an even chance that he lives through tomorrow.

Henry Anthon was with him today and is firmly convinced of his innocence. But it's clear that his sympathies have been most powerfully wrought upon. The sheriff asked him today to ask Colt at what hour tomorrow he would be executed; he could not do it himself, he said. Dr. Anthon did so, and Colt flung himself on the bed and rocked there in agony for a moment or two, and then named "sunset." I thought there was some limitation as to the hour.

It's a curious trait in the man's character that while he expresses himself with the utmost bitterness against the penny press, he cannot yet refrain from getting all the papers and reading them, his craving is so strong to know what the press and the public say about him. . . .

November 18. . . . This has been a day of memorable excitement and agitation, for it has witnessed the last act of the tragedy that has thrown everybody into fits every now and then since it began with that frightful murder. And the end has been worthy of the beginning and of the extraordinary character of the whole affair from its commencement.

Colt's second application to the Chancellor was met by a peremptory refusal to allow the writ of error, and as there was no hope of success with the Governor, his last chance was gone. From eight o'clock this morning the Tombs were literally besieged by a mob, blocking up every street around it, all assembled not with the hope of getting admission, but

to gaze eagerly at the walls that contained the miserable prisoner and to
catch what rumors they could of what was going on within them. All
over the city a like feeling seemed to prevail. The approaching act of
justice seemed to be a weight on people's minds, to be constantly present
to them, and painfully so, though very little sympathy, if any, was expressed for him and a reprieve would have raised a storm of indignation.
Indeed, the sheriff assigned as one reason why he could not comply with
the very ill-judged protest or remonstrance that Colt's counsel addressed
to him that he'd inevitably be lynched if he did.

Dr. Anthon was at the prison all the morning. He married Colt to
his mistress Caroline Henshaw, and Colt was as he has been since Monday,
deeply penitent to all appearance, and this morning or yesterday he
protested most solemnly to Dr. Anthon that he had no intention of committing suicide. At two o'clock the Doctor went into his cell; the execution was to take place at four. Colt himself prayed most fervently and
poor Dr. Anthon went into the next vacant cell and counted the minutes
till four o'clock. (N.B. *He was the last person who was alone with Colt.*) At
five minutes to four, the sheriff and Westervelt made their appearance;
the procession was formed (Colt had requested after Dr. Anthon left him
to be left alone till the hour arrived). They opened the door, and there
lay Colt on his bed with one hand holding a dirk which he had driven into
his heart and had the resolution to *twist* as he did it, to make the wound
more sure.

By a strange coincidence, the great cupola of the Tombs caught fire at
this moment somehow or other, the alarm was given, the cupola, made
of wood, was soon in a blaze, and the row among the mob outside reached
its height. They knew nothing of the suicide and thought it was an attempt
at a rescue—and it looked very like it, to be sure—though it was doubtless no such thing, or Colt wouldn't have sent himself out of the world
in such a hurry.

As to the suicide, when the rowdies heard of it of course they didn't
believe it—it was all a trick to secure Colt's escape—and I suppose that
there'll be a prevalent tradition among the vagabonds of the city for a
long time to come[9] that Colt's alive and all sorts of rumors of his being in
this place and that.

Well, my conclusions from all this are, first, that the sheriff should be
indicted for leaving Colt alone and unsecured in any way without searching his person and his cell, especially when the probability of his com-

[9] There is—1859. (Strong's note.)

mitting suicide was the common talk of everybody even while they were waiting for four o'clock, and such a result was expected even by the sheriff himself, for "as I thought" was his exclamation on seeing what had occurred. And no longer ago than last Monday, Colt had asked Macomb for a work on anatomy, and when that was refused, tried to pump him as to the arteries that could be most easily reached and which would, on being reached, produce the speediest death. And secondly, that notwithstanding, this is the best result for the community that could have taken place. Had Colt been hanged, there would soon have been a strong feeling of sympathy got up for him, for he would have protested his innocence under the gallows itself, and great use would have been made of the case by the silly people who are seeking the abolition of capital punishment.

I went to Post's office after dinner and was astounded to hear this story from him. Didn't believe it, indeed, till an Extra *Herald* confuted my *a priori* arguments against his views.

George Anthon didn't come. He'll be rather chop-fallen at this termination of the career of the penitent, contrite, sincere, innocent man who was to be legally murdered at four o'clock. And I'm really sorry for his father, who I know will be very much distressed at the event, his feelings have been so wrought upon during the past week. . . .

November 19. . . . Saw George Anthon this morning. His father is ill with distress and excitement arising from this horrid business of Colt's. He "fainted" on discovering what had taken place, was just able to reach the next vacant cell, and there he remained some ten or fifteen minutes unnoticed in the confusion, the fire having broken out in the meanwhile. And when he recovered his senses and heard the bells ringing, the noise and bustle within and the cries of the firemen and the mob outside, his impression was that the mob had risen and were storming the Tombs.

The affair's in everybody's mouth, and everybody seems really glad, relieved as it were, at the result. People would have been infuriated at his escape, but still they could not make up their minds fully that it was quite right to hang him. They knew an example must be made, for the security of life in the city, that Colt must die for the public good, yet they could not satisfy themselves altogether that he deserved to die, and so the public in its magnanimity seems rather pleased that Colt saved them the responsibility by taking it on his own shoulders. . . .

November 21. . . . Saw Dr. Anthon this morning. He's disposed to think that Colt was sincere in his penitence and expressions of right feel-

ing all through the week but was carried away by the temptation to
suicide when he found himself so near a death on the gallows. I hope it's
so, and I'm inclined to think it must be.

Read his notes this evening. Like them. He seems to have dealt
plainly with the man and to have done the best he could for him. No man
could have done more.

George Anthon was very mysterious and ominous this morning and
talked portentously of something that was to come of this yet, which he
couldn't possibly communicate. Feeling a little malicious, I didn't gratify
him by pressing my inquiries. Some mare's nest or other, I suppose.

November 22. George Anthon called this evening and we discussed
divers matters, among other things the standing topic, viz., John C. Colt,
and he mentioned some things that have come to light since his death
and which, if the inferences he drew from them are well founded, as
there's certainly some reason to think they are, make the termination of
the affair a blacker business than I thought it. The facts are certain expressions in certain letters received by [*crossed out*]—one from Colt: the
inference is shocking enough—that the man never abandoned his intention of suicide, not even during his intercourse with Anthon, and worse
still, that he was reluctantly *persuaded into it to spare his family!* This was
George's mystery of yesterday morning. . . .

November 24. . . . Spent the evening at home. Dipped into Chaucer.
The most delightful thing about his books is his love of spring, of green
fields, and flowers, and the song of birds, and of everything in nature
that's fresh and bright. He's a fine old fellow, and despite his crabbed
orthography and his diction of five centuries old, better worth reading
than very many of his more fashionable successors. I don't know whether
to think him uncatholic, as well as disloyal to the church of his time, or
not. Many of his cautious attacks on it are founded on the right principle
—an appeal to the primitive rule. But the fact is that it's more the temper
of a man's mind than accurate premises and sound reasoning, or even
existing abuses, that put him into a hostile attitude to the church, and
I'm afraid that if Chaucer had lived in these days he'd have been no good
churchman. . . .

November 25, FRIDAY. Evacuation Day. But it a'nt the evacuation
day of ten years ago—its glories have departed and nobody thinks about
it now. . . .

November 26. . . . Webb's sentenced to two years' imprisonment.
Now we shall see whether Seward will be able to sustain the reputation

he got by steadiness and firmness in Colt's case. It's more important to the public, if possible, that Webb should suffer for his sentence than that Colt should have suffered his. Seward can't interpose without directly contradicting the rules as to the exercise of the pardoning power, in his opinion in the latter case, and if he *does*, the blackguards on trial at White Plains for the murderous prize fight in September can come forward and demand impartial justice, and a pardon *of right.* . . .[10]

December 17. . . . News arrived this morning of a shocking affair on board the brig *Somers,* Lieut. Mackenzie.[11] A mutiny was discovered, it seems, headed by one of the midshipmen, Philip Spencer, one of John C.'s sons. He and a couple of confederates were arrested and kept in irons for three or four days, and then, as it was believed that the mutiny was not thoroughly suppressed and that a rescue was meditated, and as a large majority of the crew were thought to be disaffected, the three ringleaders were hung at the yardarm. Various opinions seem to be entertained as to Mackenzie's conduct, and no opinion can be safely formed till we know more of the facts. This much I think is pretty clear—that to justify himself, Lieut. M. must show a case of absolute necessity, that he cannot protect himself by setting up his authority as commanding officer, but must show that it was a matter of life and death for the officers and the well-affected part of the crew, such a case as would bear out the captain of a merchant vessel in ordering summary execution on some of his men. But I think this case will turn out to have been of that character, not only because it's so generally stated, but because Lieut. M., from all accounts, is a man not likely to act either in a passion or in a panic, and it's not likely that he'd take this step except as a last resource—that he'd assume such a very undesirable responsibility if he could avoid it. . . .

December 20. . . . Looked this afternoon into Longfellow's new slavery poems. Very fair generally, but the professor has done better. I fancy

[10] Colonel J. Watson Webb had been indicted in New York for his duel with Congressman Marshall in June; he pleaded guilty, and was pardoned by Seward two weeks later.

[11] Philip Spencer (Union 1843) was the son of the Hon. John Canfield Spencer (Union 1806), then Secretary of War and later Secretary of the Treasury. The *Somers* affair has many literary ramifications. James Fenimore Cooper, who had been engaged in a controversy with Mackenzie over the latter's published account of the Battle of Lake Erie, wrote a long review which was affixed to the *Proceedings* of Mackenzie's court martial (1844). *The Cruise of the Somers* (1844), attributed to Cooper, was probably not by him, but he did use an incident from the *Somers* in his book *Ned Myers* (1843). Lieutenant Guert Gansevoort, who brought news of the mutiny on the ship to Captain Mackenzie and was one of the investigating officers, was a cousin of Herman Melville, who late in life used the *Somers* affair as a source for *Billy Budd.*

these were written and published for the sake of defining his position and
not from the natural unsought impulse which alone produces real poetry.
The second of them is perhaps the best: describing how a nigger who
was a great potentate and a mighty man at home went to sleep, and how
he had a dream, and how he dreamed that his "dark-eyed" royal consort
was with him again, and that he was riding along the banks of the "lordly
Niger," and so on, and then how he died in earnest—and "Dat de end of
dat ole nigger long time ago."

The rest are generally stuff. It's a puzzling subject, this same Abolitionism; there is but one question involved in it: Is slavery morally right
or wrong? And that's a question which I can't answer.

The readiest answer of course is *wrong*—a national sin, and the future
parent of national curses and calamity. But the Bible and the church are
silent—and most unquestionably were there such moral guilt in slave-
holding as its opponents insist on, the primitive church would have
entered its protest against it and overthrown it with the overt corruptions
of the old world. Let it be shown that there are any indications even of
such a feeling in the remains of that period, and I will call myself an
abolitionist most gladly. But I'm suspicious of all the religious improvements of the nineteenth century.

December 22. . . . What shall I do to find some agreeable novelty?
Take to drinking? or to politics? or to amateur woodsawing? or to Society?
I'm getting to be a very stupid humdrum kind of character. I think I
should enjoy a whaling voyage before the mast. Is running away on some
scrape of that kind altogether impracticable? Alack, I fear so. I don't
know but I'll turn popular lecturer—that's fashionable now—deliver a
series of lectures before the Sixth Ward Library Association or the Com-
munipaw Lyceum on the life and times of Sir John Snooks, the History of
the Steam Engine during the fourteenth century or the peculiar features
of the farthingales of the Elizabethan era.

I shall gradually stultify myself into an inanimate block if I go on
without something to give a relish to the countless enjoyments that I
have now, but which a'nt enjoyments to me for the want of something
else—what, I can't say. If I were to go furiously into Society I believe it
would rid me of my bluenesses, but that I won't do. No matter, I think
I can rid myself of them.

December 29. . . . Had myself Daguerreotyped this morning. I tried it
yesterday, but for some reason or other they failed signally at every
attempt. It's a great bore—one doesn't know till he has tried how hard

it is to sit without moving a muscle for two minutes. I fancy that a like-ness taken when one was reading would be much more successful than any I've yet seen; a book would divide one's attention from the process and enable one to keep still naturally without any conscious effort. As it is, the portrait of a man staring intently into vacancy and striving desper-ately to keep still must be unlike his usual appearance.

Went to Niblo's after tea with Anthon to hear Horn's *Christmas Bells* again. It's decidedly a good thing—many passages remarkably neat and graceful—and I enjoyed myself highly. Mr. Rogers, the guitar man, made his appearance again with another patriotic song in the second part, like an insane troubadour, and was received with the same inextinguish-able laughter and the same uproarious applause as on the former occasion. The passages where he thumps the guitar and drums on the strings after an extraordinary manner seem to produce the greatest sensation. . . .

It was snowing when I got out at eleven and there was a great fire burning downtown, and never was anything more splendid than the effect it produced. The whole sky was lit up with a bright soft crimson glow, almost of uniform brilliancy. The snow reflected it back—streets and roofs were all tinted with the same color. It had a most magnificent and unearthly appearance. I was told the fire was in Wall Street, and started off on a run, expecting to find the office on fire and the old gentle-man wringing his hands in front of it. The snow was deep and my run soon subsided into a trot, and then I took the first cab I could find and came downtown. Found that the fire was on Water Street, five or six stores blazing, and a fine sight it was. It was the worst fire we've had for a long time. The wind was very strong at N.E. The engines were retarded by the snow—the hydrants were many of them frozen—and at one time the fire crossed both Maiden Lane and Water Street, but it was checked in that direction. The walls kept each other up for some time but at last one gave way, and then four or five large stores came thundering down with a prolonged roar that seemed to shake the ground, and the change from the blaze and brightness of active conflagration to smothering smoke and comparative darkness, only lit up by a perfect hailstorm of sparks and cinders, and then to see great masses of thick smoke light up as the flames rose again among the ruins and eddy round and sweep off before the northeast wind till the glare of the burning buildings was fully dis-played again, was very fine. . . .

1843

THE MILLERITE DELUSION · ARTHUR CAREY'S ORDINATION : VISITS TO ALBANY AND THE CATSKILLS · THE CROTON WATER CASE

The great events of the year 1843 in New York were to be the trial of Commander Alexander Slidell Mackenzie, captain of the U.S.S. Somers, for his summary execution of certain alleged mutineers—Mackenzie being defended by George Griffin; the visit of President Tyler to the city on his way to the Bunker Hill jubilee in Boston; and the appearance of the eminent English actor William Charles Macready and the violinist Ole Bull before metropolitan audiences. It was a quiet year, for city and nation were again prosperous, Webster had exorcised the principal international difficulties, and sectional antagonisms did not as yet run high. On New Year's, Governor Seward retired in favor of a Democratic executive, William C. Bouck.

For some weeks Strong, who was kept drudging long hours by his office duties, had little of importance to chronicle. "I'm getting disgusted, misanthropical, and savage," he wrote on January 4. He thought he might be happy in some magical retreat of the sort pictured by Washington Irving—a cavern far underground, with a vaulted roof, a bright fire, a few ponderous volumes, and an enchanted ring by which he could call up his dinner or other comforts whenever he wanted them. "Marine court suits and verdicts with exemplary damages would never annoy one in such a blissful retreat."

January 2, MONDAY. New Year's Day proper. Cold, overcast, and occasionally snowing, to which comforts may be added that the streets are as slippery for pedestrians, and as hubby and dirty and perilous to those who prefer sleighs, as they well can be. Heard of six tumbles

[197]

among the former class, and saw one grand jettison befall a party of the latter. It was very fine—cloaks and buffalo robes and three or four well-dressed bipeds all rolled out of the sleigh in a confused conglomeration, their hats rolled into the gutter, and horse and sleigh vanished up the street.

I paid no visits. Went to the office and enjoyed myself, smoked and read and did up one or two small matters. Perhaps, though, to be candid, it was a little dull at the office this morning; and I certainly did think once or twice that if I had only got fairly under way in my career of calls I should enjoy the process, hard as it might be to start, more than sitting there over Betts's *Admiralty Practise.*

If I could have more favorable accounts of the tone of society, I think I'd try the experiment of going into it a little. But it's too bad. For instance, there's one place where if I visited at all I would be glad to make my appearance occasionally—they're sensible people, not very gay, and profess to be somewhat superior to the follies of their neighbors. Yet their intimate friends, near neighbors, and everlasting associates are certain ladies whom common rumors describe as among the most ridiculous, frivolous slaves of fashion in the city, living in and for the sake of society, belonging to a class that I can't tolerate.

March 6.   Mackenzie's court-martial is slowly progressing and they are trying to get up an indictment. (May they succeed; for if ever there was a case of cold-blooded lynching, that *Somers* tragedy was one.)

March 17. . . . Went to Madam Otto's concert tonight. I had an ugly headache, but the orchestra was splendid and the selection of music good, so I enjoyed myself rather than otherwise. Confound those two overtures, *Oberon* and *Der Freischütz*; they stick in one's head to the exclusion of everything else.

I wonder whether the other arts, when one's taste for them is developed, can excite the same feeling that music does.

The comet that the Millerites are in such a stew about shone out in great glory tonight. His nucleus was hid below the horizon, but his tail streamed up, a long riband of pale transparent light, like that of an aurora, from the horizon nearly to the zenith. The question of comet or zodiacal light is warmly discussed, but there can hardly be a doubt, I think, but that it's really a comet. If it be the zodiacal light, the respectable functionary has certainly placed itself in a new position before the public.

I believe I lost my pocketbook at that confounded concert. Either my pocket was picked as I came out or else I lost it in some inconceivable way

when I tumbled down in a slippery place on my return. It's rather a good
haul for the finder, though very fortunately I had taken out of it and put
in a safer place a roll of bills that I should have been disgusted at losing.
So much for French tailors and incontinent pockets.

March 21. Fine weather, but most unseasonably cold. Another
"sign," the Millerites say it is, and I suppose a most superb meteor I saw
on Saturday night was still another. It was a most beautiful sight, sailing
slowly down the sky, the meteor itself like a large ball of bright bluish
flame and the broad train behind it red and scintillating. It lasted nearly
half a minute, I think, and I could scarcely believe at first that it was not
some sort of rocket running the wrong way.

Wonder how these meteors are to be explained. They're somehow
connected, no doubt, with aerolites and moonstones, and my notion is
that the same variety prevails in the regions of space that we see on the
surface of the earth, that besides the vast masses of matter that constitute
planets and suns there may probably be myriads of small bodies shooting
about in the universe, *worldlings* in the literal sense of the word, perhaps
independent from the beginning, perhaps splinters of some big planet,
smashed by a mischievous comet. They may have their regular orbits,
or be erratic and dissipated in their habits, but at any rate if one should
accidentally come within range of the fascinations of this earth, down it
would come to its surface in the shape of a "meteoric stone"; if its sub-
stances should be inflammable, it would blaze into a meteor as soon as it
got within the earth's atmosphere.

Talking of Miller,[1] though—he ought to be locked up. Very few religious delusions have led to so many cases of insanity and crime as this
of his, of late years at least. But the ludicrous side of it appeared the
other day at Brooklyn, where a nigger troglodyte, an inhabitant of a
cellar in that city, was buried under a snow bank, completely blocked up
by a drift. On being dug out and restored to the light, he demanded

[1] William Miller, farmer of Low Hampton, New York, sometime captain in the
War of 1812 and deist, after conversion to Baptist tenets and an exhaustive study of
the Bible, concluded in 1831 that there would be a second appearance of Christ some
time between March 21, 1843, and March 21, 1844, followed by the end of the world.
He went about preaching this theory, with great charts presenting mathematical
proofs. Some fifty thousand people became converted, and as the fateful days approached there was vast excitement throughout the country, though the tales of
ascension robes and believers giving away their worldly property are not well authenticated. Although the world did not come to an end, Miller and a large proportion
of his following remained convinced, and there is still an Adventist sect.

whether "the end had come" and added that "he thought they'd forgotten dis saint altogedder."

Old Betts has decided that the civil courts have no jurisdiction over the *Somers* murder (we may as well call things by their right names). Confound him, I think his decision's right enough, but it's a pity that he should have accidentally gone right in this particular case. . . .

April 8. John Jay has been writing some very flippant and foolish articles in the *New World* about church matters and abolitionism. As he is possessed of but one idea himself, he thinks it queer that the church is not equally limited in its range and can't understand that it should have other objects in view besides that of educating gentlemen of color. Well, if a man has a penchant for niggers, he has a perfect right to indulge in it.

April 9, SUNDAY.   Fine weather. Heard "Orlando Harriman, Ju-nior," as poor old Prex used to thunder out his name on commencement days, this morning. Liked him much. He was brought over from Dutch Deformity by the Oxford Tracts and is evidently a thorough-going churchman.

April 11, TUESDAY.   The Whigs, if rumor be an honest woman of her word, are totally routed, notwithstanding the high moral influence exerted in their favor by my vote this morning. Never saw National Hall look more chop-fallen, and never heard Tammany more vociferous.

April 14.   Horrid rainy weather—a great nuisance at any time and especially at this present, for the erection of our back building was begun the day before yesterday and this rain is an effectual stay of proceedings. There's nothing of the building yet, by the way, but a vast and dreary excavation in the back yard, and if this cataract of rain don't hold up pretty speedily, we shall have a nice fish pond perhaps, but a very ineligible building spot.

April 15, SATURDAY.   Hawks has exploded.[2] St. Thomas's Hall has suspended payment. Just what might have been anticipated. Why will clergymen run into such miserable money-making schemes, leave their parish, neglect their legitimate duties, and meddle with speculations and projects, and blow up bubbles that are sure sooner or later to burst? For they never have worldly wisdom enough to secure their success. I cannot see any prospect of strength to the church, any hope that she can free herself from the liability to injury by such failures as this (for they

---

[2] The Rev. Francis Lister Hawks, rector of St. Thomas's Church in New York, had established a church school, St. Thomas's Hall, at Flushing in 1839; after this enterprise failed for $30,000, he found it expedient to transfer his talents to Mississippi; he was elected bishop there, but declined the office.

always do great harm), till we have an *unmarried clergy*—a little rank popery. Then, without children to leave wealth to and bring forward in the world, the clergy will live and work for the church *alone*. As it is, they can always delude themselves into the belief that such schemes as this of Hawks's are within the line of their duty. And then let us have monastic institutions in their full force and full vigor—vows and all. I'm strongly inclined to believe in the whole system as it existed A.D. 500. If they were "failures," so was the church. If celibacy exposes to temptation and has given rise to atrocious crimes, so has wealth, so has everything else.

Didn't go out tonight. Stayed at home and read: Shakespeare and Webster—*Hamlet* and *The Duchess of Malfy*. It's a curious psychological fact, but I'm just beginning to appreciate the matchless power of the former.

April 20. Nothing new except the news from England. Southey is dead. It's not much after all, for he's been morally dead for a year or two past. He was a great man, but his writings never will be popular; he never will take the rank, I think, in English literature to which his intellect and his attainments entitled him.

April 23, SUNDAY. The world was to have come to an end today— but, doubtless to the great disgust of Miller & Co., it seems to be going on at present much as usual. There don't seem to be any indications as yet of a demand for "ascension robes." It's so foggy and overcast that people can't even look out for "signs in the heavens."

April 25. . . . The *palazzo-vulgo*, the rear building, progresses during this clear weather, and I hope in the course of a couple of weeks to see it under roof. . . .

Came down to 108 with Anthon and then walked up with him to the Church of the Redemption, where they'd done us both the honor to elect us vestrymen. Attended to our parochial business very successfully. They are in spirits there, though there's still a pretty serious weight of debt to discharge.

April 28. Fine day, enlivened by the inspiriting cry of *"mor-tar"*— and the peculiarly cheering sound produced by the tapping of brick with a trowel. That is, the salon has progressed prospiciously, and Mr. Somebody Smith, the Vitruvius of Greenwich Street, thinks I'll be under roof in a fortnight.

April 29, SATURDAY. Went to the Academy of Design this evening. The collection is uncommonly good. Durand has two beautiful landscapes there, both purchased, I see, by the Apollo; [William Sidney] Mount one rather clever piece, not new, however. There's a really fine painting of Columbus brought home in chains—forget the painter's name, but it's the best thing in the room. Huntington has one good picture at least, and to go no farther, it's worth six of last year's exhibition. There's a deficit of portraits, though there are some severe enough to make it up. [Charles] Welford's there, Jonathan Miller, [Lindley Murray] Hoffman the auctioneer, Dr. Channing—unquestionably the face of a man of acuteness and habits of thought; the portrait gives one a favorable impression of the man's personal character.[3]

May 1, MONDAY.   Promenaded the Battery before breakfast. It's a fine bright May Day, but those who would celebrate it must go to their greenhouse for the wherewithal—unless they'll put up with green grass and budding dandelions. Either London springs are vastly ahead of ours, or Herrick and his fellows are addicted to poetic license, or to green spectacles. If his Corinna had turned out early to go a-Maying on the Battery this morning she'd have gone back in disgust to finish her nap.

May 2. . . . Tonight went to the [New-York] Historical Society, whereof I've been duly elected a member. Full meeting, Gallatin, the president, in the chair. It reminded one of Poole's antiquary in *Little Ped-lington*—with his disquisition of the antiquities of the ruined pump and his helmet of the time of Richard I, so strongly resembling a saucepan of the time of George IV. A letter was read from Crosby enclosing an "interesting Revolutionary relic"—breathless expectation—namely a button cut from the coat of a spy—I forget on which side—during the most momentous struggle. [John Lloyd] Stephens is trying to get up a great work on the Antiquities of Central America. Hope he'll succeed. The society resolved that they hoped so too—but subscribing for a copy at $100 is another matter. Got tired and came off early.

May 8. . . . Saw George Anthon this afternoon. Bull's in great tribulation. The trustees of Alma Mater are acting in a very eccentric way. Among other practical jokes of theirs, they've cut down all the salaries. I think the faculty had better strike for higher wages as the sailors here have been doing, and march up and down Park Place in procession, with Bull at the head playing on the accordion and Mack carrying the banner. As to the former, he of all men can't get along on half allowance, and for the latter, he'd resign if he could, but high moral positions are expensive

---

[3] The portrait of William Ellery Channing, the great Boston Unitarian leader who had died the previous October, was painted by Charles Cromwell Ingham.

luxuries and half a loaf's better than no bread, half a salary preferable to the New Workhouse on Blackwell's Island.

May 11, THURSDAY.   Went to the Hall after tea, to see the attorneys' examination. Found Anthon there and went—of all places—to the American Museum to see an instrument they have there, a kind of barrel organ on a large scale, the same, I think, that Maelzel had here years ago, in the times of the carrousel and the Conflagration of Moscow and the Automaton Chess Player. It plays overtures and so forth very nicely, and if the reed stops were a little better would give them quite effectively.

May 13.   Heard the *Messiah* performed last night, a selection from it, I mean, and most villainously performed, by the Sacred Music Society. The choruses were endurable, but the solo and orchestral parts most atrocious. . . .

May 16.   Nice weather to economize fuel in. Yesterday and today have brought all the indicia and appurtenances of July into full activity: straw hats, light breeches, ice cream, and open windows. How I wish I could spare one day for a country ramble, but it's not to be dreamed of. . . .

They say opium chewing prevails here extensively, much more so than people think. I know the consumption of it has greatly increased since the blessed Temperance Movement began. Nothing more natural— a "movement" of that sort never moved away the *principle* of any vice, though it may drive this or that development of it into the background for a while. . . .

May 17, WEDNESDAY.   Fine weather, rather cooler than yesterday. My villa, bungalow, *schloss*, *château* or whatever may be its appropriate name, progresses well. It's quite independent of weather now, for the roof's on and they're nailing up lath vehemently.

> In Greenwich Street did G.T.S.
> A stately backbuilding decree,
> Where clear the Croton Water ran
> Through pipes impervious to man—
> Up to the third stor*ie*.
> So *x* square feet of useless ground
> With fair brick walls were girdled round.

Errors excepted, viz., for "third" read—*meo periculo*—"second," there being no third story *in rerum natura*, at least not in the backbuilding, and the contemplated bath room being in the second. And for *x* read the correct number of square feet, which that unknown quantity is intended to symbolize, and which if inserted would convert a harmonious iambic dimeter into a choliambic pentameter hyper-paralytic with a "tail out of joint" like Pope Alexander's wounded Alexandrine Snake.

The bath room! *"C'est un notion magnifique—supairbe!"*. . .

May 27.   Looking into a desk [at the office] this afternoon in pursuit of certain stray papers, what should I find there but a "novel" of Paul de Kock's—I forget its name—one of the shilling publications that by their unexampled cheapness are going to give a new impulse to the present age, spread light and intellect and knowledge over the world, and so on. . . . Well, I had the curiosity to look through it and came to the conclusion that Dr. Johnson was perfectly right when he described the people among whom Paul is not only tolerated but popular as "possessing the manners (and the mind) of a dancing master and the morals of a whore": for the book is just as shallow and contemptible in point of all that constitutes literary merit as it is execrable and profligate in sentiment. And in *that* it exceeds any production that I ever met with yet. It's the first French novel I ever read and it shall be the last.

May 29.   If Quakerism brought such calamities to New England in the days of the "Pilgrim Fathers" as it does to New York in these times, I don't wonder it was persecuted and proscribed. My first thought, on waking this morning and looking at the dingy sky and the wet streets, was "the Quakers are in town"—and sure enough, they are so. There is certainly some occult sympathy, some mysterious relation of cause and effect between Yearly Meetings and northeast storms.

The weather is shocking bad. I think the Little Master in Fouqué's *Sintram* must have been one of the "people called Quakers," from his faculty of brewing foul weather. . . .

June 1, THURSDAY. . . . Bulletin from the palace. Floor laid. Encouraging symptoms of dryness about the "scratchcoat" and diagnosis on the whole decidedly favorable. . . .

June 4, SUNDAY. . . . The Common School election comes off tomorrow. The Romanists are going, it is said, to exert themselves, and if they do they'll probably succeed. Now, which ticket should one vote? It's not a clear case by any means. In the abstract, I prefer the positive errors of Romanism—or rather the system with its errors—to the miserable negative syncretism of the other side. But as a practical matter, considered in reference to the 5th of June, 1843, and the proper conduct of my very important self at the epoch, I think it's safer, better, and altogether more discreet to vote the Protestant ticket. For I believe Protestants are right in insisting on the use of the Bible in the schools; and notwithstanding Romanism is far more to my taste as a creed, or a theory, than Protestant-ism, there's very little to choose between them in their practical develop-ments.

June 12. . . . The Tyler made his triumphal entry today and was re-ceived with fuss and parade enough to make him comfortable, it's to be hoped. From eleven o'clock this morning till ten tonight everybody has been in everybody else's way, and everything upside down, and every-where except Broadway and the other streets along the line of the pro-cession deserted. I was at the corner of Wall Street and Broadway when the procession turned out. The crowd was considerably dense and the whole scene remarkably absurd. The grand army was out in force, and with the "Repealers" and the "Spartan Band" and a numerous deputation from the Rag and Tag and Bobtail formed the principal part of the pro-cession. Everybody stared at the President much as they would have stared at the Emperor of China and displayed about as much enthusiasm and good will towards him as if he had actually been that potentate.

June 14.   Been reading some of Fredrika Bremer's novels—the first I've sat down deliberately to amuse myself with for a long time. Like 'em—clever sketches—and now and then a really individual, tangible character standing out of the canvas; and independently of that, the tone of feeling throughout is quite unexceptionable. One fault, though, is a sort of Frenchified fondness for situations and surprises and effects that don't tell well in novels of domestic life. Domestic life: if it were such a rosy affair as she paints it, there'd be some sense in making an investment. It's rather comical, too, such a blending of passion and enthusiasm and purity and loveliness, with great practical talent for the darning of stock-ings and getting up of dinners. A full-blown angel darning a pair of pantaloons would make a very good frontispiece for any one of her pro-ductions.

June 22, THURSDAY.   Fried to death, nearly, and quite broiled besides. It's as hot as an oven tonight, and I'm constantly looking at myself in-voluntarily, to see whether I've begun to turn brown. But this weather's no joking matter.

And here I'm sitting—positively steaming and stewing—and afraid to open the window and let in what little cool air there may be stirring, for this murderous influenza is going about like a raging hyena, seeking whom it may—not devour exactly—but give a vicious clawing that leaves its victims in a sufficiently pitiable case a week or so. Never knew such an epidemic. I believe three out of four of my acquaintances are more or less unhappy from its visitation. . . .

I went to Albany on the 20th—left at five in the *North America*. Beautiful afternoon it was, and while daylight lasted the time passed rapidly enough. Lydig Hoyt was on board, and as evening came on he, as a newly-married man, only a few months old at least, felt himself bound to talk sentiment and to express various novel and original views about the self-sacrificing spirit, beautiful devotion, angelic ministration and all that of womankind, to all which I assented, and we talked at each other and it was very fine till we began to get very prosy and I fairly ran dry of variations and synonyms, when we reached Hyde Park and went ashore there. Walked the deck vehemently, smoked cigars and drank brandy and water to keep off the influenza, and thought I'd keep it up all night, but I didn't. Got tired and went below and took off my coat and tumbled into a berth. Couldn't stand it more than a couple of hours, tumbled out again and tumbled upstairs feeling as if I'd been used to make soup of. Found daylight just beginning to glow in the East and the prettiest possible moon shining faintly overhead. I never saw the moon at such a time before. It was a phenomenon. Walked about and watched the dawn as it brightened slowly—a kind of sunset backwards—another rare curiosity that was quite interesting to look at, and at last reached Albany. Not a soul stirring. Nobody else seemed disposed to leave the boat, but I was tired of it and marched ashore and found my way to Congress Hall by some mysterious instinct. All shut up and my ring answered first by a great brute of a bull dog that seemed, by the demonstrations he made, disposed to be carnivorous, and then by a somnambulistic waiter who showed me to a room and then, not having slept a wink all night, I found myself inclined for a nap and enjoyed one till breakfast time. Breakfast very good and I sallied forth refreshed, and from then till two o'clock there was an unspeakable chaos of fuss, fidget and dissension between Pruyn and Martin and Van Vechten and Ryckman himself and a gang of people that I didn't know. Had it all my own way, as I held the balance of power in my own hands, and finally at the earnest prayer of all parties came into an arrangement that I think will prove safe and satisfactory. Left in the same boat in the afternoon.

The run down the river as long as daylight lasted was exquisite. The scenery below Albany is tame to be sure, compared with the Highlands, but the beautiful wooded banks, with the fields undulating gracefully upwards in the background, the snug little hollows here and there with their quiet substantial-looking farmhouses and now and then a bright slip of meadowland, an island but almost a peninsula, with a group of tall feathery elms at one end and a little rocky hill at the other its original nucleus—all this in the light and shadow of a most resplendent sunset was very pleasant to look at. To look at a green lane now and then winding along the shore and consider where it went to and what beautiful rambles there must be in its course, and as it grew dark, to look even at a solitary light on the shore and wonder whether the people found it warm—and whether they were "up to" ice cream—and whether it was a pleasant family party or not—was quite an interesting occupation for a while, but at length the last faint glimmer of sunset faded behind the Catskills—it stood out till after 9 and then it grew rather dull.

Went below awhile. Read [G.P.R.] James's *Forest Days*—the old story made up after the receipt of the Knight of the Burning Pestle: "Be sure you call every field a desert and every horse a palfrey." Sad stuff, it seemed, but perhaps the strange compound of gases I was breathing made me obtuse. Then looked about the deck awhile—went through the imagination with a brilliant vocal and instrumental concert—but found myself growing sleepier every minute and watching the churning of the engine in a kind of fascination.

Entered into conversation with a man who told me he'd never been on board a steamboat before—rather an intelligent person, too, from Delaware county. Hitherto "father had gone down to York, but father was gittin' old." Such greenness in an enlightened American I'd never dreamed possible and I involuntarily felt my pockets, in doubt whether he wasn't a wolf in sheep's clothing, bent on abstracting my valuables. Had a curiosity to ascertain the sensations of the subject on first experiencing this novel kind of locomotion. He said it make him kind o' dizzy. Considering our nomadic habits as a people, I regard this person as a curiosity deserving the attention of the scientific world.

Home at last and after sleeping awhile and changing my dress I felt renovated. . . .

June 28. A dismal day. I heard before I got up that poor Aunt Jane Templeton had passed a wretched night and that Dr. Neilson had called before six o'clock and thought it doubtful whether she'd live through the day, but I wasn't prepared to expect such a speedy issue. She died at half-past eight this morning. And so, it's all over and a thousand quiet pleasant recollections from my earliest childhood till now are made mournful. How one's life saddens with its progress! There never lived a human being more completely made up of kindness and good will towards all created things, more watchful for opportunities of giving happiness. And poor Aunt Olivia! What is she to do, with no one now to care for and watch over as she did over her? . . .

July 2, SUNDAY. . . . They are in great trouble, by the way, at the [General Theological] Seminary. Two of the graduating class, a man named [Benjamin B. J.] McMaster and my old acquaintance Arthur Carey are accused of Romanistic tendencies and subjected to visitations and special examinations and conference and made the subjects of protests and resolutions and fierce discussions of every sort in the Board of Trustees. The former, I'm told by [John Ireland] Tucker, is a very excellent person but, it would seem, of the character that Paget depicts in the *Warden of Berkingholt*—one of those whom he speaks of as "full of crude crotchets of nonsense which they call Catholicism," etc. I only infer this, though, from some indiscreet practices and expressions of his of which I've been told and which may be distorted and exaggerated. He has been refused ordination, but on the plea of deficiency—unfounded, . . . and if so, it seems rather an unworthy way of getting around the difficulty. Carey's case . . . is still worse, since his difficulties are not those of a man run away with by his imagination and by an impractical fondness for the many excellent things that Rome has retained and which we can't at once recover, but the fruits of hard reading, unsettled opinions on certain points, I don't clearly know what. Whether he was ordained with the rest this morning, I don't know.

It's a very great pity: these are the men we want—ultraism, unless it's too ultra, is desirable in the church now, and I suppose it'll end in McMaster's going over to the Church of Rome at all events, and Carey's following him, in case he has not been admitted to orders in his own church. It is a very great pity indeed.

July 5, WEDNESDAY.   Returned from Lloyd's Neck this morning, having gone down *cum paterno* on Monday. Had a very agreeable time of it. Let me see, Monday afternoon we walked across to the Northside, chased woodchucks, investigated swallows' nests in the cliffs, had a personal controversy with a big snake, and met with divers other important adventures. Tuesday I started solitary and alone—had a grand ramble and a beautiful bath in the clear salt water, sparkling like so much champagne, on the north beach. Got myself fairly lost in the woods at last, tried all the points of the compass consecutively without coming anywheres and finally got home by some complicated process which I've unhappily forgotten. Then after dinner we had a grand sail in the *Sportsman*—with a nice fresh south-west wind coming through the West Neck hills in flaws and gusts that made us dance about after a very lively manner.

Left for Huntington last evening—saw nothing remarkable except a Temperance "tea party," "pic nic" or whatever may be the specific name of that cold-blooded variety of the Tea Squall. The attempt to get up the proper amount of enthusiasm and conviviality seemed discouraging. Occa-sionally two men would give three cheers very vehemently when some-thing striking was said or done—and some stray loafer just returned from Commack (where they'd been celebrating the 4th on *anti*-temperance prin-ciples) would wind up with a prolonged howl. But generally people seemed very cold-blooded. . . .

It appears that on Sunday at St. Stephen's Church, Rev. Henry Anthon and Hugh Smith read formal protests against Arthur Carey's ordination, and on the bishop's announcing his intention to proceed marched solemnly out of the church. In very bad taste indeed. They had already stated their objections to the bishop; he had called in eight presbyters (including the two protesters) and six of them had then reported favorably after a full conference with the accused at which the other two were present and in which they participated. Their protest, therefore, was not what I suppose the rubric contemplates—the announcement of an obstacle to ordination then first made known—but a piece of gratuitous, uncalled-for interference in a matter wherein they'd no more concern than anybody else. I don't like it a bit, and the dignified exit from the church was a piece of disrespect for which the gentlemen in question, much as I respect 'em both, ought in my judgment to be brought up. . . .

The Arthur Carey affair was important in Episcopal Church history since it brought into the open the controversy between the High and Low Church groups which had been going on for decades and had been intensified recently by the publication of the Oxford Tracts. Carey, a gifted, ascetic, retiring, consump-tive young man, was caught in the cross-fire; Strong had known him slightly in college, where he had been graduated at the head of the class of 1839. At the Seminary he had read and studied himself into a firm belief in High Church principles as Strong had done in his private reading. A bitter warfare of pamphlets and articles ensued, upon which Strong commented at length. Bishop Onderdonk incurred the fierce hatred of the Evangelical, or Low Church party, which was to result disastrously to him the following year.

Carey became assistant to the Rev. Samuel Seabury, but his health broke down, and early in 1844 he died at sea on a trip to Havana.

McMaster was refused graduation and ordination; joined the Roman Catholic church, and according to George E. DeMille in The Catholic Movement in the American Episcopal Church *(1941), "quarreled with Archbishop Hughes and Orestes Brownson, was jailed for disloyalty during the Civil War, and died an utterly discredited old man."*

July 9, SUNDAY. . . . Tried our new bath room last night for the first time, and propose to repeat the experiment this evening. It's a great luxury—worth the cost of the whole building. . . .

July 10. . . . Rather succumbed to the weather today—couldn't do much. Saw Cram and Anthon. Read awhile at the library tonight. Read an article by Mr. [Orestes] Brownson in the last *Democratic Review.* It don't come natural to praise anything in that review, but this is excellent; and slightingly as he speaks of "Puseyism," I shouldn't be surprised if he were to work himself into a strong churchman some day. Stranger things have happened.

July 11. . . . Must see about getting the bookshelves put up in my room tomorrow. I've altered my intentions in regard thereto, and propose leaving out the glass doors. They'd only stick in damp weather like this, and would ruin my temper irretrievably in six months.

July 15, SATURDAY. . . . I've led rather an amphibious life for the last week—paddling in the bathing tub every night and constantly making new discoveries in the art and mystery of ablution. Taking a shower bath upside down is the last novelty. A real luxury, that bathing apparatus is. . . .

July 17. . . . Mr. Derby's going to England on the first, to be gone for two months. The idea flashed on my mind after dinner that I might go, too, and for an hour and a quarter I luxuriated in it, walked through London, looked into Payne and Foss's, fancied myself gazing for the first time on Westminster Abbey, obtained a realizing sense of the first glimpse of St. Paul's and the Tower and Windsor and a dozen places beside, and imagined myself driving into Oxford on top of a big stage with the tower of Magdalen and St. Mary's Church and the dome of the Radcliffe Library and the pinnacles of All Souls and Christ Church College rising above the rest, and worked myself into an eager desire to push out of doors instantly and buy carpet bags and mackintoshes and patent pills to keep off sea sickness. But at last the thought of 56 Wall Street came down on me like a shower bath and the shadows fled away. If it were not for the disarrangement that my absconding would cause there, I *would* abscond most assuredly. Well, I must console myself by reflecting on my own personal importance and, on the other hand, on the discomforts of sea sickness. *Illi robur et aes triplex*, as the Ethnick poet hath it. "O what a row, what a rumpus and a rioting those folks endure, you may be sure," and so on. It must be a dreadful thing to go to sea.

July 19. . . . There are just two cool places in the city of New York at this present time, to wit, the Fountains in the Park and Union Square. As to the great pile of stones in the Bowling Green, it's the most calamitous failure that ever a public-spirited attempt at getting up something ornamental eventuated in. In the first place, it's a monstrosity that Renwick must have conceived in the inspiration of a nightmare—so hideous that the people who got up the subscription to build it are talking of another subscription to pull it down again—and what's worse, the sewer that carries off the water has proved too small and all the cellars in Beaver Street are inundated. One man had a cellar full of brown sugar turned into a cellar full of *eau sucrée* to the damage of the said plaintiff of $2000, and I shall send fifteen threatening letters to fifteen public-spirited tort feasors tomorrow morning warning them of an action on the case. I suppose they'll settle it— but at all events there'll be a considerable sum for them to make up. . . .

July 24, MONDAY. . . . Saw George Anthon tonight. Just back from Newburgh. Tells awful stories of the popular excitement there concerning the Ordination and the Protests. Hope it won't terminate in a No-Popery riot, or a civil war, or a Protestant St. Bartholomew's. It's a bad business, though, in sober earnest, I fear—not that the agitation of the enlightened public is a more serious matter than the disturbance of any other puddle in a gale—but I fear it may lead to action, to practical results of some sort or other, though I can't see very clearly what.

August 1, TUESDAY. . . . Got myself a perfect Bolivar of a meerschaum tonight—picked it up cheap in Chatham Street. It's a Paixhan among pipes—fit to solace the leisure moments of cloud-compelling, or "cloud-blowing" Jupiter Nicotianus himself. . . .

August 3. Very tolerable weather for the season. Mustn't encourage a querulous temper, but I should like it better still if there weren't so many mosquitoes. Verily I believe that the King of the Gallinippers held his court in my room last night. They're such a sagacious animal that there's no circumventing them. It's utterly visionary to think of seducing them into this room out of mine by opening the door and calling their attention to the light. They argue that somebody must probably sleep in a room with a bed in it and conclude to wait for their supper and take it in a comfortable way. Then they see in the dark, confound 'em, well enough to dodge all hostile demonstrations at least, for I don't believe there's a case on record of a man having hit one of them after the candle's blown out, unless he waited till the brute's suction pump was two inches deep in his cellular tissue, so as to operate as a detainer. . . .

September 7, THURSDAY. . . . This abominable damp weather, flooded cellars, and all that began to treat my books very unhandsomely this morning. Have forgot to chronicle the fact, by the way, that the greater part of them are in their new quarters, and an imposing figure they cut there, though their emigration was mournful. From their ancient seats "with sighing sent" they left the old shelves looking like the ruins of the Great Fire, or the Monasteries after Henry VIII cleared out their books. Well, this morning I found divers of them decorated with a mossy growth of mould, mildew, fungus, or some other vegetable production neither useful nor ornamental that would have made Dr. Dibdin perspire with agony to behold and the first glimpse whereof put me into a violent state of activity. Had a January fire of hard coal built forthwith and rubbed the books all off during the day. No damage done, I believe.

September 11. . . . News is there not much. Rumor that William [Colford] Schermerhorn is engaged to Miss C[ottenet], descendant of the Crusading Emperors of Constantinople. Matrimony is epidemic just now. There's young King, and—of all people—my amiable classmate Tom Cooper!—if newspapers tell the truth—married to some nymph of the Backwoods. She'd best keep her nails sharp, that's all. . . .

September 12. Fine weather, but dubious and uncertain, the wind sticking hopelessly at N.E. Saw Pete Strong this afternoon and we're bound for the Kaatskills tomorrow in utter spite and defiance of whatever may betide in the way of weather. I *do* hope it won't rain, though, for that don't tend to enliven a journey. . . .

Further matrimonial developments: little Lord—Danielissimus, or Daniel Minimus—the "juniorest" of the three happy proprietors of the name—is off after Miss [Mary Howard Butler, daughter of] Benjamin F. Butler. The epidemic certainly rages to an awful extent. All prudent men should avoid danger of infection, and if I find any eligible females at the Mountain House (on the hypothesis that I get there) I'll incontinently colonize myself and camp out on the most inaccessible peak (Hibernically speaking) that I can get up to.

September 18, MONDAY. . . . One can't put the Catskills into a private journal, but the expedition was too pleasant to be allowed to pass into oblivion unchronicled.

Very pleasant run up the river, Wednesday, and very comfortable drive up the mountain. Got to the house at seven, having opportunely encountered Sam Whitlock at the village. Hotel pretty much deserted, and no wonder: weather cold and dubious. Thursday: Rambled off with Pete to the Catskill falls proper and spent an hour or two loafing and loung- ing about the rocks and ravines. Be it remembered that the pictures one sees of those falls don't give one the remotest idea of their effect; and that even finer than the view of the falls from below is that from the little shanty that hangs over them, looking down the superb wooded ravine (through which the stream takes itself off) to the stately hills that form the back- ground: emblems of everything that's true and unchangeable, of the Awful Realities below and amid which the little noisy Stream of Life goes fretting onward and disappears. (Rather fine, that last sentence?)

After we got back, effected a breakneck excursion to the South Moun- tain and after dinner it rained, and Pete was disappointed of a coon hunt by moonlight whereon he'd founded great expectations and which he'd got up with the counsel and acquaintance picked up in the course of the morning's ramble, name unknown.

Sam Whitlock came up in the evening, and highly comfortable we were over a good fire with the rain and the wind making a row outside. Mon- archs of all we surveyed—house all to ourselves. Friday morning opened savagely, rain and wind reduplicated and intensified. We were comfortable enough though within doors. But at eleven or twelve o'clock the wind shifted and the dense mass of fog that had prevented one's seeing ten yards from the house began to eddy about and change to clear sky over- head and a tempestuous rolling chaos of clouds below that hid everything below the mountain.

Gradually they swept off here and there, giving glimpses of the river and of the landscape; then everything was invisible again. I never saw so magnificent a sight before. Sam and I adjourned to the South Mountain and there the sight was unsurpassable. One long and broad column of clouds kept constantly pouring round the foot of the mountain, in close order, like the march of an endless army, onward and onward unceasingly, while beyond the edge of the current of air that drove them on the dense masses of fog kept rising and falling and eddying about in every direction, sometimes banking up into great mountainous masses that seemed to rival the Catskills, and as they did so leaving little well-defined breaks or gaps in the cloudy covering of the lowlands through which, far below, we could see patches of bright landscape, like miniatures. In short it was the grandest sight I ever beheld. After dinner we took a substantial stage that could stand rough going and drove off to the falls again—couldn't walk it, for the "lakes" had risen about three feet and covered the road. The falls were in great glory of course, ten times the body of water that came down the day before.

Saturday morning, though, and its sunrise were about the most glorious sight I saw after all. All the low country was completely covered with a sheet of clouds, dense and fleecy and undulating like a rolling country, or like an ocean suddenly frozen in the midst of its highest rage and tumult; for they were perfectly motionless till the sun rose over them in a cloudless sky tingeing this sea of clouds below with all kinds of lights and colors, and then they gradually began to move off towards the north, slowly and majestically, not eddying about and changing every moment like their predecessors of yesterday, but floating steadily away with their grand and graceful outlines and proportions varying slowly as they went. It was inexpressible altogether. Pete had resolved to go down and had got all ready and paid his bill, but the splendid morning overcame his good resolutions and he stayed. It was very fine altogether. I don't know when I've felt so entirely happy as on that Saturday morning. . . .

Sunday morning. . . . took a walk to the falls. . . . Got through it somehow and got home at last. Found some visitors, among the rest that great loafer, Mount the artist. . . .

After dinner. . . . Pete and I put ourselves on board the steamboat and came down as comfortably as could be expected. And here I am! back again —among the "stern realities of life"—mosquitoes included. . . .

After the entry of October 2 there is a note, added subsequently by Strong, that henceforth—till October 1848—he was domiciled in the new rear building at 108 Greenwich Street.

October 8, SUNDAY. . . . So here I am, fairly established in great comfort in this, my new abiding place, with a long row of books—shelf upon shelf of the great and mighty of past days looking down on me. Health to the New Library. May it witness neither folly nor frivolity nor inaction; may it be the scene not of wasting and perishing faculties, of time passing away unimproved, of evil feebly resisted and the good and true gazed after in admiring indolence, but of a quiet and diligent and steady effort for knowledge and strength to fulfil the duties set before me, in all things to see the right clearly and to do it earnestly, and utterly to vanquish and overcome its deadly opposite that is ever seeking to paralyze and corrupt, to degrade and destroy. *Omnes insidias Inimici ab eâ longe repelle. Angeli Tui habitent in ea—qui nos in pace custodiant, et benedictis rua sit super nos semper. . . .*

October 20, FRIDAY.   *Nil* save a feminine irruption tonight into this, my peaceful retreat, which has just subsided. Its devastating progress may be traced in the chaotic disorder of my penates at this present writing—bookshelves especially left in great confusion. However, sensible women who can appreciate handsome books are not to be spoken of irreverently.

October 23, MONDAY. . . . Got in some nice books tonight and I'm better disposed to overhaul them than to potter over this journal. Can't even stop to chronicle Prof. Bull's last practical joke—and the biography of "Cromalibus Howitz, Bishop of Pulk" and his medal commemorative of the conversion of eighty thousand Turks and its solemn interment in the mason-work of Trinity Church steeple.

November 18, SATURDAY. . . . Felt as lazy all the morning as was naturally to be expected in such a state of weather; took tea in Murray Street and went with Templeton to the *First Philharmonic.*

Great crowd: all the aristocracy and "gig respectability" and wealth and beauty and fashion of the city there on the spot an hour beforehand. For myself, being superior to such vanities I selected the little side gallery where I could look down in a calm and philosophical manner on the splendors below, and especially upon George Anthon making very strong love apparently to one of the ——s! and upon Schermerhorn making himself generally ornamental, and Fanning Tucker trying to devise outlets for his legs and barking his knees on the bench next in front of him, and Mr. Wilmerding dozing off regularly at the soft passages and waking up with a jump at the loud ones, and so forth.

Beethoven's Symphony in A was the *opus magnum* of the evening. The first movement isn't very striking, though there are two or three brilliant passages in it; the second is extremely beautiful, and the third, the minuet, includes a long slow movement which is one of the most majestic and magnificent things I ever heard. The last movement is showy enough, but don't compare with what preceded it. If all the stuff about Orpheus and Eurydice tacked to the programme was even dreamed of by Beethoven, this last movement was certainly intended to be descriptive of Orpheus fallen into habits of intoxication and become quite drunken and dissipated and half-cracked in his efforts to drown his grief.

I hold this the finest symphony I've heard yet—finer than even the C minor; it was intelligible to me almost throughout, which I've found symphonies apt not to be, and it was well played except one or two difficult cadences in which the trumpets failed signally.

Then Castellan sang some trash or other—superb voice she has, but "very uncultivated" everybody says, so I suppose it is, though I didn't find it out. That ended the first part.

Then came the Overture to the *Zauberflöte*—very fine of course, but I never appreciated it. It was too classical and lame altogether to come between Beethoven and Weber. Then something or other of Donizetti's by Castellan, and then the unspeakable *Jubilee* Overture—encored, of course. The slow movement at the opening thereof is grand; never observed half its beauties before. On the whole I decidedly never enjoyed a concert half so much before.

November 19. . . . Walked fiercely uptown tonight—it makes one tingle to recall some of that music of last night.

Mozart is too artistical, it appears to me—too *Addisonian* and elegant for my taste. Except some of his mass music, I've heard very little of his that I could get up any enthusiasm for. But the man who wrote the "Gloria" and "Et Resurrexit" and "Quoniam Tu Solus" of the Mass No. 12 and the first movement of the "Dies Irae" in the *Requiem* is not to be lightly found fault with.

If I had to name the composer, though, whose genius stood highest in my estimation, setting Handel and Haydn out of the question, I think it would be Weber. Little comparatively as he has written in quantity— and little as I've heard of that—there are more passages in what I have heard that stick in my memory and recur over and over again and are untiringly delightful than in all the works of all other composers (barring the two H's) together. He has this merit in common with Handel, I think, that his greatest effects are produced by simple means—his finest passages are his least elaborate. I wonder whether he couldn't be compared to Coleridge, and Beethoven to Carlyle. There's the same simplicity and intense, deep, feeling in his music that one finds in the best of Coleridge's poetry. And for Beethoven I think the parallel is very fair—and I mean no disrespect to him by any manner of means.

November 25, SATURDAY. . . . Got in quite a snug little lot of books this evening—*inter alia* Hawkins's edition of *Ignoramus*.[4] His notes are

---

[4] George Ruggle (1575–1622), M.A. Cantab. et Oxon., wrote *Ignoramus*, a Latin comedy ridiculing pettifogging lawyers; Strong had a copy of the edition of 1787 with elaborate notes, glossary, etc. by John Sidney Hawkins, F.S.A.

perfectly admirable, the finest specimens of ponderous gravity, solemn absurdity and asininity in general that the commentator genus ever produced. "A late friend of mine (distinguished for critical acumen and profound research) informs me that his grandmother stated to him that she had on one occasion been told that the Hobby Horse, by a certain mechanism of the fauces, was made to produce the sound of 'snoop-snoop.' It may not be an unreasonable hypothesis, that if this mechanism were worked with an increased degree of liveliness and spirit, the sound emitted would become 'snip-snap,' which thing it is truly consoling to the critical reader of the Prologue to Ignoramus to reflect upon and know and inwardly digest, whenever his thoughts recur to the Hobby Horse therein brought before an enlightened public." . . .

This sort of scrap work—cinder-sifting—is only worth any thing at all, when facts are thereby preserved, which enable us in some degree to realize and understand past times and the great men of those times— when the times are worth understanding and the men truly great. One such fact perhaps compensates for its worthless tribe.

Wonder whether Posterity will treat us in the same way. If I thought so I'd be tempted to make my journal worth something to the Sir John Hawkinses of the twenty-third century—and chronicle small beer most indefatigably. Just think of the value of a minute detailed journal of one year only in the twelfth century!

However, what with novels and newspapers and magazines, the future investigators of the antiquities, manners and customs of the nineteenth century won't want my help. In all probability they'll be blinded with excess of light—and die off ingloriously from plethora and over-feeding on the abundant feast that we shall bequeath them and so the race will become extinct. Which is certainly one good effect that I never thought of before, of an enlightened Public Press and the universal dissemination of knowledge among us.

Just think of a Jim Crow Society for the republication of the *African Minstrelsy of the Nineteenth Century*—patronized by H.R.H. the Prince of Pottowattomy, and Field Marshal the Duke of Paixhan, Viscount Patchogue—or *Historic Doubts concerning the Protest of St. Stephen's*, dedicated by permission to his grace the Lord Bishop of Texas—or *Selections from "The New York Mirror," a "Periodical" of the Nineteenth Century*, with notes critical and antiquarian and a dissertation on the probable situation of its printing office and a biographical essay towards the life and military exploits of its supposed Editor—Published under the auspices of the

Webb & Bennett Society. One hundred copies printed for private circulation—or *Prize Essay*, read April 1, 2156, before the Tweedledum
Association of New York, establishing the identity of the Strong who
was professional adviser to the "Vocal Society" of Antiquity with Strong
hanged for murder in Albany by Lord Chief Baron Duer in the early part
of the nineteenth century—by Philalethes.

November 26, SUNDAY. Fine weather. Heard a good sermon this
morning from Mr. Higbee and *did not* hear a good one this afternoon
from Dr. Wainwright, for I had a toothache in a carious molar that
nearly drove me out of church. Tried to reflect on and take comfort at
Carlyle's "what difference does it make whether thou art Happy or
not?" but couldn't convince myself of the indifferent nature of the point. . . .

December 7, THURSDAY. . . . Not much today that's any wise new.
The *Acadia* hasn't brought anything to signify. Daniel O'Connell con-
tinueth rampant; the Anti-Cornlawites are still more and more vociferous
and belligerent: they'll carry the day sooner or later, I doubt not. It
can't be prevented—perhaps it may be wrong to try—looking at the unspeakable abyss of destitution and misery and starvation that's to be
effected by the result. But if they're to end in making England the seat
of a triumphant Mercantile and Manufacturing Aristocracy, that result
will make England hide her dim, discrowned head and sink a century
sooner under the punishment that her unquenchable thirst for wealth has
already made inevitable. Corn Law repeal will give temporary relief, I
think very likely, to the physical suffering of the nation, but it will give
tenfold energy to the causes that have produced that same suffering. It
will return in greater intensity and with the only aristocracy that can
inspire reverence weakened or destroyed, a church deprived of a strong
temporal bulwark—and Chartism and Benthamism and a dozen other
-isms in some new shape and a tyrannical upstart race of "merchant
princes"—there will be some very effectual ingredients for a hurricane in
the land. And then perhaps the air will be purer.

Let church principles triumph, and let the present aristocracy do their
duty, and the nation may live—the noblest empire the world has ever
seen; but another hundred years of shallow quackery, like the last, will
see results of a highly decisive character.

December 11, MONDAY. . . . Just got back from Vieuxtemps' first concert at Washington Hall—perfect jam and the audience wrought up at
last into a state of furor. He's by all odds the greatest performer I ever
heard; his mechanical effects are most wonderful: but I found very little

that I cared for till his last piece, and in that he certainly threw a feeling and expression that made the instrument almost speak and enabled me to realize the accounts one hears of Paganini's marvels.

Tomorrow the great fountain case comes in, and I anticipate a defeat —our evidence isn't as clear as it ought to be, and the enemy are wide awake. . . .

December 12. Those amiable hydraulic cases were to have been tried today but Counselor Griffin was in one of his accustomed fidgets, and after everything was ready—lists prepared and the combat about to be commenced—some misunderstanding as to which should be first tried knocked everything up and the cases were at last set down for tomorrow, with the understanding that ours is then to be tried. I suppose its result will determine both. . . .

Now for the fight tomorrow—Griffin and Lord are the champions— David and Goliath reversed, I trust, in the issue. The nymph of the fountain may be supposed to sit by in a white sheet while her guilt or innocence is determined by wager of battle. Two to one on Griffin and Bidwell. The "old red horse" and the Canadian Pony against the field.

December 13. Bitter cold day—the severest yet. In court all the morning. Got through with an evidence and opened the defendant's case before we adjourned. Our case came out beautifully—we worked it out much cleaner than I expected. The defense relies, I think, mainly on the point of law—the question of Wilmerding's liability under any circumstances—but whatever may be the fate of that question above, the court here is clearly with us on it. Vanderpoel overruled their motion for a nonsuit on that ground, very peremptorily. Besides that, however, there are various minor points that they're going to bring up with a view, I suppose, of muddling the matter as far as they can. They've a legion of witnesses in court.

Went to Ole Bull's concert tonight. Such a jam I believe was never known before; 4,000 tickets were sold and the Tabernacle was as full as it could by physical possibility be. Had to stand all the evening, though I was on the ground an hour and a quarter before the time—and very disgusting it was. Didn't regret it though, for he is a most transcendent player—far superior to Vieuxtemps. His harmonies are admirable, and nothing can be purer and more beautiful than his very high notes; they've all the peculiar quality of the sound of the Eolian Harp. In fact, the instrument loses its character entirely in his hands—the violin's the last instrument one would expect to hear some of his tones from.

December 14, THURSDAY.   Fine weather. Thanksgiving Day. Went to church this morning and heard a sermon from the Bishop. Went to the office. Had a visit from Counsellor Griffin who came downtown for the express purpose of talking *fountain*—and accordingly sat there for two hours propounding doubts, starting difficulties and imagining all sorts of impossible perplexities, always ending, "Now, my dear sir, what is the answer to that?" I played my part with exemplary gravity and decorum —sympathized, suggested, and made myself as serenely sagacious as I conveniently could on short notice—and the Counsellor listened to all my stock of erudition with great condescension. Seriously, with all the Counsellor's eccentricities, I've always found him very kind and attentive in listening to what one has to say about a case; he always treats one's suggestions, whether they're worth anything or not, with great respect.

Visit from George Anthon after dinner. Went to Murray Street and with Mary and Julia and Templeton to the great concert at the Tabernacle. Rossini's *Stabat Mater* was the first part—smashing orchestra— near seventy I should think—and a very heavy chorus—and Miss Flandin, Castellan, Antognini, and Brough for principals. It went magnificently, of course, though the orchestra was not very well drilled and rather overdid the matter. Antognini's splendid tenor solo was nearly overwhelmed— and the grand "In die judicii" chorus must have almost blown the roof off.

The second part was Beethoven's *Battle of Waterloo* symphony. What pleased me most in it was the lovely way in which "Rule Britannia" and "Malbrough" were brought out. "God save the King" too, with a curious accompaniment of hurrahs at intervals, went very nicely. On the whole the piece is a little inferior to what I supposed Beethoven would make it, but I've had Malbrough singing in my ears ever since—the effect that was given the simple old tune by that orchestra was spirited and glorious beyond all description.

December 15.   In court all the morning and again from half-past five till near eight. Testimony closed on both sides. They've brought out some very pungent testimony today that will tell heavily against us I fear—for though it don't really meet our case by a great deal, Lord will contrive to mystify the jury with it somehow.

On Wednesday I thought the case was won beyond all hazard but Nicoll didn't shew his whole hand in opening, and from the present aspect of things, the issue's quite a matter of uncertainty. Like enough the jury will disagree—though from the questions jurors have put I should incline to think them with us.

It a'nt much matter how they find, for we've exceptions enough to old Vanderpoel's extraordinary rulings on matters of no very great importance to get us a new trial for the asking. . . .

December 16.   Got a note from Griffin announcing that he was sick and couldn't turn out, so the summing up of the case of Croton Water *vs.* Brown Sugar was postponed to Monday. I've deliberated myself into a perfect conviction that we're entitled to a verdict there; whether we get it is another question. . . .

[Edward] Hodges [organist of Trinity Church] has succeeded at last in his stern chase after Miss Sarah Moore—they're to be married. How the Professor [Clement Clarke Moore] reconciled himself to the misalliance, as he was pleased to consider it a year or two ago, don't appear. He said then that he'd expatriate himself if it took place—fly the country—take apartments in one of the Pyramids, I suppose, like Peter Schlemihl when he lost his shadow. Hodges, from all I can learn, is a very worthy person and a good churchman besides—not to speak of his being a man of genius and a regular grand Maestro of the Prosy school—so I don't see that "the family" need give themselves any airs on the subject. . . .

December 18, MONDAY. . . . In court all day. Bidwell and Lord occupied the morning, till four o'clock, in summing up. Griffin closed this evening and Vanderpoel is to charge tomorrow morning. Bidwell's opening was a very good one, very clear, very minute, and covering the whole ground. Lord's speech struck me as not a very happy effort—terribly labored and not very clear. He relies mainly, I think, on the obstructions proved in the Broad Street sewer; that seems to be their whole case, barring the botheration they've raised about the main points of ours. Griffin's reply was the ablest argument I ever heard from him—in fact he has excited himself prodigiously throughout the case. It was clear and cogent almost to demonstration. I'm in doubt as to the result. There's no calculating on old Vanderpoel, and the jury have got a perfect wilderness of facts to deal with. I shan't be at all surprised at a verdict for the defendant or a disagreement. Well—we'll see tomorrow.

December 19.   Poor Judge [Smith] Thompson *is* dead at last; there seems to be no doubt of the matter any longer. Griffin announced it in Court this morning after old Vanderpoel had delivered his charge and the Court thereupon adjourned, leaving the jury to bring in a sealed verdict tomorrow morning.

Vanderpoel charged in our favor on all the law points, and then by way of impartiality, I suppose, reviewed the facts pretty strongly against us, giving a very undue prominence to several miserable matters of no importance at all that the defense had raked up. I was a little afraid the jury might disagree; but they have agreed, it seems—which way remains to be ascertained. For my own part I'm pretty sure they'll hand in a verdict in our favor.

December 20. We've come off victorious in the Fountain Case—got a verdict this morning for the whole amount—and it now remains to be seen whether we can keep our verdict, for they're undoubtedly going to fight it out to the last ditch.

December 26, TUESDAY. Elias Hasket Derby made his appearance this morning. He's made his appearance in the literary world by publishing in pamphlet form the letters[5] he wrote to some newspaper in Boston while in Europe last summer—transcripts of his notes apparently, for I've but just glanced at them—and no doubt worth more than many books of more pretension, for he's not a man to travel with his eyes shut. . . .

December 29. . . . Father and Mary left for Boston this afternoon, and from present prospects they'll have a pleasant journey.

Pete's grand soirée—party—rout—row—fête or whatever it is, came off tonight. Didn't go, though I was so badgered to be civil that I was almost tempted to rush to my artiste's and order a dress coat and resign myself to the worst. Walked past there tonight; most imposing aspect of things—house brilliantly lighted and the lights in the hall door reflected back by the pile of bricks on the other side of the street, crowd of three loafers and two watchmen gazing in awe and admiration on the scene. Pete and Jem within, no doubt, feeling that the great crisis—the decisive moment of their respective lives, the era towards which their previous existence had been but a sort of apologetic preface—had come at last.

December 30, SATURDAY. . . . Spent the afternoon hunting up New Year's presents—no easy job. Agreeably disappointed, though, in one purchase—a musical box that turned out after it came home to play some pet music of mine instead of what it was represented to play. . . .

[5] *Two Months Abroad; or, A Trip to England, France, Baden, etc.* (Boston, 1844).

1844

NATIVE AMERICAN RIOTS IN PHILADELPHIA · NIAGARA FALLS · OLE BULL · POLK DEFEATS CLAY · TRIAL OF BISHOP ONDERDONK

*T*wo *immortal books,* **Dickens's** Christmas Carol *and* William Hickling *Prescott's* Conquest of Mexico, *claimed universal attention as the year began; and it is interesting to note that Strong paid the same tribute to them as his fellow-diarist, Philip Hone. For a few weeks no great events claimed notice. Then came the horrifying disaster on the steam frigate* Princeton, *when a great wrought-iron gun, the "Peacemaker," exploded, killing the Secretary of State, Upshur, the Secretary of the Navy, Gilmer, and other men of note who had boarded the vessel for a short Potomac excursion. On the heels of this tragedy came the announcement that the annexation of Texas was contemplated by the Tyler Administration. The campaign of 1844—a campaign in which James K. Polk, the first "dark horse," faced Henry Clay—was soon begun under circumstances which suggested that a conflict with Mexico might be near, and that an intensification of sectional antagonism might follow it.*

January 1, MONDAY. . . . There seems to have been an unusual turn-out today; the shrines of Wall Street were left desolate for the ten thousand temples of womankind. . . . For my own part, I did no homage to Juggernaut. Went to the office as usual and worked away famously, wrote and whistled and chalked out a week's work for Deane. . . .

Read Prescott's *Mexico* this afternoon. Very clever book it is, and it can't help being among the most interesting of histories. There's a little striving after fine writing now and then visible that's rather a nuisance, but on the whole I like the book much.

[223]

January 5. Just got to the end of a visit from Pete. His chief and engrossing topic at present is the atrocious conduct of that ungentlemanly ruffian the Vicomte Bertrand at the soirée last Friday, where he had the cold-blooded villainy to call for a cigar and some brandy and adjourn to the kitchen to enjoy them. He's the Cesare Borgia of the nineteenth century. Well, if people will invite these fancy characters to their houses because they're counts, it serves them right to meet with a little cavalier treatment. People who look on their entertainers as low-bred republican *canaille* are apt to show it. . . .

January 6. . . . Read Kent assiduously on the delicate and inflammatory subjects of tenancy by the curtesy, reduction into possession of choses in action, and other collaterals of the *vinculum matrimonii*, exposing myself to that combustible course of reading mainly in reference to that amiable and amatory intestate Mr. Vyse, whose vicious old concubine is going to make herself as troublesome as she conveniently can and will probably try to make herself a dowager by brevet, prove herself a widow by prescription, or kind of post mortem Mrs. Vyse, connubialized *nunc pro tunc.*

January 21, SUNDAY. . . . Visit from George Anthon. I shouldn't be astonished if he were to wake up some cloudy morning and find himself multiplied by two, for I surmise that, like the immortal Panurge, he "hath a flea in his ear and desireth to be married." . . .

From what [Anthon] tells me, there's reason to fear that the next diocesan convention in September and the General Convention in October will be scenes of renewed attacks on Catholicism and church authority on the part of those who disgraced themselves at the ordination last July and of their backers and fellows in faction at the subsequent convention; and that they are organizing and straining every nerve to secure a triumph for their party at the next. Shame on them! —a party whose only common principles and bonds of union are personal hostility to their bishop and a fidgety antipathy to everything that implies submission, humility, and reverence. Many of its members are governed by very different motives, to be sure; but to think that clergymen should condescend to associate themselves as leaders of a "religious party" with such men as John Duer, a swindler to the extent of $200,000, and "Sir Pandarus Dogdraught" Webb, the unblushing and notorious author of more outrages on honesty, morality, and public decency than any man I at this moment remember. . . .

January 27. . . . Last night I found myself growing blue again, but the unexpected entry of Coryat's *Crudities,* arrived per the last steamer,

set me all right again, and with that most comical book and with Dickens's
clever (but mighty absurd) extravaganza, the *Prose Christmas Carol*, I've
been very comfortable and strong of heart ever since. *Dissipantur inimici;*
the blue devils are scattered, and I trust that I shall "live to my dying
day in despite of mine enemies."

Delightful book is Mr. Dickens's. He's not dead yet, though *Martin
Chuzzlewit* is flat and the *American Notes* a libel on this model republic of
enlightened freemen.

February 2. . . . Read the article attributed to Dickens in the *Foreign
Quarterly* on American poets, over which all the papers are going into
severe paroxysms of patriotic wrath. Don't see why they can't keep cool.
That we have no national school of poetry is very true, but it's our misfortune and not a fault, for we've no materials to make one out of. We've
neither a legendary past nor a poetic present. Large mountains, extensive
prairies, tall cataracts, long rivers, millions of dirty acres of every cos-
mographical character don't "constitute a state" for purposes of poetry;
but "men, high-minded men" and their memories. . . . That except Halleck and Bryant and Longfellow, we've no poets is a fact that the *Foreign
Quarterly* man seems to regard as a great critical discovery and which our
independent press in general are calling heaven and earth to witness is a
most foul and bare-faced slander begotten by British envy, but which I
suppose to be a very undesirable matter. I think that in the course of time,
when the various hostile and prosifying causes that are enumerated in the
article in question (and certain others) have ceased to operate, we shall
have our poets, and that we have as fair a chance of producing the next
Dante or Milton or Shakespeare as any other nation, in the course of the
coming five centuries, which is about a reasonable period to assign for
the advent of the next of that stamp.

February 15. . . . Have been reading with delight and astonishment
the argument in the Supreme Court of the United States in the Girard
will case delivered by—(silence for two minutes and a half, followed by
a flourish of trumpets and three claps of thunder in G-sharp)—DANIEL
WEBSTER!

How long is it since I've seen or heard anything from any one of our
quacking flock of "statesmen" and politicians that I cared to read again
or to remember? This, I do believe, is the first, and though the immortal
Daniel is said to be slightly heathenish in private life, and though it is but
a forensic argument after all, it gives one hopes of the republic to find a
man wide awake to his political reputation and thoroughly conversant

with the thoughts and feelings of the Sovereign *Demos*, the dispenser or withholder of his highest earthly good, venturing to leave legal technicalities and deal with a subject in the light of realities and truths that I thought were most odious to the taste of the free and enlightened masses.

How it must have bored Horace Binney to hear truths that he doubtless recognizes from the bottom of his heart, hurled at him to the demolition of the argument he'd been building up, by authorities ingeniously dovetailed, and his own convictions diligently smothered into silence.

Likewise I have been reading Macaulay. He's a clever humbug—a fluent, plausible, elegant, perspicuous sophister. His review of Gladstone is in some points unmatchable. Whether his profound ignorance of the views of Gladstone's friends on church matters as exhibited in his confident crowing over the state arguments that would disgrace a boy of fifteen who had a clear view of the battleground, or his presumption in daring to tamper in such a spirit of meddling vanity with the awful truths or diabolical falsehoods (whichever they are) that his subject embraces be the more stupendous is a full, great, doubtful question. I'd like to ask the man, just for my own satisfaction, what he means by being such a lying idiot. Such was the man whom Rabelais (or somebody else) didn't wish to hear repeat the Creed, lest it should weaken his faith. . . .

February 17, SATURDAY.   Croton water bathing pipes just burst, to the consternation of the household who are engaged in solemn consultation somewhere in the basement, up to their necks in water, I suppose. It hasn't flooded my premises, though I think the fatal breach is somewhere inside the wall thereof, which will probably lead to the destruction of my domestic peace and literary seclusion by an irruption of hod-carrying, plaster-mongering Goths, vandals, and Mongrel Tartars. Shall I sue the architect, the plumber, or the Mayor, Aldermen & Co.? . . .

February 22, THURSDAY.   Today the nation celebrates "Pa's birthday" —a fact of which I received very early notice, having been waked by the brazen uproar of a vigorous military band under the window, out of my precious morning nap, doubly precious from my having sat up near all night to despatch an urgent injunction bill. . . .

February 28, WEDNESDAY. . . . Saw Fowler this morning and M. M. Backus this afternoon—both well and in good health and sound condition —no expression of "hang you, you think yourself better than me, but you a'nt a bit of it" about either of 'em, which is a gratifying thing. It's very hard that a man can't lead an eremitical life and decline making a pig of himself at claret and whiskey punch parties and a donkey of himself by philandering with his friends' wives without being set down for a super-fine piece of stolid self-conceit that thinks himself too good to associate with other people.

February 29, THURSDAY. News this afternoon of a frightful occur-rence at Washington: the explosion of one of the *Princeton's* Paixhans, killing Upshur, Secretary of State; Gilmer, Secretary of the Navy; Virgil Maxcy, Solicitor of the Treasury; Commodore Kennon, a high officer in Gilmer's department; David Gardiner of Southampton, and others of less note. I suppose there's scarcely an instance on record, of late times at least, in which so many high official characters under one government have been destroyed by the same blow. James II of Scotland died alone. And after all the brag that's been made touching those guns, which were lallied about as if they were sufficient alone to defend the nation against the English navy, it's a most dismal issue for the invention. Col. [Thomas Hart] Benton and [Commodore Robert Field] Stockton were both badly hurt.

March 1, FRIDAY. . . . It was this atmosphere of laziness that set me to reading Tennyson, I suppose; but apart from that, he's on the whole a favorite of mine, and if they'd publish an edition of his poems expurgated of their spooneyism, affectation, and grimace, I'd import a large paper copy with india proofs (for a collection of "dainty" little vignettes would be indispensable to make it a complete thing) and have it bound in very light green morocco and it would be quite a nice little pet book. In fact, of the English *Di Minorum Gentium* he's about the cleverest. . . .

March 16. . . . The Vestry of Trinity Church have concluded to com-plete the tower, to put on the spire, I mean, at once. So saith gossip rumor. *Vivat* said vestry.

The College Green is to be cut up into city lots on College Place and Murray Street, on some authority. The trustees should be bound over to keep the peace without delay. Goths are they, and vandals and a horde, or board, of barbarous blackguards. If they think of cutting down those trees, I'll assassinate 'em in detail or blow up the president's room at their next meeting.

March 19. . . . United States stocks are *down* "full fathom five" on the strength of the rumors touching the Texas project. No wonder. If consummated it may probably lead to war, and if its opponents are dis-posed to make trouble, to a Dissolution of the Union. For that it's an utterly unconstitutional measure, there can be no doubt. It is not an exercise of the treaty-making power and cannot lawfully be done by that power—nor is it within the compass of both Houses; it can be legitimately accomplished only by direct action of the People, from whom the powers of those bodies and the Constitution under which they act, are derived. To say that President and Senate have power to *incorporate us with another nation*, because they've power to make binding treaties with foreign powers, is to say that one member of a partnership can add a dozen members to it, of his own free will, *because* he can bind the firm by signing notes and making bargains. It's an act of Sovereignty of the most fundamental character, which in a Popular government that has not expressly clothed its Representatives with the power, can be done only by the fundamental authority, the People itself.

April 10, WEDNESDAY. Hurrah for the Natives! They've elected Harper by a majority of 4,000 and stand two to one in the Common Council. Such a revolution is unheard of; the Locos are perfectly stunned and the Whigs not much better off. Such a blow hasn't fallen on the Hibernian race since the days of Earl Strongbow or Boynewake at the latest.

I'm just from the Native Headquarters, the Aboriginal gathering place. Not an exile of Erin ventures to show his nose in the neighborhood and the row and the bonfires and the popping of small arms of every denomination and the incessant whizz of rockets from the roof of "Military Hall" are altogether imposing and tremendous. . . .

April 24. . . . Got in a fine copy of Holinshed (first edition) this afternoon. I've strong hopes of Purchas's *Pilgrims* through Bartlett & Welford, and then I shall consider myself to have laid a very fair foundation for an Englysshe Librarie.

As for the bibliomaniacal introuvables of Caxton, DeWorde, Pynson & Co., it's idle to think of acquiring anything more than a specimen or so of each of them, and not even that unless chance throws cheap copies in one's way. The technical bibliomania, the pure, abstract *Delirium Dibdinianum* that rages after those things simply as book varieties, independently of any interest attaching to the edition, I never was smitten with to any great extent, and if I had Earl Spencer's fortune I never should have got together Earl Spencer's library. . . .

Yet are some Caxtons and Pynsons genuine black diamonds that I'd bleed freely for. The *Morte d'Arthur* for example, Pynson's Froissart (mine's imperfect) and divers other stars that twinkle far beyond human reach in the profoundest depths of the book firmament, I should enjoy greatly. But a sale catalogue of these books with the prices is generally a mere monument of folly, for there's nothing to recommend nine-tenths of them but the childish merit of rarity. They are rare now because they were always worthless. Rarity adds to the value of what's good, but alone it's nothing.

Went to the anti-annexation of Texas meeting tonight at the Tabernacle. It was very full and much more interesting than I'd expected to find it. Albert Gallatin presided and spoke with more force and more physical strength than one would have anticipated from his appearance, for he's very old and looks very infirm. Sedgwick and Field also spoke, neither of them with any very startling degree of eloquence. The principal source of fun arose from Mike Walsh and a tail of about twenty who had come down express to make a row and did all they could to provoke one. They were in a decided minority, however, and their impertinent blackguardism only made the meeting applaud the louder and feel the more magnanimously hostile to Tyler Texas. . . .

April 25, THURSDAY. . . . Started for the Greenwood Cemetery with Templeton at four o'clock and walked there, traversed the grounds, and walked back by half-past seven, a pretty fair afternoon's walk, and I confess to a pair of feet a little exacerbated and one or two extensor muscles a little sore. Beautiful place it is, and they're hard at work improving it, putting it all in good order. When it's brought to the same high state of civilization with Mt. Auburn, it will far surpass it. I'm glad to see that what Pugin calls the "revived Pagan style" doesn't prevail very extensively there. I only noticed one pair of inverted torches and not a single urn or flying globe or like silliness, only not profane because it may be supposed to be unmeaning. This recurrence to heathen taste and antichristian usage in architecture or art of any sort is or should be unreal and unnatural everywhere, but in such a place as that, it's disgusting. But when churches are modelled after Parthenons—even to the bulls' heads and sacrificial emblems on the frieze—of course it's not wonderful that people will cover their tombs with the symbols of Paganism.

I used to be very indignant at any assaults on classical literature, and to be sure one may well be so at the pseudo-utilitarianism that generally prompts the attack. Anything that may be said about waste of time, useful knowledge, greater advantage of familiarity with living languages and all that, is sheer twaddle. But whether their cultivation and study may not be objected to on other grounds entirely, whether it's not an utterly false basis for education that they supply, whether it's not wrong to poison the minds of boys of fourteen with Ovid and Lucretius, whether much of the degeneration of Christendom is not traceable to the revival of their study, are questions that it might be worth while for people to think about.

April 27.   If John Tyler originated this Texas project, he's a more sagacious shepherd of the people than I gave him credit for being. There's no chance of the annexation's being effected just now, I think, but it may well bring about a general moving of the waters that will upset all calculations as to the coming election and knock all the existing "interests" into hotchpot. I give the immortal John a chance of making himself conspicuously absurd for another four years. Stranger things have happened since Adams's time than even the reëlection of John Tyler would be.

After all, while Mississippi and Pennsylvania and certain other sovereign states continue to be stars in our galaxy, I don't know that we need turn the cold shoulder to Texas—or New South Wales (*that's* colonized with a strong infusion of Anglo-Saxon blood and there's some of the superlative ichor of Anglo-Americanism there, too).

A general act of amnesty to all our expatriated citizens in the new member of the Confederacy would remove one serious obstacle.

The Treaty now before the Senate was published this afternoon. If I were a senator, as unfortunately for the republic I'm not, I should insist on the following supplementary or additional clauses:

I. The Republic of Texas shall, at its own proper cost and charges, procure to be printed a sufficient number of copies of *The Whole Duty of Man*, Paley's *Moral Philosophy Abridged*, *God's Revenge against Murder and Adulterie*, *Fichte on the Distinction between the Ego and the Non Ego*, as applicable to questions of Meum and Tuum, and some approved practical treatise on the law of larceny, swindling, embezzlement, and the picking of pockets, and shall cause the same to be distributed gratuitously among its citizens within six months from the ratification of his treaty.

II. The Republic of Texas shall, within the same period, enact a statute making assassination with the bowie knife or repeating pistol to be felony, and no person shall receive from the Executive of said Republic more than fifteen pardons for offences against such statute, but on the sixteenth conviction for violation thereof, shall be punished by fine or imprisonment in the discretion of the jury by whom he is convicted.

III. The Republic of Texas shall build her own penitentiaries, treadmills, and other penal establishments.

IV. The Republic of Texas shall not be entitled to send any Representative to Congress who shall have become a citizen thereof after having been sentenced to be hanged in any state or territory of the Union.

With those improvements and one or two more, the Treaty would deserve a more respectful consideration unquestionably than it is now entitled to. . . .

April 30.   Splendid night it is, clear, cool and everything glowing in a flood of moonlight. Walked uptown by irresistible necessity. No one can stay in the house under such circumstances. Went to the Academy of Design this afternoon. This year's exhibition is but a shabby affair; more than the usual number of libellous portraits, and a decided preponderance of the signpost school of art in the other pictures. There are two or three good landscapes by [Asher Brown] Durand and a very nice portrait by [Henry Peters] Gray of Mrs. Kem[ble] Paulding, I believe, and at this moment I can think of nothing else that's worth walking up that interminable flight of stairs for.

That reminds me that the Generalissimo of No. 56 is going to have his portrait taken by Mount, the artist selected for the sake of Suffolk County, I s'pose, for I don't think much of his powers in that line.[1] Gray's the best portrait painter we have. It should be a grand historical piece representing an examination on Graham's *Practice* with a bevy of future chief justices and attorney generals, *videlicet* our hopeful students, as examinees, including that last most precious addition to our numbers Mr. somebody Phillips[2] (son of the parson's) who is in sober sadness the most unadulterated snob I ever met: a perfect "artist's dream" of snobbiness, snobblaginous in all his details of blackguardism. I've known blackguards before that were perhaps equally hircine and porcine, but none that could stand comparison with him for a moment as to the *in toto attingunt* of the combined elements of blackguard, spooney and snob.

May 1.   Fine weather, to the great comfort of the locomotive public. Never knew the city in such a chaotic state. Every other house seems to be disgorging itself into the street; all the sidewalks are lumbered with bureaus and bedsteads to the utter destruction of their character as thoroughfares, and all the space between the sidewalks is occupied by long processions of carts and wagons and vehicles omnigenous laden with

[1] George Washington Strong's portrait by William Sidney Mount was exhibited the following spring at the National Academy of Design.

[2] This seems to have been John Mason Phillips (New York University 1841), son of Rev. William Wirt Phillips, D.D., minister of the First Presbyterian Church.

perilous piles of moveables. We certainly haven't advanced as a people beyond the nomadic or migratory stage of civilization analogous to that of the pastoral cow feeders of the Tartar Steppes.

May 7, TUESDAY. . . . Just back from another visit to the Academy of Design. That man [Francis William] Edmonds is certainly a most clever painter. Durand's pictures improve on acquaintance; so do Montgomery Livingston's landscapes. The rest is stuff.

> Hey-hey - de country's risin'
> For Henry Clay and Frelinghuysen.

Good nomination was Frelinghuysen's, astute decidedly; Clay, being by the admission of his friends a good deal of a runner, will run none the worse for having a deacon to ride him. But the Democracy is in a most "unhandsome fix." Their convention meets on the 27th, and if Van Buren's science in wire-pulling and managing the mechanism of the party procures his nomination, the game's up for them, and barring accidents, Clay's as sure of dining in the White House on the 4th of March in the year of grace 1845 as ever he was of doing his man at brag or poker. If they select any other champion, it's a matter of hopeless uncertainty to calculate the chance. Yet whom can they bring out except Van Buren, but at the certain sacrifice of the electoral vote of New York? In short, their game's very extensively disorganized, their pieces don't support each other, and their only salvation will be in sacrificing a castle and risking everything else in some desperate demonstration from an unexpected quarter. . . .

Well, I don't think I shall allow myself to suffer much anxiety or distress of mind, whatever the issue may be.

> In the year Eighteen hundred
> And forty and four
> There are darkies as many
> As ever before.

May 8. . . . Great row in Philadelphia. Queer city that, the most anarchical metropolis on this side the Atlantic. The military won't do anything because they're afraid they won't get their pay; the fire department won't do anything because the military won't help them; and as for the police, if one of them gets a rap in the row he's trying to quiet he treats it as a personal matter and throws himself into the arms of the party that's opposed to his man, and lays about him like a trump. . . .

This breeze was Natives *vs.* Hibernians, and the latter had the best of it: seem to have been decidedly gamey, and to have shot down their men with as little compunction as a sportsman lets slap into a mob of black-birds, and to have been desperate and sanguinary and savage enough to do anything. I would not live in such a hornets' nest as the City of Brotherly Love appears to be. One can't look out of his window without the risk of being knocked down by some stray bullet or other that was intended for somebody else entirely, or fired on speculation, without meaning anything against anybody in particular.

This'll be a great thing for the Natives, strengthen their hands amaz-ingly if judiciously used. It wouldn't be wonderful if it should lead to some flare-up here. There's latent irritation enough which won't be much mollified by the exaggerated versions of this business, bad enough at best and in matter of fact, but magnified into a second St. Bartholomew's on both sides that will be recounted and expatiated on in every alley and bar-room and ganglion of rowdyism from Madison Square to the Bat-tery. . . .

May 11, SATURDAY. . . . The City of Brotherly Love is reduced to a state of quietude by dint of hostile demonstrations from the Governor of the Commonwealth and eloquent appeals to the public by the Fathers of the City. Such a pitiable scene of feebleness, irresolution, and old-grannyism in general as the civic potentates of that place have enacted for the amuse-ment of posterity isn't to be found anywhere, unless in Dickens's descrip-tion of the No-Popery riots in *Barnaby Rudge*. Captain Fairlamb and General Cadwalader must settle it between 'em which is to succeed Henry Clay, for the country never can forget the services of those great military chieftains. The charges of the "City Troop," first up the street, second down the street, and third off the ground entirely, form a com-bination of manoeuvres that outsaxify Saxe's wildest "reverie." An amusing commentary on the whole affair is the resolution adopted by acclamation at the grand meeting held after all the damage had been done, that the majority of rioters consisted of small boys too young to know how naughty they were; and that all parents and guardians were re-quested to keep said small boys at home, send 'em early to bed or hide their stockings. Doubtless it was a sensible practical person that moved that resolution.

It's some consolation that Philadelphia is worse governed than we are. Some apprehensions are entertained of a flare-up among our own virtuous and independent masses, but every precaution's taken to put a stop to any such proceeding at a very early stage and I don't think our shepherds of the people would think it discreet to wait for an opinion in writing from the Attorney General before they authorized the military to fire on the mob. . . .

May 12, SUNDAY. . . . Walked uptown tonight. Looked at Grace Church. They won't consecrate it this fall, I think, from present appearances. [James] Renwick [Jr.] is a clever fellow and his church looks very well on paper, but I fear the practical embodiment of his conception, the church itself, will be a botch. He's hampered for money and the plan's an ambitious one and the effect of the structure will probably be that of an attempt at the sumptuous on slender means, which is always undignified, and generally unsuccessful. . . .

May 13. Went through Trinity Church this morning with George Anthon. The spire is commenced and rising rapidly; that steam engine shows its true value now that the stone has to rise 140 feet. From the wilderness of cunningly carved stones that lie about I infer that the spire is to be more ornate than was at first designed, as an innovation which will be generally conceded to be an improvement. The tower has settled to a considerable extent and produced some ugly starting, springing and gaping about the south front window, but Upjohn's a man of unlimited resources, and he'll remedy that somehow; if he has to shove up the tower again with jackscrews. The stained glass so far as it's yet visible does very well for native American manufacture.

May 19, SUNDAY. Feel today neither particularly happy nor particularly unhappy, I can't certainly determine which, for did I not last night hear the Symphony in C minor by one Ludwig Van Beethoven, No. 67, played *ad unguem* by the Philharmonic? Haven't I been fairly tingling all day with the remembrance of that most glorious piece of instrumental music extant, the second movement? (Twice played, by the by, the first *encored* symphony on record.) . . .

The first movement, with its abrupt opening, and the complicated entanglement of harmonies that makes up the rest of it, is not very satisfactory or intelligible to me as a whole, though it abounds in exquisite little scraps of melody that come sparkling out like stars through a cloudy sky, but the second and fourth movements (the third a'nt much) are enough to put Beethoven at the head of all instrumental composers if he'd never written another note. They're just one succession of points and yet each is as perfect, each seems as if it had been a single effort of the composer's genius that gave it birth. There's nothing in them like the mere aggregation of distinct though original and beautiful passages that one notes in Rossini's music, for example.

GEORGE WASHINGTON STRONG

EEL-SPEARING AT SETAUKET

BOYS CAUGHT NAPPING IN A FIELD

PAINTED FOR G. W. STRONG BY WILLIAM SIDNEY MOUNT

The introduction of the subject of the second movement by the violins and its instantaneous ringing repetition by the full orchestra is matchless; so is the stately opening of the fourth. But it's idle to write about it. If I were asked for an explanation of the symphony, and to tell the exact train of thought that produced it, I should be at a loss. The first general purport of its story would seem to be, for the first movement, weariness, sorrow, and perplexity; energies preying on themselves for the want of an object for life and the disheartening sense that earnest minds feel at a certain stage of their development of the worthlessness of all that they're doing and living for, and their need of something that may wake them up to real and energetic existence. Then, in the second, is the glorious birth of the new principle of love, ambition, or some yet higher element and its exulting and triumphant progress in freshness and vigor, on to the victory and full function of the end and aim which seems to be the subject of the finale. . . .

Between the second and third parts Vieuxtemps made his appearance and played variations on themes from *Norma*, on one string with the orchestra, about the most satisfactory piece of violin music I ever heard. "Casta Diva" in particular was most exquisitely played, and with a delicacy and expression beyond what I ever heard the voice give it.

The second part was Mendelssohn's *Midsummer Night's Dream*, beautiful thing it is; some trash or other by Vattelina, and Weber's *Ruler of the Spirits*, a very effective overture. . . .

May 27. . . . I find that Mrs. Lewis L.'s anticipated offspring has flashed in the pan and proved a total failure likewise. The story is that some castoff Unfortunate Female of that most unfortunate male, her husband, recently made her appearance with much clamor and obstreperousness and several small children at the residence of that gentleman during his absence and threw an entirely new light on his ante-nuptial habits and practices, new to his wife at least, and that the vexation and annoyance thereby occasioned brought to pass the result aforesaid. Isn't it execrable? Yet if pretty, amiable, intelligent, and accomplished women will condescend to unite themselves with men who've led such lives as common fame and his own hard face give Mr. L. the credit of having led, they've not much to complain about; they must make the most they can of the fashionable name and the foreign graces that formed the consideration of the contract. . . .

Wonder how the grand Democratic Palaver is getting on at Baltimore about this time. They've a pretty tangled skein to wind and I suppose the consumption of cobblers and brandy smashes, loud lying and hard swearing throughout today has kept the dealers in those commodities pretty actively employed. On the whole, two to one on "the little red fox of the Empire State." He's about as available as anybody they can put forward, and if the Texas plot be really knocked on the head, which blessed consummation of the scheme there's reason to hope has taken place, the sole shadow of a chance of nomination that John Tyler ever possessed is gone. Don't much care; "country's risin', Clay and Freling-huysen, quite surprizin', give the Loco pisen," and so on. It don't matter much which Loco is selected to be made a martyr of. . . .

Whether the jacobinical spirit and the antipathy to law and order and the overthrow of everything worth preserving, which is the un-conscious principle of the one party, and the temper and final result of its unchecked development, be worse than commercial, speculating, bank-swindling, money-worshipping *primum mobile* of the other is a question.

Certainly since the downfall of Federalism there has been no con-servative party in the country which has ventured to avow any higher aim than the cultivation of tariffs and credit systems, trade and manu-factures.

Its unchecked development would make us a commercial aristocracy which is mean enough everywhere, but here 'twould be a fluctuating mushroom aristocracy and the meanest the world has seen yet.

May 28, TUESDAY. . . . Came across a bibliographical black swan this morning: a copy of [Daniel] Horsmanden's quarto concerning the nigger plot of [1741–1742], fine copy, too, and uncut (though I never could appreciate the importance of that), the only copy of the book I ever saw or heard of. Gave orders to have it bought in; hope I may get it.[3]

Started after dinner with Templeton for a walk to Weehawken. . . . Hoboken's a good deal cut up and built up, but pleasant still; pity it's haunted by such a gang as frequent it; its groves are sacred to Venus and I saw scarce any one there but snobs and their strumpets. Walked on in momentary expectation of stumbling on some couple engaged in what Schroeder would call "the commission of gross vulgarity."

Crossed the dyke and walked out to Weehawken. The "William Tell

---

[3] This book, *A Journal of the Proceedings in the Detection of the Conspiracy founded by some White People, in Conjunction with Negro and other Slaves, for Burning the City of New York in America, and Murdering the Inhabitants. . .* (New-York, 1744), fetched $300 at the sale of Strong's library in 1878, the highest price paid for any book in the sale.

Cottage" of Mary Rogers memorability is shut up and deserted, probably found to be haunted.

Nothing decisive yet from the Baltimore council fires. Van Buren stock seems rather down and the "Jack Casses," as the adherents of that very great statesman are disrespectfully termed, are understood to be full of hope and hilarity. *He'd* be beat most signally if nominated; his Louis Philippe toadying would kill him dead the first month of the campaign.

May 30.   News arrived this morning of the issue of the Baltimore Convention, the result of the agonizing throes of the last three days. For President, James K. Polk and for Vice-President, Silas Wright.

There's no telling what a day may bring forth, *a fortiori*, no telling what the chance and change of the next six months may result in, but I can't think that the nominees will get much good of their nomination.

Poor Martin Van Buren! It's his final exit from the busy scene of politics, there's no doubt of that. He's laid on the shelf for good. The tidings went northward by this evening's boat and they'll reach the cabbage gardens of Kinderhook in an hour or two. Doubtless Matty received a dismal and ominous letter from Ben Butler last night, telling him to keep up his spirits, but expatiating largely on the ingratitude of party men, the demoralization of the Democracy and the great blessings of private life and rustical retirement: and now he's waiting for the decisive news that the night boat will bring in a fever of fidgety desperation.

June 3. . . . Item: Silas Wright's backed out of his proffered Vice-Presidency, disgracefully declining the crown of martyrdom, and [George Mifflin] Dallas of Pennsylvania is the chosen victim. . . . Item: Polk and Dallas are a severe dose for the Northern Democracy; if Van Buren would consent to run, as he certainly won't, I believe they'd be tempted to make a schism in the party.

June 16. . . . Bad business, this, in the Diocese of Pennsylvania. They say that in the Philadelphia bar-rooms some new modifications of mint julep have become popular under the name of "Onderdonks." I do believe that Philadelphia lies in some special manner under the dominion of the "Prince of the Power of the Air." Everything goes wrong there: insolvent government, swindling banks, burnt churches, drinking bishops, rapes, murders, and riots all seem to flourish and abound there as in their appointed abiding place and own natural home. As for the Bishop [Henry Ustick Onderdonk], if the reports that are current here as to certain eccentricities of his be true, he'll unquestionably be refused permission to resign and his career will be terminated by a degradation, and probably that is the best course for the church that can be adopted. . . .[4]

June 17. . . . Looked in at Trinity Church. They're pushing it fast; possibly next Easter may see it consecrated, but I profoundly doubt the probability thereof. . . .

The present taste for . . . pointed architecture and the other increasing "retrograde" tendencies in art and literature that one sees the signs of every day may be very important matters if they're not a mere temporary caprice of popular taste and one of the phases of fashion. But even if they are so, and their result should be but trifling, it must be good so far as it goes. All things are bound together, and the study of medieval art must tend, at least, to revive some of the medieval habits, thoughts, feelings, and principles, an infusion of which the age is sadly in want of. . . .

June 23, SUNDAY. . . . What I've read and thought on the subject of late has led me to the conclusion that the present Catholic movement in England and in this country cannot produce any permanent and important changes except as a transition state towards the higher positions which alone can produce a lasting Reformation, as preparing the way for a movement the first principle of which shall be the abjuration and utter defiance of everything that appertains to enlightened Protestantism, without apology or circumlocution. Catholicism can't be built up again without offending the prejudices of the nineteenth century, and it's idle to think of a compromise.

June 26. . . . I've just heard a rumor that infatuated old John Tyler was married today to one of those large, fleshy Miss Gardiners of Gardiner's Island. Poor, unfortunate, deluded old jackass; it's positively painful to think of his situation, and the trials that lie before him. . . .

June 29. . . . Went up to Pike's this morning with Anthon to look at some electromagnetic apparatus of his that's reported to be sovereign for sick headache, and we shocked ourselves and sent currents of the mysterious fluid marching and countermarching through our several systems with most scientific gravity and perseverance. It's certainly a very nice and ingenious contrivance, but whether a sick headache will bow before it is a doubtful question. It may have been fancy, or the fine weather, or

[4] The Right Reverend Henry Ustick Onderdonk (1789–1858), A.B., A.M., M.D. and D.D. (Columbia), M.R.C.S. (London), Bishop of Pennsylvania, wrote to the House of Bishops in 1844 confessing his habitual use of intoxicating liquor and offering his resignation, which was accepted. They also voted to suspend him from the ministry, but two years before his death the suspension was removed.

unaccustomed eupepsia, but I certainly felt extremely fresh, vigorous, and bright after my dose of magnetism.

Had a call from [Mancer Mark] Backus this afternoon: he's in better health and spirits than I've seen him for some time, all which he devoutly attributes to matrimony, and like most foxes who've lost their tails, he counselled me with much earnestness to do likewise and lose no time about it. It seems he's not studying for the "ministry" at all, but is an associate editor of a certain weekly organ of some schism or other called *The Evangelist*, the critical and literary department whereof would seem to be entrusted to his special care and conduct. To such base uses may we come at last. . . .

Went to Pike's again, with Backus, and bought one of his machines and have just been galvanizing all my finger joints nearly out of their sockets. It's a most mysterious effect to come of such slight means.

June 30, SUNDAY.   Heard a certain Mr. Southard[5] this morning, good sermon of its kind, but I'm not partial to the sentimental style of pulpit oratory that always has such an effect on the soft-hearted tailor that sits on the other side of the aisle, and always makes him to blow his sympathetic nose so fervently. It's an especially unhappy way for a young clergyman to get into; they can raise such a fuss among all the young women and old women so easily that they're in danger of adopting it to the exclusion of all manlier tones: and they get so petted and coddled up for it that unless some signal good fortune save them, they're apt to sink into clerical coxcombs—"pet parsons"—and they are without any exception the most miserable creatures on earth. Heard Wainwright this afternoon, and took a long walk tonight. The air is like October's.

Tried the galvanic apparatus again this afternoon, for the premonitories of a headache. The headache took itself off, but whether I'm to thank Pike for the deliverance must be resolved by future experiments. If it can vanquish a well-developed assault of that my fiercest and fellest temporal foe, I'll present Pike with a gold snuff box and a duly authenticated certificate of the most surprising cure on record.

July 2, TUESDAY.   Walked uptown tonight. Stopped at the Society

---

[5] The Rev. Samuel Lewis Southard, Jr. (Princeton 1836), who erupts later into this diary, was the son of the Hon. Samuel Lewis Southard (Princeton 1804), sometime U.S. Senator, Secretary of the Navy, and Governor of New Jersey. The son went to the General Theological Seminary, was ordained to the Episcopal ministry in 1842 and became rector of Calvary Church in New York. After the big row there in 1849, he was located in Boonville, Missouri. Deposed from the ministry in October, 1859, he died December 7, 1859, at St. Louis from an overdose of chloroform.

Library. Read the July number of *Brownson's Quarterly Review*. He's a strange being, but he has two most uncommon characteristics that redeem a multitude of sins. He has a proper estimate of the relative values of Truth and Trade, and furthermore, when he's satisfied he's in a false position he's not ashamed to confess it and seek a better. I shall certainly subscribe to his *Review*.

In this number he avows himself to be (for the present) a Roman Catholic and seems to have satisfied himself (for the present) that the Anglican Church forfeited its claim to the title of Catholic at the Reformation.

July 6. . . . Isaac Greene Pearson is the architect of Phillips's new schism-shop in the Fifth Avenue [the First Presbyterian Church], and from what I can hear of the plan, it's going to prove an abortion, and just such a travesty of a Gothic church as one might expect from a bankrupt Unitarian amateur builder of meeting houses.

Another rumpus in the Protestant city of Philadelphia. Extras out, and "at the time our reporter left" the church of St. Philip Neri beleaguered by a mob of Natives. If the people facetiously called "authorities" of that city permit a recurrence of the late outrages without shooting down at least a hecatomb, they richly deserve to be hanged by some special act of *ex post facto* legislation. . . .

July 8. . . . Joe Smith's killed. Wonder whether that'll kill Mormonism; probably not. Jolly fight in Philadelphia, civil war raging, mob pelting the military, not with paving stones, but with grapeshot and scrap-iron out of ten-pounders; the state of things in that city is growing worse and worse every day. I shan't be caught voting a "Native" ticket again in a hurry.

July 14, SUNDAY. A most stewing night this is; if I were not a counsellor I would be a salamander.

Attorneys *are* poor creatures, a most inferior order of creation. What a snob I've been for the last three years without knowing it!

¶ Will be published shortly a New Work of great interest entitled: "Incidents of Travel, by a Counsellor at Law." In three vols. 8vo. price six cents.

CONTENTS: *Chap. I,* TUESDAY. Steamboat *Troy.* Reflections on the progress of science and the march of steam. Leave at seven. Gardiner Howland, Ogden Hoffman, his friend Dorr, and Clarence Livingston, nice party. . . . Beautiful run up the river. Overslaugh in a disgusting state.

Proposal to erect a statue of John Tyler in the act of writing his last veto, on the shallowest spot. Albany: Congress Hall. Noyes. Bad supper of doughy bread and a muddy fluid humorously termed coffee. Adjourned to the piazza for a comfortable smoke, and retired after being composed into a proper frame therefor by two several orations delivered by me.

Chap. II, WEDNESDAY. Journey through the great desert from Albany to Schenectady, thence to Utica. Climate torrid exceedingly. Weather showery. Railroad in every respect shockingly bad. Utica at two; feeding time; piggish character of the car dinner. Joe Blunt and Clinton DeWitt the lovely representatives of the New York bar. John Astor,[6] F. Cunningham and Emott of Poughkeepsie. Dalliba and Dick Varick.

Call on Mr. Clerk Denio and take an evening saunter with Dorr and Clarence Livingston out to "Deerfield."

Chap. III, THURSDAY. . . . At court. Examiners appointed: Noxon, Hand of somewhere, and Benton of Little Falls. Spend the day in lounging and loafing. Attorneys examined after dinner . . . Listened to it for an hour; pretty sharp work—too minute entirely. Forty-nine, all admitted. Evening. . . . Examination [for counsellor] commenced at eight in one of Baggs's parlors: class of twenty-five. Hand and Benton both examined rather lightly; one asked me some questions about uses, the other about trespass on the case—all very smooth and I thought that was the end of the matter, but it was only the beginning, for old Noxon took up the thumbscrews and I quaked with exceeding fear when I found what kind of an ordeal he was going to make us pass. His way of doing things was severe and searching enough. My share of his attention related chiefly to pleading and evidence and though I answered one or two questions somewhat at random, I believe I got through fairly enough, so I judge at least from the remarks that he and Comstock and somebody else were reported to me to have made touching and concerning my distinguished self and my profound acquirements.

Got through a little before twelve and went to bed with a headache. Friday. . . . Went to court. Everybody admitted. Took a pretty warm walk a couple of miles out on the railroad and then along the beautiful Mohawk.

---

[6] John Jacob Astor (1822–1890), the son of William Backhouse Astor, was educated at Columbia (A.B. 1839), Göttingen and the Harvard Law School, and practised law briefly, but his lifework was the management of family real estate in New York. For a decade he was a Columbia trustee whom Strong rated highly.

Start for home at half-past eight; fine night. Took the Troy road at Schenectady and found it a decided change for the better. Got on the *Empire* at half-past three and, having been wide awake all night, roused the captain and got a stateroom with Dorr and enjoyed a sound nap till breakfast time. Good breakfast, the effect whereof was refreshing in a high degree. Some talk with John Astor; agreeably surprised to find him a sound, sensible man. Pete Strong & Co. came on board at Catskill; made a profound obeisance to his womankind and kept at the boat's bow thereafter. Got home at six.

* * * *

August 22, THURSDAY. Came down to town in the morning [from Flushing] through a rather foggy atmosphere with certain unpromising clouds overhead. Clouds gradually develop themselves into a steady rain, and the weather becomes a bore. Leave at seven, however, in the *Albany* in defiance of the elements, and after a pretty substantial supper we fortified ourselves against the weather's worst and walked the forward deck and smoked our cigars as we traveled through the Tappan Zee and the Highlands. Before we left New York, Stoughton introduced to Templeton a little Spanish officer with a truculent moustache who had heroically started for Niagara without knowing a word of English. Templeton did his best for him, in execrable French. Very decent person he seemed, though my acquaintance with him was limited to certain telegraphic communications and the interchange of civilities and cigars. . . .

August 23. Tumble up just before reaching Troy. Weather rather dubious and showery. Troy to Schenectady, Schenectady to Utica and dinner, Utica sustaining its character as the slop-bowl of creation by a pouring deluge of rain that lasted all through the hour we spent there. Begin to discover that I'd made a fatal error in starting with a pair of new boots. Sufferings growing to severity as we move on. Utica to Syracuse, swamp and forest alternating and more log huts than civilized residences. Rome, Oriskany, and Oneida Depot. Nothing very important at any of them. Take tea at Philo Rust's; clever place is Syracuse and a very nice house is Rust's. Pick up Haswell of the Naval Engineer corps as we're leaving and find him an acquisition. Rig on a platform car and establish ourselves on a few extempore seats made of firewood, and pass Cayuga Lake and Seneca Lake and Geneva, riding thereon in great comfort, with a bright moon to help our vision. Resume our seats inside at Auburn. The tortures of the boots at their acme; had their maker been within reach, he might have suffered. Reach Rochester at three in the morning, about as completely jaded as ever was mortal in this world of suffering, and after a long walk through the dark and desolate streets to the hotel and all sorts of botheration and desperation about our luggage after we got there, turn in for a nap.

August 24.   Daylight impressions of Rochester as unfavorable as the previous night's. Very "common doings" for breakfast. Leave at seven for Buffalo. Road bad, country desolate. One endless forest on either side, sometimes at a mile's distance but more frequently crowding up to the track and looking as primitive as it did three hundred years ago. Acres of thickly-standing tall black stumps. Trees that had fallen carrying their surface roots and a great cake of earth with them to stand on edge till time rots them down. Forest, half-burnt clearing, swamp and loghut, and then at every ten miles a "depot" with a one-story erection of pine boards and a counter inside covered with pea coffee and putty pies where everybody rushes out of the cars to eat against time for ten minutes.

Had one queer set of fellow passengers, more 'specially an Eastern party who talked high philosophy, discussed aesthetics, and quoted Carlyle. "Shade of Attica! what a miserable place," said the belle, the Corinne of the company, as we stopped at the town that has the imposing name of the state she apostrophized.

Reach Buffalo at about one. It looks raw and half-finished, as it has good reason, but the streets and by-ways around the wharves are filthy enough for the most revered Oriental antiquity. 'Twill be a fine city some day, doubtless; as it is, there are some good points. There's a fine view "out to sea" and it was delightful to look over the same beach from the upper deck of one of the large steamers (splendid boats they are) and see and hear the surf rolling and roaring on a shore as sandy and weatherbeaten as if the Atlantic itself broke against it.

Leave Buffalo at five. Jolly conductor. Ride from Buffalo to Niagara in baggage car and on platforms. Road very fair and passes through a lovely country, the river always in sight. Black Rock. Tonawanda (Tánawanty). Grand Island—Schlosser, and Niagara at seven.

Get rooms, and good ones, and a very substantial supper before doing anything else. Thereafter turn out in search of the picturesque. Weather overcast, moon trying in vain to throw a little light on the subject. My feet in a horrid state and my frame of mind a dogged desperation that made me view the contingency of my tumbling over the cliffs in the dark with surprising serenity.

Bath Island and Goat Island. The rapids between them and the shore took me by surprise and waked me up partially. Thence to the falls successively. Two large masses of something white very indistinctly seen, and "that's Niagara." Trifling sensation of disgust. Try to return by a short cut, which proves a long one. Home at last, try to sit up awhile, fail signally, and retire in disgust unspeakable.

August 25, SUNDAY. No church, here nothing but meeting houses, any quantity of them. The evangelical privileges seem to be as great as the water privileges. Try the boots and find them as far from being broken in as ever. Mount a pair of Templeton's old shoes at last, about six sizes big for me, but I'm past attaching any weight to such trifles. Breakfast, write home, start for a walk with Templeton and "the Cid." Spent the morning on Goat Island and the Terrapin Rocks. No time to write a critique on Niagara. Each point of view in succession seems the grandest yet. Most striking features on a first acquaintance: the depth and emerald green color of the water as it passes over the Horse Shoe Fall, just beginning to be beautifully clouded with white, before it's lost behind the storm of mist that rages at the foot of the fall, the unmatchable tints of the river below the American Fall seen from near the foot of the Ferry Stairs, where a little spur of ground hides the lower part of it and the fall seems to rush down from the sky.

Noise of the fall less than I expected. *Query*: if the vibration of so large a body of water does not produce a sound below the compass of audibility? The "roar" one hears is lost but a little distance above the falls and seems a mere superficial splashing compared with the thunder such a fall should produce.

Walk down the Biddle Stairs and along shore, parlous place rather, the loose rocks over head decidedly threatening. It was here Dr. Hungerford of Troy lost his life in '39.

Spend the afternoon partly on Goat Island and partly at Robinson's Observatory ("Pagoda" he calls it). Very beautiful view of both falls. Camera obscura and two young "barr." Evening. Rather tired with the day's rambling and scrambling, especially being regularly foundered with the inflictions of that son of a shoemaker Cullen, who'll never have the satisfaction of sending me another pair of boots. I'm strongly inclined to make him eat this pair. Considering the propriety of a retreat to bed when the moon makes her appearance from among a bank of clouds and we march off once more to Goat Island. Rapids by moonlight and superb lunar bow springing from the centre of the Horse Shoe. From the tower on Terrapin Rocks it was an arch with the farther extremity reaching nearly to the American Fall.

August 26. Weather so-so-ish. Furnish myself with a pair of boots and cross to the British side with Templeton and the Cid. That's the grandest place for a general view of the Falls, though on the whole the American side with its rapids and its thousand varying pictures of each fall is decidedly better. Perhaps, too, one better appreciates the transcendent power and sublimity of the centre of the British Fall where the water rushes over, they say twenty feet deep, on Table Rock than anywhere else. Determine to try an expedition under the sheet. Disrobe and put on a costume that's something between a French smuggler's and that of some semi-monastic order. Descend the stairs and follow our leader. The Cid backs out and bids us an affectionate adieu. For the scene "behind the veil" it's quite indescribable: wind exploding from all quarters at once, spray whirling into one's eyes, nose, and mouth, the rock on one side hanging far over, evidently destined to tumble sooner or later, and on the other side the wall of water, whether it's half a mile off or within arm's length one's eye can't determine, not descending slowly as it seems to, when seen from without, but speeding down with a rush and a power that it makes one dizzy to look at. The shower bath one gets is exhilarating and glorious—never felt better than I did after it.

August 27. Drive to the Whirlpool. Very striking distant view of the Falls seen unexpectedly on the road. Expected to find a large surface of water going round and round very fast, with a small hole in the middle where everything's sucked down. Did not find anything of the sort and pronounce the Whirlpool, *as* a whirlpool, a gross imposition. Descend the bank by a long stairs made slippery by the late rain and find the view up the river (literally *up*), and the whole aspect of things, decidedly worth looking at. The foot of the bank a decidedly pokerish position, and scrambling along over the rocks, with the deep black water rushing past, somewhat perilous for a nervous man. Some prodigiously "ugly" spots in that same Whirlpool, where the water seems all alive and crawling about, with tough, wiry, little eddies. It's a most savage looking place, with its rugged precipices and perilous waters.

Start this evening with Moore in quest of a lunar bow and get a splendid one from the Terrapin Rocks.

Took a pleasant afternoon ramble round Goat Island. Rapids above the Horse Shoe Fall between Goat Island and the Sisters. Standing on the Tower a gust of wind drove the spray over us and inside the Terrapin Rocks, and as we turned to make a hasty retreat we saw that the afternoon sun had formed on the cloud of spray the most brilliant and beautiful circle conceivable, the upper edge rising far above the bank and standing out bright and well defined against the clear sky, and the lower resting on the water at our feet.

August 28. Morning weather dubious. Cross to the British side. Decided and unmistakeable rain, the best-humored man going couldn't have called it spray. Shocking state of the highways in her Majesty's dominion. Loaf about Table Rock awhile and return. Spend an hour or so on Terrapin Rocks after dinner, sunshine having resumed its reign. Find myself feverish and unwell and make my way home and lie down for a nap, with serious misgivings as to my bodily health and some apprehensions that my scrambling and amphibious mode of life might have brought on a Western Fever. Take some tea and retire early.

August 29.   Fine day. Take a boat at the Ferry and row about a half a mile down the river and then commence a scramble up the bank through running water, rotten trees, and obstacles of all sorts. Reach the object of our search at last, viz: "Catlin's Cave," the same being a sort of rat hole in the side of a rock. We'd taken Catlin (the discoverer) with us and he helped us in by a system of boosting and pushing. Inside after much exertion on all sides. Position a remarkably novel one, being in the inside of a cavity too small to let one stand up, sit, lie down and extremely humid and astonishingly dark. Admired the wonders of nature for a while and then I stuck my feet out of the rat hole and Catlin, who's rather a muscular man, pulled them forcibly and thus by degrees pulled me out. Wonderful place, Catlin's Cave!

Come back and hold a grand consultation as to the propriety of returning the way we came or via Montreal. Finally resolve on the former course, pack up and make off in the half-past two o'clock train. Buffalo straight ahead. Rochester some time in the night; don't quite remember the hour. Invasion of the cars by a deputation of drunken vagabonds from a Loco Foco mass-meeting at Rochester. One of them tries to canvass the car and gets knocked down. N.B. The same experiment in the car going up last week. Result: Whig forty odd, Loco Foco one, viz: Mr. Andrew Jackson Polk, a brother of Mr. J.K.'s.

August 30.   Utica at eleven, having gone over the ground so far in fine style. Therefore commences the slow stage, continuing till we reach Schenectady, where we put ourselves on board the Troy cars and shoot into the waspish little city with great expedition.

Make the best of my way on board the *Albany* and secure a state-room and that point being settled and a tolerably hearty supper on board and one or two (rather bad) cigars indulged in, I found myself quite comfortable and altogether in a better frame of mind and body than I'd enjoyed all day. Turn in early, however, and albeit I knew my stateroom was on top of the boiler, sleep like a stone.

August 31, SATURDAY.   Wake up as the boat's entering the dock. Dress in a very leisurely way and walk home. . . .

October 14, MONDAY.   Back from the City of Brotherly Love and Burnt Churches this morning. Had on the whole a very passably pleasant visit save in one particular: my liver or lower intestine, I'm not sure which, has been guilty of gross malfeasance, flagrant breach of every obligation of duty and friendship, for the last few days, and I have been and now am really unwell and uncomfortable.

As to a detailed chronicle of this my late tour, I'm too tired to under-take it. How I went to [the General] Convention and how I heard Dr. Hawks's great Apologetic oration, and how I came off with the most exquisite sick headache I ever experienced, how though unhappy I bore it with equanimity as it formed an impregnable position and tower of strength against all solicitations to go to a tea squall. How I went to Fairmount, all over the Mint with Major Roach and saw the battlefield and the still extant bullet holes of Southwark, and saw all the little lions of Philadelphia, and how I went to Christ Church Sunday morning and St. Peter's in the afternoon and how the former has the best organ I ever heard, and all that, must fade into oblivion, beyond the reach of the Journalistic Muse.

Hawks's speech, by the way, was the ablest piece of Old Bailey elo-quence, the cunningest web of crafty sophistry with its adroit *suppres-siones veri* and its malicious *suggestiones falsissimi* (as against Muhlenberg, for example), its artistical blending of pathos and trenchant sarcasm with the conversational tone of a candid reasoner, its air of disinterested advocacy of justice, honest and humble admission of venial error and calm expostulation against hasty or prejudiced judgment, its occasional outbreak of something really like eloquent indignation, its cool shuffling aside of strong points and its triumphantly plausible attacks on weak ones altogether made it the greatest effort in that kind of dishonest word-monger-ing that folks call forensic eloquence I ever heard. Result doubtful. Bishop Whittingham told me he thought he would *not* succeed. So I hope it may be.

October 16, WEDNESDAY. . . . Looked in upon Trinity Church this morning. They've got up the first flying buttress on the south side of the chancel, very light and pretty it is; also, I observe indications of cleaning up dirt and carting off rubbish that give hopeful promise of the commencement of paving and finishing inside. The church looks like Westminster Abbey, or the Cathedral of Cologne completed on three times the original scale after the churches I've been looking upon in Philadelphia, the city of ugly buildings *par excellence*. There's not a church in it but's downright *hideous*.

October 19. . . . Whether this attack that's now going on in Philadelphia against our diocesan [Bishop Benjamin T. Onderdonk] with such strange and ominous stillness comes from the same quarter or not, I don't know. I rather suppose it does not. It's the office I respect and not the man. I don't know him personally and if these charges be sustainable, in the name of heaven let things take their course. But I devoutly hope the matter will pass over quietly and be dismissed by the House of Bishops and that we shall be spared the excitement and pain of a second edition of the Pennsylvania case.

October 23, WEDNESDAY. . . . Looked in at Trinity; got hold of the tower key by a lucky chance and went up into the spire with Anthon, second time I've been up. It's now rather over 200 feet, I believe; glorious view of the city and parts adjacent. Terrible breakneck process getting up and rather worse coming down again. Found one way on the upper scaffolding above the aisles of the nave where for the first time we had a view of the ceiling of the nave and the clerestory windows as far as completed, eight, I think, in the north side, and four or five on the south. Both are lovely. . . .

October 27. . . . The movement against our bishop, whatever it may precisely be, still kept very close. A paragraph in the *Express* of Friday morning alluding to it, contradicted "by authority" in yesterday's paper and in the *American*. Were there anything in it, the Bishop has enemies enough who'd be too happy to push matters to a crisis, so I'm disposed to hope the best from their inactivity. . . .

November 8, FRIDAY. The verdict's against us, and a new trial can't be got. The state's given up, now, and to be sure it's time, for Polk's majority is running hard on 5,000. It's no use to think about the matter any longer. There's a bare possibility that Delaware and the other states yet to come in may alter the aspect of affairs, but it's hardly worth considering, and the vote of New York has settled the question and the illustrious Polk is President-Elect.

And the Whig Party is defunct, past all aid from warm blankets, galvanic batteries, and the Humane Society; it's quite dead and the sooner it's buried the better. What form of life will be generated from its decomposition remains to be seen.

Two causes have mainly brought all this to pass: Native Americanism, and the great difference between the candidates in conspicuousness and vulnerability. Everybody could talk about Clay's long career as a prominent politician and find something in it to use against him fairly or falsely, while his opponent was impregnable from the fact that he'd never done or said anything of importance to anybody and the attempts made by the Whigs to injure his personal political character only recoiled on their own heads. Henceforth I think political wire-pullers will be careful how they nominate prominent and well-known men for the Presidency; they'll find it safer to pick up the first man they may find in the street. . . .

November 10, SUNDAY. . . . I omitted on Wednesday to chronicle the fact that Bishop Onderdonk was on that day "presented" in due form by Bishops Otey, Polk, and Meade for (*sit venia loquendi* the lying charge) "licentiousness," the presentment, or charges, served on him, and the House of Bishops notified to assemble for a judicial session in this city thirty days hence.

The "actor" seems to be the Reverend Mr. [James Cook] Richmond. He was left off the missionary committee at the last Convention and was weak enough to let his irritation and wounded vanity show themselves most plainly in all he said and did thereafter till the adjournment. This has made him just fit for the purpose of the Reverend Henry Anthon, who, I can't doubt after what I've heard, is the real mover in the matter, and with him [Thomas J.] Oakley, [John] Duer, John Jay!!! and I fear the whole of that unhappy minority.

It is in short, and really and truly painful is it to believe the fact so, the last desperate effort of the malignant, bitter, partisan hostility of those people to the Bishop that has brought this false and foul accusation into the light of day, and Richmond is the tool used for work too dirty even for Dr. Anthon, and after his attack on McVickar in the last convention I thought nothing was too mean and miserable for him to put his hands to when the Bishop or the Bishop's friends could be injured by it. But this dirt is to be thrown at a higher mark and may fall on the head of him who aims it, and a prudent man is the doctor.

That the accusation is a lie I fully believe and assuredly most fervently hope, but be it true or false, and should it be proved by a mathematical process or by the confession of the accused, it would not alter my opinion of those who, with all the facts in their possession, for six years took no steps to procure an investigation till three signal defeats in three successive conventions had shown them that they could not break down the Bishop's office, and that in a sudden fit of zeal for the purity of the church, this most pitiful attack on the Bishop's personal character was their only chance of victory and vengeance.

November 24, SUNDAY. . . . Can learn nothing more about the progress and prospects of those amateurs in stink and stercoration, the prosecutors of the Bishop. The session of the House of Bishops commences on the tenth of December and we shall soon have the state of the case then.

All I dread is that some silly slips of sickly virginity, whom the Bishop may have shaken hands with, looked at, or (shocking to relate) actually *kissed* (the ungentlemanly old ruffian!) will be brought forward, with some imperfect recollections, distilled by vanity, party feeling skilfully wrought on, prejudice, self-importance and their own impure suggestions, to swear to—heaven knows what—of an attempted rape and a heroic resistance.

That creature [Rev. Henry M.] Beare, I'm told, is in the business. With what satisfaction the Reverend Chief Cook of this precious stew must survey his forces and concoct his charity materials! . . .

December 13. . . . There's not much new to write about now, except that we're going to war with Mexico as fast as possible for the extension of "the peculiar institution" and the glorious privilege of paying the debts of Texas. That will bring John Bull down upon us, of course, and then probably the "natural enemies" on the other side of the Channel will get their backs up and from swearing get to fighting, and then Russia will pitch into 'em both on her own private account, and a very pretty little motion will grow out of the matter and a very pretty mess will John Tyler, John C. Calhoun, and Wilson Shannon contrive to get us, the people, into. . . .

December 20, FRIDAY. . . . The Bishop's trial is still in progress. [David Bayard] Ogden and David Graham for the defense and that foolish fat bag of unfragrant flatulence, Hiram Ketchum, Esq. (who thinks himself like Daniel Webster), and [Henry] Anthon's priggish little *fidus Achates*, Gerardus Clarke, Esq., for the prosecution. Saw Mitchell this morning; he's staying with Bishop Gadsden and knows all about the position of things, and he's very confident the affair will turn out as it should do. I'm sure I hope he's right, but it's hard to tell, and to make matters straight before the world, an acquittal's not enough: the case must be such as to bear publication; and it must be published, or the charitable and enlightened public will consider its enlightened self at liberty to believe all sorts of things.

Beare's wife was to be examined today, and with her testimony it's understood that the Presenting Bishops rest their case. In reference to that most miserable and despicable matter, it's expected to show the utmost cordiality, warmth, and seeming confidence to have existed on the part of the injured and insulted female toward the Bishop till it occurred to certain people that something might be made of it.

Certain "Miss Rudderows" (from St. Mark's) have testified and some ominous remarks are made about the impeachment of their evidence. A certain Mrs. [Clement Moore] Butler, one of the mainstays of the prosecution, seems to have met a terrible discomfiture and to have utterly come to naught on the cross-examination. On the whole, the aspect of affairs is brighter, decidedly, but the sky is not quite clear yet.

December 23. . . . Can learn nothing more touching the trial that's in progress. I'm sorry to hear some people talk rather gloomily and unfavorably as to its issue, Gerrit Van Wagenen for one. However, I suppose one man's predictions and impressions are about as good as another's. For my part I'm unable to form any sort of opinion as to the result or the course things will take in either event. Harm must come of it, however it ends. Dirt can't be thrown at any man without some of it sticking to him, and so far doubtless these blackguards will triumph and claim a victory.

December 24. . . . Rumors from the Secret Tribunal: various, contradictory, and generally in a high degree nonsensical and absurd. But I went into Appleton's shop this afternoon and there happened to hear, pretty directly, from Bishop Whittingham one degree removed, a very felicitous statement of the position of things. May it prove true!

The Avocato del Diablo has rested his case. How long the defense will occupy no one seems able to guess. I predict that it will not be very protracted.

December 25, CHRISTMAS DAY. . . . To church as usual, and heard Higbee. Mama couldn't go; she had an unlucky fall yesterday that produced a certain discoloration about one eye, not altogether ornamental. Adjourned to St. Peter's and heard the finale of one of Mozart's masses. Looked in at Appleton's and got a copy of *Martin Chuzzlewit* wherewith I've been making myself comfortable, for the book's far better than I expected and Mr. Dickens's tone of coloring is exactly in harmony with Christmas, though it won't do for everyday use. . . .

1845

BISHOP ONDERDONK CONVICTED · ACADEMY OF DESIGN · DOWNTOWN FIRES · PROFESSOR LONGFELLOW

*T*he annexation of Texas, much desired by the South but opposed by many Northerners, had been certain ever since the election of Polk; and Tyler took steps in the last weeks of his administration to gain the glory of the measure. A joint resolution of annexation passed the House by a large majority and the Senate twenty-seven to twenty-five. Strong briefly but emphatically records his disgust. Mexico at once broke off diplomatic relations and warned the United States that the admission of Texas as a state would mean war. Though efforts were made to conciliate the Mexicans, Zachary Taylor was sent with 1,500 men to the new frontier. The diarist remained preoccupied, however, with home affairs—with the completion of the new Trinity Church, with the great midsummer fire that destroyed nearly three hundred buildings, and with concerts and fashionable balls.

January 3, FRIDAY. Sad news this morning that spoiled my breakfast: *the Bishop convicted by a vote of 11 to 6.* And it seems not to have been a party vote. Brownell at least voted with the majority. Went into Templeton's office and held an ecclesiastical council with him and Winthrop and one or two more and was half talked into the belief that there was something in all this. But I can't and won't believe it. But I'm too much mystified and astonished and disgusted to discuss the matter. One thing I'm surprised at, I confess: the very general feeling of sympathy for the Bishop that seems to exist even in quarters where one would least expect it.

News of the sentence tonight. "Indefinite suspension," by 9 to 8, a very indefinite sentence in every respect, and one that will give rise to a good deal of doubt and disputation, I think, before its exact meaning is settled.

January 6. . . . Went with John Parish to the Tabernacle and heard Ole Bull. Heard "Niagara," "The Solitude of the Prairie," and "The 78th Psalm"; which of the three is the greatest humbug I've not decided. He's a great player undoubtedly, but that he's no composer one may see by his orchestral parts, of which one can judge better than of the solos. They are thin and miserable beyond expression, mere noise, perfectly trivial and utterly without musical ideas. His theory of the sublime in music would seem to be that it rests in a happy combination of brass and kettledrums.

In the opening of "Niagara" one might discover (if he knew the subject) the image of a flowing river gradually quickening its current and becoming broken with rapids. Then came a grand explosion from the orchestra, intended to express a cataract, and after that I could recognize no meaning in the piece unless the *artiste* meant to express that he'd gone over the falls with the crash that described them and was drifting about in a fragmentary state below. . . .

January 15, WEDNESDAY. . . . Commenced German Monday night with Charley [Strong] for fellow student and Hempel[1] for *magister*. What with the cultivation of gutturals and the desperate complication I'm getting into in Wall Street, I find my hands pretty full.

The report of the Bishop's trial is to be out on Saturday. James [Cook] Richmond has been publishing the most extraordinary piece of crazy blackguardism on the subject that ever came from a man who was allowed to go at large. His pamphlet's[2] a curiosity which I shall carefully preserve—if only for its most keen and lively expression of the insolent exultation of a mean and malignant man who thinks he has triumphed beyond his hopes. A Bowery loafer who had licked somebody he's long had a grudge against would talk in the same tone in which this production's written. . . .

January 28. . . . Got a copy of the Bishop's trial this afternoon by special favor. Been diligently reading the same tonight. Won't say anything about it till I've read it through. . . .

[1] Charles J. Hempel (1829–1897) was a student at the medical college of New York University; he took his M.D. later in the year and was subsequently professor at the Homœopathic Medical College in Philadelphia.

[2] *The Conspiracy against the late Bishop of New-York unravelled by One of the Conspirators.*

February 12. . . . Read Richmond's Pamphlet No. 2, also John Jay's.[3] Confound that most miserable business from the beginning to the end thereof! I do believe that the Bishop is guilty of no conscious impurity or moral offence of any kind, and that the witnesses have perjured themselves by exaggerating, distorting, and forgetting, perhaps unconsciously, too, from mere spite; that at all events, these facts if admitted should not have been followed by such a sentence. . . .

February 16, SUNDAY. . . . It's not so very long since I used to shrink with a mental spasm of indignation and disgust, as one draws back his fingers from hot iron, from the thought of the silly scruples and restraints which had conspired, with my own want of energy, to keep me out of the world and ignorant of so much that's in it, to prevent my gaining confidence, energy, manliness, and self-reliance, the way I've been through my whole life watched and cared for and kept at home. And still I believe such a system of education and discipline to be, for most boys and young men, on the whole ruinous. For most of them are better able to be their own masters than I am, and when they know a course to be right and true, are more likely to follow it than I should be if left to my own governance.

But though this same imprisonment and espionage has, I suppose, rendered me pretty thoroughly unfit for the practical uses of active life, and settled conclusively that I am never to acquire wealth, eminence, or station, still with perfect sincerity do I thank God that so He has ordered it. Were I now to find myself my own master, free to do and go what and where I pleased without fear of inquiry, or remonstrance, without any of the restraints and checks that I've so often (and so naturally) been out of temper by, I should tremble for myself. Had I been so emancipated in my college days or for a long while thereafter, I should have gone bodily to the Devil in a month, and if preserved in any way from utter destruction, I should have gathered for myself a load of offences of which the imagining and half-conscious guilty intention is more than sufficient without the overt acts.

February 23, SUNDAY. . . . Loder's long-expected concert came off last

[3] *Mr. Richmond's Reply to the "Statement" of the late Bishop of New York.* John Jay's pamphlet was titled *Facts Connected with the Presentment of Bishop Onderdonk.* The authorized record of the trial, *The Proceedings of the Court Convened under the Third Canon of 1844, in the City of New York . . . December 10, 1844, for the trial of the Right Rev. Benjamin T. Onderdonk, D.D.* . . . published by Appleton, ran to 333 pages. A scurrilous parody appeared on the streets soon after: *More Disclosures in the Feeling Career of the Right (Wrong) Reverend Overdone Overdrunk.*

night, and thither I went, with Charley. Well attended it was, despite the discouraging weather, and Loder probably pocketed a very satisfactory surplus. As usual, three-fourths of the assembly were children of Israel: the author of *Coningsby* certainly right in claiming for his brethren a higher development of the musical sense than is common to mankind. Had any one suddenly ejaculated last night "Norwich and Worcester's *down!*" or "Farmer's Loan and Trust Co. has just executed an incoherent assignment!" the announcement would have had an appalling effect on the hook-nosed and black-whiskered congregation. . . .

March 3, MONDAY. . . . I instituted a minute examination this afternoon into Renwick's new church [Grace Church]. It will certainly look well when completed and the pipe-cleaners of columns that support the clerestory will tend to impress the congregation with a sense of the uncertainty of human life and suggest profitable meditation of the instability of things temporal. It's positively frightful to behold them, and they'll be but very little stronger, I reckon, when plastered over and made to look substantial. A Samson who can grasp two of them at once would have but little to brag of in bringing the whole clerestory down with one jerk.

Texas is annexed. I believe I'll expatriate myself.

March 13. . . . Had a visit from Tom Griffing. He's shortly going to New Orleans, and thence west, with some thoughts of making a permanent settlement there, if the *genius loci* shall make fair promises. Fred Anthon's going with him; his papa, I hear, has resolved to ship him off for a season to try what change of air will do toward the eradication of some rather erratic propensities on the part of that most hopeful young gentleman. Those two fellows—young Van Rensselaer, Phil A.—and a Bostonian named Swett, a most bitter blackguard, as Yankees commonly make severe cases of blackguardism when they're once fairly inoculated with the distemper, have been leading for the last year or so about as hard a life as any set of boys about town, in one perpetual and unintermitting spree morning, noon, and night. A temporary rustication may help matters. But what prodigy of paternal stupidity could have chosen a place more entirely malapropos than New Orleans, with its drinking shops and its quadroon girls and its atmosphere of dissipation and money-making and nothing at all besides, where every young man who's not slaving at a countinghouse desk or over the cotton bales outside is almost driven to be a roué for the want of something else to do? Are there not Labrador and Nova Zembla, and an extensive tract of Arctic and Antarctic wherefrom to choose, in which the blood may gradually be cooled down to a certain degree of staid sobriety? . . .

March 16, SUNDAY.   The next time Hempel comes here, I'll endear myself to him by becoming his first patient and renounce all things on which he lays his veto, and dose myself diligently and obediently with decillionths of belladonna or anything else and give homœopathy a fair trial, for that allopathy is no match for a sick headache, whatever else it can do, I've satisfied myself.

March 23, EASTER SUNDAY.   Very fine day this, but I'm in no humor for enjoying it. One very sufficient reason is that I'm but just emerging from a frightful headache that beset me in great force on Friday morning.

So when Hempel came here last night I surrendered myself formally into his keeping, underwent a vigorous cross-examination as to symptoms attendant and symptoms premonitory, and expect my first homœopathic dose at our next meeting. So now we'll see what the children of Hahnemann can do. The old lights—Galen, Hippocrates & Co.—are but blind guides in this matter. . . .

Got a note from William C. Schermerhorn yesterday on some business. He announced his adhesion to homœopathy and says it has saved his life. Well, if it can touch these abominable headaches of mine I'll renounce allopathy with all my heart and become a zealous convert. Certainly if there be any substitute for the old system, that dispenses with emetics and cathartics and blistering and bleeding and all the horrors anticipation of which makes "the Doctor's" entry give me such a sinking of spirit, it's worth trying.

March 28, FRIDAY. . . . That animal P[hillips] grows more and more odious and intolerable every day. I dreamt about him last night and awoke feeling uncomfortable in consequence. I'll sprinkle some bed-bug poison about the premises and see if it don't lead to his speedy disappearance. There are not many men for whom I've ever felt an antipathy, but this is one of them. And it's not the kind of feeling with which one shrinks back from such a face as Ben Butler's, for example, the feeling that you're looking at a smooth, dangerous clear-headed scoundrel (all which Mr. B. *looks like*, at least). But it's the peculiar sensation with which one steps aside when he has nearly trodden on a coprolite *before* petrifaction. That's as cleanly a circumlocution as I'm master of.

March 31.   Heard a good story today of old Myles Cooper, D.D., LL.D., etc., quondam of Columbia College. "I once knew," said someone in his company, "a very good, pious, honest old Presbyterian, who—"

"My dear sir," interrupted the Doctor in great excitement, and hurrying out his notebook, "*Will* you have the goodness to give me his name?"

And another facetious remark of the immortal [James] Harper, the Mayor that wants to be, but won't be after his present term runs out. Somebody was recommending Anthon and him to get out a Greek Testament with English notes mainly for the benefit of Harper's friends of the Methodist clerical corps, who, being generally men of rather limited education, would find it much more convenient than the Latin notes and commentaries that belong to most standard editions. "Don't," said Harper; "they're nice people, they are—but they all think the New Testament was written in English, and it would only unsettle their minds and throw them into horrid perplexities to be undeceived; they do very well as they are—let 'em alone."

April 1, TUESDAY. *Festum omnium stultorum.* The only performance intended to honor the day that I've witnessed was the publication in the *Courier* of a notice of the death of Prof. [Nathaniel Fish] Moore concluding with

None knew him but to love him
Nor named him but to praise—

Doubtless the work of some most witty-conceited Sophomore, and a repetition of the facetious performance of somebody in our class who announced in like manner the demise of Renwick.

April 9, WEDNESDAY. . . . Election came off yesterday and resulted as generally anticipated in the rout and utter overthrow of Whigs and Natives both. [William F.] Havemeyer's mayor, and the Locos have swept nearly every ward in the city. As for the Natives, they may be looked upon as politically dead, for though they've polled far more votes than the Whigs, who scarcely tried to do anything, new parties require tender nursing and propitious influences of all kinds to keep them in a state of cohesion, and the Natives have suffered a run of bad luck ever since their exploits at Philadelphia last summer that will rather tend to break them up. So the Sect of the Ecclesiocausts may be considered as verging fast toward dissolution. . . .

April 20. . . . The annual exhibition of the Academy of Design has opened, and I've been twice to look at it. It's vile. One or two good landscapes there are, by Cole and Durand. Edmonds has a couple of clever pieces in his peculiar style, "Facing the Enemy" and the introduction of a small boy to his first schoolmaster, and possibly half a dozen tolerable productions might, on a searching and exhaustive analysis, be raked out of the several hundred square feet of spoiled canvas that cover the walls of the exhibition room. But Mount has been very far from successful. Gray has produced nothing that's anywhere within sight of what he has done and ought to do. Inman is shocking bad, and so on through the whole artistical catalogue. There are some tolerable portraits: there's my father looking facetious, and Hugh Maxwell looking fidgety, and old [William P.] Furniss looking pecuniary, and Mrs. Edward H. Ludlow looking brazen—her portrait, by the way, the work of a man named Wenzler, or something like it, is a most amazing piece of minute, high-finished Chinese miniature-painting, and a good variety besides. . . .

April 25. . . . Coming down Broadway [with Templeton], we heard an alarm of fire, and a most volcanic cloud of black smoke came suddenly sweeping over the sky from the northeast. I thought it could be nothing less than the gas works on fire that could produce such a portentous phenomenon, and as Templeton had a tea squall to dress for . . . and couldn't go, I detached myself as a reconnoitering party and rushed down Franklin Street. Before I was two blocks from Broadway, the smoke was suffocating and blinding, and when I reached the scene of the performance and stationed myself at the head of Elizabeth Street, the scene was strange enough. The Bowery Theatre was on fire, burning inside. Everything was wrapped almost in darkness by the dense smoke that was pouring out of every window and every crevice of the building; you could scarce see across the street, and only now and then as a gust of wind swept off the smoke was the outline of the theatre distinguishable, running through the block from the Bowery to Elizabeth Street and rising high above the low two-story houses built around it. Then came a flicker of deep red flame streaming up under the cornice in the rear, and subsiding again, then another and another, and at last it caught on the roof, one or two dazzling little streams of fire ran like lightning along the cornices, and in one minute the whole area of the building was a mere furnace, sending high up into the air such a mass of intense raging flame as I never saw before. It was blowing pretty smartly and everyone said the whole block would go, and it would have gone but for the strength of the side walls of the theatre which kept the flames above the roofs of the adjoining houses. As it was, they took fire again and again, and some of the roofs were pretty well demolished by repeated lightings and snuffings out. All the people were evacuating their houses with great despatch, and a motley tribe they were—French and German and Irish and unadulterated

Native American Bowery Boys, flashy supernumeraries and scene-shifters, members of the whore-archy in most slatternly *deshabille*, despairing housekeepers whose furniture had been moved to parts unknown, and patrons of the theatre who looked on and moralized melodramatically in ungrammatical English over its downfall, and loafers of most unquestionable genuineness on the lookout for anything they could lay their hands on. It was a funny assemblage and I had hard work to make my way out of the mob. . . .

May 11, SUNDAY. Walked this evening. Saw Cram and Pete. Pete was rushing down to his "Club." Those establishments should be visited by some kind of legislative discouragement. They are mere Institutions for the Doing of Nothing—systematically; places where a parcel of boys have larger facilities than elsewhere for lounging and loafing, and where they may meditate, as they sip their brandy and water, on their precocious attainments as "men of the world" and knowing fellows, and try to look like a Sanhedrin of Pelhams and Vivian Greys.

I've heard considerable jaw about this "knowledge of the world" of late, and the phrase as commonly used seems to mean the habitual avowal of the belief that everybody (the present company tacitly included) is a quack and a humbug, and that he's the best man whom it's hardest to find out, a certain practical familiarity with the Flesh and the Devil being implied at the same time as indispensable to give a final polish to the "knowing" character. It's the Mephistopheles philosophy, diluted and made *flat*.

And half these people are such well-meaning fools, such really good-hearted, kindly, and amiable puppies, that it's truly lamentable to see them going out of their way to trade in mere affectations of this kind. . . .

May 15. . . . Pete paid me a visit tonight; he brought a bulletin from the City Hall where the May examination is going on, our most promising *élève*, Mr. Phillips, being one of the candidates. He had flunked fearfully "up to the time our reporter left." May he *only* get through! Another three months of his endearing sociality and high refinement would be more than we deserve.

May 16, FRIDAY. . . . That animal Phillips, it seems, got through by grace of a second examination. His narrative was the most irresistibly convulsionific, the most intensely funny, tale of woe I ever listened to. Cutting was admitted counsellor.

Went to Castle Garden tonight with Pete and Carolus to hear *Semiramide* as a concert. Came off before the end. It's quite pretty music, but wanting, it seemed to me, in the freshness and vividness and exuberance of a certain kind of genius that I supposed belonged to Rossini's opera.

May 22, THURSDAY. [After a long fit of melancholia.] All right again, I believe. I consulted Hempel, whom I chanced to meet, on Monday, and he exhibited certain infinitesimals which I swallowed with great gravity—and, "imagination" or not, I was quite sound the next morning. Homœopathy's a strange business. . . .

I met Erben yesterday or day before in Wall Street, and as visitors have been for some time past vigorously excluded from Trinity Church, I took the opportunity to go in under his convoy. The scaffolding is nearly all down, so that for the first time one could see something of the general effect of the interior, which has hitherto been visible only in parts and parcels at a time. It is altogether the finest interior I ever saw, the only Gothic interior that ever seemed natural and genuine and not the work of yesterday. How far the pews and internal arrangements will spoil it remains to be seen. . . .

May 28.   Pleasant weather. Treated myself to a shower bath this morning before breakfast, a laudable procedure which, with the permission of Morpheus, I'll repeat tomorrow. His sway is usually most tyrannous from five o'clock to seven so that no pledge on the subject may be lightly given.

May 29. . . . Took my ablutions patiently and underwent a shower bath with fortitude this morning, but unless the thermometer bounces back to summer heat during the night, I shall spare myself the like affliction tomorrow morning. It's a serious matter to tumble out of a warm bed, pull on a dressing gown, rush to the bath room, and have all the breath knocked out of one's body by the first crashing shock of that instrument of torture. . . .

May 31, SATURDAY. . . . Rumor of the projected alliance of "Piggy" Bedell [Rev. Gregory Thurston Bedell] with the Beata of No. 1 [Waverley Place—Miss Julia Strong] still vociferous and uncontradicted. I have not the smallest objection to its being "justified by works," verified by the event. On the contrary, I hold it to be altogether desirable that $150,-000 more or less should come into the church instead of being pouched by some sprig of Dutch Deformity. For that the lady in question, if she ever look favorably on mortal man, will strike her colors to a white cravat and nothing else, I consider a sure thing. It's a subject that scientific men have unaccountably neglected to investigate, the mysterious influence of white cravats over womankind. . . .

June 14. . . . Trinity spire is nearly at its climax—only one or two courses of stone yet to ascend and then comes the cross, of copper. Upjohn did not like to venture on a stone cross of magnitude corresponding to the height of the spire. The church, he says, will be ready for consecration by Christmas, but so he said last year. There was a great pow-wow and parochial jaw in the vestry touching the cross—Philip Hone made a great speech against papistical innovations.

June 15, SUNDAY. . . . Walk tonight through devious paths and byways perilous on the west side of the town. Encountered Dorr and lounged up the Fifth Avenue and across to Gramercy Park. I'm thinking more and more of buying there contingently. For this section of the metropolis is beginning to pass all toleration, and I think we shall be forced to become emigrants before we're much older. Certainly if Pine Street should be cut through or Thames Street widened, and one or the other's certain to be done in a year or two, Greenwich Street will be utterly untenable. There's a nice lot on the corner of Twentieth Street and the anonymous little street that bounds Gramercy "Park" on the west whereon I've fixed my regards.

This being Sunday night, our neighbors in the rear are comparatively quiet—there's only the average choir of cats, a pulmonary horse (stabled within twenty-five feet of this room) afflicted with a periodic cough of great severity at regular intervals of about fifteen minutes, and a few drunken Dutch emigrants singing what I've no doubt's a highly indecent Low Dutch canticle, fortunately unintelligible, with a chorus like a house on fire. That's all. It's quite a "Sabbath stillness," for an ordinary evening; there are two Dutch lust-houses in Washington Street that keep an orchestra apiece—one has nothing but some kind of a tumtuming instrument and a cracked clarinet, but t'other exults in a very violent cantatrice accompanied by a piano and two trumpets. . . .

June 16, MONDAY. . . . Rumor tonight that General Jackson's dead— probably a speculation of some loafing editor's to make money by an extra—though not very unlikely, the Old Hero having been declining and decaying in strength for some time. Well—*de mortuis nil nisi bonum* —so before it's settled that he's actually dead, I'll take this opportunity to say that he's done the country more harm than any man that ever lived in it, unless it may have been Tom Jefferson.

Walk tonight. Gramercy Park looks like a comfortable place—must make further inquiries touching real estate in that vicinage. . . .

June 17. The "Old Hero" is dead—beyond all gainsaying—and today all flags are at half mast and the nation is, in the language of oratory, supposed to weep. Well, with all the man's transgressions, it should also be borne in mind that he was at least thoroughly in earnest in all he did. There was neither hesitation nor humbug in his composition, and what his hand found to do, he did with such might as was in him. . . .

July 7. . . . It's frightfully hot this Monday evening, so hot that I can scarce summon energy enough for the chronicling of our Eastern journey. However, I'll try, for it's but just nine o'clock and it's certainly too hot to do anything else—and then for the bathing tub.

Leave Friday morning and go through to Greenport very comfortably in three hours and ten minutes, being thirty minutes inside the regular running time. So far the journey was very well and things looked promising, but then (after waiting half an hour on the wharf) we got on board the *Traveller*, our ferry boat, and she was crowded with an extensive selection of raff and ragamuffins of every color and degree, all more or less tipsy and riotous, who had come out on a day's spree in honor of the Fourth from all the neighboring parts. Then the sun was warm as it's apt to be in July, and the feed was vile, and everything was all wrong, and the voyage across was a bore. Reach New London—delayed half an hour there by their blundering way of coming alongside the wharf—and dump part of our live lumber there and take the Norwich & Worcester train at Allen's Point and go through in comfortable style, stopping at Newton by special permit between six and seven. Find Haskey and George at the depot, and five minutes' drive brings us to Mr. Derby's *Schloss*—very snug place with some thirty acres attached, on which he's farming most enthusiastically. Eloise and the children all well.

Saturday morning, after a walk with Mr. Derby and an inspection of divers miraculous potato patches and unrivalled displays in the rutabaga line, drive to Waltham and go into Boston by the Fitchburg road. Boston looks very knowing, bustling, thriving, and pecuniary. Walk about a little, without finding certain books I was in quest of. Drive to Charlestown with Mr. Borland and my father. Ascend the monument *solus*, go with them through the Navy Yard—ropewalk, dry dock and all that, very fine—come back and take a nap after dinner, while the rest of the folks are rushing off to Mt. Auburn. Sunday: To church with Mr. Derby and the boys at Newton —something—Falls, upper or lower, I forget which, nice village, said to be the only village in the state where there's *nothing but* an Episcopal church. Not very rubrical there, certainly, but the congregation was large and looked well. Afternoon: . . . saw Henry Andrews and he told me that Texas had concluded that the United States *should* be annexed if it wanted to.

This morning: rise at half-past four, breakfast, cut over to Newton. The train comes along like a chain of paixhan-shot preceded by a congreve so that for a moment the thought—they won't stop for us after all—suggested itself vividly, but the red flag and Derby's personal presence recalls the permit to the conductors, and the train heaves to in beautiful style. 'Twas really a fine sight to see the immense line of cars that had come rushing and thundering down upon us brought up so easily, and at the conductor's signal standing fast almost in a moment. In and off—run to Norwich in grand style—on board the *Worcester*—weather fine and water quite still and the voyage across very pleasant but for one drawback—that my father complained of being quite unwell and couldn't go down to dinner. From Greenport to New York was hot, tedious, and uncomfortable. . . .

July 10. . . . Wish there wasn't any such thing as money in the world, or that every one was comfortably supported by the state; wish I was a good-tempered, amiable, and accommodating kind of person and wish I could find somewhere a small epitome of feminine perfection still unengaged and open to competition. I'd seriously consider *then* the propriety of following Templeton's example and trying on myself the medicine that's dissipated all his causes of complaining and fairly made a different person of him. But there must be a revolution both pecuniary and personal, and good luck most rare in one's search and enquiry, before such a notion can be entertained: and were I to fall in with an Angel incarnadine tomorrow and to prosper in my wooing, I should probably be more desperately out of humor in six months than I am now.

July 19, SATURDAY.   Rather a notable day. Was waked at half-past three this morning by a couple of explosions in quick succession that shook the house like an earthquake and must have blown me out of bed, I suppose, for I was at the window before the roar had fairly died away. And the last remnants of sleep were pretty well knocked out of me by the aspect of things out of doors. The moon was shining full and bright; the dawn just beginning to show itself, and to the southeast there rose into the air a broad column of intense red flame that made the moon look pale and covered everything with a glow and glare that passed every effect of artificial light which I'd ever witnessed. Didn't stop to analyze the phenomenon but hurried my clothes on, gave the alarm downstairs, and rushed out of the house as fast as possible. Hadn't far to go—the fire was in New Street and Exchange Place, and burning most fiercely. Everything in New Street as I looked down from Wall seemed withering away and melting down in absolute white heat. Only a few people assembled, and no engines visible. The explosion that had just taken place had taught people to keep at a deferential distance—shown them that fire was not to be played with. . . .

Whereupon I went home to report the position of affairs, as I'd been requested to do. Came back to the scene of action, and seeing that all Broad Street on both sides from about No. 20 down was one grand solid substantial flame, most glorious and terrible to look at, and that the two or three fire companies on hand and hydrants open were likely to make about as much impression on it as His Honor the Mayor would have made by a singlehanded attack on the conflagration à la Captain Gulliver, I pelted home very expeditiously to tell my father that the days of '35 had returned and that he'd better turn out and see the sport.

When I got back the fire was crawling down Beaver Street and Exchange Place toward William, quite unchecked, and then I came into Broadway just in time to see the iron shutters on the stores three or four doors south of Exchange Place beginning to grow hot, and the Waverley House beginning to disgorge occupants, furniture, and smoke from every convenient outlet—they said 'twas already on fire in the rear, but I didn't believe it, and thought it could have been saved had any body made much exertion to save it. One of St. John's people whom I knew met me and told me awful stories of the Croton giving out and the fire having it all its own way. Soon a few snaky little curls of flame made their appearance in the stores on Broadway—the Waverley, abandoned to its fate, was burning slowly down, story after story, beginning at the top—fire appeared in great activity lower down Broadway and the engines were playing on the west side of Broadway where the house fronts were hissing hot already, and I began to consider where the fire was likely to stop, in a very serious kind of way, as a matter wherein I should soon have some personal interest. And I believe I went home and reported my apprehensions. Indeed, it was shocking to watch the fire at this point—building after building taking fire, not in regular order, but as they caught in the rear, from New Street, where it was raging among stores and carpenter shops.

Saw Cram and walked about with him, and at last went on top of one of the new Wall Street stores where his office is, and where we had as good a view of the burned and burning district as the smoke would allow. This was at about *seven*, and I then came to the conclusion that the fire was beginning to find its match, and that the worst was over. . . . Everything between Broadway and Water Street, where active combustion was still going on, was covered with a uniform cloud of dim smoke which prevented our discovering that there was still terrible mischief in progress to the south and enabled me, therefore, to go home and eat a comfortable breakfast. Came out directly afterwards and found out my mistake: the fire had reached the Bowling Green, all the east side of Broadway from Exchange Place to Whitehall Street was burned or burning. The Adelphi Hotel was a magnificent sight, blazing from roof to cellar—Whitney and Wilmerding and all those people moving and cordons of police crossing Broadway to keep people off. At the south end of Broad Street the sight was grand. Everything was going down before the fire and the wind rising. One side of S. William Street was burning fiercely, with every prospect of its crossing the street. Everybody in Water, Front, Pearl, and the other streets about those parts moving out in frantic haste—the fire will go from river to river, a sure thing in all men's mouths. Stone Street and the narrow streets to the north of it, absolutely impenetrable, arched with fire, and the throngs of people in the streets all working for their lives, hurrying back for fresh loads—the indications of desperate terror and haste in every store one passed seen in the boxes and barrels that were tumbling out of doors in such utter recklessness—the universal consternation that prevailed made even the streets that were yet untouched by the fire most exciting and rather perilous places.

Went once or twice to the office, where my father was mounting guard, and returned by a circuit on the east side of the fire. Saw with dismay on reaching the Bowling Green that it had *crossed Broadway* near Morris Street. Couldn't get through the line of police to see exactly the extent of the mischief, but went home and to Wall Street two or three times before I could get all parties possessed with the very disagreeable fact. Very disagreeable it was, for the wind was getting round to the south—the fire would probably soon cross Morris Street and the houses on the west side of Broadway, thoroughly heated by the fire opposite them, would soon communicate it to one of the stables on Lumber Street in the centre of the block running parallel with Greenwich and Broadway. Nothing of course could be done to stop them from going, and they would make short work with the east side of Greenwich Street up to Rector, which would bring the fire into most unpleasant closeness to No. 108 Greenwich. Got through the line of police by special favor of one of them and went down Broadway. Five houses, beginning at the south corner of Morris Street, were burning, among them Ray's and Brevoort's, old acquaintances of mine. Never shall forget the aspect of things there—the street wholly deserted, save by two

ELIAS HASKET DERBY AND HIS SON RICHARD HENRY DERBY

TREADING IN THE FOOTSTEPS OF MY ILLUSTRIOUS
PREDECESSOR

STRONG AND PROFESSOR ANTHON IN THE COLUMBIA CHAPEL

THE ATT'Y

DRAWINGS BY G.T.S. FROM THE DIARY

or three firemen, all one side of it a mere chaos of ruin and smoke and flame still flickering over the wreck and here and there a single front wall still standing with the background of smoke visible through its naked windows. . . . Everybody in Greenwich and Washington Streets as far up as Rector moving out in hot haste, the crowd, confusion and panic worse if possible than on the east side of the city.

At about half-past ten I thought the crisis had come, for the southeast corner of Greenwich and Morris *"took"* on the roof. But by dint of cutting off burning fragments and sending a stream into the building it was stopped, and about the same time the five houses on Broadway having burned themselves out without communicating the fire on either side to any great extent, the danger was pretty much over—to my great satisfaction, for the last hour had been one of more excitement than was altogether pleasant.

By half-past eleven the fire was stopped at all points, having burned near three hundred buildings and done only not quite so much damage as the great fire of '35. . . .

July 20, SUNDAY. . . . Not much thought of or talked of but this fire. Everyone still rigorously excluded from the burnt district by a cordon of the National Guards—very sensible arrangement. Much more so than Havemeyer's first move, in ordering out a troop of horse; a specially fit arm of service is cavalry for checking a conflagration. Not knowing how to charge the burnt district, feeling that they ought to be doing something on so momentous an occasion, they merely made themselves ridiculous by rampaging about on the sidewalks and putting themselves in everybody's way.

August 1, FRIDAY. . . . Spent the day pretty busily, and took a long walk this evening: an Architectural Tour. First there's the new Unitarian meetinghouse, on Crosby Street's show front on Broadway—Gothic in the Chinese style, and a more deplorable exemplar of infatuated vulgarity trying to look venerable and medieval. Then comes Grace Church—there are faults enough there, even to an unpractised eye, not to speak of the unhappy straining after cheap magnificence that seems to color the whole building, but the upper windows of the tower, which I'd supposed were going to be some preposterous kind of lancet, are now nearly finished and are coming out very differently from my anticipations. They're to be very elaborate specimens of the flamboyant and add much to the effect of the tower. Potts's Meetinghouse (Enterprise Chapel) is undergoing embellishment by the addition of something elongated, in front: but whether it be some anomalous kind of spire, or the tower run to seed, I can't determine. Phillips's show [the First Presbyterian Church] grows uglier and uglier, and when its tower is finished it will resemble a corpulent Chinese gander with its neck rigid, stout and tall, and its square-built rump and broad expanse of back, sturdy, squat, and not easily to be shaken. A deeply engaged tower in such a dumpy body as this, and a tower of such height and breadth won't improve, as if risen.

November 4. . . . The Boston steamer in today brings news of the total failure, or something nearly as bad, of the potato crop in Ireland. A frightful amount of misery will be caused by it, I'm afraid, coupled as it is with bad harvests in England. It's also stated positively that the Rev. John Henry Newman has reconciled himself with the Church of Rome and been formally received into that communion. Every steamer for the last year or so has brought some kind of "information from a reliable source" that that reverend gentleman had done so, or was about to do so next week, which I've commonly charged to the account of the natural appetite for lying and slandering that belongs to the canting crew whose special scourge and terror he is. But this statement looks rather more definite and trustworthy than its predecessors, and I'm afraid it's true. As for the tempest of clamor and bad language about apostacy and all that which will rise up as naturally as poisonous vapors rise up from a stagnant pool when one throws a stone into it, that of course will be entitled to about as much consideration as the scolding and swearing of a badly-educated parrot. But the Anglican Church and the cause of true Catholicism have received what looks to me like the worst blow that has been inflicted on them for many a year. It is the solemn declaration, by a deliberate and momentous act, of one whose equal it would be hard to find in the Church of England, that she is not a member of the church Catholic, that Catholicity is not to be found on earth except in dependence on Rome. The leader and master-spirit of the only hopeful movement toward the establishment of a fully-developed Catholic communion that should be free from the corruptions of that communion which claims an exclusive Catholicism that has been seen for near two centuries abandons the effort as hopeless. Well, the impulse he has given remains behind him, and if I read the signs of the times aright, it will remain in spite of this heavy check and discouragement.

November 29, SATURDAY. . . . Mr. Moritz Eitheiler, our new German teacher, made his first appearance Thursday night, looking like an incarnate nightmare, or one of Hoffmann's outré imaginings introduced into real life, and delivered us an inaugural lecture as remarkable in its

way as its author in his. Not particularly clear, perhaps, but very comprehensive in its range, and presenting in one view a new system of
philology, the Croton Aqueduct, Chimborazo, John Ronge, "Mother
Germany and Her Infant Humanity," Fourier, and "St. Margaret Fuller,
of the *Tribune*." His audience (Charley and I) found it rather a trial of control over our risible muscles. He gave us our second sitting tonight, read
us an "appendix," and we went ahead with *Wilhelm Tell*.

November 30. . . . Looked into Longfellow's poetry last night, in the
new edition (a much better book than I'd hoped to see—the illustrations
nearly all passably good and none of them outrage decency as our engravings are apt to do). He's the first native American poet who promises to be
remembered a century hence, for Halleck and Bryant themselves, and much
more the smaller fry, won't stay very long in the minds of men, and (not
counting Wordsworth, who properly belongs to the last generation) is
there any living English poet who stands above him? I think not, even if
one omit to take into account the purity and healthiness of his tone of
thought, the solemn, earnest, inspiring notes that give to almost everything
he has written a character and feeling like that of some austere piece of
sacred music. I presume he's a Unitarian, and that Unitarians are beginning
to think and write as he does is one of the signs of the times that's worthy
to be had in remembrance. For my own part, if I were to make my own
poetical private judgment and individual likings the rule of my poetical
faith, I should say something a good deal more emphatic about the merits
of Mr. Longfellow, for very few of the brethren of his craft have given
anything to the world that I think of so often and enjoy so much as some
of his productions.

December 23, TUESDAY. . . . Well, last night I spent . . . at Mrs. Mary
Jones's great ball. Very splendid affair—"the ball of the season," I
heard divers bipeds more or less asinine observe in regard to it. Two houses
open—standing supper table—"dazzling array of beauty and fashions."
Polka for the first time brought under my inspection. It's a kind of insane
Tartar jig performed to a disagreeable music of an uncivilized character.
Everybody was there and I loafed about in a most independent manner and
found it less of a bore than I had expected. Mrs. Jones, the hostess, is fat
but comely; indeed, there's enough of her to supply a small settlement
with wives. Came home with Charley at about half-past one, but didn't
get asleep all the rest of the night—an abominable wooden kind of cadence
upside down in one of those polka tunes haunted me like an evil spirit, and
came jerking and creaking into my head whenever I began to subside into

a doze. On the whole, the ball room, with a waltz raging in the midst of it, was really a showy spectacle. Modern civilization has achieved thus much, that people making fools of themselves do it in an ornamental way.

And tonight I'm irrevocably booked for Mrs. Baker's rout—or whatever its name may be in the dialect of the élite—given, I believe, to the honor and glory of Mrs. Lynch[4] and confidently expected to be a jam unprecedented, the invitations out being reported by some as one thousand and by others as 2,500. . . .

December 24. . . . The ball last night was a bore, more crowded than the Jones rout, and people say not so successful. Can't pretend to decide, myself —one seemed to me about as afflictive as the other and common sense equally remote from both. Perhaps No. 2 was rather the more irrational transaction, the whole house from garret to cellar being turned upside down and the third story consecrated to the waltz and the polka, whereas at No. 1 they were able, by reason of their greater command of room, to get along with the basement and drawing rooms alone and were therefore able, I suppose, to go comfortably to bed at such hour of the night or morning as the departure of their guests might permit. But where Mrs. Baker's people slept last night I can't conceive unless they went to the Police Station house near by and solicited accommodations at the public expense as homeless and destitute folk turned out of their own house by the aristocratic public generally. . . .

The practical lesson I've learned from my experience of the last two nights is that if this be "going out," I shall come in again and stay in; that if going into Society consists in habitually participating in such comfortless, joyless, insipid exhibitions of extravagance without results and folly without amusement, I have shewn more wisdom in staying at home hitherto than I gave myself credit for. Dissipation it is in the strictest sense of the word. Rational speech there is none, and none is expected; people leave their common sense in the dressing rooms with their cloaks and hats, and one finds himself the next day unfit for business and wholly stupified and done up without having had anything in the way either of amusement or edification to show for it. So I'll go to no more balls. May people who give them bear the painful announcement with resignation!

December 28, SUNDAY. . . . This life of Cromwell by Carlyle I've been dipping into last week is a very unaccountable kind of thing. I had thought that to a certain extent I understood his position, and that it was one from

[4] Elizabeth Jane Strong, Peter's sister, had been married on the 9th of December to Edward Livingston Lynch.

which he looked down in a patronizing kind of way on all forms of faith as developments more or less enlightened of the same religious principle and equally entitled to respect when held in earnest, that he included Anselm and Becket and John Knox and Mahomet with equal honor in his muster roll of "Heroes." But in this book he seems to identify himself with Puritanism, and to treat his subject with as blind a zeal and as resolute a determination to see one side of the question only as any contemporary partisan pamphleteer. One would suppose that if there were instances in history of upholders of a Catholic system of faith who were not quacks, the defenders of such a system in the seventeenth century might possibly have been as sincere as their adversaries. But Carlyle has evidently no notion of any such thing.

Idolatry of power seems to lie at the foundation of his philosophy of history—very visibly in this book and still more in his dealings with the character of Napoleon. Your hero was a rebel and a usurper, says the Legitimist. He governed, replies Mr. Carlyle, because he was the only man then extant who could govern—"to the workman belong the tools." Or translating from Carlylese into English, Mr. Carlyle means to say that might makes right and that man rules *divino jure* to whom God has given ability to take the reins of government and to keep them. A very significant doctrine, and a very fruitful one in results yet to come. For democracy being a mere transition state in the progress of a people, and the idea of a government by the grace of God being very rapidly on the decline, along with all recognition of a divine presence and influence in the affairs of the world giving them sanctity and majesty and a title to veneration, we may perhaps even in this age see the new dynasty of rulers reigning in their own strength by grace of themselves and giving glory to their own arm which has itself placed the crown on their head. And woe to those over whom the sceptre is held by that title!

December 29, MONDAY. . . . War panic still dominant. Stocks down. What does the politician deserve who makes the question of war or peace the servant of his personal ambition, and uses his dirty cunning and meretricious oratory and faculty of talking sophistry and lies with a face of brass—the elements of all his statesmanship—for bringing once more on earth the crimes and horrors of war, that he may work his way to higher political station?

December 31. . . . Spent the morning in a general investigation of Tiffany & Young's stock of gimcrackery and the selection of divers New Year's presents therefrom. . . .

1846

TRINITY CHURCH CONSECRATED · NEW HAVEN AND THE
WINTHROP WEDDING · THE ANTI-RENT MOVEMENT

———————•⌣•———————

*A*s the year opened, tension between the United States and Great Britain
over the Oregon boundary dispute had become a threat to peace. Strong
fully expected war, but was not greatly alarmed at the prospect. Although he
was undoubtedly pleased at the settlement of the dispute by a friendly accept-
ance of the forty-ninth parallel, he does not mention the event. He writes little
of the war with Mexico that began in April, albeit the country heard of
Taylor's first victories at Palo Alto and Resaca de la Palma with great
excitement. Strong, with most Northern Whigs, utterly condemned the con-
flict. His diary for the year contains much less than usual about public affairs.

January 1, THURSDAY. . . . Started with my father and got pleasantly
through with our legitimate list of calls . . . in company with him. Then
left the carriage and went off on my own private account to Mrs. Isaac
Jones's, William Samuel Johnson's,[1] Mrs. Baker's, Berrian's, Griffin's, and
so forth. It wasn't so very bad after all. Bedell's turnout was quite imposing
and aristocratic—made a very satisfactory call there and another at
William Aspinwall's. His arrangements, by the by, house and furniture
both, are really magnificent. One can't make a satisfactory guess at the
amount he's invested in rosewood and satin, mirrors, cabinets, and vertu.
And they say that Langdon, William B. Astor, and Penniman go beyond
him in display and costliness. One don't readily see spending money on

---

[1] William Samuel Johnson (1795–1883), Union 1816, the grandson of the U.S.
Senator and Columbia president of that name, was a New York lawyer and politician; his wife was Laura Woolsey.

one's self in its true light till he sees it done on a large scale in luxuries of this sort. Langdon's arrangements are said to have cost not much less than eighty thousand dollars. Paid a glacial sort of visit to Mrs. George Griswold. . . .

January 5. . . . War fever up again at its hottest. Calhoun's unexpected intervention as peacemaker has quieted matters considerably, but old John Q. Adams has taken his stand on the other side, and he's a formidable element in the calculation of chances. One good result, though, will come of his course. It tends to separate the question from party considerations so that the Democracy will make but little capital by pushing things to a crisis and can't drive their measures through to their own exclusive glory.

January 8.   Really, I'm beginning to find myself plunging into dissipation to an extent that would have made my hair stand on end if I had dreamed of it a year ago. Last night was spent at a small tea fight at Mr. William Samuel Johnson's, and tonight I met the same set at Waverley Place; and having just returned therefrom, I devote the five minutes that remain before the rule for going to bed becomes absolute in chronicling this miraculous revolution in myself. There's a puzzling sense of doubt about my personal identity that comes across my mind now and then when I find myself in a drawing room with the clatter of feminine tongues going on about me, and I look in despairing bewilderment at my white gloves. Confusion between the ego and the non-ego is embarrassing.

Well, the little women are really quite charming little creatures altogether. Only it's a pity that some of them are so supernaturally ugly, and so wooden in their stupidity where they don't think it worth while to try to make themselves agreeable. On the other hand, there are several— three at least—with whom I'm already quite heroically in love, and with any one of whom I'm fully prepared to elope at a moment's warning. And then if their respective relatives will kindly place me in funds for the erection of an Elizabethan mansion fifty feet by ninety-five, with furniture and establishment to match, on the Fifth Avenue, with an income of fifteen to twenty thousand per annum, what a felicitous arrangement, what a happy match it would be! . . .

January 10, SATURDAY.   Went last night with Parish and Charley to see the Keans in *Richard the Third,* as the same has been brought out at the Park with the scenery, dresses, and so forth that were used in England two or three years back with so much *éclat.* . . . This is the third time in my life that I've seen the inside of a theatre. The last time I was at the Park was just about fifteen years ago, in January, '31, to see little Master

Burke as Shylock. The second time was at Boston, during my first visit to that great metropolis in '35. . . .

January 19. . . . Great news from England. Sir Robert Peel out, and the Whigs in, with that pig-headed Lord Palmerston for Foreign Secretary, I presume, though that don't seem settled yet. The Corn Laws are going, of course, and with their abolition the existing system of things in England that's been growing up for so many centuries and has reached its appointed stage of decrepitude and ricketiness receives the final shove and shock that will soon prove fatal.

War we've got to have, I suppose, and if I had a wife to look after and a family to support I suppose I should feel bored at the prospect. . . .

January 25, SUNDAY. . . . The anxiously expected *Hibernia* has come at last. News arrived yesterday. Rather more pacific than people expected. And to everybody's great surprise, the Whigs are out again. Lord John Russell couldn't get a cabinet together and Sir Robert had to be called back. Whether he'll have a long lease of power remains to be seen. I can't get the hang of their maneuvering at all. . . .

January 27. Tonight my evil destinies render it imperative on me to go to Mr. [Henry] Parish's big party in all the pomp and vanity of white waistcoat and dress coat. Certainly I should stay away, for I'm in no humor for nonsense tonight, but from appearances there won't be so many there as might be, and one's absence may be noted and found fault with, especially as this is my first invitation there. . . .

Strongly tempted I am to pull back the one foot I've ventured into this treacherous bog of Fashionable Womankind and peremptorily to cease from being one of the soirée-suffering aristocracy: to bore myself neither with call nor party more, and to resume my strong position as an implacable and unexpugnable woman-hater.

I think I should do so without further ceremony or delay, but I'm desirous of getting out of my system somehow or other the absurd something which I can't describe or define or analyze, which makes me so miserable at these places. Whether it's sheepishness or nervousness or envy or self-conceit I can't determine, but I want to be rid of it whatever it is. . . .

January 28, WEDNESDAY. . . . Been reading Schiller and Hoffmann— homœopathic doses of both: for I'm particularly sleepy, thanks to my late hours of last night. Went to Parish's—very pretty party and much people there. Everything in good taste and very successful, though Pete [Strong] was sure there would be no "existences" there. Found it but indifferent pleasant myself, but gave myself very little concern about the matter—didn't try to make myself either useful, ornamental, or agreeable, for there was nobody there I cared to cultivate, but being in a magnificent fit of the sulks, established myself in a corner, and watched other people making asses of themselves. . . . Not a pretty woman—really honestly and sincerely pretty, that is—on the premises. They all look unhealthy on close inspection, and no wonder, making Pandemoniums of their viscera as they do night after night with oysters and ice cream and pâtés and charlotte russe and all sorts of abominations and ruining themselves with late hours. . . .

February 10. . . . Feel myself to a certain extent redeemed and disenthralled from the scrape I've been getting myself into for the last few weeks. I am a decidedly great fool, even greater than I've been in the habit of admitting myself to be, and if I'd followed my first impulses in this ridiculous business a very pretty picture of desperation and disappointment should I have made a month or two hence. Shall assuredly expose myself to no more of these very perilous influences.

February 28, SATURDAY. . . . At the first "Bee" last night at Mrs. William Samuel Johnson's. Not very different from any other party so far as I could see: about sixty people on hand, including a few outside barbarians —*Fan-kwei* or "foreign devils" who don't belong to "the Bee" but were specially invoked for this occasion. Spent a very particularly pleasant evening, though they say the affair won't work so well this year as it did last. The evening has been changed to Monday, which is an improvement.

News from Washington a little squally. The administration seems to be bent on blundering us into a war, and why everybody here is so supremely indifferent to the prospect, so very sure that it'll all be peaceably settled, I can't imagine. . . .

March 6. . . . Friedrich Schlegel has taken up most of my leisure this week. Beyond all doubt or question, he's a magnificent fellow and I shall fight my way through his books with the least possible loss of time.

There was our Bee on Monday night at Dr. Smyth Rogers's—rather pleasant. Made Lieutenant Townsend's acquaintance; very good fellow he seems. On the whole, I'll patronize the Bees. It's entertaining to see the manoeuvering and intriguing and Machiavellianism that go on whenever you create a little community of any sort; plotting and counterplotting seems a natural instinct of man, to be exercised on all occasions in little matters and great. . . .

War prospect much the same. Nobody knows and nobody seems to care, and I'm sure I don't care much. Probably the bombardment of New York would be the first historical event that would succeed the declaration of war, for our fortifications at the Narrows, though quite picturesque of a summer afternoon, are still, considered strictly as defenses, worth about as much as a line of squirtgun batteries, and so long as falling ruins will hurt people, they are like to be more dangerous to those inside of them than to anyone else in the event of its coming to hard knocks, paixhan shot, and improved projectiles. . . .

March 10. . . . Chimes in Trinity commenced operations this morning, much to the delight and astonishment of the giddy and excitable populace, who stood and stared at the church steeple with eyes and mouths in a state of dilation. The interior of that edifice hasteneth toward completion; they're beginning at an elaborately-carved reredos, and St. John with his eagle has been added to the group in the west window. . . .

April 17. . . . Tonight went to the Academy of Design with Anthon and Charley. Much people there. Spent most of the evening looking about with Jem Strong. Exhibition the best I've ever seen. Plenty of damaged canvas, of course, but quite an unprecedented proportion of really very good pictures: e.g., a very lovely thing by one Blaas, belonging to Henry Parish—St. Catharine carried to heaven or to Mt. Sinai, I forget which, by angels. Paintings that so delight one at first sight are apt to lose their place in one's affections when they've been seen several times, and this may be but a meretricious affair after all; but one's first impulse on seeing this is to pronounce it perfect and most beautiful. "Master and Pupils" by Huntington, in his best style. "Landing of the Northmen" by Leutze —very striking and effective piece, a little exaggerated and very inconsistent and faulty in the details, but on the whole extremely good. Several matchless specimens of Chinese facsimile portrait painting by Wenzler, in particular one of Dr. Berrian.

Mount's picture ["Fishing along Shore"]² for my father is there; I like it no better than when it hung in the back parlor. Capital landscape by Durand, and so on. . . .

April 18. . . . West window of Trinity finished at last, and the scaffolding all down, effect very good and ecclesiastical—better than one had a right to hope. People find great fault with it, though; there's that wise woman Mrs. B. [who] objects to the "improper preferences." She goes

² This excellent canvas, now called "Eel Spearing at Setauket," painted for George W. Strong in 1845, is owned by the New York State Historical Association, Cooperstown, N.Y.

for 54° 40'—"all the Apostles or none." Others complain that one grand "Scripture piece" was not put there, filling up the whole window, and indulge in other profound bits of criticism of the same sort which show that they know nothing of the uses and capabilities of stained glass.

German tonight, then to the Academy of Design. Saw Jem Strong there, and Hamilton Hoppin. Abide still by my first opinion that the exhibition is good beyond all precedent and example. Blaas's picture bears looking at—people say that one of the Angels looks like Miss Christine Kean—can't see it myself. Huntington's "Master and Pupils" is excellently good—the girl's face, looking down on the book her instructor is illuminating, is the loveliest face I've seen on canvas for a long while. Confounded be the whole generation of pretty faces—on canvas and off it.

> *. . . es ist mir worden leid.*
> *Ich hab in meinem Sinne*
> *O Venus, edle Jungfrau zart,*
> *Ihr seid eine Teufelinne*

What were they made for, and why do they put themselves pertinaciously forward to perplex, hinder, and delay "rational folk" in the doing of their lawful business? . . .

April 21. . . . *Caledonia* in today: news of no moment on the engrossing question of peace or war. The Sikhs seem to be finally routed; I suppose Sir What's His Name the English general will be created Viscount Sutledge, Baron Punjaub, or some such thing. Sorry for it. I should like to see our Uncle Bull get the drubbing which fifty years of iniquity in the Indian Peninsula have fairly earned him.

The threatened riots at South Brooklyn around the Atlantic Dock seem to have come to nothing. The *Oregon* is not yet got off from her very awkward position on the Gridiron in Hellgate, and I begin to think she won't be, except in pieces. What prognostication does her very singular catastrophe afford one touching the other Oregon and the catastrophes and calamities that may spring up from that quarter?

May 19. . . . News from Mexico—great battle: seven hundred Mexicans killed and *one* of the free and enlightened—on the whole, a highly improbable lie. . . .

May 21. Today Trinity Church was consecrated. Went there, found place for the sole of my foot, but as for a seat, I might as well have looked for a live phoenix. . . . The services were quite imposing, and all the arrangements judicious and good. Near two hundred clergymen in surplices entering the church in procession and filling the chancel and the space around it gave quite a novel character to the ceremonies. The choir was full, and though the organ is not more than a third finished, it answered very well indeed. But the music was generally rather ponderous, as under Hodges's regimen one was prepared to find it.

May 24. . . . Great news from the frontier: two great victories; the Mexicans smitten hip and thigh and General Somebody taken prisoner. "Nothing equal to it," said my extra, "in all Napoleon's campaigns." Hurrah, hurrah, crow and cackle . . . and no end to the glorification. I do believe we're the windiest people extant. . . .

June 8. . . . Pleasant prospect before me is this: to go to that detestable little Yankee "kraal," New Haven, make myself agreeable to a few score of its Hottentot denizens, and officiate as groomsman at Templeton's wedding. What my precise duties are the Goddess of Etiquette knows; certainly I don't. If there could only be a preparatory rehearsal! . . .

After a long and nervewracking courtship, many of the ups and downs of which were recorded by Strong, his cousin William Templeton Johnson had won the hand of Miss Laura Winthrop, daughter of Francis Bayard Winthrop (Yale 1804) of New Haven, formerly a merchant of New York, and they were to be married June 10 in Trinity Church on New Haven Green.

June 13, SATURDAY. Back again; got home last night, Templeton being duly swung off according to the letter of the rubric and everything having been transacted in the most prosperous way.

Left in the *Globe* on Tuesday. . . . Wednesday very propitious; walk about town with Henry [Rogers] Winthrop and afterwards with Templeton into Hillhouse Avenue to see "the magnificence of New Haven"; sat on a fence and moralized on the chances and changes of things temporal. Certainly New Haven can brag of a show of vegetation in general and elms (the aborigines call them "ellums") in particular that beats all my experience of foliage; nothing like it, except in pictures, have I ever had the happiness to see. If the houses were all carefully removed, New Haven would be a lovely place. But I won't speak disrespectfully of it, for though they're a queer set of men and women who live there, yet the "barbarious people" showed us no little kindness; they're "gentle savages" —civil barbarians—an amiable and well-disposed native population. After dinner there were divers things to be done. My father came up by the morning boat; Mamma's cold kept her at home, most unluckily. Drove to the seat of war at eight o'clock with Templeton. Found the *prima donna* of the evening looking very nice, and after a few minutes the curtain rose, and Dr. [Harry] Croswell did the business in no time. The little lady was as cool as a little cucumber, steady and self-possessed, and did her part of the business beautifully, and as there were no mysteries or nonsense of any sort, and as everybody seemed in good trim, the whole transaction was highly successful. Congratulations and so forth—and then made myself generally agreeable. . . .

Thursday morning was miscellaneously spent. . . . Looked in on the Winthrops; was lionized about town by little Theodore Winthrop, a very pleasant, intelligent person whom I shall cultivate.[3] Spent an hour in the new [Yale] library. Building a preposterous caricature of King's College Chapel [at Cambridge]. Books badly chosen—ninety per cent mere lumber; indeed, except in modern Italian and French literature, in which it's rather strong, the collection is on the whole rubbish—old Puritan divinity and the like. [Edward Claudius] Herrick, the librarian, seems a good-natured sort of priggish little man. Took a dinner at the hotel that was meant for a lunch and went off at three to Mrs. Salisbury's big dinner party—very magnificent affair—*no wine*. May it not be written in the Book of Destiny that I'm ever to undergo the like affliction again. I feel it in my bones yet—such a piece of stately stupidity is without parallel in the experience of most mortals. Was released at about eight, and then ordered some tea to drive off the exhaustion and stupefaction that were brought on by the suffering of the afternoon, and found myself mechanically stuffing bread and butter and cold ham, so that I was eating from one o'clock till about nine. Nice place is New Haven for a man who wants to gormandize himself into an apoplexy.

Friday morning visited the library and the Gibbs Cabinet [of minerals] with H. Winthrop—most superb affair is the latter. . . . Came off in the *New York* at one o'clock. Rather pleasant run home. . . .

June 21, SUNDAY. Twice to Trinity. It continues to draw full houses; crowd today was extensive and miscellaneous. . . . That west window will bring an epidemic ophthalmia into the parish. With a bright afternoon's sun full upon it, it's a formidable thing to look at, as my eyes still testify by their tingling.

June 27, SATURDAY. . . . Went to Fort Hamilton last night and came

[3] In the margin Strong later wrote "*Big Bethel*"—*1861*. Theodore Winthrop, brother of Miss Laura, was then an undergraduate at Yale; his career as traveler, author, and lawyer was cut off by a Confederate bullet fifteen years to a day after the Johnson-Winthrop wedding.

in this morning. Spent part of my time there in a survey of the fort, which, being garrisoned just now by a lieutenant, two corporals, sixteen recruits, and a black cat, is probably not impregnable, though perhaps better able to stand a siege than Fort Lafayette, which is manned by *an* American soldier. Saw the drilling of half the garrison, i.e., eight very dirty and lubberly scapegraces caught three days ago—better fun for me than for them was the performance. . . .

August 11. . . . Not much news today. William Price blew out what brains he had left this morning.[4] The *Great Western* brought me some clever German books yesterday and we had a thundershower and squall last evening that blew off a cat's tail—that is, my unfortunate black and white friend was trotting in at the door to get out of the rain when a gust whisked the door suddenly shut and slammed off about three inches of Puss's finale. Mercy on us, how she ran!

Legend of Swedenborg's Ghost—how it had a long conversation with one Mr. Davis on a hill north of Poughkeepsie one rainy morning a fortnight since. Saw Mr. Davis's MS *procès verbal* of the conference. The Ghost's views probably profound, but wanting in precision and not remarkable for clearness. He quotes his own books (particularly the *Arcana Cœlestia*) with a perfect looseness. John R. Bartlett and Professor Bush believe all this stuff and Mr. Bartlett looks awful when he talks about it and ponders the Ghost's sayings and reads 'em forward and backwards and upside down and all sorts of ways to find out what they mean and what the Ghost's sentiments really are, but he hasn't succeeded yet.[5]

August 18, TUESDAY. . . . Back from Montauk last night. Very glad I've been to Montauk, just as I'm glad to have had the measles and the

[4] William M. Price (Columbia 1804), one of "General Jackson's pets," U.S. District Attorney for the southern district of New York, had absconded on the *Liverpool* December 6, 1838—"a defaulter to heaven knows what amount."

[5] Andrew Jackson Davis (1826–1910), the "Poughkeepsie seer," was just beginning his career as a spiritualist. Originally he had been a mesmerist, and although an uneducated man, had discoursed freely, while in a state of trance, on medical, philosophical, and theological topics. He was the author of more than a score of books. John Russell Bartlett (1805–1886) was at this time a partner of Charles Welford in the book-importing business in New York; he became Secretary of State for Rhode Island in 1855 and had a distinguished career. He wrote *A Dictionary of Americanisms* (1850) and edited the Colonial Records of Rhode Island and the first catalogue of the John Carter Brown Library. The Rev. George Bush (Dartmouth 1818) was professor of Hebrew and Oriental Literature at New York University; in 1847 he published a book arguing that the doctrines of Swedenborg were corroborated by the developments of mesmerism.

whooping cough: it's gone through with, and a recurrence of the thing isn't likely. Not but that I've had a very positively pleasant expedition—it's a joyful thing to be out of sight of the brick walls and out of hearing of the newsboys wherever one may be—but Montauk is not the terrestrial paradise.

Reached Greenport Thursday morning at a little before eleven and Sag Harbor at twelve. Queer place is the latter, with a very imposing Presbyterian meetinghouse which the inhabitants contemplate with much pride and affection. I'd give a trifle for a drawing of the edifice. . . .

Chartered a conveyance; left at two. East Hampton, Amagansett—and then all signs of civilization disappeared. Long trail of beach and then the Montauk Hills: miles and miles of monotonous desolation . . . neither tree nor shrub nor any green thing but the short grass, no object visible by which one could determine whether any given hill were as big as Mont Blanc and a hundred miles off or within a stone's throw and fifty feet high at the outside. . . . Sunset—here and there a big pond. Driver afraid of losing his way if night overtook him (there's no road through this blackguard territory) and went pelting over the hills and far away, like mad. Reached Gould's a little after seven. . . . Mr. and Mrs. William Seton arrived just before us, and there were two or three anonymous snobs besides in the way of our being comfortable. All three of us had to sleep in one room about as big as a cigar box. Next night, however, we were much more comfortably lodged. Friday: Very comfortable surf bath and the morning spent with Pete and George Anthon outlying after snipe, the plover being altogether apocryphal. . . . Morning chiefly spent in lying on our stomachs in a sand hill east of the "Oyster Pond," Pete and George busily whistling a dismal kind of tune consisting of three notes, over and over and over, "a Greek invocation to call snipe into a circle," like the "duc dame duc dame duc dame" in *As You Like It*. Snipe came and were knocked over. Pete was indefatigable—rampanged around the Oyster Pond like a kind of Dismal Wild Huntsman in a dirty shooting jacket. Phenomena of Montauk nowise numerous; when one has seen the first acre of undulating hill and the first hundred yards of beach and the lighthouse and a group of cows, he has seen it all. Cows said to be ferocious at times; no wonder. Noticed a kind of sponge on a small scale about the beach. Found no mosquitoes. George Anthon says that if Columbus had stumbled on Montauk, he'd have gone quietly home again and said nothing about it. . . .

Saturday: Drs. [Samuel M.] Elliott and Granville [Sharp] Pattison.

Dr. Elliott is a snob perfumed with musk like a wagonload of polecats. Amused ourselves during the morning by hurling pieces of lead armed with a hook and attached to a string into the surf and then pulling them back again. It is said that blue fish have been known to allow themselves to be caught in this way. . . . After nearly dislocating my shoulder blade and scarifying my fingers and knocking my lead about in all sorts of ways to my great bodily peril, I got tired, sat down, watched Pete and Professor Pattison and Anthon and Theodore Gould throwing themselves into calisthenic attitudes and dancing about the strand like people demented with a perseverance truly wonderful. Smoked cigars and drank raw brandy out of a pocket flask. Blue fish clearly not to be imposed upon, so Anthon and I went and took a glorious surf bath. Sporting privileges of Montauk clearly a good deal exaggerated. . . .

Sunday morning an eligible smack presented itself and we put ourselves on board at half-past nine for Plum Island. . . . Reached there at half-past three, landed and found that Conklin, at whose house we contemplated putting up, was sick and couldn't take us. . . . Came off and reached Greenport at seven after a pleasant day's sail. Peconic Hotel very full. Tolerable supper. To bed early, in something that was rather a case than a room, so very little bigger than myself was it.

Monday morning: drove over to the north side, took a boat and went out after ten-pound blackfish. . . . Caught more porgies than blackfish, none that were of extra size. After dinner put myself into the Brooklyn train; the two sporting characters concluded to wait till morning and then go to Babylon. Long detention, rain, smoke, dust, cinders, headache again, all sorts of botheration—home at half-past nine and went straight to bed doubting whether I should ever enjoy the blessing of a clean face again, for the abominable dust from the pine wood they burn on that road had mottled my countenance till it looked unearthly and my first ablutions didn't more than half remove it. . . .

August 23. . . . Reading of late a little Schiller, a very little Burke, a good deal of the *State Trials*, and considerable Schlegel, to wit the *Philosophie des Lebens*. A little diffuse, perhaps, is the last, but on the whole most beautiful and earnest and true. Lecture on Art especially admirable. Looked into Dumas' *Monte Cristo*. The secret of that school of novels consists simply in narrating and describing the most extravagant events and the most impossible characters in such a way that the reader, when two-thirds asleep, may not be more than half-conscious of their extravagance and impossibility. They aim at nothing higher than to astonish, and attain that end by the mere brute magnitude and monstrosity of their conceptions, the prodigiously surprising nature of their story. Kit Marlowe's *Tamburlaine* and *Jew of Malta* are legitimate specimens of the same school, and a very vulgar, semi-barbarian school it is.

September 25. . . . Ham Fish up for Lieutenant Governor. John Young for Governor. He's an anti-renter and I'll sooner vote for the d——l himself. Fish is well enough, though a mere bundle of negatives, but *noscitur a sociis*, and he should keep better company if he looks for the support of people who want to be held indifferent honest.

The toleration that this Anti-Rent movement meets among people who profess to be decent and to have souls above larceny is a very pregnant token of the indifference with which right and wrong are looked on by people in this land and generation, of their insensibility to the truth that there's any distinction between the two that can't be excused and palliated and diluted and done away with. These leases are a "hardship" on the tenants, they operate injuriously, they're against public policy, the tenants conscientiously think themselves aggrieved, they take a mistaken view of their rights and obligations, they're a very numerous body—such twaddle is the answer one gets to the question: why are not these people put in prison for forcibly withholding the property of others and hanged for murdering those who are charged with the execution of the law. And that they're patronized in an underhand way and courted and indirectly encouraged with hopes of "redress"—impossible except by a legislative robbery—by the Whig party shows pretty conclusively that the salvation of the country will never come from that quarter.

September 28, MONDAY.   I won't go to Trinity Church again in the afternoon, that's flat. My eyes are still tingling and smarting from the effects of that glaring west window. I was wiping them, as they watered and ran over, all through Wainwright's sermon, and my neighbors probably thought me under conviction and much exercised.

Talking of Trinity Church, the old feud between [Henry] Erben and [Edward] Hodges has ripened into a row which resulted in Hodges being tossed *vi et armis* out of the organ loft and left sitting on his hinder end in the lobby calling for the sexton and the rector. Erben wants to have an "exhibition" of that instrument (which is finished at last), but the spiritual authorities won't allow it. Erben appealed to the precedent of the exhibition of St. John's organ, and when Berrian gently insinuated that "we'd improved in churchmanship since then," he pointed to the Eagle Lectern and ejaculated, "I suppose you call that turkey buzzard an improvement in churchmanship!" . . .

[Daniel] Huntington's "Master and Pupils" installed over my mantel on Saturday afternoon; lovely picture it is, as I always thought it, and it improves on acquaintance.

October 29. . . . Went with my mother this afternoon to Catlin's in Brooklyn; saw my little friend Miss Helen—sweet little thing she is. She is a "member" of the "Academical Institute" or some swell, ineffable humbug, in the city aforesaid, and she learns all the Ologies—and Latin besides—and I don't know but Chaldee, too. Pity that what might so easily be left to grow up into a natural, simple-hearted, beautiful woman, with sense enough for all reasonable requirement, should be puffed up and spoiled with the conceited superficiality that such places generate and soured with the strifes and envying and emulations that grow out of "intellectual rivalry" in algebra and the theory of composition and Dugald Stewart's philosophy and somebody else's constitutional law! . . .

November 4, WEDNESDAY.   Election yesterday. John Young has carried the state by storm. I prefer Locofocoism to Anti-Rentism and voted for Silas Wright. There's said to be a strong vote against the New Constitution in this city, but I suppose there's scarcely a hope of its being rejected, though if everybody who thought it a bungling piece of radical legislation had taken the trouble to vote accordingly, it would have been laid on the table two to one. . . .

November 17, TUESDAY. . . . The Van Duzer tragedy complicating itself and increasing in interest daily. List of "young men about town" suspected of liability in damages said to cover two pages of foolscap— double-columned. Old Selah Van Duzer here last night and at the office this morning seeking for proof of Edward Potter's handwriting with a bundle of letters under his arm as big as a roll of carpet. Didn't meet with much success. Everybody was quite surprised, on coming to think of it, to find that he'd never happened to notice what Mr. P's hand was like. For my own part, Potter has been so little in the office, and done so very little when there, that I could not honestly swear I'd ever seen a line of his. Old Van Duzer breathes fire and slaughter, and there's a *crim. con.* suit coming, and no mistake—possibly a batch of them. It's a queer case. If the fortieth part of the stories afloat be half true, this woman must have led the life of a common whore for the last two years without her husband's suspecting what was going on. It would seem as if there were reason to suspect that the husband has been winking at the game and waiting for some eligible person of unquestionable solvency to begin trespassing on his grounds before incurring the expense of a suit. Doubt much whether he'll get heavy damages.

November 19. . . . Nothing new about Mrs. Van Duzer except that it's said that a Mass-Meeting or General Convention of the parties implicated is to be held in the Tabernacle tonight to arrange about a defense by subscription and to apportion the damages equitably between themselves.

December 20, SUNDAY. . . . Called at Henry Winthrop's with Cram Wednesday night. Never knew half the capabilities of the human tongue as a vehicle of gossip before. I was informed "positively" . . . "on very good authority" that I had the honor to be engaged to Miss [*name blotted out*], which thing I contradicted with fervor. But somebody or other has set the same story circulating, and I've had to disclaim the honor forty times since, and people are so very sure they're right that I get bewildered and uncertain myself sometimes. I believe I'll go and ask the lady whether it's so or not. Well, it's not so bad as it might have been. My fiancée is rather good-looking, quite pretty at times, good figure, and moderately sensible, plays nicely, paints a little I believe (at least I think I saw at her Papa's last winter a very unearthly-looking landscape attributed to her), has been abroad, talks about Switzerland, and has seen Cologne Cathedral. Other accomplishments, charms, virtues, and eligibilities no doubt in great number, but I've never found 'em out yet and haven't seen the lady for six months. Perhaps she's improved since that time; but if not, I humbly hope the report is wrong. If it's right, I shall fly the country. . . .

December 27. . . . Poor Giles Hillyer [Columbia '36]; his career since he left college has been sadly unlike what we all expected. What with his academic glories and his celestial urbanity, he was cock of the walk then, was *primum mobile* and first violin in everything, and his admirers said he'd be President, or governor of the state at least. He got married and his wife's immense fortune turned out a delusion. He bet ridiculously beyond his means that Clay would be elected, and that turned out a delusion. He went over head and ears into politics and neglected his business and went utterly to ruin, and Waters tells me he was for some time in absolute want, for his family couldn't help him—lived for a week,

I believe, on fifty cents and finally got tired of that and made for one of the southern states, Georgia or Alabama, where he is now. Poor fellow! After all, if he'd been the rogue that a good many pious and respectable people here think proper to act like, he'd be living here still very comfortably and snapping his fingers at his creditors. . . .

1847

CAMPAIGNS IN MEXICO · CENTURY CLUB · NORTHWARD
GROWTH OF CITY · WHIG VICTORY IN NEW YORK

The year 1847 witnessed the complete victory of American arms in Mexico, General Winfield Scott reaching the capital in September. California had meanwhile fallen to Frémont and Kearny. The crowing of Democrats and Southerners over the new conquests irritated Strong, who had no taste for an expansion of slavery. Already the sectional quarrel was becoming bitter; the Wilmot Proviso, designed to maintain freedom in the territories won by the war, was passed by the House but smothered in the Senate under a storm of Southern denunciation. Strong continued to be occupied with city and home affairs; and he became more of a New Yorker than ever when he bought a horse to explore the town and its environs, and when he joined the newly-formed Century Club.

January 24, SUNDAY. . . . Began our Teutonic Saturday with Adler,[1] and began (also with Charley) *French* under the guidance of a hard-featured Gaul named Buffet, Wednesday. I'm ashamed of myself for complying so far with popular prejudices as to have aught to do with so despicable a dialect.

January 26. Italian opera last night—*Lucia di Lammermoor*—certainly it's a capital company, but the opera, glorified though it is, seems to me a weak affair. But there's a furor on the subject just now and some

[1] George J. Adler (1821–1868), professor of German at New York University, was just completing his great *Dictionary of the German and English Languages* (1848); shortly afterwards his mental health failed, and until his death he was intermittently insane, though he published several other scholarly works written in Bloomingdale Asylum.

reason to hope it may bear fruit in the building of a new opera house. The little Chambers Street concern is quite too small; 'twas more than full last night. The aristocracy were present *en masse*—Washington Irving among the rest, with Mrs. Mary Jones. On the whole Donizetti is inferior to Mozart.

Have got to go to Mrs. Hamilton Fish's tonight.

January 27. The Fish rout last night was decidedly a "fast affair," the pleasantest party of its dimensions that I've seen yet. Everybody there nearly. . . .

January 31, SUNDAY. . . . Going to be sick, I think, so specially wretched have I been today with every sort of horrid dyspeptic sensation. My little black friend Teufelchen—or whatever is his proper style and title—I mean my black squirrel, is an invalid too, and has been sitting grunting on my lap all the afternoon in great affliction. . . .

Robert Weeks's big party Friday; went thither through the great waters of a most rainy evening. Pleasant affair, rather. Wonder why people always look so solemn when they dance a quadrille. Perhaps it originated in the Homeric funeral games.

Calvary Church—it's now complete enough for us to judge of its exterior. It is a miracle of ugliness. Cheever's meetinghouse [The Church of the Puritans on Union Square] gives hopeful indications of being somewhat worse. Happily there's reason to believe that the monkey who built them [James Renwick, Jr.] will not be allowed to build the Smithsonian Institution after all.

February 8, MONDAY. . . . Call on Mrs. Cruger tonight; pleasant evening, rather. Letters from Miss Edgeworth about the horrors of famine in Ireland. All accounts concur in a most frightful picture of suffering and destitution and every imaginable feature of physical misery. Yet some people dare to talk of probable exaggeration and the danger of being too hasty with relief! Mrs. Cruger showed me a letter she sends Miss Edgeworth tomorrow, begging her to write an "appeal to the ladies of America." Such things are commonly in bad taste, but this is a case that sets all ordinary rules at defiance.

Talked of Scott and Coleridge and Wordsworth and Southey and so on—'tis a rare thing to meet one who has known them all, spent days and weeks at Abbotsford and Keswick. . . .

What is the matter with me and why has my life for the last few years been so wretched, so utterly and uncontrollably dreary and miserable? Surely every external influence is in favor of its being as tolerable as is the average lot of mankind. Positive happiness I don't expect, or seek for; it can't be sought as an end and made an object without forfeiting deservedly the chance of meeting it. But this dreary succession of listless, unsatisfying days, varied now and then by fits of intense and bitter disgust at myself and everything about me, deadness to all that's good, paralysis of every right feeling and impulse, I protest against most stoutly. . . .

February 19, FRIDAY. . . . Hudson River Railroad. Monday next is the last day for filling the subscription and saving the charter. Gardiner Howland and his brother Sam and some other very good men are making the utmost exertions; otherwise I should think the case hopeless.

February 21, SUNDAY. . . . Was done yesterday by Gardiner Howland, who took me by the button, lugged me into a broker's shop, and made me subscribe $500 to the Hudson River Railroad. No matter; the road ought to be put through without further delay, and I'm magnanimously content to lose half my subscription.

The *Cambria* in; price of grain a little down. That'll damp the enthusiasm of the Irish relief movement somewhat. Very creditable, by the by, is the spirit and liberality that we, the people, have shown in that matter. To be sure, all that's done is little enough, and to have neglected doing it would have been mere unnatural inhumanity: but this general spontaneous movement is a thing I like to look at. It's so different from most of our popular excitement. Rather different, too, from the relations between us and Great Britain that were fairly to be expected a year ago. It will please John Bull, too, and perhaps its remembrance may do both nations good service if there should ever be another Oregon question between them. But our neighbors on the other side will have something to say about Mississippi bonds and repudiation and being just before one's generous.

Still busy at German and French. The former I despair of talking grammatically unless the great happiness of spending some time in Germany is hereafter to be vouchsafed me. As to the latter miserable dialect of monkeys, hyenas, and man-milliners, it's easy enough, fortunately, for time and labor expended on it are all but quite wasted. But I can find nothing in it to read. Must try Molière. As to taking up Eugène Sue and George Sand and so forth, I'd as lieve spend my time in a museum of morbid anatomy done in wax; to make the comparison hold, however, it should not be a collection of copies of nature, but of the fancies of a crazy anatomist depicting impossible ulcers and inflammations and gangrenes that never existed in any human subject. It's only for its modern historical productions that I want to know anything of French literature.

February 22. . . . News by the *Cambria*: horrible, most horrible, is the story it tells of famine and pestilence in Ireland. The misery there eclipses all that in Northern Scotland and on the Continent that would otherwise be a most fruitful subject for sympathy and a most potent call for help. . . .

February 27. . . . News from Mexico—guerrilla parties and yellow fever. Polk said to be going off to the seat of war in person. Nobody believes it. Hope he'll go, and like Don Sebastian of Portugal, never come back again. . . .

March 5, FRIDAY. . . . Saw Adler at the University and spent a pleasant hour or so with him. With an interesting and engrossing subject of study and labor, I should greatly enjoy a life of solitude and stillness like his. And there are but three choices: 1. his career, or something like it; 2. conjugality, which is a bore, a vexation; 3. loaferism more or less genteel, respectable, and ornamental. Give me No. 1.

March 6. . . . Philharmonic last night. Beethoven's Symphony in A; not very perfectly played, but it would take very serious defects in the performance to outweigh the freshness and spirit and strange fascination of the piece and I never had my attention held faster by music than it was by this. The "Orpheus and Eurydice" story that they always put on the programme when this symphony is played was as far from Beethoven's thoughts when he wrote it as the story of Puss in Boots, or The Dairyman's Daughter. . . .

Tom Griffing appointed to a second lieutenancy and going to Mexico. He'll make a good officer, and anything is better than idling here among roués and blacklegs, "leaving his clothes at the Woodcock and sleeping out." . . .

March 11. . . . Tom Griffing looks taller than ever; he'll be the Goliath of the hosts of Columbia, and if they want a champion to determine the war in a single combat, he's qualified to lick any one they can produce on the other side.

"Extrees" this afternoon: great battle near Monterey and Santa Anna discomfited. Story not generally credited, but there's probably some foundation for it. . . .

March 24, WEDNESDAY. . . . Chief topic of debate and discussion the Mexican news. Nobody knows the facts yet with any certainty, so there's ample room for all sorts of inferences and conclusions. Thus much is certain, that Santa Anna has moved from his position at San Luis Potosí with an overwhelming force on our line from Saltillo to the Coast, originally far too extended and now deprived of half its strength for the attack on Vera Cruz, and that Taylor's communications are interrupted and that he's shut up either at Monterey or the Rinconada Pass. Whether it's the wish of the administration to sacrifice Taylor or it's only their imbecility that's brought this about, it's like to undo all that's been accomplished since the campaign began, to destroy the prestige of the American arms and unite all Mexico in confidence and determined resistance. Taylor will do all that can be done, but he's in a tight place and can't expect to be reinforced in any reasonable period. Great reason to fear he may be used up altogether.

Scott writes like a coxcomb. Polk and his Divan are all imbeciles together. If the next news should be that Taylor and his force are prisoners of war and that we're driven across the Rio Grande (and I can't see what's to hinder), what a unanimous howl of rage there will be through the country! . . .

March 31. News from Mexico looking a little more direct and authentic than most of the legends that have been in circulation for the last two weeks. "Battle of Buena Vista," and General Taylor hath prevailed against the Mexicans and Santa Anna hath fled into the wilderness with more or less of loss and damage. Victory not bought very cheaply; heavy loss on our side, and the Mexicans would seem for once to have stood up to the scratch like men. . . .

April 4. . . . News from Mexico. Battle of Buena Vista confirmed: complete victory. 'Twould seem to have been against five to one, and after hard fighting. Very creditable to Taylor and the volunteers, even if it be true that the Mexican Army were fighting on empty stomachs and that Santa Anna had to use his cavalry to keep his infantry from running away. Also Vera Cruz is invested, Scott having made his landing without loss or serious opposition. Probably it has fallen before this, and a march on the City of Mexico will be the next movement. *Vive la République!*

April 11. News came yesterday of the fall of Vera Cruz after but a feeble sort of fight, it would seem. Miserable race, the Mexicans must be. All accounts make this a strong place (independently of the Castle) and had they kept it for two or three weeks longer, our troops would have been decimated daily by the vomits. I thought they were going to make

it another Saragossa; to let Scott approach as regularly and breach as
effectively as Engineer Corps and paixhan shot could do, and when all
that was done, to begin in earnest and give him an unscientific fight in
the breaches and from house to house. But it isn't in them, and they are
to Scott and Taylor's unpractised regulars and green volunteers just
what those who occupied the soil before them were to Cortez and his
handful of Spaniards. . . .

April 15, THURSDAY.   An hour yet before 'tis time to dress for the
Ruggles soirée, so I'll devote it to autobiography—"*Wahrheit und Prosa
aus meinem Leben.*"

Don't remember anything about Monday beside a long loaferine
evening walk and the illumination of Florence's two oyster shops in
honor of the downfall and capture of Vera Cruz—and that I remember
chiefly because I came considerably nearer being squeezed to an inglorious
death by the mob of unwashed spectators than was pleasant.

Tuesday: Election. Hill's concert—fair selection of music, the best
pieces from Rossini's *Stabat Mater*, overtures to *Gazza Ladra* and the
Jubel and that lovely chorus from *Preciosa*, but all played in rather a
slovenly way. Went off to National Hall and the Broadway House with
Parish and Benson thereafter, looking for news; found the Whigs drunk
and vociferous and glorious exceedingly, as they might well be on the
strength of so unlooked-for a victory. . . .

And now I *am* bored and this Bee that is to come off tonight won't
make matters any better. I am in manifold danger there of something
unpleasant and in the meantime I'll take up Richter.

April 16, FRIDAY. . . . At Ruggles's soirée last night—spent part of
the evening pleasantly. Walked down with that most windy of all the
bags of conceit and coxcombry that ever dubbed themselves Architect,
Jemmy Renwick [Jr.], and most entertaining was the monologue with
which he favored me—all about the "points" of Grace Church and Calvary. If the infatuated monkey showed the slightest trace or germ of feeling for his art, one could pardon and pass over blunders and àtrocities so
gross as to be palpable even to my ignorance; but nature cut him out
for a boss carpenter, and the vanity and pretension that are endurable
and excusable in an artist are not to be endured in a mechanic, and especially not in one who is a mechanic in spite of his ennobling vocation, and
degrades, vulgarizes and pollutes every glorious idea and form of the
successive eras of Christian art that he travesties and tampers with, as a
sacrifice to the stolidity of building committees and his own love of fat

jobs and profitable contracts. But he may improve and I hope he will: for as yet he has only done harm to the growth of true principles and right feeling in church architecture.

Ich bin nicht verliebt, but I don't care to be nearer it than I am. There's a beautiful sunshiny face making itself visible to me every five minutes here and in Wall Street and at the Hall and in all sorts of inappropriate places. It's quite a novel kind of hallucination to me, and I must reform it altogether. So I say with the scribe of the German MS. of the fifteenth century which I picked up t'other day as he records his name at the end of his labors:

> *"Henricus de Wildenholtz*
> *Got behut mich vor den frauwen stolz."*

April 25. . . . Saw Tom Griffing yesterday; he obeys his country's call on Monday, leaves for Point Isabel as second lieutenant in Col. Temple's regiment, with the prospect of an adjutancy. . . .

May 2. . . . Equestrian performances continued prosperously. Shall give instructions tomorrow for the purchase on my behalf of a sober Bucephalus. . . .

News from Mexico: Scott has probably settled Santa Anna before this, at a place called Cerro Gordo this side of Jalapa.

May 7, FRIDAY.   All but tired to death, for I've been spending the evening with Parish and Charley in struggling and pushing through the crowded streets to see the illuminations in honor of our Mexican victories. And the streets were absolutely swarming, alive and crawling with the unwashed Democracy. It was a fine sight and worth some trouble, especially seen from the Park: the City Hall, Tammany, the Park Theatre, the hotels and nearly every building in Chatham Street and Broadway lit up and glittering, rockets and Roman candles whizzing and popping in every direction, fireworks blazing away on the Astor and the American and half a dozen other places, and every side street that one looked down glowing, sparkling as far as its houses could be seen from the Park. All the hotels, club houses, principal shops and so forth lit up and some private residences.

Rumor tonight, very apropos, of another battle somewhere near Jalapa—probably at Cerro Gordo, where Santa Anna was said to be occupying a strong position in great force and the Mexicans discomfited, of course. . . .

Came near buying a horse since last entry—a subdued sort of Bucephalus that suited me very well. Trotted him as far as Washington Square on Wednesday morning, and took a refreshing ride with him out to Manhattanville yesterday afternoon, and concluded to take him; but the vagabond of a Scotch Presbyterian carpet dealer who owned the brute sold him to someone else before the time came when I was to have given him an answer. Any horse would have acquired low habits in the service of such a snob, and I'm very glad not to have bought him. . . .

May 8. April weather. Mexican news of last night confirmed: defeat of Santa Anna quite total; everything lost, even to that hero's wooden leg. Six thousand prisoners taken, and the rest of the army disorganized and dispersed so there don't seem much to hinder Scott from marching straight to the City of Mexico.

May 11. . . . Thurston sent me down a very good-looking piece of horseflesh this morning that promises to answer my purposes, and if I find he does, I'll get him.

May 16. Well, I tried the "piece of horseflesh" and find myself better suited with him than with the carpet seller's Rosinante; but the brute's been and got a cold in his head and I've been unable to give him the second trial I must have before I finally take him. . . .

May 23. . . . Can't remember anything important in the last week unless it may be the sudden development in the domestic circle of a taste for uptown—the recognition to the fullest extent of the principle I've been long proclaiming, that a street of emigrant boarding houses and dirty drinking shops is not a pleasant place to live. So I shall not be greatly surprised if an emigration to the north is effected at last. I'm going to take the first step tomorrow morning by pricing some lots on Gramercy Park. Yet I'm silly enough to feel very nervous on the subject at times— a superstitious kind of notion on the subject has got into my head. . . .

Theodore Winthrop in town and here last night.

May 25, TUESDAY. . . . This afternoon Parish and Charley and I went off riding together. Crossed at Hoboken and rode by the Weehawken hill out nearly to Fort Lee. . . . Glorious afternoon it was. The country was lovely; yesterday's rain and today's warm sun had made everything resplendent and brought spring forward into summer with a rush. Crossed the Rubicon when I got to the stable again and told my knowing friend that I'd take the beast at two hundred, for better or for worse, so there's one job disposed of. He's a pretty animal, with pleasant paces and a gentlemanly sort of deportment, but he pulls like a newly-bitted mastodon, or megalosaurus, and has got to be rode with a curb whether it frets him or not. . . .

May 31. . . . Rumor of a defeat in Mexico: "Col. Doniphan" licked somewhere near Chihuahua and the "astonished eagles," as Napoleon would have called them, compelled to run away with the loss of their artillery and baggage. Hope it's true, for the only way of bringing the war to a close is to prosecute it *totissimis viribus*, and a little defeat or two will open up the administration to send on men and means, which are grievously wanted, if I'm not mistaken.

June 2. Loveliest of all possible summer days. Improved the afternoon by a long, rambling ride through all sorts of shady lanes and winding by-roads somewhere in the state of New Jersey, turning up at last unexpectedly on the road north of Weehawken. It's a bore to ride by one's self, in general, but this cruise was delicious and faultless in all particulars. . . .

June 7, MONDAY. . . . Judicial election today—slender vote polled—voted a split ticket myself, but with a Locofoco preponderance, for the Whig nominations were mostly despicable. . . .

I voted for the Free Academy, though additional sources of taxation are not specially needed just now. It will be at first a contemptible affair no doubt, its professorial chairs places of refuge for emigrant Irish hedge schoolmasters, and the whole institution a hospital for impoverished sciolists and decayed political hacks, like those erected by an enlightened charity for diseased monkeys in Bengal—a Brahminical Asylum for vermin, more especially for such as are too weak to grapple with the rough realities of the out-of-door world and gain an independent living by bloodsucking, and therefore need some shady retreat where they can live on the public generally in learned leisure. But it's not often we're called on to appropriate money for such purposes—and it will form a nucleus for donations and legacies, and may some day be valuable.

The Free Academy, opened for instruction in a brick Gothic building at Lexington Avenue and Twenty-third Street, early in 1849, turned out to be something very different from Strong's prophecy. In 1866 the name was changed to The College of the City of New York.

June 10, THURSDAY. Hot solo ride yesterday afternoon and another with Charley this afternoon over nearly the same ground—both quite delightful—the byways and back roads of New Jersey are paths of pleasantness, shady and quiet, and not without glimpses of real picturesqueness at times—views of the river and of Newark meadows and so on. Very well suited with my four-legged friend; he improves as I become intimate with him. Except an occasional display of alarm at some sight or sound that he's not used to, and a strange propensity to be constantly turning round imaginary corners, I've found no faults in him as yet. . . .

Visited Anthony's Daguerreotype shop with George Anthon this morning.[2]

Provided myself a pair of spurs, but haven't assumed 'em yet. Tornado'll run away with me the day I do. In the blessed Middle Ages people won their spurs by hard knocks and severe contusions and fractured arms and legs, but in these beggarly days when everything is the antipodes of what it was in the "ages of Faith," I fear that usage has been inverted with the rest and that I shall win a bad bruise and a compound fracture by my spurs.

June 27, SUNDAY. . . . President Polk reached the city in the course of his progress on Friday morning. Did not feel myself called upon to undergo any fatigue or put myself into a heat on his account, so I was not a witness of his entry. The lieges received him decently but without much enthusiasm. The crowd was extensive, and I dare say bigger than any Mr. Polk had ever seen before, so he probably felt himself complimented; but some charitable person ought to tell him that if Pat Molloy or Henry Marx or Sherman Brownell or N. P. Willis or Tom Thumb, or any other blackguard or fool or prodigy of insignificance were President, the crowd would have been no smaller. . . .

July 16. Quite demoralized by the hot weather and the New [State] Constitution. . . . I wish no severer punishment to the fools, quacks, and demagogues who brewed that precious instrument and the Judiciary Act than to be compelled to write notes and commentaries on the work of their own dirty hands till they can show that it had some good points somewhere and is not shallow and slovenly and incoherent and contemptible even beyond what sensible people had a right to expect from its authors.

Paper constitutions are the grand delusion of the nineteenth century. Alchemy, witchcraft, and astrology are obsolete, and an infatuated faith in this paltry paper and parchment machinery has taken their place and

[2] Strong's classmate, Edward Anthony, had accompanied Professor Renwick to Maine in 1840 and taken daguerreotypes for the surveying party which assembled data used in determining the North East Boundary. Later he had studios in New York and Washington, but disliking excessive competition, turned his attention to the manufacture and importation of daguerreotype (and afterward, photographic) materials. His brother Henry T. Anthony '32 joined him as a partner in 1852, specializing in chemicals, and the firm of E. & H. T. Anthony became highly successful.

bids fair to keep it. . . . The great problem of the statesman is: to devise
an ingenious system of political checks and balances on paper! Solve that,
and we shall have "What makes a nation happy, and keeps it so" in
pamphlet form, price only six cents and a liberal allowance to wholesale
dealers, at all the stationers'.

When those wise men of France discovered that man was only an
improved monkey, the next thing for them to do was to define accurately
wherein the improvement and difference lay. And I believe they settled
at last that it consisted in man's being "able to construct constitutions."
A constitution-mongering monkey isn't a bad definition of a French
philosopher of '89; they showed knowledge of themselves by adopting it.
But if applied to mankind at large and not to French philosophers exclu-
sively, the position seems to me altogether wrong: and I should prefer
saying that the man who had faith in nothing but constitutions and went
about manufacturing them to order and supplying organizations for any
given people on a month's notice, with a grave face, had ceased to differ
in any essential particular from the baboon and monkey tribe except that
his foolery was much less entertaining and might be much more mischievous.

I've taken no oath to support this constitution, fortunately. It gives
one a taste for the crime of treason generally and in the abstract to read
the thing.

News there is but little. "Century Club" got up by Verplanck and
Daniel Seymour. Elected; went there last night; things look rather well
for a beginning.[3]

Washington Monument Association. Looked at the plans submitted;
all on a scale of impracticable splendor and magnitude, and with two
exceptions, all execrable. One by [Minard] Lafever, a combination of
obelisk, church steeple, and gas house chimney intended to look Egyptian,
and five hundred feet high, is horribly ugly, but has a sort of knowing
original preposterous nightmare look that's rather taking, and I'd rather
see it adopted than any of its competitors but one, a gigantic nondescript
structure amplified and magnified from the Scott monument (as are most
of them) and put in, I think, by Arnot. It is late perpendicular Gothic,
abundantly faulty in proportion and detail but looking very rich and
effective on paper. The rest are beastly.

[3] The Century Association was organized January 13, 1847, by forty-two New
Yorkers, including twenty-five members of the Sketch Club and ten from The Column.
Strong's name does not appear on the list of founders.

August 2, MONDAY. . . . Have been vibrating between here and Flushing for the last week (we went there on the 23rd). . . . Riding every evening. . . .

August 6, FRIDAY. . . . Rode into town, but Tornado got somehow wrong just after I left Newtown, and began to be lame in his near shoulder —had to ride but slowly and didn't get home till two o'clock.

August 19, THURSDAY. . . . Am going to Boston this afternoon—don't know why or wherefore or for how long—to do a little premeditated lounging and lazing.

Peter [Gerard] Stuyvesant [Columbia 1794] died at Niagara Monday. Everybody—that is, some thirty people at least, that I heard speak of the matter—delivered themselves to the following effect: "What a great thing for the improvement of uptown." Except one, who remarked that it was a very imprudent procedure for a man who was worth two millions to take a cold bath directly after dinner. He was an awful old screw, I'm afraid. Walter Langdon's also dead—didn't live to get his library from Frost, the cabinet-maker who's finishing it (not the cases but the books) in deal with morocco backs. It was to have been very fine, but the illiterate idiot had made everything in three volumes 8vo. Historical Society is to turn out in force at Stuyvesant's obsequies. George Gibbs suggests an eulogy at the grave after the manner of the French Academy. I'm in favor of funeral games after the manner of the Greeks, with real estate brokers for the combatants.

Nothing further from Mexico; everybody waiting with mouth wide open for the first reliable statement of what Scott's doing; there are about three new lies every day.

August 31, TUESDAY. . . . Went to Boston on the 20th and returned thence last Saturday morning, after a longer sojourn there (or rather at Newton) than I anticipated. Very pleasant week of profound, stupendous laziness. Haskey and George Derby fully developed into a brace of ill-bred ungoverned little cubs, but Henry, who's hardly old enough yet to be spoiled, is a noble little fellow, the most engaging little compound of docility and self-will, the prettiest specimen of affectionate obedience softening down all sorts of small whims and obstinacies that one can well imagine. Spent Tuesday at Nahant and on Monday I had two big grinders dug out in three pieces by Dr. Keep[4] while I was under the

---

[4] Nathan Cooley Keep, M.D. Harvard 1827, afterward dean of the Harvard Dental School, by identifying the false teeth of Dr. George Parkman (Harvard 1809), who had been murdered by his colleague Professor John White Webster (Harvard 1811), sent the latter gentleman to the gallows in 1850.

THE GREAT FIRE OF 1835: BURNING OF THE MERCHANTS' EXCHANGE

THE GREAT FIRE OF 1845: VIEW FROM BROAD AND STONE STREETS

BISHOP JONATHAN MAYHEW WAINWRIGHT

BISHOP BENJAMIN TREDWELL ONDERDONK

influence of ether. The operation was so pleasant that I'd be glad to have it repeated. . . .

September 3, FRIDAY. . . . Still nothing of moment from Mexico except the daily report that Scott is marching on Mexico and Taylor on San Luis—or positively going to march tomorrow.

September 7, TUESDAY. . . . Prime, Ward & Co., in serious trouble— nothing has saved them from a smash but King's personal exertions with the Barings, which prevented a whole ream of bills from coming back on them. Very creditable to King, especially considering the circumstances under which he went out of the concern, and that he's now leader of a rival banking house. Common report says that the Barings did a clean thing and accepted all the bills that were out. But I know of one batch ($15,000) that's come back. In the case of any other house, I should say the diagnosis was very unfavorable, but these people are strong enough to weather a good deal.

September 10. . . . News from Mexico—seemingly reliable: Scott at the gates of Mexico after two battles in which he settled Santa Anna and Valencondres respectively. Doesn't march in and take possession from a sense of delicacy and a reluctance to aggravate the Mexicans into rejecting the peace propositions said to be under discussion in their enlightened congress. Suspension of hostilities also said to have taken place, so that there's hope of peace; Heaven grant it's well founded.

Prime, Ward & Co. stopped yesterday morning. John Ward retires from his house, a bankrupt, the other partners carrying on the firm as best they may. Wonder who'll go next. . . .

September 19, SUNDAY. . . . The most novel feature in my social position just now is that I'm enjoying the society of Collins's long-expected present, a giantly black Newfoundland cub. He's stretched out over many a rood of carpet by the side of my chair and snorting and sighing at intervals like a bull buffalo.

Back from Catskill this morning. Reached there Saturday night, after a rather rainy journey, but a very pleasant one. Dr. Stevens and his wife, Fox and his people, and George Cornell and Swipes [N. W. Chittenden]. Swipes has been roaming as usual from Maine to Monterey. Unless he's a relative of the Wandering Jew, or privately engaged in some line of peddlery, it's difficult to account for his locomotive propensities and the mystery in which they're always wrapt up.

Catskill. George Griffin, Jr., and his wife, one McWhorter (a relative of the Bruens) of Oswego and a very nice little Mrs. McW., Wenzler,[5] who turns out one of the pleasantest fellows I ever met, and the Rev. Brother Maffit and his wife—both snobs, and the former somewhat of a blackguard. All Sunday it rained ruefully. Monday was pleasant, though a little showery, and I spent the day in a drive with Griffin in the Platte Kill and a walk nearly to its foot. It's the grandest place—the head of this "clove"—that I ever beheld, finer even than the clove of the Cauter-skill, and the falls in the ravine are well worth the scramble that's necessary to reach them. After the rain of Sunday the streams were all in full life and energy, and from the woody side of the south mountain waterfalls were springing out 1,800 feet above us, flashing and gleaming among the pines, till one leap after another hid them in the darkness of the ravine below.

Tuesday was dubious, Wednesday clear and cold with a savage north-west wind. . . . It was too windy for Wenzler to work at his landscape (a very promising view of the south mountain), so we walked and played tenpins and practised pistol shooting and got along very comfortably. Charley came Thursday morning—he'd been detained by getting aground in the Genesee River—and specially glad I was to see him. We devoted Friday to a grand ramble down the Clove Road and left with Wenzler yesterday after dinner. . . .

One walk I musn't forget to commemorate: it was to the Falls with Wenzler on Wednesday afternoon. What made everything so transcen-dently beautiful I don't know, unless it was the clear autumnal sunlight and the foliage in its first golden stage of fall coloring that harmonized so as to produce the maximum of beauty. . . .

[Francis] Marion Ward, I hear, is dead of yellow fever at New Orleans. . . .

September 22, WEDNESDAY. . . . Long pleasant ride in New Jersey this afternoon—the pleasantest possible for riding. Then walked uptown with Charley. Powers's "Greek Slave" (the same that John Jay is said to have got out a habeas corpus for, by mistake) very pretty production and I suppose that I don't know enough about sculpture to see that it's anything more than that.

Marion Ward's case was a pretty severe one—left his office as well as usual at eleven and was dead at six the same day. It wasn't yellow

---

[5] A. H. Wenzler (also known as Henry Antonio Wenzler, Jr.), a native of Den-mark, was a highly regarded miniature and portrait painter in New York who also produced a number of successful landscapes.

fever, but some of their "country fevers"—a kind of congestive arrangement which they say is worse. . . .

Schuyler Hamilton very seriously hurt—two bayonet thrusts—in a
reconnaissance the day before the Battle of Churubusco, or Contreras, or
Mexico, whichever its proper style may be. His party encountered a
superior force of Mexicans also on the lookout and in charging through
them he got separated from his men. [Phil] Kearny, Jr., lost one of his
arms in the battle by a grapeshot—buying glory dear, that.

September 28. . . . Report of the Commissioners on Practice and
Pleading indicating the course of their intended reformation, which is to
be root and branch work, all existing law and usage to be swept away
and a new system created *in vacuo* by these enlightened and modest jurists.
Rather like their plan. I shall know as much law as Daniel Lord the moment
it's adopted, or rather I shall know more, for I won't have so much to
forget. And with such a bench as we're likely soon to have, this reduction
of legal practice to a Hottentot standard of simplicity and despatch is
indispensable. Being ignorant, our elected judges will be thereby preserved from blunders; being inclined to be mischievous, they'll not be
protected in partisan decisions and wilful injustice by mysteries and formalities unintelligible to the public at large. *Vive la République* and *à bas*
the Common money courts! To the Lantern with John Doe and Richard
Roe, and let there be a *noyade* and a *fusillade* and a general extermination
done upon all extant reporters and writers of treatises.

October 1, FRIDAY. . . . Very satisfactory ride with Johnny Parish this
afternoon from Hoboken to Fort Lee by the way of the "English Neighborhood" and returning by the shore road and Bull's Ferry. Have been
riding before breakfast a little of late also, but that's a hungry sort of
arrangement. This afternoon's expedition was unexceptionable in every
particular and there are few rides about New York equal to the river
road from Fort Lee.

October 3, SUNDAY. . . . Went to the Century Club last night. Verplanck,
Seymour, Gray, Van Winkle, and so on. Spent a very comfortable evening. . . .

News by the *Hibernia* this evening: black catalogue of failures on
t'other side; crisis fully developed there, and another crisis very like to
be brought about here. Wall Street will be in a state of excitement tomorrow. . . .

Awful noise outside. I believe it's Hector eating up a cat, and the
Irish females remonstrating with him. Hope the cat will agree with him.

News from Mexico very important but fragmentary, inconsistent, and not very intelligible. Armistice broken off and several days more of hard fighting in and about the capital; that seems unquestionably true. Loss of 600 men at one place, and of 1,700 at another; repulse of the Americans from the Mill of something. Riley and his crew of deserters hanged. Pillow and Smith killed. Worth blown up by an ammunition wagon and not certainly known to have come down again. Hard fighting in the streets of Mexico. City stormed and the Anglo-Saxon race in the Halls of Montezuma at last. All that and a great deal more of the same sort is less authentic and credible. Don't see why Scott should have engaged a perilous street fight, necessarily at great disadvantage, unless he was out of shot and shell, and don't see where the Mexicans so soon after two or three hard drubbings got pluck enough to make fight again.

October 5. . . . Rode this afternoon out to Manhattanville. The city is spreading north on the Bloomingdale Road out of all reason and measure. Curb stones laid out to its junction with the Sixth Avenue. Ambitious little row of houses starting up in Forty-second Street—everywhere signs of progress. Several new palazzos rising in the Fifth Avenue; it is built up without any very great gaps nearly to Twentieth Street.

Recommenced French tonight with Buffet and Charley.

October 7, THURSDAY. . . . French tonight. I've always despised that people and reviled them on all occasions and they are a pitiful breed of men; but they deserve credit for having preserved any traces of human nature and any shadow of the dignity of man in spite of the degradation they have suffered so long in their abject jargon of a language. Anybody compelled to use and hear that base and beastly compound of cackle and whine during his whole life would be found on dissection, one would suppose, to have assimilated fearfully to the lower orders of creation, and to have at least the rudiments of a prehensile tail.

October 10, SUNDAY. . . . Century Club last night. Huntington, William Hoppin, and others.

Johnny H. Parish tells me that his sister's engaged to Robert J. Dillon. He's a humbug, and probably a wooer of the lady's expectations.

N.B. If Hector is going to make a habit of ululating in this way—long deep intense wailings, very slow, rising and falling at intervals and sounding "like woman wailing for her demon lover" or like the complainings of a dyspeptic ghoul wandering around the lonely burial place where he has just been making an overhearty supper by moonlight or like Madame Fleury Jolly vainly endeavoring to sing *Casta Diva*—he will have to be hanged or sent off in disgrace to board. His presence here has in a measure interfered with the performances of the company of feline artistes who used to do such full justice to the opera of the Katzenjammer every night, but if this kind of thing is to last it will be a change for the worse.

Sorry to hear from George Anthon tonight of Sam Whitlock's having been hit in the eye at the Racket Club and that the eye is lost, as Suydam's was a couple of years ago. Heartily hope it's an exaggerated account of the affair. . . .

Nothing more from Mexico. No despatches—communications cut off probably—and Scott and his army of *conquistadores* revelling in the Halls of Montezuma because they can't get out. Hope he'll soon be rein-forced. . . .

My poor little black squirrel expired after a tedious illness Friday night, poor little thing; he was so weak and unable to move that he couldn't have enjoyed life much. Wonder what the matter with him could have been. It's very unpleasant to see a pet animal sick, especially when it's quite tame and gentle and seems to appeal to one for help and comfort.

October 12, TUESDAY. . . . The worst is true about poor Sam Whitlock: vision destroyed and probably the eye itself lost.

Sam Raymond told me this morning that I was elected to supply somebody's place in Trinity Church vestry last night. Extraordinary if true, as it can hardly be, seeing that I've heard nothing about it from anybody else, and though very much of a compliment coming from such a corps of respectable old fogies, not at all a desirable thing to me at this present time. . . .

October 14. . . . Rumors from Mexico that Scott has been wounded in a street fight with the "leperos" of the capital, a class that corresponds in some respects, I suppose, with the b'hoys of this metropolis; that Santa Anna on hearing the news plucked up a spirit, stopped running away, and marched back again to eat up the Americans. Don't believe the story, nor does anyone else. If the mob of Mexico should proceed to get up a disturbance after the surrender of the city such as could only be put down by a murderous warfare in alleys and among houses each of which is a stronghold, I think Scott would be justified, after a bona fide attempt to restore order had failed, in setting fire to the city at its four corners and getting rid of the leperos as people get rid of fleas in a straw bed.

October 17, SUNDAY. Heard Bishop McCoskry this morning. Collection taken up; turned pale at the sight of the plates, for it occurred to me forcibly that the sexton might see fit to make me useful as a vestryman, but he didn't. . . .

October 18. Bored. As I dismounted from Tornado on board the ferry boat, out of pure good nature to the brute, he trod on my toe; intentionally, as I'll make affidavit—haven't examined the toe, but it feels as if it was a total smash. . . .

October 21. Washington Monument corner stone laid the 19th; monument destined to be a gigantic deformity if the present plan's adopted. Some architecture is "music turned into stone": this might be poetically described as the creak and whizz and pounding of a big steam engine petrified, so angular and stiff and prosaic is it. A large telescope drawn out and then set upright on its big end is the nearest approach to it that has ever met my eyes. The architect seems to have had some vague unconscious feeling that prompted him to try to give an upward tendency to its lines, a dreamy sense that some such character should belong to it without knowing why, but he has only produced a nest of boxes with the biggest on the ground and the smallest on the top of the pile and sealed himself for the decision of posterity with but two chances of being forgotten: the abortion may never be built, and it may tumble down again if it is—either quite likely.

N.B. General Scott has not been ate up by the rabble of Mexico after all. There has been a deal of very murderous fighting, but his hand has prevailed against his enemies and Santa Anna has run away, like Sisera or Johnny Cope, to parts unknown. As to peace, there's not the smallest chance of it.

October 26, TUESDAY. . . . Further particulars of the Mexican Iliad arriving in daily driblets, to the great delectation of all newspaper editors. Probably, by the by, the Mexicans would prefer describing the transaction as the fall of another Rome before barbarians from the North. It's an unpleasant business for them, and they are pardonable for hating and abusing the parties concerned in it. If they've any patriotic poets, it opens a splendid field for lyrics after the manner of Tyrtaeus and lamentation after the manner of Jeremiah. The former ought to command fancy prices at the office of the Mexican Secretary of War, for they might possibly inspire the grand army and its generals and officers of every degree with a little more pluck than they've shown yet. . . .

The march on Mexico really seems to me the most brilliant piece of victorious audacity I ever heard of, beyond the daring of Cortez. It will do us harm, for our tendency to brag and bluster and give glory to

ourselves needs no encouragement and no stimulus, and unless the Mexicans be sunk to depths of imbecility below all historical precedent, this
performance is what any nation might be proud of.

For the last fortnight I've been engaged in the innocent folly of quacking myself homœopathically, without the slightest serious expectation of
success, with reference to this blighting, paralyzing, disgraceful, hideous,
unspeakable disease of nervous dejection and instability that has been
down upon me like ten thousand tons of granite for the last two years.

And today for the first time in all that period I verily believe I've felt
perfectly well—the oppression about my chest that's always accompanied
and perhaps caused the other feeling totally gone. If I should be disen-
chanted—but I can scarcely hope it—if it be so, God make me thankful
for it.

October 29, FRIDAY. . . . Ride to the High Bridge, now nearly finished,
Wednesday afternoon. Very great piece of work is the bridge, and very
great city is this with all its absurdities. That fact is forcibly impressed
on one after riding miles of crowded streets and bad pavements to get
out of town. What will it look like one thousand years hence? Perhaps
just as it did a thousand years ago. . . .

[J. R.] Bartlett very great on [A. J.] Davis's "Revelations," a little
unwilling to avow that he considers the new patent Apocalypse destined
to run the old one out of the market and supersede it altogether, but evidently rather inclined to think so. He says the statements of the book
coincide exactly with the latest discoveries in philology, physical science,
astronomy, ethnology and so forth, that have been made abroad and are
as yet known to but very few in this country. Remarkable, if true, and to
my mind conclusive evidence that the author, though he may be a "psychological phenomenon," is not an apostle or a messenger of truth. Had his
revelations coincided in part with modern opinions and in part with obsolete notions, and been in part altogether novel and unheard of, they would
not perhaps have been stamped with falsehood on their face; but if they
embody and endorse the discoveries of the year 1847, and profess to
reveal as absolute truth the prevailing system of any one period, with or
without new matter, they are discredited as effectually as they possibly
can be. . . .

October 30. . . . Concocted a letter for Adler this afternoon; he has nosed
the vacant Gebhard Professorship in Columbia College and would like the
appointment, and I hope he may get it; but I fear he won't, for he's a little
too late with his application. . . .

Adjourned to the club and smoked and drank beer and talked aesthetics with Leupp and political philosophy with Gourlie and German literature with Dan Seymour.

November 7, SUNDAY. . . . Political news: Whigs have swept the state. William Samuel Johnson and John L. Lawrence are senators, and Hamilton Fish lieutenant governor.

At the Century last night. Parish and Charley elected. Pleasant evening with Cozzens, Seymour, Gray, and so on. Wenzler's Catskill picture at the Art Union[6] room; very creditable I think, especially for a first landscape, with a very trying and repulsive subject, and executed without any humbug or artificial concealment of slovenly work in a downright, literal, vigorous fidelity to nature. Other people, however, abuse it.

New "Free Academy" to be built by Jemmy Renwick after the manner of Flemish *Hôtels de Ville*; not a bad notion, if Jemmy were capable of building anything. . . .

November 9, TUESDAY. . . . Last night went to a Trinity Church vestry meeting; was most patronizingly received by all and singular the "porochial" Conscript Fathers. Thereafter chessed in haste and betook myself with Charley to the great wedding of Woodbury Langdon and Miss Helen Jones, or rather the grand reception-polka party that followed the wedding. Very noisy affair; both houses open, all the wealth, beauty, and fashion and so forth. . . .

November 21, SUNDAY. . . . At Dr. Stevens's soirée in honor of Henry Lloyd's intended on Friday night; reasonably pleasant it was. Didn't go to the Jones soirée No. 2. Talking of that, they say that when old [Walter] Langdon found out, to his surprise, that he was going to die, and that pretty soon, he summoned all his family round his bed to receive his last paternal counsels and benediction. All were there but Master Woodbury, and the affectionate father felt that he should not see his son again in this world. "I shan't be able to bid Woody goodbye," said the departing

[6] The American Art Union, an outgrowth of the Apollo Association, was incorporated in 1840 to foster American Art, and for several years had extraordinary success. A gallery was maintained in New York, and the work of American painters, sculptors, engravers, and medallists was purchased and exhibited. Membership ran as high as 16,000, and for a $5 annual fee all subscribers received a large steel engraving, four small ones, and a monthly *Bulletin*. As new paintings were acquired for the gallery, old ones were retired and these were distributed to the members by lot. Enemies of the association invoked the state lottery laws in 1851, the annual distribution was banned, and in 1853 the remaining works of art were sold at auction; nevertheless, during its existence 2,400 paintings and other works had been distributed, and the institution had successfully stimulated great interest in the fine arts.

patriarch, "but give me one of my cards." And they gave him a card and he wrote under his name "P.P.C." and said, "Hand that to Woody," and so died, in the odor of gentility.

December 5, SUNDAY.   Church as usual. My "porochial" duties involve *one* bore: marching down the north aisle on Communion Sunday in a mendicant capacity with an exaggerated soup plate that looks suspiciously like German silver and is a deal too big for what it has to hold—a kind of practical satire it is on the liberality of that side of the church, for the reception whereof a teaspoon were the more suitable utensil. Mine's a most beggarly beat. I never knew I had this business to go through with. What an important element of the circulating medium is the five-penny piece! . . .

December 7, TUESDAY. . . . St. Nicholas [Society] dinner last night. Instead of sitting down at five, it was half-past six before feeding commenced, and as I'd been ass enough to omit my usual dinner, my gastric juice was by that time eating up the coats of my stomach and I was in that disgusting state of faint, headachy misery to which a postponement of pabulum always reduces me, for dinner deferred maketh the stomach sick. And then sitting down with an omnivorous appetite and filling myself up with 1. oysters, 2. soup, 3. fish, 4. turkey, 5. venison, 6. canvasback duck, 7. miscellaneous trifles, the enumeration of which under seventeen several subdivisions I omit for the present, this promiscuous kind of abundant pasture, moistened by a little hock and a little champagne and a tolerable sufficiency of sherry and a few sips of vitriolic Schiedam—all this swinery, or hoggishness, or whatever it may be called, gave me a shocking sick headache, which I deserved.

Alderman Benson was the best thing I saw last night. I left him in a very shiny state. He says the bottle of whiskey disinterred under one of the Park gate posts was tasted and commented on by all the city fathers and generally pronounced to have a queer kind of flavor, and he thought it well before taking a mouthful to make a thorough investigation of the contents of the bottle. The dismay of the Common Council may be imagined when this investigation brought out a man's *little finger* preserved in the bottle. There's a tradition that it was the finger of George Frederick Cooke.

1848

POLK'S PEACE TREATY · MISS ELLEN RUGGLES · COURT-
SHIP, MARRIAGE AND HONEYMOON : TWENTY-FIRST
STREET HOUSE · CALIFORNIA GOLD MANIA

*The happiest year of Strong's life begins gloomily enough in his record. On
the 26th of January the name of Miss Ellen Ruggles appears in the diary
for the first time, although it is almost certain that the "beautiful sunshiny
face" that haunted him at the office and around town on April 16, 1847, after
the Ruggles soirée of the night before, was none other than hers. Strong remarked then that he was not in love but didn't care to be nearer to it than he
was. Nevertheless he took plenty of time to think it over, and confided nothing
to his journal. The party at Mrs. John Austin Stevens's December 28, 1847
(barely noted at the time but vividly recollected a decade later) and the soirée
in January of this year evidently revived the whole matter, but still he wrote
nothing until March 4, when the situation was well in hand. From that point
we let him tell his story in full.*

*This was an eventful year; the year of a formal peace with Mexico, of the
organization of the Free-Soil Party, of the great Whig victory in electing
Taylor to the presidency, and of the discovery of gold in California. To Strong,
however, it was a year of one event which transformed his life.*

January 26, WEDNESDAY. . . . Have been dissipating on chloroform
lately. It seems an innocent kind of amusement not followed by any reaction
or other unpleasant symptoms. N.B. I think it altogether probable that its
use may be instrumental in bringing to light important truths in the science
of "psychology," or rather in that department of physiology which relates
to the connexion between mind and matter, the functions of the nervous
system and so forth.

Nothing else new except the opera and the people one sees there—the "Ruggleses" and so on. Miss Ellen Ruggles is *rather* worth cultivating. . . .

January 27. . . . Am sitting here waiting for Sam Whitlock who promised to come and see me tonight—poor fellow, what a bore it must be for him, this condemnation to a black patch over one eye for life.

January 29. . . . George Jones[1] looked in to turn over engravings, then walked up and had an hour or two at the club. Tayler Lewis, Verplanck, Hoppin, Dorr, Leupp and Gray, *cum multis aliis.* Walked downtown with Verplanck. Legend of the corner of Canal Street and the woodchuck killed there one moonshiny night in June, 1815.

January 30, SUNDAY. . . . *"Lassati sumus in via iniquitatis"* and of all its paths and byways this is surely the most rugged and the least attractive. But it is well for me that I have got into this rather than another. A taste for wicked *pleasures* I might find myself too weak and worthless to resist or even wish to conquer. But sinful self-denial and ungodly sorrow, penance and mortification and the renouncing of worldly pleasure for the sake and service of evil, I think I am able to contend against. Christian asceticism may look unpromising, but this *dämonische ascese,* this cutting off the right arm and plucking out the right eye in order to be as wrong and unhappy as possible, this renouncing the happiness of earth because one thinks it probable he can't get the moon, is unreasonable, intolerable, and not to be endured.

Think I'll write "confessions of a chloroform-smeller" some of these days after the manner of the English Opium Eater, though I've as yet but little to confess. It's curious stuff, is chloroform—and very curious indeed are its temporary effects on one's system. The dreams are so strange it fills one's mind with, the apparent duration of its effects so much longer than one's watch indicates. The sensations of a week are crowded into two minutes.

Last time I dosed myself I heard most distinctly the performance of a part of Mozart's *Requiem*—the "Dies Irae" chorus and part of the "Tuba Mirum" accompaniment by an orchestra and, as I noticed at the time, not a very good one. I remember listening most attentively and noticing that in

---

[1] This is probably George Frederic Jones (1822–1882), who was in college with Strong, married Lucretia Stevens Rhinelander, and was the father of Edith Wharton; and not George Jones (1811–1891), then of the *Tribune* and later a founder of the *Times.* The Centurions mentioned are Professor Tayler Lewis of New York University, Gulian C. Verplanck, William Jones Hoppin (Yale 1832), Henry Crawford Dorr (Brown 1839), Charles M. Leupp and Henry Peters Gray, the artist. Dorr was a younger brother of Thomas Wilson Dorr (Harvard 1823), the Rhode Island insurgent.

many points my memories of the music were wrong. I may add, as showing that perchloride of formyle is not a power of inspiration or a supernatural means of arriving at truth (like Mesmerism) that as compared with the dream concert my memories of the music were right.

February 1. . . . Consulted a horse doctor about Tornado this morning. Tornado, I fear, has chronic podagra. Rather think I've got or am getting a typhus fever, for I'm uncomfortable to a degree and can't sleep at night. Longfellow's *Evangeline*, quiet and beautiful; under obligations to the "recommender" of it, confound her.

February 5, SATURDAY. . . . Just in from the Mendelssohn "Commemoration" Concert at Castle Garden. Went with Charley and Pedrillo and Johnny Parish. It was unparalleled in one respect—the crowd. Tickets had been sent out gratis, and I suppose eight thousand people availed themselves of the opportunity of testifying their musical taste and their respect for the departed composer. There were just as many people as the place would hold, and it was a fine sight to behold. Almost a compensation for the heat and press and prodigious discomfort of the whole transaction. Certainly there was no other compensation, for though the music was very discreetly selected (including the second movement of the *Eroica* and the glorious "Sleepers awake—A voice is calling" chorale from *St. Paul*) it was played so vilely that I scarcely cared to listen to it. . . .

February 10, THURSDAY. . . . Opera: Biscaccianti. The Bostonians may puff her till they crack their cheeks, demonstrate till they're tired that she's taller than Jenny Lind and prettier than Jenny Lind and acts better than Jenny Lind and is therefore a fitter subject for a furor than Jenny Lind, but it's altogether of no use. She's excessively slow, sings and acts with visible effort and painful straining for effect, and has been provided by nature with a voice and a face and a manner that Bostonians may admire but I do not. Habicht seems to have constituted himself her especial champion and defender.

At the club frequently of late in the course of my walks downtown from the opera; pleasant hour there last night.

Reading, last two volumes of Campbell's *Chancellors*—gossiping and pleasant. Queer novel, *Jane Eyre*—not a book I *like* at all, but very full of cleverness and character. Lamb's books—haven't yet got them home. Application from Duyckinck on behalf of Professor [Henry Hope] Reed of Philadelphia for leave to print some of Coleridge's marginal scribblings.

Visit from Dr. Berrian today with divers data and statistics to show the propriety of building a new chapel of Trinity Parish uptown—doubtless a desirable thing to do, for the tide of uptown emigration has left the church and its present chapels almost bare of parishioners. . . .

February 13, SUNDAY. . . . Not much to write that's new or entertaining just now. Remsen party Thursday night: great crowd—found the transaction a bore. "Evangeline" dancing the polka most indefatigably.

I do hate to see women who are worthy of better things, who have heads at least if not hearts, whirling and spinning and ricocheting across a ball room, profaned by the touch and breath and look of somebody who's not worthy to come within a hundred yards of them. For the *real* "dancing girls," whose organs of saltatory locomotion have been cultivated to such a development and perfection as to render the head and heart quite secondary and subordinate parts of their physical organization, if not to obliterate and destroy them quite (like the stamina and pistils of an artificial hot-house rose), it don't matter at all. They are merely fulfilling their vocation, acting out the part in life they've chosen and for which they've laboriously qualified themselves. But for those who are fit for better things, it's a sin and a shame. Neither brains nor hearts. I wonder why those J. people, for instance, don't decompose as other people would if deprived of those important viscera. Probably they avail themselves of antiseptics. . . .

Darley's outlines to the Rev. Mr. Somebody's *Margaret*[2]—spent an hour yesterday in Maunsell Field's office examining them. Very exquisite indeed, as good in their way as anything of Retzsch's, possibly better in respect of the character and individuality of all the faces and figures, and the "native Americanism" of the accessories and still life. Admirable as Retzsch's productions undoubtedly are, most of them look like a series of tableaux by the same people in different costumes. That's a dictum of Hoppin's and the most sensible thing he ever said, for though I denied it stoutly at first, it is, on consideration, perfectly true.

February 17. . . . Lamb's book home at last. Coleridge's notes are quite interesting, at least when read in Coleridge's autograph. Duyckinck has acknowledged my civilities in the premises by the present of a copy of *Arcturus,* so I've just been writing him a letter expressing my gratitude,

[2] Rev. Sylvester Judd (1813–1853), Yale 1836, Unitarian minister of Augusta, Maine, had a brief but important career as a humanitarian preacher and lecturer; his religious and social views were set down in his two novels, *Margaret* (1845) and *Richard Edney and the Governor's Family* (1850). F. O. C. Darley's book, *Compositions in Outline . . . from Judd's "Margaret,"* was not published until 1856. Maunsell Bradhurst Field (Yale 1841), New York lawyer and diplomat, was co-author with G. P. R. James of a novel, *Adrian; or, The Clouds of the Mind* (1851), and wrote a valuable book of memoirs.

as I conscientiously could for his good intentions—and for nothing else—
the contents of the periodical as a whole, and with the exception of one or
two piquant articles by Dr. Hawks, being very great stuff, indeed. Literature pursued as an end, for its own sake, and not for the truths of which it
may be made the vehicle, is a worthless affair, and those who cultivate it
for itself alone are always unreal, and unless they have ability and originality far above their fellows, are pretty sure to degenerate into puppyism and
pedantry. Where such a litterateur is feeble himself and is dealing with and
laboriously commenting on and striving to magnify the writings of people
like himself, his productions are apt to be among the most pitiful specimens
of human infatuation that are to be found anywhere. And Mr. Duyckinck
and Mr. [Cornelius] Mathews, criticizing and comparing and weighing
with the nicest accuracy the relative merits and demerits of the small fry
of authors, foreign and domestic, exhibit and illustrate in their own persons
the ridiculous side of humanity with painful force and clearness. However,
there are some principles maintained in the book; it is pervaded by the
cant of progress instinct with the lies of "liberality" and enlightenment
and the like twaddle.

Arcturus would unsex woman and destroy the Idea of Womanhood
on Earth by removing their "disabilities" and "elevating" them into a race
of disagreeable, effeminate men in petticoats. It holds capital punishment
cruel, barbarous and unnecessary, the diffusion of useful information a
panacea for all social evils, and so forth—anybody can gulp its doctrines
on all other subjects from those specimens.

February 22, TUESDAY. . . . Rumors of a peace with Mexico made by
Scott on his own responsibility—generally credited. Senate will probably
ratify it in a hurry and be glad to be done with conquering. . . .

News that John Quincy Adams has been seized with paralysis.

February 24. J.Q.A. died yesterday. The indomitable old boy has
been put down at last. Other news is there but little. Peace rumors confirmed—ratification of some sort of treaty thought to be certain, though
no party is quite satisfied with the terms and conditions of the preliminaries
said to have been agreed on. There strikes seven, so I must go and array
myself for an evening in Union Place to meet some Boston woman or
other whose name I don't remember, and enough people besides, I suppose,
to make up some sort of tea squall.

February 27. . . . Lamartine—*Harmonies Poétiques*—the first French
Poetry I've yet read with respect. In spite of the difficulty of giving dignity

and earnestness to anything written in that dialect, these poems express solemn and pious feeling with reverence and sincerity. Just finished "Le Retour"—"*On regrette la vie avant d'avoir vécu.*" Fine enough.

March 4, SATURDAY. Afternoon, 26 minutes and 1/2 past three P.M. Bright sunshine and a lovely day, though somewhat sloppy and slushy under foot, for we'd quite a heavy little snowstorm Thursday night. Thermometer 34° at this present writing. Rather particular as to the details of the current half-hour for I find myself just now in an Abnormal State, very new and strange. Have thought once or twice on former occasions that I was experiencing this sort of thing, but it was all a mistake. I've never had the disorder before but in a mild form; it's been slowly coming on for the last three months and has now assumed a very threatening character. Perhaps I shan't journalize any more, for if this bubble should burst (as I hope and sometimes believe it will not) I think I should die on the spot. At least I should not want to survive the rage, mortification, and bitter disgust of such a state of things. Never mind that, however, just now. . . .

March 6. Eleven P.M. Just in from my expedition to Union Place and I sit down here to write in the first flush of real happiness and joy I've known for years—the first I've *ever* known—that I may have something tangible to recall it by hereafter.

Walked downtown nearly wild. Heaven help me if I'm under a delusion, and make me grateful if this be real and true; for if so, I believe the game can and will be won and I shall be—there are no words in the English or any other language to express this.

God bless, keep, preserve, protect, and defend her forever!

"Fashionable" and "artificial"!!!!! The sagacity of some people is marvelous.

Case stands over till Thursday night—possibly Friday. What an idiot I was not to settle it tonight. But if–if–if–if–if–if–if—IF this be all a dream of mine!

March 13, MONDAY. Here endeth the life and history of the G.T.S. hitherto known in the pages of this journal. Another person bearing the same name and residing at the same place here beginneth the Chronicle of his Life—and humbly hopes that it will be a very different kind of life from the dreary, desolate, objectless, worthless existence the shabby details whereof are contained in the miserable pages that go before.

Reminiscences of the Transition period and new birth.

March 7, TUESDAY.   Pleasant morning, gradual assault of the blues, nervousness, uneasiness, and all kinds of horrors. Evening. Buffet. Madame de Staël. Walk up with Charley, stop at Florence's, eat oysters, drink ale—if possible, more desperate than before. Conclusion that I'm a presumptuous fool settled in my own mind irrevocably and without appeal. Came home, read Longfellow, conscientious effort to be philosophical and heroic ending in total failure.

March 8, WEDNESDAY.   Warm, mild, lovely day, which I thought at the time disgusting. Call from Jem Strong. Appleton's, last *Dombey*, great doubt and perplexity whether 'twould do to send it up. Another chase after an English *Jane Eyre*—unsuccessful. Rush up to Colman's to look for an engraving mentioned by Jem Strong; couldn't find it; back to Wall Street. Wilbur and Brush, intense desire to throw 'em out of the window. J.Q.A.'s funeral—disgusting crowd. Home. Mrs. Stevens: walk her and M. to Trinity Church. Afternoon: sat in Wall Street, did nothing but boil inwardly till I nearly burst. Evening: walked on the Fourth Avenue to nobody knows where and back again; considered the question of cabling— decided against it. Half moon over Cheever's meetinghouse; very pretty, quiet, mild spring evening it was. Met Samuel B. Ruggles, Esq., as I came down Broadway. Club: "Delineators"—Ellsworth—Dorr—Charley. Long and very distrait talk with old Verplanck on a variety of subjects. Home.

March 9, THURSDAY.   Rain and wind—very desperate state of things. Terribly grand, gloomy, and peculiar conversation with Charley which makes me laugh now, though I didn't perceive how funny it all was at the time. Evening: carriage to Professor Nicoll's lecture at the University; found my friends by special good fortune and joined 'em. Lunar surface, great craters, Tycho, lunar mountains upside down, "innate depravity of human nature." Walk home through the rain in a consolatory frame of mind.

March 10, FRIDAY.   Morning. Master's office, Maurice, James J. Jones, W. T. J., Raddi and Garrigue after German duplicates. Evening: to Union Square. Fouqué—Hoffman—Tennyson—*Couriers*—St. Peter's— Raffaello—*pieta curia advisari vult*—"continuance" to tomorrow night.

Saturday March 11th A.D. *1848*.   Call at No. 8 Wall Street at eleven-thirty—at Bank of Commerce at twelve-thirty. Long conference and cross examination. Frank Griffin referee. Afternoon: Wall Street—to the *Herald* office and back. Evening: Union Square. *Victoria!* God make me grateful enough for it and enable me to bear myself henceforth as becomes the depositary of so precious a trust and so unspeakable a blessing.

Yesterday: church in the morning. Charley and Johnny Parish. Haight preached, I believe. Walked a little way up Broadway thereafter. Afternoon: sat still in this chair and did nothing. Evening: walked to Union Square. Overtook Johnny Parish and he joined me, evidently in great wonder as to where I could be going. Mr. and Mrs. Tighe—Mr. and Mrs. Henry R[uggles?].

Today: announcements. Carried two round to Delmonico's and took his breath away with the news. Walter Cutting—Henry Cram—walked with him on the Battery from eleven to twelve in sheer reckless, indolent happiness, spurning Wall Street with my heels. George Gibbs—letters—dinner—Mamma in great felicity, for she went to Union Square this morning; my father was there tonight and he's as happy and pleased as possible. That was all that was yet wanting to make this *perfect.*

* * * *

April 9, SUNDAY.   Have been meaning to take out the journal every day since my last entry, but my efforts have been unavailing. Not that there has been anything to chronicle—there has been nothing but a monotony of happenings. But this state of things is so new and strange, this last month of my life has been so utterly different from all the months that have gone before it, and worth so much more than all of them together, that I have felt as if I ought to preserve some trace of it for my journal.

Perfect, entire happiness—so new and strange to me that I dread day to day and almost from hour to hour that it must end. Happiness that teaches one gratitude to God and faith in him, and so enables me to shake off my nervous fear that it cannot last. Happiness that I can dwell upon and luxuriate in freely and unrestrained, because it includes the anticipation of a life no longer cold and selfish and objectless and indolent, but henceforth to be built on joyful self-denial and hearty labor for a worthy end. Happiness that it bewilders me to look upon—that I know I do not even yet fully realize and appreciate—the happiness of loving and being generously loved by a beautiful, high-principled, noble-hearted, frank, affectionate, good girl possessed of everything that refinement and cultivation and taste and intelligence can adorn womanhood withal.

Who'd have thought this six months ago? Even yet I can scarcely believe it myself.

I've not had much to journalize about. For the mornings, I've spent them in diligently dodging all work and labor that was not inevitable. . . . Home at half-past five regularly; dress and omnibus to Union Square. Back again rather late than otherwise—quite too late to cultivate the journal.

Of course I'm not such an ass as to look forward to the life before me as one of mere abstract felicity. There are chances and changes to be feared, and at best there will be oceans of cares and anxieties that I'm an utter stranger to as yet and of which I am like to be more than commonly sensible—the care about money matters first of all—to be fought with and to be mastered.

That same care about the *Diva pecunia* is the only one that besets me at present, though I know that as far as human calculations and arrangements are worth anything, I've a right to feel at ease on that score. But it has become so momentous all of a sudden, after having always been so entire a matter of indifference, about which I never felt anxiety, fear, or foreboding that I can't quite yet treat the matter rationally and philosophically. Till a month ago I don't think it would have given me three days' abiding unhappiness to have a cypher for my worldly estate in possession and expectancy; on some accounts I should rather have enjoyed the perfect Diogenes independence of such a state of things. Now things are rather changed. And our start in life will probably be on rather a larger and more expensive scale than I should have wished, if my tastes alone had been in question.

Never mind—I think we may fairly count on things coming out right.

At Grace Church this morning Ellen confirmed by Bishop [Alonzo] Potter of Pennsylvania. After dinner walked downtown, and here I am, and I shall march uptown again presently, so I must be expeditious with my chronicling.

Plenty of news of late. French Revolution No. 3. Democratic influenza running through Europe. French provisional government—absurdity, sentimentality, and melodramatic monkeyism of every kind; decrees that "everybody shall have everything, and secondly everything else is hereby abolished." Louis Philippe run away. Lamartine, Louis Blanc, Ledru-Rollin, and so on in his shoes. Wish all this could have been postponed a year, for it has nipped in the bud our projected summer expedition to the Old World. Death of old [John Jacob] Astor. William B. his grand residuary legatee. Affliction has fallen on the Oxonian Bristed, and great tribulation on all the tribe of the Langdons.[3] Henry Cram engaged to Miss [Katherine] Sergeant at last!

April the 15th A.D. *1848:*   I sometimes think it can never be—something will befall before then. But even at the worst, one era of my life has past and is gone and can never return. I never again can return. I never again can be what I have been.

If this were all to come to naught, I should never return to the quiet, desolate, vacant, objectless, "respectable" life of the last five years. I should either die at once or leave the country instantly, no matter how, and go no matter where and never return. I'm waked up now, for good or evil, according as the event shall show (for I dare not think of the event as certain), and I shall doze and dream and stupefy no more.

I'd sooner join a settlement of the gregarious blue baboons of South Africa than live on in the dismal way I've been living of late.

Half-past four, and I must stop scribbling. Heaven prosper this to us both and give me the will and the power henceforth to fulfil aright my new obligations to show myself worthy of being its instrument and make the life of her whom its mercy has given to me as beautiful and happy and honored as it ought to be.

April 20.   12 M., "noon of night," that is. Just in from Union Square. Ancestors called there this evening. Also Mr. and Mrs. Abbott Lawrence of Boston "happened in"—both possessed of a full appreciation of their own estimable qualities. Out this morning with my glorious little Ellen making calls on divers people. Mercy on us: I'm terrified at that "my" in the last line. Things temporal are uncertain—"many a slip" and so forth. I dread to tempt the destinies to mischief by a premature use of the pronoun possessive.

Prussia's a republic and Europe generally has gone mad.

April 24, Monday night or Tuesday morning—uncertain which, for my watch is wrong and as to my clock, it ran down somewhere about the 11th of March last and has not been wound up to this day. "In" from Union Square. Isn't my little Ellen Ruggles a noble little girl!

I'm horribly bored. Mrs. Mary Jones, the "Madame Josephine Weiss" of polite society—the female impresario of the "dancing girls"—has sent

---

[3] The "Oxonian Bristed" was the Rev. John Bristed (1778–1855), physician, lawyer, author, and cleric, who married Magdalen (Astor) Bentzon, daughter of John Jacob Astor. Fitz-Greene Halleck lampooned Bristed in *Fanny* with the foregoing title, but the reverend gentleman's name does not appear on the rolls of that university. Col. Walter Langdon of New Hampshire married Dorothea, another of Astor's daughters.

us cards for tomorrow night's saltatory *soirée*. That don't seem as if it were a sufficient reason for my feeling prompted to shoot myself or take passage for New Holland or write a note uptown to announce that our —— must be —— yet I feel as if I could do any one of them. Brooded over the prospect in constantly increasing blackness of spirit all the way downtown, and I'm now boiling over with wrath and disgust and desperate ill humor. But I know the notion or prejudice or vexation or dislike or whatever it may be called is unreasonable and that I'm a fool. Whatever Ellen does is right, *ipso facto*. But I wish Mrs. Mary might be seized with apoplexy tomorrow morning and recover and be restored to perfect health just two minutes after her invitations had been irrevocably countermanded.

Yesterday was Sunday. At Grace Church: very momentous day it was, of the transaction whereof I will not write while I'm in my present most unchristian frame of mind. Prussia isn't a republic after all.

Wish I had the man here that invented the polka—I'd scrape him to death with oyster shells. Probably, though, he's dead already, and polking everlastingly through another and a *worser* world, and so beyond my vengeance. . . .

April 28. At Wenzler's studio this morning. Portrait prospers, and gains ground daily, and will be a good portrait exceedingly. Poor little Ellen quite unwell and obliged to end the séance prematurely—better though this evening. . . .

Jones *soirée* was not honored by either of us. Broadway Theatre last night. *Romance and Reality* and *Used Up*—much fun in both. Still suffer from the debilitating effect of excessive cachinnation. . . .

Orders given to commence excavating in Twenty-first Street Wednesday night at 23 minutes past seven P.M. Hibernia came to the rescue yesterday morning; twenty "sons of toil" with prehensile paws supplied them by nature with evident reference to the handling of the spade and the wielding of the pickaxe and congenital hollows on the shoulder wonderfully adapted to make the carrying of the hod a luxury instead of a labor commenced the task yesterday morning.

What the object may be of putting us into a forty-foot house, and how soon such an establishment is going to reduce us to an insolvent state, and whether it is or is not absurd in me to acquiesce in this lamblike way I've not yet clearly settled in my mind. All that deliberation and consideration on those and other cognate subjects I've left to the Two Governors, on whose judgment I perfectly luxuriate in relying, for it saves me a deal of perplexity and anxious thought.

The wedding is to be noisy to a degree—perfectly vociferous. I don't care tenpence. If any one had told me six months ago that I should be utterly indifferent to such a prospect I should have looked at him with serene incredulity, and if he'd repeated the statement offensively, should have kicked him with violence for his impudent mendacity.

It's a shame I should so neglect my journal *now*, for though I've a right to expect and do expect that hereafter will be a happier time than this (rather), still I know that I shall always dwell on the memories of this time and cherish them most dearly, even as I now think of the month or two that preceded the 11th of March and try to remember every little matter connected with their history, and half wish I could live through the same scenes again—anxious and unhappy as I was then.

If I could but rid myself of this dead weight of responsibility that so presses on me, even when I'm happiest! Yet I know I need feel no special uneasiness, that I've less reason than most men for forebodings about embarrassment and difficulties and anticipatory cares about expense and pecuniary perils, that I'm (at the worst) as competent as most men to care for a household and fight my way through life without "prospects" or assistance *ab extra*. My own personal tastes, views, and wishes are sufficiently modest and subdued, and work and vigilance, with the help of Heaven, will enable me to gratify the *additional* tastes and wishes that I'm now bound to look after and provide for. Ellen isn't one of the people who live by satin and rosewood alone, but she likes elegance and comfort, and she has got to be suited and satisfied, and she shall be if I can bring it to pass. For myself—I've spent money on myself lavishly enough heretofore and I'm tired of that kind of thing; "there's nothing in it," as Sir Charles Coldstream says, and I can make my precious self comfortable enough on $250.00 a year and rather enjoy the novelty of the proceeding.

April 30, SUNDAY AFTERNOON.   Sixteen days yet. Grace Church this morning—dinner—downtown with George Gibbs. Dr. Wainwright preached.

Just striking five and I'm in a fidget to be back in Union Square, and here's a whole fortnight (and more, too) to be got rid of somehow before the 15th of May shall make its advent on this earth. It strikes me that I'm in love—a little. And tomorrow I've got to do some work—that there's no escaping from—and I'd rather take a dose of physic. Never mind—I'll live through it all in some way or other, I suppose.

May 3, WEDNESDAY AFTERNOON.   Bright and clear, after a rainy

morning. Indefatigably busy (comparatively speaking, that is). Collins—
Maurice—Prince—Dickinson—Peck—Glover and so forth. Tomorrow I
must spend at Flushing superintending a foreclosure where there is going
to be vexation and bother without end, fifty things probably going
wrong, for all which I don't care tenpence. At Mrs. Rebecca Jones's
party last night with Ellen, Heaven bless her.

May 8.   Home an hour earlier than usual, for I had to leave Union
Square at eight and come down to a most prosy vestry meeting of Trinity
Church, which I should have cut if Bishop [William Heathcote] De
Lancey and Dr. [Benjamin] Hale hadn't both called to urge my attendance for the sake of Geneva College, which has sent in a humble "sifflica-
tion" to Trinity Church to be "liberally endowed"—they are not particular
how, as long as it's arranged "liberally," but they'd rather prefer un-
encumbered improved real estate in the city of New York.

It has been fearfully hot and showery for the last few days. Sunday
was perfectly withering. I've got a slight cold too, which is a bore, as
the cards are out today for the 15th.

Poor dear, good, innocent little Ellen, thinking so much of me and so
grateful for every little attention I'm able to show her. It really seems
incredible that I should have gained such an unprecedented combination
of all sorts of excellence as she is and entirely and absolutely. Thank
Heaven that she thinks of me as she does, and long may she think so—
but that she should condescend to love me is marvellous. It's the unspeakable and most undeserved blessing of heaven and I must show my
gratitude for it by making her happiness the one great object of my life.

Enter conscience and common sense with a bucket of cold water and
a knout. "Mr. G. T. S., you are more thoroughly in earnest in what you
have been thinking and writing than ever you were on any other subject
in all your life, we believe and admit. But don't you know what a miserable, selfish, thoughtless, good-for-nothing vagabond you really are?
Don't you know that five years hence or ten years hence your Wife will
be an everyday affair and not the lovely novelty that she is now; and that
there will be cares and anxieties and worriments and vexations and
temptations to bad humor or little unkindnesses or nameless neglects or
little insignificant unamiabilities that you would *now* die sooner than
admit the possibility of your committing? Won't you be lazy and tempted
to neglect her, bored and cross and careless about her feeling it, selfish
and unaccommodating and unwilling to sacrifice your comfort to hers?

Now if you forget your feelings of this time and of the months that have passed, and all that you have said and promised—and all that she has done and is to do for you—if you ever forget this and cease to keep it all fresh and a living spring of action in your heart *we shall not forget a bit of it.* And if you ever thoughtlessly or willfully, by look, word, or deed, slight or neglect her or ever cease for one minute to think of her as she deserves or treat her as you are bound to treat her, then look out for yourself; for as we have thrown cold water on your dream of a whole life of uninterrupted and undiminished fervent, romantic adoration, so we shall come down with the knout of retributive vengeance on one solitary failure of the care and gentleness and kindness and affection that you've promised and are ever bound to show."

Very sagacious and true, but I survive the cold water and I believe I shall not incur the knout. If Ellen's face and form were her chief excellence, I could well fear that I should gradually find my love growing less fervent as time fades her beauty, and cares and anxieties unfelt before might make me less mindful of my pledge to cherish and care for her; but thank Heaven it is not so, and if ever I fail in my duty to make her comfort and happiness my daily care, may Heaven abandon me as I shall most justly deserve.

May 13, SATURDAY. Half-past three P.M. So one era of my life is ending—all the old ways and habits and associations are obsolete now and to be laid on the shelf.

In all the happiness of this time there's now and then something like a feeling of self-reproach. "How *can* I abandon all these old usages and leave this dirty, rat-infested loaferine Greenwich Street and everything that I've grown up among and got used to, and yet feel no sorrow about it; give up all my old friends here, the row of houses on the opposite side of the way that I've known so long, the lookout on shabby brick walls from the windows of this room, this inconvenient old house where alone I can remember living, and yet change cheerfully?" It seems to me as if I were parting from my oldest and best friends for ever and ought to be unhappy about it: but somehow I a'nt a bit. Which, under the circumstances, is not so very remarkable after all.

This morning was bright and pleasant, but clouds have come back now, and there's reason to fear more rain. Improved the sunshine by a walk uptown to Mantello's and Dunlap's, bouquet-hunting, and then went to Wall Street and looked sagacious and did nothing at all.

Preliminary mass meeting of *bridesmaids and groomsmen* came off

Thursday night. Monday at twelve-thirty all hands reassemble at No. 24 Union Place.

Now may Heaven help me to do my duty and bear myself as I should in my new estate! That's all I ask—with that blessing I may reasonably count on every other as its necessary consequence.

Miss MARY C., only daughter of Chester Childs, Esq., of this city.
On Monday, the 15th inst., by Rev. Dr Taylor, GEORGE TEMPLETON STRONG, to ELLEN, daughter of Samuel B. Ruggles, Esq.
On Monday evening, the 15th inst., by the Rev. Dr. Fisher.

Gloria Deo in Excelsis — et in Jenâ Pax

July 26, WEDNESDAY.   I've been too busy and too happy to journalize of late, but there's a leisure hour of warm weather before me just now, and it seems natural to take out my journal—though I hope and believe it will never again seem natural to cover its pages with the morbid, monotonous, melancholy whinings and maunderings of the last two or three years. There's too much to do and too much to enjoy to admit of any philosophizing and sentimentalizing about my nervous system and the other favorite and pleasing topics of the pages that go before.

Retrospect. May 15th. Defection of Walter Cutting by reason of the death of his brother-in-law Wilson. Jem R[uggles] took his place. Grace Church. Rev. Thomas H. Taylor. Reception—slight *déjeuner* and *soirée dansante*. All very jolly and very brilliant and very preëminently successful. Mrs. Dillon and Madame Trobriand. Day was unsurpassable —bright sunshine and cool. Church quite full; poor little Ellen behaved like a Joan of Arc, or any other heroine. Tuesday at eleven we took a carriage and drove over to Mrs. Post's; left there Saturday afternoon. Particularly pleasant time—several nice drives; one stampede of three cows, two horses, one heifer, and a cat. Poor Ellen sick on the Saturday, to my unspeakable dismay, but able at last to come to town. Monday was the day of Mrs. Davis's party in honor of Mrs. Rives; then came the Kean blowout in honor of Mrs. S. June 13th was our expedition to Lydig's at West Farms. Sunday afternoon, drive to High Wood (James Gore King's) [at Weehawken]. June 18th to Mrs. James Strong's place

—memorable as an awfully hot time. Poor Ellen sick the day after and confined to her bed for two or three days. Divers pleasant sprees in a small way at the Broadway Theatre: *School for Scandal, Romance and Reality, Old Heads and Young Hearts*, etc.

Friday afternoon last we went to Rockaway, where Jerry V[an] R[ensselaer] got us a very nice room. Maj. Gen. Scott and Mrs. Scott and the (rather pretty) young ladies—Mrs. Brooks, Tucker, the Hamersleys, Mrs. Robert Cutting, and so on. Very nice time, including one surf bath and two drives, one of them (with Charley and Mrs. V. R. on the beach) it is consolatory to remember in this warm weather. To town yesterday at three P.M.

Letter from Sharon announcing that a room is engaged for us, so thither we go next Monday. Tomorrow afternoon we may perhaps betake ourselves to Whitestone (Powell's) for a day or two.

The house-building plans have undergone a series of mutations. First there were to have been three houses on the four lots. Then Aunt O[livia Templeton] concluded that she would not live in anything so big, and insisted on a single lot. Then the remaining three lots were to have been divided between the two other houses, but when plans and estimates came in my father became refractory and struck for a single lot, too. Now our architectural arrangements are ordered as follows.

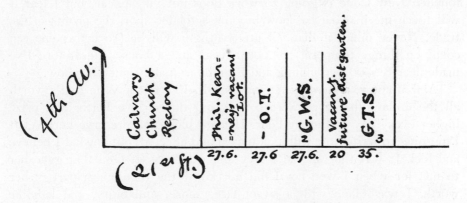

Nos. 1 and 2 have got the start and are going on fast. No. 2 advances more slowly. Mr. Ruggles very kindly gives us a stone front and a kind of architectural bay window for Ellen's boudoir or snuggery on the west side. The house will cost a clean $25,000, of which fact I don't think my father has yet a full realizing sense. As to furnishing, I've called in a little $2000 investment which will do something, and for the balance I trust to economy of income during the coming year, and those comprehensive words "somehow or other."

Going into so large a house and starting on so grand a scale is not in accordance with my "private judgment." But they tell me I'm safe and I hope it will prove so. If I had not the most prudent, sensible, economical, managing little wife that ever was heard of I should be in despair.

In all my happiness there's but one drawback—a sad kind of indefinite foreboding that it is too great to last, a feeling that in this world people cannot expect more than a short interval of contentment and prosperity and perfect happiness like what I'm now enjoying.

Our first plan for the winter was life at a hotel, but we found the extravagance and discomfort of that system quite too severe, and so to housekeeping we go in October in a house of Mr. Ruggles's on the Fourth Avenue till our own shall be finished. . . .

Very hard at work in Wall Street ever since I was married; last great job a partition bill for the benefit of the Beekman estate, which nearly drove me demented. No longer listless and weary and bored in Wall Street—there's need of work now, and I have worked, diligently and with all my heart, and have found comfort in working. How this confounded New Code is going to work does not yet appear, but I fear it will touch me in what has now become a tender spot, the profits of the trade. Never mind, if that fail utterly there will be (so far as one can count on things temporal) $3,000 a year and a house. Heretofore I've made near $2,500 per annum, and I ought to make something now.

And anyhow, and whatever may befall, I've got a Wife that's worth all the dollars that ever were coined and that I love better and prize higher every day and every hour. Heaven bless and preserve her! What I'm going to write now will look unreal and affected, but is what I believe and feel. It was the especial mercy and goodness of God that gave her to me, for when I won her I did not know the thousandth part of her worth. I was taken with a sweet face, sense, amiability, and ladylike manners, and knew of nothing more. And a couple of months' experience of married life has shown me that there might well have been, along with all this and nowise inconsistent with it, fifty terrible drawbacks that would have made me by this time utterly wretched. Some of them I took it for granted I should find, and should have to bear with, and I supposed then that they would be trifles though, and see *now* that they would have been calamities I ought to have dreaded. I supposed I should have fashionable extravagance to contend against—in the place of the sound practical sense and economy I've found—and though I knew she had a kind of reverent feeling for religion and things connected with it, I never suspected her of the piety and high principle that put me to shame every day. No, it was no wisdom and prudence and sagacity of mine that picked her out from the crowd of people that filled Mrs. Stevens's drawing rooms on the night of the 27th of December last, but the special mercy of Heaven that gave me infinitely more than I hoped to find and gave me withal the *duty* and happy, honorable labor, of watching over her to the end of our lives—the office of its minister to make all her days to come as cheerful and contented and bright as they ought to be.

July 29, SATURDAY. Went to Whitestone with Ellen Thursday evening, in the *Washington Irving*. She stays there till Monday and I am going up and down as of old. As of old, and yet I hardly know the place or recognize myself, for I see everything with different eyes now. For the last three summers I've looked on that region with downright disgust. The miserable depression that haunted me in town overwhelmed me there, where I had no resource but a solitary lounging walk and a cigar, and nothing prevented my putting a decisive stop to my daily and nightly voyagings and my dismal evenings and more dismal monotonous listless Sundays but the certainty that our people would go nowhere else, and that if I stayed away, Mamma would abridge her sojourn or perhaps spend the summer in town. But I don't think I could have borne it this summer. Now I see things rather differently. Ellen seems to be pleased and happy there—contented everywhere, she is. Mr. and Mrs. Binney and the infant B. and the Johnsons. . . .

We go to Sharon Tuesday. Would give at least one joint of my little finger to stay away—not only because I've no great surplus of time and am ravenous to be working, but for other reasons. It will be a useful trial, however, of a fault of temper that I'm very conscious of, and it shall be submitted to with as good grace as may be.

July 31, MONDAY. In from Flushing with my dear little wife this morning. Spent yesterday there very pleasantly. . . . Today is drizzly and foggy and warm and the air of the city generally and of Greenwich Street in particular is not aromatic. Bidwell off tomorrow morning for the Red Sulphur. I'm off P.M. for that rendezvous of rheumatic old men and fortune-hunting young ones, Sharon Springs. . . .

September 2, SATURDAY. Month's rustication at Sharon has just

ended. Left yesterday morning at eight and came down the river in the
Oregon last night. Have found my unwonted holiday pleasant decidedly,
though toward its end I began to feel a yearning for Wall Street like
that of a banished patriot for his native land. Not without some apology
neither, for I wanted to be working again, and moreover Charley has
been stewing in town all through the month and my conscience smote
me a little for not relieving him sooner. One or two bores there were,
especially in the earlier part of the season, due mainly to my own faults
of temper. I'm wanting in the easy good nature that carries me pleasantly
through a month's companionship with all sorts of people good and bad.
. . . D'Oremieulx of West Point—capital person; said to be engaged to
Miss Laura Gibbs. Miss Chanler, very lively; Miss Kean with her
rueful admirer Gerry, and Lieut. Griffin; Hamilton Fish and his whole
ichthyological collection; Brandegees big and little; Henry Lloyd and
wife, the latter quiet and rather nice; Parishes, Johnny P. included;
Vanderpool; Johnstons—Miss Margaret J. clever but not particularly
agreeable—something wrong in her composition, I don't know what.
Christie and Lupp, very conversable; Penningtons, very fast; Beldens
very nice, except that fat piece of usurious vulgarity vainly striving to
look virtuous and to be elegant, viz., the papa, and except also the mamma,
who has plenty of sense and of seeming good nature, but is entirely too
strong-minded, too long-headed, and too long-winded for my taste. Miss
Teresa Griffin; Major Van Buren and Mrs. V. B. and little Matty; O'Sullivan elder and younger; old Dr. Rodgers and Miss Fanny, painfully slow;
Mrs. Borland, very nice; Clement Moore & Co., the sons a compound of
imbecility deep beyond all fathoming, with an appetite for chambermaids
beyond all precedent—the two Miss M's very nice indeed; Dr. and Mrs.
Mütter; Kennedy of Baltimore, very pleasant; Mr. and Mrs. Van Rensselaer—the W. Rhinelanders, Giacasso Rhinelander included; Hudson
and Munson, *Arcades ambo*; the Fowlers—loquacious mamma, daughters
that I didn't exactly like, and De Grasse (2d son) a very fine fellow; James
Suydam; Col. Duane, sublimely slow; Remsen and wife; Mr. and Mrs.
Wurts; pretty little Miss Marié and her very nice mamma and brother;
Mrs. Habicht, and others. I can't remember any more just now.

Sharon's a pretty place, in the midst of a pretty country. The natives
seem to be a primitive race: they crowded up to the Pavilion on "hop"
nights to see the dancing, and flattened their noses hour after hour against
the windows with a patient perseverance in admiration worthy of a party

of South Sea Islanders paying their first visit on board a man-of-war. My own amusements were limited. Was with Ellen a good deal—God bless her. She gave up waltzing, except with the girls, because she thought I didn't like it, the first day we reached Sharon. Indeed, I shouldn't have liked it, by a great deal. I walked about the country a little and we took a drive every now and then, to Prospect Hill or the "Palisades"—one drive with Griffin and Miss K. was highly entertaining—and one moonlight expedition, with little Miss Marié, on a most sultry night was refreshing. There was a good deal of music. Ellen was principal performer and was persecuted to sing to the utmost limit of her good nature. One of the Boston Bigelow girls played nicely and Major Searle accompanied himself on the guitar occasionally, to his own great delectation.

September 10, SUNDAY EVENING.   Have walked downtown this beautiful moonshiny night to see how Mary is getting on in her solitude here in Greenwich Street, for all the balance of the household and Aunt Olivia beside betook themselves to Whitestone again yesterday afternoon. So here am I once more of an evening in this my little library and at the same old table, and everything looking so natural and as it used to look that I might almost fancy the last six months a pleasant delusion, only that instead of the lamp that used to be lit so punctually for me I've a couple of candles, and that the table is lumbered up with all sorts of things and in such an entirely chaotic condition that it is apparent that some unwonted cause has been at work and reduced it to its present state of neglect and confusion.

"No more that clock repeats the hours," for it has run down. Its seven used to be the signal for Hempel, Eitheiler, Adler, and Buffet; at eight I used to look out for the boys coming down from the law examination in the library upstairs and wonder whether some of them wouldn't come in for a cigar; half-past nine—Charley, if he was here, would insist that he must go uptown; ten I used to make the signal for going into the front room for a few minutes, to try experimental chords and fancy modulations on the organ; half-past eleven generally found me at this journal and warned me to shut it, lock it up, and march off to bed.

All that's over. It was a dreary monotony enough, and one or two years more of it would have ruined me utterly; my faculties were rusting, temper souring, feelings preying on myself for want of a dinner, and oh, how wretched I was for the past two or three years and how happy I am now! But it's strange how the thought that it's gone and over and never can come back makes one feel toward any period of past life; what a beautiful melancholy light it sheds over times and things that were insignificant, dull, or downright disgusting while they lasted. It's like the change that distance works in the clouds—mere uncomfortable masses of damp, dingy fog, but when seen from far off, inaccessibly distant, becoming exquisite in form and glorious in coloring, beyond any object of this lower earth.

Great fire in Brooklyn last night and this morning—some three hundred houses burned. At Calvary Church twice today. Poussin, the minister of Republican France, taking tea in Union Place when I came off —quite an agreeable kind of person. At the Astor Place Opera House twice last week, *Elisir d'Amore* and *Fille du Régiment*, both pleasant— Donizetti's comic music lively and pretty—those operas worth a dozen *Lucias* and *Lucrezias*. Gramercy Park houses prospering, and I shall be in the little Fourth Avenue establishment in two or three weeks. How I shall furnish the *Schloss am Square* when it's finished, without borrowing, is an inscrutable problem about which I think it prudent not to trouble my head at present. This New Code is going to *tell*, I think, most powerfully, on "the Law and the Profits" and to reduce all professional incomes to a standard of Arcadian simplicity corresponding with the unsophisticated and primitive rudeness of the system introduced by it. . . .

September 14. . . . Took dear little Ellen to Flushing in the *Washington Irving* last night, came down this morning, and am going up again at five. . . .

September 18, MONDAY. Pleasant fall weather. Spent Saturday and yesterday at Flushing. Weather was cool and autumnal, and we were very comfortable, barring a sick headache on Saturday, and the charcoal and magnesia treatment to which I resorted in order to get rid of it. . . .

Charley in town this morning: he has been having a grand time at Catskill. How I wish we could have gone! I never appreciated the *maladie du pays* before, but the memories of the Mountain House and the region around it haunt me perpetually now, I suppose because it's the only place I'm familiar with where nature's to be seen in something like ruggedness and mountain grandeur. The drive up the Mountain House road in the shadow of the mountain rising high and almost perpendicularly on the right with its dark growth of pines and hemlocks, and far up, hundreds of feet above, a single tree just catching the last rays of the

sun that's setting behind the mountain and glowing there like a mass of
arborescent gold, relieved against the clear autumnal blue sky and giving
deeper gloom by the contrast to the solemn shadows that have settled on
all the woods below—it seems to me as if I'd give a year of life to be
traveling up there with Ellen this evening and to have her quite well and
strong enough for a little rambling and scrambling on the mountain for
two or three days of sunshine and pleasant weather. . . .

September 20. At Niblo's last night (Astor Place). *London Assurance*, clever comedy, played middling well. Driven nearly desperate by
the mosquitoes all the rest of the night as the small hours drew on. I
commenced promenading the room with my eyeglass on my nose, candle
in one hand and handkerchief in the other, "deer stalking" on a small
scale. Game shy—bagged three mosquitoes and one cockroach and
finally sunk into slumber a little before four. Desperately tired and altogether good for nothing all today; superintended the removal uptown of
sundry household gear, sweeping out most of the chairs from this apart-
ment and the bureau from my dormitory on the second story. We shall
soon be in our little Fourth Avenue house. Ellen's rooms at No. 24 Union
Square are being stripped and dismantled and most of her furniture is
already removed to our future quarters. It made me quite unhappy to
see the rooms sacked that have always looked so bright and comfortable. . . .

September 25, MONDAY AFTERNOON. So tired that I feel as if rising
from this chair were a physical impossibility. Poor little Ellen is decidedly
ill: no worse thing the matter than influenza, I hope, but that is no mild
affliction when it comes with fever and restlessness and all pervading
weariness and pain for its symptoms. She wasn't well on Saturday, but
the indomitable little woman would be up and busy with her little household arrangements at No. 54 Union Place, so yesterday she had to lie
still and suffer for it, and today she's no better at all. Spent all yesterday
at No. 24 with her except a short walk to Twenty-first Street and up the
Third Avenue in the morning and an expedition to this place and back
in the evening, and as I had little sleep for the past two nights (only an
hour or so last night) I feel most abjectly tired just at present. Dr. Johnston has been invoked, and I trust he'll do his office so far as to alleviate
her troubles and give the poor little girl the comfortable, refreshing
sleep that her feverishness has denied her for the past two days. . . .

Haven't been very energetic this morning, though I tried to get my-

self into working order by a stimulating cup of coffee at Delmonico's—
the first time I've so sinned against my liver for some months. . . .

Bought a pew in Calvary Church, Saturday, of Isaac S. Hone—$550.
Poor old Jesse Oakley unaccountably blew his brains out Saturday in the
little room adjoining the Supreme Court clerk's office. Inspected the
little Fourth Avenue house t'other day—the area of the future domestic
circle, if two points can constitute a circle. Furnishing nearly completed
and everything looking supremely spruce. We were to have taken possession Thursday, but poor Ellen's indisposition will probably retard us.

September 30, SATURDAY AFTERNOON. My little wife not well yet—
better and worse by turns all through the week—and this morning better
decidedly than she has been since her illness began, but I'm afraid that
when I go uptown this evening I shall find her down again and as wretched
as ever. . . .

Tom Griffing I saw yesterday. He seems improved by his campaign,
though it was not a very eventful one and involved little consumption of
powder except in Mexican snipe shooting. . . .

Thackeray's *Vanity Fair*. Not a "work of genius," as some people
call it, by any means, but a remarkable book written on a new principle
and likely to have many imitators in this age—the principle being the
exclusion of any sort of *idealism* in character, plot, or catastrophe. Its
title is an apt one, "a novel without a hero." And now that "heroism,"
in every sense but the melodramatic, is at a discount, people will naturally
feel best satisfied and most at home with a class of fiction that has no
characters or features or notions in its structure that rise much above
their own experience of the world themselves; they will prefer a Hogarth
to all the romantic scene painters in the world. And it is a preference
that no one need quarrel with. Every commonplace man, woman, and child
on earth has hopes and fears and destinies and trials and latent powers of
good and evil that no human artist can do justice to. The elements of
what we called Romance are but a cheap substitute, after all, for the
awful interest of everyday realities. The greatest painters of the most
glorious period of art found their noblest ideals in portrait, and the considerations which explain their triumphant use of individual portraiture
of the human face in their greatest and most strictly ideal works, and their
infinite superiority over our modern painters with their (so-called)
original insipidities of their own creation apply for aught I can see with
tenfold force to the painter of character in novel or drama. *Every* character
is ideal. . . .

SECOND EDIFICE, 1788–1839

PRESENT EDIFICE, BUILT 1842–1846

TRINITY CHURCH

MRS. PHILO RUGGLES (ELLEN BULKLEY)
ELLIE'S INDOMITABLE GRANDMAMMA, JANUARY 1864

MRS. GEORGE TEMPLETON STRONG
JULY 1864

The Twenty-first Street palazzo coming on fast. In the name of the Sphinx, *what* will I do with it when it's finished and possession delivered? Carpets and mirrors and Louis Quatorze chairs and Buhl tables and ormolu gimcracks cost money, and unless I happen to pick up a large roll of $100 bank notes in the street and fail in discovering the loser, or find myself unexpectedly remembered with a bouncing legacy in the will of some one of my numerous clients who may have been struck with an admiring appreciation of my talents, virtues, and accomplishments, or commit a brilliant and successful bank robbery, or am somehow favored with some sort of unprecedented good luck, I don't see but that I'm likely to find the question of ways and means complicated and embarrassing.

October 7, SATURDAY AFTERNOON.   Fine weather. Ellen is better and would be tolerably well, only she can't eat—and how the poor little woman supports life is a marvel. On Thursday afternoon, the long-expected emigration took place, and we became housekeepers. The experiment thus far has been eminently successful: the two breakfasts, two teas, and one dinner which have been produced at No. 54 have prospered and have left fragrant memories behind them. Our visitors the first night were Charley and Mr. Ruggles. Last night we had quite a soirée, except that there wasn't anything to eat and drink: Mr. and Mrs. Curtis, George Anthon, the grandmamma, and Mrs. Bostwick. On the whole things look encouraging. I've taken to rising at seven and only want to acquire the faculty of going to market to become a model Head of a Family.

Saw Macready Wednesday night in *Macbeth*. Very finished and forcible performance. Went with one Fortescue, a Member of Parliament—younger son of the Earl of Something—and a very nice person withal. Macready was at No. 24 Tuesday, where a small gathering was got together to meet him, and where I got a sick headache from my father-in-law's sherry.

October 17. . . . Macready last night in *Julius Caesar*. Very pleasant evening. Macready as Brutus, Vandenhoff [as] Mark Antony. Macready's conception of his part was very beautiful and Vanderhoff played better than I've ever known him play. House but thin.

Domestic life comes on famously. It's cheaper than I expected. Mutton chops are not expensive, and I fare sumptuously enough for me on a most reasonable daily outlay. If it were not for the houseful of rosewood and red satin that's got to be bought and paid for in a year or so, I should feel quite pecuniary and comfortable. We've got very good servants; Ellen seems to glory in her new vocation and everything thus far has gone on most swimmingly. Thank God for giving me such a wife and for enabling me to take care of her in a way that she's contented with, though I don't think it a quarter good enough for her. May I only be able to keep her always in comfort and with something of the elegance and luxury about her that she deserves. That's all the temporal happiness I ask for. . . .

October 21.   Bank account is $690.00, which has got to pay for divers furnishing bills and two season seats at the opera and to last till January 1. I shall turn Socialist, Fourierite, Free-Soiler, and Red Republican. . . .

October 24.   Bright sunshiny day after a rainy yesterday. Got downtown late today. Had to stop at No. 24, then at Dr. Johnston's and then at the Astor Place Opera House. Ellen is down again with another attack of feverishness and so forth—the same sort of thing, it would seem, with her illness of September—only promising, I hope, not to be quite so severe. Engaged a couple of seats at the Astor Place Opera House on the memorable old sofa. They open on Wednesday next with *Norma* and some say that they'll bring out *Don Giovanni* thereafter. Hope they will. . . .

Europa just arrived. News important. . . . Cholera in Edinburgh and London—doubtless it will reach us in two or three months. France has decided to elect her President by universal suffrage. Never did delirium create a more unsubstantial dream than that of their being able to carry on a government on such a basis. But democracy is epidemic now and even Austria has gone mad: the mob of Vienna are erecting barricades, driving out their Emperor, and murdering obnoxious ministers in style quite worthy of Paris itself. The latest rumor is that the Emperor is bombarding his capital. But I don't believe it. Providence seems to have a period of storm and revolution in store for all Europe, and to have blinded the eyes of its legitimate rulers, put confusion into their councils, and the panic fear that comes on fated men into their hearts. Indecision, imbecility, and groveling fear of their subjects are the prominent features of King and Kaiser all over the continent; they shrink from before the cowardly and clamorous mobs that have suddenly risen up to dispute their rule as if a supernatural enemy had appeared against them. The rôle of Louis XVI seems assured to them all, and if one may judge from these proceedings in Vienna it would seem as if the scenes of the National Convention might be destined to be re-enacted through Europe and Paris might lose the bad eminence it has held so long. To be sure, the bears of Germany must exert themselves to surpass or even equal the tiger monkeys of France, but there's an element of brutality in the Teutonic character that is capable of great things in the way of sullen carnage and slow, stupid atrocity and heavy feeding on horrors of every sort. . . .

October 27. . . . Had Macready and Mr. Ruggles at No. 54 last night. Cram and Charley also happened in and we had quite an aesthetic evening.

October 28. Party at Mrs. Sidney Brooks's last night: not very fast, but pretty well, considering. Went to Greenwich Street this morning. Find the household just starting for Whitestone, there to spend Sunday, influenced, I strongly suspect, by the desire to provide a haven of refuge if the cholera comes—and come it will I predict, within the month. Prudent proceeding, for Greenwich Street has got to be a most promising location for plague and pestilence of every sort. . . .

October 31, TUESDAY. . . . Long talk last night with Mr. Ruggles about Atlantic Dock—most brilliant operation, in his judgment, now on the eve of most brilliant success—but he is rather inclined to be sanguine, and I shall wait till I see the mortgage disposed of and the stores bringing in their annual $60,000 rent before I put full faith in his calculations. . . .

Political enthusiasm rather torpid, although the crisis is so near. Taylor stock rather declines as the day of battle approaches, and in the absence of any extraordinary excitement such as that of '40 I always augur infavorably for the Whigs from the discipline and steadiness that their opponents always bring into action. The election of Cass, by the by, would introduce a rather serious disturbing element into the chances and the prospects of the Atlantic Dock concern, for he hates England as fervently as a French Jacobin or an Irish Repealer, and according to common belief would jump at any chance of running us into a war. . . .

November 4, SATURDAY. . . . Opera last night *Lucrezia Borgia*—house jammed and performance spirited. Miss Laura Gibbs went with us. Cultivated the Rhinelanders, Jaudon, and V. R. and C. C. Moore's little daughter. Today has been rather busy, for I got downtown late. Hereafter I must make it part of the "Organic Law," my first and firmest rule, to leave No. 54 at half-past eight even if I've nothing on but my shirt.

Came downtown with Osgood Field. He and Maunsell Field and David B. Ogden are all staying at Peteler's, opposite to us. Duyckinck called—tells me that Macaulay's long promised *History of England* will appear in December. . . .

Wish I had a great deal of money—say $12,000 a year. But I won't let myself worry on the subject if I can help it. Bating accidents and casualties, I have a reasonable right to expect to get along somehow and that's more than I deserve.

November 6, MONDAY. . . . Yesterday was a very rumbustious kind of day—violent storm. Went to church in the morning, and my indomitable little wife armed herself with cloaks and clogs and went likewise. Cleared off splendidly toward night and I had a pleasant walk down Broadway and up again. Called at No. 108.

For this morning, nothing very special. . . . Old Mrs. Hamilton came in. I don't believe that old lady has the slightest intention of ever going to a better world: such a specimen of juvenile antediluvianism I never encountered. . . .

News from Europe by the *Hibernia* and the *Washington*. It would seem as if the Austrian Empire were to be the great battlefield of democracy against the institutions of the past age. At present the imperial prospects don't look bright at all, but if anything like a protracted struggle should follow, Russia will probably pitch into the fray from one side and France from the other, and there will be a general war. England might possibly be drawn in it, and she's more likely, I think, to ally herself with Russia than with the champions of the New Light system, but if she does not, and Russia has to fight the battle singlehanded against all the strength of Western Europe, I think the Great Northern bear will probably have to return to his den with a skinful of sore bones. He's invincible at home and can laugh at invasion, but his powers of attack are limited and all the energy and youth and spirit and enterprise of the rest of Europe have deserted the conservative side and are clamoring for innovation and ready to fight for it, especially when backed by the ignorant, brutal, degraded masses who are ready not only to fight but to rob and murder in the glorious cause. . . .

November 9.   Feel nervous, cross, anxious, annoyed, and insolvent. Whether it be the prospective operation of the New Code on all legal emoluments or one or two recent visits to the Twenty-first Street house that has produced my present state of mind, I can't certainly say, but I experience today a gloomy, superstitious foreboding of duns, a mournful presentiment of a bank account pumped dry, and impertinent creditors to be bullied or dodged. Perhaps it's because I went into Tiffany's with Ellen this morning and saw a great many things I wanted but could *not* afford to buy. But Ellen's a heroine. The way she turned away her eyes from beholding vanity and calmly defied the insinuating attacks of a whole bevy of most eloquent and argumentative salesmen, conceded that various gimcracks were beautiful, were immensely cheap and *would* suit her exactly, but concluded with the avowal that she should not buy them or let me buy them was delightful to behold. It reminded me of the superhuman firmness of some Christian matron of the times of Diocletian quietly repelling all the entreaties and persuasions of a whole gang of Priests of Jupiter-Flamens and Arch Flamens, heroically holding fast her faith and refusing to burn incense on any terms before any heathen deity whatever. . . .

November 20. . . . Walked about a little and contemplated the progress of uptown. The Fourth Avenue is so far built up as to have a city look as far as Thirty-first Street. All the cross streets have rows of houses starting up in them, and ten years more of this growth will carry the city beyond the Lower Reservoir. Looked at Tyng's church [St. George's] which was opened yesterday (but not consecrated because he and his flock don't like Doane and Whittingham, who are performing episcopal functions here). The building is fatally short and squat, but the front and the towers are among the finest things in the city, and it's consoling, after Renwick's pasteboard abominations, to see the massiveness and solidity of the whole structure. The church stands in a howling wilderness at present, but the streets around Stuyvesant Square will soon fill up. [Hamilton] Fish proposes to build a fine house on the north side, I believe. . . .

Ellen's better and was at breakfast this morning. Twenty-first Street house is advancing slowly. I'm tending gradually to insolvency. Have been reading the *Trois Mousquetaires*—amusing trash, which one can get along with very pleasantly by putting his moral sense and his common sense both in a state of suspended animation *pro hac vice* and consenting to be entertained in their absence. It is really, and in fact, profligate nonsense, but I must acquire a little more French than I've yet obtained, and reading such stuff as this is part of the necessary process.

November 30. Well, the boys have gone, the Old Gentleman has gone, and Field Marshal Bidwell has gone, and it's three o'clock, and I've done a tolerable morning's work; and so I put up my papers "In the matter of John Borland" and lug out the journal.

It's a mild, warm, humid Indian summer kind of day that began with sunshine and a bright sky, but a dull cloud has gradually established itself over all the heavens, and a change of weather's coming. Such a state of things always makes me feel heavy, depressed, and anxious, and I feel most particularly so just at present with a foreboding of fifty nameless evils—want of money first of all.

Then I'm plagued and worried about this house-building business. I do wish our numerous kind and disinterested friends would let us alone, to build as we see best. I shall now do what I might better have done before—put down my foot, and prohibit any more trifling additions and insignificant alterations. . . .

Row at the Opera last night—the Manager *vs.* Benedetti. Wasn't lucky enough to see the fun, for having heard *Lucrezia Borgia, ad nauseam,* we stayed at home, and had a visit from my jolly uncle Philo Ruggles. Divers parties in prospect, to some of which we shall have to go, I suppose. One at that amiable Mrs. Baxter's tomorrow night that I shall shirk, one at Mrs. Fearing's and one at Abraham Schermerhorn's. The Penningtons give a fancy ball at Newark next week. . . .

December 2, SATURDAY. . . . The operatic row that was anticipated came off last night; house crowded full, hundreds of people turned away, and excitement prodigious. Benedetti was silenced by a hurricane of sibilation as soon as he shewed himself; he had plenty of friends in the house, but their applause could not drown the hisses, and the combined uproar made it hopeless for him to proceed, so he marched off, the curtain fell, Fry appeared, and after divers futile attempts succeeded in saying what he had to say to an obbligato accompaniment of mingled hisses and applause from the boxes and parquette, and of squeals, shrieks, and yells from the Third Estate in the amphitheatre. Then the curtain rose and Benedetti was allowed to proceed. It was upon the whole a victory for Mr. Fry, though the battle was hard and the disapprobation of Benedetti's presumption less overpowering than it should have been. The indomitable little Laborde was received with huge applause and did very well, indeed, and was in a white rage and sang superbly, and the Norma and Pollio, being in a state of mind fully adequate to reciprocal manslaughter, there was a reality about their acting whenever they came near each other that was delicious to witness. I trust the fire of discord will be fanned, and that this row won't be suffered to subside; the present state of things gives a pleasing animation to an evening at the opera and greatly promotes the pecuniary health of the concern. There was $1,300 in the house last night. . . .

December 4, MONDAY. . . . Had a long conference with Mr. Ruggles. . . . He is just at the last step of his long series of operations in

Atlantic Dock property, and by a series of disappointments that seem
to have a fatality about them, finds more difficulty in raising this $25,000
than he has had with all the $300,000 that has gone before it. He
is annoyed and anxious and not without some reason, where there
is so important a stake depending on the issue of his negotiations, but
I think he can hardly fail to be successful in following up one of the
numerous tracks he has opened. I've been at work this morning to see if
I could manage anything, but it's business I'm very raw at and then I
don't feel authorized to say anything definite or to use anybody's name.
The Seamen's Bank have got about $150,000 there and don't wish to go
farther: the Chambers Street concern is in hostile hands and won't act.
The James Lloyd estate won't invest in Brooklyn, on principle. . . . Poor
little Ellen, in her ignorance and simplicity, was terribly distressed by
what her father told her of the matter. . . .

December 5. . . . Interrupted by Mr. Ruggles, with whom I have had
another long discussion. His position is critical, and one day of this epidemic
influenza or of any other indisposition would probably involve a smash, so
close has he run down upon the payments to be made within a week or
two. I've been racking my brains to devise some way of being useful in
the premises, but as yet without success. In the meantime I've entire
confidence in his pushing through and coming out right, but the present
posture of affairs is one that should be terminated as soon as possible. It's
a shame that he of all men should be condemned to a life of toil, perplexity, and corroding care over the details of bonds and mortgages and
bank extensions.

December 11. . . . Tolerably energetic morning. . . . The [California]
gold mania is rising fast and may lead to important results. There are
already signs of an inflation and rise in prices, and if one is to believe a
quarter of the newspaper stories, gold is going to fall to half its value
within a year. People talk in the calmest way about adding a thousand
millions to the circulating medium.

December 14. . . . Tuesday night was the great Grinnell party. Shoals
of people, splendid house, sumptuous supper, of which I partook not
wisely but too well. Talked to N. P. Willis and Charles Bristed and Mrs.
Hills and Mrs. Fearing and Butler King, and so forth. . . .

California gold fever raging furiously. Cholera cases still occurring
at Staten Island, but not so malignant a type as at first. One case on Monday in a pestiferous emigrant boarding house No. 136 Greenwich Street
—the man died, but whether the cholera has the credit of that result or

the mustard plasters, the cayenne pepper and the twenty grains of calomel per hour, is questionable.

Wolcott Gibbs is very ill: in the fourth week of a slow fever caught in the copper regions of Lake Superior, where he was geologizing all summer. . . .

December 21. . . . Prodigiously busy. Dined on a shilling's worth of oysters at George W. Brown's. . . . I'm working like a California gold digger who has just come on a specially rich stratum of auriferous mud. . . .

Ellen rather better this morning; poor girl, she has a hard time of it. She's sadly disappointed not to be able to go out this evening and see three or four of her friends arrayed for Mrs. Stevens's fancy ball, and I'm afraid she'll be still more disappointed in being obliged to spend her Christmas at home instead of going down to No. 24 and having the pleasant day that she'd set her heart upon.

Saw Henry Cram. Wolcott Gibbs worse; his recovery now very doubtful. He's just been elected to the chemical professorship in the Free Academy. . . .

December 26, TUESDAY.   Yesterday was Christmas. Lucky it's essentially an indoor and domestic festival, for the weather was of a kind to suffocate rejoicing and to make all festivity a hopeless thing except in the house and with the blinds closed. A warm stifling fog had settled down on the city, a fog so dense that the rain drops seemed to fall lazily and with difficulty down upon the snow that covered the streets and which rain and fog and warmth together were converting into streets of mud and nastiness inexpressible. One could scarcely see across Broadway, spectral omnibuses loomed up through the fog, splashed the weary passengers with a volley of superfluous mud and vanished. Pedestrians went walloping restlessly through mud and muddy water, and were blind to the attractions of the shopwindows. Never was weather more perversely wrong and more ludicrously and pitiably out of place. . . .

After church I put my most imprudent little wife into a carriage and sent her down to No. 24, and then put myself into an omnibus and went ploughing and lunging down to Greenwich Street. The driver was drunk and the progress of the vehicle was like that of a hippopotamus through one of the quagmires of South Africa. Came back, dined at No. 24, and was knocked down directly after by a pounding sick headache of the first magnitude, so I spent the evening on a sofa in the library in a most unchristian and unChristmas-like frame of mind. We made a night of it, for

it was thought imprudent for Ellen to journey home through such execrable weather, and breakfasted there this morning.

Gibbs is a little better. Southard succeeded on Sunday morning, much
to my regret, by dint of thirty-five minutes of absurdity, affectation, and
melodramatic monkeyism delivered from his pulpit, in demonstrating
himself to be an incontrovertible noodle. . . .

Today is a delightful specimen of genuine winter weather, with its
legitimate sunshine and frosty air. Have been very indefatigable notwithstanding my night of headache and feel in tolerably good condition and of
a joyful spirit: only every now and then the thought of the bills that will
come in after January 1, and nearly eat up that quarter's income, descends
upon my spirit with an awful weight.

Ellen's Christmas presents numerous and nice, some of them novel
and peculiar and pointing toward the future. . . .

December 28. . . . Deposited my quarterly $750.00 in anticipation of
January 1, for I was cutting my bank account painfully close, and then sat
down and considered how far it was going to be reduced by the coming
bills; but my under jaw began to settle so awfully before I was half
through my estimates that I finally concluded to let the morrow care for
the things thereof and to shut my eyes to the probable approach of insolvency.

December 30. Another snowstorm commenced yesterday morning
and continued till an hour ago, with the exception of a few hours last
evening, when people bound to and from the Opera House were indulged
with a moderately severe rain. Went there with Ellen and her mother;
the *Barber* again and rather better sung than on Wednesday. Most de-
·licious music it is from overture to finale; few things can be pleasanter
than its performance by people at all adequate to their work. House was
reasonably full considering the weather. . . .

Eighteen hundred and forty eight will have departed before I make
another entry here. Heaven carry us safe through 1849! I'm looking forward to several things that may happen before another 30th of December,
and I can't help feeling a little anxiety for the future and a little of that
sadness for the past that the dying out of a year always awakens. There
are several things to happen before this time next year. Among the least
important of them are: the farther prosecution of our experiment of
living; the probable completion and occupation of the new house; the
coming of the cholera (it's now making havoc in New Orleans); the possible rupture between North and South on the slavery question; the action

of the legislature on matters of moment to all who practise law, and so forth. But it's not worth while to worry oneself with moping over the melancholy possibilities of the future. I'm contented and happy now, and they are fools who taint present happiness by looking forward to chances of evil which may not come, and which Man cannot avert if its coming be ordained. *Spero meliora!* Among the more important is——!!!

1849

MACAULAY'S *ENGLAND* · PECUNIARY WORRIES ·
ELLEN'S ILLNESS · THE ASTOR PLACE RIOT ·
CHOLERA EPIDEMIC · A HOUSEWARMING

Domestic bliss—with one all but tragic interruption—was the staple of Strong's diary for the year. His delight in his wife, in the rapid completion of his "palazzo" on Twenty-first Street, and in his circle of friends, fills these pages with a sunny glow. But as he records, there were two weeks when he suddenly aged by years; the fortnight in which Ellen so narrowly escaped death. Happily, Rockaway and West Point soon restored her to health. Of the national events of the time—the inauguration of Taylor, the rising threat of sectional collision, the demand of California for admission and so on—he makes but brief mention. Only the gold rush, which caught up his brother-in-law John Ruggles, and which seemed likely to inflate prices disastrously, enlisted his close interest.

January 2, TUESDAY. Spent yesterday most indefatigably. Turned out with Charley in a carriage and made about eighty calls, closing the day's work at six o'clock, then went up to Mr. Ruggles's, where Ellen spent the day, and got home at last, tolerably tired. The day was not so very disagreeable as I expected to find it. At some of the places I had rather an agreeable time. But there was one very radical change everywhere. To quote Mr. Hood, "it used to be the females first, but now it's furniter," and I busied myself much more with the rosewood and the red satin and with the estimated price of the carpets and the mirrors and the gas fixtures and the Dresden china than with the fascinations of any of the angelic beings with whom I exchanged views on the weather.

January 4. . . . Opera last night. Went with Mr. Ruggles and my little wife, resplendent in opera hat, pink satin, and bouquet, and looking prettier than any six women in the house.

January 8, MONDAY. . . . Century Club Saturday night; my first appearance there for six months. Find that they've spoiled the concern by bringing into it a herd of new people, some of whom I don't know, and who may be very nice but look rather seedy and very slow, and others whom I do know—so well that I don't want to know them any better. Such men as Evarts and Prichard and Gilbert Speir and Brown are very well in their way. I know nothing against them, but know nothing so much in their favor as to make it an object to belong to the same club with them or to cultivate them as associates. I can find fifty people exactly as good anywhere. I was provoked, moreover, at the turn some business took in the course of the evening, and made up my mind to quit.[1]

Opera Friday night—my little wife and little Miss Rosalie with me. Heard that lovely *Giuramento* again, or rather heard two acts of it and then came off compulsorily in the bitterness of sick headache.

Church yesterday. Southard talked about astrology and quibbled and played tricks with the Star that led the Wise Men of the East to Bethlehem, and emitted cunning conceits and quaint prettinesses on his subject till I was tired. He's an ecclesiastical Euphues—a Friar Gerund of the nineteenth century. The man has sense: why don't he show it by talking plain truth when he's in his pulpit, instead of dressing up his ideas with tropes and figures and exquisite similitudes, most [in]tolerable and not to be endured, like a sonneteer of 1620?

January 15. . . . Reading Macaulay's *England*, a clever book and likely to be popular beyond its deserts. His introductory view of domestic life and manners in England in the latter part of the seventeenth century is valuable, and his views of the great Parliamentary struggle that led to the fall of Charles I are more reasonable and moderate than I expected to find them; but the book can hardly claim the credit of an impartial

[1] Strong thought better of this decision, for he remained a member of the Century until his death. At least two victims of his attack of snobbism made their mark in the world: William Maxwell Evarts (Yale 1837) was a lawyer of great learning and distinction, Attorney General of the U.S. in Strong's lifetime and subsequently Secretary of State; and Gilbert McMaster Speir (Union 1832) was a justice of the superior court of New York City. William Mackay Prichard (Harvard 1833) was a law partner of William Emerson (Harvard 1818), R. W. Emerson's elder brother, and afterward of William Gardner Choate (Harvard 1852). Thompson S. Brown, an engineer, died in 1855.

record of events or a just and philosophical view of their causes and consequences. It is a lively and readable narrative and nothing more: and even
that recommendation is due in some degree now and then to its writer's
imagination, and to little bits of adroit coloring skilfully introduced with
a single word for which I suspect Mr. Macaulay would find it hard to
quote book and page. . . .

Miss [Margaret] Johnston is engaged to John Bard:[2] a fashionable
fool purchased with the profits of thirty years' successful ironmongery.
The more I see of the way in which marrying and giving in marriage is
conducted in this city, the more profoundly and sincerely am I thankful
for my own great good fortune.

January 25.   Ellen better, thank Heaven; that's one bright spot at
least. Wretchedly nervous, anxious, and uneasy for the past few days,
gloomy and oppressed, with a perpetual fifty-pound weight of foreboding
on my breast, looking forward to all sorts of nameless calamities, and
first and worst that standing bane of man's existence on earth—the fear
of the want of money—tenfold worse than the reality, bad as that would
be. Perfectly without any tangible reason, too; that makes it still more
unworthy of a man who ought to have faith and hope in something beyond
dollars. But it's a periodical disease with me, a causeless attack of insane,
gnawing, corroding, burning, suffocating anxiety and despair about my
own resources and prospects, my ability to fight my way through the
world and carry my little wife through it in comfort and honor. When
the disease is upon me I'm a pitiable case, sick at heart, disgusted with
myself, and able to exist only by working hard and drinking coffee.

This California business worries me sadly, though I hope and believe
that the stories afloat are nothing but the wildest exaggerations. But
suppose they should prove in any degree true, and the circulating medium
of the world should suddenly be increased by a third or a quarter? Where
should I be then? Of course, without any loss whatever, one-third or one-
fourth poorer. But it's disgraceful to allow one's self to be tormented by
dreams on that subject.

---

[2] John Bard of Hyde Park, New York, was the son of William Bard (Columbia
1797), pioneer in life insurance, and grandson of Dr. Samuel Bard (Edinburgh 1765),
the famous New York physician; in 1860 he was the founder of St. Stephen's College
at Annandale, New York, now Bard College. Margaret Johnston was the daughter of
John Johnston of New York, ironfounder, and sister of John Taylor Johnston (New
York University 1839), railroad executive, art collector, and first president of the
Metropolitan Museum of Art.

January 26. Went with Charley last night to Robert Ray's[3] big party, a flagrant case of domestic tyranny and oppression, for I felt very vilely and did not experience any call to go off through the mud and fog to the Northwest settlements somewhere between Twentieth Street and Lake Champlain which Mr. Ray has the bad taste to inhabit and to call Fitz Ray Place. Some speculator has run up a row of sixpenny shanties in the neighborhood and, his name being Martine, has dignified his handiwork by the name of "Lamartine Row."

But the party was a very magnificent one. The size and style of the house, and the conservatory, and the uncommonly good dancing, music, and so on, made it one of the most successful affairs I ever attended. As I did not feel in a humor for enjoying myself, I retreated to the library, sat down with Charles King, and looked over Audubon's foxes and squirrels and skunks for an hour,[4] and then came home, supperless, with a headache.

Hector, who has been missing since Sunday morning, and whom I advertised in the *Sun* yesterday, has returned to his afflicted family. Bob Benson is going to California, also Frank Winthrop; in short, there's no end to the emigration. I don't wish any harm to all these people, but it would give me considerable satisfaction if a sudden rise in the waters of the Pacific would overwhelm the gold region and the gold diggers, being provided with life preservers, could be floated off to the Sandwich Islands.

January 27. . . . Saw William Pennington. He's off for California next week. It's a most weighty and momentous business, this California furor. Either it will be an era in the monetary concern of the world like the discovery of America, or posterity will have another chapter of delusion and mania and ruin and distress to wonder over, almost equal to the history of the Mississippi scheme and the South Sea bubble. . . .

January 29. . . . *Crescent City* arrived from Chagres; brings us gold. The frenzy continues to increase every day. It seems as if the Atlantic Coast was to be depopulated, such swarms of people are leaving it for the new El Dorado. It is the most remarkable emigration on record in the history of man since the days of the Crusades; and as the country fills up

[3] Robert Ray (Columbia 1813) was a member of the banking house of Prime, Ward & Co. and married a daughter of Mr. Prime. He was a trustee of Columbia and also clerk and treasurer of Grace Church, from which he resigned in protest when Dr. Thomas House Taylor, the rector, married Tom Thumb in that edifice.

[4] John James Audubon's *Viviparous Quadrupeds of North America* was in the course of publication at this time; two volumes of plates had come out, but the text was not completed until 1854.

with adventurers from every part of the world, and as they begin to crowd each other, some strange results will be seen. There is neither law nor social system there, scarcely a nucleus of civil order is yet visible at one or two points, and the rest is mere chaos. Everyone is resolved to make a fortune and every one will soon begin to feel pressed for the necessaries of life, and then crime and violence and disease and starvation will make a Pandemonium of the whole region.

January 30. . . . Saw Harriot & Henry about the Palazzo Strong— "Strong's Folly," I suppose posterity will call it. . . .

Constantly annoyed and anxious about my pecuniary prospects, with or without good reason. Can't help it. There's only one resource or help in my perplexity, and that's so commonplace that it sounds like cant to write it down, but I rather think that if one can realize it fully, it's worth relying on, and I find, thank Heaven, that I do realize it more and more. It is to trust in God and to take no thought for the morrow, in reliance on His promises, to do my duty as diligently as my worthlessness will permit, and to leave the issue with Him.

February 2. . . . I believe I'll emigrate to Typee with my family, live on bread fruit and bananas, and teach the parrots and paraqueets to swear at the New Code of the Supreme Court in every language of which I am master. . . .

February 19. . . . Weather bitterly cold. Croton water frozen tight. I have been dining downtown for the last few days and walking up at six or seven in the evening, and I'm able to state it as a fact within my personal observation that a walk from 108 Greenwich Street to No. 54 Union Square when the thermometer is below 10° and the wind is from the northwest is a very cool kind of transaction. Commenced on Friday the melancholy business of taking down the books from my shelves in Greenwich Street and boxing them up for removal to the basement of No. 54, where they are to remain till the Twenty-first Street house is ready for them. It's mournful work pulling them down from the places where I've been so happy in putting them and from which they've looked down on me through so many long desolate winter evenings, the shelves where I've watched them accumulating and multiplying so long. As yet I've made but little impression on the job before me, but after the first ten minutes of removal there was a great gap left that will never be filled up again. I believe my sense of local attachment must be very strong, for it made me feel quite disconsolate to look at the breach I had made.

March 1, THURSDAY. First day of spring. . . . Operations recommenced on the Twenty-first Street Palazzo and the stairs now going up. I feel as if I never should get fairly settled in that house—as if something would certainly happen to upset all my calculations before we can be finally established there. . . .

March 5, MONDAY.   [Zachary] Taylor has a day of sunshine for his inauguration—a specially good omen in this era of fog and foul weather. Spent half an hour this morning in inspecting the Palazzo where they are vigorously at work once more, and have spent the rest of the day pretty busily between Wall Street and my poor little deserted room in Greenwich Street where the book-packing job proceeds as fast as I can push it, but still not very rapidly. . . .

March 16, FRIDAY. . . . Prosecuted the book-packing job yesterday afternoon and got my thirteenth box packed full. I shall send up the first division of the library before long. . . . Meantime I'm nervous about them and apprehensive, not of moth and rust, but of rats and damp, and I shall feel fidgety and uneasy till they are fairly disinterred and ranked on their new shelves.

I look in at the Palazzo Strong almost daily now, and my heart is rejoiced by the sight of some daily progress—small but consolatory as far as it goes. The stairs is now up and rampant; the "white finish" is establishing itself in the third story; certain bold creations of carpenter work that look like window frames are accumulated in the parlor, and the aspect of affairs is much more encouraging and hopeful than it was during the long winter period of entire inactivity. I wish the house was finished. I wish the furniture was bought. I wish the furniture was paid for. I wish we were settled in our domicile, Ellen in good health, and everything disposed of and settled.

News about town. . . . Curious attempt to extort $50,000 from William B. Astor—as arduous an undertaking as extorting its hide and tallow from a flint. None but a genius in rascality, a Michael Angelo of swindlers, could have conceived so sublime an idea. . . .

March 21. . . . Conferences with Harriot & Henry touching doors, stained glass, "cornishes," centerpieces, and "enrichments." Heaven be praised that I'm in the hands of honest people, for my stupendous ignorance and my capability of being imposed on would be tempting and irresistible facilities to a knavish builder. As it is, I sometimes think that that house will hurry me into an early grave. It is not particularly pleasant to be running up big bills for one's self to pay, but it's ten times worse to be running them up in this way; and though I know that my father won't breathe a syllable of dissatisfaction at any of these expenditures, yet it's bitterly annoying to feel that I'm incurring them for him, and I sometimes seem to feel my hair turning gray as I meditate on plumber's bills, extra finish, and dealings with workers in marble. And sometimes I feel inclined to execrate my own folly for having been so pliable and so easily induced to acquiesce in building the concern. But it's not worth while to think about that now.

March 22. . . . My malediction on marble mantels! How much more simple, how far less expensive, how inexpressibly superior in dignity, comfort, cheerfulness, and artistic effect was the fire in the middle of the floor and the hole in the middle of the ceiling wherewith our respectable Anglo-Saxon ancestors warmed the wall of the grange and the Refectorium of the Mynchery! Why should we shrink from the smoke which so many illustrious Ethelwalds and Ethelberts, not to speak of their more illustrious Norman invaders—De Veres and Taillefers and Courterrais—not only tolerated but snuffed up with enjoyment. . . .

March 27. . . . Jem Ruggles still unwell and thinking of a summer visit to Europe. John [Ruggles] off for California on the 20th. Sorry he's made up his mind to go, for he's a very valuable kind of person to whom I don't think his friends and the public do justice. Wonder whether we're all going to be ruined and undone by this California business. There are times when I feel very blue and uneasy on the subject. I'm bothered and bored still, moreover, about the expense of finishing and furnishing this plaguey Palazzo in Twenty-first Street. But Heaven bless that little wife of mine, how she has been working and toiling and managing and studying and combining and calculating to accomplish the result that's wanted without imprudent expenditure, and to make our parlors and dining room look as nice as they ought without costing one superfluous dollar. Confound the word *Dollar*, and especially confound the necessity that exists of paying such deference to the word! If I hadn't spent money like an extravagant fool in my bachelor days I should have enough now to be able to tell her to march down to Baudoine's and order right and left whatever pleased her fancy, and so spare herself all this trouble and worry and fatigue.

March 30. Palazzo is advancing rapidly; arches run in the hall, cornices commencing in front parlors and second story. . . .

Old Daniel Appleton died the other day, probably from the dyspepsia, of which he has long looked like the incarnate type and symbol. . . .

April 4. . . . News from California: lots of gold coming—"200 millions next year," says the *Herald. Tant pis. Auri sacra fames.* Such a movement as that of the past winter has not been seen since the sixteenth century and the gold-hunting emigration to Mexico and Peru. What would be the effect of the discovery of so much gold as to lower the article to the level of iron and lead? Would it cease to be the conventional stand-ard of value? Or would the nominal value of land and the other subjects of sale and transfer rise so as to correspond with the depreciation of the standard?

April 13. . . . Went with Mr. Ruggles to see Howland & Aspinwall about some arrangements for John's convenience and comfort when he gets to San Francisco and for the facilitating his getting away from there, if he shall want to come. Didn't settle the details of the arrangement, but I think it can be managed. That firm was always magnificent, but of late they have come to be like Brama, Veeshnoo & Co.—their operations in the Pacific and their Isthmus railroad scheme and all their other grand and mighty transactions have tumefied them and made them to wax great in their own conceit. John L. Aspinwall talked about government aid in a tone of sublime indifference. He couldn't say now whether they'd let the government come into the arrangement or not. He didn't know that I was aware that the firm is now in a posture of supplication before Curtis for his influence with Uncle Sam and that their relations with Butler King are those of mendicancy. . . .

April 26, THURSDAY. Down town first today since April 14, and I feel as if I'd lived ten years in that time. Ellen had some trouble on Satur-day and Sunday with a cold and feelings of general indisposition, but not much more than she has felt every day or two for some months. Sunday Jem and Charley dined with us. Ellen went upstairs after dinner and took tea in her room. I read to her a little and there seemed nothing of impor-tance the matter. She slept badly and complained of headache, but toward daylight we both fell asleep. I woke first, turned to take up my watch, and saw that it was a quarter to eight, and then turned toward Ellen, who was just waking and raising her head from her pillow. I spoke to her, and she looked toward me with an expression of pain, and at that instant her eyelids began to twitch and her mouth to work. It is too horrible to think of.

I sent off the servants as fast as I could for help, and then held her, we two alone together, for near twenty minutes. Some of the ladies came up from No. 24. She was quiet then, only half-conscious, clinging to me and now and then looking at me with a bewildered, appealing kind of gaze. I was telling her that I really would not go downtown at all that day when came more of the same dreadful convulsions that began the illness, and then Dr. [Francis Upton] Johnston and Dr. [Abel Bellows] Robeson came in together. They instantly bled her freely, for congestion had set in; and then it appeared that labor had commenced but was proceeding slowly and seemed to be checked by the convulsions. The convulsions kept on, held in check by chloroform but not prevented from returning by anything they could do. Total insensibility. Dr. [John Cummings] Cheesman sent for, and at ten minutes before seven a dead child born—a little girl—and still the insensibility, the convulsions, the sterterous breathing. At two Tuesday morning came the announcement from Johnston and Robeson that it was hopeless—pulse failing, inability to swallow.

I can't write about it. At seven I made one last effort with ice and some brandy and water from a rag, and she swallowed—and the tide had turned. I believe that rubbing of her rigid lips and the inside of her mouth with ice saved her life—if God will yet spare it—for they had ceased to do anything and said she could not live two hours, that her speedy death was inevitable. Since then there has been steady improvement. . . .

The serious and prolonged illness of his young wife was the most severe blow that Strong had had to meet, and he wrote at great length not only of the details of her illness and recuperation, but of his own dreadful anxieties and miseries. That his wife should be at death's door was enough for any man to bear; but on top of this he had to look after the construction of his house and worry about the financing of it during an exceedingly hot spring and summer in which New York was visited by a severe cholera epidemic. His constitution was good and his faith was deep; these together with a temperamental resilience carried him through his "Via Dolorosa." It should be added that Mrs. Strong survived this illness and many more, and outlived her husband.

An obbligato running through most of this year was inflicted on Strong by his cousin Charley; the latter was relentlessly pursuing Miss Eleanor Fearing, and the endless ups and downs of his courtship were discussed and duly recorded in the diary.

April 30.   Ellen continues better, but I rejoice as yet with trembling. Her cough diminishes but is still severe.

I'm beginning to feel jaded now, for I've not been in bed for a fortnight and have made a full change of my clothes but once—and have slept but little.

Moving from Greenwich Street nearly over. I was there this morning for the last time. If I hadn't so much else to think of, it would make me feel sad to see the household gods vanishing from their ancient shrines, the whole house in confusion, every well-remembered room a scene of dirt and desolation.

As to the Twenty-first Street Palazzo, it seems to be advancing pretty well. Poor little Ellen. Heaven send her health and strength to live happily in it. . . . I told her on Saturday that she had been confined, of which, strangely enough, she was totally ignorant. We had kept it from her, lest the news of the loss of the child should produce some kind of shock. The expectation of her speedy confinement had kept her anxious and excited ever since her return to consciousness, and as she had made up her mind that the child must be dead, the news gave her no distress, was rather a relief.

I am older by years since that awful Monday morning, the 16th. A few such days and nights open one's eyes to many things before unseen and make one to realize many truths that had been held only in words. . . .

May 1. . . . Went to bed last night, but I've got out of the habit of sleeping in bed. Had to take some morphine to quiet myself withal, and am this morning utterly knocked up with a thousand things to do and a painful sense of the utter impossibility of doing one of them.

The emigration from No. 108 took place last night. I walked around to the Twenty-first Street house in time to do the honors of uptown and "receive" my father and mother.[5] Comfortless, desolate, and uninhabitable is the aspect of the house, everything out of order, every place cumbered with the precious rubbish that has been painfully carried up from No. 108. They are all nearly tired to death. That some of them are going to be seriously ill from this, I've no shadow of doubt.

May 2. . . . It's perfect misery to have to come down here to Wall Street while things remain thus, but there's nothing for me to do uptown, and it would only disturb and alarm her to see me hanging around the house. . . .

May 3. . . . All this, and the feeling that I'm oppressed with work that I can't bring myself to take hold of, and the wearing anxiety about money matters, from the indefinite expenses lately incurred and from this house-building business which has now begun to return upon me continue

[5] Strong's parents moved into the house at 70 East 21 Street.

to weigh me down with a despairing kind of gloomy dejection that's intolerable. However, if my poor little wife will only get better, I shan't mind insolvency much, and if she don't, why I shan't mind it at all.

I see from Tyler Smith's treatise that a cold water douche to the face is an important means of removing the spasm of the throat that was preventing poor little Ellen from swallowing on that Tuesday morning. So that it may very well be that my liberal use of ice on her poor rigid, distorted lips and on the inside of her mouth, after which she was first enabled to swallow, did actually produce the change and save her life, for her pulse had then become unperceptible and she was in *articulo mortis.*

May 4. . . . Looked through the Twenty-first Street house with Charley yesterday afternoon. Front stoop finished, everything advancing with tolerable rapidity; but I don't take a particle of interest in the concern now.

May 8. . . . Well, I have had one year of what comes as near to perfect happiness as I suppose exists in this world, and only tainted by an occasional foreboding that it was too great to last. And now when the shadow of its Destroyer is darkening everything and turning our thoughts to the terrible possibilities of another day or another hour it is bitter to look back, bitter to look forward, and the present is as gloomy as past or future. Only God has promised to hear our prayers and I ought to find certainty of help in His promises.

I have not thought much of myself—Heaven knows I'd gladly give my life this moment to secure her delivery from present danger—but it's mournful enough sometimes to think of thirty or forty years of objectless, dreary life such as may be before me, listless and worthless, without a future on earth and with one black curtain shutting off all the past. Disgraceful it is, to be sure, that any selfish thought of myself should come sprouting up even now. . . .

May 11, FRIDAY. Ellen "materially better," say the doctors. God be praised therefor, and let us not tempt Fate by premature rejoicing.

Row last night at the Opera House, whereof I was a spectator. Mob fired upon, some twelve or fifteen killed and four times as many wounded, a real battle, for the b'hoys fought well and charged up to the line of infantry after they had been fired upon. Prospect of a repetition of the performances tonight on a larger scale, for the blackguards swear they'll have vengeance. The houses of the gentlemen who signed the invitation to Macready to perform last night threatened. Judge [William] Kent and Mr. Ruggles and some six or seven others of them live on Union Square and that will, therefore, very probably be a scene of disturbance. I'm going up now to clean my pistols, and if possible to get my poor wife's portrait out of harm's way. Mr. Ruggles is making every arrangement and is a good deal alarmed. Don't think myself that there will be much serious mischief.

The Astor Place Opera House riot was the culmination of bitter professional rivalry and personal quarreling between Edwin Forrest, the great American tragedian, and W. C. Macready, the brilliant and powerful English actor, which dated back a number of years. This quarrel had been much in the press, and nationalistic prejudices had been stirred up; sides were taken along social lines, the rank and file and the Bowery boys making a hero of Forrest. On the 7th of May, Forrest's following had broken up Macready's performance of Macbeth *by the conventional means of hissing and egg-throwing, with the addition of certain refinements: the hurling of chairs and the release of a deluge of asafoetida from the gallery. Macready announced the abandonment of his engagement and prepared to leave for England, but a number of leading citizens, headed by Washington Irving and including Mr. Ruggles, published an appeal to him to carry out his original plan, relying on the good sportsmanship of his audiences for the avoidance of further demonstrations. Macready acceded, and undertook to play* Macbeth *again on May 10. Feelings had been inflamed meanwhile by the appearance of placards announcing that the British crew of the Cunarder* America *were resolved to sustain their countryman with arms, and the Mayor had ordered out the militia. Wild disorder broke out inside and outside the theatre as soon as the play opened, and before the riot was over twenty-two had been killed.*

May 12. . . . Yesterday afternoon was a very hurrying time, what with hunting the doctors and running about between my house and No. 24 to make arrangements for the night. Mrs. Ruggles was brought up to our front parlor, where an extempore bed was rigged for her. She hadn't left her room for two or three months before. Poor Ellen's portrait and some other precious things were sent up.

Spent the night till about one partly with Mr. Ruggles and Judge Kent and partly in reconnoitering the view of operations at Eighth Street and Astor Place. Everything looked much in earnest there—guns loaded and matches lighted—everything ready to sweep the streets with grape at a minute's notice, and the police and troops very well disposed to do it whenever they should be told. The mob were in a bitter bad humor but a good deal frightened, and the only overt acts that were committed, on the Bowery side, were met by prompt measures and with instant success. Some of the cavalry were badly hit with paving stones, but as soon as the Unwashed were informed that unless they forthwith took themselves off they'd be treated with a little artillery practice, they scampered. . . .

May 25. . . . The Twenty-first Street house coming on fast. Most reckless expenditure of plaster in the hall; a grand frieze runs around it like that of the Parthenon depicting a sort of procession of *Testaceous Mollusca.* I shall name it the "Battle of the Bivalves." My poor wife says, "We can't have everything." This sickness is perhaps a set-off against her handsome house, poor girl. Heaven grant she may be restored to live in it, in health and happiness. I've never prized her half enough. Through all her pain and weariness and distress, I don't think I've heard one word or one accent of peevishness or impatience, and her first thought when she's relieved from any temporary uneasiness seems to be that it will make us glad to hear of it. It is dreadful to feel that we've as yet no right to rejoice, that the sword still hangs over her. . . .

May 28. Better, I hope—certainly stronger, for she was able this morning to walk as far as the window and to take a survey of the omnibusses and the railroad cars and the green grass that has sprung up in the vacant ground opposite while she has been lying between life and death. . . .

June 4, MONDAY. . . . Cholera looking up as the weather grows warmer. Twenty-five cases reported yesterday and twenty-three today. I've laid in a supply of camphor and paregoric, calomel, pepper, and mustard and am now waiting silently, "hushed in grim repose" for the first symptom of diarrhea to let slip the dogs of war, to ravage my interior with calomel and opiates, and to scarify my outward man with mustard and cayenne. Very nasty disorder is *cholera asphyxia,* but I can't say that I feel any uneasiness about it on my own account. We shall have it among us pretty severely, I dare say, but I don't think it will take such a hold on the community as it did in '32.

Meeting of pewholders of Calvary Church called for Wednesday night. There's an annual deficit of $1,800 at present, and no prospect of diminishing it. If I'm applied to I shall decline all donations or subscriptions; and if I'm pressed for a reason I'll give it and tell the enquirer that the ship cannot be kept afloat without throwing the rector [the Rev. Samuel L. Southard, Jr.] overboard. His antics have driven out half his congregation. . . . He is a standing proof that Catholic principles, good intentions, and respectable abilities may be made worse than useless by egotism, vanity, and indiscretion. He used to be a sensible and rather promising young man, it's said, but people told him that his tropes were beautiful and his rickety periods of loosely-linked, incoherent rigmaroles long drawn out were "eloquent," and so he took to preaching firework sermons, all glitter and sputter and pop, that leave nothing behind to remember them by but a few most commonplace sticks and a great quantity of transitory smoke and stink. . . .

June 5. . . . Carried Ellen downstairs to tea last night, in triumph. She spent an hour there, received a visit from Charley, sat a few minutes at the piano, and looked and acted as if she were well once more. . . .

June 6, WEDNESDAY.   Beautiful weather and a very triumphant day for Ellen. At half-past ten we put her into a carriage, and with her father, her grandmother, and myself she went over the Third Avenue and the old Cats Road some three miles out and back, without apparent injury or fatigue. . . . The country was looking lovely in its new June dress, even in despite of the ruinous encroachments of suburban filth and deformity which have extended themselves over almost all the region through which our expedition lay. Few rides were ever half as pleasant to me. . . .

They're going on fast in Twenty-first Street, laying marble in the hall, getting up Ellen's pretty boudoir window, mantels in the second story, and so forth. What a relief it will be when it and its furniture are paid for and settled!

Ruskin's book on architecture: much in it that I like, much deep thought, many positions taken that I've had a sort of glimmering half-perception of before. Rather more fine writing and *figgers* in it than are necessary, but the man treats his subject with an earnestness and positiveness and intensity of love and hate according as he finds things to be good or bad that are rare and refreshing in this age of eclecticism, indifference, miscalled charity, and heartless, vapid dilettantism. It is not dogmatical, though most folks would say so. . . .

June 7. . . . Thirty-eight cases of cholera reported, and nineteen deaths. John Jay said to have the disorder—probably nothing but an aggravated paroxysm of wind. . . .

June 13. . . . Ellen still convalescing like mad, astonishing us daily by some new achievement. Heaven be praised therefor! At Brooklyn two hours this morning closing a foreclosure; came back with $27,000 in my pocket—unhappily somebody else's money. Palazzo gets on but slowly.

N.B. If I had foreseen the annoyance that house was to give me, I'd never have had it built. The rashness of so heavy an expenditure, and its uselessness for so small a family are serious items of disagreeable reflection; and then the endless additions and alterations over and above the contract, each a trifle in itself, but making together a formidable sum total. Some of these, by the by, have been put in by Messrs. Harriot & Henry contrary to my positive directions, but the parties interfering did so out of pure good nature and inability to keep from devising and improving and arranging. However, it must be stopped. . . .

June 15. . . . George Anthon walked into the office this morning to my great amazement. Drowned out of New Orleans by the waters of the Crevasse. Spent half an hour at Delmonico's with him and Wolcott Gibbs. He gives a dismal account of the filthiness of the great water flood that has come on the city and of the insolvent state of business people there resulting from the various drawbacks it has undergone this past winter. Saw Templeton—breathing out slaughter against Southard. It's questionable even yet whether his excision be practicable. If he stays there the church will sink—perhaps it will whether he stays or not. In which event I lose my investment of $550 in Pew No. 108. Wish I had the money in my pocket. Some reason for wishing I had ten times the amount, when there's that prodigious Twenty-first Street house staring me in the face, and saying from every one of its drawing rooms and boudoirs: "We shall have to be furnished next fall." . . .

It's a terrible daily source of anxiety and depression, which I'm ashamed to say that I can't throw off even now when Ellen's unhoped-for improvement gives me so much ground for joy and gratitude. Ruskin is right—no man's happiness was ever promoted by the splendors of rosewood and brocatelle and ormolu and tapestry carpets; they never give pleasure to their possessor or to those who come and see them, except as a perfect suit of tattooing gives pleasure to a Sandwich Islander. The tyranny of custom makes the one agreeable to us in spite of the expense, and the other agreeable to the scarified savage in spite of the pain of his acquisition. It is a slavery to which we submit in the meekest silence, though it darkens life with needless cares and shuts us out from other and real enjoyments that might be purchased with the wasted cost of this pernicious trumpery. . . .

June 21. Four P.M. Screaming hot—thermometer at 95°—the hardest day yet. Rather jaded after the sufferings of last night, which I spent on a sofa that's too short, with my legs curled over the back to keep me from sliding off. Our movement into the basement was unavailing—it's just as hot sleeping there as anywhere else. So last night we took possession of the parlors, beds and bureaux and so forth carted down, and with every window staring open, and contrived to gasp our way through the sultry night to the sultry morning. I found Ellen asleep when I got home and could not bring myself to the inhumanity of waking her, so I camped out on the said sofa till five A.M. We live next door to a very vociferous mocking bird that talks in its sleep. . . .

June 25, MONDAY.   Back from Rockaway by the early train this morning after a pleasant visit and a season of coolness refreshing to look back upon from the heat of the city. Ellen is not doing as well as I wish. . . . But I don't think this little expedition has made matters worse. We were a party of four, including the grand-mamma and Doctor Robeson, and yesterday Mr. Ruggles came down with Henry Ruggles and his wife, and as the latter gentleman was knocked down with a slight attack of cholera, or "cholerine" as they call it now, immediately on reaching the pavilion, they stayed all night and came down this morning with us.

The house is filling pretty fast. There were the Whites, Jerry Van Rensselaer, one of the Glovers, Charles Aug. Davis, Dr. Smith of Bleecker Street, and Tony Robertson and John Van Buren with a most suspicious "Mrs. Jones" generally concluded to be a chattel held in joint tenancy by those gentlemen. They abandoned the premises, however, last night, and so escaped the gathering cloud of public indignation. . . .[6]

June 27. . . . Poor Ira Whittelsey died at Wallingford on Saturday of the hereditary taint of consumption under which he had been slowly sinking for three years past. There were no very strong points about him: he was a person of considerable information, fair talent, and refined tastes, without much force or brilliancy, but there are few living that have as much purity and simplicity of character as he possessed and act on unselfish motives and generous impulses as habitually and as unconsciously as he always did.[7]

June 29, FRIDAY. . . . Plan of the Astor Library: examined it yesterday

[6] Anthony Lispenard Robertson (Columbia 1825), son of Archibald Robertson, the New York artist, had been assistant vice-chancellor of New York State, and was later chief justice of the Superior Court of New York City. "Prince John" Van Buren (Yale 1828), tall, handsome, and elegant son of the President, briefly attorney general of the state, was a gay widower.

[7] Ira Day Whittelsey (Yale 1843) had studied law in the Strong office and been admitted to the bar in 1846; the following year, because of impaired health, he went on a voyage to Cuba and New Orleans, but returned to the family home in Wallingford, Connecticut, unimproved, and died there June 24, 1849.

with Mr. Ruggles. Devised by one [Alexander] Sältzer, who calls it "Byzantine." I should call it Romanesque or Lombard, but all those terms seem to be very loosely employed. Design promises well on paper. . . .

July 12. . . . What can I do for poor little Ellen? Think I'll run up to West Point tomorrow night and see what kind of rooms Rider can give us. Cozzens's is too fast, too exhilarating and pulse-accelerating.

July 14. . . . West Point last night in the *Columbia.* Boat crowded, loaferine, slow, dirty, inconvenient, and uncomfortable. Strong breeze of tepid, sickening air in our faces. Point at nine or thereabouts. Rider's: engaged rooms, went to bed, slept little, made the pleasant discovery that there were mosquitoes in those latitudes. Up at six—things looked very bright and beautiful, for though it was still hot, there was a lively wind sweeping down the river. On board the *Roger Williams* at eight. As we passed Piermont, Alexander Wyckoff of the Hudson River R. R. Co. came to me and said he was very sick and wanted me to take care of him. Swore he had the cholera, which I doubted; but when I found he could scarcely stand, his hands cold, scarcely any pulse at the wrist, eyes muddy, mouth filled with ropy saliva that one could plainly see in strings when he opened it to speak, and when he told me he'd had seventeen passages since three in the morning, I began to consider it not impossible he was right. So I made him as comfortable on some chairs as I could and went racing about the boat for a doctor. None on board, and what in Heaven's name was I to do, for that he was desperately ill there was no question, and he'd not an acquaintance on board but myself. Resolved to take the responsibility; got him into the cabin with some pillows, gave him a horn of brandy, had my pocket handkerchief converted into a colossal mustard plaster, and then fired away with camphor (which I had with me) and laudanum (which I got from the bar) at short intervals. This stopped the diarrhea, and then he began vomiting pailfulls. Kept on, and the mustard plaster on his abdomen seemed to give relief. Reached New York, sent for a carriage, had him carried ashore, and drove uptown with all convenient speed. Stopped at Kearny Rodgers's—out; Neilson ditto, Johnston ditto, Robeson ditto, and all this time he was lying in the carriage pretty near collapse, almost convulsed with cramps, and as I thought like enough to die at any minute, which was not pleasant, for independently of other considerations, I didn't want to be indicted for unlicensed medical practice and perhaps for manslaughter. Caught R[obeson] by good luck at Mersereau's shop and then got Wyckoff to his house. All his family out of town and everything out of the way and inconvenient. Stayed till one, when some of his friends and Dr.

Dubois appeared. The doctors said it was a full-blooded case of Asiatic cholera and they fully approved of what I did for him. When I left, the cramps continued and total prostration, but the corrugated blue look of his hands was diminished and they said the pulse was better. I never want to have such a job again, and if he don't get well I shall feel very uncomfortable about my share in the transaction, though I suppose I did nearly right. . . .

July 26. Cholera the all-pervading subject and has been so for the past fortnight. Increase considerable, especially as shown by the Inspector's Weekly Report, the only reliable authority. That report shows a hundred deaths and upwards daily for the week ending Saturday last.

David B[ayard] Ogden died on the 16th of something like cholera; John L. Lawrence the day before yesterday, a well-defined case of the disease. Those two cases startled and alarmed me not a little.[8]

Poor Wyckoff died between four and five in the afternoon of the day I brought him to town. There was a partial reaction, but he began to sink about an hour after I left him and went straight down. The doctors approved of what I did for him, and his family have been pleased to be very grateful for my attention and care, though I did nothing more than the merest common humanity required. . . .

Ate too much dinner three or four days ago, a hot voyage in town and back on Monday made things worse and brought on a savage sick headache, and that left me in a state of intestinal commotion and brought on what I've scarce ever experienced before—a diarrhea last night. I cannot get up much anxiety about myself in reference to the disease, and I took a cigar and a stroll last night with a feeling of interest and curiosity about the possible results and consequences of the phenomenon, but certainly with no feeling of fear or personal uneasiness.

This morning I'm nearly free from derangement, but as weak as water. Got some opium pills as I came downtown and shall open a battery on my lower intestines the moment they become riotous again.

We went to West Point on the 16th in the *Alida*. Mrs. Ruggles and Miss Mary Bostwick joined us on the 18th. We've nice rooms; the hotel is well enough kept, and we're comfortable. Ellen took the indomitable grandmother with her and her Abigail or tiring-woman, and is well cared

[8] These deaths were a hard blow to Columbia College. Ogden (Pennsylvania 1792), a distinguished lawyer noted for his arguments before the Supreme Court, was chairman of the board of trustees, and Lawrence (Columbia 1803), lawyer and state senator, was treasurer of the college.

for and happy. There's morning and evening parade with the music and the drum major, and artillery practice on the plain and at the target under Cro' Nest, and mortar practice, and walks to the library and among the cedars that skirt the bank, drives to Cozzens's, to Fort Putnam, Weir's lovely little church, etc.

Professor Bartlett. Observatory, big telescope night before last—lunar surface looks as if pockmarked with craters big and little. Lieut. Buckner, Professor Mahan, General Scott and his two military nymphs; Robert Ray, C. C. Moore, and so on.[9]

Long ramble among the hills last Saturday. To town on the 18th, 20th, and Monday last and up each night; but it's too hot and too tedious, so yesterday morning I came down leaving Ellen desolate and inconsolable, and am to go up tonight. . . .

July 30, MONDAY. To town this morning for first time since last entry. Ellen has been doing delightfully well till this morning, but I think she hurt herself a little—God grant it's only a little—by an imprudent promenading of the piazza last night, and there was a little cough and a little distress about the chest when she woke today that make me uneasy about her. I left at eight in the *Roger Williams* and don't go up again till Wednesday night. Poor little Ellie refused to be comforted and was in bitterness of spirit over the prospect.

Have enjoyed the last few days much. Visit to Professors Bailey and Agnel[10] and walk through the laboratory and the cabinets and the other notabilities of the academic department. Weir's studio:[11] spent a pleasant hour there on Saturday among pictures and carved cabinets and ancient, uncouth furniture and arms and rusty armor, all carelessly disposed and lumbering up the room, yet whether by accident or design so grouped as to make the room itself, with all its rubbish and litter, a perfect picture.

[9] William Holmes Chambers Bartlett (U.S.M.A. 1826) was professor of natural and experimental philosophy at the U.S. Military Academy. Simon Bolivar Buckner (U.S.M.A. 1844) became a lieutenant general in the Confederate army and was later governor of Kentucky; even though he surrendered Fort Donelson to him, he never broke off personal relations with his classmate Grant, and was a pall-bearer at his funeral. Dennis Hart Mahan (U.S.M.A. 1824) was professor of civil and military engineering at the Academy, and the father of Admiral Alfred Thayer Mahan (1840–1914). Old "Fuss and Feathers" was relaxing after his Mexican honors.
[10] Hyacinth R. Agnel was professor of French at West Point; Jacob Whitman Bailey (U.S.M.A. 1832), professor of chemistry and mineralogy, and a noted microscopist, became a close friend of Strong.
[11] Robert Walter Weir (1803–1889), professor of drawing, who had instructed Whistler as well as Grant and Lee, was a famous, prolific, and beloved artist.

One or two unfinished paintings promise well. To church yesterday and after dinner took a ramble among the woods on the slopes of Cro' Nest— struck a little ravine, or rather the dry bed of a stream that runs like a deep groove or scratch down the hillside, and went up clambering over the big boulders that line it till I reached the summit. The view was most magnificent, but I had no time to enjoy it; hurried back as I came and reached the hotel at seven after four hours of intense heat and active gymnastics, fairly dripping with perspiration. . . .

It is strange how perceptible the effect of the atmosphere of the city is on me. At West Point my appetite is ravenous and I feel as if I could run down a deer and eat it up afterwards. Here my appetite deserts me; I shouldn't eat any dinner but for the awe in which I stand of sick headache, and though I've worked hard this morning, it has been with an effort and without any feeling of energy.

July 31.   Last night was a cruel time. Went to bed in the third story of No. 70 and soon discovered that I had merely set myself out as a supper for a lively soirée of mosquitoes. Fought 'em awhile, then jumped out of bed, lit a candle, and read *Hawkstone*. Went back to bed—case hopeless, and after waking and worrying till the second cockcrow and the first glimmer of dawn and the recommencing rattle of the carts, I constructed an extemporaneous pavilion on the floor with four chairs and a sheet and contrived under its shelter to accomplish an hour's comfortless and unrefreshing slumber. . . .

Visit from Henry. "*Hast du das Schloss gesehen, das hohe Schloss am Square?*"

A terrible business will be the tottle of the bills growing out of that charming specimen of domestic architecture. The primal curse that condemned man to earn his bread by the sweat of his brow was heavy, but far heavier is the curse that man has laid upon himself by the artificial habits and conventional necessities and social fictions of the system of luxury and extravagance and ostentation to which he has bound himself in these latter days. Toil and labor may be happiness; they are so to a healthy mind; but there never is aught but wretchedness in the bitter, corrosive cares and sickening anxieties of debt, of position too expensive for the real abilities of its occupant. Now and then I'm very uneasy and disconsolate.

But I ought not to be so. God has given me a little treasure in my little wife, and He will defend her and enable me to maintain her in comfort, home, and happiness.

In the *Schloss* the doors are hung in the third story and basement, library advancing, and door trimmings in progress in parlors. Henry concedes that it may be a *little* later than September 1 before it's quite finished.

August 3, FRIDAY.   Fast day, pursuant to the President's proclamation. Very generally observed, so far as the cessation of business goes. I've not seen an open shop, except Delmonico's, where I've just lunched, for I take it that in these cholera times a literal compliance with the proclamation would generate wind, dyspepsia, sick headache, and tendencies to cholera.

Got into the *Schloss* last night by the back window, by help of a step ladder, and inspected its progress, which has been tolerably rapid of late, then took a walk with George Anthon and spent an hour in the Düsseldorf Gallery. It was very like old times, and as we walked into Palmer's Hotel to take a prophylactic drink, it seemed to me as if the last eighteen months must be a dream, as if George must be still an inmate of a Wall Street office, and it couldn't be that I had a little wife at West Point.

August 7. . . . Saw Mr. Ruggles. Dined with him at Frederick's on the never-varying beef and brandy, our regulation diet of cholera times. That distemper seems tending toward its decline and fall. The last weekly report showed a further diminution, though a small one, and the daily returns since Saturday have been below a hundred cases for each day.

August 15, WEDNESDAY.   Went to West Point Saturday night. Mrs. Henry Ruggles and Mrs. Samuel B. Ruggles on board, but I spent most of the three long hours between New York and the Dunderberg in a state of sick headache recumbent on a settee in the forward cabin. Found Ellen delightfully well, and Sunday she was still better; took a really long walk with me after breakfast. . . .

For an hour or so on board the *Roger Williams* I was in great bitterness, for it seemed as if it was our destiny to be always making progress *toward* the shore—always getting better, but never well—and I was in that mood in which one hates the sun for shining bright and the hills for looking beautiful. In the midst of it all I came across a sad spectacle enough: an Irish woman of thirty or thereabouts who might have been good-looking once, held by a couple of laboring men from the line of the railroad and almost struggling out of their hold, in a paroxysm of furious mania. People seemed to think her drunk, but on enquiry it turned out that she had been ill with what was probably a mild attack of cholera, and while recovering had seen her husband and three children die of that disease. Her last child had died on Monday and this brain fever, or mania or whatever it was, was the result. Looked about with Mr. Ruggles till we found a physician on board, and obtained from the captain, not very willingly by the by, the use of a mattress in the forward cabin and then ice on the head and so forth, pursuant to the doctor's directions, seemed to give her relief, and when we got to town she was quieter, and if she was not injured by being carried to the hospital, was likely to do well. It was a dreadful exhibition enough, and I shan't soon lose the painful impression it made on me. . . .

August 20, MONDAY. . . . To West Point Friday afternoon in the *Roger Williams*. Find Ellen pretty comfortable. Saturday: walked with her, saw artillery drill, then walked to Fort Putnam with George Anthon, who's spending a few days at the Point. Afternoon: didn't go to Mrs. General Scott's *fête champêtre*, but called on Mrs. Agnel and Mrs. Bartlett and then walked along the "Flirtation Path" as far as Dade's monument. Sunday morning spent an hour or two with Bailey and his microscope, and I've been wild on the subject ever since. I shall get out my big compound Chevalier tonight and go to work with energy and perseverance, in the hope of producing some results a little like his. Fossil infusoria—and living ones—in the *Bacillaria* something, *Proteus* something else, exquisite shells in the fluviatile mud of the Hudson, some lovely experiments with polarized light, etc.

August 21. . . . The mortality in the city is large and don't diminish very fast. . . . Spent last evening partly in a lounge with Charley and a look at those lovely Düsseldorf pictures, and partly with my microscope over the specimens of fossiliferous earth that Bailey gave me. Result very satisfactory; defining power of my instrument equals his for all ordinary purposes at least. . . .

September 3, MONDAY. General swarming from West Point this morning. We all came down together, for good. . . .

September 6. . . . Cholera so far fallen off that the Board of Health are to make no more reports. . . .

Schloss am Square "making very rapid strides toward completion." I advance *pari passu* toward insolvency and shall probably bust up for the benefit of my creditors when the last finishing touch is given to that elegant and commodious mansion. . . .

September 14, FRIDAY. Very abject and jaded today, not without apology and excuse. Tuesday night was signalized by a sick headache, and as I had a visit from Bailey of West Point, I sat up longer than I should and was scientific to the best of my abilities—microscopicized and talked infusoria—and went to bed at last with my head feeling as if the devil were in it. Wednesday and yesterday were consecrated to the library;

worked like a dog from morning till night in arranging books, lugging about boxes, shifting shelves and so forth, and got through with the more pressing part of the job last night, leaving plenty of work yet to do, however, and a large surplus of literary rubbish for which there is no room in my cases. . . .

September 21. . . . The Palazzo comes on fast. Furniture will soon begin to appear and the wilderness and the solitary places will blossom like the rose, with gilt gas fixtures, furnaces, and yellow brocatelle. One carpet indeed has already defined its position, in the third story, and tomorrow the furnaces are to be fired up and the gas turned on. My books, that is that part of them that reposed in the little Fourth Avenue basement, are looking lovely from behind their plate glass, and nothing remains to be done in that department but to provide for the quartos that are stowed away at my father's. Certainly the Palazzo is handsome, well arranged and well built; there's not a house in the city I'd prefer to live in. . . .

September 28, FRIDAY. No. 54 was abandoned last night. We were to have slept in the Palazzo, but the house had a raw, uninhabited, unwholesome shade of chilliness in its atmosphere, so I turned Ellen out of it, took tea at home for the last time, slept at my father's, and breakfasted there this morning—board and lodging gratis and no additional charge for mosquitoes, of which vermin I killed four under the net this morning. . . . The Palazzo is beginning to look as if it might be habitable and comfortable at no remote period. The organ is going up in the third parlor. Dining room carpeted, second story all finished and filled with furniture, a mighty maze and quite without a plan, a chaos of chairs and tables. Certain females called Smack have got through with their appointed task—that of making covers for parlor furniture—and the parlors will be carpeted next week.

October 1. Friday night I spent at my father's in a state of sick headache unparalleled and unexpressible. All Saturday I was most nerveless and wretched. Spent the afternoon in putting up and getting rid of the last arrearages of my library. Took our first meal in the new house that evening: a very satisfactory tea with Mr. and Mrs. Ruggles, my father and mother, and Charley as accessories thereto. Slept there that night—and now we are fairly established in *The Palazzo.*[12]

Had been feeling wretchedly ill for the last three or four days and as

[12] The "Palazzo Strong" at 74 (after 1868, No. 113) East 21 Street appears to have cost $30,427.94. In his will George W. Strong bequeathed his estate in equal parts to his three surviving children, and the foregoing sum which had been "advanced for his house in 21st Street" was to be deducted from the share of his son George T. Strong without interest.

soon as we are sufficiently settled in Twenty-first Street to allow of my dining there at five after the fashion of former times, I shall be rejoiced and shall give up all this ruinous business of lunching at Brown's and dining at Delmonico's and trespassing on my viscera in all sorts of ways and shall begin to lead a righteous and sober life once more.

October 28, SUNDAY. . . . We are beginning to look more like a habitation for Christian men and women now, and less like a deserted garret or the ruins of Palmyra or any other type of unfurnished desolation and loneliness. The indomitable grandmother has been rusticating in Western New York till Friday, and during her absence the three parlors remained stationary in uncarpeted nakedness. Yesterday, however, the work of organizing chaos began and carpets are now down and furniture partly in its place. The music room is furnished and the dining room likewise, but it's melancholy to look at the two parlors and see how much is yet to be put into them before they will be presentable. The vast "middle room" especially is as sparsely settled (with chairs and sofas) as the Great West. Never mind, we shan't want to give a great many big parties this winter and we can get along, I suspect, pretty comfortably. . . .

November 26. . . . Reading German with Ellen, who is coming on rapidly with the language—Schiller and Fouqué. Visitors of late have abounded. . . .

Looked in at the laboratory of the Free Academy. [Wolcott] Gibbs has it arranged very well and seems well enough satisfied with the place for a beginning.

December 3. . . . Col. [J.Watson] Webb has just married Miss Laura Cram and gone off to Liverpool en route for Austria, where he's been nominated *chargé*, but won't be confirmed. He'll get his outfit and that's all he wants. He borrowed largely of Blatchford, Prescott Hall, and all that set, and then made a moonlight flitting, leaving a batch of letters for his creditors in which he went largely into the merits of his matrimonial arrangements, but said nothing about his debts.

December 4. . . . Great rumpus in Boston—one Dr. Parkman killed; strong evidence against Professor Webster of Harvard.

December 11. . . . Webster and Parkman affair in Boston remains where it was. Evidence against Professor Webster rather fading away, though some awkward points still stand out against him. I don't believe him guilty.[13]

---

[13] Dr. John White Webster, Erving Professor of Chemistry and Mineralogy and lecturer in the Medical College connected with Harvard University, an improvident

December 31, MONDAY EVENING. Sit down to write this evening in dress coat and state breeches—not as of old to announce that I've got to go to a party, but to certify to incredulous generations yet to come that I'm going to have one!!!

Or rather Ellen is, for I've no part nor lot in the matter. Twenty people or so are cited—how many will appear is uncertain as yet. Doubtless it will be very nice, provided the ice cream don't make default or the boned turkey forget to come or all the champagne prove bad, or some other contretemps happen. . . .

Quarter to eight: the tocsin of the street door bell will soon begin to sound the alarm. Very strange that I never used to appreciate or realize the awful state of mind in which people have been who have received me on various occasions at parties little and big, notwithstanding their beaming countenances and nonchalant demeanor. . . .

---

man, had become heavily indebted to a colleague, the wealthy and penurious Dr. George Parkman; when the latter found that Webster had disposed of a mineralogical collection pledged as security he accused him of dishonesty and threatened him with ruin. By prearrangement Parkman went to Webster's laboratory in the Medical College on November 23, 1849, and was never seen again. When the janitor of the school discovered portions of a recently-dismembered body in the waste-disposal vault and a set of false teeth in the furnace (later identified as Parkman's by Dr. N. C. Keep, the dentist who made them), Webster was indicted for murder, and at the end of a sensational trial before Chief Justice Lemuel Shaw, involving the testimony of many highly-placed Bostonians, was convicted by a perfect chain of circumstantial evidence. He subsequently confessed the murder and was hanged August 30, 1850.

INDEX

Abolitionism, 62 n., 94, 124 n., 194–195, 200

Academy of Design, 25–26, 27, 60–62, 69, 85, 161–162, 178, 201–202, 231, 232, 258–259, 276, 277

Acadia, 218

Adams, John Quincy, vi, xxxviii, 80, 103–104, 173, 230, 273, 312, 314

Adams, Samuel (murdered 1841), 168, 173

Addison, Joseph, 216

Adelphi Hotel, New York, 266

Adler, George J., 287, 290, 305, 327

Adventists, 199 n.

Aeschylus, 36, 49, 60, 68, 75

Agawam, 144

Agnel, Hyacinth R., 359

Agnel, Mrs. Hyacinth R., 362

Agnew, Cornelius Rea, xxxiii, xxxvi, xxxviii

Akerman, John Yonge, 37

Alabama, 286

Alaricus (Latin salutatory of G.T.S.), 87–88, 90

Alarm clock, 86

Albany, 77, 163, 165–167, 206, 241

Albany, 162, 165, 242, 247

Albany Basin Rattlers, 151

Albert, Prince Consort, 132

Albert Edward, Prince of Wales (King Edward VII), 171

Alexander, Pope, 204

Alida, 358

All Souls College, Oxford, 210

Allopathy, 257

Alpers, W., 179

Alpha Delta Phi, xlix, 25, 35, 41, 42, 53, 57, 59, 61

Alton, N.H., 32

Amadis de Gaule, 171

Amagansett, L.I., 281

America, discovery of, 88

America, 352

American Art Union, 306

American Colonization Society, 86

American Historical Association, 12 n.

American Museum, 203

American Notes (Dickens), 189, 225

American Red Cross, v

American Revolution, 1, 2, 18, 40, 202

American Tract Society, 62 n.

Amherst College, liii, 31, 181

Anderson, Henry James, xx, xxx, xlix, 2, 5, 17, 29, 37–38, 48, 77, 79, 87

Andover Theological Seminary, 175 n.

André, John, 154

Andrews, Henry, 264

Anglo-Saxons, 152, 347

Animal magnetism, 178, 181, 182

Annuals, literary, 42, 46

Anselm, St., 271

Anthon, Charles, xviii, xx, xxvi, xlix, 2, 3, 5, 7, 9, 10–12, 17, 22–24, 29, 36, 39, 42, 54, 56, 60, 63, 75, 77–79, 84, 87, 88, 91, 93 n., 115, 149, 202, 215, 258

Anthon, Charles Edward, 59

Anthon, Frederic, 13–14, 28, 29, 59, 90, 91, 256

Anthon, George Christian, xxvi, xxxviii, xlix, 34, 37, 46, 54, 56, 64, 65, 73, 86, 90, 103, 110, 127, 129, 131, 134–137, 142, 158, 161, 162, 170, 178, 183, 184, 189, 192, 193, 196, 201, 202, 210, 211, 215, 220, 224, 234, 238, 248, 281, 282, 296, 303, 331, 355, 361, 362

Anthon, Henry, xxvi, 110, 189–193, 209, 249, 250, 256

Anthon, John, 29

Anthon, Joseph, 144

Anthon, Philip Hone, 256

Anthony, Edward, 51, 85, 90, 296 n.

Anthony, Henry T., 296 n.

Antiquarian Book Store, Boston, 18, 20

Antiquarianism, 202, 217–218

Anti-Rent War, 117–118, 283, 284

Anti-Slavery movement. *See* Abolitionism

Antognini, Cirillo, 220

Apollo Association for the Promotion of the Fine Arts in the U.S., 202, 306

Appleton, Daniel and his bookstore, 12–17, 21, 22, 24, 25, 29, 34, 41, 43, 46, 49, 65, 107, 169, 181, 182, 251, 252, 255, 314, 347

Appleton, William, 19
Archer, 95
Arcturus, 311–312
Areopagitica (Milton), 66
Argenti, 122
Aristophanes, 3, 68, 76
Arnold, Benedict, 154
Arnot, David H., 297
Arnoux, A. & G. A., 34, 118, 119
Aroostook War, 97, 99–100
Arthur, Chester Alan, xxv
Arthur, King, 161
Ascension robes, 199 n., 201
Asceticism, 309
Aspinwall, John L., 348
Aspinwall, William Henry, x, 152, 174–175, 272
Astor, Dorothea (Mrs. Walter Langdon), 317 n.
Astor, John Jacob (1763–1848), xi, xv, 131, 316, 317 n.
Astor, John Jacob (1822–1890), xxxviii 241, 242
Astor, Magdalen (Mrs. John Bristed), 317 n.
Astor, William Backhouse, xix, xxxix, 55 n, 241 n, 272, 316, 346
Astor House, x, 107
Astor Library, 356–357
Astor Place Opera House, 328, 332; riots (1849), 351–353
Astronomy, 37, 69, 314
Athenaeum Hotel, New York, 59
Atlantic Dock, Brooklyn, xxviii, 277, 333, 337
Attica, N.Y., 243
Attorney, G.T.S. admitted and sworn as, 165
Aubrey, John, 152
Auburn, N.Y., 242
Audubon, John James, 174; *Birds of America*, 27, 174; *Quadrupeds*, 344
Augusta, Ga., 87
Augusta, Me., 311 n.
Aurora borealis, 48
Austria, Revolution of 1848, 332, 334
Automaton Chess Player, 203
Awful Disclosures of Maria Monk, The, 92 n.
Aymar and Aymar *v.* Astor, xv

Babylon, L.I., 282
Bach, Johann Sebastian, xl
Bache, Alexander Dallas, xxxiii

Backus, Mancer Mark, 34, 36, 46, 52, 54, 65, 66, 74, 78, 79, 81, 85–90, 104, 163, 165, 226, 239
Bacon, Francis, 49
Bagg's Hotel, Utica, 164, 241
Bailey, Jacob Whitman, 359, 362
Baker, Mrs., 270, 272
Ballistics, 77
Balloon ascensions, 39–40, 109
Ballston Spa, 166
Baltimore, 17 n, 235, 237
Bancroft's bookstore, 21
Bangs & Co., 10
Bank for Savings *v.* Field, xxxvi
Bank of America, New York, 65
Bank of Commerce, New York, 314
Bank of the Manhattan Company, New York, 65, 103, 131
Bank of the United States, 107
Bank of the United States, Philadelphia, 156
Baptist tenets, 199
Bar examinations, xxiii, 162, 163, 164, 165, 167, 241
Barber, John, 36, 41, 50
Bard, John, 343
Bard, Mrs. John (Margaret Johnston), 326, 343
Bard, Samuel, li, 343 n.
Bard, William, 343 n.
Bard College, 343 n.
Baring Brothers, 299
Barnaby Rudge (Dickens), 233
Barnard, Frederick, Augustus Porter, xxxv, xxxvii
Barnard, George G., xxxvi
Bartlett, John Russell, 12 n., 280, 305
Bartlett, William Holmes Chambers, 359
Bartlett, Mrs. William H. C., 362
Bartlett & Welford, 12 n., 228
Bashfulness of G.T.S., 135–136, 186, 255, 274, 275
Baskerville, John, 55
Bath Island, 244
Bath room, new, 204, 210; bathing in, 210, 261
Battery, New York, x, xiv, 26, 40, 42, 46, 84, 86, 140, 202, 315
Baxter, Mrs., 336
Bayle, Pierre, 14
Bayside, L.I., 73
Beach, Moses Yale, xxvii
Beare, Henry M., 249
Beare, Mrs. Henry M., 251
Beaumont, Francis, 87
Beckmann, John, 152

Bedell, Gregory Thurston, 261, 272
Bedell, Mrs. Gregory Thurston (Julia Strong), 261
Bedell, Gregory Townsend, 27
Beecher, Henry Ward, 47
Beekman estate, 324
Beethoven, Ludwig van, xi, 169, 215–216, 220, 234–235, 290
Belden, Mr. and Mrs., 326
Belknap, 32
Bell, Edward Rogers, 59
Bellows, Henry Whitney, xxxiii, xxxv, xxxvi, xxxix
Belmont, August, 168
Benedetti, S., 336
Bennett, James Gordon, x, 51, 131, 218
Benson, Robert, 292, 344
Bentham, Jeremy, 218
Benton, Thomas Hart, 227
Bentzon, Magdalen (Astor) (Mrs. John Bristed), 317 n.
Berkeley, George, 83
Berrian, William, xxxi, xxxii, 103, 104, 272, 276, 283, 310
Berthemy, Pierre-Augustin, 29–30
Bertrand, Vicomte, 224
Betts, Samuel Rosseter, 13, 198, 200
Betts, William, xxx, 58
Bible in schools, 204–205
Bibliomania, 187, 228
Biddle, Nicholas, 107
Biddle Stairs, Niagara Falls, 244
Bidwell, Barnabas, xxii
Bidwell, Marshall Spring, v, xxii, xxiv, xxviii, xxxvi, xxxvii, xxxviii, 88, 92, 102, 111, 129–131, 139, 148, 219, 221, 326, 335
Bidwell, Mrs. Marshall Spring, 121
Bigelow, Katherine (Mrs. Abbott Lawrence), 317
Bigelow girls, 327
Binney, Miss, 185
Binney, Horace (1780–1875), 88, 226
Binney, Horace, Jr. (1809–1870), 88, 105, 175, 185, 325
Binney, Mrs. Horace, Jr. (Eliza Johnson), 88, 105, 185, 325
Birds of America (Audubon), 27, 174
Birthday of G.T.S., 157
Biscaccianti, Signora, 310
Blaas, C., 276, 277
Black, Jeremiah Sullivan, xxxii
Black, Sylvia, viii
Black Rock, N.Y., 243
Blackstone, Sir William, xxi, 93, 147, 164, 170

Blackwell's Island, 203
Blake, William, xl
Blanc, Louis, 316
Blatchford, Alexander Warfield, 364
Blatchford, Samuel, 36, 41, 43, 74
Bloomingdale Asylum, 287
Bloomingdale Road, xvi, 302
"Blues" (melancholia, depression, dejection), 195, 225, 261, 288–289, 305, 318, 319, 324, 325, 343, 351
Blunt, Joseph, 241
Boethius, 24, 25
Bombardment of New York, 175–176
Book auctions, 24, 25, 65, 84, 100, 106
Booth, Junius Brutus, x
Borland, John, 263, 335
Borland, Mrs. John (Rebecca Nelson Woolsey), 122, 123, 326
Boston, xi, 17–20, 30–32, 43, 71, 98, 104, 105, 108, 109, 130, 143, 144, 146, 149, 175, 186, 197, 222, 263, 274, 298, 310, 317, 364–365
Boston (racehorse), 181
Boston Athenaeum, 71, 186
Bostwick, Mrs., 331
Bostwick, Mary, 358
Boswell, James, 42
Bouck, William C., 197
Boustrophedon inscriptions, 12
Bowery, New York, 7, 46, 56, 86
Bowery boys, 260, 352, 353
Bowery Theatre, x, 259
Bowling, 143
Bowling Green fountain, 211; lawsuit, 219–222
Braham, John, 170
Brandegee, Clothilde Angeline Caroline (Mrs. Henry Lloyd), 306
Brandegee family, 326
Bremer, Fredrika, 205
Brevoort, 266
Brevoort, Henry, xx
Brevoort, Margaret Ann (Mrs. James Renwick, Sr.), 23
Brinckerhoff, 163
Bristed, Charles Astor, 337
Bristed, John, 316, 317 n.
Bristed, Mrs. John (Magdalen Astor Bentzon) 317 n.
Britain, U.S. relations with, 97, 99–100, 153, 156, 157, 160, 175–176, 272, 289, 333
Britannia, 143
British Queen, 136, 160
Broadway, New York, 150, 176 n., *et passim*

Broadway House, New York, 292
Broadway Tabernacle, New York, 152, 169, 179, 219, 220, 229, 254, 285
Broadway Theatre, New York, 318, 323
Bronson, Isaac H., 100
Brontë, Charlotte, *Jane Eyre*, 310, 314
Brooklyn, 199, 277, 284, 328, 354
Brooklyn Navy Yard, 134
Brooks, Mrs. Sidney, 323, 333
Brough, W. F., 220
Brougham, Henry Peter, Baron, 93
Brown, 123
Brown, George W., 338, 364
Brown, Julia, 162, 170
Brown, Thompson S., 342
Browne, Hablot Knight (Phiz), 92 n.
Browne, Sir Thomas, 64, 69–70
Brownejohn, William, 106
Brownell, Sherman, 296
Brownell, Thomas Church, 253
Brownson, Orestes Augustus, 149, 210, 240
Brownson's Quarterly Review, 240
Bruen, 115, 127, 300
Bruen, George W., 94
Brush, 314
Bryant, William Cullen, x, 58, 225, 269
Buckingham, George Villiers, second Duke, 87
Buckner, Simon Bolivar, 359
Buena Vista, Battle of, 291
Buffalo, N.Y., 243, 246
Buffet, J. F., 287, 302, 314, 327
Bulkley, Charles H. A., 66
Bulkley, Ellen. *See* Ruggles, Mrs. Philo
Bull, Ole, 197, 219, 254
Bull's Ferry, 301
Bunker Hill, 18–20; Monument, 19 n.; Jubilee, 197
Burchard, Jedediah, 83
Burgess, John William, xxvii
Burke, Edmund, 282
Burke, Master, 273–274
Burney, Charles, 100
Burns, Robert, 116, 174
Burr, Aaron, 82
Burton, Robert, 25, 26
Bush, George, 280
Bush & Hillyer, 62
Butler, Benjamin Franklin (1795–1858), xiv, liv, 158, 190, 212, 237, 257
Butler, Mrs. Clement Moore, 251
Butler, Mary Howard (Mrs. D. D. Lord), 212
Butler, Nicholas Murray, vi

Byrnes, The Reverend, 83
Byron, George Noel Gordon, sixth Baron, 16 n., 52–53, 60, 96, 122, 169

Cabot, Eliza Lee (Mrs. C. T. C. Follen), 124
Cade, Jack, 149
Cadwalader, John, 233
Cadwalader, John Lambert, v
Calculus, 77
Caledonia, 277
Calhoun, John Caldwell, 250, 273
Caliban, 158
California, 287; discovery of gold in, 308
California gold rush, 55 n., 337, 341, 343–345, 347–348
Calvary Church, New York, 239 n, 288, 292, 323, 328, 330, 353–354
Calvinism, 117, 174
Cambria, 289, 290
Cambridge, University of, 279
Camden, William, 64
Camera lucida, 52
Camera obscura, 244
Cameron, Simon, xxxiii
Campbell, John, first Baron, 310
Canada, 97, 100, 105, 130, 245, 246; Mackenzie-Papineau rebellion in, xxii, 79–82, 88
Cape Ann, 144
Capital punishment, 26, 312
Cardozo, Albert, xxxvi
Carey, 100
Carey, Arthur, 208–210
Carlyle, Thomas, 91, 110, 132–133, 216, 218, 243, 270–271
Caroline, Queen, 93
Caroline affair, 80–82, 156, 175
Carter *v.* Taylor, xxxvi
Cary, Alice and Phoebe, xxv
Cass, Lewis, 333
Castellan, Jeanne Anaïs, 216, 220
Castle Garden, New York, 27, 32–33, 39, 72, 74, 86, 88, 260, 310
Cathedral for New York, 105–106, 111, 182–183
Catlin, Mrs. Charles Taylor (Lucy Ann Derby), 71
Catlin, Helen, 284
Catlin's Cave, Niagara Falls, 246
Cats, 280, 301
Catskill Mountains, 162, 163, 207, 212–214, 299–300, 328, 329
Catullus, 64
Caxton, William, 228
Cayuga, Lake, 242

Cedar Street Church, New York, 40, 51
Celibacy for clergy, 201
Cellini, Benvenuto, 152
Center Harbor, N.H., 32
Central America, 202
Century Club, xxvi, 287, 297, 301, 302, 306, 309, 310, 314, 342
Cerro Gordo, Battle of, 293
Chambers Street Opera House, New York, 288
Chancery, Court of, 106
Chandler, Charles Frederick, xxxvii
Chanler, Miss, 326
Channing, William Ellery, 124 n., 202
Chapman, George, 181, 182
Charles I, 342
Charles II, 145
Charleston, S.C., 86
Charlestown, Mass., 18, 31; Navy Yard at, 263
Chartism, 218
Chasers' Lodges, 80
Chatham Square, New York, 160
Chaucer, Geoffrey, 193
Cheesman, John Cummings, 349
Cheever, George Barrell, 288, 314
Chelmsford, Mass., 32
Chelsea, 140
Chepachet, R.I., 184
Chess, 133, 136, 139, 161, 175, 181, 306
Chihuahua, Mexico, 295
Chillingworth, William, 93
Chilton, 13
Chimborazo, 269
Chittenden, Nathaniel William, xlix, 6, 15, 21, 25, 28, 34, 36, 37, 41, 42, 46, 51–54, 57, 60, 61, 66, 73, 74, 79, 83, 90, 92, 95, 101, 103, 140, 187, 299
Chloroform, 308–310
Choate, William Gardner, 342 n.
Cholera, xvii, xviii, 332, 333, 337, 339, 349, 353, 354, 356–358, 361, 362
Christ, second appearance of, 199 n.
Christ Church College, Oxford, 210
Christie, 326
Christmas, 45, 154, 251–252, 338; observance of, 171
Christmas Carol, A (Dickens), 223, 225
Chrystie, Albert, 108
Church, The. *See* Protestant Episcopal Church
Church music, 169
Church Music Association, xxxvii
Church of England, 268. *See also* Oxford Tracts

Church of the Annunciation, New York, 180
Church of the Holy Cross, Troy, 74
Church of the Messiah (Unitarian), New York, 78, 104, 175 n., 267
Church of the Puritans, New York, 288, 314
Church of the Redemption, New York, 201
Churchill, Winston, 17 n.
Churchman, The, 180 n.
Churubusco, Battle of, 301
Cicero, xli, 36, 42
Ciphers, 71
Circumstantial evidence, 16, 365 n.
Cisco, John Jay, xxxviii
City Bank, New York, 103
City Hall, New York, 94, 147, 150, 173, 203, 260, 293; fire bell, 70–71
City Hall Park, New York, 27, 160, 186, 188, 189, 211, 293, 307
Clairvoyance, 182
Clapp, Judge, 30
Clarendon, Edward Hyde, first Earl, 29, 46
Clark, Aaron, xxi, 63
Clarke, Gerardus, 250
Clarke, McDonald, 176
Classical literature, 68, 229, 230
Clay, Henry, 121, 223, 232, 233, 236, 249, 285
Cleopatra, 186
Clergy, flattery of, 114, 239
Clermont, xii
Clinton, Charles, 73
Clinton, De Witt, 73
Clubs, 260
Coddington, David Smith, 92
Coenties Slip, New York City, 110
Coins, 3, 6, 8, 12–14, 18, 37, 38, 84
Coit, Mrs. Henry Augustus, 122
Coke, Sir Edward, xxi, 96, 170
Colden, Cadwallader David, xiii
Cole, Thomas, 85, 161, 258; and the Stream of Life, 152–153
Coleridge, Samuel Taylor, xli, 79, 84, 114, 122, 134, 139, 216, 288, 310, 311
Coles, 95
College of the City of New York, 295, 306, 338, 364
Collins, 299, 320
Colman, William A., 15, 49, 75, 157, 314
Cologne Cathedral, 248
Colt, John C., 173, 189–194
Columbia (ship), 157; (steamboat), 357

Columbia College, ix, xviii–xx, xxvi, xxix–xxxi, xxxv, xxxvii, xxxix, xl, xlix–liii; G.T.S. at, 1–91; Alumni Association, 48, 112, 187; College Green lots, 227; commencement, 2–3, 34–36, 74, 89–91, 112, 149, 168, 187; examinations, 11, 14, 27–29, 48, 71, 81, 87, 89; faculty, 2, *et passim*; Gebhard Professorship, 305; King's College, 1, 40; Law School, xxxi, xxxvii; Library, xx, 3, 40–41, 45, 60, 77, 81, 82, 174; matriculation, 2, 37; Peithologian Society, 7, 26, 35; Philolexian Society, xlix, 6, 7, 14, 16, 21, 27, 34, 35, 41, 44, 57, 59, 74, 79, 81, 84, 87, 96, 138; presidency, 180, 182, 185; salaries cut, 202; School of Mines, xxxi, xxxv, xxxvii; Semi-Centennial Celebration (1837), 40, 48, 56–59.
Columbia Grammar School, xviii, xix, xlix, 36, 43, 79
Columbus, Christopher, 202, 281
Column, The, 297 n.
Comet, 198
Comet, 88
Commack, L.I., 209
Comines, Philippe de, 83
Comstock, 164, 241
Concord, N.H., 32
Confucius, 13–14
Congress Hall, Albany, 163, 206, 241
Coningsby (Disraeli), 256
Conklin, 282
Connecticut charter, 145
Connecticut River, 144, 145
Connecticut State House, Hartford, 145
Consecration of bishop, 168–169
Constitutions, 296–297
Conti, Jean (Webber), viii
Contoit, John H., 183
Contreras, Battle of, 301
Cooke, George Frederick, 307
Cookie Hill, 73
Cooley's, 65
Cooper, James Fenimore, xi, xxii, 53, 92, 93 n, 194 n.
Cooper, Myles, 40, 257–258
Cooper, Peter, xxv
Cooper, Thomas Colden, 27, 45, 57, 59, 89, 90, 139, 212
Cooper, Mrs. Thomas Colden (Catherine Augusta Richmond), 212
Copley, John Singleton, 71
Copps Hill Burial Ground, Boston, 19
Corlears Hook, New York City, 91

Corn Laws, 218, 274
Cornelius Agrippa, 24, 25
Cornell, George James, 299
Cornell University, 54 n.
Cortez, Hernando, 292, 304
Coryat, Thomas, 224
Coster, Washington, 117, 139
Costume balls, 98, 170
Cottenet, Annie Laight (Mrs. W. C. Schermerhorn), 212
Counsellor, G.T.S. admitted, 241
Court, Strong's debut in, 178
Cow Harbor, L.I., 141
Cow Island (Lake Winnepesaukee), 32, 130
Cox, 139
Coxe, Arthur Cleveland, 35, 61, 153–154
Cozzens, Abraham M., 306
Cozzens's Hotel, West Point, 357, 359
Cram, Henry Augustus, 1, 139, 148–149, 154, 170, 210, 260, 265, 285, 315, 317, 333, 338
Cram, Mrs. Henry Augustus (Katherine Sergeant), 317
Cram, Jacob, 139
Cram, Laura (Mrs. J. Watson Webb), 364
Cranmer, Thomas, 130
Crescent City, 344
Criticism, literary, 312
Cro' Nest, West Point, 359, 360
Cromwell, Oliver, 90, 270–271
Crosby, 154
Crosby, John Player, 202
Crosby Street Synagogue, New York, 82
Croswell, Harry, 279
Croton Aqueduct, 269
Croton Celebration, 188–189
Croton Reservoir (42nd St.), 335
Croton Water, 184, 186, 203, 221, 226, 265
Cruger, Mrs. Harriet (Douglas), 288
Crumby & Draper, 131
Cullen (Shoemaker), 244
Culprit Fay, The (Halleck), 52
Cunard, Sir Samuel, 105, 143
Cunard Line, x
Cunningham, F., 241
Curtis, 30, 348
Curtis, George William, xxvi
Curtis, Mrs. and Mrs., 331
Cutting, Francis Brockholst, 98, 113
Cutting, Mrs. Robert Livingston, 323
Cutting, Walter Livingston, 98, 127, 129, 136, 166, 178, 181, 315, 322

Dade (Francis Langhorn) monument, West Point, 362
Daguerreotypes, 157, 162, 195–196, 296
Dallas, George Mifflin, 237
Dalliba, 241
Dancing, 78, 311, 317–318, 327
Daniel, Peter Vivian, 157
Dante Alighieri, 225
DaPonte, Lorenzo, 11
Darley, Felix Octavius Carr, 311 n.
Darling, 24
Darwin, Erasmus, 53
Davies, Charles, xxxvii
Davis, Andrew Jackson, 280, 305
Davis, Charles Augustus, 356
Davis, Mrs. Charles Augustus, 322
Day, Thomas, xvii
Deal, N.J., 185
Deane, William, 92, 223
Dearborn's, 81
De Behr, Charles, 11
De Bonneville, mesmerist, 181
Deerfield, N.Y., 241
De la Bèche, Sir Henry Thomas, 68
De Lancey, William Heathcote, 320
Delaware, 248
Delaware County, N.Y., 207
Delirium Dibdinianum, 228
Delmonico's, 74, 91, 315, 330, 361, 364
De Mille, George Edmed, 210
Democratic party, 77, 94, 121, 159, 197, 232, 235–237, 273, 287
Democratic Review, 210
Denio, Hiram, 163, 241
Denning, Hannah Maria (Mrs. W. A. Duer), 61
De Quincey, Thomas, 309
Derby, Elias Hasket, xxi, 1, 18, 19, 31–33, 67, 71, 72, 92, 104, 105, 108, 109, 119, 130, 142, 144, 157, 210, 222, 263, 264
Derby, Mrs. Elias Hasket (Eloise Lloyd Strong), xiv, xvii, xxi, 1, 20, 31, 32, 50, 71, 72, 92, 98, 108, 129, 130, 142–144, 147, 186, 263, 363 n.
Derby, George Strong, I (1837–1837), 50, 72, 79; II, (1838–1875), 92, 105, 109, 186, 263, 298
Derby, Mrs. George Strong, v
Derby, Hasket, 31, 147, 186, 283, 298
Derby, Hasket, II, v, vi
Derby, John Clark, 118–119, 123
Derby, Lucy Ann (Mrs. C. T. Catlin), 71
Derby, Martha, 122, 123
Derby, Mrs. Richard, 19, 71, 98
Derby, Richard Henry, 298

De Trobriand, Mme. Régis Denis de Keredern (Mary Mason Jones), 322
Dewey, Orville, 78, 104, 125, 175
De Witt, Clinton, 241
Dial, The, 169
Diary of G.T.S., v–viii, ix–x, 24, 37, 48, 119, 152, 168, 217, 313, 315, 316, 319, 322, 327
Dibdin, Thomas Frognall, 45, 49, 100, 212, 228
Dickens, Charles, 146, 175; *American Notes*, 189, 225; *Barnaby Rudge*, 233; *A Christmas Carol*, 223, 225; *Dombey and Son*, 314; *Martin Chuzzlewit*, 225, 252; *Master Humphrey's Clock*, 136; *Nicholas Nickleby*, 113, 173; *Oliver Twist*, 113, 173; *Pickwick Papers*, 53, 60, 75, 82, 173
Dickinson, 320
Digamma, Grand Order of, 57
Dillon, Robert James, 302
Dillon, Mrs. Robert James, 302, 322
Diogenes, 316
Disasters, 76, 123–125, 227
Disraeli, Benjamin, first Earl of Beaconsfield: *Coningsby*, 256, *Vivian Grey*, 83, 152
Dix, John Adams, xxxii, xxxviii
Doane, George Washington, 335
Dogs, 98, 165, 299, 301–303, 344
Dombey and Son (Dickens), 314
Dongan, Thomas, 101
Doniphan, Alexander William, 295
Donizetti, Gaetano, 216, 288, 328
Donne, John, xli
Dorr, Henry Crawford, 240–242, 262, 309, 314
Dorr, Thomas Wilson, 182, 184, 309 n.
Dorr's Rebellion, 180, 182–184
Douglass, Brainard, 45
Douglass, Major, 100, 114
Douglass, Richard Henry, 5, 6, 8, 24, 39, 45, 50, 57, 60, 89, 90, 185
Douglass, Stephen, 34
Dover, N.H., 31
Dow, 72
Dow, Richard W., 123
Drake, Elias Guion, Jr., xxxvii, xxxviii
Drake, Samuel Gardner, 20
Drawing, 78
Drinking, 59–60, 68, 73, 86, 91, 100, 115, 140, 144, 165, 195, 227, 237–238, 256, 260, 307, 338
Drowned Meadow, L.I., 141
Dry Dock Bank, New York, 63, 64
Duane, Colonel, 326

Dubois, Abram, 358
Dubois, John, 43, 103, 104
Dudley, Thomas, 20
Duels, 82, 168
Duer, Eleanor Jones (Mrs. George T. Wilson), 87
Duer, Frances (Mrs. H. S. Hoyt), 85
Duer, John, xiii, 90, 224, 249
Duer, John King, 28, 34, 39, 43, 90
Duer, William Alexander, xx, 1, 2, 4, 5, 16, 26, 27, 29, 35, 36, 38, 42, 43, 45, 56–61, 65, 66, 74, 75, 78, 81, 85–87, 89, 90, 96, 103, 149, 159, 168, 180, 200
Duer, Mrs. William Alexander (Hannah Maria Denning), 61
Dugan, Thomas, 4, 6, 9, 59, 88
Dumas, Alexandre, 282–283; *Trois Mousquetaires*, 335
Dumbbells, 70
Dunderberg Mountain, 361
Dunlap, 321
Durand, Asher Brown, 201, 231, 232, 258, 276
Düsseldorf Gallery, New York, 361, 362
Dutch, 163
Dutch Reformed Church, 111, 169, 200, 261
Duyckinck, Evert Augustus, 3, 310–312
Dwight, Benjamin Woodbridge, 157
Dwight, Theodore William, xxxi, xxxvii
Dwight, Timothy, xxxi, 41

East Boston, Mass., 143
East Hampton, L.I., 281
East Lexington, Mass., 124 n.
Eastburn, Manton, 58
Edda, 161
Edgar, Newbold, 35
Edgeworth, Maria, 15, 288
Edmonds, Francis William, 232, 258
Edwards, Jonathan, 116
Egleston, Thomas, xxxi, xxxvii
Ehninger, John Whetten, xxvi
Eitheiler, Moritz, 268–269, 327
Elbert, coachman, 13, 34
Elections and political campaigns, 93–94, 101, 121, 151, 160, 177, 223, 228, 248, 249, 258, 292, 295, 306, 333
Electro-magnet, 70
Electromagnetism, 238–239
Elizabeth, Queen, 18, 71
Elizabethtown, N.J., 11 n.
Elliott, Samuel M., 281–282
Ellsworth, 314
Elm Street Synagogue, New York, 82
Emerson, Ralph Waldo, 47, 342 n.

Emerson, William, 342 n.
Emmet, Richard Stockton, 59
Emmet, Thomas Addis, xiii, xiv
Emott, James, 241
Empire, 242
Engagement of G.T.S., 314–315
England, 101–102, 150, 210, 218, 250, 274, 277, 334, 343
English drama, 87
English Neighbourhood, N.J., 301
Entomology, 34
Erasmus, Desiderius, 24
Erben, Henry, 133, 135–138, 149, 152–155, 261, 283
Erie, Lake, 243
Erie Canal, 163
Erie Railroad, xi
Ether, 299
Euripides, 68
Europa, 332
Evacuation Day, New York, 6, 42, 43, 193
Evangeles, Christodoulos Leonidas Miltiades, 16, 35
Evangeline (Longfellow), 310
Evangelist, The, 239
Evangelistic meeting, 83
Evarts, William Maxwell, 164, 342
Evelyn, John, ix, xxxviii, 13, 46

Faerie Queen, The (Spenser), 68
Fairlamb, Captain, 233
Fairmount Park, Philadelphia, 247
Fanny (Halleck), 21, 25, 38, 317
Fashion (racehorse), 181
Fast days, 161, 361
Fawcett, 152
Fearing, Mrs. 336, 337
Fearing, Eleanor Burrill, 349
Federalist party, 236
Fessenden, Henry Partridge, 50
Fichte, Johann Gottlieb, 101, 230
Field, David Dudley, 229
Field, Eleanor Kingsland (Mrs. John Jay), 12 n.
Field, Maunsell Bradhurst, 311, 333
Field, Osgood, 333
Financial worries of G.T.S., 316, 318, 319, 324, 327, 331–332, 334–337, 339, 343, 345, 347, 349, 350, 355, 360
Finley, Clement Alexander, xxxiii, xxxv
Fires, 8, 10–11, 14, 32, 34, 44, 66–68, 70, 78, 111, 124, 126–129, 134, 153, 166, 181, 191, 196, 253, 259, 260, 264–267, 328
Firman, Judge, 84

First Presbyterian Church, New York, 240, 268
Fish, Hamilton, xxvii, xxx, 283, 306, 326, 335
Fish, Mrs. Hamilton (Julia Kean), 288, 326
Fish, John Beekman, 39, 45, 46, 51, 90
Fish, Preserved, xi
Fishing, 108, 144, 282
Fitchburg R.R., 263
Fitz Ray Place, New York, 344
Flandin, Miss, 220
Fleming, John, 62
Fletcher, John, 87
Fleury Jolly, Mme., 302
Flirtation Path, West Point, 362
Florence's, 292, 314
Florida Indians, 31
Flushing, N.Y., 115, 168, 200, 242, 298, 320, 325, 328
Flushing Bay, 168
Fogruni, 42
Follen, Charles Theodore Christian, 124, 125
Follen, Mrs. Charles Theodore Christian (Eliza Lee Cabot), 124
Foot ball, 65, 66
Forbes, John Murray, 159
Ford, John, 87
Foreign Quarterly, 225
Foresti, Eleuterio Felice, 49
Forests of western New York, 243
Forrest, Edwin, 352
Fort Hamilton, Brooklyn, 279–280
Fort Independence, Boston Harbor, 31
Fort Lafayette, Brooklyn, 280
Fort Lee, N.J., 294, 301
Fort Meigs, Battle of, 137–138
Fort Putnam, West Point, 359, 362
Fortescue, Member of Parliament, 331
Fountains, 186, 187, 188, 189, 211, 219–222
Fouqué, Friedrich, Baron de la Motte, 364; *Sintram*, 204, 314
Fourier, François Marie Charles, 269
Fowler, Isaac Vanderbeck, 85, 86, 90, 91, 226
Fowler, Orson Squire, 46, 47
Fowler family, 326
Fox, 299
France, government of, 184–185; Academy of, 298; Revolution of 1789 in, 94, 100; Revolution of 1848 in, 316, 332–333
Frankenstein, 54
Franklin, Benjamin, xli

Franklin House, New York, 149
Frederick's, 361
Free Academy. *See* College of the City of New York
Free-Soil party, 308
Freemasons, 43, 160
Frelinghuysen, Theodore, 232, 236
Frémont, John Charles, 287
French church, New York (L'Eglise du Saint-Esprit), 38 n., 111
French language, study of, 38–39, 287, 289, 302, 335
French people, 204, 259, 297
French poetry, 312–313
Froissart, Jean, 46, 77, 228
Frost, William, 298
Froude, Richard Hurrell, xxxi, 101
Fry, Edward R., 336
Fuller, Margaret, 269
Fuller, Thomas, 96, 147
Fuller's gymnasium, 22–25
Fulton, Robert, xii
Furlong, 23
Furniss, William P., 259

Gadsden, Christopher Edwards, 251
Gaines, Edmund Pendleton, 31
Gaisford, Thomas, 3
Galen, 257
Gall, Franz Joseph, 19
Gallatin, Albert, 108, 202, 229
Gambling, 175
Gansevoort, Guert, 194 n.
Gardiner, David, 227
Gardiner, Julia (Mrs. John Tyler), 238
General Theological Seminary, li, 159 n., 167–168, 183, 187, 208–209
Geneva, N.Y., 242
Geneva College (afterward Hobart), 320
Gentleman's Magazine, 55
Geology, 16, 68
Georgia, 286
Gerard, James Watson, xiii
German, study of, 254, 268–269, 274, 275, 277, 280, 282, 287, 289, 364
German literature, 68
Germans, 259
Germany, 269
Gerry, 326
Gibbons *v.* Ogden, xv
Gibbs, George (1776–1833), 279
Gibbs, George (1815–1873), 298, 315, 319
Gibbs, Laura Wolcott (Mrs. T. M. d'Oremieulx), 326, 333

Gibbs, Wolcott, xxvi, xxx, xxxiii, xxxvi, xxxviii–xl, 338, 339, 355, 364
Gilmer, Thomas Walker, 223, 227
Girard (Stephen) will case, 225
Gladstone, William Ewart, 226
Glentworth, James B., 162
Globe (bathing establishment), 140
Globe, 278
Glover, 320, 356
Goat Island, 244, 245
God's Revenge against Murder and Adulterie (Reynolds), 230
Godwin, Mary Wollstonecraft, 54
Göttingen University, xxxi
Goethe, Johann Wolfgang von, 50
Goodwin, 133
Gordon, Theodore, 34, 39
Gould, Theodore, 281, 282
Gourlie, John Hamilton, 306
Gowans, William, 84
Grace Church, New York, xxv, 234, 256, 267, 292, 316, 318, 319, 322, 344 n.
Graduation of G.T.S. at Columbia, 89–91
Graham, David, 250; *Practice of the Supreme Court of the State of New York*, 92, 93, 106, 112, 116, 124, 127, 128 133, 153, 164, 231
Graham, James, 117, 189
Graham, John, xxi, 35
Gramercy Park, New York, xxv, xxvii, 262, 294, 328
Grand Island, 243
Grant, Ulysses Simpson, xxxiv, xxxviii, 359 n.
Grattan, Edward, 143
Grattan, Mrs. Edward, 143
Gray, George Griswold, xxxix
Gray, Henry Peters, 231, 259, 301, 306, 309
Great Britain. *See* Britain
Great Western, 84, 86, 101, 132, 280
Greek drama, 75–76
Greeley, Horace, xxv
Green, The Reverend, 142
Green, William, 17
Greenport, L.I. 263, 281, 282
Greenwood Cemetery, Brooklyn, 111, 229
Gridiron, Hellgate, 277
Griffin, Edward Dorr, 65
Griffin, Francis, xxi, xix, 314
Griffin, George, xiii, xxi, xxiv, l–li, 58, 107, 142, 143, 176–177, 197, 219–221, 272
Griffin, George, Jr., 299, 300
Griffin, Mrs. George, Jr., 299

Griffin, Teresa, 326
Griffin, William Preston, 326, 327
Griffing, Thomas Strong, li, 78, 137, 141, 142, 150, 256, 290, 293, 330
Grinnell, Moses Hicks, xi, xxxi, 337
Griswold, Edward, 83
Griswold, Mrs. George, 273
Guizot, François, 71
Gunnery, 77
Gurley, Royal, 24, 25, 64

Habicht, Claudius Edward, 310
Habicht, Mrs. Claudius Edward, 326
Hahnemann, Samuel, 257
Haight, Benjamin Isaacs, 138, 315
Hale, Benjamin, 320
Hall, Jonathan Prescott, 107, 364
Hall, Thomas, 133 n., 135, 154, 155
Halleck, Fitz-Greene, 58, 225, 269, 317 n.; *Fanny*, 21, 25, 38, 317; *The Culprit Fay*, 52
Halley's Comet, 70
Halsey, Anthony, 34
Hamersley, Andrew Gordon, 323
Hamersley, Mrs. Andrew Gordon (Sarah Jones), 323
Hamilton, Alexander, xiii, 2, 40, 82, 98 n., 154–155
Hamilton, Mrs. Alexander (Elizabeth Schuyler), xxiii, 98, 121, 154–155, 174, 334
Hamilton, Schuyler, 301
Hamilton College, xxxi
Hammond, William Alexander, xxxv
Hampden House, Springfield, Mass., 144
Hampton, N.H., 31
Hand, Augustus C., 241
Handel, George Frederick, xl, 203, 216
Harleian Miscellany, 49, 107
Harlem, 162
Harlem Bridge case, 95
Harper, James, 228, 258
Harriman, Edward Henry, 3
Harriman, Orlando, Jr., 3, 200
Harriot & Henry, 345, 346, 355
Harris, Elisha, xxxiii
Harrison, William Henry (Tippecanoe), 121, 137–138, 145, 147, 151, 156, 159–60
Hart, Eli, 51
Hartford, 145; Hartford Convention, 145
Harvard University, xxvi, 31, 124 n., 143; Dental School of, 298 n.; Divinity School of, 124 n.; Law School of, l; Medical School of, 31, 364–365
Harvey, Captain, 12
Hastings, Hiram P., 139

Haswell, Charles Haynes, 242
Havemeyer, William Frederick, 258, 265, 267
Havens, Rensselaer, 8
Hawks, Francis Lister, 81–82, 94, 115, 155, 200, 201, 247, 312
Hawkins, John Sidney, 216–217
Hayden, 127
Haydn, Joseph, 58, 179, 216
Haywood, Miss, 73
Head, Sir Francis Bond, xxii, 102, 130
Headcheese, 129–130
Hector (Newfoundland dog), 299, 301, 302–303, 344
Hellgate, 34, 277
Hempel, Charles J., 254, 257, 261, 327
Hempstead Plains, 33, 167
Henricus de Wildenholtz, 293
Henry, George, 360, 361
Henshaw, Caroline, 191
Herodotus, 4, 29
Herrick, Edward Claudius, 279
Herrick, Robert, 202
Hewitt, Abram Stevens, xxv, 187
Heyward, 113
Heyward, Edward, 168
Hibernia, 274, 301, 334
Hicksville, L.I., 99
Higbee, Edward Young, li, 76, 81, 98, 105, 112, 134, 174, 218, 251
Higgins *v.* Nostrand, xxiv
High Bridge, New York, 305
Highlands of the Hudson, 242
Hill, 164
Hill, Thomas Henry Weist, 292
Hilliard, Captain, 125
Hills, Mrs., 337
Hillyer, Giles Mumford, 21, 35, 36, 41, 42, 58, 62, 189, 285–286
Hinman, Royal Ralph, 145
Hippocrates, 257
Hobart, John Henry, 91, 179 n.
Hobart, John Henry, Jr., 35, 179
Hobart, Mrs. John Henry, Jr. (Elizabeth Riggs), 179
Hobart College, Geneva, N.Y., 320
Hobbes, Thomas, 64
Hoboken, N.J., 72, 236, 294, 301
Hodges, Edward, 221, 278, 283
Hodges, Mrs. Edward (Sarah Ann Moore), 221
Hoffman, Charles Fenno, 58 n.
Hoffman, Edward, 35
Hoffman, Josiah Ogden, xiii
Hoffman, Lindley Murray, 202

Hoffman, Ogden, xiv, xv, xxvi, xxix, 240
Hoffmann, Ernst Theodor Amadeus, 268, 274, 314
Hogarth, William, 330
Holbrook, Schoolmaster, 66, 88
Holden, Horace, 148
Holinshed, Raphael, 228
Home, 76
Homer, 88, 181, 182
Homœopathic Medical College, Philadelphia, 254 n.
Homœopathy, 257, 261, 305
Hone, Henry, 73, 113
Hone, Isaac S., 6 n., 330
Hone, John, 6, 85
Hone, Philip, Sr., x, xxxvii, xxxviii, 6 n., 15 n., 54–55, 61, 93, 103, 112, 168 n., 223, 262
Hone, Philip, Jr., 6 n., 28, 85, 89, 90
Hone, William, 152
Hood, Thomas, 112
Hooker, Richard, 111
Hoppin, Hamilton, 277
Hoppin, William Jones, 302, 309, 311
Horace, 17, 25, 60, 69
Horn, Charles Edward, 196
Hornett, Edward, 95
Horse (Tornado), purchase of, 287, 293, 294
Horse racing, 180, 181
Horseback riding, 33, 72, 88, 287, 293–296, 298, 301, 302, 304, 305
Horsmanden, Daniel, 236
How, Nehemiah, 20
Howard, 142
Howe, Julia Ward, 55 n.
Howland, Edgar, 152
Howland, Gardiner Greene, 240, 289
Howland, Samuel Shaw, 289
Howland & Aspinwall, 348
Howland observatory, 34
Hoxie, Joseph, 15 n., 23
Hoyt, Mrs. Henry Sheaff (Frances Duer), 85
Hoyt, Lydig, 206
Hubbard, William, 20
Hudson, 326
Hudson, Hendrick, 163
Hudson River, xvii, 47, 162, 165, 166, 167, 206–207, 213, 240–242, 326
Hudson River R.R., 289, 357
Hughes, John, 83, 102, 177, 210
Hull, 57
Hungerford, Dr., 244
Hunters' and Chasers' Lodges, 80, 97

Huntington, Daniel, 60–61, 161, 202, 276, 277, 284, 302
Huntington, L.I., 188, 209
Hyde Park, N.Y., 206

Ice cream, 181, 203
Incendiarism, 127–128
Inclined planes (railroad), 163
Incunabula, 4, 24, 25
India, 277
Indians, 20, 31, 72, 100, 150
Influenza epidemic, 205–206
Ingham, Charles Cromwell, 202 n.
Inglis, William, 112
Inman, Henry, 61, 259
International law, 86
Ipswich, Mass., 31
Ireland, potato crop failure in, 268; famine in, 288–290
Irish (in U.S.), 44, 94, 105, 150, 151, 177, 184, 228, 229, 232, 233, 259, 301, 318, 361
Irving, Washington, x, xii, xix, xxv, lii, 168, 197, 288, 352
Italians (in U.S.), 94
Ivanhoe (Scott), 142

Jackson, Andrew, xxi, 49, 65, 262, 280 n.
Jacobinism, 149
Jalapa, Mexico, 293
Jamaica, L.I., 33
Jamaica Plain, Mass., 71
James, George Payne Rainsford, 207, 311 n.
James I of England, 159
James II of Scotland, 227
Jane Eyre (Charlotte Brontë), 310, 314
Japhet in Search of a Father (Marryat), 17
Jay, John (1745–1829), 12 n.
Jay, John (1817–1894), 12, 35, 200, 249, 255, 300
Jay, Mrs. John (Eleanor Kingsland Field), 12
Jay, Peter Augustus, Sr., 170, 187
Jay, Peter Augustus, Jr., 170
Jay, William, 12 n.
Jerome, Leonard W., 17 n.
Jerome Park race course, New York, 17 n.
Jersey City, 53
Jewett, Helen, xv, 15 n.
Jews, 256; religious services, 82–83
John Carter Brown Library, 280 n.
John Mason, 166
Johnson, Eliza (Mrs. Horace Binney, Jr.), 88, 105
Johnson, Julia, 105, 185, 220

Johnson, Reverdy, 17 n.
Johnson, Samuel, 42, 70, 204
Johnson, William, li, 325
Johnson, Mrs. William (Maria Templeton), li, 325
Johnson, William Samuel (1727–1819), 272 n.
Johnson, William Samuel (1795–1883), 272, 273, 306
Johnson, Mrs. William Samuel (Laura Woolsey), 272 n., 275
Johnson, William Templeton (cousin), li, 85, 105, 113, 215, 220, 236, 242, 244, 245, 253, 259, 264, 278–279, 314, 355
Johnson, Mrs. William Templeton (Laura Winthrop), li, 278, 279
Johnson, Wilmot, 23, 24, 34, 39
Johnston, Francis Upton, 329, 332, 349, 357
Johnston, John, 326, 343 n.
Johnston, John Taylor, xxxviii, 343 n.
Johnston, Margaret (Mrs. John Bard), 326, 343
Joinville, Prince de, 170
Jones, 179
Jones, Mrs. 356
Jones, Mrs. Cave, 110
Jones, David Samuel, 176–177
Jones, George, 309 n.
Jones, George Frederic, 309
Jones, Mrs. George Frederic (Lucretia Stevens Rhinelander), 309 n.
Jones, Helen (Mrs. Woodbury Langdon), 306
Jones, Mrs. Isaac (Mary Mason), 269, 272, 317–318
Jones, James J., 314
Jones, Mary Mason (Mme. R. D. de K. de Trobriand), 322
Jones, Mrs. Rebecca, 320
Jones, Samuel, xiii, 122, 123
Jones, Sarah (Mrs. A. G. Hamersley), 323
Jonson, Ben, xli, 102
Judd, Sylvester, 311 n.
Jung-Stilling, Johann Heinrich, 161

Kane, Mrs. John Innes, liii
Kean, Christine A. W., 277, 326, 327
Kean, Julia (Mrs. Hamilton Fish), 288
Kean family, 273, 323
Kearny, Philip, Jr., 301, 323
Kearny, Stephen Watts, 287
Keats, John, xl
Keble, John, xxxi, 101

Keep, Nathan Cooley, 298, 365 n.
Kemper, Jackson, 27
Kendall's band, 35
Kennedy, of Baltimore, 326
Kennon, Commodore, 227
Kent, James, xiii, xiv, xv, xxi, 105, 106 n., 122, 146, 154, 224
Kent, William, xv, 173, 351, 352
Kermit, 139
Kernochan, William Seymour, 187
Ketchum, Hiram, 250
Kinderhook, N.Y., 138, 237
King, 149
King, Charles, xix, xxx, xxxv, xxxix, 92, 96, 344
King, James Gore, xix, 299, 323
King, Rufus, xix
King, Samuel Ward, 183
King, Thomas Butler, 337, 348
King's College, Cambridge, 279
King's College, New York. *See* Columbia College
Kirk, Edward Norris, 134
Kissam, Benjamin Tredwell, 28, 90, 163
Knapp, Jacob, 134
Knickerbocker Magazine, 92, 93 n., 149
Knowles, James Sheridan, x
Knox, John (1505–1572), 271
Knox, John (1790–1858), 29, 103–104, 169
Knox, John Mason, 13, 34, 78, 90, 91
Koberger, Antony, 24
Kock, Charles Paul de, 204
Komroff, Manuel, 15 n.
Koster, Gerard, 141
Kraft, Virginia, viii

L_____, Mr. and Mrs. Lewis, 235
Laborde, opera singer, 336
Lafever, Minard, 297
Lagrange, Joseph Louis, 55
Laight, Edward Huger, 35
Laight, Edward William, 48
Lake, James Phillips, 36
Lake Erie, 243; Battle of, 194 n.
Lalla Rookh (Moore), 54
Lamartine, Alphonse de, 312, 316
Lamartine Row, New York, 344
Lamb, Charles, xli, 57, 58, 310–311
Lambert, 8
Lambert, David, 60
Lambert, Henry, 60
Lane, Miss, 71
Lane Theological Seminary, 62 n.
Langdon, Walter, 298, 306, 317 n.

Langdon, Mrs. Walter (Dorothea Astor), 317 n.
Langdon, Woodbury, 272, 273, 306–307
Langdon, Mrs. Woodbury (Helen Jones), 306
Larocque, Jeremiah, 90
Latin drama, 76
Laud, William, 21, 101
Laurens, Henry, 154
Lauriat, balloonist, 39, 40, 109
Law, study of, 72, 87 ff.
Law Association, 96, 115, 131, 151
Law schools, 92
Lawrence, 121
Lawrence, Abbott, 317
Lawrence, Mrs. Abbott (Katherine Bigelow), 317
Lawrence, Cornelius, x, xxi
Lawrence, Isaac, 131
Lawrence, John B., 163
Lawrence, John L., 138, 306, 358
Lectures, popular, 195
Ledru-Rollin, Alexandre August, 316
Lee, Alfred, 168
Lee, Charles C., 44
Lee, Gideon, xi
Lee, Robert Edward, 359 n.
Legendre, Adrien Marie, 13
Lemprière, John, 75
Lenox, James, 154
Lenox, Robert, xi
Lenox Library, 176 n.
L'Estrange, Sir Roger, 64
Leupp, Charles M., 306, 309
Leutze, Emanuel, 276
Lewis, Tayler, 309
Lexington, 71, 72; disaster, 123–125
Library of G.T.S., xli, 10, 14, 16 n., 53, 62, 64, 70, 169, 187, 210, 212, 214–215, 228–229, 327, 345, 346, 362–363
Lincoln, Abraham, xxxii–xxxv, xxxix–xl
Lind, Jenny, xl, 310
Liszt, Franz, xl
Literature, 312
Little Neck, L.I., 72
Little Neck Turnpike, 145
Little Pedlington (Poole), 141, 202
Littleton, Sir Thomas, 95
Liverpool, 105, 280 n.
Livingston, Clarence, 240, 241
Livingston, Edward, xx, 1
Livingston, Montgomery, 232
Livingston, Robert Swift, 137
Lloyd, 25
Lloyd, Angelina (Mrs. G. W. Strong), xiv, 158

Lloyd, Henry, 306, 326
Lloyd, Mrs. Henry (Clothilde A. C.
    Brandegee), 306, 326
Lloyd, James, 186; estate of, 337
Lloyd, John, Jr., xiv
Lloyd, John Nelson, xvi, 157–158
Lloyd's Neck, L.I., 21, 188, 208
Locke, John, 93, 146
Lockhart, John Gibson, 73, 77, 86–87,
    93 n.
Lockwood, 67
Locofocos, 57, 62, 77, 138, 145, 147, 151,
    177, 228, 236, 246, 258, 284, 295
Loder, George, 255–256
Lodge, Henry Cabot, 155 n.
London, 210
London *Times*, 55 n.
Long Island R.R., 111, 188, 263
Long Room (auction house), 65
Longfellow, Henry Wadsworth, 55 n.,
    113–114, 124, 194, 195, 225, 269, 310,
    314; *Evangeline*, 310
Longinus, 36, 39, 75
Lord, Daniel, xiv, xv, xxii, xxiv, 219–
    221, 301
Lord, Daniel De Forest, 60, 212
Lord, Mrs. Daniel De Forest (Mary
    Howard Butler), 212
Lorton, mesmerist, 181
Louis XIV, 28
Louis XVI, 332
Louis Philippe, 184, 316
Loutrel, Alfred Mersan, 90
Low Hampton, N.Y., 199 n.
Lowell, Mass., 32
Lucian, 24
Lucretius, 74, 230
Ludlow, Mrs. Edward Hunter, 259
Ludolfus, Hiob, 106
Lupp, 326
Luther, Martin, 114
Lydig, 323
Lyell, Sir Charles, 68
Lynch, Edward Livingston, 270 n.
Lynch, Mrs. Edward Livingston (Eliza-
    beth Jane Strong), 270
Lynch, Harrison, 35–36
Lynn, Mass., 31, 109

Macaulay, Thomas Babington, 226, 333,
    342–343
McClellan, George Brinton, xxxiv, li
McCoskry, Samuel Allen, xxxii, 303
McCoun, William T., 165
McElroy, Joseph, 22, 41, 60, 100

Mackenzie, Alexander Slidell, 194, 197,
    198
Mackenzie, William Lyon, xxii, 80, 102,
    105
McLeod, Alexander, 80, 156, 175
McMaster, Benjamin B. J., 208, 210
MacMullen, John, 14, 37
Macomb, Dr., 192
Macready, William Charles, 197, 331,
    333, 352
McVickar, Henry, 36
McVickar, John, xx, xxxi, li, 2, 4, 5, 9,
    13, 14, 18, 22, 28, 37, 42, 56, 59, 65,
    75, 78, 84, 87, 122, 132, 149, 180, 202,
    249
McWhorter, Mr. & Mrs., (of Oswego),
    299–300
Maelzel, 203
Maffitt, The Reverend and Mrs., 300
Magdalen College, Oxford, 210
Mahan, Alfred Thayer, 359 n.
Mahan, Dennis Hart, 359
Mahomet, 271
Maine, 145. *See also* North East Boun-
    dary dispute
Maine, Sir Henry, xx
Malcolm, Sir John, 106
Malory, Sir Thomas, *Morte d'Arthur*,
    161, 171–172, 228
Manhattanville, 294, 302
Mansfield, William Murray, first Earl of,
    xvi, 105
Mantello, 321
Manuscripts, 169–170; illuminated, 66
Marblehead, Mass., 109, 110, 144
Marco Polo, 175
Marié, Miss, 326, 327
Marine Society Museum, Salem, 31
Marlowe, Christopher, 283
Marriage, 131, 162, 175, 206, 212, 239,
    343
Marryat, Frederick, 55, 124; *Japhet in
    Search of a Father*, 17
Marshall, John, xv, 183 n.
Marshall, Thomas Francis, 183–184,
    194 n.
Martin, Henry Hull, 206
Martin, John, 153
Martin Chuzzlewit (Dickens), 225, 252
Martine, Theodore, 344
Maurice, 314
Marx, Henry, 296
Mary, Queen of Scots, 28
Mason, John, 111–112
Mason, Mary (Mrs. Isaac Jones), 269,
    272

Mason will case, 112
Masonic Hall, New York, 170
Masons, 43, 160
Massachusetts, 15, 17, 25, 142
Massachusetts Regiments, 6th, xxxiii
Massachusetts State House, 20, 71
Master Humphrey's Clock (Dickens), 136
Mather, Cotton, 43, 147
Mather, Increase, 20
Mathew, Theobald, 150–151
Mathews, Cornelius, 312
Mathews, James M., 16 n., 61 n.
Maurice, 314, 320
Maverick House, East Boston, 143
Maxcy, Virgil, 227
Maxwell, Hugh, 13, 151, 259
May Day, 202
Mayo, Maria D. (Mrs. Winfield Scott), 323
Mead, 181
Meade, William, 249
Mechanics' Bank, New York, 62
Meerschaum pipes, 133, 211
Melville, Herman, 194 n.
Mendelssohn-Bartholdy, Jakob Ludwig Felix, 235, 310
Merchants' Bank, New York, 65, 103
Merchants' Exchange, New York, 8, 93, 103, 147
Mercantile Library, New York, 53
Mergenthaler, Virginia Katherine, viii
Merrimack River, 32
Mesmerism, 178, 181, 182, 280 n., 310
Meteor, 199
Methodism, 115
Methodist clergy, 258
Metropolitan Museum of Art, 76 n., 343 n.
Mexican War, 272, 275–278, 287, 290–295, 298, 299, 301–305, 308, 312
Mexico, 223, 250, 253
Mexico City, 291, 294, 299, 301, 302
Microscopy, 38, 362
Middle Ages, 115, 296
Middle Dutch Church, New York, 103, 112, 187
Militia, 65, 72, 113, 117–118, 147, 160, 189, 267, 352, 353
Miller, Mrs., 114
Miller, Jonathan, 202
Miller, William, 198–199, 201
Millerite delusion, 198–201
Milton, John, 68, 70, 122, 140, 225; *Areopagitica*, 66
Mineral water, 167
Minerals, Gibbs cabinet of, at Yale, 279

Mirage, 144
Mississippi, 200; state bonds, 289
Mitchell, 250–251
Mohawk & Hudson R.R., 163
Mohawk River, 163, 165, 241
Molière, Jean Baptiste Poquelin, 289
Molloy, Pat, 150, 296
Monastic calligraphers, 170
Monk, Maria, 92 n.
Monocle, 65, 66, 69, 161
Montauk, L.I., 280–282
Monterey, Battle of, 290, 291
Montezuma, Halls of, 302, 303
Montfaucon, Bernard de, 41, 42
Montreal, 246
Moore, 245
Moore, Clement, 326
Moore, Clement Clarke, xxix, 29, 140, 221, 326, 359
Moore, Katharine Van Cortlandt, 328
Moore, Maria Theresa Barrington, 328
Moore, Nathaniel Fish, 77, 81, 82, 180, 185, 187
Moore, Sarah Ann (Mrs. Edward Hodges), 221
Moore, Thomas, 130, 179; *Lalla Rookh*, 54
Moore, William Taylor, 326
Mormons, 240
Morpeth, Lord, 170
Morris, Robert H., 117, 177
Morse, 61
Morse, Samuel Finley Breese, 61 n.
Morte d'Arthur (Malory), 161, 171–172, 228
Morton, Jacob, 43
Morton, Nathaniel, *New-England's Memorial*, 20
Moscow, Conflagration of, 203
Mosquitoes, 73, 148, 211–212, 214, 329, 357, 360, 363
Mott, Valentine, 99, 170
Mott, Mrs. Valentine (Louisa Dunmore Munns), 170
Mount, 182
Mount, William Sidney, 61, 161, 202, 214, 231, 259, 276
Mount Auburn Cemetery, 19, 111, 186, 229, 263
Mount Misery, L.I., 99, 141, 142, 171
Mount Pleasant, 31
Mount Pleasant Classical Institute, Amherst, 16 n.
Mountain House, Catskill Mts., 212, 213, 328

Mountain House, Ossippee Hills, N.H., 32
Moving day (May 1), 231–232
Mozart, Wolfgang Amadeus, xl, 11 n., 58, 156, 179, 216, 252, 288, 309
Muhlenberg, William Augustus, 247
Munns, Louisa Dunmore (Mrs. Valentine Mott), 170
Munson, 326
Musical box, 222
Musical notes, G.T.S. learns, 152
Mutter, Dr., and Mrs. 326

Nahant, 31, 71, 108–110, 142–144, 298
Nairne, Charles Murray, xxxvii
Napoleon I, 28, 184, 271, 278, 295; Russian campaign of, 29–30
Narragansett, 71, 108
Nashua, N.H., 32
National Academy of Design. *See* Academy of Design
National Bank, New York, 105
National Hall, New York, 151, 200, 292
National Theatre, New York, 111, 162
Native-American party, 228, 249, 258
Native-American riots, 177–178, 232–234, 240
Naturalizing, 94
Navy Island, 82
Negroes, 100, 194–195, 199, 200, 217, 232, 236
Neilson, John ("Esculapius"), 50, 129, 174, 183, 207, 357
Nelson, Samuel, 164
New England, 169
New-England's Memorial (Morton), 20
New England Historic Genealogical Society, 20 n.
New Era, 100, 160
New Hampshire, 31–33
New Haven, Conn., 145, 278–279
New Haven, 145
New Jersey, 295; turnpike, 95
New London, Conn., 263
New Orleans, 49, 256, 300, 339, 355
New Testament, 258
New World, 125, 136, 200
New Year's calls, 48, 121–122, 174, 197–198, 223, 272–273, 341
New York American, 248
New York Athletic Club, 17 n.
New York City: bombardment of, 276; Common Council, 307; Negro plot, 236; sanitary conditions, 110
New York Commerical Advertiser, xxii, 92 n.

New York *Courier*, 258, 314
New York Evening Post, x, 94, 149, 160
New York *Express*, 248
New York Herald, x, 24, 29, 94, 192, 314, 348
New-York Historical Society, 16 n., 103, 202, 298; G.T.S. elected a member of, 202
New York Journal of Commerce, 160
New York Mirror, 27, 217
New York Public Library, 176 n.
New York Review, 81, 82, 94, 119, 149
New York Society Library, 83, 86, 169, 181, 210, 239–240
New York *Standard*, 160
New York State: Constitution of 1846, 106 n., 284, 296–297; Historical Association, 276 n.; Supreme Court, New Code of Procedure of (1848–1849), 301, 324, 328, 334, 345 (*see also* Graham, David); University, 48
New York Sugar Refining Co., xiii
New York *Sun*, 24
New York Times, 309 n.
New York Transcript, 24
New York Tribune, 309 n.
New York University, xx, xxi, 3, 16 n., 34–35, 57, 61 n., 78, 280 n., 287 n., 290, 309 n.; Chapel, 66; Law School, 92; Medical College, 172, 254; Philomathean Society, 66
Newark Meadows, 295
Newburgh, N.Y., 77, 162, 167, 211
Newburyport, Mass., 31
Newman, John Henry, xxxi, 115, 162, 268
Newport, R.I., 18, 20
Newton, Mass., 263, 264, 298
Newtown, L.I., 72, 298
Niagara Falls, 80–82, 242–246
Niagara River, 243–246
Niblo's Garden, New York, 138, 196
Niblo's Theatre, 329
Nichol, J. P., 314
Nicholas Nickleby (Dickens), 113, 173
Nicoll, Henry, 220
Nitrous oxide, 81
No-Popery riots. *See* Native-American riots
Normans, 347
North America, 206
North American Review, 149
North East Boundary Dispute, 97, 99–100, 150, 153, 296
Northport Bay, L.I., 141
Norwalk River, 163

Norwich, Conn., 186, 264
Norwich & Worcester R.R., 256, 263
Nott, Eliphalet, 152
Noxon, 241
Noyes, 241
Numismatics, 84
Nuremberg Chronicle, xli

O.K., 137, 138, 151
Oakley, Jesse, 330
Oakley, Thomas Jackson, 103, 249
Oberlin College, 62 n.
O'Connell, Daniel, 218
O'Conor, Charles, xxiv
Ocracoke, N.C., 76
Octagon houses, 47
Odd Fellows, 187–188
Ogden, Abraham, 57
Ogden, David Bayard, xiii, 250, 333, 358
Ogden, Gouverneur Morris, xxx
O'Haggerty, 131
Oldfield, 186
Oliver Ellsworth, 85
Oliver Twist (Dickens), 113, 173
Olmsted, Frederick Law, xxvi, xxxiv, xxxv
Onderdonk, Benjamin Tredwell, lii, 56, 140, 171, 209, 220, 248; trial of, 249–251, 254–255; conviction of, 253
Onderdonk, Henry Ustick, lii, 237–238
Onderdonk, John, lii
"Onderdonks" (modified mint juleps), 237
Oneida Depot, N.Y., 242
Opera, 287–288, 310, 328, 332, 333, 336, 339, 341, 342
Opium chewing, 203
Oregon, 277, 326
Oregon Boundary Dispute, 272, 277, 289
Oremieulx, Theophile Marie d', 326
Oremieulx, Mrs. Theophile Marie d' (Laura Wolcott Gibbs), 326, 333
Organ, parlor (Goliath), 133, 135, 136, 137, 138, 149, 152, 153, 154, 155, 363
Oriskany, N.Y., 242
Orleans, Ferdinand P. L. C. H., duc d', 184
Osborn, Laughton, 93 n., 96
Osborn, Samuel, 93 n.
Ossipee Hills, N.H., 32
O'Sullivan, 326
Otey, James Hervey, 249
Otto, Mme., 198
Overslaugh, 240
Ovid, 230

Oxford, University of, 210, 317 n.
Oxford Tracts, xxxi, 101, 111, 112, 119, 179, 200, 209, 238

Paganini, Nicolò, 219
Paget, Francis Edward, 208
Paixhan guns, 185, 227
Paley, William, 230
Palgrave, Sir Francis, 152
Palmer, 130
Palmer, William, 101
Palmer's Hotel, New York, 361
Palmerston, Lord, 274
Palmieri, Joseph, 107
Palo Alto, Battle of, 272
Paltock, Robert, *Peter Wilkins*, 152
Panic of 1837, xxi, 49, 55–56, 60, 62–65, 80, 97
Papineau, Louis Joseph, 80
Paris, Matthew, 152
Parish, Mr. and Mrs. Daniel, 326
Parish, Henry, xxxviii, 274, 276
Parish, John Harris, 254, 273, 292–294, 301, 302, 306, 310, 315, 326
Park Theatre, New York, x, 88, 99, 273, 293
Parkman, George, 298 n., 364–365
Parsons, Theophilus, xv
Pasor, George, 18
Patrick, St., 83, 150
Pattison, Granville Sharp, 281–282
Paulding, Philip Kemble, 90
Paulding, Mrs. Philip Kemble, 231
Pavilion, New Haven, 145
Payne & Foss, 169, 210
Peale's New York Museum, 178, 182
Pearsall, Thomas, 101
Pearson, Issac Greene, 240
Peck, 320
Peconic Hotel, Greenport, L.I., 282
Peel, Sir Robert, 274
Penniman, James F., 272
Pennington, William, 326, 336, 344
Pennoyer, Captain, 141
Pennsylvania, Diocese of, 237
Pepys, Samuel, ix, xxxviii
Percy, Thomas, 21, 77
Pergolesi, Giovanni Battista, 179
Perkins, Thomas Handasyd, 144
Peteler, Alois, 333
Peter (servant), 129
Peter Wilkins (Paltock), 152
Phi Beta Kappa, 25
Philadelphia, 49, 157, 175, 232–234, 237, 240, 247, 248, 258
Philharmonic Society, xxxvii

Philharmonic Society concerts, 215, 234, 290
Phillips, John Mason, 231 n., 257, 260
Phillips, William Wirt, 231 n., 240, 268
Philostratus, 64
Phiz (Hablot Knight Browne), 92 n.
Phenix Bank, New York, 158
Phoenix, Jonas Phillips, xi
Phrenology, 19 n., 46–47
Physicians and Surgeons, College of, 44 n.
Pickens, Francis Wilkinson, 160
Pickersgill, Mrs., 124
Pickman, Benjamin, Jr., 31
Pickwick Papers (Dickens), 53, 60, 75, 82, 173
Pike, Benjamin, 238, 239
Pilgrim Fathers, 119–120, 156–157, 204
Pillow, Gideon Johnson, 302
Pillsbury, 130
Pinckney, Charles, xv
Pindar, 74–75
Pius IX, Pope, 159 n.
Plato, 88
Plautus, 3, 28, 68
Plum Island, 282
Pneumatology, 161
Poe, Edgar Allan, 168 n.
Poets, American, 225, 269
Point Judith, 17
Political economy, 84
Polk, Andrew Jackson, 246
Polk, James Knox, 223, 237, 246, 248–249, 253, 290, 291, 296
Polk, Leonidas, 249
Polka, 269–270, 311, 318
Poole, John, *Little Pedlington*, 141, 202
Portland, 19
Portsmouth, N.H., 31
Post, Jehiel Jaggar, lii, 115, 116, 135, 138, 149, 152, 153, 157, 170, 178, 181, 182, 184, 192
Post, Rosetta, Mrs., 322
Potter, Alonzo, 316
Potter, Edward, 284
Potts, George, 267
Poughkeepsie, N.Y., 280
Poussin, French Minister, 328
Powell, "Admiral," 73
Powell's (Whitestone), 323
Powers, Hiram, 300
Powers, John, 44, 83
Practice of the Supreme Court of the State of New York (Graham), 92, 93, 106, 112, 116, 124, 127, 128, 133, 153, 164, 231
Predestination, 117

Presbyterian Hospital, New York, 176 n.
Presbyterianism, 95, 100, 171, 176 n., 257–258
Prescott, William Hickling, 83, 223
President, 17
Prester John, 106
Price, William M., 280
Prichard, William Mackay, 342
Prime, Nathaniel, 152, 344 n.
Prime, Ward & King (*later* Prime, Ward & Co.), xi, 299, 344 n.
Princc, 320
Prince, John, 131
Princeton, U.S.S., 223, 227
Princeton College (College of New Jersey), xiii, l, lii, 139, 176 n., 239 n.
Princeton Theological Seminary, 176 n.
Prior, Matthew, 64
Prize fighting, 185, 186, 194
Protestant Episcopal Church: doctrines and liturgy of, 21, 37, 95, 101, 112, 115, 154, 168, 209; General Convention, 168–169, 247; High Church-Low Church controversy, 209–211, 224, 248–251; House of Bishops, 248–251
Protestantism, 204–205
Providence, R.I., 18, 20, 32, 144
Providence, 20
Prussia, 317
Pruyn, John Van Schaick Lansing, 206
Psychology, 308
Pugin, Augustus Welby Northmore, 229
Purchas, Samuel, 228
Puritans, 147, 156–157, 171
Pusey, Edward Bouverie, 101, 210
Pynson, Richard, 228

Quackenbos, Henry Feltus, 26, 34
Quackenbush, Daniel McLaren, 35
Quadrupeds (Audubon), 344
Quakers and Quakerism, 147, 161, 204
Quevedo, Francisco de, 64
Quincy, Josiah, 143

Rabelais, François, 130, 226
Racket Club, New York, 303
Radcliffe, Ann (Ward), 7
Radcliffe Library, Oxford, 210
Railroads and railroad travel, 108, 163, 241, 242, 246, 263, 264, 282
Rathbone, Mary Rosalie. *See* Ruggles, Mrs. Samuel Bulkley
Ray, Robert, 266, 344, 359
Raymond, Samuel G., 303
Realism in literature, 289–290
Red Mountains, N.H., 32

Reed, Henry Hope, 310
Rees, Abraham, 16 n., 17, 71
Reeves, John, 147
Religious beliefs of G.T.S., 95, 100–102. *See also* Oxford Tracts; Protestant Episcopal Church
Renwick, James, xx, lii, 2, 3, 5, 7, 10, 15, 16, 22–24, 26, 29, 37–40, 42, 43, 50, 51, 58, 59, 70, 77, 85, 87, 150, 153, 187, 296 n.
Renwick, Mrs. James (Margaret Ann Brevoort), 23
Renwick, James, Jr., lii, 12, 20, 22, 187, 211, 234, 256, 288, 292, 293, 306, 335
Repealers, 205
Resaca de la Palma, Battle of, 272
Residences of G.T.S.: 50 Franklin Street (1820–1822), 157 n.; 108 Greenwich Street (1822–1843), 2, 87, 124, 321, 345, 346, 350—rear building, Palazzo-vulgo (1843–1848), 200, 201, 203, 204, 214, 215; 54 Union Place (Fourth Avenue) (1848–1849), 324, 329, 331, 333, 363; 74 (later 113) East Twenty-first Street, at Gramercy Park, Palazzo Strong, Schloss am Square (1849–1875), xxvi, 318, 323, 324, 328, 331, 334–336, 339, 341, 345–347, 349–351, 353–355, 360–364
Retzsch, Moritz, 311
Reynolds, 93
Reynolds, John, *God's Revenge against Murder and Adulterie*, 230
Rhinelander, Lucretia Stevens (Mrs. G. F. Jones), 309 n.
Rhode Island, 280 n. *See also* Dorr's Rebellion
Rhode Island, 33, 109
Richard & Platt, 106
Richard III (Shakespeare), 273
Richards, 22
Richmond, Catherine Augusta (Mrs. T. C. Cooper), 212
Richmond, James Cook, 249, 250, 254–5
Richter, Jean Paul Friedrich, 292
Rider's Hotel, West Point, 357
Riggs, Caleb B., xiv
Riggs, Elizabeth (Mrs. J. H. Hobart, Jr.), 179
Riley, 302
Rinconada Pass, Mexico, 291
Rio Grande River, 291
Roach, Isaac, 247
Robertson, Anthony Lispenard, 356
Robertson, Archibald, 356 n.
Robertson, William, 14, 28

Robeson, Abel Bellows, 349, 356, 357
Robinson, Richard P., xv, 15 n., 22, 23, 24
Robinson's Observatory, Niagara Falls, 244
Rochester, N.Y., 243, 246
Rockaway, L.I., 72, 73, 323, 341, 356
Rodgers, Fanny, 326
Rodgers, John Kearny, 326, 357
Roger Williams, 357, 359, 361, 362
Rogers, 196
Rogers, Henry, 140
Rogers, John Smyth, 275
Rogers, Mary Cecilia, 168, 237
Rollin, Charles, 145
Rolph, John, 102
Romaine, Benjamin, 45–46, 90, 91, 163, 172
Roman Catholic Church, 43–44, 81–83, 93, 102–103, 112, 114, 154, 159 n., 171, 177–178, 204–205, 208, 210, 211, 240, 268
Rome, N.Y., 242
Ronge, Johannes, 269
Roosevelt, 45
Roosevelt, Theodore (1858–1919), xxv
Rosebery, Archibald Philip Primrose, fifth Earl of, 55 n.
Roscoe, William, 65
Rossini, Gioachino Antonio, 179, 220, 261, 292
Round Hill School, Northampton, 55 n.
Rubeta, The Vision of, 92, 96, 153–154
Rudderow, Helen, 251
Rudderow, Jane O., 251
Ruggle, George, 216 n.
Ruggles, Ellen Caroline. *See* Strong, Mrs. George Templeton
Ruggles, Henry Joseph, 315, 356
Ruggles, Mrs. Henry Joseph, 315, 356, 361
Ruggles, James Francis, xxvii, 322, 347, 348
Ruggles, John Rathbone, xxvii, 341, 347, 348
Ruggles, Mrs. Philo (Ellen Bulkley), grandmother of Mrs. G.T.S., 331, 356, 358, 364
Ruggles, Philo Taylor, 336
Ruggles, Rosalie, 342
Ruggles, Samuel Bulkley (father-in-law), xi, xxv–xxvi, xxviii–xxxi, xxxiv, xl, 292, 308, 309, 314, 318, 322, 324, 331, 333, 336–337, 341, 351, 352, 356, 357, 361, 363
Ruggles, Mrs. Samuel Bulkley (Mary

Rosalie Rathbone), 339, 352, 358, 361, 363
Ruskin, John, xl, 354, 355
Russell, 142
Russell, John, Lord, 274
Russell, William Howard, 55 n.
Russia, 100, 250, 334; Napoleon's campaign in, 29–30
Rust, Philo, 242
Rutherford, Lewis Morris, xxvi
Ryckman, 206

Sacred Music Society, 151, 203
Sag Harbor, L.I., 281
St. Ann's Church, New York, 159 n.
Saint-Esprit, L'Eglise du, New York, 38 n., 111
St. George's Chapel, New York, 168
St. George's Church, 335
St. George's Manor, L.I., 142
St. John's Chapel, New York, xi, 3, 27, 34, 35, 58, 74, 88, 149, 284
St. John's Park, New York, 17, 58
St. Luke's Church, New York, 159 n.
St. Luke's Hospital, New York, 153 n.
St. Mark's Church, New York, x, 110, 168, 251
St. Nicholas Society, 307
St. Patrick's Cathedral, New York, 43–44, 83, 177
St. Paul's Cathedral, London, 210
St. Paul's Chapel, New York, xiii, xxxi, 16, 34, 40, 41, 45, 63, 69, 104, 168, 171
St. Paul's Church, Troy, 166 n.
St. Peter's (P.E.) Church, Chelsea, 140
St. Peter's (R.C.) Church, New York, 81, 102, 171, 252, 314
St. Petersburg, Russia, 30
St. Stephen's Church, New York, 209, 217
St. Stephen's College, 343 n.
St. Thomas's Church, New York, 169, 200 n.
St. Thomas's Hall, Flushing, 200
Sale, George, 21
Salem, Mass., 31; witchcraft delusion, 147
Salisbury, Mrs. (of New Haven), 279
Salmasius, 68
Saltillo, Mexico, 291
Sältzer, Alexander, 357
San Luis Potosí, Mexico, 291, 299
Sand, George, 289
Sandy Hook, 85, 86
Sanitary Commission. *See* United States Sanitary Commission
Sanskrit, 12

Santa Anna, Antonio Lopez de, 290, 291, 293, 294, 299, 303, 304
Saragossa, Siege of, 292
Saratoga Springs, 165–167
Saxe, John Godfrey, 233
Schaeffer, George Christian, 75, 78
Schenck & Co., 61
Schenectady, N.Y., 163, 167, 241, 242, 246
Schermerhorn, Abraham, 95, 336
Schermerhorn, Cortlandt, 163
Schermerhorn, William Colford, xxxviii, liii, 212, 215, 257
Schermerhorn, Mrs. William Colford (Annie Laight Cottenet), 212
Schieffelin, Richard Lawrence, 177
Schiller, Johann Christoph Friedrich von, 274, 282, 364; *William Tell*, 269
Schlegel, Friedrich von, 275, 282
Schlosser, Fort, 243
Scholarship, life of, 290
Schroeder, John Frederic, 63, 69, 115–116, 236
Schuyler, Elizabeth. *See* Hamilton, Mrs. Alexander
Schuyler, Philip, 98 n.
Scot, Reginald, 84
Scotland, 290
Scott, Sir Walter, xvii, xx, 28, 30, 33, 72, 73, 77, 86–88, 93 n., 122, 288; *Ivanhoe*, 142; Monument (Edinburgh), 297; *Woodstock*, 147
Scott, Winfield, 31, 97, 103, 287, 292–294, 299, 302–304, 312, 323, 359
Scott, Mrs. Winfield (Maria D. Mayo), 323, 362
Scott family, 88
Scribner, Charles, 12 n.
Scribner & Welford, 12 n.
Seabury, Samuel, 154, 180, 182
Seals in Boston harbor, 31
Seamen's Bank, New York, 337
Searle, Major, 327
Sebastian, King of Portugal, 290
Sedgwick, Theodore Jr., 107, 229
Seneca, Lake, 242
Sergeant, Katherine (Mrs. H. A. Cram), 317
Setauket, L.I., 125, 141
Seton, Mr. and Mrs. William, 281
Seward, William Henry, 97, 113, 118, 189, 190, 193, 194, 197
Seymour, Charles, 21, 26, 35, 92
Seymour, Daniel, 297, 301, 306
Shakespeare, William, 21, 22, 88, 152, 158, 201, 225; *Richard III*, 273

Shannon, Wilson, 250
Sharon Springs, N.Y., 323, 325–327
Shaw, Lemuel, 365 n.
Shea, Charles Edward, 43, 44
Shea, James, 43 n.
Shelley, Percy Bysshe, 42, 52–54, 122
Shelley, Mrs. Percy Bysshe, (Mary Wollstonecraft Godwin), 54
Sheppard, William, 170
Shirley, James, 152
Shirreff, Jane, 116
Shot Tower, New York, 56
Siddons, 85, 86
Sidney, Sir Philip, 52, 152
Sikhs, 277
Silliman, Benjamin, 13, 16, 21
Simson, Sampson, xxx
Singleton, Angelica (Mrs. Abraham Van Buren), 326
Sintram (Fouqué), 204, 314
Sir Robert Peel, 80
Sirius, 84, 85
Sismondi, Jean C. L. de, 52
Sixth Ward Hotel, New York, 177–178
Sketch Club, 297 n.
Slavery 194–195, 287, 339
Smack, Misses, 363
Smallpox, 151, 172
Smith, 201
Smith, 302
Smith, Dr., 140, 356
Smith, Augustus F., 164
Smith, Hugh, 187, 209
Smith, Joseph, 240
Smith, Thomas H., 114–115, 126, 133
Smith, Tyler, 351
Smithsonian Institution, 288
Smollett, Tobias, 60
Snipe-shooting, 281
Snobs (Thackerayan variety), 231, 236, 240, 281, 282, 300
Snowballing, 78
Society, 195, 198, 269–270, 273, 274
Socinianism, 169
Solicitor in Chancery (G.T.S. admitted), 167
Somers mutiny, 194, 197, 198, 200
Sophistication, 260
Sophocles, 68, 75, 76
South Dutch Church, New York, 16 n.
Southard, Samuel Lewis, 239 n.
Southard, Samuel Lewis, Jr., 239, 339, 342, 353–355
Southern Literary Messenger, 113
Southerners, 173, 287

Southey, Robert, 49, 60, 122, 140, 156, 172, 201, 288
Spartan Band, 177, 205
Spear, Charles, 6
Speculation, 65, 132, 200
Speir, Gilbert McMaster, 342
Spencer, George John, second Earl, 228
Spencer, Jesse Ames, 34, 46, 140
Spencer, John Canfield, 194
Spencer, Philip, 194
Spenser, Edmund, 88; *The Faerie Queene*, 68
Spiritualism, 280 n., 305
Spring, Gardiner, xxix, 148
Springfield, Mass., 144
Spurzheim, Caspar, 19 n., 47
Squirrel, pet (Teufelchen), 288, 303
Staël, Anne Louise Germaine de, 314
Stanton, Edwin McMasters, xxxii, xxxiv, xxxv
Star, 33, 88
Staten Island, 3, 71, 104
Stebbins, 65, 66
Stephanus, Robert, 22
Stephens, John Lloyd, 202
Stevens, Alexander Hodgdon, 157, 174, 299, 306
Stevens, Mrs. Alexander Hodgdon (III), (Phoebe Coles Lloyd), 299
Stevens, John Austin, liii
Stevens, Mrs. John Austin (Abby Wild), 308, 314, 325, 338
Stevens, Mary Emmeline, liii, 314
Stewart, Dugald, 284
Stockton, Robert Field, 227
Stone, William Leete, xxii, 92, 96
Stonington, Conn., 108, 109
Stoppani, Charles G., 140
Story, Franklin Howard, 144
Story, Horace, 144
Story, Joseph, xv, 143, 157
Stoughton, 242
Stoves, base-burning, 152 n.
Strong, Benjamin (uncle), 63, 64, 93, 142
Strong, Charles Edward (cousin), v, xxviii, xxxvi, liii, 181, 254, 255, 260, 269, 273, 287, 293, 294, 300, 302, 306, 310, 314, 315, 323, 326–328, 331, 333, 341, 344, 348, 349, 351, 354, 362, 363
Strong, Elizabeth Jane (Mrs. E. L. Lynch), 270
Strong, Eloise Lloyd (sister). *See* Derby, Mrs. Elias Hasket
Strong, Emily (still-born daughter of G.T.S.), xxv, xxvi, 349, 350

Strong, Mrs. George Templeton (Ellen
    Caroline Ruggles), xxv, xxvi, xxxvii,
    293, 308–311, 313–325, 327–339, 341–
    343, 346–365
Strong, George Templeton, Jr., xxvi
Strong, George Templeton, III, vi
Strong, George Washington (father), v,
    ix, xii–xviii, xxi–xxv, xxviii, xxxi, 7,
    8, 17, 18, 22 n., 29, 31, 32, 36, 43, 48,
    58 n., 62, 63, 66, 72, 84, 88, 95, 98, 99,
    102, 108, 111, 118, 119, 124, 126, 127,
    129, 137, 144, 148, 157 n., 158, 175,
    183, 208, 222, 231, 259, 265, 266, 272,
    276, 278, 315, 318, 323, 333, 335, 350,
    363, 363 n.
Strong, Mrs. George Washington (first
    wife, Angelina Lloyd), xiv, 158
Strong, Mrs. George Washington (second
    wife, Eliza Catharine Templeton,
    mother of G.T.S.), ix, xiv, xvii, 27, 71,
    88, 129, 142, 251, 278, 284, 315, 325,
    333, 350, 363
Strong, James, 277, 314
Strong, Mrs. James, 122, 323
Strong, James Henry, 222
Strong, John (Elder), 157 n.
Strong, John Ruggles (son), v, vi, xxvi
Strong, John Wells, xiv
Strong, Julia (Mrs. G. T. Bedell), 261
Strong, Lewis Barton (son), xxvi
Strong, Mary Amelia (sister), ix, xiv,
    22, 39, 46, 71, 100, 102, 108, 129, 220,
    222, 327, 363 n.
Strong, Peter Remsen (cousin), liii, 154,
    158, 174, 212–214, 222, 224, 242, 260,
    270 n., 274, 281, 282, 310
Strong, Selah (1737–1815), xii
Strong, Selah, 142
Strong, Thomas (uncle), 99, 134
Strong, Mrs. William M., 174
Stuart, Alexander, 176–177
Stuart, Gilbert, 145
Stuart, Kinloch, 176 n.
Stuart, Mrs. Kinloch (Agnes), 176–177
Stuart, Robert Leighton, 176–177
Stuyvesant, Peter, xi
Stuyvesant, Peter Gerard, 103, 122–123,
    298
Stuyvesant Institute, New York, 172
Stuyvesant Square, New York, 335
Success Pond (Lake Success), 33
Sue, Eugène, 289
Sullivan, Yankee, 186
Sun, 141, 142
Superior, Lake, 338
Sussex, Duke of, 132

Suydam, 303
Suydam, James, 326
Swedenborg, Emanuel, 280
Swett, a Bostonian, 256
Swimming, 142, 165, 185, 281
Synod of Dort, 117
Syracuse, N.Y., 242

Taft, Henry Waters, v, vi, 112
Talbot, Olyphant & Co., 62
Tammany Hall, 77, 118, 160, 200, 293
Tappan, Arthur, 62, 131
Tappan Zee, 242
Taylor, Bayard, xxv
Taylor, Jeremy, 79
Taylor, Moses, xxiv
Taylor, Nathaniel William, xix
Taylor, Thomas House, 322, 344 n.
Taylor, Zachary, 253, 272, 291, 292, 299,
    308, 333, 341, 346
Tecumseh, 121
Temperance movement, 188, 189, 203,
    209
Templeton, Eliza Catherine. *See* Strong,
    Mrs. George Washington
Templeton, Jane (aunt), 88, 129, 207–208
Templeton, Oliver, xiv
Templeton, Olivia (aunt), 88, 129, 208,
    323, 327
Tennyson, Alfred, Lord, 227, 314
Terence, 36, 68
Teufelchen (pet squirrel), 288, 303
Texas, 7, 217, 223, 227–231, 236, 250,
    253, 256, 264
Thackeray, William Makepeace, *Vanity
    Fair*, 330
Thames, Battle of the, x
Thanksgiving Day, 7, 43, 220
Theatres, G.T.S. at, 273–274
Thomas à Becket, St., 271
Thompson, 162
Thompson, Benjamin Franklin, 107
Thompson, Smith, 221
Thompson, William, 36
Thomson, Poulett, 130
Thorn, 108
Thurston, George, 294
Tic douloureux, 99
Tiffany & Young, 271, 334–335
Tighe, Mr. and Mrs. Richard, 315
Tilden, Samuel Jones, xxv
Timm, Henry Christian, 179
Todd, John, 53
Tom Thumb, 296, 344 n.
Tombs Prison, New York, 104, 118, 190–
    192

Tonawanda, N.Y., 243
Tooke, John Horne, 106
Tornado (horse), 296, 298, 304, 310
Toronto, 79
Tower of London, 210
Townsend, Lieutenant, 275
Townsend, Rosina, 15 n.
Tractarian Movement. *See* Oxford Tracts
Tracy, 164
Trade unions, 14
Transcendentalism, 146, 169
Travers, William Riggin, 17, 90
Travers Island, 17 n.
Tremont House, Boston, 18
Trevett, Russell, 6, 21, 37, 38, 74, 82, 167
Trigonometry, 16
Trinity Chapel, New York, 310, 311
Trinity Church, Boston, 18
Trinity Church, New Haven, 278
Trinity Church, New York, xxi, xxxi–xxxiii, xxxvi–xxxix, li, 10, 34, 76, 81, 88, 89, 103, 179 n., 303–304, 306, 307, 314, 320; third edifice (torn down 1839), 105, 111; fourth edifice (built 1842–1846), 111, 177, 182, 215, 227, 234, 238, 248, 253, 261, 262, 276, 279, 283; consecration of, 277–278; chimes, 276; G.T.S. elected to vestry of, 303
Tripler, Charles Stuart, xxxiv
Trois Mousquetaires (Dumas), 335
Trollope, Frances (Milton), 124
Troy, N.Y., 166, 242, 244, 246
Troy, 165, 240
Troy House, 166
Tübingen, University of, 55 n.
Tucker, Fanning Cobham, 116, 154, 215, 323
Tucker, John Ireland, 42, 74, 85, 208
Turner, Joseph Mallord William, xl
Tweed Ring, xxxvi
Twenty Questions, 143
Tyler, John, 19 n., 106 n., 151, 156, 168, 185, 197, 205, 223, 229, 230, 236, 238, 241, 250, 253
Tyler, Mrs. John (Julia Gardiner), 238
Tyng, Stephen Higginson, 335
Typee, 345
Tyrtaeus, 304

Underwood, L.I., 188
Union Bank, New York, xiii, 103
Union College, 20 n, 152 n.
Union League Club, xxxv
Union Race Course, 180, 181

Union Square, New York, xi, 115, 186, 188, 211
Unitarianism, 125–126
Unitarians, Unitarian Churches, 78, 104, 124 n., 144, 175 n., 202 n., 267, 269, 311 n.
United Nations, 33 n.
United States Army, 160
United States Hotel, Hartford, 145
United States Hotel, Saratoga, 166
United States House of Representatives, 173
United States Marine Corps, 160
United States Mint, Philadelphia, 247
United States Sanitary Commission, xxxii–xxxvi, xxxix
United States Subtreasury, 147
United States Supreme Court, 225
Universalism, 21–22
University Place Presbyterian Church, New York, 267–268
Upham, George Phinehas, 144
Upjohn, Richard, xxxii, 177, 234, 262
Upshur, Abel Parker, 223, 227
Utica, N.Y., 156, 163–165, 241, 242
Utica Academy, 104, 164

Valencondres, 299
Van Buren, Abraham, 326
Van Buren, Mrs. Abraham (Angelica Singleton), 326
Van Buren, John, 356
Van Buren, Martin, xiv, xxi, 65, 77, 97, 121, 138, 145, 151, 158–160, 232, 236, 237, 356 n.
Van Buren, William Holme, xxxiii
Vandenheuvel, R. M., 45
Vandenhoff, George, 331
Vanderbilt, Captain, 123
Vanderbilt, Cornelius, xi
Vanderpoel, Aaron, 219, 221, 326
Van Duzer, Mr. & Mrs. Selah, 284–285
Vanity Fair (Thackeray), 330
Van Rensselaer, 256
Van Rensselaer, Jeremiah, 323, 326, 333, 356
Van Rensselaer, Mrs. Jeremiah, 323, 326
Van Rensselaer Manor, 117
Van Vechten, 206
Van Wagenen, 137
Van Wagenen, Gerrit, 251
Van Winkle, Edgar S., 301
Van Zandt, The Reverend, 34
Varian, Isaac L., 101
Varick, Richard, 92, 241
Vattelina, Attilio, 235

Vera Cruz, Battle of, 291, 292
Ver Bryck, Cornelius, 61
Verdi, Giuseppe, xl
Vermilye, Robert George, 29
Vermont, University of, 72
Verplanck, Gulian Crommelin, 180, 297, 301, 309, 314
Verren, Antoine, 38, 111, 113, 162
Victoria, Princess Royal, 157, 171
Victoria, Queen, 71, 132, 157
Vienna, 332
Vieuxtemps, Henri, 218–219, 235
Villiers, George, second Duke of Buckingham, 87
Vincent of Beauvais, 25
Vinton, Francis Laurens, xxxvii
Virgil, 3, 14, 68
Vivian Grey (Disraeli), 83, 152
Vyse, William, 224

Waddell, 115
Wainwright, Jonathan Mayhew, 18, 155, 180, 218, 239, 283, 319
Wall Street, 60, 62–64, 91, 103, 105, 106, 161, 171, 188, 223, 314, 315, 324, *et passim*
Wallace, Horace Binney, 105
Wallack, Henry, 117
Walsh, 179
Walsh, James William, 59
Walsh, Mike, 229
Waltham, Mass., 263
Walton, Isaak, 100
Walworth, Reuben Hyde, xxiii, 106–107, 167, 190
War, 99–100, 135, 153, 157, 160, 175–176, 253, 271, 272, 273, 275, 276, 333, 334. *See also* Mexican War.
Ward, Francis Marion, 61, 75, 85, 91, 189, 300–301
Ward, Henry, 29, 36, 75, 148
Ward, Henry Hall, 29, 61, 85, 90, 91, 189
Ward, John, 299
Ward, Samuel (1786–1839), xi, 16 n., 29, 55, 116, 131, 153
Ward, Samuel (1814–1884), 131; Library of, 55
Warren, Mercy (Otis), xvii
Warren, Samuel, 146
Washington, George, xl, 2, 6 n., 56, 145, 226
Washington, D.C., 157
Washington, 334
Washington Hall, New York, 218
Washington Irving, 325, 328

Washington Monument, New York City, 297, 304
Washington Square, 61 n.
Waterford, Marquis of, x
Waterford, N.Y., 166
Waters, George Gilfert, 14, 21, 35, 36, 38, 187, 285
Waverley House, New York, 265
Webb, James Watson, 51, 86, 183–184, 193–194, 218, 224, 364
Webb, Mrs. James Watson (Laura Cram), 364
Weber, Karl Maria von, 89, 198, 216, 235
Webster, Daniel, xv, 1, 7, 19 n., 100, 121, 143, 147, 156, 197, 225–226, 250
Webster, John, 87, 201
Webster, John White, 298 n., 364–365
Webster-Ashburton treaty, 97
Wedding of G.T.S., 319–323
Weed, Harvey Augustus, 36
Weed, Thurlow, 106 n.
Weehawken, N.J., 236–237, 294, 295, 323
Weeks, Edward, 99
Weeks (afterward Weekes), John Abeel, 110, 114, 116, 154, 181
Weeks, Robert, 288
Weir, Robert Walter, 16 n., 359–360
Weiss, Josephine, 317
Welford, Charles, 12, 14, 71, 77, 115, 202, 280 n.
Wells, 122
Wells, John, v, xiii, xv
Wenzler, Henry Antonio, Jr., 259, 276, 300, 306, 318
Wesley, John, xxxviii
West Farms, N.Y., 323
West Indies, 100
West Neck, L.I., 188, 209
West Point, xvii, 341, 357–362
Westervelt, 191
Westminster Abbey, 210, 248
Wharton, Edith Newbold (Jones), 309 n.
Wheeler, John 72
Whig party (U.S.), 77, 93, 94, 97, 101, 112, 113, 118, 121, 137, 151, 156, 177, 185, 200, 228, 232, 236, 246, 249, 258, 272, 283, 292, 306, 308, 333
Whistler, James Abbott McNeill, 359 n.
White, Mr. & Mrs., 356
White, Richard Grant, xxvi, xxxix
White, Robert, 105, 131
White Mountains, 32
White Plains, N.Y., 95, 194
Whitehall (New York City), 85

Whitestone, L.I., xvi, 17, 27, 33, 72, 76, 87, 88, 111, 161, 323, 325, 327
Whitlock, Samuel H., 85, 139, 213, 303, 309
Whitney, Mrs., 33
Whitney, Stephen, xi, 266
Whittelsey, Ira Day, 356
Whittingham, William Rollinson, 247, 251, 335
Whole Duty of Man, The, 230
Wickersham, George W., v
Wickham, 164
Wilbur, 314
Wiley & Long, 50
Wiley & Putnam, 52, 69, 100, 130
Wilkin, Simon, 70
Will, Freedom of the, 116–117
Willetts, 145
William IV, King of England, 71
William Tell (Schiller), 269
Williams College, 65
Willis, Nathaniel Parker, 296, 337
Wilmerding, 215, 219, 266
Wilmot Proviso, 287
Wilson, 322
Wilson, George Templar, 87
Wilson, Mrs. George Templar (Eleanor Jones Duer), 87
Wilson, James Willis, 35
Wilson, John, 116
Wilton, Conn., xvii
Windsor Castle, 210
Winnepesaukee, Lake, xxi, 32, 75
Winthrop, Francis Bayard, 278–279, 344
Winthrop, Henry Rogers, 122, 253, 278–279, 285
Winthrop, Laura (Mrs. W. T. Johnson) 278–279
Winthrop, Theodore, xxvi, liii–liv, 61n., 279, 294

Wise, Henry Alexander, 173
Wolfe, Catharine Lorillard, 76 n.
Wolfe, John David, 76–77
Wollstonecraft, Mary, 54
Women, 63, 74, 103, 110, 114–116, 131–133, 135–136, 139, 150, 162, 170, 171, 176, 185, 186, 206, 215, 224, 227, 235, 236, 256, 260, 273–275, 277, 284–285, 311, 312, 326, 356; Strong's *beau idéal*, 179–180
Wood, Fernando, xxxii, xxxix
Woodforde, Parson, xxxviii
Woodstock (Scott), 147
Woolsey, Charles W., 124
Woolsey, George, 123
Woolsey, Laura (Mrs. W. S. Johnson), 272 n.
Woolsey, Rebecca Nelson (Mrs. John Borland), 122, 123, 326
Woolsey, William, 123
Worde, Wynkyn de, 228
Wordsworth, William, xx, 65, 122, 269, 288
World, end of, 199 n.
Worth, William Jenkins, 302
Wright, Silas, 237, 284
Wyckoff, Alexander, 357, 358
Wyeth, Cripps & Co., 133
Wynne, James, xli

Yale College, xii, xiii, xviii, xix, xxxi, li, liii, 279; Library, 279; Law School, 92
Yankee servant girls, 109
Yellow fever, 110
Young, John, 283, 284

Zoological Institute, New York, 46

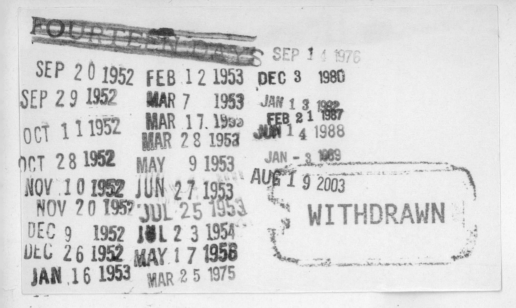